Fiscal Reform in Spain

STUDIES IN FISCAL FEDERALISM AND STATE–LOCAL FINANCE

Series Editor: Wallace E. Oates, *Professor of Economics, University of Maryland and University Fellow, Resources for the Future, USA*

This important series is designed to make a significant contribution to the development of the principles and practices of state–local finance. It includes both theoretical and empirical work. International in scope, it addresses issues of current and future concern in both East and West and in developed and developing countries.

The main purpose of the series is to create a forum for the publication of high quality work and to show how economic analysis can make a contribution to understanding the role of local finance in fiscal federalism in the twenty-first century.

Titles in the series include:

State and Local Finances under Pressure
Edited by David L. Sjoquist

The Property Tax, Land Use and Land Use Regulation
Edited by Dick Netzer

Restructuring Local Government Finance in Developing Countries
Lessons from South Africa
Edited by Roy Bahl and Paul Smoke

Reforming Intergovernmental Fiscal Relations and the Rebuilding of Indonesia
The 'Big Bang' Program and its Economic Consequences
Edited by James Alm, Jorge Martinez-Vazquez and Sri Mulyani Indrawati

Competition in the Provision of Local Public Goods
Single Function Jurisdictions and Individual Choice
Alexandra Petermann Reifschneider

Decentralization in Asia and Latin America
Towards a Comparative Interdisciplinary Perspective
Edited by Paul Smoke, Eduardo J. Gómez and George E. Peterson

The Politics and Economics of Regional Transfers
Decentralization, Inter-Regional Redistribution and Income Convergence
Fabio Padovano

Fiscal Reform in Spain
Accomplishments and Challenges
Edited by Jorge Martinez-Vazquez and José Félix Sanz-Sanz

Fiscal Reform in Spain

Accomplishments and Challenges

Edited by

Jorge Martinez-Vazquez

Professor of Economics and Director,
International Studies Program,
Andrew Young School of Policy Studies,
Georgia State University, USA

José Félix Sanz-Sanz

Professor of Public Economics,
Universidad Complutense de Madrid, Spain

STUDIES IN FISCAL FEDERALISM AND STATE-LOCAL FINANCE

Edward Elgar
Cheltenham, UK • Northampton, MA, USA

Published by
Edward Elgar Publishing Limited
Glensanda House
Montpellier Parade
Cheltenham
Glos GL50 1UA
UK

Edward Elgar Publishing, Inc.
William Pratt House
9 Dewey Court
Northampton
Massachusetts 01060
USA

A catalogue record for this book is available from the British Library

Library of Congress Cataloguing in Publication Data

Fiscal reform in Spain : accomplishments and challenges / edited by Jorge Martinez-Vazquez, José Félix Sanz-Sanz.
p. cm. – (Studies in fiscal federalism and state/local finance series)
Includes bibliographical references and index.
1. Fiscal policy–Spain. 2. Taxation–Spain. I. Martinez-Vazquez, Jorge. II. Sanz-Sanz, José Félix.
HJ1244.F57 2007
336.46–dc22
2007000737

ISBN 978 1 84720 079 2

Printed and bound in Great Britain by MPG Books Ltd, Bodmin, Cornwall

Contents

Contributors

Emilio Albi Universidad Complutense de Madrid

Francisco Comín University of Alcalá, Madrid

Laura de Pablos Escobar Universidad Complutense de Madrid

Alberto Gago REDE and Department of Applied Economics, Universidade de Vigo

J. Salvador Gómez Sala Universidad de Málaga

José Manuel González-Páramo European Central Bank

Pablo Hernández de Cos European Central Bank

Xavier Labandeira REDE and Department of Applied Economics, Universidade de Vigo

Julio López Laborda Universidad de Zaragoza

Jorge Martinez-Vazquez Andrew Young School of Policy Studies, Georgia State University

Carlos Monasterio Escudero Universidad de Oviedo

Jorge Onrubia Universidad Complutense de Madrid

Raquel Paredes Gómez Universidad Complutense de Madrid

Francisco Pedraja-Chaparro Universidad de Extremadura

Fidel Picos REDE and Department of Applied Economics, Universidade de Vigo

Miguel Rodríguez REDE and Department of Applied Economics, Universidade de Vigo

Desiderio Romero Jordán Department of Applied Economics, Universidad Rey Juan Carlos

Javier Salinas-Jiménez Instituto de Estudios Fiscales, Universidad de Extremadura

José Sánchez Maldonado Universidad de Málaga

José Félix Sanz-Sanz Department of Applied Economics, Universidad Complutense de Madrid

Javier Suárez-Pandiello Universidad de Oviedo

Ignacio Zubiri University of the Basque Country

1. Introduction

Jorge Martinez-Vazquez and José Félix Sanz-Sanz

The Spanish tax system started an extensive period of reform from 1977 onward, two years after the death of General Francisco Franco. This reform process, ongoing for the last three decades, has put Spain's public finances on a sound footing and it represents the most identifiable key factor behind the "Spanish economic miracle." In 1975 total tax revenues as a percent of GDP in Spain stood at less than 20 percent. By comparison, the OECD average country was collecting in tax revenues 31 percent of GDP. By 2002 Spain had converged to the OECD average with total tax revenues representing over 25 percent of GDP. This improved fiscal performance allowed Spain to close significant deficits in capital infrastructure and social programs, without risking any significant macroeconomic imbalances. Even though the budget deficit was in the neighbourhood of 7 percent in the middle 1980s and again in the middle 1990s following international macroeconomic shocks, by 2002 Spain was operating with a balanced budget. This significant increase in tax effort was largely accompanied by a fairer distribution of tax burdens and the elimination of large tax distortions that had affected the efficient operation of the economic system. But not everything worked well. Despite the rapid process of reform, Spain's tax system has continuously played catch-up with that of its European neighbours and it may still be lagging in international competitiveness.

However, we believe that the largely successful tax reform in Spain contains valuable lessons for other countries, such as Argentina and Mexico, which in recent times have struggled with bouts of economic crisis. These crises can be largely traced to tax systems that have failed to either yield adequate revenues for the desired expenditure programs or do so in an efficient and equitable manner.

This volume is a collection of original essays that attempt to shed light on the fiscal reform process in Spain in the last thirty years. Although some of the topics covered in this volume have been analysed elsewhere, most of the previous work has been written in Spanish and has been unevenly disseminated. In addition, this volume provides an overview of the whole reform process up to the most recent times and in all its dimensions: tax policy reform, the modernisation of tax administration, and a deep decentralisation process.

The volume focuses on four major themes. The first theme is the political economy of tax reform in Spain; a fundamental part of the success story is that political forces and economic interests were able to form alliances at some key junctures of the process to keep the reform moving forward. The second theme is an in-depth look at the main instruments of the tax system including the evolution of income taxation, the big role played initially by wealth taxes, and the introduction of a VAT upon Spain's accession to the European Common Market. The third theme focuses on the interaction between tax reform and another major institutional transformation of Spain's fiscal systems over the last 30 years: the rapid fiscal decentralisation process that led Spain from being one of the most centralised countries in the world to being one of the most decentralised. The fourth theme is the modernisation of the tax administration system in Spain. A more effective and efficient tax collection and enforcement system has been the critical ingredient for the overall success of fiscal reform in Spain. The volume closes with some reflections and lessons that one can extract from the experiences in Spain for successful fiscal reform in other countries. In the following paragraphs we describe in more detail the contributions of the different chapters in the volume.

Chapter two, written by Francisco Comín, analyses the political environment surrounding Spanish tax reform from the early seventies, during the last years of Franco's dictatorship, to the present, with the peaceful democratic succession of government coalitions from the right and the left. In the mid seventies, after Franco's death, Spain faced two fundamental challenges: the transition from a dictatorship to a democracy and the modernisation of the economic institutions. Addressing both issues required a high degree of social and political consensus. Despite the fact that almost 35 years had passed since the end of the Spanish civil war, Spain was still a deeply divided country in ideological terms where for many generations the deep wounds brought by the civil war had not healed. A significant part of this chapter is dedicated to analyzing how the necessary political consensus was generated. The chapter gives particular attention to the *Moncloa Pacts*, where very early in the transition to democracy the main parties form the entire political spectrum, from those aspiring to a continuation of Franco's legacy to the communist party and others on the left which had been illegal and persecuted for decades.

Remarkably, they sat together and came up with the key political principles that permitted the introduction of a democratic Constitution and the radical transformation of Spanish institutions, not the least of which was the transformation of its fiscal system. The rest of Comín's chapter takes us on a journey through the main political milestones up to recent times highlighting the symbiosis between political change and fiscal reform.

Chapter three, by Emilio Albi, focuses on the role played by one economic group which, surprisingly, is normally forgotten when analyzing the reform of the Spanish fiscal system: the business community. Albi, as a first-class witness due to his double role as academician and tax advisor, describes the major reform issues during the last thirty years from the viewpoint of entrepreneurs and investors. He highlights, as one of his main conclusions, the social benefits derived from the cooperation during practically the entire period between policy makers and business organisations. However, his chapter stresses some important problems still pending in the tax reform agenda, such as the complete elimination of double taxation of dividends and international regulations regarding corporate income.

Chapter four by José Manuel González-Páramo and Pablo Hernández de Cos, takes a comprehensive view of the fundamental role played by the European integration process in the evolution of the Spanish tax and budget policies. Their point of departure is the early 1960s when Spain formally applied to join the European Common Market until its definitive accession on January 1, 1986. González-Páramo and Hernández de Cos also examine the impact on Spain's fiscal policies of the European Union expanding agreements, including the creation of a Single European Market in 1993 and the reinforcement of the European convergence as a first step towards the creation of the Economic and Monetary Union (EMU), now in operation. There is little doubt that the developments taking place in Brussels at the European supranational level have had clear and strong influences on the economic and fiscal reforms undertaken in modern Spain over the last three decades. Their chapter concludes with an exploration of the important challenges that the participation of Spain in the EMU still poses for the future of its fiscal and budgetary policy.

The next six chapters pay close attention to the reform process of each of the main taxes in Spain's tax system. Chapter five, by Desiderio Romero Jordán and José Félix Sanz-Sanz, studies the important role played by the Personal Income Tax (PIT) in the modernisation of the Spanish tax system. This chapter describes the introduction of the modern PIT in 1978 (prior to that, under Franco, personal income taxation had been fragmented with a variety of scheduler approaches) and its major reforms implemented in 1991, 1998 and 2002. As is the case in other countries, the PIT is definitely among the most relevant taxes in the Spanish tax system, both in terms of revenue power as well as in terms of the number of taxpayers it affects. In addition, as the PIT is self-assessed and filed regularly on an annual basis, it is clearly perceived by taxpayers. As a result, the design and structure of the PIT has remained one of the main concerns of policy-makers, both at a national and at a regional level. This visibility was confirmed when in 1989 Spain's Supreme Court ruled as unconstitutional the use of the "household" as the unit of taxation prompting quite a radical reform of this tax in 1991. Personal income taxation in Spain has followed—with some lags—international trends, from highly progressive and narrower bases in the earlier years to simpler and flatter rate structures and wider bases in more recent times.

In chapter six, Raquel Paredes Gómez analyses the role and evolution of the Corporate Income Tax (CIT). This tax, together with the personal income tax, burst onto the Spanish tax scene for the very first time in 1978 and rapidly became one of the most important taxes in the Spanish fiscal system. The continuous fine tuning of the CIT has been a process of making good on the tax principles behind the 1978 reform. These principles included: competitiveness, international tax coordination, neutrality and coordination with accounting rules and with the personal income tax. Paredes Gómez' analysis highlights the increasing importance played by open economies, globalisation and international competition in informing the most recent reforms of this tax.

Taxing personal wealth was a fashionable public policy in the decades of the sixties and seventies of the last century. As a result, the Spanish tax reform initiated in 1978 was strongly imbued with this principle. Chapter seven, by Laura de Pablos Escobar, aims at analyzing the role played by wealth taxation in Spain's tax system. Her analysis focuses in particular on three different tax instruments levied on personal wealth: the net wealth tax, and the taxes on inheritance and gifts. These taxes were advocated mainly on the grounds of improving vertical equity, and, also important for the case of the net wealth tax, on the grounds of enhanced administrative control and enforcement of other taxes, especially the PIT. Although the net wealth tax was indeed instrumental in getting a sharp increase in taxpayer compliance in the PIT, Laura de Pablos Escobar concludes that the Spanish experience on the redistribution side has been clearly unsuccessful. De Pablos Escobar strongly advocates for a more prominent role of wealth taxes in modern tax schemes but, extrapolating from the recent Spanish experience and international trends, she conveys a feeling of hopelessness about their future. The decline of their role and importance in Spain was signalled by the re-assignment of wealth taxes at the sub-national government level, where although initially they represented key financing instruments, their use has also been in decline.

Chapter eight, by José Sánchez Maldonado and J. Salvador Gómez Sala, studies the reform and evolution of consumption taxes in Spain over recent decades. Their paper pays special attention to the introduction of the value added tax (VAT) adopted upon accession of Spain to the European Common Market in 1986. This represents one of the most important, if not the single most important, development in Spain's tax system over the last thirty years. The VAT substituted for a system of turnover taxes that had been highly distortionary and with low revenue yield and quickly became the workhorse of Spain's tax system. The accession of Spain to the European Community also demanded further harmonisation of the indirect taxes. Sánchez Maldonado and Salvador Gómez Sala further study the reform of excise taxes during the 1990s to bring the Spanish tax system into compliance with European legislation in this area. Their chapter carefully studies the comparative performance of indirect taxation in Spain in an international context.

Social security taxes and the system of social protection are analysed by Ignacio Zubiri in chapter nine. By practically all measures the system of social protection in Spain at the beginning of the democratic transition was quite defective. This "social deficit" was one that the central government moved quickly to close. The chapter carefully evaluates the rapid development of social protection in Spain in the last thirty years. During this period, the Spanish social protection system became one of the more advanced ones in the world. At present, the Spanish Pension system is, in terms of replacement rate, one of the most generous, health services are free for everyone, and unemployment benefits are substantial in comparison with other countries in the same economic area. The evolution of social expenditures and the way they have been financed is described in detail in this chapter. The achievement of a welfare state in Spain did not come without costs in terms of labour market rigidities and unemployment and it came late, at a time when Spain's European neighbours and international trends had already turned in the other direction emphasizing competitiveness and labour market flexibility.

The role of environmental taxes in Spain's tax system is analysed by Alberto Gago, Xavier Lavandeira, Fidel Picos and Miguel Rodríguez in chapter ten. These authors conclude that environmental taxes have not been used much in Spain, and this has been a clearly wrong policy. However, a certain interest in this type of taxation does now exist at the regional government level, although that interest so far has been focused more on the revenue capacity of these taxes than on the environmental impact they may have. The authors provide a careful analysis of the existing "green" taxes in Spanish regions and their potential. For the near future, these authors forecast an increased use of environmental taxes in the areas of transport, tourism and solid waste.

Chapters 11 and 12 are dedicated to the study of fiscal federalism in Spain and the important role fiscal decentralisation has played all along in the reform of Spain's tax system. Decentralisation still remains one of the fundamental issues in current tax debate in Spain.

In chapter 11, Julio López Laborda and Carlos Monasterio Escudero provide a comprehensive overview of the fundamental issues arising from the process of territorial decentralisation that has been taking place in Spain since the restoration of democracy in 1978. This process resulted in the emergence of the so-called "Autonomous State". They describe in depth the asymmetric approach to fiscal decentralisation adopted in the 1978 Constitution with two radically different systems established to finance regional expenditure: the "common system" which applies to all Spanish regions but two, and the "special or 'foral' system", which applies exclusively to the Basque Country and to Navarre. This system of intergovernmental finance is of critical importance for understanding the essence of the Spanish Public Finance in the last thirty years and, probably, for those interested in what will happen in the next thirty as well. López Laborda and Monasterio Escudero focus their attention on the assignment mechanisms, for both revenues and expenditure competences, between central and regional governments. In this respect, they dedicate special attention to assess the use of the "effective (historical) cost" criterion employed throughout the intergovernmental finance system to evaluate vertical and horizontal imbalances. The chapter also analyses the current system of transfers and sub-national borrowing. Some initially fiscally irresponsible behaviour has been followed by strict limits and discipline partly imposed by European Union rules on allowed deficits and debt levels at the overall national level.

The system of local government public finance is analysed in chapter 12 by Francisco Pedraja-Chaparro, Javier Salinas-Jiménez, and Javier Suárez-Pandiello. The most important message in this chapter is the confirmation that local government decentralisation is clearly the "forgotten child" in the vigorous process of fiscal decentralisation initiated in the late seventies. The focus on decentralisation reform in expenditure assignments and tax revenue autonomy has been almost exclusively focused on the intermediate level of government, the regions or "Comunidades Autonomas," as they are known in Spain. A very telling figure provided by Pedraja, Suarez, and Salinas is that in 1978, prior to any decentralisation and as a result of the centralist Franco regime, Spanish local authorities managed around 13 percent of total public expenditure. Currently, this figure remains under 15 percent of total public expenditure. This is a clear indication that the intense fiscal decentralisation process that has been carried out in Spain during the last thirty years has been driven by political considerations, in large part trying to manage centrifugal political forces, and much less by economic efficiency considerations traditionally associated with decentralisation reform. The chapter provides a clear picture of where local communities stand in the recent Spanish public finance experience and proposes options and mechanisms to improve decentralisation at this local government level.

Jorge Onrubia in chapter 13 provides an in-depth look at the state and evolution of the Spanish Tax Administration from 1977 until the present. The regaining of democracy in Spain together with the need for considerably increased revenues for developing Spain's infrastructure and improving its welfare system not only led to the tax policy reforms initiated in 1977 but also acted as a trigger for a new way to understand the relationship between taxpayers and the tax administration. Not only did taxpayers see that government now was on their side but there was strong political consensus for criminalizing tax offences, a first in Spanish history, and early achieved out of the Moncloa Pacts. In addition, successive governments invested heavily in human and capital resources, especially in information technology, which led to the rapid and effective modernisation of the tax administration system. Added flexibility for employment and compensation policies was provided by making the Spanish tax administration a semi-autonomous agency. Some other events that influenced the development of a more modern tax administration were the fiscal decentralisation process and the adoption of modern taxes such as a global PIT and the VAT. However, not everything has gone according to plan. Onrubia concludes by reviewing the lights and also the shadows of the tax administration reform in Spain and provides recommendations for improving tax enforcement and taxpayer services in Spain. The last chapter of the book, by Jorge Martinez-Vazquez, takes a retrospective view of Spain's experience with successful fiscal reform in the context of overall budgetary and economic policy in the country. Martinez-Vazquez reflects on the changes in tax morale in the country, with citizens becoming more approving of their government policies. The chapter also reviews the process of convergence in the performance of the Spanish tax system to that in OECD countries and it draws lessons for fiscal reform in other countries.

2. Reaching a Political Consensus: The Moncloa Pacts, Joining the European Union, and the Rest of the Journey

Francisco Comín*

INTRODUCTION

After the death of Francisco Franco in November 1975, the political transition was adversely affected by the concurrence of a deep economic crisis and intense social conflict. The hesitant economic policies of the last Francoist and the first transitional governments—up to the 1977 elections—made the economic depression even worse. Therefore, economic imbalances were more serious in Spain than in most other European countries. There were higher levels of inflation, unemployment, balance of payments deficit, public sector deficit and a larger drop in profits and investment.

Two fundamental challenges facing Spain, in the midst of such a serious situation, had to be resolved together. The political challenge called for the transition to be guided towards democracy via peaceful means, while the economic challenge required the economic depression to be lessened and the economic institutions modernised. Both problems required an incomes policy orchestrated by means of a political pact that would permit a constituent process to set up democracy, at the same time several reforms would modernise disfunctional economic institutions. The consensus amongst various political parties made the Moncloa Pacts, signed in 1977, and the Constitution, approved the following year, possible. That exceptional situation led to political and economic agreements unknown in Spain before and after that date. This chapter focuses on the economic pacts that allowed the beginning of tax reform in a democratic setting.

Many factors contributed to the success of the Moncloa Pacts. Firstly, the situation of 'social emergency' created by the economic crisis, the political uncertainty and ongoing social disturbances were decisive. In the midst of such a complicated situation an 'inspection effect' arose that led citizens—and their political representatives—to show altruistic behaviour that benefited the community and permitted a tax increase. The *Unión de Centro Democrático* (Centre Democratic Union, UCD) government managed to reach a national political consensus in 1977–1979. The extreme circumstances that existed led all of the parliamentary parties to sign the Pacts.

Secondly, the Spanish society had become more modern thanks to the economic growth of the two previous decades. A large middle class capable of offering stability to the democratic regime already existed in the 1970s. This middle class was against political adventure, be it revolutionary or totalitarian. Thirdly, within that context of risk of social collapse, the historical memory, especially the memory of the Civil War and the long ensuing dictatorship, weighed heavily. Fourthly, Spanish politicians stated their intention to move towards the economic and political model of the European democracies.[1] In fifth place, a factor that was as fundamental as all of the others was the presence of some economists who were familiar with the European experience and reached an agreement to implement it.

Unfortunately the agreement that was reached for the Moncloa Pacts only lasted until the Spanish Parliament, the *Cortes* (formed by the House of Representatives and the Senate) approved the Constitution in November 1978. Party differences became obvious later on, within the context of the elections in March of 1979. The various UCD governments that followed applied their own economic policies without reaching any kind of general pact. The short–lived period of political consensus prevented the structural economic reforms—including tax reform—from developing according to the plan set out in the Moncloa Pacts and consequently ended up stretching them out in time. In particular, the short life of the Moncloa Pacts frustrated the tax reform as this process would have required a longer lasting consensus. Actually, the tax reform lost support after the 1979 elections. The weak government of *Unión de Centro Democrático*, harassed by both social and political groups, was not able to correct the initial defects of the reform; it was not able to either strengthen the Tax Administration, or map out the direction for future reform.[2] So tax reform had to wait for better times to be completed.

The tax reform of the transition therefore embraced quite an ample period of time. The Moncloa Pacts and joining the European Economic Community were the fundamental axes of the tax reform in democratic

Spain. As a matter of fact, the first law passed democratically in the country was precisely the Law of Urgent Tax Reform Measures passed on November 14, 1977. This law got the tax reform process started. The following year was fundamental for the tax reform process as in that year new income tax and corporate tax were introduced. We could say that the tax reform reached its highest point when the Value Added Tax (VAT) became effective on January 1st, 1986—the same day that Spain joined the European Economic Community. These are two significant dates because both facts, democracy and integration into Europe, were the corner stones on which the most important tax reform of the 20th century was built.

Actually, before democracy, the tax system that existed in Spain had secular roots as the tax principles had been established in 1845 during the reform carried out by Alejandro Mon.[3] The reforms of 1957 and 1964 carried out by Navarro Rubio, during the Francoist period, respected those tax criteria. By contrast, the Spanish fiscal system changed radically in a relatively brief time between the establishment of democracy and the entrance to the European Economic Community. In that period, Spain managed to incorporate the fiscal principles of the tax model established in Europe after the Second World War.

Given the time delay, the problem that faced the new Spanish fiscal system was that Spain had finally adopted the European tax system at the same time it began to be questioned in the most modern European countries. Therefore, just as it was taking its first steps, the new Spanish fiscal system had to start adapting itself to the new trends in public finance that were spreading throughout Europe. For that reason, the Spanish governments had to make adjustments to the tax system right from the moment when they had completed its full structure with the introduction of the VAT in 1986.

These are the questions that are dealt with in this chapter, which is divided into five parts. In the first part, I will study the fiscal legacy the Franco regime left to democratic Spain; its anachronism, injustice and inefficiency was so obvious that no relevant political party opposed the tax reform. This explains, as we will see in the second part, why all of the parliamentary political parties and the social forces approved a tax reform that was based on the principles spread throughout Europe over the previous decades by signing the Moncloa Pacts. In the third part I will analyse the immobilisation of the tax reform process during the period of weak UCD governments that followed the 1979 elections. In the fourth part I will examine the culmination of the tax reform proposed in the Moncloa Pacts under the first Socialist governments and the repercussions of joining the European Economic Community on taxation. Likewise, I will try to explain how the delay and the haste with which these reforms were applied soon led to criticism of the new tax system, which led the Socialist Party to amend the system as of 1989. Finally, in the fifth part, I will briefly point out the new tax doctrine applied by the Popular Party governments starting in 1996. This doctrine tried to adapt the Spanish fiscal system to new worldwide trends where the competitiveness demanded by globalisation required more efficient taxation.

ORIGINS OF THE REFORM: CRITICISM OF THE ANACHRONISTIC TAX SYSTEM OF THE PERIOD CORRESPONDING TO THE FRANCO REGIME

The authorities of the Franco regime practised a conservative and anachronistic tax policy, reflecting the image of the dictatorial regime itself inside a democratic Europe. That policy corresponded to the interests of the social groups that supported the regime and to the economic ideology of the politicians and parliamentarians of the Spanish *Cortes*. Actually, in the first place, the Franco regime always favoured the middle and upper classes through a tax system that exercised a low tax burden and that was clearly regressive. High level civil servants and Ministers of Finance were recruited amongst the privileged classes thereby explaining their reluctant attitude towards tax modernisation. The natural exceptions to this attitude were, of course, the corps of technical civil servants.[4] In the second place, between 1957 and 1969, the technocratic ministers linked to the Opus Dei applied a liberal strategy of economic growth centred on companies and private investment which did not prevent the National Industry Institute (*Instituto Nacional de Industria*, INI) from continuing to bail out economically unviable private companies. That strategy pursued the following tax objectives: (a) keep the tax burden low, (b) obtain a balanced budget to avoid issuing public debt that could crowd out private investment, (c) maintain the stability of prices and currency, (d) grant subsidies to private enterprises through budget expenditures and tax expenditures and also through soft loans financed through the financial repression of individual accounts in banks, and, above all, in savings banks, (e) give state owned enterprises a secondary role versus the lead role they had in the industrialising programme during the autarchy (1939–1959), and (f) increase infrastructure and education expenses—public complements essential for stimulating private investment as prescribed in the indicative planning approach of the National Development Plans.

The Flaws of Franco's Tax Reforms

This last point was crucial because the main goal of the tax reforms of the Franco regime was to obtain sufficient resources to finance public investment. Given the inadequacy of the tax system at the time, the Ministry of Finance headed by Mariano Navarro Rubio put forward the tax reforms of 1957 and 1964. However, the technical limitations of these reforms prevented the Ministry of Finance's tax collection from increasing sufficiently. Therefore, the public investment that was foreseen in the National Development Plans could not totally finance itself. Consequently, at the beginning of the 1970s the deficiencies in public services, the insufficient endowments of infrastructure and human capital were evident and led to a collapse of economic growth. In that situation, as we will see, some Finance Ministers of the Franco regime (like Monreal Luque and Cabello de Alba), were obliged to sponsor a new tax reform. But in order to obtain a larger tax collection, it would have been necessary to introduce a minimum amount of progressivity into the public finances. The privileged classes of the Franco era attacked the attempts at tax modernisation from this angle and caused their failure.[5]

The tax immobility of the Spanish dictatorship concurred with the tax advances in Europe. The Spanish Stabilisation Plan of 1959 put an end to the autarchy and to the regulations that had collapsed economic growth at the end of the 50's but the public sector did not undergo big transformations. Several reforms, especially those of José Larraz (1940) and Mariano Navarro Rubio (1957 and 1964) had changed legislation and created some new taxes.[6] The names, types and ways of managing old taxes also changed. These reforms temporarily increased tax collection but they did not contribute to modernising the principles of fiscal burden sharing in Spain. So, the economic Stabilisation Policy of the late 1950s and the Development Plans of the mid 1960s were implemented without any outstanding improvement in the tax system. The Stabilisation Plan of 1959 was a wasted opportunity, as taxes were not updated. The same thing occurred with the 1964 tax reform, which accompanied the approval of the First Development Plan. This time, again, the system failed to establish a modern income tax or a technically acceptable sales tax, like the VAT.[7]

The absence of a modern tax reform during the Franco regime kept a backward, inefficient, insufficient, unjust and not neutral tax system alive. However, its obvious technical defects did not provoke a tax reform because the traditional factors that bring about tax changes in Spain—grave revenue insufficiency, acute inflation and above all political impetus[8]—had not yet been triggered. The sufficiency of the tax system during the 1960s was an illusion. The Finance Ministers used control budgeting (or budget sequestering)—that is the expenses were limited to the receipts regardless of the economic and social needs. Franco's regime preferred to live in budgetary penury rather than carry out a tax reform.[9] The ideological questions were also deciding factors. Despite the proposals of economists and even some Finance Ministers, the sociological and political sectors which supported Franco's regime never admitted the modern taxation criteria based on the progressivity of direct taxation and on the generality of indirect taxation. The social groups that enjoyed the favour of the regime also hindered the improvements in tax collection that would have fought against the tax fraud and tax evasion that was commonly admitted and allowed by the Ministry of Finance. The only taxes that were actually collected were those using withholding schemes, such as payroll tax. The figures show that at the beginning of the transition to democracy, tax schedules (the old non–personal or product taxes) still dominated Spanish taxation despite their technical and economic obsolescence. Public finance experts recognised the failure of non–personal taxation but the two Navarro Rubio reforms were not able to substitute personal taxation for it.

As a consequence, taxpayers only had to endure low tax burdens but, these were unequally distributed.[10] During Franco's regime the tax burden shows a rather peculiar evolution when compared to European experience. The government of Burgos (Franco established the government of the national army in Burgos during the civil war) paid the main part of the bill of the Civil War after they had won it.[11] That meant approving some special taxes and fees. This is the reason why the tax burden (defined as the ratio of fiscal revenue to National Income) increased in the post–war period. But once the payment arrears of the war were paid the tax burden receded immediately. Unlike what happened in democratic Europe, Franco's autarchy did not use the State budget as an instrument of economic policy—neither for financing public works in order to promote economic reconstruction and recovery, nor for funding social spending in order to create the Welfare State. Unlike in European democracies, the political consensus was not needed in the Spanish dictatorship and public spending did not increase. That's why an increase in tax collection was not needed. So the tax burden (10.6 percent) in effect during the pre–war period was not recovered until 1959. In 1969, the fiscal revenue /National Income ratio was still at 12.1 percent.[12]

Logically, the tax burden associated with the entire Public Administration (General Government) was greater than the one corresponding to the State (Central Government). (See Figure 2.1.) But this tax burden also grew moderately during Franco's regime. The main reasons were the failure of Navarro Rubio's first reform in 1957,[13] and the fact that the increase in social insurance contributions during the 1960s after the Bases Law on

Social Security was passed in 1963, did not go into effect until 1967. The General Government's tax burden did not rise towards levels closer to those in the rest of Europe until the death of General Franco and the beginning of democracy. General Government's current revenue as a percentage national income grew from 15.6 to 40.5 between 1959 and 1992. This growth took place between 1959 and 1962, in 1967 and especially from 1977 onwards. The consolidation of the Welfare State—that took place as a result of the Moncloa Pacts—demanded more taxes and social insurance contributions to finance its new budgetary functions.

As a result, after 1966, the Central Government current revenue /General Government ratio decreased due to the boom of the *Seguridad Social* (Spanish equivalent of the British National Insurance or the US Social Security) until 1982. Between 1958 and 1966 the Central Government absorbed between 60 percent and 65 percent of the General Government's current revenue while social insurance collected between 20 and 24 percent. The change came after 1967 when the Central Government's current revenue share decreased to 53 percent and that of the social insurance grew to 35 percent. The Central Government continued to be the public agent with the largest resources. Ten years later the outlook was different because, in 1978, the current revenue of the social insurance system exceeded that of the Central Government. In 1982 the social insurance collected half of the General Government's current revenue while the Central Government barely retained a third. The decentralisation of the democracy's Public Sector Administration became evident through the rise at the subnational level of the Autonomous Communities' current revenue. Nevertheless, the financing of the autonomous communities (regional governments) suffered from insufficient tax autonomy that made them dependent on transfers and taxes from the Central Government.

The Backwardness of Spanish Taxation in the Twilight of the Franco Regime

During the final years of Franco's regime the growth of the tax receipts was slowed as much by the regressivity of the tax system—which caused the collection to grow less than the national income—as it was by tax fraud which reduced the effective collections by the Ministry of Finance. The Spanish taxation system continued to be regressive because the average tax rate diminished as the taxpayers' income grew. This regressivity occurred both in indirect taxation and in social insurance contributions. These effects more than offset the moderate nominal progressivity of direct taxation. The implementation of the tax system was even more regressive than its legal

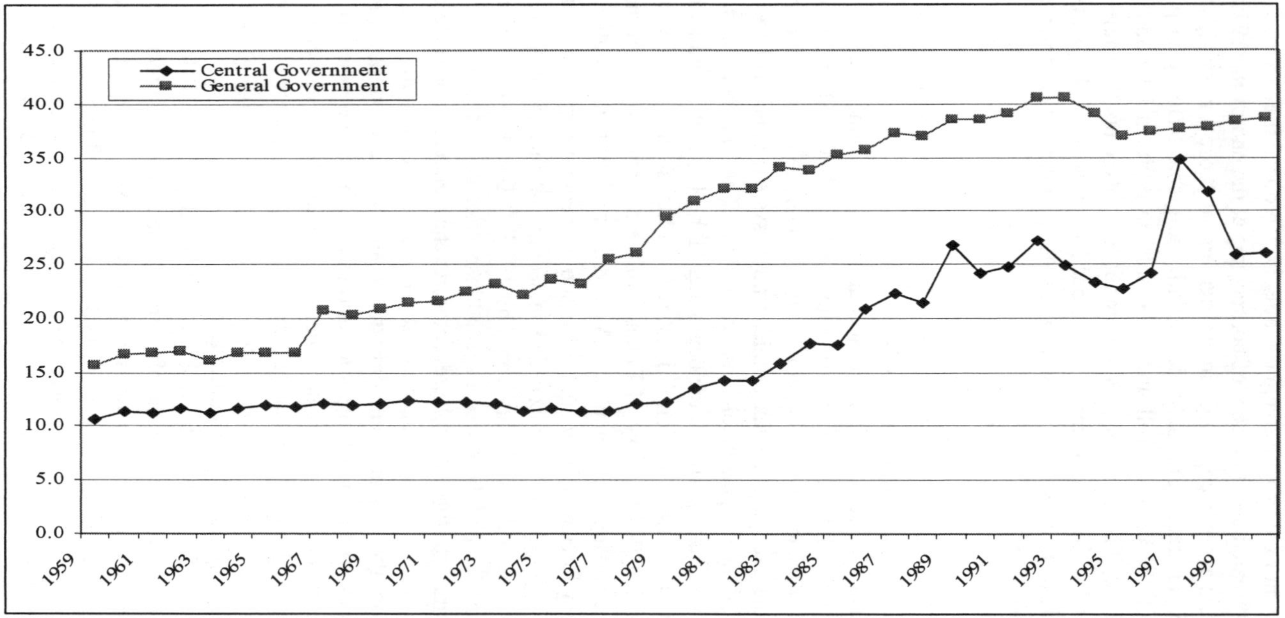

Figure 2.1 Tax burden (1959–2000)

Source: Comín and Díaz (2004) and Prados de la Escosura (2003).

configuration. The system became more unjust as tax evasion spread. This was so because evasion tended to be more common in taxes that were, theoretically, somewhat progressive, no matter how reduced they were. Tax evasion was estimated at 40 percent of tax receipts at the end of the 1970s. The Spanish taxpayers recognised (in 93 percent of those surveyed) the existence of fiscal fraud. The individuals with the greatest ability to pay were left out of the taxpayer roll and there was no political intention to pursue fiscal fraud. The opportunities to commit fraud were not the same—it was calculated to be 70 percent in the upper income level.[14] Wages tax fraud was difficult because the tax was withheld at source. This form of collection procedure was not used for other revenues, not even for corporate tax which was assessed as a presumptive tax. It was obvious that Franco's regime was not interested in stopping fiscal fraud at all as supported by the following facts: (a) fraud was not standardised as a criminal offence, the defaulters only received small administrative sanctions; (b) bank secrecy on current accounts was sanctioned, (c) there was a ban on publishing taxpayer lists and finally, (d) the Ministers of Finance kept a deficient tax collection system.[15] Deficient tax collection derived from the fact that the tax administration system continued to be poorly endowed with personnel and resources. The number of tax administrators was quite small. At the beginning of the 1970s the number of civil servants in tax administration did not reach a thousand. Probably not only taxpayers, but the Ministry of Finance officers themselves were not interested in increasing their numbers. As a matter of fact, although the 1964 tax reform foresaw the creation of a sub–inspectors corps, pressure from the Tax Inspectors corps succeeded in seeing that there was not one single civil servant in this auxiliary corps by 1975.[16] Besides, inspections lacked co–ordination and there was a special inspection corps for every tax. The lack of administrative control prevented revenue increases because of the widespread fraud. It also allowed abuses in the accounting of tax expenses due to the misrepresentation that companies carried out with impunity thanks to the many exemptions, allowances and bonuses set up in the Development Plans and in the *acciones concertadas* (State agreements with firms). This loss of revenue for the Ministry of Finance was not compensated by an increase in the firms' investments as that type of incentive was not efficient in promoting it.[17]

Other features of backward tax systems persisted along with low tax burden during Franco's regime. One of them was the fact that indirect taxes brought in larger revenue collections than direct taxes. Revenues from indirect taxes were as well more variable over time (Figure 2.2). In addition, the number of indirect taxes was larger than that of the direct taxes and their legislation was not systematic at all. The collection of

Contribución de usos y consumos (Excise tax) fell from 27.7 percent to 18.3 percent of the Central Government's non–financial revenues in 1958 because of the tax reforms of that year. Later on, it fell to 11.9 percent in 1964 as a consequence of the 1959 Stabilisation and Liberalisation Plan.[18] After the liberalisation of foreign trade, the Customs tax replaced excise taxes as the main tax during the 1960s, reaching the ceiling of 21.4 percent in 1966. The 1964 tax reform intensified the decline of excise taxes and collection fell to 7.6 percent of the total tax receipts in 1965 and to 1.6 percent in 1979 (Figure 2.3). Likewise, from the 1964 reform carried out by Navarro Rubio, the collection of the *Impuesto sobre el Tráfico de Empresas* (ITE, turnover tax) grew. This turnover tax was an obsolete form of cascade tax, brought into Spain at the time when Europe had already introduced the Value Added Tax, which was technically superior.[19] The turnover tax represented 15.2 percent of Central Government's receipts in 1974.

Another fundamental trait of the backwardness of Spanish taxation in this period was the absence of a genuine Income tax. The largest part of the receipts from direct taxation came from tax schedules (the non–personal or product taxes). From 1964 onwards there were several precursor taxes of the general income tax. The tax levied on salaries stood out. The Wage tax bore a heavier tax burden than the tax on capital income. Before the 1979 tax reform, the wage tax had become the Central Government's main tax. Its growth during Franco's regime was remarkable. In 1959 Wage tax contributed 7.2 percent of the Central Government's receipts; in 1971 it became the most important direct tax (8.3 percent) and in 1978 it had made up a 22.7 percent share (Figure 2.4). The receipts from the tax on capital income decreased from 3.5 to 2.9 percent between 1959 and 1974 but later it rose again to 6.1 percent in 1978. Corporate income tax increased its yield from 5 percent to 10 percent between 1941 and 1953. Later on, it decreased to 7.7 percent in 1965 and after that it recuperated to represent 9.5 percent in 1979. During Franco's regime the Personal Income tax was nothing more than a minuscule, subordinate appendix of product taxation. The percentage of income tax in total receipts still was 1.5 percent in 1978 (Figure 2.4). The reason for this was its deficient technical definition ever since the *Impuesto complementario sobre la renta* (Surtax) was established in 1932. Along the same lines, the *Impuesto general sobre la renta* (General personal income tax), introduced in 1964, was not a genuine income tax but rather a schedular income tax where the prepayment of tax schedules continued to bring in the largest receipts for the Ministry of Finance. These were a far cry from personal taxation since joint taxpayer incomes were not taken into consideration nor were the tax payers' personal

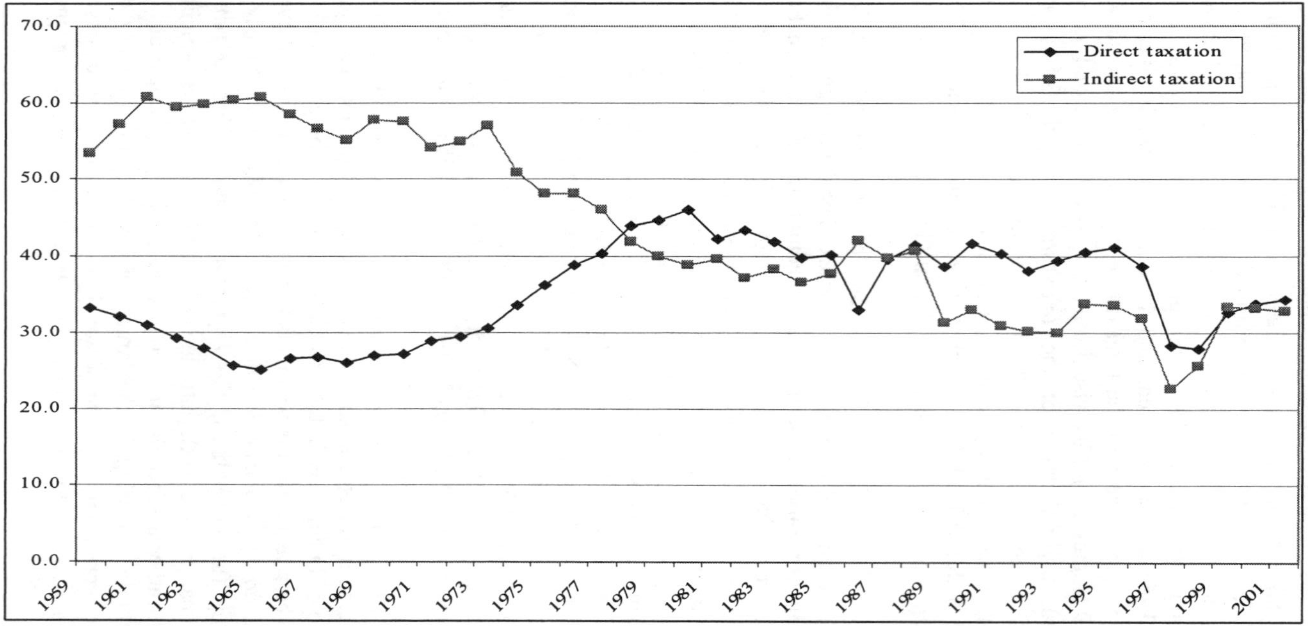

Figure 2.2 Percentage of central government tax revenue (1959–2001)

Source: Comín and Díaz (2004).

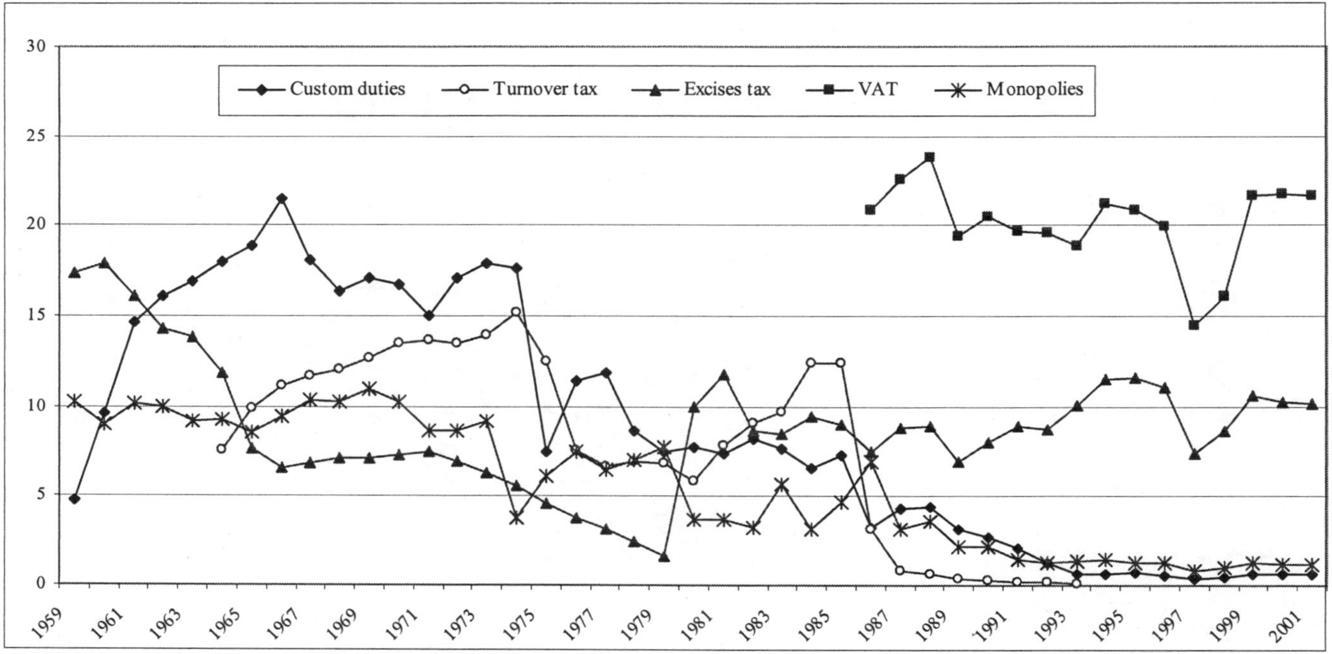

Figure 2.3 Indirect taxation. Percentage of central government's tax revenue (1959–2000)

Source: Comín and Díaz (2004).

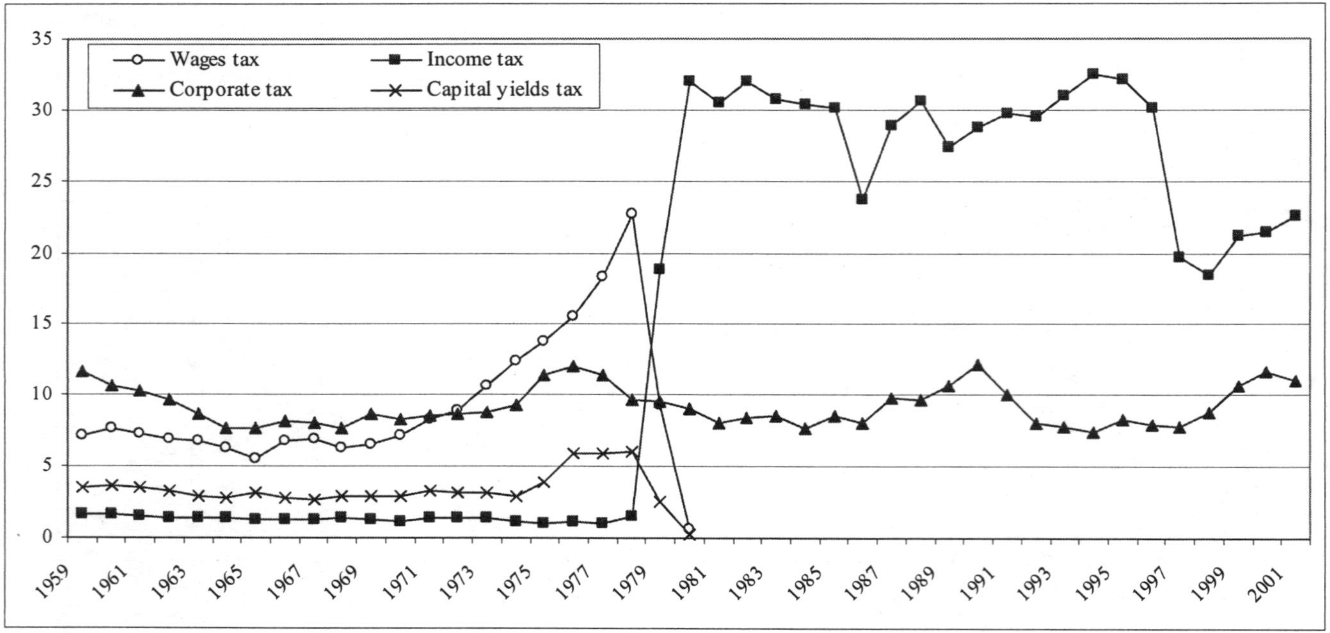

Figure 2.4 Direct taxation. Percentage of central government's tax revenue (1959–2000)

Source: Comín and Díaz (2004).

circumstances. The obstacles to implement personal taxation (income tax) in Spain were as much a political factor (Franco's Dictatorship) as a technical tax deficiency of the schedular income tax—the tax that had been chosen by Spanish reformers. Other European countries that tested this type of schedular income tax, such as France and Italy, also underwent similar difficulties in the consolidation of their personal income tax.[20]

Consequently, in the twilight of Franco's regime, old forms of taxation continued to disrupt the development of the national economy. It did not bring in enough resources for the State to provide the public goods and services (basically education, health and infrastructure) demanded by an economy that needed industrialising. Likewise, that tax system, rooted in the 19th century, represented a real risk for social stability because it did not contribute to improving income distribution. On the contrary, this taxation system generated ostensible tax injustices that fed into the existing general social unrest, which Franco's authoritarian rule continued to repress. Besides, from the 1960s onwards, economic growth, more powerful labour unions and a fast urbanisation process were changes that were starting to transform the Spanish society. Among other things, social forces were starting to demand policies that would redistribute income. However, this was not feasible with the taxation system in effect because it did not allow for progressivity in the distribution of tax burdens and because the Ministry of Finance's scarce fiscal resources did not allow the supply of merit goods with significant redistribution potential—such as education, health or housing—to grow. The economic crisis that started in the mid 1970s showed, even more, the gap between the Spanish taxation system and the economic and social structures. The rigidity of the taxes hindered any attempt to stabilise the crisis and the revenue inadequacy of the tax system did not allow the budget transfers necessary to alleviate the results of the economic depression.

The Preambles of the Democratic Tax Reform

Given the deficiencies of the traditional taxation system, fiscal economists had been outlining tax reform plans ever since the mid 1960s. As a matter of fact, Public Finance experts were paving the way for reform in different ways. These ways included: criticising the standing tax system and especially the 1964 tax reform, incorporating the European Union's principles of tax harmonisation into their academic values, studying the obstacles that had always interfered with past tax reforms in Spain and by preparing a tax reform project that would be ready when political demand for reform arose. The role of the fiscal economists became institutionalised in 1969 when Enrique Fuentes Quintana was appointed Director of the

Institute for Fiscal Studies with César Albiñana as his Assistant Director. The main lines of the reform proposals worked out in the Institute for Fiscal Studies consisted of substituting comprehensive personal taxation for schedular taxation, and Value Added Tax for Excise Duties and Turnover tax. In 1970 the Institute for Fiscal Studies worked hard on the reform and the publication of a double issue of the review *Hacienda Pública Española* in June and July 1970 showed this work. Herein the guidelines of tax harmonisation (that the Neumark Committee was putting to use in the European Economic Community) were used to systematically analyse the necessary changes for taxation in Spain. From the point of view of the Minister of Finance, the matter of tax reform could not still be raised because it was considered politically risky. The Institute could not start the reform project openly so public finance experts decided to collect ideas and experiences from other countries.

In the last years of Franco's regime, policy makers were also very aware of the Spanish taxation system deficiencies. What worried them most was its revenue insufficiency. The technocratic Opus Dei ministers tried to increase the State's revenue to finance the growing infrastructure and education expenses that economic growth policies were demanding, right from the moment they took office in 1957, but even more so after the National Economic Development Plans got started in 1964. However, they came up against political restrictions that vetoed any modern tax reform that implied that in order to collect more revenues the system had to be progressive. Therefore the technocratic ministers could not solve the buried problems of a Ministry of Finance that was apparently healthy. While its budget showed no debt, what was really happening is that the Ministry had given up on fulfilling the purpose of a modern Ministry of Finance. At the beginning of the 1970s the tax system inadequacies were so noticeable that a Minister of Finance of Franco's Government asked the Institute for Fiscal Studies to carry out the preparatory work for the Spanish tax reform.[21] Laureano López Rodó, the Commissioner of the Development Plan, backed the tax reform programme. The reason was that the lack of resources of the Ministry of Finance did not allow the financing of the large public investments foreseen in the development plans. Only genuine tax reform would have allowed the necessary increase in public investment to accompany the big growth in private investment. Those studies were condemned to failure because the declining Franco regime opposed fiscal reform just as it would later veto political liberalisation.[22]

As a matter of fact, the first political support for the reform came from Alberto Monreal Luque, the Minister of Finance. In July 1972, the Minister decided that it was time for the Institute to begin working on the tax reform programme. The report was finished in April 1973 which made it possible to hold meetings with the Minister, the technical general secretary, Francisco Fernández Ordoñez and the general directors of the Ministry of Finance. At the beginning of June 1973 the Report, called the 'green paper', was the topic of discussion in the *Comisión Delegada de Asuntos Económicos* (Delegate Commission for Economic Affairs).[23] This document was even presented to the Head of State, General Franco, and handed out to be discussed in the Cabinet meeting. But, the day after that presentation, Minister Monreal was relieved of his duties. The attempts at tax reform were aborted. His successor in the Ministry of Finance, Barrera de Irimo, did not urge for the reform and any ideas about tax reform were completely forgotten. The assassination of the first President of the Government (Franco was still the Head of State) since 1938—Admiral Luis Carrero Blanco—in December of 1973 planted the seed of uneasiness in Franco's regime. The *Caudillo* (one of the names by which General Francisco Franco was known) was no longer of sound mind and body and Carrero Blanco had been planned by some accounts to be named his successor. Finally, the economic crisis in Europe—brought about by the oil crisis—was starting at this same time. These factors all had some influence on the paralysation of the tax reform.[24]

Work on the fundamental technique of tax reform continued in the Institute for Fiscal Studies. They also worked on making the various political forces, including the political opposition (semi–clandestine since the beginning of 1976) aware of the need for tax reform but putting it in the framework of both an extensive programme of economic readjustment to face up to the crisis and general economic reform. In this way, when Minister Cabello de Alba tried to urge for the Ministry of Finance's reform programme again in 1976 the team of the Fiscal Studies Institute unenthusiastically started drafting a new report (the 1976 'white paper') with no hope whatsoever of seeing it turned into legislation. Public finance experts at the Institute thought that tax reform was no longer possible unless set in the framework of a programme of far–reaching economic and political reform that would require widespread political agreement to work, something that was not yet possible. Enrique Fuentes Quintana and his team left the Institute for Fiscal Studies because of their differences with the Ministry over the extent of the reform. These incidents all show that tax reform was possible neither under the regime that Franco and the *Cortes*, elected by organic democracy, had established nor before the democratic general elections. Once the Dictator had died, the first two transition governments – already under the reign of King Juan Carlos I and presided over by Carlos Arias Navarro and Adolfo Suárez respectively—did not change the tax system. Together with the fact that their energies were concentrated on transforming the political regime, there was another reason consisting of the fact that the reformer economists themselves thought that it was better to wait until there was a parliamentary democracy so that the new tax system could command more legitimacy. To sum up, when the first democratic elections were held in 1977 and Adolfo Suárez formed his second government while Enrique Fuentes Quintana held the Vice Presidency of Economic Affairs, the Spanish taxation system had barely changed since Mariano Navarro Rubio's 1964 reform. This fact reveals that the 'liberal tax principles' established in 1845 were still in effect.[25]

THE NEED FOR THE REFORM: THE APPARENT UNANIMITY IN THE MONCLOA PACTS

The Origins of the Pacts

Therefore tax reform had to wait until the first democratic government. In 1976 the best Spanish economists advocated applying the generalised incomes policy, already in use in the main countries of Western Europe, in Spain. The economic crisis in the continent had provoked social tensions so European politicians were looking for a consensus remedy. The traditional Keynesian policies based on discretionary monetary and tax instruments had not been able to resolve a crisis characterised by the two basic imbalances of inflation and unemployment. In view of the absence of alternatives, practically all of the political parties that competed in the 1978 elections—from *Unión de Centro Democrático* (Union of Democratic Centre, *UCD)* and *Alianza Popular* (Popular Alliance, AP*)* on the right to the *Partido Socialista Obrero Español* (Spanish Socialist Workers' Party, PSOE*)* and the *Partido Comunista* (Communist Party, PC*)* on the left[26]—included social and incomes policies in their election programmes. *Unión de Centro Democrático* won the general elections in June of 1977. Consequently, the *Cortes* entrusted Adolfo Suárez with the task of forming a government. Enrique Fuentes Quintana was named Vice President of Economic Affairs and Francisco Fernández Ordóñez was named Minister of Finance. These appointments were not fortuitous. Both men had been committed to the prior projects of tax reform. On July 11th the government presented an economic project that included economic adjustment measures (devaluation, monetary restriction, wage control) together with structural reforms in the budget area (taxes and public expenditure) and financial system reforms (liberalisation of financial markets). The first measure adopted by Fuentes Quintana, in this sense, was the July 23rd 1977 Ministerial Order which set up a plan to reduce obligatory investment coefficients of the banks, liberalise some interest rates and increase the rates applicable to special regulation loans.[27]

Economic and tax reforms were more complicated, by nature, than financial market reforms. The negotiations between the Government and the social organisations – employers' associations and unions—had not made progress by August of 1977. So the Government decided to try to reach an agreement among all the political parties represented in Parliament. In September, a team led by Fuentes Quintana developed an Economic Reparation and Reform Programme that convinced Suárez and the rest of the Government of the need to reach a political pact in order to carry it out. In the Moncloa Palace (the office of the Presidency of Government) on October 8th Suárez convinced the political parties to negotiate and to use this programme as a basis. Therefore, when the agreements were signed on October 25th, they were called the Moncloa Pacts. They were later approved by the *Congreso de los Diputados* (House of Representatives, on October 27th with only one vote against the bill) and by the Senate (on November 11th, with only two abstentions). The incomes policy put into practise, in many ways, was more thorough than the one that was applied in the rest of Europe. Given the institutional delay and the longevity of the Franco dictatorship, the Moncloa Pacts had to include very thorough public sector and market structural reforms, which western democracies had established after World War II.

The Content of the Pacts

The Economic Reparation and Reform Programme contained three objectives. The first one was to correct the basic imbalances of the Spanish economy through a set of preparatory measures already established by the government. The second one was to fairly distribute the costs of the crisis and of economic reparation measures through tax reform, social insurance, and education and housing policies. The third objective was to adapt the Spanish economy to the principles of a market economy through financial and employment policies, industrial relations reforms and modern sector policies referring to agriculture, industry and commerce. The key to success of the Moncloa Pacts was, on the one hand, the subordination of the collective negotiation to price stability and, on the other hand, the use of tax and public expenditure policies as an instrument of income redistribution.

The negotiating strategy of these economic agreements set the principles of dialog between the political parties that led to a consensus for the 1978 Constitution. The Constitution, approved in the *Cortes* on November 17th, defined 'a social, constitutional and democratic State subject to the rule of law'. In such a way the Welfare State, set up, in fact, in the Moncloa Pacts, was constitutionally consolidated. The main objective of the Pacts was the redistribution of income through progressive taxation and social spending. Nevertheless, the Moncloa Pacts showed temporary asymmetry in their development. The stabilisation policies were successful because the immediately relevant instruments could be applied. In contrast, the short–lived consensus did not allow enough time for the structural reforms to be carried out. As a matter of fact, the short–term objectives of the Pacts were reached in 1978 and 1979, when wage stability and inflation control were reached and when corporate benefits were recuperated. Once the Constitution was approved, the consensus was lost and this prevented the structural reforms that had been approved in the Pacts—especially those that referred to creating the Welfare State—from being completed. In exchange for wage control the unions and the left wing parties got concessions in other labour and budget policies in addition to social and political legitimacy.

Three things stand out among the successful ideas of the democratic tax reform: its inspiration in the European taxation system, the approval of urgent measures that paved the way to tax reform itself, and the exploitation of the unique opportunity for consensus that was not only exceptional but very short–lived.[28] Tax reform was incorporated into the global reforms of the Moncloa Pacts and meant the modernisation of the Spanish tax system along European lines where the Neumark Commission had defined the model at the beginning of the 1960s. Its essential principles were: the importance of direct and very progressive taxes, very high marginal rates, notable flexibility and potential tax–collection, and finally, moderate use of indirect taxation.[29]

The main part of the democracy's tax reform strategy was already included in the Institute for Fiscal Studies' 1973 and 1976 reports.[30] It clearly explained the principles as follows: (1) Integration of public spending into the tax reform as a way to justify and rationalise it. (2) A modernisation of the tax administration to prevent the reform from turning into a 'fiscal pipedream' that offered no practical results whatsoever. (3) Imitation of the tax system operating in Europe—not in vain did Spanish democrats aspire to integrate into the European Economic Community. (4) Institutionalisation of the tax reform through a special organisation and a previously fixed calendar to assure fulfilment independent of changes in government. The three first principles were applied in the Moncloa Pacts more or less successfully but the tax reform was not institutionalised, which meant its paralysation as of 1979. The reform plan prepared by the Institute for Fiscal Studies was incorporated into the Moncloa Pacts especially into the Urgent Measures Law of 1977 and into the 1978 Personal Income Tax and Corporate Income Tax configurations. Nevertheless, only the following measures of the UCD government's anticipated reform projects were approved: (1) Law 50/1977, November 14th which approved the Urgent Measures for Tax Reform; (2) Laws 44 and 61 of 1978 which approved Personal Income Tax and Corporate Income Tax; (3) Law 30/1979 which modified the assessment of the special taxes, and (4) Law 32/1980 which approved the new Tax on Capital Transfers and Documented Legal Proceedings.

The Resistance and Amendments to the Tax Bills

After the June 1977 elections, democratic change finally created a political mood that was well disposed to the admittance of modern taxation. The previous work explained that at a date as early as July 11th 1977, the Government's programmatic Statement on economic policy could already be made public. Tax reform was an important part of it. Despite Suárez's support, the reformers (led by Fuentes Quintana and Fernández Ordóñez) met up with opposition within the government itself—among the Liberal and Christian Democrat ministers—as well as with the doubts of the *Confederación Española de Organizaciones Empresariales* (CEOE), the Spanish Confederation of Business Associations. This resistance explains the delay in the presentation of the Urgent Tax Reform Measures Bill until August 9th 1977. The delay to pass the Bill in the Cortes and the Senate was much longer—it wasn't passed until November 14th. This law of urgent measures sought to pave the way for tax reform via the following measures: (a) voluntary regularisation of taxpayers, removal of banker's duty of secrecy, declaration of tax fraud as a crime, and regulation of interposed companies for fiscal transparency; (b) establishment of wealth tax that would serve as a control measure to facilitate establishing and collecting personal income tax; (c) reform of sumptuary tax, and (d) concession of tax allowances to create employment.

To overcome the aforementioned business resistance as well as the left wing parties' resistance to the project, three key alterations were made. They were: (1) a generous tax moratorium was granted, which obviously benefited the previous tax defrauders, but also improved tax compliance after the reform; (2) a regularisation of the accounting of companies was authorised; and (3) progressivity was introduced in the wealth tax.[31] These corrections of the original project fell within Suárez's strategy of using pacts and reaching consensus. They also explained why the 1977 and 1978 tax reforms had barely met with any public criticism or discussion despite the fact that they radically changed the principles of tax burden distribution in Spain—at least in the law. Before 1979 neither the centre nor the right wing parties (*Unión de Centro Democrático* and *Alianza Popular*) nor the business organisations (neither the *Círculo de Empresarios*—Businessmen's Circle—nor the CEOE) objected openly to the tax reform. The explanation is that their amendments to the tax projects were considered by the government while drafting the articles of the laws. Only a few discrepancies were aired publicly with respect to the excessive speed with which the tax reforms were being established and to the rather dubious moment chosen for their establishment given the economic crisis.[32] The lobbying methods and delaying tactics of the right wing groups, in direct contrast with the left wing's haste, slowed down the negotiation of the tax reform.

The Personal Income Tax bill was sent—together with the Inheritance and Wealth Taxes—with considerable delay to the Cortes in January 1978. This delay reveals that beyond general matters, the party confrontations were about particular articles of the law. The ample consensus on tax principles and the left wing's desire to pass the new taxes, as quickly as possible, explain the absence of an in–depth public debate on the reforms. Nevertheless, there was buried opposition to the Government's projects. Due to extra–parliamentary pressures, changes were made to the tax projects before they were publicly debated in the Cortes. These modifications were a more favourable tax treatment of capital returns and gains as well as the annulment of the mechanisms for cross control between the various taxes thereby leaving the door wide open to tax evasion of unearned income. Everything considered, disagreement on tax reform finally became known when some UCD MPs used the Press to show their opposition. The case is that Fuentes Quintana resigned shortly after February 24th 1978. One must look for reasons in the pressures of some business organisations and some leaders of UCD who opposed some of the structural reforms proposed, albeit substantially changed.[33] Bills related to Corporate Tax, Capital Transfers and Documented Legal Proceedings Tax, VAT and Temporary Regulation of Indirect Taxation reached the Cortes even later, in July. Of all these bills, only two were passed. The first was the Personal Income Tax Law passed on September 8th 1978 and the other was the Corporate Tax Law passed on December 27th. This demonstrates that beyond agreements on the general principles, an obvious resistance to the tax reform proposed by the UCD Government existed.

This resistance explains why tax reform in the transition was slightly distorted with respect to the Government's original bills. There are three reasons. First, opportunities for tax fraud and tax avoidance were left in the actual legal texts. Second, the approval of some taxes was delayed, which left the tax system unbalanced. Three, the administrative reform indispensable to put the legal change into effect was not done. Some of these problems also arose out of the haste with which the government wanted to establish the reform contrary to the gradual strategy foreseen in the initial reform plans. The precipitate writing of the tax laws led to formal deficiencies. All of this broke the balance of the reform project, made the later introduction of tax reform more difficult and made it necessary to make various corrections in the legal texts.

Regarding the first point, the 1977 and 1978 tax laws, which were an historic reform in Spanish taxation, suffered from certain technical deficiencies and left some legal gaps. As I already mentioned, that was due to the fact that the consensus of the political parties—regarding the general tax principles—in the Cortes hid a certain resistance to the tax reform. The clearest reflection of this is seen in the amendments that the right wing AP presented. Public opposition was very moderate but there was more decided negotiation to attain certain apparently technical amendments. Those who defended the corrections justified them saying that they were necessary to protect investment and to provide legal safeguard for taxpayers. These amendments had real consequences on the efficiency and equity of the tax laws that were passed. The concessions that the UCD Government made were not so much in the explicit exemptions to payment of tax on certain earnings but rather in the legislative looseness to tax avoidance as well as the blocking of the measures that could help in fighting tax fraud.

The doorways to tax fraud and avoidance were the following. (1) The application of a wealth assessment system to calculate the capital gains that allowed the accumulation of big capital losses when selling assets in the context of a declining stock market. This allowed high incomes to escape income tax payment up until 1985 and what is more, many in fact got big refunds back from the Ministry of Finance. (2) Fiscal transparency in income and corporate taxes meant paying less for many well to do families. (3) Corporate accounting regularisation allowed reducing profits for tax effects and therefore smaller payments for corporate tax. And (4) the incorporation of multiple tax exemptions and allowances on investment that led to reducing the taxable base for those taxpayers that were in the upper income brackets.

The pressure exercised on the government by various groups also led to deductions and excessive and arbitrary tax exemptions. Their propagation allowed taxpayers to abuse these tax abatements in view of the absence of efficient fiscal management that generated elevated fiscal expenses. The fight against tax fraud that had been a main objective of the initial plans of the UCD Government was cancelled for a series of reasons. On one hand, the restrictive interpretation of the lifting of the banker's duty of secrecy until 1985 meant that in practise, this secrecy existed until that year. On the other hand, the development of certain fiscally opaque financial assets became a shelter for dirty money. Finally, wealth tax did not work at controlling taxpayers' income because the parliamentary proceedings excluded the wealth tax on legal persons. Besides, the tax was granted to the autonomous communities which did not develop legal measures because such a tax could become an instrument of control, as the delay in the update of the cadastre registry reveals. These loophole concessions to tax payment were, without a doubt, related to the fact that the left wing requested that high rates be established for the wealth tax.

Regarding the last points, the problems arose because the tax reform was not institutionalised. By that I mean that the Cortes approved neither a technical commission nor a calendar that would guarantee the implementation of the reform no matter what the political circumstances might be. The absence of this organisation hindered the fulfilment of the indirect tax reform (indirect taxation took too long to reform generating an imbalance in the tax system), the modernisation of fiscal administration and the correction of the technical deficiencies of some of the tax laws. Likewise, the implantation of the new taxes was more difficult. In practise, personal income tax was not generally applicable to the entire population of taxpayers because there was no institution in charge of keeping watch over tax fraud. Consequently, tax fraud remained commonplace especially where there were large fortunes or unearned incomes. It was less common in low–income brackets where wage taxes were withheld at source. So, just like in the last years of Franco's regime, salaries were still the basis of direct taxation. Not institutionalising the reform brought about the weakness of the tax management and deficient statistical information that obstructed efficient tax collection.[34] This prevented tax audit from expanding the tax bases (due to their lack of knowledge and consequent fraud). The fiscal insufficiency led the government to raise tax receipts by keeping nominal rates of the personal income tax fixed in the presence of inflation that made taxpayers' nominal income grow. Against all of the initial plans, the reform of public expenditure policy was not adequately integrated into tax reform so the taxpayers noticed degradation of the public spending/paid taxes ratio. Inadequate public expenditure policy together with evidence of tax avoidance and fraud in the high–income brackets made it difficult to legitimise the new taxation system and to increase fiscal pressure on those taxpayers who fulfilled their obligations with the Ministry of Finance. The initial speed and the lack of continuity afterwards in the tax reform created other imperfections such as the deficient handling of international taxation as well as careless use of fees and public pricing as receipts for the Ministry of Finance and as a means to rationalise consumption of public services.[35]

THE TAX COUNTER–REFORM OF THE WEAK UCD GOVERNMENTS (1979–1983)

After approval of the new Constitution on December 6th 1978, the UCD Government's political reform was postponed, especially regarding tax matters. Clear evidence of this is that the government withdrew from the commitments it had made in the Moncloa Pacts. The reform of indirect taxation was blocked and the same thing happened to the tax management's modernisation projects and to efforts to repress tax fraud. On the contrary, tax advantages to those in the upper income brackets grew. Consequently, the results of the reform in terms of equity, neutrality and efficiency fell far behind what had been foreseen back in 1977. At the same time, advances in public expenditures characteristic to the Welfare State were curbed. Given such a situation, it is not surprising that talk about a tax counter–reform started to emerge. Bringing the reforms to a standstill was a consequence of several factors. These included the departure of Fuentes Quintana from the Government, the March 1979 elections that gave a scant majority to UCD and the internal fragmentation of the centre party itself, the difficulties raised by the reappearance of the economic crisis and the disagreements among the social and business groups, reinforced criticisms of the Welfare State.

The consensus reached in the Moncloa Pacts had already begun to fall apart in February 1978 with the departure of Fuentes Quintana from the Government. His was a resignation related to his tax reform proposals, but also to his attempts to restructure the electricity sector.[36] Once the bill creating the Constitution was passed by the Cortes in November 1978, and legalised by the constitutional referendum on December 6th, the political parties ended the consensus and began to compete against each other in the legislative elections that took place in March 1979 after which the period of 'Weak UCD Public Finance' began.[37] The party that won the elections, *Unión de Centro Democrático,* did not reach the absolute majority in the Cortes needed to impose the reform. Moreover, the internal confrontations in the aforementioned party lessened the already weak Government. The UCD leaders were not even able to keep the party together. Dissension arose among the various groups that held differing ideological positions within the party. The social democratic faction—that had run the taxation reform—lost power in the very heart of UCD which contributed to its paralysation. As if this were not enough, the political instability coincided with a worsening of the economic crisis in 1979. This double crisis stopped the economic sector rearrangement and the institutional reforms that both the economy and the Spanish society demanded. The political costs for the UCD Government for continuing with structural reforms grew because differences arose among the social and business groups that, until then, had supported the centre and right wing parties.

In fact, ideological positions of the right wing parties and the business associations shifted. After 1981, the strengthening of *Alianza Popular* and the CEOE secured criticism against the new tax system. These organisations argued that the effects of the reform had been very detrimental to the business because of UCD's excessive left–wing ideas. These opinions fell within the framework of criticism which also arose in the United Kingdom and the United States of the Welfare State that was spreading throughout Spain starting that year. In Spain, therefore, criticism of the Fiscal State began before there had been time to develop it. The CEOE openly criticised the 'enormous growth of public expenditure', which was only true because of the low initial levels and 'the demagogic and inadequate tax reform started in 1977'. In 1982, this critical opinion of the Welfare State was widespread among businessmen who censured the 'fiscal voracity' of the Spanish State. That same year the centrifugal forces that finally divided the *Unión de Centro Democrático* into pieces strengthened the *Alianza Popular* (AP) party, which was politically further to the right. AP ran in the 1982 general elections with an electoral programme that promised 'reform of the taxation reform' thereby accepting, as their own, the new taxation speech of the CEOE. The fact that the tax reform agreements of the Moncloa Pacts were only half–completed posed no obstacle to proposing that the new tax system be dismantled. The needs of the Spanish society and the interests of the voters went in another direction, as the results of the elections showed: The *Partido Socialista Obrero Español* (PSOE) won an absolute majority at the general elections, as we will see.

Consequently, between 1978 and 1982 fiscal legislation barely advanced. The Law of November 30th 1979 suppressed some special taxes such as those on sugar and chicory. It reformed the taxes on alcohol and alcoholic beverages and maintained those on telephone services, the price compensation on industrial alcohols and tobacco growing. The Law of December 25th 1979 on the transitional regulation of indirect taxation corrected some technical aspects of the Turnover and Sumptuary Taxes. Law 21 of June 1980 reformed Capital Transfers and Documented Legal Proceedings Tax. These small reforms left the indirect taxation picture practically the same. As we will see, the implementation of a Value Added Tax (VAT) had to wait until Spain joined the European Economic Community and it was obligated to implement it.

The UCD finance ministers (and also the first PSOE finance ministers) justified keeping Turnover Tax by arguing four reasons: (a) the inflationary effects VAT would have, (b) the losses the disappearance of hidden subsidies of the Turnover Tax would represent for exporters, (c) the complete reform of the tax administration that the implementation would demand, (d) the business organisations' opposition to the VAT, and (e) the strong increase in fiscal pressure that its implementation would mean. The postponement of the indirect taxation reform threw the new taxation system off balance thereby impeding fiscal neutrality, increasing its regressivity, and maintaining widespread tax avoidance and fraud.

The centre party government also stopped normative development of the laws that had already been passed in 1978 and 1979 and, above all, they did not attempt any administrative reforms at all. The result was that the number of people in charge of tax enforcement did not grow. In 1981 the total number of personnel working in the Ministry of Finance was the same as in 1972. Logically, the tax reform could not run adequately with such a lack of civil servants.

The inadequacy of the Administration regarding tax audits demanded by the new taxes was the main reason why taxpayers' tax appeal claims collapsed the *Tribunal Económico Administrativo Central* (Central Economic Administrative Court). Other reasons also contributed to this collapse: (1) the end of global agreements with taxpayers, which meant the demand for individual income tax returns grew, (2) the increased number of taxpayers especially for the personal income tax, (3) conflicts that arose from the application of the new taxation regulations and their technical imperfections, (4) lack of available jurisprudence for the Court, and finally (6) deficient legal standardisation of tax fraud and institutional and judicial tolerance. The lack of political decision to fight fraud contributed to the growing tax fraud culture inherited from the Franco regime.

Some political parties approved the 1977–1979 tax reforms in exchange for some legislative amendments that left wide opportunities for tax avoidance.[38] Later, the change in government permitted a tax counter–reform and paralysed the modernisation process of the tax enforcement apparatus thus allowing some social groups to openly commit tax fraud. This looseness in tax legislation and the Government's negligence regarding fraud conserved social inequality regarding the possibilities of fraud. The tax reform of the transition to democracy period therefore, in practice, hardly changed the incidence of tax burdens in the distribution of income. The Personal income tax carried on as being merely a tax on salaries. Unfairness was strengthened by the persistence of the old indirect taxation until 1985. A transfer of the tax burden from companies to consumers—via indirect taxation—and to the salary earners (who could not commit fraud because their taxes were withheld at source) went along with the growth of fiscal pressure during the transition to democracy. The extent of tax fraud impeded increasing the tax bases discovered by the Ministry of

Finance. So, to increase public revenue, the governments had to resort to the procedure of not adjusting the income tax rate schedule for inflation, which meant doing something that went against the theoretical principles of the reform planned since 1973. This lack of adjustment for inflation, in practice, meant an increase in the tax burden, but it was logically applied only on the incomes that could not escape taxation—fundamentally salaries.[39]

CULMINATION OF THE TAX REFORM OF THE TRANSITION CARRIED OUT BY THE PSOE AND THE SUBSEQUENT CORRECTION

In 1982 the general or legislative elections gave power to the Socialist party who had promised to complete the tax reforms; and they did. On December 2nd 1982 the first government of the Socialist party (PSOE) was formed with Felipe González as President and Miguel Boyer at the Ministry of Finance. From 1985 to 1993, the Minister of Finance was Carlos Solchaga. This party obtained sufficient political power to enable them to undertake all of the economic reforms that had been postponed since 1979, mainly the industrial reorganisation and the modernisation of the public sector. The comfortable majority that the PSOE obtained in the 1982 general elections allowed the 'reform trail'—that had started in 1977 and that the right-wing[40] political and social powers had opposed—to be retaken.

The First Socialist Tax Reforms

The first Socialist tax reforms, between 1983 and 1987, completed the tax system that had been programmed in the Moncloa Pacts. The VAT was passed, progressivity was emphasised via the partial reform of Personal Income Tax and the administrative reforms foreseen by the teams led by Fuentes Quintana in the Institute for Fiscal Studies were introduced. This prolongation of the tax reform had two elements. In the first place, from 1983, the PSOE carried out an extensive reorganisation of the tax administration in its various elements: territorial administrations or regional offices, management was computerised and the tax auditor corps was created. In second place, the indirect taxation reform was carried out through Law 30/1985, which introduced VAT. International pressure was decisive in adopting the VAT, because this tax was an indispensable condition for Spain to enter the European Economic Community. In third place, they set up the instruments to fight tax fraud and to generalise the tax system to the entire population, through the following regulations: Law

10/1985 modifying the General Tax Law, Organic Law 21/1985 reforming the Criminal Code in matters of Crime against the Ministry of Finance, Law 14/1985 regarding the Tax System of certain financial assets, and Law 48/1985 that partially reformed Personal Income Tax. In the fourth place, Law 29/1987 incorporated the new Estate and Gift Tax (or Capital Transfers Tax).[41]

As had happened in Spain in previous historic situations, when the Socialists completed the tax model of the Welfare State, Europe was already consolidating new tax options. On the one hand, the conservative governments of Ronald Reagan in the United States and Margaret Thatcher in the United Kingdom were already using new tax guidelines that were extending to the majority of the member countries of the Organisation for Economic Co–operation and Development (OECD). The objectives of high tax yields and tax progressivity passed to a second line of interest and were replaced by other objectives such as efficiency, reduction of tax rates, expansion of the tax bases and greater prominence of indirect taxation.[42] On the other hand, joining the European Economic Community and globalisation imposed restrictions on the tax treatment of capital that did not exist in 1977. These new taxation trends quickly became part of the Spanish public finance experts' background. Already in 1987 the new, available tax options were published in *Papeles de Economía Española.*[43] Therefore, the public finance experts began proposing new tax reforms that were considered necessary because the tax system, established in the democracy, was full of imperfections that were a result of the historic circumstances in which it had developed. Hence, at the end of the 1980s, Spanish public finance experts began criticising the standing tax system basing their criticisms as much on the new international tax trends as on the deficient practical results of the tax reform of the transition to democracy. It could not be denied that the most obvious defects of traditional taxation inherited from the Franco's regime had been corrected, but it was also evident that some of the old problems persisted and new ones had also appeared. The evaluation that public finance experts made of the reform of the democracy can be summarised in the following points.

The Criticism of the Tax System and the New Reform Proposals

First, taxation in Franco's Spain was chaotic and outdated. The taxation picture was simplified by the new democratic regime and tax harmonisation with the European Economic Community (EEC) was also reached by introducing modern tax principles such as the personality and progressivity of direct taxation and the neutrality of indirect taxation. Nevertheless, in practice, the delays and imperfections of the reform had penalised direct taxation excessively. Taxes on families (personal income tax and wealth tax) and on businesses (corporate tax and Social Insurance contributions) increased their share in the Central government's receipts. In contrast, consumption taxes had grown less than the balanced taxation system foreseen by the reformers in 1977. Besides, taxes on capital income had stayed in the small percentage points on the tax receipts prior to the reform. The latter was the objective sought after by the legislators to link up with European tendencies foreseeing free movement of capital within the EEC. As we have seen, the three main direct taxes introduced by the reform that had started in 1977 were: Personal Income Tax, Corporate Tax and Temporary Wealth Tax that despite the name had become a permanent tax. Personal Income Tax had changed the panorama of tax collection, substituting the old tax schedules (non–personal taxes) that had been introduced in times so far back as 1845 and 1900. After being established, the revenue that Personal Income Tax supplied had grown during the first two years but the collection of Personal Income tax slowed down during the tax counter–reform of 1980–1982. It delayed the technical corrections that public finance experts were demanding until 1983.

The experts had been reporting the notorious flaws of the initial 1978 tax legislation and demanded the modernisation of the tax administration to reduce tax avoidance and to detect the wide tax bases hidden from the Ministry of Finance. As Table 2.4 shows, until 1979 no authentic personal income tax existed.[44] That year the collection of Personal Income Tax jumped to 18.8 percent of the Central government's revenue and in 1980 it was already over 32.0 percent, but later its relative growth came to a standstill. In 1985 it was 30.1 percent and logically after setting up Value Added Tax the share of Personal Income Tax revenues in total central fiscal revenue decreased to 23.7 percent in 1986. Afterwards, income tax receipts recovered to a ceiling of 32.5 percent in 1994. The comparative receipts brought in by Corporate Tax after the tax reform (Table 2.4) stayed around 8 percent to 10 percent of the Central government's fiscal revenue.[45] The figures show that the tax reform of the political transition to democracy alleviated the tax burden on companies and overloaded the families.[46] The reform of the democracy rested indirect taxation mostly on the VAT—which offered collection capacity advantages and economic neutrality. The VAT receipts represented around the 20 percent of State fiscal revenues from its inception in 1986 (Table 2.3). Nevertheless, together with this essential indirect tax of the new system, the tax reformers maintained the traditional excise taxes (on oil and its derivatives, alcohols, beer, wine and tobacco). In fact, some of them only replaced the old fiscal monopolies that were incompatible with European Community membership. These excise duties continued to provide a remarkable 10 percent of public revenues

(Table 2.3). The indirect taxation harmonisation with EEC also implied raising the rates of these excise taxes which previously were lower in Spain than in the rest of Europe. Consequently, around 1990, the Spanish tax structure was much closer to Europe's: direct tax on personal income and corporate profits collected 29.6 percent, social insurance contributions brought in 36.2 percent and VAT and the excise duties brought in 29.3 percent. Therefore, 95.1 percent of the public revenue at the beginning of the 1990s was based on these three basic pillars, achieving the tax simplification objective pursued all along by the democratic tax reform.

Secondly, tax management had been perfected but moderately and insufficiently. That is why, although there was less tax fraud compared to times of Franco's regime, there were still some professional and economic sectors where widespread fraud persisted. This is where the principal problem in implementing the reform was located given the permissiveness of the UCD governments in the fight against tax fraud. In 1980 there was a big improvement in the number of taxpayers who met their obligations and filed their Personal Income Tax returns. Over the following two years the number of new taxpayers barely grew and the differences between earned income and declared income hardly improved. After 1983, especially in 1985 and 1986, the fight against tax fraud intensified,[47] and noticeably improved the levels of compliance. The tax administration's efforts to control the so called 'other earnings' with the help of VAT were noticeable. The Commission for Tax Fraud Evaluation's estimates revealed widespread tax evasion in almost all taxes. In 1985 the percentage of incomes declared to the Ministry of Finance with respect to the incomes that should have been declared in Personal Income Tax, estimated from macroeconomic variables, was 44.9 percent. Half of the Spanish people's income did not pay this tax. On the other hand, in 1986, 27 percent of the workers did not contribute to the *Seguridad Social.*[48] Finally, in VAT, fraud was around 28 percent of the collection in 1986 but if we exclude imports that were very controlled by Customs, the level of fraud raised to 39 percent.[49] This widespread fraud reduced the theoretical advantages of the tax system of the democratic regime regarding equity. In principle, the larger revenue yield from the Personal Income and Wealth taxes after 1977 revealed a fairer distribution of the tax burden in relation to the one that was in effect during Franco's regime. In fact, widespread tax fraud was still the main problem of Spanish taxation at the end of 1980s. Because it was applied on the taxpayers unfairly due to the asymmetry of tax fraud, the high tax rates worsened the distortions and the defects of the existing taxation.[50]

Nevertheless, despite the high index of fraud in some sectors, social acceptance of the income tax had improved with democracy in Spain. The radical reform of the Personal Income tax in 1978 implied a change in the levels of tax compliance and in the number of tax returns filed to the Ministry of Finance. But with time, at the end of the 1980s some tax resistance reappeared demanding a lesser tax burden, especially because the citizens thought they were getting fewer public services than the sacrifices they made by paying taxes. They also appear to have thought that the State Administration squandered the public resources it had.[51]

Thirdly, the criticisms of the tax system that was implemented since 1977 were general a decade later. Public finance experts argued that the system had not met the basic principles of the tax reform package because: (a) it was not revenue sufficient in any year, (b) it was not equitable, neither horizontally nor vertically, (c) it was not easy for the taxpayer to fulfil his/her obligations or for the Administration to collect, and (d) it was not neutral with respect to economic activity because it had distorted the allocation of resources. The critics emphasised that the increased tax burden had not even worked to achieve sufficiency, given the larger growth of public expenses. The rapid growth of tax receipts was as much due to the tax reform as it was to mere growth of the nominal incomes of taxpayers, as I remarked above, the Personal Income Tax rates had not been corrected for inflation. The insufficiency obliged the Ministry of Finance to resort to borrowing from the central bank, the Bank of Spain, setting up the inflationary tax through 'seignorage'. It was estimated that the public revenue from seignorage grew between 1980 and 1990 to reach a yield of nearly 1.7 percent of the Gross Domestic Product (GDP).[52] As we have already seen, the distribution of the tax burden by rent groups and by economic sectors was considerably unfair given the generalised tax fraud. On the other hand the excessive complexity of the Personal Income Tax provoked rejection of the tax by the taxpayers, continued pressure by the taxpayers to obtain more tax abatements and special tax treatments, and high compliance costs for taxpayers and for the Tax Administration.[53] Likewise, the odd creeping up of the effective marginal rates and the proliferation of allowances did not allow an adjusted system of Personal Income Tax withholding to appear, which made it difficult to spread this tax.[54] Finally, the disincentives that high marginal rates of Personal Income Tax usually produce on the supply of the factors of production and the consequences of the excessive proliferation of deductions on the efficiency of the economy also made their presence felt. At the beginning of the 1990s the high IRPF rates and the complexity of its rate schedule hindered the achievement of the goals of simplicity and efficiency. Likewise, public finance experts already foresaw that the internationalisation of taxation would end up making Spain adjust its tax treatment of savings to that of the EEC countries to prevent savings from leaving the country.[55]

In fourth place, there were other critical considerations of the tax system that needed to be addressed. In the case of the corporate income tax, one criticism was, at the beginning of the 1990s, that burdens were higher (by 40 percent) than those in effect in the EEC with values near 12 percent. This was explained by the higher weight of employers' social security contributions in Spain. It was also argued that the corporate income tax and the personal income tax should be better integrated to avoid the double taxation of dividends. Some public finance experts recommended that social insurance contributions should be replaced by indirect taxes (a VAT increase) because of its favourable effect on foreign trade.

An interesting proposal that dates back to 1987 was the flat tax, characterised by a single tax rate and no deductions or exemptions except for minimum level of personal income to provide the tax with the desired degree of progressivity. It was argued that the flat tax promised to improve simplicity, efficiency and equity—three objectives sought after by taxation versus the problems really raised by Personal Income Tax in effect in Spain: too many tax rate brackets and too many allowances.[56] As always happens with the most radical tax proposals, the political parties only defended the flat tax while they were in the opposition.

The Socialist Governments' Amendments to the Tax Reform

All this criticism of the tax system established as of 1978 led to some guidelines to correct the reform, some of them implemented by the Socialist governments themselves. At the end of the 1980s there were two tax changes that were imposed on the Ministry of Finance: (1) the February 20th 1989 ruling of the Constitutional Court forced a reform of Personal Income Tax and Wealth Tax and Legacy Duty; (2) the European Market forced tax harmonisation, essentially in taxation of capital yields to prevent it from flying to other countries.

As a matter of fact, one of the first proposed amendments referred to the concept of the taxpayer. The 1978 reform had identified family as a taxable unit but the Constitutional Court declared the obligatory joint tax returns unconstitutional in February 1989. A transitory regime was established for the years 1988 and 1989 and extended to 1990 in order to adapt the tax to this court ruling. This allowed the taxpayers to choose among separate and joint returns depending on which of the two was most beneficial. It also established that investment yields could be divided between the spouses while salaries could not. Later Laws 18 and 19/1991 definitively adapted the personal income tax and wealth tax to ruling 45/1989 of the Constitutional Court on taxation of the family unit.

In mid 1989 the authorities of the Ministry of Economy and Finance were very clear on the taxation objectives but they could not always put their intentions into practise. The Ministry publicly undertook a campaign to spread the need for the reform of the personal income tax. The proposed guidelines were as follows: (1) reduce the direct tax burden and increase the indirect tax burden (VAT), (2) obey the Constitutional Court ruling to not discriminate against families but to maintain progressive formulas, (3) promote family savings but not only by reducing direct taxes, (4) discourage home buying, (5) make dirty money surface but without offering a tax amnesty; (6) reduce public spending and the budget deficit while continuing to invest in infrastructure, (7) reform the presumptive assessment of VAT for shop owners and independent professionals to reduce fraud, and (8) progressively reduce the withholdings on investment yields to take Spanish regulations closer to those of the EEC.[57]

On the other hand, in 1990, the Ministry of Finance considered that, although the Spanish public sector was inferior in size to those of the other European countries, they had to stop its growth in the future for the following reasons: (1) the inconvenience of increasing individual tax burden, which would reduce private savings—already quite deteriorated, and (2) macroeconomic stabilisation objectives did not allow the public spending to GDP ratio to increase further. The objective here was to eliminate the public deficit in 1992 by increasing revenue, intensifying the fight against fraud and perfecting tax management without increasing the tax burden of those who honestly met their obligations to the Ministry of Finance.[58] The increase in budget revenue would have to come from increasing the assessment bases, from economic growth and from the fight against tax fraud.

The Royal Decree Law of December 29, 1989 on urgent measures in Budget matters (replaced in its entirety by Law 29 of June 1990) contained the core of the measures on taxation for 1990, intended to annually adjust the taxes to the new economic and social reality. The 1990 Budget asked the authorities in charge of tax policy to prepare a tax reform under the following guidelines: approximation to the tax systems of the EEC countries, search for indirect tax harmonisation, increase the VAT and Special tax rates and reduce the tax burden from the Personal Income tax.[59]

THE REST OF THE JOURNEY: THE 'POPULAR' GOVERNMENT'S NEW TAXATION CONCEPT

The delay in introducing the tax reforms implied, yet again, that the Spanish tax system of the democratic regime went in the wrong direction when compared to the new trends in more economically advanced countries.[60] The question that should be introduced is whether, in the field of tax reforms, it is possible for a country to skip stages. The Spanish case demonstrates that it is only possible to make rapid progress through them. The tax reforms of the UCD and PSOE governments were inevitable because they imitated a tax model that was already consolidated in Europe and that was also really the only one available in 1977 when the reform was carried out in Spain. The governments of the transition could not run any risks with tax experiments. The establishment of democracy in Spain could not avoid the fulfilment of the demonstration effect that the Welfare State developed in Europe between 1942 and 1980 had on Spain during the dictatorship and the transition. What they could not have done was to try to skip stages by adopting some of the proposals of the new taxation models before consolidating the one established as of 1977. Criticisms from the right wing politicians and businessmen came before the taxation system of the democracy was consolidated. The Welfare State had still not been developed in Spain, and they were already criticising the 'excessive' tax burden imposed by the public sector.

The criticisms of the tax system of the democracy from academia came at the end of the 1980s after the new tax model had been spread throughout most OECD countries and when the problems of the taxation system established in Spain were very evident, given the new international experiences. The Socialist governments themselves raised some of the corrections and proposed innovation at the end of the 1980s. Consequently, the golden age of the Welfare State, that had lasted four decades in Europe, lasted only one decade in Spain. In 1995 the contrast between the tax system of the OECD member countries and the Spanish one were very marked. Spain continued to be anchored in the model that had been established in Europe in the post–war period: high marginal rates, tax schedules with many income brackets, narrow tax bases, high Personal Income Tax share and low VAT share in the structure of public revenues, and high importance of social insurance contributions. In the mid 1990s the tax burden supported by the majority of the taxpayers who did not commit fraud could already be termed overwhelming. The political reaction of right wing parties was to offer voters tax reductions and this was very likely one of the reasons for the victory of the *Partido Popular* (PP) in the 1996 elections.

Therefore, some of the new proposals of the public finance experts were introduced only after 1996, by the Popular Party government led by José María Aznar, with Rodrigo Rato and Cristóbal Montoro in the Ministry of Finance. The PP's arrival to government in Spain almost coincided with the Stability and Growth Pact, outlined in the European Summit in Dublin in

December 1996 although it wasn't formalised until June of 1999. The budget orthodoxy followed by the Spanish government allowed a noticeable reduction of the budget deficit and of the outstanding public debt. The restrictions on fiscal policy imposed by the Stability Pact were reinforced by the economic globalisation that demanded the search for efficiency in the Spanish economy. All of this, within the tax reform framework, meant accepting the principle of efficiency in the allocation of resources as the fundamental one, since the PP government had assumed the limitations of very formal progressive taxes as a means of income redistribution. Therefore, the gradual tax reform was imposed in 1996 with the objective of reducing the tax rates to foster economic growth and employment, to stimulate savings, to strengthen small and medium sized firms and to help internationalise Spanish corporations. The main measures implemented by the first PP government were: (a) in 1996 capital gains tax rates were reduced,[61] (b) in 1998 a new tax regime for small and medium sized companies was passed, and (c) in the same year the Taxpayer's Statute *(Estatuto del Contribuyente,* Law 1/1988) was passed. Once the Maastricht objectives were met and Spain joined the European Monetary Union, the PP government went on to reform Personal Income Tax via Law 40/1988 to incorporate new international trends in the Personal Income Tax including the following: tax burden reduction especially on low incomes and salaries, decrease in marginal tax rates to avoid its negative consequences on savings, labour supply and investment, encouragement of long term savings, tax protection for families and simplification in the tax return forms for many taxpayers. The reduction of the tax burden in Personal Income Tax (10 percent of disposable personal income) allowed an increase in tax receipts (4 percent) in 1999 versus 1998. It also had the expected improvements in the distribution of tax burdens and the reductions in taxpayer compliance costs.

The next reform of the Personal Income Tax in Law 6/2000 tried again to promote the internationalisation of Spanish companies, to facilitate the adoption of new technologies strengthening of small and medium size enterprises, to protect the family unit and the most disfavoured social classes, and to encourage long–term savings. The 2002 *Ley de Acompañamiento a los Presupuestos Generales del Estado* (the Law accompanying the State's General Budget) introduced a new tax reform in the direction indicated by the Commission for Personal Income Tax Reform created in January 2002, chaired by Manuel Lagares. The objectives of the reform this time were to improve the tax treatment of the families and the disabled, reduce taxation on the lowest salaried incomes, improve the stability and mobility of employment, stimulate the supply of rental homes, improve neutrality in savings products and favour retirement savings, reduce tax rates (with a maximum rate of 45 percent) and the number of brackets (to five), safeguard the principles of progressivity and sufficiency, and rearrange the taxation of professionals. The PP Government reformed the corporate tax.[62]

The results of the Popular Party's tax reforms can be evaluated on the basis of collection figures. The general Government's tax burden peaked in 1992 at 40.5 percent. It stagnated the following year, falling to 37.0 percent in 1995. As of 1996, the general tax burden recovered and reached 38.6 percent in 2000. For its own part, the central government's tax burden grew from 22.7 percent to 26 percent from 1995 to 2000 (Table 2.1). From 1995 to 2001, the share of the central Government's direct taxes fell from 41.1 percent to 34.4 percent, while indirect taxes only decreased from 33.5 percent to 32.9 percent over this time. As such, during the Popular Party Administrations, revenues generated by direct and indirect taxes were about the same (Table 2.2). The collection of income tax reached its peak with respect to total public revenues at 32.5 percent in 1994. In 1996, this percentage was at 30.1 percent, but in 2001, income tax accounted for only 22.6 percent of the central government's total tax revenues. To the contrary, the corporate tax increased from 7.3 percent to 11.1 percent from 1994 to 2001 (Table 2.4). Excise taxes were 11.1 percent in 1996, and declined to 10.1 percent in 2001, while value–added tax increased from 20 percent to 21.6 percent over this time. Consequently, the most remarkable feature of this period was the decrease of the relative collection of income tax and the increase of receipts generated by other indirect taxes, which still allowed for an increase of the tax burdens.

CONCLUSIONS

The Spanish case clearly shows the relevance of political factors in the evolution of its tax systems. The Franco Dictatorship posed an insurmountable obstacle to tax modernisation in Spain. That created a lag in the establishment of modern taxation emerging across Europe after the Second World War. Despite sharp economic growth from 1960 to 1973 and the projects presented by the Treasury and the Ministerio de Planes de Desarrollo (Ministry for Economic Plans), Spain could not approach the European taxation norm, which included two basic taxes: progressive personal income tax and value–added tax. When the tax reform of 1977 was undertaken after the democratic elections, the taxation principles established in 1845 by the liberal State were still in effect in Spain.

In Spain, one had to wait for democracy to create a series of economic reforms. Most noteworthy among these changes were the modernisation of the public sector via tax reform and increased spending by the welfare state, and the liberalisation of markets (foreign, financial and labour). The end of the Franco regime also allowed Spain to enter the European Economic Community. That entailed the introduction of value–added tax, completing the tax reform that brought the Spanish tax system closer to the European model. The taxation principles adopted by Spain between 1977 and 1986 were similar to those adopted by Europe after the Second World War. By 1986, the main taxes in effect in Europe had been established in Spain.

However, some of the European taxes that Spain copied were being reformed in Europe. Furthermore, the legal definition of the Spanish taxes and their administration presented problems that needed attention at the end of the 1980s. That required the creation of new tax reforms that updated the taxes introduced between 1977 and 1986. Although these new reforms were important, they did not include new taxes or changes in the taxation criteria. Instead, all that was changed were the technical characteristics of the taxes established during the transition to democracy.

As had occurred in the reform of 1845, which established the taxation of the liberal State, the reform begun in 1977 entailed such a radical change in the taxation principles that it required political consensus for its approval. The magnitude of the changes and the need to cater to conflicting social interests in order to achieve the consensus resulted in a reform with flaws which later had to be corrected. Moreover, once the consensus was finalised and the reform went through, the subsequent governments first paralysed and afterwards accelerated the implementation and generalisation of the new taxes and even changed some technical points.

As such, tax reform in Spain did not take place overnight, once and for all, but was rather the result of several reformatory impulses pursued by different governments. Because of this, the tax reform under the democracy needed more time to be established and consolidated, and to adapt gradually to the permanent international advances in taxation. Sure enough, a decade after the reform of 1977 started, new international trends in the composition of direct taxes were spreading, both within the framework of globalisation and out of the necessary improvement in the productivity of national economies. Additionally, the reforms of the taxes established as of 1977 also required adjustments in the different taxes due to the changes of government. However, these tax modifications were not so extensive, given the restrictions imposed by Spain's membership in the European Union and the growing international movement of capital.

Table 2.1 Public revenue/PIB (1959–2000)

	Central Government	General Government
1959	10.6	15.6
1960	11.3	16.7
1961	11.2	16.8
1962	11.6	17.0
1963	11.1	16.2
1964	11.6	16.8
1965	12.0	16.8
1966	11.8	16.8
1967	12.1	20.7
1968	11.9	20.3
1969	12.1	20.9
1970	12.3	21.4
1971	12.2	21.5
1972	12.2	22.5
1973	12.1	23.1
1974	11.4	22.2
1975	11.6	23.5
1976	11.4	23.2
1977	11.4	25.5
1978	12.0	26.1
1979	12.2	29.5
1980	13.5	30.8
1981	14.3	32.0
1982	14.2	32.1
1983	15.8	34.1
1984	17.8	33.8
1985	17.6	35.2
1986	20.8	35.7
1987	22.2	37.2
1988	21.4	36.9
1989	26.7	38.5
1990	24.1	38.5

Table 2.1 Public revenue/PIB (1959–2000) (continued)

	Central Government	General Government
1991	24.8	39.1
1992	27.1	40.5
1993	24.9	40.5
1994	23.2	39.2
1995	22.7	37.0
1996	24.1	37.4
1997	34.7	37.7
1998	31.7	37.8
1999	25.8	38.4
2000	26.0	38.6

Source: Comín and Díaz (2004) and Prados de la Excosura (2003).

Table 2.2 Percentage of central government's revenue (1959–2001)

	Direct Taxation	Indirect Taxation
1959	33.3	53.2
1960	32.1	57.1
1961	31.0	60.7
1962	29.2	59.3
1963	28.0	59.8
1964	25.6	60.3
1965	25.0	60.6
1966	26.6	58.4
1967	26.7	56.5
1968	26.0	55.0
1969	27.0	57.7
1970	27.1	57.5
1971	28.9	54.1
1972	29.4	54.9
1973	30.6	56.9
1974	33.6	50.8
1975	36.2	48.1

Table 2.2 Percentage of central government's revenue (1959–2001) (continued)

	Direct Taxation	Indirect Taxation
1976	38.9	48.1
1977	40.4	46.1
1978	44.1	41.9
1979	44.8	40.0
1980	46.0	38.8
1981	12.3	39.6
1982	43.5	37.3
1983	41.9	38.4
1984	39.8	36.6
1985	40.2	37.8
1986	33.0	42.0
1987	39.7	39.9
1988	41.5	40.8
1989	38.7	31.4
1990	41.7	33.1
1991	40.4	30.9
1992	38.2	30.1
1993	39.4	30.0
1994	40.5	33.7
1995	41.1	33.5
1996	38.7	31.8
1997	28.3	22.5
1998	27.8	25.6
1999	32.6	33.4
2000	33.7	33.1
2001	34.4	32.9

Source: Comín and Díaz (2004).

Table 2.3 Indirect taxation percentage of central government's revenue (1959–2001)

	Customs Duties	Turnover Tax	Excise Tax	VAT	Monopolies
1959	4.8	–	17.4	–	10.2
1960	9.6	–	17.9	–	8.9
1961	14.6	–	16.1	–	10.1
1962	16.1	–	14.3	–	9.9
1963	16.9	–	13.8	–	9.2
1964	17.9	7.6	11.9	–	9.3
1965	18.8	9.9	7.6	–	8.5
1966	21.4	11.2	6.6	–	9.4
1967	18.1	11.7	6.8	–	10.3
1968	16.4	12.0	7.1	–	10.3
1969	17.1	12.7	7.1	–	11.0
1970	16.7	13.5	7.3	–	10.2
1971	15.0	13.6	7.4	–	8.6
1972	17.1	13.5	6.9	–	8.6
1973	17.9	13.9	6.3	–	9.2
1974	17.6	15.2	5.6	–	3.8
1975	7.5	12.5	4.6	–	6.1
1976	11.4	7.6	3.8	–	7.4
1977	11.9	6.7	3.1	–	6.4
1978	8.6	6.9	2.5	–	7.0
1979	7.4	6.8	1.6	–	7.8
1980	7.8	5.8	10.0	–	3.7
1981	7.3	7.8	11.8	–	3.7
1982	8.2	9.1	8.6	–	3.2
1983	7.7	9.7	8.4	–	5.7
1984	6.5	12.4	9.4	–	3.1
1985	7.3	12.4	9.0	–	4.6
1986	3.3	3.1	7.5	20.8	6.9
1987	4.3	0.8	8.8	22.6	3.2
1988	4.4	0.6	8.9	23.8	3.6
1989	3.1	0.4	6.9	19.4	2.2

Table 2.3 Indirect taxation percentage of central government's revenue (1959–2001) (continued)

	Customs Duties	Turnover Tax	Excise Tax	VAT	Monopolies
1990	2.7	0.3	8.0	20.5	2.2
1991	2.1	0.2	8.9	19.7	1.4
1992	1.3	0.2	8.7	19.6	1.3
1993	0.6	0.1	10.1	18.8	1.3
1994	0.6	–	11.5	21.2	1.4
1995	0.7	–	11.3	20.9	1.3
1996	0.5	–	11.1	20.0	1.3
1997	0.4	–	7.4	14.5	0.8
1998	0.5	–	8.6	16.1	1.0
1999	0.6	–	10.6	21.7	1.3
2000	0.6	–	10.2	21.7	1.1
2001	0.6	–	10.1	21.6	1.1

Source: Comín and Díaz (2004).

Table 2.4 Direct taxation percentage of central government's revenue (1959–2001)

	Wages Tax	Income Tax	Corporate Tax	Capital Yields Tax
1959	7.2	1.6	11.7	3.5
1960	7.7	1.6	10.7	3.6
1961	7.3	1.4	10.2	3.5
1962	6.9	1.4	9.6	3.3
1963	6.8	1.4	8.7	2.9
1964	6.3	1.4	7.6	2.7
1965	5.5	1.3	7.7	3.1
1966	6.8	1.2	8.2	2.7
1967	6.8	1.2	8.1	2.7
1968	6.2	1.3	7.7	2.8
1969	6.5	1.3	8.6	2.8
1970	7.2	1.1	8.3	2.9

Table 2.4 Direct taxation percentage of central government's revenue (1959–2001) (continued)

	Wages Tax	Income Tax	Corporate Tax	Capital Yields Tax
1971	8.3	1.4	8.6	3.2
1972	8.9	1.3	8.6	3.1
1973	10.6	1.4	8.8	3.2
1974	12.4	1.1	9.2	2.9
1975	13.8	1.0	11.5	3.9
1976	15.6	1.1	12.0	6.0
1977	18.4	1.0	11.4	6.0
1978	22.7	1.5	9.7	6.1
1979	9.3	18.8	9.5	2.6
1980	0.6	32.0	9.0	0.2
1981	–	30.5	8.0	–
1982	–	31.9	8.5	–
1983	–	30.8	8.5	–
1984	–	30.4	7.7	–
1985	–	30.1	8.5	–
1986	–	23.7	8.0	–
1987	–	28.8	9.8	–
1988	–	30.7	9.6	–
1989	–	27.3	10.7	–
1990	–	28.8	12.1	–
1991	–	29.8	10.1	–
1992	–	29.5	8.1	–
1993	–	31.0	7.7	–
1994	–	32.5	7.3	–
1995	–	32.1	8.2	–
1996	–	30.1	7.9	–
1997	–	19.6	7.8	–
1998	–	18.5	8.8	–
1999	–	21.2	10.7	–
2000	–	21.5	11.6	–
2001	–	22.6	11.1	–

Source: Comín and Díaz (2004).

NOTES

* University of Alcalá, Madrid

1. In the end, what they did in 1977 and 1978 was very similar to what the European democracies had managed to do after the Second World War. They set up a democratic system and created a consensus for the creation of a Welfare State as well as the development of fiscal, monetary and tax policies that would contribute to political, economic and social stability. The political parties tried to imitate the European model but without specifying the characteristics of the model. The generalities of this objective permitted them to reach a political consensus that would have been impossible if they had not avoided the obvious differences that existed among the various European States.
2. This was at least the opinion of Fuentes Quintana (1983 and 1990a), who would become later the chief architect of the tax reform.
3. See Comín and Vallejo (2002).
4. See Gunther (1980, pp. 64–67)
5. See Fuentes Quintana (1978 and 1990a) and Comín, Martínez, Martorell and Vallejo (2005).
6. See Fuentes Quintana (1997) and Fernández Clemente (1997).
7. Fuentes Quintana (1961) and Comín (1991).
8. See Fuentes Quintana (1964), Albiñana (1974), Albiñana and Fuentes Quintana (1966).
9. See Gunther (1980).
10. Following Fuentes Quintana (1991). See Valle (1974) and Lagares (1975).
11. See Comín and López (2002).
12. See Comín (1996a, pp. 156–162) and Comín (1996b, pp. 43–47).
13. Minister Rubio refused to switch tax collection procedures from the collective taxpayer agreements to individual filings; this practically brought collections to a halt.
14. See Fuentes Quintana (1983), Comisión para la Evaluación del Fraude (1986), Comín (1991) and Lagares (1991).
15. See Biescas (1980, pp 116–123).
16. Gunther (1980, p. 95)
17. Fuentes Quintana (1973 and 1978) and Comín (1996b).
18. The excise tax came out of Larraz's reform and had brought between 18 percent and 28 percent of the ordinary income of the State between 1941 and 1960; during the autarchy (1939–1959) foreign trade was subject to contingent regime which reduced customs receipts to 4 percent to 6 percent.
19. As Fuentes Quintana (1964) already pointed out the same year.
20. See the references to the Latin tax system in Fuentes Quintana (1991) and Comín (1996a, pp. 205–224).
21. See the excellent description of the entire process that led to the creation of the tax reform programme in Lagares (2002, pp. 586–600).
22. In the reports prepared by the team led by Enrique Fuentes Quintana (1973 and 1976), a reform plan was presented that implied getting rid of taxes in effect in Spain from the 1845 reform and highlighted the previous requirements needed to establish the tax reforms in Spain. These reports were the basis of the reform that was started in 1977. Enrique Fuentes Quintana—who had studied the work of Ramón Santillán and Antonio Flores de Lemus—played a key role in the tax reform that started in 1977, similar to the one public finance experts carried out in the 1845 reform and the one that was programmed between 1910 and 1932.

23. The members of this commission were the 'subsecretarios' (deputy secretaries) of the economic ministries. The commission met before the weekly Cabinet meeting presided over by Franco himself in order to discuss and prepare the issues and bills to be approved by the Government.
24. The mere existence of the 'green paper' supposed such a threat to the Franco regime that the government made the document secret. For these matters see Valiño (1989) and Pan–Montojo (1996, pp. 267–299) and Lagares' evidence (2002, pp. 586–600). See also Fuentes Quintana (2004).
25. See Pan–Montojo (1996 pp. 266–275). In 1977, Spain and Portugal were the only Western countries that still did not have a real personal income tax. See Comín (1991) and Fuentes Quintana (1991).
26. See Pan–Montojo (2002, pp. 236–240), Bermejo and García Durán (1994), and Trullén (1993, pp. 60–63). For the political events see Juliá (1991 and 1995) and Tusell (2003).
27. As explained by Lagares (2002).
28. See Lagares (2002, pp. 586–600). For the evolution of expenses see Pan–Montojo (2002, pp. 230–235).
29. According to Fuentes Quintana (1993).
30. They are the Institute for Fiscal Studies reports prepared under Enrique Fuentes Quintana (1973 and 1976b) and entitled 'Report on the Spanish Taxation System', presented in 1973 and 'Spanish Taxation System. Criteria for their reform' completed in 1976.
31. See Trullén (1993) and Valiño (1989).
32. See Pan–Montojo (1996) and Cabrera and del Rey (2002, pp. 339–349).
33. Lagares (2002 and 2004).
34. Nevertheless an important step was taken with Law 40/1977 on September 7th which created the *Cuerpo Especial de Inspectores Financieros y Tributarios* (Special Corps for Financial and Tax Inspectors) that unified the old tax inspection corps.
35. See Fuentes Quintana (1991).
36. See Pan–Montojo (1996 and 2002).
37. See Fuentes Quintana (1990a) and Comín (1990).
38. There was a precedent in Spain for this in the 1845 tax reforms. See Comín and Vallejo (2002).
39. See Pan–Montojo (1996, pp. 275–296).
40. According to Fuentes Quintana (1991).
41. See Albi and García (2001, pp. 61–64).
42. See Gago et al. (2002, pp. 257–265) and Albi (2004).
43. See the articles of numbers 30–31 of *Papeles de Economía Española,* 1987.
44. Complementary income tax (surtax) was created in 1932 and in 1964 it became General Income Tax but direct taxation was still focused on prepayment of traditional tax schedules, because General Income Tax still was a schedular tax. Although the 1964 reform expanded the name of the income tax by substituting the adjective 'general' for 'complementary', it reduced its receipts from 1.5 percent to 1.2 percent of the Central government's revenue.
45. Corporate Tax appeared in 1920 with tariff III of *Contribución sobre las utilidades de la riqueza mobiliaria* (the taxation of the utilities of movable wealth was a tax on salaries, capital yields and corporate profits created in 1900) and it became an independent tax in 1957 during Navarro Rubio's first tax reform.
46. See Albi (1987 and 1994) for the taxation on companies that was not heavy because of Corporate Tax but rather because of the employers' contribution to social insurance. See González–Páramo (1990c).

47. The Public Administration's capacity to enforce taxes and impose sanctions improved as of 1983 and from 1986 onwards because they had the help of VAT as an element of control for the Personal Income Tax, especially the incomes of professional and small businesses. Sanctions on tax fraud also increased in 1986.
48. Comisión para la Evaluación del Fraude (Commission for Tax Fraud Evaluation) (1986), Instituto de Estudios Fiscales (1989), Lagares (1991), Díaz and Romero (1994), Fuentes Quintana (1990a) and Zubiri (1991).
49. Statements of the Secretary of State for Public Finance in the *Cortes*, *El Independiente*, October 4, 1990; *El País* October 4, 1990.
50. Fuentes Quintana (1990, pp. 264–265 and 558–577).
51. Alvira and García López (1981 and 1987). The levels of coverage of public services appear to have been quite insufficient at the end of the 1980s. See Lagares (1988).
52. See Repullo (1991 and 1986).
53. The information available for the mid 1980s shows, on the one hand, that almost two thirds of the taxpayers needed external help to complete their income tax returns. On the other hand, the high number of taxpayers' appeals against the collection of Personal Income Tax indicated that the Tax Administration also had problems managing it. Inflation, the accumulation of income in married couples and irregular incomes, all circumstances that were present in Spain as of 1979 complicated even more the enforcement of the Personal Income Tax (Fuentes Quintana, 1990b).
54. In 1985 half of the people filing tax returns asked for a return and the differential quotas that are withheld when the tax is paid were around 12 percent of the collection.
55. Fuentes Quintana (1990a, pp. 569–573).
56. See Enrique Fuentes Quintana (1991), González-Páramo (1987, 1990a and 1990b), Albi, Rodríguez and Rubio (1987), Albi, Rodríguez and Rubio (1993) and Valle (1989).
57. The withholdings on capital yields were progressively reduced to 25 percent (in 1990) until it reached 10 percent in 1993; see the Statement of Mr. Borrell, Secretary of State for Public Finance, *El País.* May 20, 1990.
58. See Ministry of Finance (Ministerio de Hacienda,1990a and 1990b).
59. Ministry of Finance (1990 a, pp. 37–41). See Borrell (1986 and 1990) and Boyer (2004).
60. See Comín (1996b).
61. Nevertheless, with the system implemented in 1991, capital gains could be fully exempted. From 1996 on, every capital gain pays taxes whereas before 1996 this could not be the case.
62. See Rubio (2002, pp. 300–307), Lagares (2004), Lagares and Castellano (2004), Castañer, Romero and Sanz (2003), Sanz, Castañer and Romero (2004), González-Páramo and Sanz (2003a and 2003b), Onrubia and Sanz (2003) and Albi (2001).

REFERENCES

Albi, E. (1987), 'La empresa española ante la Hacienda Pública', *Economistas*, 26, 19–24.

Albi, E. (1987), 'Propuestas tributarias actuales: la experiencia internacional', *Papeles de Economía Española*, 30–31, 37–53.

Albi, E. (1990), 'La reforma fiscal', in E. Albi (dir.), pp. 27–54.

Albi, E. (dir.) (1990), La Hacienda Pública en la Democracia, Estudios en homenaje al profesor Enrique Fuentes Quintana, Barcelona: Ariel.

Albi, E. (1991), 'Elusión y evasión fiscales: la investigación económica', *Hacienda Pública Española*, 115, 251–263.

Albi, E. (1994), 'Hacienda Pública Internacional: un panorama', *Hacienda Pública Española*, 2, 253–266.

Albi, E. (1994), *Fiscalidad y Empresa Familiar*, Barcelona: Planeta Agostini.

Albi, E. (2001), 'Líneas de reforma en el Impuesto sobre Sociedades', *Hacienda Pública Española*, Special Issue.

Albi, E. (2004), *Sistema Fiscal Español*, Barcelona: Ariel.

Albi, E., and J. L. García (1987), *Sistema Fiscal Español*, Barcelona: Ariel.

Albi, E., J. A. Rodríguez, and J. J. Rubio (1987), *Nuevas Reformas Fiscales: una experiencia para España*, Madrid: Instituto de Estudios Económicos.

Albi, E., J. A. Rodríguez, and J. J. Rubio (1993), *Fiscalidad y PYME*, Madrid: IMPI, Ministerio de Industria.

Albiñana, C. (1974), 'Apariencia y realidad del sistema tributario español', *Revista de Economía Política*, 66, 7–46.

Albiñana, C., and E. Fuentes Quintana (1966), *Sistema fiscal español y comparado*, Madrid: Facultad de Ciencias Económicas.

Alvira, F., and J. García López (1981), 'Los españoles después de la reforma fiscal', *Hacienda Pública Española*, 72.

Alvira, F., and J. García López (1987), 'Los españoles y la fiscalidad; la pérdida de la ilusión financiera', *Papeles de Economía Española*, 30–31, 90–105.

Bermejo, N., and J. García Durán (1994), 'Spain: Dual Transition Implemented by Two Parties', in S. Haggard and S. B. Webb, *Voting for Reform. Democracy, Political Liberalization and Economic Adjustment*, Oxford: Oxford University Press/World Bank, pp. 89–127.

Biescas, J. A. (1980), 'Estructura y coyunturas económicas', in Manuel Tuñón de Lara (dir.), *España bajo la dictadura franquista (1936–1975), Historia de España*, vol. X, Barcelona: Labor, pp. 13–164.

Borrell, J. (1986), 'Dos leyes para un sistema fiscal más eficiente y justo', *Hacienda Pública Española*, 99, 15–24.

Borrell, J. (1990), 'De la Constitución a Europa: una década de política fiscal', *Información Comercial Española*, 9–37.

Boyer, M. (2004), 'El segundo ajuste económico de la democracia española (1982–1985)', in E. Fuentes Quintana (dir.), *Economía y Economistas Españoles, 8, La economía como profesión*, Barcelona: Galaxia Gutenberg y Círculo de Lectores, pp. 239–303.

Cabrera, M., and F. del Rey (2002), El poder de los empresarios. Política y Economía en la España contemporánea, Madrid: Taurus.

Castañer, J.M., D. Romero, and J. F. Sanz (2003), 'La nueva reforma del IRPF: valoración de sus efectos recaudatorios y distributivos', *Economistas*, 96, 196–203.

Círculo de Empresarios (1979), Aspectos fundamentales de los trabajos del Círculo en 1978, Madrid.

Comín, F. (1988), *Hacienda y Economía en la España contemporánea*, Madrid: Instituto de Estudios Fiscales.

Comín, F. (1990), 'Presentación', in E. Fuentes Quintana, *Las reformas tributarias en España. Teoría, historia y propuestas*, Barcelona: Crítica, pp. VII–XXXIX.

Comín, F. (1991), 'Raíces históricas del fraude fiscal en España', *Hacienda Pública Española*, 1, 191–206.

Comín, F. (1993), 'Reforma tributaria y política fiscal', in J. L. García Delgado (dir.) (1993), *España. Economía*, Madrid: Espasa Calpe, pp. 1073–1121.

Comín, F. (1994), 'El fraude fiscal en la Historia: un planteamiento de sus fases', *Hacienda Pública Española*, 1, 31–46.

Comín, F. (1995), 'Public Finance in Spain during the 19th and 20th Centuries', in P. Martín Aceña and J. Simpson (eds.), *The Economic Development of Spain since 1870*, Aldershot: Edward Elgar, pp. 521–560.

Comín, F. (1996a), Historia de la Hacienda pública. I. Europa, Barcelona: Crítica.

Comín, F. (1996b), Historia de la Hacienda pública. II. España (1808–1995), Barcelona: Crítica.

Comín, F. (2002), 'La Hacienda Pública entre 1940–1959', *Hacienda Pública Española*, 1, 169–190.

Comín, F., and D. Díaz (2004), 'Sector Público', in A. Carreras and X. Tafunell (eds.), *Estadísticas Históricas de España. Siglos XIX y XX*, Bilbao: Fundación BBVA (forthcoming).

Comín, F., and S. López (2002), 'Las dos Haciendas Públicas y la financiación de la Guerra Civil (1936–1939)', *Hacienda Pública Española*, Monografía No. 1, 127–168.

Comín, F., E. Martínez, M. Martorell and R. Vallejo (2005), *La Hacienda Pública del Franquismo (1936–1977)*, Madrid: Instituto de Estudios Fiscales, (forthcoming).

Comín, F., and R. Vallejo (2002), *Alejandro Mon y Menéndez (1801–1882). Pensamiento y Reforma de la Hacienda*, Madrid: Instituto de Estudios Fiscales.

Comisión para la Evaluación del Fraude (1986), *Evaluación del fraude en el Impuesto sobre la Renta de las Personas Físicas (1979–1986)*, Madrid: Instituto de Estudios Fiscales Librery (C–1015. N 18241).

Confederación Española de Organizaciones Empresariales (CEOE) (1979), *Memorándum de la CEOE al Gobierno*, Madrid.

Cortezo, J., M. Azcárate, M. Boyer, F. Fernández Ordóñez, M. Sánchez Ayuso, and N. Aguado (1976), *Programas económicos de la alternativa democrática*, Barcelona: Anagrama.

Díaz, D., and D. Romero (1994), *Evolución del fraude en el Impuesto sobre el Valor Añadido, 1986–1992*, Madrid: Instituto de Estudios Fiscales, Documento de Trabajo 4/92.

Fernández Clemente, E. (1997), 'Mariano Navarro Rubio', in E. Fuentes Quintana et al., *La Hacienda en sus ministros: franquismo y democracia*, Zaragoza: Prensas Universitarias de Zaragoza, pp. 53–90.

Fuentes Quintana, E. (1961), 'Los principios del reparto de la carga tributaria en España', *Revista de Derecho Financiero y de Hacienda Pública*, 41, 161–298.

Fuentes Quintana, E. (1964), 'El impuesto sobre el volumen de ventas: perspectivas de una idea fiscal española', *Anales de Economía*, 5, 3–159.

Fuentes Quintana, E. (dir.) (1973), *Informe sobre el sistema tributario español*, Madrid.

Fuentes Quintana, E. (1976a), 'La ideología de la reforma tributaria silenciosa', *Hacienda Pública Española*, 42–43, 105–144.

Fuentes Quintana, E. (dir.) (1976b), *Sistema tributario español: Criterios para su reforma*, Madrid: Instituto de Estudios Fiscales.

Fuentes Quintana, E. (1978), 'El estilo tributario latino: Características generales y problemas para su reforma', in J. L. García Delgado and J. Segura (eds.), *Ciencia social y análisis económico. Estudios en homenaje al profesor V. Andrés Alvarez*, Madrid: Tecnos, pp. 195–279.

Fuentes Quintana, E. (1983), 'Hacienda democrática y reforma fiscal. Notas para un balance de la reciente experiencia histórica española', in G. Anes, L. A. Rojo, y P. Tedde (eds.), *Historia Económica y pensamiento Social*, Madrid: Alianza, pp. 475–521.

Fuentes Quintana, E. (1990a), Las reformas tributarias en España. Teoría, historia y propuestas, Barcelona: Crítica.

Fuentes Quintana, E. (dir.) (1990b), La reforma fiscal y los problemas de la Hacienda Pública española, Madrid: Civitas.

Fuentes Quintana, E. (1991), 'La Hacienda Pública de la democracia Española frente al proceso de integración europea', *Papeles de Economía Española*, 48, 2–34.

Fuentes Quintana, E. (1993), 'La tardía e inacabada modernización del sector público español', *Papeles de Economía Española*, 57, 194–232.

Fuentes Quintana, E. (1997), 'José Larraz', in E. Fuentes Quintana et al., *La Hacienda en sus ministros: franquismo y democracia*, Zaragoza: Prensas Universitarias de Zaragoza, pp. 1–14.

Fuentes Quintana, E. (2004), 'Los Pactos de la Moncloa y la Constitución de 1978', in E. Fuentes Quintana (dir.), *Economía y Economistas Españoles, 8, La economía como profesión*, Barcelona: Galaxia Gutenberg y Círculo de Lectores, pp. 163–197.

Fuentes Quintana et al. (1997), *La Hacienda en sus ministros: franquismo y democracia*, Zaragoza: Prensas Universitarias de Zaragoza.

Gago, A. et al. (2002), 'La política fiscal en España durante el período 1982–1996', *Hacienda Pública Española*, 1, 253–187.

González, M. J. (1979), La Economía Política del Franquismo (1940–1970). Dirigismo, mercado y planificación, Madrid: Tecnos.

González–Páramo, J. M. (1987), 'Tendencias de la fiscalidad en la OCDE y en España', *Papeles de Economía Española*, 30–31.

González–Páramo, J. M. (1990a), 'La Hacienda Pública de fin de siglo: desarrollos recientes y direcciones de estudio', *Hacienda Pública Española*, 115, 265–287.

González–Páramo, J. M. (1990b), 'Tres lustros de cambios estructurales en el sector público' , in J. L. García Delgado, *Economía española de la transición y la democracia*, Madrid: GIS, pp. 245–272.

González–Páramo, J. M. (1990c), 'La imposición empresarial en España: evolución, efectos y tendencias', in E. Albi (dir.), *La Hacienda Pública en la Democracia, Estudios en homenaje al profesor Enrique Fuentes Quintana*, Barcelona: Ariel, pp. 75–90.

González–Páramo, J. M. (1991), 'Fiscalidad personal y composición del Ahorro en España', *Papeles de Economía Española*, 48.

González–Páramo, J.M., and J. F. Sanz (2003a), '¿Quiénes se beneficiaron de la reforma de IRPF de 1999?: una evaluación desagregada de sus efectos sobre la oferta de trabajo, el bienestar y el coste marginal de los fondos públicos', Bilbao, Fundación BBVA, Documento de Trabajo 1.

González–Páramo, J.M., and J. F.Sanz (2003b). 'Beneficio marginal de la reforma de IRPF de 1999 a través de un ejercicio de microsimulación con comportamiento laboral. ¿Quién gana y quién pierde?', in J. Onrubia y J. F. Sanz (dirs.), *Redistribución y bienestar a través de la imposición sobre la renta personal*, Madrid: Instituto de Estudios Fiscales, pp. 91–130.

Gunther, R. (1980), Public Policy in a No–Party State. Spanish Planning and Budgeting in the Twilight of the Franquist Era, Berkeley: University of California Press.

Instituto de Estudios Fiscales (1989), *Informe sobre el fraude fiscal*, Madrid.
Juliá, S. (1991), 'Sociedad y Política', in M. Tuñón de Lara (dir.), *Transición y Democracia (1973–1985)*, Barcelona: Labor, pp. 26–186.
Juliá, S. (1995), 'Liberalismo temprano, democracia tardía: el caso de España', in J. Dunn (ed.), *Democracia, el viaje inacabado (500 a. C.–1993)*, Barcelona: Busquets, pp. 29–186.
Lagares, M. J. (1975), 'La distribución de la carga tributaria: algunos aspectos de interés para la política fiscal', *Hacienda Pública Española*, 33, 141–159.
Lagares, M. J. (1982), *Déficit público y crisis económica*, Madrid: Instituto de Estudios Económicos.
Lagares, M. J. (1988), 'Niveles de cobertura del gasto público en España', *Papeles de Economía Española*, 37.
Lagares, M. J. (1991), 'Fraude fiscal y aceptación social del sistema tributario', *Moneda y Crédito*, 192, 127–156.
Lagares, M. J. (2002), 'La Hacienda pública en las facultades de ciencias económicas y en la sociedad española durante la segunda mitad del siglo XX', in E. Fuentes Quintana (dir.), *Economía y Economistas Españoles, 7, La consolidación académica de la economía*, Barcelona: Galaxia Gutenberg y Círculo de Lectores, pp. 571–617.
Lagares, M. J. (2004), 'La modernización del sistema fiscal español durante la democracia', in E. Fuentes Quintana (dir.), *Economía y Economistas Españoles, 8, La economía como profesión*, Barcelona: Galaxia Gutenberg y Círculo de Lectores, pp. 535–597.
Lagares, M. J., R. Alvarez, I. Encabo, J. M. González–Páramo y J. L. Raymond (1988), *Niveles de Cobertura del Gasto Público en España*, Fundación FIES.
Lagares, M., and F. Castellano (2004), '25 años de IRPF', *Papeles de Economía Española*, 100 (II), 2–16.
Ministerio de Hacienda (1990a), Informe sobre la reforma de la imposición personal sobre la renta y el patrimonio, Madrid.
Ministerio de Hacienda (1990b), El Presupuesto para 1990 (Ley 4/1990, de 29 de junio de Presupuestos Gnerales del Estado para 1990), Madrid.
Onrubia, J. and J. F. Sanz (dirs.) (2003), *Redistribución y bienestar a través de la imposición sobre la renta personal*, Madrid: Instituto de Estudios Fiscales,
Pan–Montojo, J. L. (1996), 'Una larga e inconclusa transición: la reforma tributaria, 1977–1986', in J. Tusell y A. Soto (eds.), *Historia de la Transición y consolidación democrática en España*, Madrid: Alianza, pp. 264–304.
Pan–Montojo, J. L. (2002), 'Política y gasto social en la Transición, 1975–1982', *Hacienda Pública Española*, 1, 229–252.
Prados de la Escosura, L. (2003), *El progreso económico de España (1850–2000)*, Bilbao: Fundación BBVA.
Repullo, R. (1986), 'Déficit, deuda pública e inflación: aspectos teóricos y aplicación al caso español', *Boletín Económico, Banco de España*, 13–24.
Repullo, R. (1991), 'Financing budget deficits by seignoriage and implicit taxation: the cases of Spain and Portugal', CEMFI, Workpaper 9105, Madrid.
Rubio, J. J. (2002), 'La Hacienda Pública Española en el tránsito al siglo XXI', *Hacienda Pública Española*, 1, 289–310.
Sanz, J.F., J. M. Castañer, and D. Romero (2004), 'La reforma de la imposición personal sobre la renta. Una evaluación de la reciente experiencia española 1998–2003', Madrid, Fundación de las Cajas de Ahorro, Estudios de la Fundación, n.18.

Trullén, J. (1993), Fundamentos económicos de la transición política española. La política de los acuerdos de la Moncloa, Madrid: Ministerio de Trabajo y Seguridad Social.

Tusell, J. (2003), 'La política', in J. Tusell (ed.), *La transición a la democracia y la España de Juan Carlos I, Historia de España Menéndez Pidal*, XLII, Madrid: Espasa Calpe, pp. 37–375.

Unidad del Fraude (1994), *Informe de la Unidad Especial para el Estudio del Fraude*, Madrid: Ministerio de Economía y Hacienda.

Valiño, A. (1989), *La reforma tributaria de 1977. Principios y realización*, Madrid: Tesis doctoral, Universidad Complutense.

Valle, V. (1974), 'La distribución de la carga monetaria de los impuestos. Una aplicación de las hipótesis de Pechman–Okner', *Hacienda Pública Española*, 26, 75–80.

Valle, V. (1989), 'La Hacienda española: perspectivas de una década', *Revista de Economía*, 1, 22–25.

Zubiri, I. (1991), 'La fiscalidad española ante el mercado único', *Papeles de Economía Española*, 48, 136–154.

3. The Business Community, Policy-makers, and Tax Reform (1977–2004)

Emilio Albi*[1]

INTRODUCTION

Over twenty-five years have passed since the original predecessors of today's Personal and Corporate Income Taxes came into force on January 1, 1979 and since the Urgent Measures on Tax Reform were published on November 14, 1977. The latter signalled the start of a major reform process aimed at modernising Spanish public finance, which continues today.

With the perspective of time, this long fiscal reform process contains elements of considerable interest for the analysis of taxation. So many years of tax reform in Spain place one in an ambivalent position. On the one hand, it is stimulating to study, with the objectives I will soon establish, such an important issue as a country's tax reforms over such a lengthy period. On the other hand, and this is slightly less pleasant, one of the possible comparative advantages I have when considering these matters is age; having been an active witness of the preparation and onset of the 1977–78 tax reform and the large number of changes made since then.

Indeed, there have been a considerable number of legislative and tax management changes for close to three decades. There certainly has been enough time for progress and reversals, for both implicit and explicit doubts, and for the economic, political and social constraints on the system to have changed quite substantially.

One analytical alternative would be to study the reforms in more or less detail in chronological order. This could be beneficial for research from a legal perspective but would evidently be lengthier than necessary. It would also be useful to consider the impact of some of the tax changes taking place in this period on tax revenue, distribution or efficiency, which would be a good subject for a doctoral dissertation. Readers should not be concerned, however, because the aim of this study is much simpler and, I trust, equally interesting.

This paper will start by analysing how this fiscal reform process came about, defining the fundamental characteristics of the 1977–78 reforms, in order to consider how these characteristics have changed over time. The purpose of this study focuses on the relationships between the policy-makers and officials who establish tax reform measures and the business community which demands or rejects them and investigates the interactions occurring over nearly three decades in certain aspects of taxation which were of special interest for businesses (organised or not in institutions) considering the economic and political changes of the period. To be more efficient, we will primarily consider the repercussion of income and wealth taxation on firms and entrepreneurs, and thus be in a better position to understand the current status of business taxation in Spain and reach reasonable conclusions concerning the types of reforms required in the near future.

A discussion of other tax reform questions would untowardly lengthen this paper. I have focused on the relationship between policymakers and the business community, regarding corporate income and wealth tax during the tax reform process starting in Spain back in 1977–78, because these are the areas where most friction and interaction existed along these nearly thirty years of reform. My aim is to provide some understanding of what has changed, and how, in Spanish business taxation in the last quarter of the 20th century and the first few years of the new millennium and to obtain an idea of possible new reforms.

Tax reforms can be contemplated from different perspectives. This paper falls within the conceptual framework of what we could call the "tax reform market" to which Alan Peacock (1979) referred some time ago. To explain why certain tax changes, and demands for them, arise, we have to consider the goals and constraints of business and economic policies in general and interpret the efficacy of certain measures in relation to others as a way of achieving these private and collective goals.

Taxes are means for collecting public funds, but they also serve other purposes under the constraint of the overall economic context. The "supply or demand of tax reform" arises when a tax instrument, or part of it, is no longer useful and indeed hinders achievement of desired goals. Basically, this can be the case because goals have changed, overall economic constraints have varied, certain taxes no longer have the same value in relation to others or, more commonly, it is considered that a different tax configuration would be fairer or more efficient. Additionally, it should be underlined that lobbies also have an impact on tax changes as the economy and power relations evolve over time.

A reform always implies changes in relation to a point of reference which, in this case, will be the original reforms of 1977–78. We will focus on direct taxation and, more specifically, on business taxes, for investigating the interrelations between policy makers and the business community. The business community includes not only business organisations, but also the tax affairs of entrepreneurs and their families. These relations have not always ended in agreements, or agreements have taken years to reach, but changes have nearly always been supported on economic grounds related to the objectives and constraints on businesses and the Spanish economy.

In the following discussion, I will attempt to establish the major issues which, from a business perspective, have dominated the tax reforms involved in this lengthy process. I will not bore the reader with many dates, legal references or details. I will rather concentrate on the major reform issues, with special emphasis on the most recent changes (during the last ten or fifteen years), the present situation and possible new demands for prospective reforms. The chapter is divided into different sections reflecting the major issues affecting the Spanish business community since the start of the reform process in 1977–78. The time has come, however, to review how this process came about and the economic approach on which it was based.

THE ORIGINS OF THE CURRENT TAX SYSTEM

Background and Reasons for the 1977–78 Reform

The tax reform process that Spain embarked upon in 1977 was preceded by discussions in some university forums and the Ministry of Public Finance itself. The previous reform, in 1964, had established a tax system that could only be described as ineffective and unfair, largely due to its narrow tax bases and the associated high levels of tax evasion.

The economic context in the 1960s, and up to 1974, was characterised by high growth rates (an average of over 7 percent a year) and an inequitable distribution of personal income. The Spanish population was making a major effort to cover its private needs.[2] At the same time, the population was demanding from the State more and better education, healthcare and pensions, together with more freedom and equal opportunities. It must be remembered that, socially and politically speaking, this was the end of the authoritarian regime of General Franco, who died in November 1975.

Criticism of the 1964 system was voiced in areas of the tax administration itself, reports by international organisations and in a few, not very widespread, Spanish business forums. In 1969, when Enrique Fuentes

Quintana was appointed the director of the Fiscal Studies Institute (*Instituto de Estudios Fiscales*—IEF), this agency of the Ministry of Finance started an important period of effective association and interaction between the Administration and Spain's universities, which eventually had a fundamental impact on the 1977–1978 tax reform. The IEF, from the early seventies to date, has been an important centre of research on tax and public expenditure matters with considerable influence on government policies.

The numerous studies conducted by the IEF on tax reform issues resulted in two main reports. The first, entitled "*Informe sobre el sistema tributario español*" (called a "green paper" because of the colour of the covers) (Fuentes, 1973), provided a thorough discussion and diagnostic of the ongoing problems with the tax system in Spain. The second report, entitled "*Sistema tributario español. Criterios para su reforma*", (Fuentes, 1976), became known as the "white paper" of the Reform, and it provided a blueprint for the reform of the entire tax system. However, the distribution of the two reports was limited. The 1973 report was never printed and all the copies were ordered destroyed following orders from the highest political level. However, some of the copies remained safe in the hands of those who collaborated in the report and in the libraries and offices of the IEF and the Ministry of Finance. The 1976 report was printed but not distributed. Both these reports were recently re-published by the IEF in 2002.

These two reports, however, had a considerable impact, and they were widely distributed. As pointed out, they represented a detailed summary of criticisms of the tax system in force at the time and presented a coherent proposal for tax reform. The 1977–78 reform may have been hidden in desk drawers, but it was ready for action.

After the democratic elections in 1977, the centre/right-wing government headed by Adolfo Suárez included professor Fuentes Quintana as the economic vice-president and Minister of Economy and Francisco Fernández Ordóñez as the Minister of Finance. The economic situation was dire, with heavy internal price disequilibrium and a severe balance of trade deficit. Needless to say, there was a need for an effective stabilisation programme and higher tax revenues. In the 1975–1985 period, after the fifteen years of high growth rates mentioned earlier, the annual GDP growth rate slowed down to only 1.69 percent; overall, this was a decade of limited economic capitalisation and falling employment rates, following the 1974 oil crisis which affected Spain severely.

The social situation was hardly appropriate for a policy programme aiming at economic stability. The Spanish Constitution was not approved until December 1978 and political consensus was precarious. Spain was not a member of the European Community and had a closed economy. Business organisations were just starting to arise. For example, the Spanish Confederation of Business Organisations (*Confederación Española de Organizaciones Empresariales*—CEOE) had just been created in 1977. Furthermore, the policies aimed at tackling the economic crisis that started in 1974 had taken too long to define, largely due to the fluid political context at the end of Franco's regime and the economic problems that had accumulated during that period.

In such a difficult situation, the only possible solution lay in obtaining an agreement between the different political parties represented in Parliament with a view to defining the required reform. This possibility arose with the Moncloa Agreements ("*Pactos de la Moncloa*")[3] signed in October 1977, in which the political parties accepted a Reform Programmeme centred on a policy of economic stability and a profound reform of the economic and social system. The costs of the economic crisis and all the adjustments to be made were to be shared among the population based on equity criteria, thus the need for reforming the tax system. In short, tax reform became an essential part of the Moncloa Pacts.

The 1977–78 tax reform arose from a social agreement or national compact in the context of a closed economy facing serious economic problems and a new democratic regime demanding widespread reforms. The studies and research work (especially in university departments and the IEF) that had been carried out some years before were now ready to be used. All these circumstances largely explain the very rare socio-political phenomenon consisting of all parties accepting the need for tax reform and agreeing to its content. Socially, including the business community, the reform also met with relatively widespread acceptance.

The Beginnings of the Reform in 1977

The first step in the Reform consisted of the Urgent Measures on Tax Reform Act ("*Ley de Medidas Urgentes de Reforma Fiscal*, Law 50/1977, of November 14). This Act was fundamentally designed to provide the ground for voluntary compliance, so that in the future, their relations with the authorities would take place in a climate of transparency. Among other aspects, it focused on:

- Granting a tax amnesty, applicable both to individuals and legal entities, in order to start afresh and foster more honesty between the authorities and taxpayers. Fourteen years later, this was followed by a new quasi-amnesty which received the euphemistic name of Fiscal Regulation of Abnormal Situations (Additional Provisions 13 and 14 of the Personal Income Tax Act—Law 18/1991, of June 6th). There have been no further widespread tax amnesties or "regularisations of taxpayers' fiscal situations."

- Including tax offences in the Criminal Code. Articles 305 to 310 of the Criminal Code (Organic Law 10/1995, of November 23) that are currently in force refer to Public Finance offences punished with monetary fines ranging from 100 to 600 percent of the evaded tax amount and prison sentences ranging from one to four years in prison.
- Eliminating banking secrecy and regulating the collaboration of banks with the tax authorities.
- Integrating the taxation of shareholders in certain types of companies in a transparent taxation regime, which we will consider later in more detail, as a way of tackling tax evasion methods that used these companies as screens between the taxpayers and the tax administration authorities.
- Establishing a tax on personal wealth ("*impuesto sobre el patrimonio*"), basically aimed at generating fiscal information to control income and wealth, with highly progressive tax rates. We will also go into further detail later on the wealth tax as well as the inheritance and donation tax.

As far as we can tell, the fundamental idea creating the basis for the 1977 Act was to establish a clearer relationship between taxpayers and the administration, which provided the former with the opportunity to start from scratch and the latter with the means required to ensure better management of the new tax system.

The 1978 Reform of Personal and Corporate Income Tax

We have already mentioned that the new system was conceptually solid and supported not only by the green and white papers of 1973 and 1976, but also by research and analyses conducted by the Administration and several Spanish universities. The approach to the 1978 reform was based on the intellectual tradition of Henry Simons (1938) and his comprehensive income taxation proposals that led up to the Carter Report (1966–67) drafted in Canada from 1962 to 1966. It also incorporated the taxation principles of Fritz Neumark (1970).

The taxation system was already designed and ready for immediate application. The reform programme followed what we could call the "tax style" of the sixties, which was a synthesis of Anglo-Saxon and Continental direct taxation and the more clearly European indirect taxation represented by VAT, so it was already, possibly, out of date in an economic context of low growth and high inflation rates. It was designed for a primarily closed economy. Its major objectives were:

- To increase tax revenue and enable the Spanish Government to finance the public services demanded by the population.
- To provide appropriate instruments with which to develop a macroeconomic, stability-oriented tax policy.
- To make the system more equitable by adding a social component to the Moncloa Agreement and its reform programme.
- To use the criterion of comprehensive taxation to increase revenue and fiscal capacity to ensure a more stable economy and a better distribution of income based on highly progressive taxes.
- To bring Spain's tax system up to similar levels reached by the tax systems of other European countries.

These objectives were achieved by January 1, 1979. Two laws on the personal and corporate income taxes were approved by Parliament (Law 44/1978, of November 8th on personal income tax and Law 61/1978, of December 27th on corporate income tax). In the field of direct taxes, income taxation was rounded up with a tax on personal wealth based on the, already in force, inheritance and donation tax. This tax would not be reformed again until 1988 by Law 29/1987, of December 18.

Major reform of indirect taxation had to wait until 1986, when Spain joined the European Community (VAT Act—Law 30/1985, of August 2, and Excise Act—Law 45/1985, of December 23, both of them amended again in 1992), with temporary systems established in the meantime. VAT has provided a considerable increase of revenue for the system over the years.[4]

The new territorial organisation of the State arising from the 1978 Constitution gave rise to the Autonomous Region Financing Act (Organic Law 8/1980, of September 22), which later would be subject to important changes. The issue of the financing of central government versus the regions is today still the centre of political disputes. The financing of local tax authorities (provinces and municipalities) was later addressed by Law 39/1988, of December 28, amended by Law 51/2002, of December 27.

Ultimately, the 1977–78 reform signalled the start of a major change in the Spanish tax system specifically affecting income taxation. This truly represented a revolution in the country's fiscal tradition. Since the mid-19th century, the Spanish tax system had maintained a basic structure of schedular taxes, which provided limited revenue, gave relatively more weight to indirect taxation, and had numerous serious technical defects. The problem of low revenue yields inherent to this system disappeared largely because of the sharp increase in personal income tax collections, followed later by VAT collections, both instruments capable of serving the purposes of a modern fiscal policy. With regard to this last point, it seems fair to say that the reform started in 1977–78 was more equitable and eliminated important distortions of the previous system.

THE ROLE OF THE BUSINESS COMMUNITY'S DEMANDS IN SUCCESSIVE TAX REFORMS

The starting point, in 1978, of the long tax reform process was well accepted by all political forces and the business community in general. This may seem surprising but is understandable given the serious economic situation and lack of political stability at the time. We have already mentioned that the 1977–78 reform took place within the framework of the Moncloa Agreements. Indeed, the new democratic regime played a fundamental role in getting the reform on its feet.

This explains why, in exchange for a tax amnesty, there was widespread acceptance of making tax evasion a crime (the so called "criminalisation of taxation.") There is no doubt that these two types of measures represented powerful aids to improving tax management and enforcement. The introduction of a tax on wealth was questioned by the business community. The new tax transparency regime, which mainly applied to "passive" corporations, drew more questions than the wealth tax. However, the initial resistance was rather weak, something to be expected given the low profile of business organisations at the time.

However, the political and social approval of the 1977 Act and the new income taxes in 1978 did not mean that the defects and shortcomings of the reform were not acknowledged, particularly those affecting the business community. The business community, in general, accepted the 1977–78 reform but they criticised the excessive academic nature of the approach and the fact that it was poorly adapted to the reality of the time with an ongoing economic crisis. The reform introduced sharp increases in the progressivity of the system, both in the personal income tax and in the taxation of wealth. In addition, personal and corporate income taxes were not well integrated in relation to the double taxation of business profits. As just mentioned above, the new "tax transparency regime" for certain corporations was also contested. Last but not least, the reform failed to appropriately tackle international aspects of taxation required for Spanish businesses to operate in foreign markets. These, among others, were the principal issues leading the business community to demand further tax reforms.

The business organisations already established during the early years of the new democracy became stronger and more outspoken, at the same time new organisations arose. They all voiced strong opinions on taxation policy over the years. To mention just a few of these business organisations, the Spanish Confederation of Business Organisations—CEOE (Confederación Española de Organizaciones Empresariales) played an important role corresponding to its status as a confederation of other organisations, especially through the members of its Fiscal Committee, primarily Javier Berruguete. In Barcelona, *Fomento del Trabajo Nacional* was always interested in fiscal affairs, with the collaboration of Alexandre Pedrós and others. In Barcelona and Madrid, and now many other cities, the Family Business Institute (*Instituto de la Empresa Familiar)* considerably influenced aspects of the taxation of entrepreneurs at the personal and household levels. In Madrid, the Institute of Economic Studies and other organisations contributed to strengthening the institutions of the market economy, including fiscal aspects. And the same can be said of other business organisations, such as the Spanish Banking Association, the Confederation of Savings Banks, the Confederation of SMEs (*Confederación de la Pequeña y Mediana Empresa*—CEPYME) or Chambers of Commerce.

It is apparent that many business organisations played significant roles for or against aspects of the different tax reforms started in 1977. It is not possible to mention all of them and the organisations listed above are mere examples. But it is important to emphasise that, in most cases, business organisations have used persuasion not only aimed at the Administration but also at the general public, increasing the awareness of policy-makers, officials and taxpayers of the economic effects of the tax system. Overall, the business community demanded lower taxes, based on the economic restraints of the time and on other arguments emphasising, especially over the last twenty years, the liberalisation of the Spanish economy, which was limited at the time of the 1970 Preferential Agreements with the Common Market and increased considerably after Spain joined the European Community in 1986. A reduction in the business tax bill was also demanded based on arguments related to desirable limits to the size of the public sector.

With regards to economic internationalisation, one solid argument aimed at increasing the competitiveness of the Spanish economy, thereby improving the ability of Spanish businesses to defend their internal markets and to grow by exporting. Different Spanish organisations also have commonly referred to the need for increased competitiveness in their demands for greater support for small or family businesses.

Most of the tax changes which have taken place in the last twenty-five years in Spain have been based on economic arguments demanding reforms in business taxation with a clear rejection of such aspects as the progressiveness of personal income tax, the taxation of business wealth, and the tax transparency regime for "passive" corporations. This is probably a good time to consider these issues in some detail, with reference to their essential aspects.

CORPORATE INCOME TAX REFORMS: BASIC ASPECTS OF THE TAX

Fundamental Reform Trends and Demands Relating to Corporate Income Taxation

With regards to the Corporate Income Tax, the tax reformers of the seventies aimed at:

- increasing the scope of the tax,
- widening its tax base,
- rationalising the tax rates and system of economic incentives,
- reducing the double taxation of business profits, and
- avoiding the use of companies acting as screens between the authorities and individual taxpayers (who were subject to a global and highly progressive personal income tax).

The Spanish corporate income tax (with a history that goes back to 1900, with the creation of Tariff III—"Taxation of the utilities of movable wealth") had reached a reasonably acceptable technical level by the mid-70s. However, widespread tax evasion continued to reduce revenues quite considerably. In addition to the evasion problem, augmented by weak tax management and inspection processes, there were other reasons for improving and strengthening the tax.

The legal regulation of taxpayers was not always appropriate. For instance, joint ownership companies were not subject to corporate income tax with regards to agricultural operations or earnings other than those derived from commercial or industrial activities. Passive companies holding securities and other assets were exempt even with regard to earned interest. Although the taxation of business holdings was legally regulated, specific regulations had not been drafted and they were not applied in practice, enabling the possibility of transferring earnings between group companies.

Another example of the limited scope of the tax was the capital gains obtained by non-residents without permanent residency. In this case, the only earnings considered to be obtained in Spain were those subject to a schedular tax on account of the corporate income tax. However, since there was no tax (on account of the corporate income tax) applied to capital gains, these were excluded from taxation for non-resident companies which were often owned by Spanish residents.

We could mention other examples of problems associated to the scope or base of the tax, and the other basic elements in any corporate income tax, but the above should suffice for now. In fact, other defects of the corporate income tax prior to 1978 will be mentioned later in this section, with an aim of understanding the solutions initially proposed. Generally speaking, these solutions involved a corporate income tax similar to that applied in other European countries that emphasised enlarging the tax base by using comprehensive taxation criteria. They reformulated tax incentives and established fiscal transparency in an attempt to tackle the use of companies acting as screens between the taxpayer and the administration. These were the fundamental aspects of corporate income tax reform in the following quarter of the century.

Business reactions to corporate income tax regulations followed clear trends in the long period we are considering. As mentioned earlier, the tax was generally welcomed initially (this was true of the tax system as a whole), although the stricter legislation and its practical application introduced in the mid-80s led to important confrontations in the second half of the decade. One example was the document published by the CEOE management board on June 6, 1989 entitled *La urgente reforma del sistema tributario español* (The urgent reform of Spain's tax system). Another example arose from an academic perspective with the publication of a report entitled *La Reforma Fiscal y los problemas de la Hacienda Pública Española* (Fuentes, 1990). Indeed, after the system became stricter in the eighties, the reforms introduced in 1991 became a turning point towards more realistic trends favouring consensus within the new personal income and wealth taxes (Law 18/1991 and Law 19/1991, both of June 6th). The less urgent changes in business taxation took a little longer. They followed after the Ministry of Economy and Public Finance issued the *Informe sobre la Reforma del Impuesto sobre Sociedades* (Report on the Reform of the Corporate Income Tax) in 1994, with the Corporate Income Tax Act (Law 43/1995, of December 27th).

Combining business perspectives and academic research proposals, or others put forward by policy makers themselves, the fundamental goals of the reform of the corporate income tax in 1995 can be summarised as follows:

- To limit (or reduce) the overall tax burden on companies, considering not only the corporate income tax, but also Social Security contributions and the income taxation of entrepreneurs (which included the personal income tax, the wealth tax, and the inheritance and donation tax).
- To achieve an appropriately neutral corporate income tax with the aim of enhancing economic efficiency related, among others, to the sources of business financing, investment projects, location or legal status, and company size.

The fulfilment of this last goal, however, was affected by the constraints represented by other goals informing the reform, such as:

- To foster saving and business investment as a means of ensuring an increase in productivity and sustained economic growth.
- Incentives to increase business competitiveness that increasingly focused on R&D activities, occupational training, small enterprises, certain intangible assets or company restructuring or alliances.
- International coordination in terms of possible harmonised lines of corporate income tax in the EU and fiscal support for the integration of Spanish firms in a more global economy.

The tendency to include fiscal incentives in the corporate income tax with the aim of making Spanish firms more competitive on an increasingly international scale has been fundamental, especially since the tax was reformed in 1995 and other changes that were made in the following years. Arguably, the overall impact of this tendency has been positive, because the competitiveness of a national economy largely depends on the competitiveness of its firms,[5] without prejudice to the beneficial effects of a stable macroeconomic framework, especially in relation to prices or interest rates, of budgetary discipline or an appropriate choice of public expenditure policies.

The consensus interpretation of the available statistical evidence is that the application of these ideas to the corporate income tax generally helped Spanish firms maintain their market shares, become more international and increase their export capabilities. Spanish corporations are open to internationalisation since the early nineties as Canals (2004) shows. However, the specific effect of corporate taxation in this process is difficult to discern since it is intertwined with the effects of the devaluations of 1992 and 1993, the competitive rate of exchange maintained after those years which led to the fixing of the peseta-euro exchange rate for Spain and the greater openness of the economic setting during the last fifteen years.

In general, trends in corporate tax reform, particularly in the last ten years, have converged, both in demands and actual changes, on the introduction of tax incentives aimed at fostering the following activities:

- R&D and innovation in products and processes
- business internationalisation
- exports
- vocational training
- support for small and medium-sized enterprise (SMEs)
- business restructuring and alliances

The effectiveness of these incentives seems unequal. For example, the international oriented incentives may have been proved as positive but R&D and innovation is still lagging in spite of very generous tax benefits. In any case, these new tax incentives, which are only a recent trend in corporate income tax and will be discussed later, have been accompanied by reforms in other aspects of the tax, which we discuss next.

Tax Rates

The reformers of the sixties proposed a reduction in the variety of tax rates applied in the corporate income tax to a single overall rate of 36 per cent, with one or two lower rates for specific cases. However, not much progress has been made since then, because in effect there are now twelve different rates plus two additional rates applicable to passive holding companies that we will be considering later.

The corporate income tax started in 1979 with an overall tax rate of 33 per cent, plus three reduced rates for specific situations (savings banks, mutual insurance companies and some cases of non-residents or exempt entities). In 1985 the overall corporate tax rate was increased to the 35 per cent, which continues to be applied today.

Until approximately seven years ago, the nominal tax rate had not been particularly questioned (except for the taxation of reinvested capital gains, which we will return to later). Actually, during the first two decades of the reform, the nominal corporate income tax rate in Spain was relatively moderate compared to that of most other countries. However, in more recent times, this situation has changed due to fiscal competition between countries in the form of reduced tax rates and other measures.

A European Commission study (2001) on corporate income taxation in the EU identified important differences in the effective taxation of businesses, which could have an impact on international competitiveness and the location of direct investment. The Commission's study provides no evidence on the impact of business taxation on economic location decisions. These decisions involve many other non-fiscal aspects such as labour or transport costs or the quality of human capital and infrastructure. However, Devereux and Griffith (1998) show that, although the decisions of North American multinational corporations to establish their production in Europe or the United States have not been significantly affected by tax reasons, such reasons did have a considerable impact on their location within Europe.

All this has become more important with the enlargement of the EU from fifteen to twenty-five countries. The average nominal rate of corporate income tax in Europe was 33 per cent in the year 2000. This average, however, has fallen considerably when taking into account the new EU members. Poland and the Slovak Republic, for instance, reduced their corporate income tax rate to 19 per cent in 2004 (from 27 and 25 per cent, respectively). Hungary applies a 16 per cent tax rate and Estonia does not tax reinvested profits. A debate concerning the convenience of reducing fiscal competition by establishing a minimum corporate tax rate, and the harmonisation of the tax base, is certainly on the cards, at least in Europe. [6]

In Spain, there are certainly reasons, arising from international fiscal competition, for contemplating a reduction (after twenty years) in the present overall corporate tax rate of 35 percent.[7] This could have a considerable impact on tax revenues and have consequences for other important issues such as the integration of corporate and personal income tax, and the accounting effects of a rate reduction in companies with advance or deferred taxes on profits, due to positive or negative time differences, or with losses pending compensation.

The EC Commission itself (2001) underlines the importance of nominal tax rates in the field of fiscal competition between member States. Future fiscal reform in Spain will probably involve a reduction in nominal corporate income tax rates. However, the tax rate is not the only issue of interest in relation to international business competitiveness. We also have to consider the principal components of the tax base.

The Tax Base

Many of the issues discussed, and confrontations between policy makers and the business community in relation to the different reforms of corporate income tax in Spain have been related to the definition of the tax base. More specifically, the discussion has focused on the relationship between accounting and taxation. In practice, the corporate income tax has logically always been based on business accounts. Although the reform reports of the seventies and the initial legislation contemplated the differences between the corrected value of fiscal capital at the start and the end of the tax period as a way of determining income, this idea was soon abandoned. Instead, the debate focused on adjusting the profit and loss account to determine the corporate income tax base.

Generally speaking, the tax that came into force in 1979 involved important differences between the accounting result and the computation of the value of the tax base for tax purposes. Evidence of this is the fact that the Corporate Income Tax regulations (Royal Decree 2631/1982, of October 15th) had more than 400 articles compared to 34 articles in the 1978 Act. The 1982 regulations contained 135 articles related to the tax base, 90 of which were concerned with accounting aspects. With these figures, it is easy to understand why the tax base differed considerably from the accounting profit and losses of the period. The situation changed radically in the new 1995 Corporate Income Tax law and, without prejudice to certain adjustments to the economic result which give rise to temporary or permanent differences, accounting-business standards are generally accepted in the determination of the tax base.

However, article 148 of the current law empowers the tax authorities to apply fiscal precepts when calculating the accounting result. I believe that this cautionary measure is meant to be used only when there is evidence that there has been failure to comply with accounting-business standards and that this non-compliance has fiscal effects. In practice, the Tax Administration does not apply this article. It is generally understood that if a firm, for instance, has been audited and the auditors have issued a favourable technical opinion, considering that the criteria followed by the firm are in accordance with accounting principles, it would make no sense and would also be a frontal attack to legal certainty, to apply this (cautionary) measure. In any case, this clause continues to be a source of friction between policy makers and the business community.

This issue of differences between fiscal and accounting criteria was a source of many disagreements and considerable controversy between the business and academic communities and the tax authorities during the initial reforms in 1978 and the most recent reform of 1995. To mention just a couple of examples, until 1996 the LIFO method was not admitted for inventory valuation for tax purposes. While this method had already been accepted in the General Accounting Plan and the 4th EU Directive, negotiations to make updates to balance sheets during periods of high inflation rates, although fiscally admissible (specifically from 1979 to 1983), were always difficult.

The trend in relation to fiscal (and accounting) amortisation over the last twenty-five years has consisted of offering Spanish firms, especially small ones, financial competitive advantages by applying higher depreciation coefficients and reducing the useful life of assets. The fiscal admission of deductible provisions was another source of confrontation between the business community and policymakers. From the initial highly restrictive positions, there is now more flexibility since the 1995 corporate tax reform. For instance, since 2002, non-financial insolvency provisions can be deducted six months after the obligation becomes due, instead of the previous twelve months.

There are other aspects of interest in relation to the corporate income tax base. On the one hand, there has been the gradual strengthening of the fiscal regulation on "not at arm's length" transactions since 1978. On the other hand, there has been application of "advance price agreements" and rules referring to the "undercapitalisation" of Spanish subsidiaries of foreign companies. We should also mention the progress made in the consolidated taxation of holdings. At the same time, business restructurings (mergers, spin-offs, transfer of assets and share swapping), courtesy of the application of Community directives, have progressed from the discretionary application of tax benefits by the authorities, to an automatic system based on deferring income for tax purposes. The reduction in the double national taxation on dividends and capital gains has continued to progress; since 1978, it has followed the trend of deductions to tax payable, either eliminating or halving the double taxation of a firm obtaining revenue from shares in national companies.[8] The business community, of course, has always been in favour of the complete disappearance of double taxation in all cases.

As for the capital gains obtained in the transfer of business assets, Spanish corporate income tax has traditionally always encouraged the reinvestment of such earnings, which could favour business capitalisation. Naturally, the greatest encouragement consists of making reinvestments exempt, and this was the case in the 1978 Corporate Income Tax Act, although it was only applicable to capital gains from the transfer of tangible fixed assets. Before 1978, the system reduced the tax base by a certain percentage of the profits allocated to the investment provision fund or the reserve for export investments, but the fact that there were no time limits to these investments meant that firms could benefit from this fiscal advantage to finance themselves without investing.

In this field, the exemption approach was followed by the alternative of deferring payment of the tax on the capital gains obtained if the transfer of fixed assets was reinvested in other fixed assets. In turn, this benefit was enlarged to include the sale of shares when total shares represented no less than 5 percent of the stock capital of other firms. With a deferral period of usually ten years, this fiscal benefit meant that the effective tax burden was 25 percent instead of the nominal 35 percent. Since 2002 (Administrative and Social Fiscal Measures Act—Law 24/2001, of December 17) this has changed again. There is now a tax payable deduction for reinvestment which, starting in 2003, represents 20 percent of the capital gains (reinvestment of a less than the total amount obtained from the transfer reduces the deduction in proportion to the reinvested amount). This deduction is applied to the tax payable for the tax period in which the reinvestment is made (which must be made between the year prior to the transfer date, in which case the deduction is effective in the year of the transfer, and the three following years, or exceptionally according to a special reinvestment plan). With this deduction, given a nominal corporate tax rate of 35 percent, the nominal tax burden is reduced to 15 percent (personal tax rate on capital gains earned in a period of over 12 months).

Finally, with regards to compensation for losses, the business community's proposal for retroactive compensation with a return of corporate income tax paid in previous years has not been admitted by policymakers. What the business community did achieve was a considerable extension to the period during which negative tax base can be compensated in the future. The five years initially contemplated in the 1978 Act grew to seven in 1995, and the current law allows fifteen long years starting with the tax period following the one in which the negative tax base was registered (for new firms and for negative tax bases derived from the operation of new toll motorways, tunnels and roads by concessionaires, the term starts with the first tax period in which fiscal income is positive).

Tax Credits and Fiscal Incentives for Investment and Other Business Activities

When referring to depreciation in the previous section concerning the tax base, we mentioned the tendency, common to many countries, to shorten depreciation periods for tax purposes in order to provide firms with financial advantages and encourage investment. Currently in Spain, although this is a temporary measure, the maximum linear coefficients established in the official depreciation tables are multiplied by 1.1 for new asset acquisitions in 2003 and 2004. Free depreciation is used in some cases, as with elements related to R&D activities (excluding buildings, which can be depreciated by tenths) or R&D costs accounted for as intangible assets. Free depreciation has occasionally been used, as was the case in 1985, in order to compensate for the effect of deferring investments until 1986, the year that VAT came into force, since the new tax treated investments better than the indirect tax it was replacing. In the previous section we also referred to reinvestment of the product of asset transfers in the form of reducing taxation on the resulting capital gains. Here, however, we will be focusing on tax credits (as opposed to deductions) as incentives for investment or other business activities.

Starting with tax incentives for investment, the basic idea of the reformers of the seventies, generally accepted by the business community, consisted of rationalising the incentive system current at the time. The idea was to replace the incentives included in the 1964 corporate income tax with other more effective mechanisms. The investment provision and export investment reserve system mentioned earlier was seriously inefficient and the chosen alternative was to provide fiscal support for investment by means of tax credits consisting of deducting a percentage (initially 10 percent in 1979) of the total investment made from the tax due in the tax period. The tax credit system appeared to be more effective, particularly because it promoted investment and not the self-financing resulting from the provision and reserve system. Furthermore, the tax credit system was easy to modulate according to the fiscal policy needs of the time.

Pressure from the business community, during the economic slowdown, prevailing since 1975, considerably increased the weight of fixed asset investment incentives, which became quantitatively significant in relation to revenue. On the other hand, as Cuervo and Trujillo (1987) showed, investment deductions were largely applied in capital intensive sectors generating relatively little additional employment.

The new corporate income tax had successfully attenuated the cost of using capital, reducing the negative impact of the high financial costs of the eighties (Espitia *et al.,* 1988). However, the short-term efficacy of the tax incentives for the investment system also had its costs. Besides generating efficiency costs on the labour market, the tax incentives had undesirable effects on the composition of investment. These effects were compounded by other aspects of the tax system, such as tax rates, loss compensation and the treatment applied to depreciation, capital gains, and sources of financing in general. These issues were studied by Sanz (1995) in relation to Spain.

For example, the tax system discriminated against investment in inventories, with special benefits for investment in vehicles, machinery and equipment. In general, effective marginal tax rates also depended on the firm's financial structure, with debt financing being the most favoured by the tax system. Throughout the eighties, the result was that the marginal effective rates on investments by small firms tended to be higher than those applied to large companies, because the latter needed proportionally lower inventories and had better access to financing, in particular debt financing.

Academic criticism of the fact that the tax system was not neutral, with important effects on the composition of investment, had a significant impact on policymakers' opinions concerning new lines of reform in the early nineties. In fact, neutrality was, in general, a priority objective of the corporate income tax reform of 1995, in which the basic criterion for investment was understood to be its own productivity rather than induced tax responses. However, the business community, now that Spain had an open economy, demanded support for international competitiveness in the form of incentives for the internationalisation of Spanish firms—which will be considered in the following section—and also demanded that the tax system benefited certain business activities. The result of the battle between the two objectives, fiscal neutrality and the promotion of certain business activities or behaviours was the disappearance of tax credits for investment and the multiplication of other credits supporting activities which the business community considered to be increasing the competitive level of Spanish firms.

According to current legislation, incentives for certain activities of the Spanish corporate income tax include, among others, the following:

- Deductions for R&D and technological innovation activities and the promotion of information technologies. This is a generous tax credit, particularly in relation to R&D, despite problems of definition of its different concepts, justification and verification. For small firms (with turnover totalling less than 8 million euros), there is a specific deduction to encourage the use of information and communication technologies.
- Deductions for investment aimed at environmental protection, the acquisition of new industrial or road transport vehicles in the part of the investment helping to reduce atmospheric pollution, or the use of renewable sources of energy.
- Deductions for occupational training costs, including the cost of providing employees with Internet connections or equipment, or grants for access to equipment, even when they are used elsewhere and outside working hours.
- Deductions for export activities, divided into two concepts: (a) for investment to create foreign branches or subsidiaries, and (b) for the cost of promoting goods and services produced in Spain and abroad. On the other hand, earnings from the export of film and audio-visual productions, books, parts of books or all educational publishing work are applied a 99 per cent deduction of the tax payable.

Policymakers and the business community are largely in agreement concerning this new tax incentive system, although the latter continues to demand direct incentives for investment in general by means of either tax credits or the fiscal policy applied to asset depreciation. For the time being, tax credits are limited to encouraging business activities other than the acquisition of fixed assets and are focused on increasing competitiveness. A careful revision of the efficiency of the current tax credits is still pending.

Promoting the Internationalisation of Spanish Firms

The objective of enhancing the competitiveness of Spanish firms has been the motivating force behind the significant fiscal promotion of business internationalisation carried out over the last ten years. Until Spain joined the EU in 1986, corporate income tax was designed for a closed economy and its only international component was a deduction for tax paid in other countries to avoid double taxation, which is logically still in force.

However, since the corporate income tax reform of 1995, the international aspects of the tax are now highly significant, largely thanks to the demands of the business community. Overall international aspects are well managed in the current Spanish corporate income tax system, which, in the wide field of business internationalisation (and the enhancing of export activities), includes:

- The exemption of dividends received from non-resident corporations (in which the holding represents at least 5 percent of the stock capital), and capital gains derived from transfer of shares in the same corporations. This exemption eliminates double international taxation and is also an improvement on the existing deduction for dividends and profit shares from foreign sources. The reason for this is that the deduction is made according to the imputation technique and limited by the Spanish tax itself. However, if the foreign tax on dividends is lower than the Spanish tax, the deduction maintains the Spanish tax burden, whereas the foreign burden is favoured with the exemption method. If the foreign tax is greater than the Spanish tax, the resulting tax burden is the same with either one of the two methods, exemption and deduction, and equal to the foreign tax. At the same time, the exemption method eliminates capital gains taxation in Spain (the exemption method is also applied to certain income obtained abroad by the permanent establishment of a firm resident in Spain).
- The special regime applicable to foreign-share holding firms. This regime benefits firms managing and administering equity of non-resident enterprises. The tax incentive consists of the exemption, applicable to the Spanish company, of income from non-resident firms in the form of dividends or net capital gains.

- The deduction from the tax base of investments for the establishment of enterprises abroad by purchasing shares in non-resident companies representing a voting majority or by establishing a company outside Spain. The effect of this tax benefit is deferred taxation, with the deducted amounts being added to the tax base, in equal parts, in the tax periods ending in the four years following the investment.
- Deductions for export activities, as mentioned in the previous section.
- The improvement and considerable enlargement of agreements to prevent double taxation signed by Spain, also benefiting non-residents who, with no agreement in place, are applied a specific tax since 1998 (Non-resident Income Tax Act—Law 41/1998).
- The application of the Advance Price Agreements system to transfer pricing.

THE FISCAL FRAMEWORK FOR SMES AND FAMILY BUSINESSES

Income Taxation

Consideration of the taxation applicable to small and medium-sized enterprises (SMEs) has been very important throughout the Spanish tax reform. We should begin by considering the personal income tax applicable to individual business owners and independent professionals, or artists. Since 1979 the general system determining taxable income for economic activities performed by these types of individuals consisted of deducting expenses and asset depreciation from total revenues. However, the tax has always contained cautionary measures. For example, payments made to the spouse or children under legal age were not deductible and neither were they classified as fiscal income of the latter. If there is an employment and social security contract, these payments are now deductible from income and taxed as earnings of the receivers. With some exceptions, there has been a tendency to gradually apply corporate income tax rules to determine net income, but with the fiscal benefits for corporate SMEs still in force. Furthermore, the capital losses or gains derived from property associated with the economic activity have traditionally been taxed as such and not as business income.

The definition of economic activity has also been subject to cautionary measures in relation to property rental or sale. For these activities to be considered "economic" for tax purposes, and for revenue not to be taxed as real estate returns, there has to be an office in charge of managing the property and at least one full-time employee. On the other hand, there is currently a simplified general regime application system for activities with a net turnover of 600,000 euros or less in the immediately previous year.[9]

However, the most radical simplification of personal income taxation for individual entrepreneurs and professionals arose with a scheme introduced in 1979. This is the voluntary return assessment system for certain economic activities performed by small enterprises and professionals, applying indices or returns established by the Administration for modules according, for instance, to turnover, number of employees, cost of purchases, surface area of premises or land, fixed assets, power consumption or capacity, etc. The quantitative limits for the application of this scheme are, according to the current legislation, 450,000 euros of total returns in the preceding year for all a taxpayer's economic activities, and 300,000 euros if they consist of farming and livestock breeding.

It is easy to imagine that both the technical and economic studies conducted to determine the value of signs, indices and modules in the different sectors of economic activity and definition of the scope of the scheme—the activities to which it applies and within which limits—have been the source of frequent confrontations between policymakers and business organisations. The system is useful and effective for the small enterprise—indeed it is not compulsory, but few waive their right to apply it—and it is simple and inexpensive for the Administration to control, although it reduces revenue on the income generated by such activities and gives way to inequalities since the tax burden of these activities is lower than it should have been (recall it is a voluntary scheme and that most entrepreneurs covered accept it).

As for corporate SMEs, we have a special corporate income regime known as "tax incentives for small firms". Fiscal support for Spanish SMEs is significant and affects firms with a turnover of less than 8 million Euros (according to current legislation) in the previous fiscal year. This is higher than the figure established in business legislation for presenting an abridged balance sheet and not being obliged to audit the annual accounts (4.75 million euros), so the definition of a "small firm" is quite broad. To prevent companies from hovering on the borderline, it would possibly be better for them to have to exceed the turnover of 8 million euros in two consecutive years in order to cease to be entitled to the special incentives for SMEs.

Both the business community and policymakers, who also have to follow EU criteria, have agreed on the need for fiscal support for SMEs. The economic reason for this is the large number of small firms capable of generating considerable employment. There is need to strengthen their competitive position, which may be negatively affected particularly by financial constraints (their lack of access to capital markets, insufficient collateral for credit institutions and limited information mean that SMEs depend on financing from banks, generally at a high cost).

SMEs receive a reduction of 5 percentage points in the tax rate applicable to their first 120,151.81 euros of profit (which is, therefore, taxed at 30 percent). This is a relatively small advantage for the firm (6,010.12 euros), although it represents a considerable loss of tax revenue.

Other tax incentives for small firms include accelerated depreciation via the doubling of coefficients, free depreciation for more situations than in the general scheme and the deductibility of global provisions for possible insolvent debtors.

Taxation on Wealth and the Family Business

It is usually thought that a family business, in which the entrepreneur is either the owner or represents a group of people with family ties, is an SME. This, however, is not the case. Individual entrepreneurs are indeed family businesses and many small firms fit into this category, but some of them are large. In fact, as Santana and Aguiar (2004) show, over half (52.7 percent) of the non-financial firms trading on the Spanish stock market are controlled by family groups.[10] Like any other businesses, family businesses and their shareholders have been affected by this long period of tax reform. However, particularly in the nineties, large family firms approached policy makers with a series of specific fiscal problems which could negatively affect the growth of their businesses and their transmission to other generations. These problems were divided into two groups. The first referred to the difficulties derived from holding shares in family firms due to the wealth tax, the fiscal transparency system, and double income taxation on dividends. All these issues will be considered in the next section. The second was related to the fiscal costs of transferring businesses, due to the effects of the Inheritance and Donation Tax. Discussions with policymakers in regard to these problems were spearheaded by the Family Business Institute (*Instituto de la Empresa Familiar*).

To begin with, the wealth tax, as we have learned above, arose from the social pact known as the Moncloa Agreements of 1977 in a peculiar political context and with the ultimate objective of generating fiscal information for the control of earnings and wealth. This objective was not achieved and was even further hindered by the transfer of the tax revenue to autonomous regions in 1984. Since that date, the better equipped central tax administration had less incentive for auditing and enforcing this tax.

Although the revenue from the wealth tax is not sizeable, it generates a burden on wealth, which can be very high depending on its mean return and can lead to family business, for instance, paying out dividends simply for tax payment purposes.

Since it was first applied in 1992, the current wealth tax (established by Law 19/1991 of June 6th, which derogated the 1977 law) has tax rates progressing from an initial 0.20 percent to 2.50 percent for tax bases in excess of just under 10.7 million Euros (according to current legislation). These tax rates, t, would have to be divided by the mean returns, r, on wealth P, to determine the equivalent tax rate, t' in terms of personal income tax revenue, accordingly: $P \cdot t = P \cdot r \cdot t'$. Thus, if the marginal wealth tax rate is 2.50 percent, with r=0.03, the equivalent personal income tax rate is 83.34 percent. The exemption minimum, only applicable to residents, is established by deducting 108,182.18 euros (unless the autonomous region in question has established a different value) from the tax base. There have also been limits to the sum of payable wealth and personal income tax, also exclusively applicable to residents, which, in the tax approved in 1991, was 70 percent of the personal income tax base, with payable wealth tax reduced accordingly. However, these reductions could not exceed 80 percent of the latter. In other words, payable wealth tax is never less than 20 percent of the assessed amount.

With this regulation, the marginal (and mean) tax rate was 70 percent and, because of the minimum assessed amount, greater than 70 percent for additions to wealth. Likewise, there were cases, relatively simple to determine, in which the tax limit was 100 percent or more, with clearly confiscating effects. At the same time, as we have mentioned, the tax was often the reason for dividend payments, causing serious problems when firms were operating at a loss, with low profits or when profits should have been retained to improve financing.

In view of this devastating taxation framework, in January 1993 the Family Business Institute presented a report (Albi, 1994), at the highest political level, referring to wealth tax, inheritance and donation tax, the fiscal transparency of the system, double taxation and other aspects of corporate income tax, suggesting several alternative solutions. It appears that the report was well accepted in general terms by policymakers at the time, but with some reluctance from Ministry of Pubic Finance officials. However, it was the political influence of the Convèrgencia y Unió party, a regional political party from the industrialised region of Catalonia (a region where the importance of family business is quite considerable) that led to certain solutions being put into practice to the satisfaction of family enterprises.

The first objective of family firms, and indeed of the entire business community, was the abolition of the wealth tax, which family firms had objected to since it was first introduced in 1977. This objective has not been achieved. However, in 1994—Law 22/1993, of December 29th —a regulation came into force exempting the personal assets required for regular, personal and direct business activities which are the taxpayer's main source of income. It also exempted shares in corporations for those individuals whose main activity was not asset management, provided that the taxpayer holds more than 20 percent of the shares, performs management functions for the corporation, and receives payment representing over 50 percent of his/her total business, professional and employment income from this corporation. Starting in 1995—Law 42/1994, of December 30th—, this 20 percent minimal shareholding was reduced to 15 percent.

In 1997—Law 13/1996, of December 30th—a new amendment was made to the minimal shareholding requirement. Taxpayers filing individually qualify for a minimum shareholding exemption of 15 percent, and taxpayers filing jointly with his/her spouse, children, parents or siblings qualify for a 20 percent exemption. This regulation establishes that the right to exemption is also applicable to shares in firms traded on the stock exchange. Holding companies with shares in other active enterprises are included in this provision if the shares they manage represent more than 5 percent of the voting rights in those enterprises. Furthermore, in 1998—Law 66/1997, of December 30th—the scope of the exemption was increased to include the assets of independent professionals.

Finally, in 2003—Law 51/2002, of December 27th—the minimum individual shareholding for this exemption to be applicable was reduced from 15 to 5 percent. In 2004—Law 62/2003, of December 30th—the scope of the exemption was again increased to include not only share ownership but also a beneficial life interest in exempt shares.

This long period of tax changes, which led to family businesses being exempt from wealth tax, has been accompanied, since 2003—Law 46/2002, of December 18th, by the reduction from 70 to 60 percent of the combined limit of payable wealth tax plus the portion of payable personal income tax corresponding to the general part of the latter's tax base. This new 60 percent limit is now calculated on the general part of the personal income tax base (which does not include capital gains generated over more than one year). Before this change, capital gains generated over more than one year (now taxed at 15 percent) could, like other income, be subject to a 70 percent tax rate, due to the combined limit. However, the minimum wealth tax payable continues to be 20 percent, so taxation may still be confiscatory.

As for the negative effects of the inheritance and donation tax on family businesses, the basic problem lies in actually paying the tax because the property transferred between generations usually consists of productive assets, without the necessary cash being available for the payment. Since inheritance and donation tax rates range from 7.65 to 34 percent (currently applicable to tax bases of just over 797.55 million euros), when taxable wealth is very large, a third of it may be paid in tax. Furthermore, depending on the taxable wealth of the acquirer prior to the transfer, coefficients are applied to increase the tax payable. For example, for an acquirer receiving a transfer from a parent, with pre-existing taxable wealth totalling just over 4 million euros, the tax increase is 20 percent, so that the total tax payable would represent a mean rate of around 40 percent and a maximum marginal rate of 40.8 percent.

Response to the demands of the Family Business Institute and other business community organisations in relation to the inheritance and donation tax took a little longer than their demands on wealth tax. Initially, in 1995, the conditions for deferral and splitting payment that were already applicable to individual businesses were also applied to family businesses exempt from wealth tax. In 1996, legislation came into force establishing a 95 percent reduction in the inheritance and donation tax—only for *mortis causa* acquisition—applicable to assets exempt from wealth tax by the family business regulation, with a series of additional conditions. The rule was redrafted in Law 14/1996, of November 30th, applicable in 1997 and, in turn, Law 13/1996, of December 30th, completed the rule by applying the 95 percent reduction to the *inter vivos* transfer of family businesses exempt from wealth tax, also with some additional requisites. In 1998—Law 66/1997, of December 30th, the reduction was also applied to professional activities and the transfer of beneficial rights on businesses. In both cases this reduction was based on compliance with the conditions for wealth tax exemption and the other requirements established for inheritance and donation tax purposes (for example, maintaining ownership for at least 10 years and, in the case of donations, the donor being 65 or over).

With the combination of the wealth tax exemption and the 95 percent inheritance and donation tax rebate (in the form of a reduction to the tax base), family businesses achieved most of their objectives over ten years of reform. This is a good example of the interrelations between policymakers and the business community, based on the economic and fiscal arguments put forward by the two sides, and ultimately the results depending on political alliances. Entrepreneurs continue to demand the elimination of the wealth tax, or at least a reduction in its high rates (only five countries in the EU have a wealth tax, and maximum rates are much lower than the 2.5 percent applied in Spain). In any case, what we have called the "minimum payable" in wealth tax (20 percent of the assessed amount) represents greater taxation than the 60 percent of the limit applicable to the sum of assessed personal income and wealth tax (which is also often exceeded in the way it is regulated). Therefore, the business community continues to demand that the "minimum payable" only be applicable in specific cases as a way of preventing attempts to evade the wealth tax (transferring wealth to the spouse or children with no income, for instance).

Finally, the regulation of family businesses in wealth tax and inheritance and donation taxes, together with other aspects of these taxes, is calling for a major reform of taxation on wealth. This reform has to be coordinated with the autonomous regions, to which these taxes and part of their regulation, were transferred in 2002. This subject is large in scope and of considerable importance. The enormous disparity in how different assets are treated—for example between family businesses and other assets—both in wealth and inheritance and donation tax is certainly not logical, and is worse in some autonomous regions. In the latter, following the traditional exemption position in the Basque Country and Navarre, the reduction was increased to 99 percent in regions such as La Rioja and the autonomous cities of Ceuta and Melilla, with different conditions applicable to *mortis causa* transfers to descendants and Cantabria, which practically suppresses the tax in some cases. This wide variety of fiscal treatments and other problems associated with the taxation of wealth require, in my opinion, an urgent study and debate on wealth taxation in the Spanish tax system.

RELATIONS BETWEEN PERSONAL AND CORPORATE INCOME TAX

Integration of Personal and Corporate Income Tax

The total integration of business profits in the personal income tax was proposed in the Carter report (1966–67), one of the intellectual foundations of the 1978 Spanish Tax Reform. Such a criterion led to various academic proposals for Spanish Reform during the 70s that would have abolished the corporate income tax. At any rate, firms must be taxed for a variety of basic control reasons, and when this is done it leads to the problem of double taxation.

The double taxation, in personal and corporate income tax, of company profits is an old problem affecting tax systems. The double taxation of dividends discourages the distribution of profits to shareholders and the issue of shares to make new investments. Debt becomes the best financing method that avoids double taxation. At the same time, it is evident that firms continue to pay dividends as a sign that they are profitable, and also to prevent managers from "over-investing", but double taxation of dividends may still be an important business and economic problem. The double taxation of profits set aside for reserves depends on how capital gains are treated in the personal income tax. We will not go into the detail of this, but the favourable treatment given to capital gains in the current Spanish tax system and the deferral of taxation until shares are transferred do mitigate the problem.

The domestic integration of personal and corporate income tax is the most general solution to the problem of double taxation of dividends. It would be costly in revenue terms to take international shareholders into account, and, in any case, countries of residency of shareholders take care of the issue through foreign tax credits or other means. Additionally, double taxation should not seriously affect the cost of capital in a small open economy, in which the returns for investors (before personal income tax) are internationally determined. The personal tax affecting a country's savings reduces savers' returns, but it does not affect the firm's cost of capital for making investment decisions if the economy is open in regard to capital markets. The double taxation of dividends does also have to be addressed both at national and international scales. Internationally, these issues can be addressed via tax treaties, foreign tax credits or other schemes provided by residency countries.

However, the issue to be considered now is the double taxation of dividends in personal and corporate income taxes within Spain. A Tax credit system was initially chosen in 1978. Shareholders were entitled to a personal income tax deduction of 15 percent of the dividends received from resident firms, which was reduced to 10 percent in 1987. In this situation, Spain was next to last in the ranking of European Community countries in relation to the degree of compensation for double taxation.

The level of compensation is easy to calculate. Since a profit unit paid 0.35 in corporate income tax and the dividend deduction was 0.1(1 – 0.35) after 1987, the degree of compensation was:

$$\frac{0.1(1-0.35)}{0.35} = 18.57\%$$

The business community demanded a reform for many years, but it only came about in 1995, and did not fully eliminate the double taxation of dividends.

The system used in Spain since 1995 is based on imputation, with domestic dividends integrated in the personal income tax base multiplied by a percentage (which "adds" the underlying corporate tax) which is, in turn, the percentage used to calculate the assessed tax deduction for such dividends. Imputation may be a good system for eliminating double taxation while maintaining the individual tax burden if one considers only dividends received by resident individuals from resident companies. Below we explain how the imputation system actually works.

Double taxation is due to the fact that corporate income tax reduces the profits from which dividends taxed by personal income tax are paid. An imputation system completely eliminates the problem of double taxation if the shareholder is returned the corporate income tax and taxed on the income from which the dividend comes. In Spain, with a corporate tax rate of 35 percent, one euro of profit is nominally taxed with 0.35 euros, with 0.65 euros left for distribution. To eliminate double taxation completely, the percentage deduction (p) to assessed personal income tax which compensates the corporate tax paid, with a nominal rate of 35 percent, would be:

$$p(1 - 0.35) = 0.35$$

$$\text{so, } p = 53.84615\%$$

The system's logic would require the return integrated in the personal income tax base to be one euro: what the shareholder receives (0.65) multiplied by 1.5384615. With this situation, the shareholder's personal income tax would apply to the profit from which the dividend comes (dividend received plus its underlying corporate tax), eliminating the corporate tax already paid by deducting it from the assessed amount.

However, the general imputation percentage currently used is 1.4, so double taxation is only partly corrected by 74.28 percent.

To discover the degree to which double taxation is mitigated in the case of the 1.4 integration percentage (p) in relation to the 35 percent nominal corporate tax rate (t), the question we have to ask is what proportion of each euro of profit before corporate tax is passed onto the shareholder before applying the personal income tax? The shareholder receives one euro less corporate tax plus the compensation for double taxation:

$$1 - t + (1 - t)(p - 1) = (1 - t)\,p$$

If double taxation were to be fully eliminated, the $(1 - t)\,p$ factor would be equal to one. That is, one euro of distributed business profit is compensated either in corporate or personal income tax to completely cancel out the corporate tax. In the case of partial correction, the uncorrected part is:

$$1 - (1 - t)\,p,$$

So, there is no double taxation per unit of underlying corporate tax in the following proportion:

$$\frac{t-[1-(1-t)p]}{t},$$

resulting in the following coefficient of attenuation of double taxation of dividends:

$$C=\left[1-\frac{1-(1-t)p}{t}\right]100,$$

Complete correction would imply $C = 1$, and with complete double taxation $C = 0$.

Applying the current Spanish system values of $t = 0.35$ and $p = 1.40$:

$$C = 74.28\%$$

Since on the other hand, if double taxation was fully eliminated:

$$(1-t)\,p = 1,$$

with $p = 1.40$ there is complete elimination of double taxation if the effective rate is:

$$t_{efec} = 28.57\%$$

Policymakers often mention the fact that this rate, 28.57%, is close to the average rate of corporate income tax actually paid, so the 1.4 imputation percentage is appropriate. However, the argument that the effective corporate income tax rate is lower than the nominal rate because of existing fiscal incentives is incorrect. If an average effective rate is used for these calculations, these incentives are not passed on to the shareholder and, therefore, cancelled. If it is thought that the effective corporate tax rate is below the nominal rate of 35 percent because of tax evasion, the correct reaction would be to prevent such evasion and eliminate the double taxation of dividends. Consequently, the business community continues to demand that the imputation system should not only mitigate double taxation but get rid of it altogether.

One difficulty associated with the proposal for complete elimination of double taxation following the imputation method, however, lies in the corporate tax reduction for reinvestment of fixed asset transfers which leaves capital gains taxed at 15 percent instead of the nominal 35 percent. With this measure, and without considering the reduced 30 percent rate for

SMEs, using g to refer to the tax rate on extraordinary profits with reinvestment (this is 15 percent) and c to refer to the percentage of distributed typical profits and, therefore, $(1 - c)$ to refer to atypical profits, the expression for the imputation coefficient is considerably more complex than the previous one, depending on t, g and c.

Following the same reasoning as before:

$$1 - tc - g(1 - c) + [1 - tc - g(1 - c)]\,[p - 1] = p\,[1 - tc - g(1 - c)],$$

so to fully correct double taxation:

$$p = \frac{1}{[1 - tc - g(1 - c)]}$$

This expression shows that it is, in practice, impossible for the imputation system to fully and precisely eliminate double taxation. We could argue that, since the reinvestment deduction is a fiscal credit, for it to remain with the shareholder, we would have to assume that the reference rate is the general corporate tax rate. Therefore, if we have a nominal rate of 35 percent, there would be nothing wrong with using an imputation coefficient of 1.5384615, even if capital gains are taxed at 15 per 100.

However, this would mean that someone who, with a marginal personal income tax rate of 45 per 100, receives a dividend from typical profits would have a 45 per 100 tax burden, and someone who receives it from capital gains would have a 28.08 percent burden, with intermediate values for dividends from profits with different proportions of typical and atypical profits. On the other hand, with regards to individual shareholders in passive holding companies, from 2003 (which we will be considering shortly), taxation remains at 40 per 100, or 15 per 100 in the case of capital gains; in other words, it is the rate that corresponds to the passive holding companies themselves. There is a manifest dispersion of the tax burden and a deterioration of the neutrality principle, which could lead, in a not too distant future, to the need to seek other solutions to the problem. These new solutions are also needed given certain rulings of the High Tribunal of Justice of the European Communities which establish that it is contrary to the EU Treaty to give different tax treatment to dividends received from domestic corporations or from corporations resident in any other EU member country. The possible solution to the problem of double taxation, in personal and corporate income tax, will be considered in the conclusion of this paper.

Fiscal Transparency and the Solution of the Passive Holding Company Regime

The fiscal transparency regime was one of the new aspects introduced by the Urgent Measures on Tax Reform Act (Law 50/1977, of November 14th) that the business community objected to from the start. It initially contained a voluntary component, since the regime eliminated the double taxation of dividends (later derogated in 1985) and a compulsory component aimed at preventing tax evasion by means of creating companies acting as screens between the taxpayer and the administration. The main objective for the screen companies was to seek a corporate income tax rate lower than the equivalent personal tax rate. An international regime of fiscal transparency was introduced in 1991, which is still in place today.

Fundamentally, the national transparency regime aimed, since its first implementation in 1978, at "passive" firms which, without performing business activities proper themselves, are concerned with the ownership of shares or assets (real estate, for instance) and firms set up by independent professionals, artists and athletes, provided they complied with a complex series of conditions. Firms classified as transparent, according to the last regulation, paid the assessed amount of corporate income tax but this amount was considered as a "payment on account" of the personal income tax of resident shareholders (non-residents were also included initially), individuals or legal entities. Negative tax bases were used to compensate positive tax bases in later periods (in the early stages of the regime, both positive and negative bases were charged to shareholders).

The national fiscal transparency system, which was subject to many changes over the years, as shown in the previous paragraph, had highly general ambitions and was too complex both for the Administration and the taxpayer. It is also true, however, that it had one major advantage in that it completely eliminated double taxation, so it was effective, for instance, for professional firms distributing all their profits.

One serious problem, among others, in relation to fiscal transparency for quite a few years concerned holding companies. These holding companies, which could be generally classified as transparent, had direct control over at least 50 percent of the voting rights in their subsidiaries, unless they managed the business activities of the subsidiaries with human and material assets. As a result of the more transparent holdings, the shareholders residing in Spain were taxed at marginal rates for individuals, and due to the effect of the wealth tax, this rate could be as high as 70 percent. Holding companies, therefore, were only able to reinvest 30 percent of their profits because they had to pay out 70 percent so that shareholders could pay their taxes. Together with other business organisations, the Family Business Institute contemplated the problem in their January 1993 report. This problem was mitigated in 1999 by reducing the holding company's share in its stock portfolio to 5 percent to be excluded from the tax transparency regime. Likewise, the transparency regime was not applied to certain firms which, in spite of performing actual economic activities, could suddenly and temporarily find themselves with a balance sheet where the majority of the assets were shares or assets unrelated to the firm's activity, ready for future investments.

The business community's proposals always emphasised complexity of the fiscal transparency regime, both from a fiscal and accounting perspective, and that the regime caused business problems and failed to serve its purpose. The system was valued, on the other hand, as a way of avoiding the double taxation of dividends. The business community also pointed out that the regime would not be justified if, as proposed, the rate of corporate income tax was to be close to a maximum marginal rate of personal income tax.

The new amendments to the national fiscal transparency regime led to its derogation in 2003 and the creation, as an alternative, of the passive holding company system which, in general, has been accepted by the business community. The system does not apply to firms set up by independent professionals, artists or athletes, and is compulsory for resident companies in Spain who passively hold assets and comply with a series of circumstances concerning the composition of their assets and share ownership. Among other cases, the composition of assets classifying a firm as a passive holding company excludes shares representing at least 5 percent of voting rights controlled by the "holding" or "controlling" firm. It also excludes shares or assets unrelated to economic activities, the purchase price of which does not exceed the amount of non-distributed profits of the year in question plus the ten previous years. This was to avoid, for instance, situations arising when profits are retained for future business investments.

Corporate income taxation on passive holding companies is configured with hybrid elements from both corporate and personal income tax. The firm's tax base is divided into two parts, a general and a special part, following personal income tax regulations. The general part consists of typical and atypical profits, excluding the capital gains and losses occurring on occasion of the transfer of assets acquired more than one year prior to the transfer date. These capital gains and losses generated in a period of over twelve months make up the special part of the tax base.

The general part of a passive holding company's tax base is taxed at a rate of 40 percent, 5 percentage points higher than the general corporate income tax rate, to discourage the use of such companies by individuals (the maximum marginal personal income tax rate is currently 45 percent). The special part of the tax base is taxed at 15 percent, the same rate applied to the special part of the personal income tax base and the rate applied to corporate capital gains when the proceeds from the transaction are reinvested.

In general, individual resident shareholders in passive holding companies are not further taxed when they receive dividends from them, but if they are firms, the dividend deduction that applies only halves the double taxation (a form of penalisation). The capital gains obtained by individuals in the transfer of shares in holding companies are not taxed as non-distributed profits. On the other hand, if the transferor is a firm or a non-resident with permanent establishment, the deduction cannot be applied to avoid the double taxation of domestic capital gains. This, in fact, penalises other firms with shares in passive holding companies.

Consequently, in many cases where such companies are used by individuals, the returns obtained are taxed at 40 percent and capital gains obtained in a period of over one year at 15 percent of non-distributed profits. The current solution would appear to be stable and satisfactory both to the policymaker and the taxpayer.

CONCLUSIONS AND FINAL REMARKS

Other varied fiscal issues have affected the relationship between policymakers and the business community over this long period of tax changes. For example, in the process of preparing for the introduction of VAT in 1986, collaboration between the authorities and business organisations was very positive. One subject that was discussed on many occasions over the following years was the reduction in the business contribution to the social security system, by means of higher VAT rates. The subnational government tax on economic activities (municipal tax, as specified in different schedules, for performance of economic activities), affecting all businesses, has always been questioned, and since 2003, this has resulted in a considerable increase in the number of exempt cases together with a significant rise in the amount due in certain cases.

With regards to personal income tax, of which we have studied several aspects earlier, of particular interest to the business community has been how capital gains from the sale of company shares are treated. Likewise, in relation to personnel benefits, one essential aspect has been the development of pension plans and retirement funds, since 1988, or the fiscal treatment given to payments in kind. Problems related to the financing of the autonomous regions have also possibly had a collateral impact on matters of interest to the business community. Finally, issues related to legal certainty and the rights and obligations involved in taxation, or the administrative costs associated with taxes, have often been at the centre of discussions between policy makers and the business community. Reasonable solutions to these questions have been included in the Statute of the Tax Payer and the new General Taxation Act that came into force in 2004.

Turning now to the main content of the paper, the Spanish business community accepted most of the fiscal measures adopted in 1977–78, but fundamentally objected to the introduction of taxation on wealth and the fiscal transparency regime. It also objected to the limited attempts to avoid the double taxation of dividends and the heavily progressive nature of personal income tax, based on the fact that, in general, economic circumstances had changed a great deal since the system was designed between 1970 and 1975. Later, due to the fact that the Spanish economy had opened up on an international scale since 1986, and especially during the nineties, the focus of attention of both policymakers and the business community shifted to reforms aimed at increasing business competitiveness and internationalisation. These goals have been largely satisfied over the last fourteen years. In fact, economic and public finance considerations and, to a considerable extent, persuasion, have been key elements in the relationship between policymakers and the business community, with a few bitter disputes, in these twenty-eight years of tax reform.

The new tax system was particularly difficult, from a business perspective, in the eighties, and the decade saw serious confrontations between the business community and policymakers. The early nineties signalled a change in attitude by policymakers, who tended to be much more receptive to the business community's demands. For example, the inclusion of incentives in corporate income tax to increase business competitiveness in an open economy has been consistently supported since the tax was reformed in 1995 and in all its more recent amendments.

As for the essential elements of corporate income tax, tax rates have not varied greatly in the period we have considered. The current 35 per cent standard rate was established back in 1985. For reasons of fiscal competition in the EU, however, the possibility of lowering the rate may need to be considered. This, in turn, would have a clear impact on the stock market because the cost of corporate taxation is "capitalised" on the stock exchange and its reduction would generate gains. In any event, it will be important to pay attention to the loss of revenue derived from decreases in nominal tax rates. In this respect, the subject of the integration of corporate and personal income tax, which we shall refer to later, would also have to be considered, together with the maximum marginal personal income tax rate.

With regards to the corporate income tax base, the discussions between policymakers and the business community have, to a great extent, been centred on taxation regulations and standards not requiring major adjustments to accounting results. The application, as of 1st of January 2005, of new International Financial Reporting Standards (IFRS), in accordance with EU regulation, to corporations forming part of a group will require fiscal changes to accommodate tax to accounting norms, and this may produce new controversies. An example is the valuation of intangible assets such as trademarks or R&D expenditure, or the financial goodwill entered into the accounts when substantial shares are acquired in other firms. The change to IFRS consists of replacing the currently applicable amortisation criterion with the depreciation concept. There will be no charge to the accounting result for the amortisation of intangible assets, but the year's accounting profits, if applicable, will be reduced by the depreciation of such assets. Other reform issues due to the IFRS are centred on the tax on profits and the advance and deferred taxes arising from differences between the fiscal and accounting value of assets and liabilities.

In relation to tax benefits, incentives for investment have tended towards accelerated depreciation and have become schemes to promote R&D activities or technological innovation, staff training, exports, more appropriate environmental conduct and, above all, support for the internationalisation of Spanish firms. Little is known about the efficiency of these tax incentives, but the foregone revenue might be more usefully used by applying lower corporate income tax rates.

Better tax treatment of SMEs was a basic component in the relationship between policy makers and the business community, both for individual enterprises and companies. Family business organisations have, in turn, concentrated on the taxation of wealth (wealth tax-inheritance and donation tax), with positive results leading to an in-depth review of this type of taxes in the future. The business community also demanded the elimination of the fiscal transparency regime, and were successful at the cost of establishing a taxation system applicable to passive holding companies.

The complete elimination of the double taxation of dividends is still a pending issue. With regards to double taxation of dividends in personal and corporate income tax the present imputation system lacks neutrality, as discussed above, and is easily subject to attack by European institutions since it only applies to dividends paid by resident corporations.

A European Commission communication dated December 19, 2003, concludes that member States should apply the same tax treatment to inbound dividends from other member States as to domestic dividends, in order to eliminate restrictions to free movement of capital (prohibited by articles 56 and 58 of the European Community Treaty). This position followed the jurisprudence of the European Community High Court in the Verkooijen case (C-35/98). This jurisprudence has continued after the aforementioned Commission communication with the Lenz case (C-315/02) and more recently—September 7, 2004—with the Manninen ruling (C-319/02) establishing that the Finish imputation system restricts the free movement of capital. Given the content of the Manninen ruling, the Spanish system preventing the double taxation of dividends should include dividends paid by corporations resident in other EU countries to personal income taxpayers resident in Spain.

The imputation system, however, is ill suited to deal with a wide array of corporate tax rates underlying the distributed dividends, as is now the case internationally and very clearly in the EU (the range of corporate tax rates in EU countries is 12.5–40 percent). To apply the same imputation coefficient to dividends distributed from profits subject to different tax burdens is unreasonable, and it is impracticable to use different coefficients or "add" to the dividend the corresponding corporate income tax paid in other countries (to be credited against personal income tax liability). This is the reason why "pure" imputation systems, which were widely used in EU countries until recently, are now very seldom applied (Spain and Malta).

The solutions chosen by EU member countries to integrate their personal and corporate income taxes are varied. Many of them follow "modified classical systems", permitting double taxation on only part of the dividends via exemption from personal income tax of, say, 50 or 60 percent of the dividends. Others simply exempt the dividend if the shareholder's share in the distributing corporation exceeds a certain percentage and apply a flat rate of 20 to 25 percent to other dividends that do not benefit from this exemption.

In fact, these solutions show that tax systems have moved away from comprehensive or global taxation—all types of income are treated in the same way for tax purposes—and back to schedular systems. Following this approach, a final and more general solution may be dual taxation. A dual income tax structure is a schedular system, taxing employment and capital income separately, although homogenously. Capital income is taxed according to a separate and lower tax schedule than labour income. This is an important departure from comprehensive income taxation, which was the cornerstone of the Spanish tax reform initiated in 1977–78. However, it represents a compromise solution not only to the problem of integration of personal and corporate income taxes, but to many other difficulties of comprehensive taxation, administrative or not.

I believe that dual taxation deserves careful consideration for a possible future reform of the Spanish tax system. If a schedular personal income tax structure was chosen, using a common corporate and personal capital income tax rate would help to solve the problem of integrating corporate and personal income taxes. It would represent a complete overhaul of the present system, initiated under a comprehensive tax approach, which would show that the road between a closed economy with severe problems in 1977–78 and Spain's fiscal situation today has certainly been a long one.

NOTES

* Professor of Public Finance, Universidad Complutense de Madrid

1. My thanks for comments provided as an assessment of the paper and the financial support provided by the Institute of Fiscal Studies, Ministry of Economy and Public Finance, Madrid. Author's contact: ealbi@retemail.es
2. This included overtime work, emigration outside the country and to other regions within Spain, and savings, which clearly supported the fast rate of growth of the economy.
3. The Palace of the Moncloa is the official residence of the prime minister (or Presidente del Gobierno) in Madrid.
4. The amendment of the Tax on Capital Transfers and Documented Legal Acts (Law 32/1980, of June 21) was prior to major changes in indirect taxation.
5. The basic assumption is that the fiscal incentives have been effective in strengthening competitiveness as opposed to protecting weaker domestic enterprises against foreign competition.
6. However, if we were to extrapolate from the United States' experience with corporate income taxation at the state level, coordination and harmonisation will be hard, if not impossible, to achieve.
7. A lower 30 percent is applicable to the first 120.202,41 euros of profit obtained by small and medium-sized enterprises, defined as firms with a turnover of less than 8 million euros in the previous year.
8. The issue of double taxation between personal and corporate income tax will be discussed later.
9. The regime follows a very simple depreciation method with provisions being estimated *a forfeit* applying a coefficient of 0.05 to net income (calculated excluding the provisions as an expense.
10. The next group of owners consists of banks and savings banks, controlling 18 percent of stock market enterprises.

REFERENCES

Albi, E. (1994), *Fiscalidad y Empresa Familiar*, Barcelona: Instituto de la Empresa Familiar and Planeta Agostini.

_______ (2005), *Sistema Fiscal Español*, Barcelona: Ariel (the twenty-seven editions of the book include all the changes that have taken place in the 1979–2005 period).

Canals, J. (2004), 'La internacionalización de la empresa española', *Papeles de Economía Española*, 100, 249–263.

Carter Report, *Report of the Royal Commission on Taxation* (1966–67), Information Canada-Décisions de Publication, Ottawa, Spanish version entitled *Informe Carter*, IEF, Madrid, 1975.

CEOE (1989), La urgente reforma del Sistema tributario español, Madrid.

Commission of the E.C. (2001), *Towards an Internal Market without tax obstacles,* COM 582 final, including Summary of "Company Taxation in the Internal Market", SEC, 2003, 1681.

Cuervo-Arango, C. and Trujillo, J.A. (1987), 'Estructura industrial e incentivos a la inversión', *Papeles de Economía Española*, 30–31, 220–235.

Devereux, M. and Griffith, R. (1998), 'Taxes and the location of production: evidence from a panel of U.S. multinationals', *Journal of Public Economics*, 68(3), 335–367.

Espitia, M., Huerta, E., Lecha, G., and Salas, V. (1988), *Inversión, coste del capital e impuestos en la economía española,* 1965–1984, mimeo, Universidad de Zaragoza, IEF.

_______ (1989), 'Impuestos efectivos sobre beneficios y rentas de los activos productivos', *Papeles de Economía Española*, 39–40, 397–413.

Fuentes, E. (dir.) (1973), *Informe sobre el Sistema Tributario Español*, 2nd edition, 2002, IEF, Madrid.

_______ (dir.) (1976), *Sistema Tributario Español. Criterios para su reforma*, 2nd edition, 2002, IEF, Madrid.

_______ (dir.) (1990), La Reforma Fiscal y los problemas de la Hacienda Pública española, Civitas, Madrid.

Ministry of Economy and Public Finance (1994), Informe para la Reforma del Impuesto sobre Sociedades, Madrid.

Neumark, F. (1970), *Grundsätze gerechter und ökonomish rationaler Steuerpolitik,* JCB Mohr (Paul Siebeck), Tübingen, Spanish version by José Zamit, entitled *Principios de la Imposición*, IEF, Madrid, 1973.

Peacock, A.T. (1979), 'Fiscal Theory and the "Market" for Tax Reform', I.I.P.F. Conference papers, Taormina, Italy.

Santana, D. and Aguiar, J.L. (2004), *Propiedad y blindaje de las empresas cotizadas españolas* , 1996–2002, National Stock Market Commission, Madrid. Monograph No. 5.

Sanz, J.F. (1995), Un análisis de la distorsiones impositivas sobre las rentas del capital en España a través del concepto de tipo impositivo efectivo, Colección Investigaciones No. 3, IEF, Madrid.

Simons, H.C. (1938), *Personal Income Taxation*, sixth edition, 1970, Chicago, USA: The University of Chicago Press.

4. Tax Reform in Perspective: The Role of the Public Sector in Spain along the Process of European Integration

José Manuel González-Páramo and Pablo Hernández de Cos *

INTRODUCTION

Over the last 25 years, the nature and role of the Spanish tax system has undergone radical changes. In the mid 70s, the tax system featured two main characteristics. First, it produced revenues representing only slightly more than half of the European average tax ratio. And secondly, its structural features—lack of personalisation, inflexibility, pervasive non-neutralities—made it unsuitable to contribute to the modernisation of the economy that was to come.

The fundamental tax reform undertaken in the late 70s by the first democratic governments helped to overcome the antiquated tax regime, kicking off a panoply of other reforms and laying the revenue foundations for the transformation of Spain's public sector. Indeed, the nature of today's tax reform dilemmas has little to do with the contents of the debates that took place in the 70s. Current policy options are placed firmly in the camp of advanced market economies. This sharp contrast can be understood only in the context of the overall evolution of the public sector along the intense process of European integration.

The single most important characteristic of the Spanish economy in the last decades has been its increasing involvement in Europe. Though the gradual opening up to the outside world began in the early 60s, after a long period of autarky, the process of adoption of more outwardly oriented policies was not definitively consolidated until Spain's accession to the European Community (EC) on January 1, 1986.

The twin objectives of creating a Single European Market in 1993 and of reinforcing policy convergence as a first step towards the creation of Economic and Monetary Union (EMU) before the end of the century radically altered the framework in which public policy was designed. Spain's participation in Stage Three of Economic and Monetary Union, from its start in 1999 after having satisfactorily met the convergence criteria, was indeed the most considerable success. The integration process has clearly broadened the possibility of drawing the Spanish standard of living closer to that in the more advanced European Union (EU) economies. However, the long-term effects of integration on the competitiveness of the Spanish economy and the welfare of economic agents will depend crucially on the adaptability of markets and the responses of public policy.

This chapter discusses the main implications of European integration for the Spanish public sector and, in particular, for those of its activities which are included in the government budget. The impressionistic analysis that follows can be succinctly summarised in four basic questions. What were the main structural characteristics of the Spanish public sector shortly before entering the Community? What policy responses were implemented to cope with the impact of entry? What policies were necessary to smooth convergence? What policies are still needed to maximise the benefits of participating in the EMU? The first of these questions is dealt with in the next section, which reviews the structural characteristics of the Spanish public sector on the eve of entry into the EC. The third section discusses the responses of the public sector between integration and 1993, when a successful fiscal consolidation process, first timid then firm, started with the aim to meet the convergence criteria of the Maastricht Treaty and to fulfil the rules of the Stability and Growth Pact. This consolidation process is described in the forth section. the fifth section concludes the work by briefly exploring the main challenges that participating in the European Monetary Union still poses for the Spanish budgetary policy.

THE SPANISH PUBLIC SECTOR ON THE EVE OF EC ACCESSION: THE POINT OF DEPARTURE

Trends in General Government Activity

The decade before Spanish accession to the EC saw an extraordinarily rapid increase in the share of the public sector in the Spanish economy. Breaking with Spain's tradition of substantial off-budget interventionism (see Comín, 1989), which caused a wide variety of rigidities and distortions, in the mid 70s general government expenditures began to grow dramatically. While in the EC public spending grew annually by an average 0.9 percent of GDP in the period 1975–1985, in Spain public spending as a proportion of GDP almost doubled, peaking at nearly 40.3 percent of GDP (Figure 4.1).

Two main factors can be identified as having triggered these spectacular rises. On the one hand, the decline in economic performance relative to the levels experienced in the previous decade brought about a sharp increase in subsidies and public transfers to the private sector. On the other, the political change to a democratic regime gave a decisive impetus to a rapid catching-up process in the welfare-state area. Thus, despite the substantial fiscal reform of 1977–1978 (the tax burden rose on average by one per cent of GDP annually), the effect of the two forces exceeded the tax revenue potential, and led to mounting public deficits and rising public debt. The ensuing increase in interest payments on the debt exacerbated these difficulties by adding to the existing commitments of public resources.

On the eve of EC membership, the role of the public sector in the Spanish economy had acquired characteristics quite different from those of the mid 70s. The initially prevailing consensus concerning the need for public-sector expansion—in order to improve living standards and to consolidate social cohesion—gradually began to break up as the detrimental effects of certain spending and revenue programmes came to bear on the allocation of resources, economic incentives and international competitiveness. What were the main characteristics of public policy during this period of transition and crisis? How did they affect the Spanish position relative to the EC member states? Both questions are briefly considered in what follows.

Budgetary Policy

The gradual deterioration of the government's financial position started in the mid 70s, moving from a surplus of 1.1 percent of GDP in 1973 to a deficit of 5.2 percent in 1982. This drastic change in public borrowing requirements was, for the most part, structural in kind. Without seeking to diminish the importance of the negative effect on public finances of the deceleration in the GDP growth rate (through the automatic reduction of tax revenue and the increase in transfers to companies and the unemployed), the worsening of the cyclically adjusted deficit was the main cause of the widening overall deficit, as Table 4.1 shows. Discretionary increases in income taxes (2.9 percent of GDP) and social security contributions (4.3 percent of GDP), together with restraint in public investment, were not sufficient to counteract the enormous increase in social expenditure (5.5

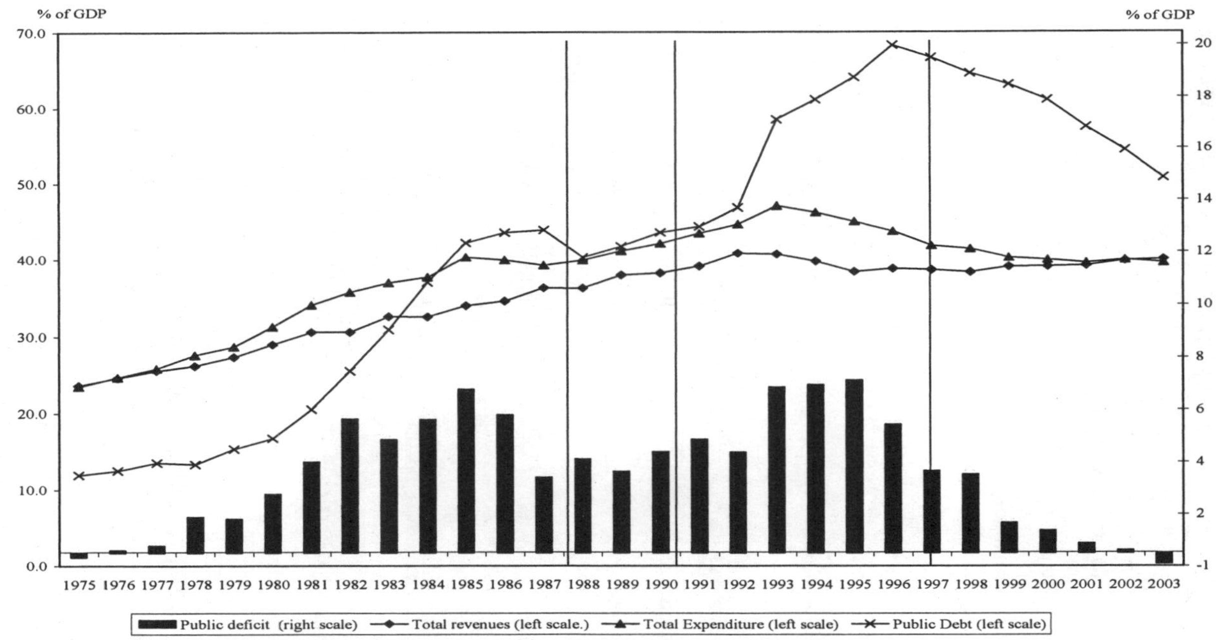

Figure 4.1 Main fiscal policy variables: 1975–2003

Source: National Institute of Statistics.

Table 4.1 General government receipts, expenditures and balances, 1973–1985 (change in percentage of GDP)

	1973–77	*1977–82*	*1982–85*
Current revenue	**3.0**	**5.0**	**3.0**
Taxes on production and imports	-1.2	1.1	1.9
Taxes on income and profits	1.0	1.9	1.5
Social security contributions	2.8	1.5	-0.2
Other current revenue	0.4	0.5	-0.2
Current transfers	**2.7**	**5.3**	**3.1**
Transfers to households	1.9	3.6	0.7
Interest payments on public debt	-0.1	0.5	2.2
Subsidies	0.5	1.1	0.0
Other current transfers	0.4	0.1	0.2
Disposable income	**0.3**	**-0.4**	**-0.1**
Public consumption	**1.5**	**2.3**	**0.5**
Public investment	**0.1**	**0.4**	**0.7**
Capital revenue	**-0.1**	**0.0**	**0.4**
Capital transfers	**0.3**	**1.0**	**0.3**
Public deficit[1]	**1.7**	**5.0**	**1.1**
Memorandum			
Cyclically adjusted deficit (EC)[1,2]	**1.3**	**2.6**	**0.8**
Bank of Spain financing	**0.4**	**3.4**	**-2.2**

Notes:
[1] A + sign indicates an expansionary change and vice-versa.
[2] Deficit corrected for the effects of the economic cycle under the ESCB methodology.

Source: National Institute of Statistics, Banco de España, and own calculations.

percent of GDP), transfers to public and private enterprises (1.8 percent) and government consumption (3.8 percent of GDP). On average, two thirds of the public deficit was funded by the Bank of Spain and by financial institutions, in large measure via compulsory ratios and other non-market instruments.

After seven years of political uncertainty, the 1982 elections produced a stable majority in parliament, an environment which facilitated a long-postponed economic adjustment. The period between 1982 and 1985 saw a break with the recent past that had two important implications for the orientation and medium-term effects of fiscal policy. The experience of the 70s lent support to a sceptical attitude towards 'fine-tuning', partly because of the negative effects of discretionary expansion on inflationary expectations and international competitiveness and partly because of the harmful effect that financing the deficit had had on investment (Mauleón and Perez, 1984), employment (Mauleón, 1986) and the dynamics of public debt (Viñals, 1985). Recognition of the importance of improving public-sector finances as a means of combating inflation, high interest rates and loss of international competitiveness, made it possible to reduce the deficit by 0.8 percent of GDP in 1983. The combined effects of reduced public investment (0.2 percent of GDP) and the substantial increase in both direct and indirect taxes and social security contributions (2.1 percent of GDP) were largely counterbalanced by the sustained increase in current expenditure; but the 1983 budgetary policy was clearly contractionary (Figure 4.2).

Perhaps one of the most notable developments of the three years prior to Spain's entry into the EC was the change, introduced by the government in 1983–1984, in the financing of the deficit. This shifted away from the Bank of Spain (Préstamos de Regulación Monetaria) by means of the creation of Treasury Notes (Pagarés del Tesoro), the purchase of which was guaranteed by the creation of a mandatory investment ratio for banking institutions. But despite the beneficial effects of this measure, high interest rates and the deceleration of monetary indicators meant that the change towards orthodox deficit financing made it more difficult to reach the objective of halting the rise of the deficit. The rapid increase in the proportion of expenditure assigned to interest payments (2.2 percent of GDP between 1982 and 1985) obscured the efforts made under other budgetary headings to slow public spending growth. Thus, despite tax increases and the considerable reduction in the growth of social expenditure and transfers to enterprises, which effectively reined in the expansion of the structural deficit, the total deficit reached the unprecedented level of 6.9 percent of GDP in 1985. At the end of that year, public debt reached 51.3 percent of GDP, i.e. three times as high as in 1979.

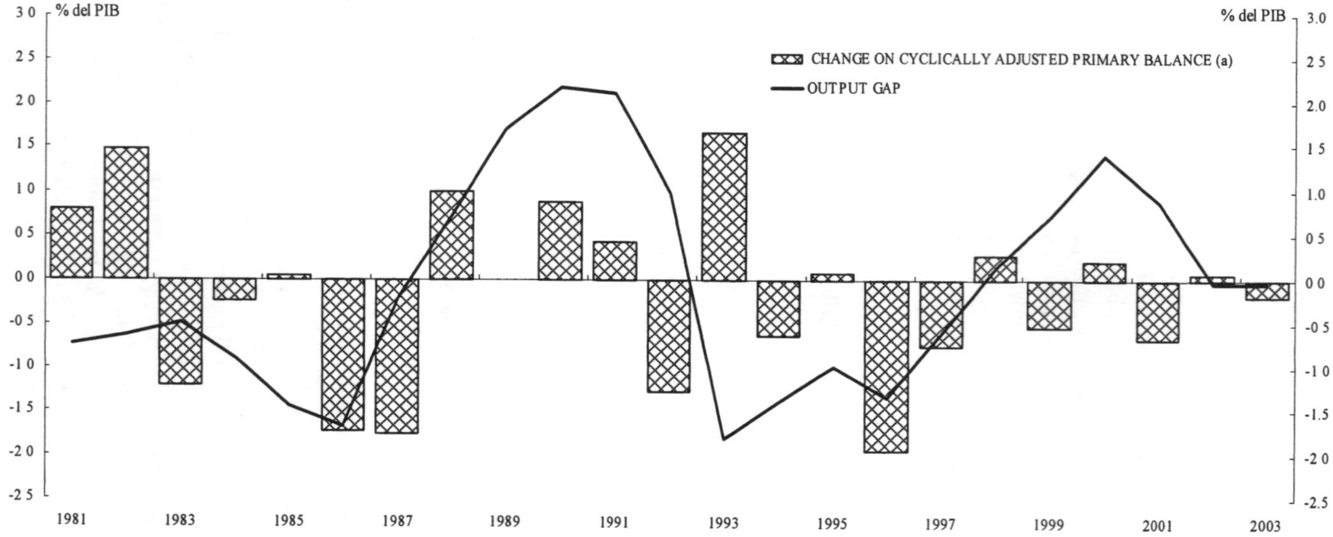

Figure 4.2 Fiscal policy and economic cycle in Spain: 1981–2003

Notes: Adjusted for transitory effects in 1997, 2000, and 2002.

Source: Own calculations.

Public Expenditure Policies

In the mid-70s, the proportion of public spending in GDP was 20 percent below the EC average. Since then and until 1986, the expansion of public spending was extraordinary but very unequally distributed among its economic components. As can be seen in Table 4.1, the item which grew most rapidly was current transfers, with an annual increase of 1 percent of GDP. The bulk of the expansion recorded in the period 1973–1982 comprised transfers to families and enterprises. During the three years up to 1985, the main factor of increase was debt service.

The growth of government consumption was more moderate (0.4 percent of GDP per annum); in the context of a notable increase in public employment, this was almost wholly comprised by wages. Data from the national accounts suggests, however, that the 'relative price effect' of current consumption was small in the late 70s, and even became negative during the 80s (Domínguez Martínez, 1988). This phenomenon reflects significant wage moderation. During the 1975–1985 period, while general government employment grew by 50 percent and its share in total employment by almost 70 percent (reaching 20 percent of the salaried population), real public wages rose very little and were outpaced by private-sector wages (López Casanovas, 1992).

In the 70s, public investment acted as an escape-valve for pressure on the government's budget constraint. As a result, the proportion of GDP accounted for by fixed public investment fell almost continuously until early in the 80s. In the same period, however, the proportion of spending that can be categorised as public capital expenditure increased as a result of the substantial increase in capital transfers to the private sector. The downward trend in public capitalisation ended in 1982; in that year public investment recovered strongly, doubling its share of GDP over five years to exceed the average public investment share in EC member states.

Broad trends in the main expenditure functions

The changes in the functional structure of public spending are summarised in Table 4.2. During the period 1975–1982, there was a major increase in public spending in the welfare-state area, as was the case in most OECD countries (Saunders and Klau, 1985). Spending on merit goods and income support rose by 5.4 percent of GDP, reaching 21.6 percent of GDP in 1982. Under merit goods, the fastest growing item was education, followed by housing and health. Income support expenditure showed considerable dynamism over this period. This was in large measure due to spending on pensions, which grew by 3.1 percent of GDP. And unemployment benefit

Table 4.2 General government spending: functional classification, 1975–1985 (percentage of GDP)

	1975	*1980*	*1982*	*1985*
Public goods	**4.6**	**5.0**	**5.4**	**6.4**
Defence	1.7	1.9	1.9	1.9
General public services	2.9	3.1	3.4	4.5
Welfare state	**16.2**	**20.4**	**21.6**	**23.5**
Merit goods	6.9	8.4	8.3	9.8
Education	2.1	3.1	2.9	3.5
Health	3.8	4.2	4.1	4.4
Housing and collective services	1.0	1.0	1.3	1.9
Income maintenance	9.3	12.0	13.3	13.5
Pensions	5.6	8.1	8.7	9.6
Unemployment	0.5	2.1	2.5	2.6
Other	3.2	1.8	2.1	2.2
Mixed economy	**4.2**	**5.8**	**9.3**	**11.2**
Economic services	3.7	5.2	7.4	7.9
Investment	2.1	1.5	2.9	3.5
Subsidies and transfers	1.6	3.7	4.5	4.4
Interest on public debt	0.5	0.7	1.0	3.2
TOTAL EXPENDITURE	**24.9**	**31.3**	**35.8**	**40.3**

Source: Fundación FIES-CECA, on data from Instituto Nacional de Estadística and Intervención General de la Administración del Estado.

spending rose fivefold between 1975 and 1982. Spending on other income maintenance categories—mainly family allowances—fell drastically.

While spending on public goods and economic services remained stable or even fell as a proportion of GDP during the 70s in most developed countries, in Spain both expenditure groups showed a marked increase between 1975 and 1982. Spending on general public services grew fastest within the category of public goods. Defence spending grew more modestly.

The single most striking difference between the broad trends of public activity in the industrialised countries and those of Spain was the rapid increase in Spanish spending on economic services, which rose by 3.7 percent of GDP. Subsidies and transfers to private and public companies accounted for the largest share in this increase, while public investment grew moderately. Lastly, spending on debt service grew by 0.5 percent, doubling its proportion of GDP.

On the basis of the data in Table 4.2, the behaviour of the main spending functions during the period 1982–1985 can be summarised as follows: (1) There was a modest deceleration in the rate of growth of public spending, which settled at 1.5 percent of GDP per annum (1.8 percent annually between 1975 and 1982); (2) Welfare-state expenditure continued to grow in line with the tendency of the previous period; (3) The upward trend in spending on economic services came to an end; (4) The growth in spending on general public services (the bureaucratic basis of the state) accelerated, in part as a consequence of the decentralisation of spending powers to the Comunidades Autónomas (Regional Governments); and (5) The interest burden of public debt grew spectacularly, finally attaining 3.2 percent of GDP.

Determinants of social expenditures

The growth in pension expenditure—the largest component under the Welfare State heading—was a consequence of demographic factors, increases in coverage and a high level of fraud. During the 1975–1985 period, the number of retired pensioners increased by almost 30 percent (550,000 new pensions) and the average pension rose by 31 percent in real terms. As regards fraud, two factors explain its high level. In the first place, laxity in the granting of invalidity pensions (fixed at 50 to 100 percent of previous earnings) resulted in an increase of 128 percent in the number of beneficiaries, to reach 30 percent of total pensioners. This surprising fact explains the reduction from 56 to 46 percent in the proportion of old-age pensions in total pensioners. Secondly, the basis for calculation of pension benefits was the wage of the two highest-paid years during the seven last years of work, and this created an incentive for increased 'pension purchase'. In 1985, the qualifying conditions were altered to make them less generous; the minimum contribution period went up to 15 years, and the reference period for the calculation of the pension benefit also rose to the last eight years.

The share of unemployment benefits grew throughout the period 1975–1985, mainly because of the increased number of beneficiaries (this was a result of the increase in unemployment rather than of the rate of coverage, which actually fell), and secondarily because of the increased real compensation per beneficiary (Fina, 1986). In 1980, the new Basic Employment Law established a link between benefit and years of contribution. The restrictive effect of this provision was cushioned via the granting of 'supplementary benefits' (75 percent of minimum wage) to a large number of unemployed workers, and by the creation in 1984 of a system of benefits for temporary agricultural workers in Andalusia and Extremadura ('empleo comunitario'). Overall, the growth rate of unemployment benefit spending as a proportion of GDP slowed considerably during the period 1980–1985, as a result of the fall in unemployment, in the rate of coverage, and in average real payment per beneficiary.

The behaviour of education spending as a proportion of GDP reflects wider coverage (especially in the non-compulsory levels) and a sharp increase in the number of teachers in state schools (OECD, 1988). This number increased by 74 percent, the payroll reaching 271,000 teachers in 1985, which translated into an appreciable increase in real spending per beneficiary. The significant increases in the number of students in secondary education, both in general education (Bachillerato Unificado y Polivalente, up 51 percent) and technical school (Formación Profesional, up 142 percent) explain the 30 percent increase in the rate of school attendance of 15-year-olds. The increase in the number of pre-primary students (22 percent) and university students (48 percent) contributed to the observed rise in the GDP share of education spending between 1975 and 1985.

The growth in the share of expenditure on housing during 1975–1985 can be attributed to the consequences of the new legislation on housing policies passed in 1978, and to the subsequent 'housing plans' of 1981–1983 and 1984–1987. These programmes, which resulted in the construction of 733,700 dwellings, were intended to reduce the housing deficit; equal access was to be ensured via personal housing benefits and housing subsidies, which were also intended to stimulate activity in the building sector. In terms of the number of dwellings completed annually during the period 1981–1985, which more or less reached the public building levels of

1975–1980, the new housing policy was not a brilliant success. Public funds nevertheless played a larger role as a result of the 1978 legislation (González-Páramo and Onrubia, 1992).

Health spending showed a modest increase between 1975 and 1985. This outcome can largely be attributed to institutional causes. Before 1986, State transfers to the social security health services took the form of credit allocations without earmarking. The effort to provide financial resources for pension increases resulted in restricted health spending, whose share in GDP was unchanged during 1980–1985. The key factor underlying the increase in the volume of health spending between 1975 and 1985 was the broadening of its coverage, which reached 96 percent in 1985. Spending was contained, thanks to a reduction in the average real benefits per beneficiary (Bandrés, 1990).

The role of economic services and infrastructure

As already pointed out, the trends of expenditure in economic services between 1975 and 1985 showed a notable difference from other developed countries during the same period. After the first oil crisis, gross public investment initiated a decline which was not reversed until 1981. Leaving aside the investment resources allocated to general public services, the GDP share of investment in education, agriculture, and transport and communications remained stable—despite the pressing need to improve infrastructure—while investment in health, housing and other sectors fell in real terms throughout the period 1976–1981 (see Lagares et al., 1988). As a result, the annual growth rate of public capital 'stock' fell from 7.5 percent (1970–1975) to 3.6 percent during the following five years (Corrales and Taguas, 1991).

Following substantial investment increases in 1982 and 1985, higher capital resources were channelled into most sectors with public participation, especially housing, transport and communications (with the notable exception of health). Investment in these sectors doubled its GDP share. The scale of this pick-up becomes clear if we note that the rise of the GDP share of public investment exceeded the average of the four largest EC countries (EC4). As a result, the average real growth rate of public capital reached 5.1 percent of GDP in the period 1980–1985.

The role of the public sector in the provision of economic services can be summarised in two basic features. Firstly, spending on transport and communications, and mining and industry accounted for two thirds of the increased GDP share of economic services. Secondly, the preferred method of state intervention in these sectors was capital transfers and subsidies to public enterprises and ailing industries under restructuring programmes initiated in the early 80s. Direct investment and payment of salaries played a modest role.

Public expenditures vis-à-vis the 'EC standard'

Table 4.3 shows the structure of total public spending in the four largest EC countries (EC4) and Spain in 1985, just before Spain entered the EC. Italy was the country most similar to Spain as regards the role of the public sector. Both countries had a high proportion of spending on economic services and relatively low spending on social security and housing compared with the EC4 average.

Did the marked progress of the government expenditure share over the 1975–1985 period succeed in raising benefits to a level similar to those prevailing in the EC? After correcting for the socio-economic and demographic differences between Spain and the other EC members, the results of the comparison of the main spending functions show that, as regards total spending, Spain had grown progressively closer to the 'EC Standard' in a stable and sustained process that reduced the difference from 37 percent to 18 percent. As regards individual spending components, the tendencies were diverse. In 1985, Spain was below the 'EC Standard' in education, housing, health, social security, general public services and defence. On the other hand, higher than proportional resources were put into debt interest payments and economic services (essentially communication media and culture).

The so-called indices of need or relative necessity show that, despite the extraordinary growth in spending throughout the decade, the spending functions with lowest coverage when Spain entered the EC were those under the welfare-state heading. These relative deficiencies, combined with those in infrastructure, which are corroborated by all available indicators (González-Páramo, 1989a), constituted both an important obstacle to and one of the fundamental challenges of the European project which Spain joined in 1986.

Decentralisation of government expenditures

The Spanish public sector as designed in the 1978 Constitution is composed of three main agents: the Central Government, the Social Security system and the Territorial Governments. The sub-national governments are the autonomous regions (Comunidades Autónomas) and the provinces and municipalities (Corporaciones Locales). Most of the resources of the territorial governments come from transfers made by the central government via three channels: unconditional transfers,

Interterritorial Compensation Fund (Fondo de Compensación Interterritorial) transfers, and public funds allocated to earmarked ends.

In 1975, the share of the territorial public sector in total public spending was very low. After the approval of the Constitution in 1979, this proportion rose continuously, slowly at first, but very rapidly after 1981.

Table 4.3 Functional structure of general government expenditure in Spain and EU 4, 1985 (percentage of GDP)

	Germany	***France***	***Italy***	***UK***	***EU4***	***SPAIN***
General services	4.4	4.3	4.4	4.1	4.3	3.9
Defense	2.9	4.0	2.0	5.0	3.5	1.9
Education	4.7	6.4	5.5	5.6	5.5	3.4
Health	6.0	6.9	5.5	4.9	5.9	4.3
Social security	19.7	22.1	15.9	13.8	18.2	14.1
Housing	1.0	3.2	1.5	3.2	2.2	1.7
Other social services	0.7	1.1	0.3	–	0.6	0.9
Economic services[1]	3.9	3.9	7.4	4.4	4.8	6.3
Other[2]	3.0	2.2	6.8	4.8	4.0	3.8
TOTAL EXPENDITURE	**46.5**	**54.1**	**49.5**	**45.9**	**48.9**	**40.3**

Notes:
[1] Includes: energy, gas, agriculture, mining, industry, transport, communications and other services.
[2] Public debt service and other non-classifiable spending.

Source: Lagares, Alvarez, Raymond, González-Páramo and Encabo (1988).

Between December 1979 and April 1983 the seventeen Comunidades Autónomas were established, which gradually acquired legislative and executive authority over economic sectors, infrastructure and social services. Over the 1979–1985 period, expenditures by Territorial

Governments as a share of total public spending increased by 12 percentage points. In 1985, the lower levels of the administration accounted for the bulk of public spending on housing, education, investment and other social services, and were assuming ever greater responsibilities in the provision of health care.

Expenditure control and deficit spending

As mentioned earlier, the rapid increase in public spending throughout the period 1975–1985 was caused essentially by the slowdown in GDP growth and the political and institutional reforms that followed the end of the Franco regime and the return to democracy. However, other factors contributed to the expansion by negatively influencing the assessment of spending needs, making rational control of resources difficult. In the first place, certain clearly identified budgetary practices made it easy for spending departments to claim larger funds than those approved in the budget. Some of these practices were (Fernández and Gutiérrez, 1987; Edo et al., 1988): (1) Automatic disposal of non-remunerated cash facilities (anticipos) from the Bank of Spain up to a limit of 12 percent of total budget appropriations; (2) Laxity in the mechanisms by which credit modifications were approved (extraordinary credits and supplementary credits), by means of which an average of 13 percent excess over initial credits was obtained during the first half of the 80s; and (3) Almost unlimited possibilities to carry forward unused appropriations, which were generated by a relatively low level of realisation of final credits (at around 90 percent on average). These practices, in combination with the lack of efficiency reviews for spending and the very limited effect of the budget management modernisation programme begun in 1983 (Zapico, 1988), all helped to void the budget's function as an instrument for limiting and assigning public spending among competing ends (Fuentes, 1988).

Secondly, the deficit itself may have caused or facilitated a higher increase in public spending than would otherwise have occurred. Causality analysis shows that there was statistical causation running from deficits to public spending (Raymond and González-Páramo, 1988). We could rationalise this finding as saying that the power of the government to create money and issue debt as alternatives to tax increases was used as a means of overcoming the tax payer's resistance to the payment of higher taxes and this, in turn, facilitated the expansion of public spending at the cost of a higher tax burden or lower public spending in the future. Empirical analysis attributes to deficit spending an explanatory power of about one-fourth of the increase in the GDP share of public spending between 1975 and 1986.

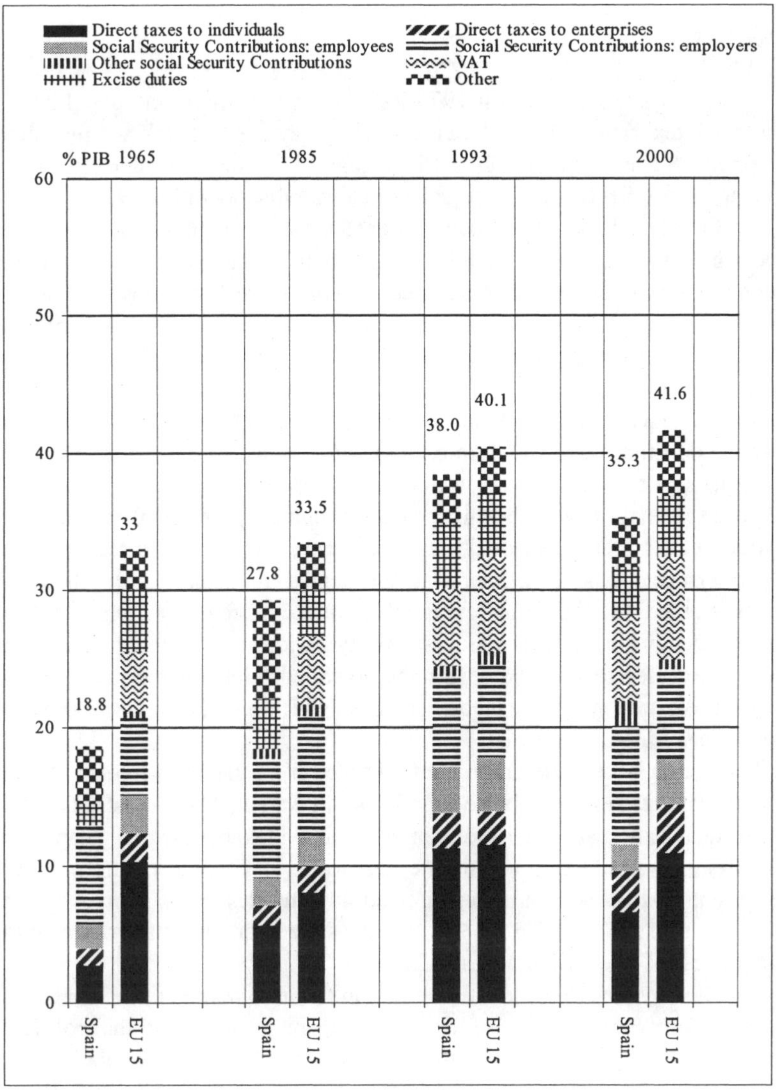

Figure 4.3 Taxations as percentage of GDP

Source: OECD.

Tax Policy

The tax system in force in 1975 had two salient characteristics. Firstly, the total tax ratio was well below the EU average. Total tax revenues attained 18.8 percent of GDP, 15 percentage points less than the EU15 average. Only Greece and Portugal had comparable tax ratios.

On the other hand, the structural characteristics of the tax system were such that they made it unsuitable to contribute to the modernisation of the economy that was to come. As can be seen in Figure 4.3, almost half of the tax revenue came from social security contributions, around 24 percent was the share of indirect taxation and 22 percent came from direct taxes on income (personal income and corporate profits). Prominent among direct taxes was a cascading-type tax on business turnover (Impuesto sobre el Tráfico de Empresas), which interfered with domestic transactions because of its lack of neutrality and distorted the pattern of foreign trade, as its lack of transparency was used to provide implicit protection to national exportable goods. Personal income taxes were collected via a 'Mediterranean-type' schedular system (Fuentes Quintana, 1976): schedular taxes worked as minimum levies which taxed different income sources independently. Presumptive assessment was widely used. Tax-payers with high incomes remained liable for the so-called 'General Income Tax', a progressive tax on gross income against which schedular tax payments could be credited.

Taken as a whole, the tax system inherited from the 1964 reform scored poorly with regard to the basic principles of taxation. The almost total lack of personalisation and the rigidity in determining taxable income meant that the system was unlikely to provide much help in funding public policies according to criteria of sufficiency, neutrality and flexibility. Moreover, the tax system in force during the 70s was considered an important obstacle to the process of integration with the EC.

Impelled by the strong social pressure in favour of expenditure increases, fiscal reform became one of the most urgent priorities of the political programme that emerged with the change of regime. In November 1977, exceptional measures designed to increase tax revenue were adopted. These included extraordinary surcharges on company profits, luxury goods and highest personal incomes. At the same time, it was announced that the tax system was to be deeply overhauled and government's stance concerning tax compliance was to be modified. The latter purpose was signalled by four measures: the concession of a tax amnesty, the abolition of confidentiality in bank operations, the creation of an 'Extraordinary Net Wealth Tax', and the introduction of heavy penalties to punish tax evasion.

One year later, Parliament approved new taxes on personal and corporate income, which were to come into force in January 1979. Schedular taxes (Licencias Fiscales) were eliminated at national level, and partly transferred to local governments. The new income tax was a modern, universal (synthetic) and progressive tax on the net accumulated income of all members of the family unit. Tax reliefs were offered as a function of family size and other personal characteristics, as were various fiscal incentives. The reformed corporation income tax was structured according to the design then being used in other European countries. The changes in the legislation about indirect taxes were relatively fewer. The principle of a cumulative burden on business turnover was maintained. Since it coincided with the break-down of political consensus in 1979, the modernisation of the tax system was sidelined.

All in all, the tax reform somewhat improved the flexibility of the tax system as a whole: the estimated income elasticity of taxes rose from 1.14 between 1955 and 1977 to 1.23 between 1978 and 1991 (González-Páramo, 1994a). The tax burden increased by an average of a 1 percentage point of GDP per annum; this was double the rate of increase of 1965–1975 and double the rate observable in the rest of the EC between 1975 and 1985. Nevertheless, it was not enough to fund the exceptional increases in spending which occurred throughout this period.

As a result of the tax reform measures, the GDP share of taxes on income and wealth rose to 7.6 percent, almost double the figure for 1975. As regards other taxes, social security contributions grew sizably until 1980, stabilising their share of GDP thereafter. The GDP share and proportion of total tax revenues of indirect taxes fell between 1977 and 1979, thereafter recovering strongly. On the whole, these changes brought the Spanish taxation structure closer to EC standards.

THE INITIAL RESPONSE OF THE PUBLIC SECTOR AFTER INTEGRATION INTO THE EC

Background

In 1985 and 1986 the existing consensus within the EC in favour of accelerating the integration process was embodied in a series of important decisions: (1) To reinforce the role of the Community institutions: Parliament, Council, and Commission, especially relative to national governments; (2) To create a European Internal Market (EIM) in 1993, for which it was necessary to eliminate obstacles to trade (border controls, national regulations, administrative barriers, differences in indirect taxation, etc), to a free market in services (financial services and insurance, notably) and to movements of capital and labour; and (3) To promote the convergence of economic policies as a first step toward the creation of Economic and Monetary Union (EMU), embodied in the Maastricht Treaty.

In what is the most far-reaching decision since the Stabilisation Plan of 1959, by signing the Treaty of Accession to the EC, by its subsequent ratification of the Single European Act and by its support for the Maastricht Treaty, Spain took on the challenge of competitiveness implied by the growing integration of markets. This challenge was of particular significance for the Spanish economy, given that its integration in international production and trade had traditionally been very limited. The potential benefits of integration were clear: more efficient markets, stable prices and, in the long term, higher income and economic welfare. Spain's share in these benefits was seen to depend on two factors: its competitiveness at the outset and its willingness to maintain the adjustment policies required to ensure macroeconomic stability and to eliminate the institutional features of 'soft-budgetism' that impair structural adjustment to changing circumstances (Rodrik, 1990); and all this in the context of progressive loss of control over monetary, tariff and exchange-rate policies. Spain's public sector had recently emerged from a crisis and was in the middle of a 'catching-up' process. It was also used to being able to intervene in the economy with considerable discretion, unrestricted by tight budgetary controls. For the Spanish public sector, the challenges ahead were extraordinary. How did the public sector behave immediately after integration?

Initial Responses of the Public Sector after Integration

Budgetary policy

If the contribution of macroeconomic policy to improve competitiveness and long-term growth consists in eliminating the imbalances that inhibit nominal stability, the policy mix exhibited by Spain in the years following integration into the EC offer an excellent illustration of how not to achieve this. The macroeconomic experience of these years clearly shows that nominal convergence can only be guaranteed if rigorous monetary policy is not treated as a pretext for allocating major budgetary aggregates to objectives inconsistent with price stability.

Since Spain joined the EC, and before the fulfilment of the convergence criteria set in the Maastricht Treaty became the core objective of fiscal policy, two very different periods can be distinguished in the performance of fiscal policy: 1986–1987 and 1988–1993. The first period, covering the years 1986 and 1987, was a phase of budgetary consolidation during which the general government deficit fell by 3.4 percentage points of GDP. As Table 4.4 shows, this was possible thanks to a strong increase in direct taxes (1.6 percent)) and to the reining in of current transfers, whose share of GDP fell for the first time since 1966 (0.6 percent). This in turn was due to the effect of the automatic stabilisers (subsidies and unemployment benefits), combined with measures adopted for the rationalisation of spending on subsidies to enterprises and on pensions, in the latter case as a result of the reform of the pension system in 1985. As a consequence of these developments, the government disposable income grew substantially (3.2 percent of GDP). When this was combined with moderation in government consumption, the fiscal policy in place produced a primary surplus (deficit less interest payments) of 1.1 percent of GDP.

A proper assessment of fiscal events in the period 1986–1987 requires us to establish the relative importance of cyclical as opposed to structural factors. The evolution of the cyclically adjusted deficit shows that the contractionary orientation of the budget recorded in 1986 was reinforced in 1987, due mostly to the improvements in tax collection and administration (partly attributable to the introduction of VAT) and the control exerted over current expenditures and public investment. The reduction of the non-financial deficit in 1986 and the strong expansion of economic activity explain both the reduction in the primary deficit, which had become a surplus by 1987, and the remarkable fall in the non-financial deficit in 1987, which reached 2.9 percent, i.e. less than half of the size of the deficit in 1985. Although a good part of this improvement is attributable to the beneficial effect of automatic stabilisers, the reduction of the structural deficit was noteworthy, and it was helped by moderate government consumption and the reduction in current transfers (Figure 4.2).

After these two years of discipline, the policy of budgetary consolidation was interrupted in 1988, and deficit figures deteriorated thereafter. On the expenditure side, social security benefits and public investment were the leading forces behind the change in the orientation of budgetary policy. Pensions recovered their strength partly as a result of union pressures which culminated in the general strike of December 1988. The acceleration of investment expenditures responded to the aim of completing major infrastructure projects, both those which had been postponed in previous years because of the high public deficit, and which the proximity of the EIM made more urgent, and those indirectly associated with the landmark events of 1992 (the World Fair in Seville and the Olympic Games in Barcelona). As regards tax developments, despite the reductions in nominal tax rates, direct taxes remained a buoyant source of revenue. This was due to the combined effects of strong economic growth and the fiscal drag associated with tax progressivity. But these extra resources were not earmarked to the reduction of the budget deficit.

In the first part of 1989, the increasingly acute conflict between monetary and fiscal policy spotlighted the need to impose a restrictive budgetary policy. This move towards budgetary contraction, partly aided by the peseta's incorporation into the EMS exchange rate mechanism and by the introduction of exchange controls and credit ceilings, took the form of extraordinary measures to increase revenue and cut investment spending.

Table 4.4 General government receipts, expenditures and balances 1985–1994 (percentage of GDP)

	1985	1987	1993	1994
Current revenue	32.3	34.8	37.6	36.9
Taxes on production and imports	11.3	10.8	9.6	10.2
Taxes on income and profits	7.6	9.2	10.6	10.1
Social security contributions	12.6	12.4	14.2	13.9
Other current revenue	0.8	2.5	3.2	2.6
Current transfers	18.7	18.1	21.7	22.2
Transfers to households	12.8	12.3	15.0	14.6
Interest payments on public debt	1.1	1.0	1.2	1.1
Subsidies	3.4	4.0	4.5	5.4
Other current transfers	1.5	0.8	1.1	1.1
Disposable income	13.5	16.7	15.9	14.7
Public consumption	15.6	15.9	18.8	18.2
Wages	10.3	10.1	11.9	11.4
Net purchases and other expenditures	5.3	5.8	6.9	6.8
Capital revenue	0.4	0.5	1.0	1.2
Capital transfers	2.3	1.7	1.8	1.8
Public investment	3.7	3.5	4.2	4.0

Table 4.4 General government receipts, expenditures and balances 1985–1994 (percentage of GDP) (continued)

	1985	**1987**	**1993**	**1994**
Public deficit	6.9	2.9	6.8	6.9
Memorandum:				
Primary deficit	3.5	-1.1	2.3	1.5
Total revenue	35.7	36.3	39.9	39.4
Tax revenue	30.1	32.6	34.8	34.6
Total expenditure	42.7	39.2	46.7	46.6
Public Debt	42.2	43.9	58.4	61.1
Change in the cyclically adjusted primary deficit	0.0	-1.8	1.7	-0.6

Source: National Institute of Statistics, Banco de España and own calculations.

Nevertheless, the orientation of fiscal policy for the year as a whole was strongly expansionary, as were the years 1990 and 1991, in relation not only to the economic cycle, but, more particularly, to budgetary targets, which were systematically overshot during these years. Only after mid-1992, when the economy was already in a deep recession, did some signs of a restrictive orientation begin to appear. However, this timid change would not have continuity in 1993, when the effects of the recession and the laxity in spending control brought the deficit back to record levels.

The pro-cyclical orientation of the budgetary policy implemented over the period 1988–1993 had very negative effects on nominal convergence. In the first place, it produced an imbalance in the mix of stabilisation policies by shifting to monetary policy—temporarily based on capital controls and credit ceilings—the whole burden of the struggle against inflation, thus undermining its effects and credibility. It was also conducted in an erratic way, marked by a variety of atypical events, such as the extension of the Budget Law, extraordinary readjustments in spending and emergency tax measures adopted in mid-year. Moreover, it can be said that a splendid opportunity to complete the process of budgetary consolidation and to gain some room for manoeuvre in dealing with the difficulties of transition to EMU was lost. The evolution of the public deficit is eloquent: with rates of economic growth well above the EC average in the period 1987–1992, the Spanish deficit was, in 1993, at 6.8 percent, well above the EC average (5.8 percent). Lastly, against the backdrop of the accelerating opening up of the Spanish economy, combined with the growing liberalisation of capital movements, it can be concluded that since 1987 the expansionary budgetary policy was probably one of the main driving factors behind Spain's exchange-rate tensions and negative external balance (González-Páramo, 1994b).

The 1993 budget year constituted the high point of this model of laxity in public spending. It was not just that the total general government deficit was twice that forecast in the General State Budget of 1993. There was also the failure to comply with the sole objective rule which established some degree of restriction on spending—Article 10 of the Budget Law of 1993—and the use of accounting criteria of a kind that prevented accurate knowledge of State actions and even of the true magnitude of the deficit (González-Páramo, 1994c).

With the onset of the recession, budgetary laxity degenerated into a problem of sustainability of debt. Since 1991 the general government accounts showed a primary deficit (budgetary balance minus debt-service charges) and since 1992 the effective interest rate of the public debt was well above the nominal growth rate of GDP. Half-way down the road toward the non-sustainability of the public debt, it was neither possible to reduce interest rates in a lasting fashion nor to base, even slightly, stable expectations on the economy's future performance. The situation of non-sustainability had only three possible solutions: more inflation in the future, an increased tax burden or a reduction in public spending.

To assess the sustainability of the public debt, the simplest indicator is the so-called 'primary gap', which is calculated as the difference between the existing primary balance, s (revenue minus spending net of interest), and the primary equilibrium balance, s^*, defined as that which would stabilise the public debt/GDP ratio. s_t^* is calculated as: $s_t^*=[(r-g)/(1+g]b_{t-1}$, where g is the nominal rate of growth of GDP, r is the effective interest rate on the debt (interest charges divided by the volume of debt in circulation), b is the debt/GDP ratio, and the subscripts t and $t-1$ indicate the current year and the previous years. A negative 'primary gap' indicates non-sustainability.

According to this indicator, the public deficit was perfectly sustainable between 1986 and 1990, despite the pro-cyclical stance of the budget after 1987. But in 1991, the 'primary gap' became negative, increasing extraordinarily in 1993, the year in which it reached -4.7 percent of GDP. To stabilise the debt/GDP ratio would have required moving from a primary deficit of 2.4 percent to a primary surplus of the same size. This non-sustainable situation explains that in only two years, the debt/GDP ratio increased from 44.5 percent to 59 percent after having been stable between 1985 and 1991 at around 51 percent.

The spending overruns of 1993 and the failure of the first Convergence Programme were the necessary outcome of a peculiar budget model, based upon the conflict between unrealistic budgeting—artificially low deficit targets and overly optimistic confidence in the revenue effects of economic growth –and the laxity of budget procedures. As an example, between 1983 and 1993, modifications of the initial budget appropriations reached an average of 25 percent, with increasing use made of credit extensions and carry-over of unused appropriations (more than 95 percent of the totals since 1985), which remain outside Parliamentary control. Since 1990, the budget laws included clauses limiting the power to make new spending commitments during the execution of the budget, but the disciplinary effect of this measure was negligible. It could hardly be otherwise, given that these restrictions affect, what are in practice, the least important forms of budgetary deviation (Edo et al., 1993).

Taxation

Between 1985 and 1993, total government revenues grew by 5.9 percentage points of GDP, a rate similar to that of the previous decade. Buoyant direct taxes underpinned this tendency, with an increase of 3.0 percentage points of GDP, a figure which contrasts with the nil growth recorded in the EC. The corporation tax increased its contribution to the tax burden by 0.8 percent as a result of the recovery of firms' profits. Social security contributions grew by 1.6 percentage points, due to the growth in employment up to 1991 and the increase in the contribution rates in 1992 and 1993.

Personal income tax (PIT) revenue growth, at 2.4 percent of GDP, was the result of a variety of factors. Although the strong increase in real income was certainly one of them, the main cause was inflation combined with the progressive nature of the tax (Argimón and González-Páramo, 1987a; Valdés et al., 1989). The heavier taxation of capital gains and financial assets imposed in the 1985 reforms, combined with the continued increase in the progressivity of the tax, were offset by the reduction in the nominal tax rates in the lower income brackets, an increase in personal allowances, and the introduction of a variable allowance for married couples. There are indications that the effect of these changes on tax collections was negative (Salas and Jiménez, 1992). In 1989, the PIT obligation to totalise income within the family unit for tax purposes was declared unconstitutional. As a consequence of this unexpected event, with an estimated revenue cost of 0.5 percent points of GDP per annum, a tax reform process was begun which culminated in June 1991. From 1992 on, the tax law provided for separate declaration, exempted from tax a large part of the financial revenues accruing to non-residents, and lightened the tax burden on residents' capital gains and financial savings.

Growth in tax revenues from indirect taxation was negative. Taxes linked to production and imports together decreased by 1.4 percentage points between 1985 and 1993. However, many changes in rules are identifiable behind this result. The most noteworthy fiscal event was the 1986 introduction of VAT, a harmonised European tax on consumption. The VAT replaced a complex and distorting set of taxes on consumption and gross turnover (Impuesto sobre el Lujo, Impuesto sobre el Tráfico de Empresas and others of lesser importance). Although it is estimated that the introduction of VAT added 2 percentage points to the 1986 inflation rate, its overall effect was highly beneficial: it substantially improved tax neutrality in relation to foreign trade and eliminated double taxation of investment. But it seems unlikely that it widened the tax base, given that the cross-checking of transactions did not operate as expected.

Excise duties and taxes on imports underwent important changes as a consequence of Spain's entering the EC. Some taxes were simply abolished (Impuesto sobre el Lujo, Renta del Monopolio de Tabacos and other smaller taxes), while others awaited a change in the law whose objective was to bring the overall structure of indirect taxation closer to that of the EC countries. The average level of tariffs on EC imports was brought down step by step till they were totally eliminated in January 1993. The elimination of customs controls in 1993 will, in the medium term, lead to an effective equalisation between VAT and excise duties across the EC.

As Figures 4.3 and 4.4 show, between 1970 and 1993 there was a noteworthy convergence between the tax structures of the EC member-states. Spain was no exception. During the integration period, the overall Spanish tax burden attained a structure similar to that of the Community average. In contrast with the position on social security contributions, there was, however, still a gap represented by Spain's relatively low taxation on income and consumption.

Public expenditures

When Spain entered the EC, total public spending initially fell as a proportion of GDP, only to rise strongly from 1987 on. The implications for the budgetary consolidation process and for macroeconomic stability have already been noted. In addition to this increase in total spending, in the years 1985–1993, events took place which affected the main spending categories, as shown by the functional classification in Table 4.5. Thus, after a short period of containment, spending on pensions again increased strongly from 1988 on. Between 1985 and 1993, the number of pensioners increased by 1.4 million (a 25 percent increase) to reach 6.8 million in 1993; this was a consequence not merely of demography but of the introduction of non-contributory pensions for the elderly and the handicapped not having contributed to the social security system in the past (December 1990). Similarly, the average pension per beneficiary grew 3 percent per annum in real terms, as a result of indexation, the higher level of new pensions, and the effort to bring pensions in line with the minimum wage. On the other hand, public investment also grew substantially during those years, reaching a level well above the Community average. Another budgetary heading that reached a particularly high level was interest on the public debt, as a consequence of both the expansionary policy implemented from 1988 on and high interest rates. Under the traditional headings of social expenditure, health showed the greatest dynamism, as a result of an increase in coverage and a higher per capita spending which has been attributed to inefficiencies and fraud (OECD, 1993). Controls on medical prescriptions were introduced in 1992 and 1993. However, waiting lists remained much of a problem, together with a system of financing that did not induce a rational use of resources by hospitals, whose debts were regularly paid for by the State once their volume was large enough. As to other spending items, education and housing remained more stable. Lastly, along with a sharp reduction in capital transfers and current subsidies (0.5 percent of GDP), the integration period saw a considerable rise in government consumption (3.2 percent), an increase related both to health spending and to the public-sector decentralisation process.

The budgetary decentralisation that began in 1979 continued during integration with the EC. In 1994, the final spending (government consumption plus gross investment) of the autonomous and local administrations exceeded that of the State. However, fiscal revenues of the autonomous regions and local governments did not grow at a similar rate. This undesirable mismatch between spending commitments and fiscal resources, which was complicated by the existence of political incentives against the funding of spending from non-fiscal current revenues, was one of the main causes behind the upsurge in borrowing requirements and indebtedness of the territorial governments.

In 1986, the Spanish economy became both a contributor to and a beneficiary from the EC budget. The majority of EC spending in Spain comprised current transfers from the European Agricultural Guidance and Guarantee Fund (EAGGF) (in implementation of the Common Agricultural

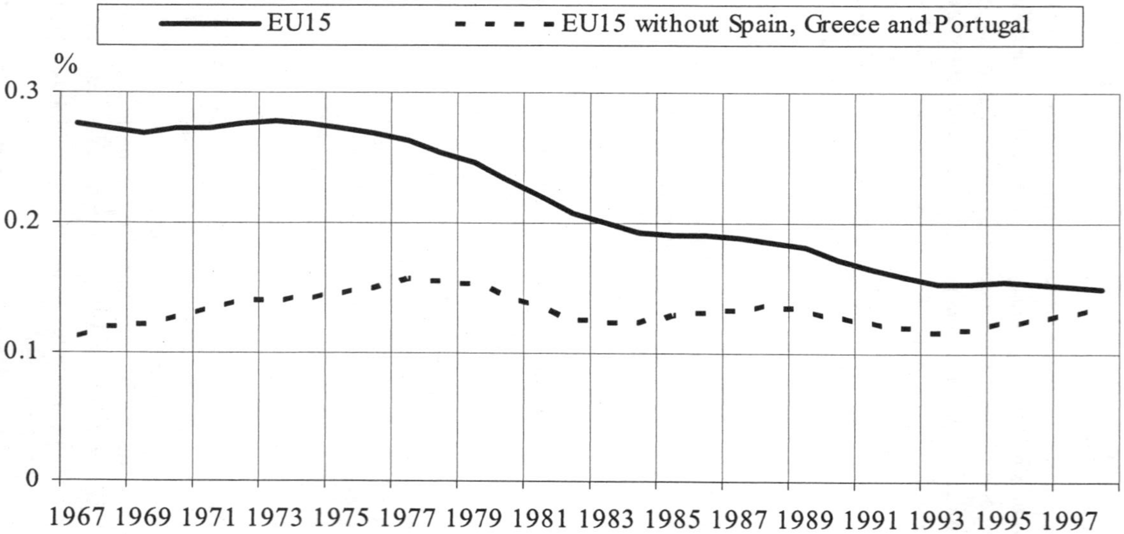

Figure 4.4 Trend in the dispersion of relative tax pressure in the European Union

Source: OECD and own calculations.

Table 4.5 General government spending: functional classification, 1985–1994 (percentages of GDP)

	1985	*1987*	*1993*	*1994*
Public goods	**6.8**	**6.7**	**6.8**	**6.6**
Defence	2.0	2.2	1.3	1.2
General public services	4.8	4.4	5.4	5.3
Welfare state	**24.8**	**24.2**	**29.1**	**28.6**
Merit goods	10.4	10.4	12.1	11.9
Education	3.7	4.0	4.5	4.4
Health	4.7	4.6	5.9	5.8
Housing and collective services	2.0	1.8	1.7	1.7
Income maintenance	14.3	13.8	17.0	16.7
Pensions	10.2	9.7	11.5	11.7
Unemployment	2.8	2.7	3.7	3.3
Other	1.3	1.4	1.7	1.7
Mixed economy	**11.8**	**11.0**	**13.2**	**12.6**
Economic services	8.4	7.0	8.0	7.3
Investment	3.7	3.4	4.2	3.9
Subsidies and transfers	4.7	3.6	3.8	3.4
Interest on public debt	3.4	3.5	5.2	5.3
TOTAL EXPENDITURE	**42.6**	**41.0**	**49.6**	**48.3**

Source: Fundación FIES-CECA, Cuadernos de Información Económica, n. 104, November, 1995.

Policy) and the European Social Fund (ESF). Of the other spending headings, the most important was capital transfers from the European Regional Development Fund (ERDF), whose total grew fastest since the structural funds reform came into force in early 1989. Since the ERDF and EFS have contributed funds to co-financed investment projects, Spain's incorporation into the EC budget can be said to have favoured investment in basic infrastructure. However, if we bear in mind the lack of sufficiently redistributive criteria between countries in the funding of projects and the limited volume of resources managed by the Community, it can be said that EC spending in Spain has not been decisive in the elimination of infrastructure weaknesses. In 1994, total EC spending in Spain reached 2.0 percent of GDP, a volume equivalent to 4.1 percent of total public spending.

A final comment should be made on the restructuring and privatisation process followed during this period. Compared to the EC average, the significance of public companies in the Spanish economy in 1985 was very small: their share in national employment and investment was between half and a third of the average of the four largest EC countries (see Myro, 1988). The share of public enterprises varied widely with sector. In terms of value added, the share of public companies exceeded 25 percent in communications, tobacco, transport (sea and air), coal, electricity, mining, and metallic minerals.

In 1985, when other liberalising measures were also being adopted (in the financial system, insurance, capital transactions with foreign countries and domestic trade), the deregulation of the public monopolies required by Community policy was carried out (in oil products, telecommunications, tobacco and television) and a programme of privatisation started. These policies complemented the rationalisation of the public sector begun in 1983 with the restructuring of the state-owned industrial group INI.

As a result of the oil crisis of the mid-60s, INI was used as an escape valve, as it absorbed employment and activities of bankrupt enterprises. Losses grew rapidly, reaching 1 percent of GDP in 1983, with the burden of financing falling largely on the government budget. The need to rationalise the public enterprise sector led to important political decisions. Absorption of private companies halted, employment was reduced, the growth of salaries was contained, financial management was overhauled, and there began a process of withdrawal from certain areas in which state participation was no longer considered essential.

Industrial restructuring and the privatisation of companies were the most salient aspects of this process (Martín Aceña and Comín, 1991). Between 1983 and 1986, restructuring plans brought a reduction in employment of almost 21,000 workers. 60 percent of these were in the shipbuilding sector, whose workforce fell by 50 percent. In steelmaking as a whole, the adjustment affected almost the entire workforce of Altos Hornos del

Mediterráneo and around 20 percent of Ensidesa. The plans also affected the special steels sector (Foarsa) and fertilisers (Enfersa).

The strong tide of privatisation that occurred between 1985 and the early 90s was not the result of a political decision, nor the consequence of a process of deliberate and technical analysis. In fact, the process itself was rather heterodox compared to those of other countries, as the variety of justifications offered in each case shows. These included the attraction to Spain of foreign technology, financial restructuring, the aspiration to upsize, and incorporation of new management criteria (De la Dehesa, 1993). As to the limited objective of curbing the drain on public funds, there is no doubt that privatisation served to soften the financial obligations of the central government. However, this is arguably a limited and probably transitory effect. Even when, as in the privatisation of major companies Repsol (in petroleum refining and distribution), Argentaria (in banking), Endesa (in steel) and Telefónica (in telecommunications), the principal objective was revenue, the Treasury in this way renounced future dividends from relatively profitable concerns. A single figure gives some notion of the limitations of this strategy: Public participation in the capital of Repsol, Argentaria, Ence, Endesa, Telefónica and Tabalecera amounted to 2.7 billion pesetas in late 1993. This sum, which represented up to 4.5 percent of GDP, would have covered only two thirds of the estimated public deficit for 1993.

ECONOMIC AND MONETARY UNION AND THE CONVERGENCE PROCESS: TOWARDS GREATER BUDGETARY DISCIPLINE

Against the previous background of deficit overruns and growing public debt, fiscal policy in Spain since 1994 assumed, as its main goal, the commitment to comply, first, with the fiscal convergence criteria established in the Treaty on European Union that regulate access to the Third Phase of EMU, consisting of a public deficit and public debt not exceeding 3 percent and 60 percent of GDP, respectively, and, following entry to EMU, with the Stability and Growth Pact, which requires government accounts to be balanced or in surplus in the medium term and for public deficit not to exceed the limit of 3 percent of GDP under normal cyclical conditions. To fulfil these goals, considerable consolidation efforts were needed.

The consolidation efforts already started with the update of the Convergence Programme for the period 1994–1997, which included a better analysis of the basic economic problems of the Spanish economy.

However, the Programme did not specify any measure to redress the laxity exhibited in the budgetary process. In fact, a large part of the fiscal adjustment was based on economic growth, while the bulk of the fiscal adjustment was postponed. As a result, the deficit stayed at 6.6 percent of GDP in 1995. A crucial change took place, however, in this period with the coming into force, in January 1994, of the prohibition of monetary financing included in Article 104 of the Maastricht Treaty. Given that the funding of budgetary imbalances had traditionally been 'privileged', thanks to the existence of mandatory cash and investment ratio requirements and

Table 4.6 General government receipts, expenditures and balances 1995–2003 (percentage of GDP)

	1995	*1997*	*1999*	*2003*
Current revenue	37.0	37.6	38.3	39.2
Taxes on production and imports	10.2	10.5	11.7	12.0
Taxes on income and profits	10.1	10.5	10.2	10.6
Social security contributions	13.0	13.1	13.1	13.7
Other current revenue	3.7	3.6	3.3	3.0
Current transfers	38.8	37.2	35.4	34.8
Transfers to households	13.9	13.3	12.4	12.2
Interest payments on public debt	1.1	0.9	1.2	1.2
Subsidies	5.2	4.8	3.5	2.5
Other current transfers	0.9	1.1	1.2	1.4
Public consumption	17.7	17.2	17.1	17.5
Wages	11.3	10.9	10.6	10.3
Net purchases and other expenditures	6.4	6.3	6.5	7.1
Capital revenue	1.4	1.0	0.7	0.8
Capital transfers	2.4	1.4	1.3	1.3
Public investment	3.8	3.2	3.5	3.5

Table 4.6 General government receipts, expenditures and balances 1995–2003 (percentage of GDP) (continued)

	1995	*1997*	*1999*	*2003*
Public deficit	6.6	3.2	1.2	0.4
Memorandum:				
Primary deficit	1.4	-1.6	-2.4	-2.9
Total revenue	38.4	38.6	39.0	40.0
Tax revenue	33.6	34.4	35.3	36.6
Total expenditure	45.0	41.8	40.2	39.6
Public Debt	64.0	66.6	63.1	50.7
Change in the cyclically adjusted primary deficit	0.1	-0.8	-0.5	-0.2
Cyclically adjusted deficit	6.2	2.9	1.4	-0.5

Source: National Institute of Statistics, Banco de España, and own calculations.

the automatic and free access to the Bank of Spain resources, this measure represented an important restriction for the future.

With the change in government after the 1996 general elections, the tightening of fiscal policy since that moment, combined at the beginning with the positive effects of the gradual economic recovery, enabled Spain to fulfil the above-mentioned EMU criteria. It was thus able to achieve its goal of being among the countries to join EMU from the start and to comply with the guidelines of the Stability and Growth Pact.

The curbing of public sector expansion was the most characteristic feature of this period. In particular, the government deficit-to-GDP ratio fell by 7.1 percentage points since 1995, recording a small surplus of 0.4 percentage point in 2003 (Figure 4.1). This reduction in the deficit resulted primarily from the continued fall in the public expenditure-to-GDP ratio, although there was also an increase in the government revenues-to-GDP ratio. Moreover, from 1996 Spain obtained a growing primary surplus that amounted to 2.9 percent in 2003.

The public debt-to-GDP ratio peaked in 1996, at over 68.2 percent of GDP, before falling by over 17 percentage points to 50.7 percent of GDP in 2003 (see Figure 4.1). This decline stemmed primarily from the existence of primary surpluses over the entire period and, to a lesser degree, from 1999 onwards, from a positive differential between economic growth and interest rates.

The Main Reforms

During this reference period, certain reforms were introduced, that affected at least four key aspects of the Spanish public sector: the decentralisation of competencies to the autonomous communities, the public enterprise sector, the control of social expenditure and the tax system.

With regard to fiscal decentralisation, in addition to the continued transfer of competencies to the autonomous communities, other changes were made that affected, in particular, the way in which the latter were financed. From 1997, a new system was put in place, which covered a five-year period (1997–2001). This new system introduced aspects of fiscal co-responsibility and financial autonomy in order to introduce greater discipline in autonomous communities' expenditure. These aspects were partly undermined, when each autonomous community was subsequently granted an increase in financing equivalent to, at least, growth in GDP.

In June 2001, the current system for financing the common regime autonomous communities was approved, coming into effect on 1 January 2002. Unlike previous models, this one was considered definitive and represented significant changes in terms of the previous financing system. First, it established a uniform system for all of the common regime autonomous communities by making all of the communities responsible for health care and placing them on an equal level in terms of their competencies. Second, the new system covered all expenditure by the autonomous communities, including the areas of health care and social services. Third, financial dependence on state transfers was reduced and the tax structure of the autonomous communities was improved by providing some normative capacity for tax autonomy and by extending revenue sharing to consumer taxes (VAT and excise duties) and by raising the revenue sharing rate for personal income taxes to 33 percent. Moreover, the new system extended the regulatory capacities of the autonomous communities with regard to taxes transferred to the state and abolished the system of guarantees relating to tax collection. Thus the new agreement included several positive new features, setting a uniform, stable and comprehensive financing system that increased the regions' financial autonomy and their level of fiscal co-responsibility (Hernández de Cos, 2002).

As a result of decentralisation, the autonomous communities currently account for over 32 percent of total central government expenditure, 17 percentage points higher than in 1995. This is primarily due to the complete transfer of competencies relating to health and education. With regard to taxation, the autonomous communities represent 37 percent of indirect and 18 percent of direct taxes, corresponding to around 18 percent of the overall tax revenues of the central government. In addition, the proportion of the autonomous communities' tax revenues to their total revenue has risen from 23 percent in 1995 to 53 percent in 2002, while the proportion of tax revenues to taxes with regulatory capacities (all except VAT and excise duties) stands at around 30 percent of their overall tax revenues.

The reform of the financing system of territorial governments also affected local entities with the amendment of the law regulating these entities (Ley Reguladora de las Haciendas Locales—Law for the Regulation of Local Entities) in 2002, which came into force on 1 January 2003. This reform included the exemption from the local income tax (IAE) of all natural persons (self-employed and employed) and companies with profits of less than one million euro per year, as well as new enterprises that have existed for less than two years, while the shares of large enterprises and mobile telephone companies increased by around 30 percent and the application of the tax on the occupation of the public domain was broadened. This reform also provided for the transfer of 1 to 2 percent of income tax, VAT and excise on beer, alcohol, tobacco and hydrocarbons collected by the state to provincial, autonomous community and municipal capitals with over 75,000 inhabitants.

In 1995, reorganisation of the public enterprise sector had already started with the dissolution of the INI (Instituto Nacional de Industria) and the INH (Instituto Nacional de Hidrocarburos),[1] and the creation of two new bodies. The first to be set up was the AIE (Agencia Industrial del Estado), which incorporated the enterprises that demanded regular public support. These enterprises were mainly in the mining, defence, ship-building and iron and steel sectors and had been subject to restructuring or rationalisation plans. The second body to be created was the SEPI (Sociedad Estatal de Participaciones Industriales), which initially comprised the TENEO group, created in 1992,[2] Repsol and the dissolved INH. In addition, the Directorate General of State Assets had grouped a number of enterprises with the Sociedades Estatales de Patrimonio I y II in order to facilitate privatisation.

The agreement adopted by the Council of Ministers on 28 June 1996 provided for a new reorganisation of the state public enterprise sector. First, the TENEO group was dissolved and integrated within the SEPI. Second, the SEPPa was created, which grouped together the Sociedades Estatales de Patrimonio I and II. Subsequently, under Royal Decree—Law No 15/1997 of 5 September 1997, the assets of the state holding company Agencia Industrial del Estado, which was also dissolved, were transferred to the SEPI. More recently, on 25 May 2001, the Council of Ministers approved the dissolution of SEPPa and the incorporation in the SEPI of its members along with another ten companies that, up to that point, had been dependent on the Directorate General for Public Assets.

This restructuring was accompanied by a heavy privatisation drive that involved a large number of enterprises. Between June 1996 and December 2003, 60 total or partial privatisation operations affecting 52 enterprises were carried out, generating €31.747 million for the state. This privatisation process significantly altered the share of the public corporate sector in the economy. On the stock markets, in 2003, only 0.52 percent of market capitalisation belonged to the state compared with 10.9 percent in 1996 (and 16.6 percent in 1992). In employment terms, the share of the public enterprise sector shrank from 3.5 percent in the second quarter of 1996 to 1.5 percent in the second quarter of 2003. In terms of added value, in line with the information from the national balance sheet office of the Banco de España, non-financial public enterprises accounted for 2.6 percent of the total added value of non-financial companies in the economy in 2002, compared with 12.4 percent in 1996 (Hernández de Cos, 2004).

The rules governing welfare payments were also reformed. With regard to the unemployment benefit system, amendments were introduced at the end of 1993 and in early 1994, whereby, among others, the conditions for access to unemployment benefit were restricted and the amount of benefit was reduced to below specific levels. Other changes were made to social security system payments, based on the recommendations made in the 'Toledo Pact'. This aimed to ensure the future financial viability of the social security system in the face of the projected ageing of the population. In 1995, temporary invalidity benefit was discontinued and incorporated in temporary incapacity benefit, which was valid for a shorter duration than the former. In 1997, decisions were taken to gradually increase the level of proportionality of the social security system, maintain the purchasing power of pensions in relation to the Consumer Prices Index, set as an objective the financing of health expenditure exclusively by means of public transfers rather than contributions, and create a reserve fund using social security surpluses. The number of years applied in determining the regulatory basis was gradually raised from 8 to 15 years and the percentage applying to this basis for the calculation of the amount of retirement pension based on contributions for a period of less than 25 years was reduced; moreover, with regard to contributions, the maximum ceiling was increased as a function of the CPI and the maximum bases were gradually harmonised. In 2001, it was decided that the surpluses in social security contributions derived from budgetary settlements would be used to finance the reserve fund. A period of twelve years was agreed in which to conclude the separation of the social security's sources of financing in relation to the permanent financing, by the state, of minimum supplements. The possibility of early retirement was extended to unemployed workers who had contributed for more than 30 years, widows' and orphans' pensions were improved and a series of measures were also approved to extend the duration of economic activity to persons aged over 65.

With regard to health expenditure, in 1994, a regulation was implemented that harmonised the key aspects of the health care financing system. Subsequently, in 1997, a new agreement was approved for the 1998–2001 period which fixed an annual increase in health expenditure in line with nominal GDP and laid down criteria for its regional distribution. In 2001, approval of the new system for financing the autonomous communities led to the transfer of responsibility for health to all of the autonomous communities. This agreement made it compulsory for the autonomous communities to allocate to health expenditure a minimum of the initial financing received, and increased in line with the growth rate of the state tax revenues. Moreover, during the first three years of the system's implementation, the state guaranteed that the growth of the revenue allocated to this item would be equal to growth in nominal GDP. In parallel, during this period, several measures were taken to rein in health expenditure, in particular on pharmaceuticals, essentially by promoting generic medicines and applying reference prices for public sector payment. In spite of all these measures, health expenditure fell only marginally by one-tenth of GDP during the period between 1995 and 2000.

With regard to taxation, the personal income tax (IRPF, impuesto sobre la renta de las personas físicas) reforms of 1999 and 2003 are of most relevance. Law No 40/1998 introduced far-reaching reforms to the structure and content of personal income tax, establishing a personal and family minimum, abolishing the distinction between regular and irregular tax bases, fixing a single taxation rate, and reducing the number of tax bands and rates. To a large extent, the 2002 reform upheld the structure and basic principles of the previous income tax law. Amendments reduced the number of tax bands to five; lowered the maximum and minimum rates to 45 percent and 15 percent respectively; reduced to 15 percent the fixed rate applicable to capital gains; introduced a number of fiscal advantages for families with children and for disabled persons; and adjusted the tax treatment of various financial instruments. The reforms were certainly a good step in the right direction with a reduction of the tax burden, an extension of the tax base, and general simplification of the tax. The progress towards greater neutrality with respect to savings was, however, quite limited, and the system continues to favour savings in the form of pension funds, insurance contracts, and housing purchases (Hernández de Cos and García Vaquero, 2003).

The Composition of the Budgetary Consolidation Process

A degree of consensus exists by now amongst the economics profession concerning the importance of the composition of the fiscal consolidation processes in ensuring their sustainability. In line with the experiences of developed countries, fiscal adjustment must focus on curbing public expenditure, since the processes of fiscal consolidation based on raising taxes generally has only a temporary effect on the deficit, as well as negative effects on productivity and economic growth. In addition, a reduction in expenditure must focus on the structural component and, within this, on current expenditure. Curbing expenditure by reducing capital expenses is ineffective, as its place is often occupied by other components of spending, and inefficient due to the positive effect of public investment on private sector productivity, and especially so as regards infrastructure.

Overall, the fiscal consolidation process implemented in Spain since 1995 seems to have followed the pattern described above. On the one hand, the reduction of the public deficit from 6.6 percent of GDP in 1995 to the surplus of 0.4 percent of GDP in 2003 can be explained predominantly by non-cyclical factors (see Figure 4.2 and Table 4.6). Even ignoring the share corresponding to the debt burden, which contributed 2.7 percentage points to the deficit reduction as a result of the reduction in the level of public debt and interest rates, there is still a significant reduction (by 3.8 percentage points) in the primary balance. This is indicative of a restrictive discretionary policy. On the other hand, this restriction has done more to decrease current structural primary expenditure (1.9 percentage points of GDP) than to increase taxes (1.5 percentage points of GDP) and/or reduce public investment (0.3 percentage point of GDP).

Public expenditure

Total expenditure fell by 5.4 percentage points of GDP to 39.6 percent of GDP in 2003. In addition to the above-mentioned fall in the interest burden, the most significant adjustment in public expenditure related to the compensation of government employees, which fell by one percentage point of GDP. This fall in staff costs was primarily due to the reduction of compensation per employee. As a result the changes in the compensation regime resulting from the decision to raise the salaries of government employees in line with forecast inflation, which ended up being continuously below actual inflation, combined with the freezing of salaries of 1994 and 1997 and better control of wage drift. This was despite the fact that public employment maintained an annual pace of growth of approximately 2 percent on average, without the restrictions on filling vacancies, which came into force at state level from 1993 on, being effective for the general government as a whole. Cuts in staff costs were not, however, passed on in their totality to the overall consumption expenditure owing to the increase in the 'other' consumption expenditure items. These have traditionally maintained strong growth inertia, a fact that remained unchanged during the recent consolidation phase. In particular, attention is drawn to the sharp increase in social transfers in kind undertaken in the market, which increased their ratio to GDP by 0.5 percentage point. Inter alia, these social transfers include pharmaceutical expenditure.

With regard to the remaining expenditure components, the fall in the ratio of social contributions to GDP (by 1.7 percentage points) stands out. This decline was mainly accounted for by unemployment contributions and, to a lesser extent, pension contributions. Unemployment contributions fell by 0.8 percentage point of GDP between 1995 and 2003 as a result of positive employment developments and the impact of the unemployment reforms of 1994 mentioned previously. In part, this improvement can be deemed to be cyclical in nature. However, a structural improvement in this expenditure component cannot be ruled out if, for example, account is taken of the most recently available estimates of the rate of structural unemployment or NAIRU, which shows a marked decline (Estrada, Hernando and López-Salido, 2002). The decline in the ratio of pensions to GDP by 0.4 percentage point is mainly warranted by a slight increase in the number of pensioners in line with prevailing demographic factors. The ratio of temporary incapacity benefits to GDP contracted by 0.1 percentage point, despite the series of reforms implemented.

The remaining current transfers rose by 0.4 percentage point of GDP. This can be explained primarily by the increase in Spain's contribution to the European Union (EU) budget in relation to GNP. This rise resulted both from Spain's relatively high levels of growth during that period, and changes to the system for financing the EU budget, and the increase in bonus payments to social security contributions (that are recorded as operating subsidies), which were partially offset by the reduction in the subsidies to public enterprises, in particular to RENFE (the national railroad system).

The moderation in capital expenditure (by 1.4 percentage points of GDP) can be explained, first, by the decrease in both capital transfers (1.1

percentage point of GDP), which was in part warranted by the state's decision not to take on new debt from public enterprises, and, second, by the fall in public investment (0.3 percentage point of GDP). It should be noted, however, that, in line with prevailing accounting methods, investment by public enterprises, which increased over the period in question, is not included under this heading. In this respect, some of the most important government programmes in the field of infrastructure policy, or under the National Plan for Scientific Research, Development and Technological Innovation, were financed by purchase of financial assets, i.e. not included in the non-financial budgetary expenditure by the state.

An important feature of the expenditure restraint experienced in Spain in this period is related to the fact that it was accompanied by changes made to budget overrun control mechanisms. Empirical studies show that successful budgetary discipline depends largely on appropriate institutional design and, in particular, the proper working of the budgetary procedure is considered to be crucial for achieving fiscal discipline. In this respect, the changes in Spain in recent years seem to have contributed significantly to the process of fiscal consolidation. In the period 1975–1995, budgetary deviations (defined as the difference between final appropriations and initially projected expenditure) stood, in annual average terms, at around 0.7 percent of GDP and 4.6 percent of the overall initial appropriations. From 1996 onwards, by contrast, the inclusion in each year's State budget of various regulations to limit expenditure overruns enabled budgetary deviations to be significantly reduced. The average for the period 1997–2002 was below 0.3 percent of GDP (1.4 percent in terms of the initially approved appropriations).

The adoption of the Budgetary Stability Law which came into force in 2003 and of the State Budget Law (the latter, inter alia, implemented certain aspects of the former) introduced new fiscal discipline mechanisms. As regards expenditure control, under these laws a Parliamentary Plenary Session must approve, in the first four months of each year, the overall general government budgetary stability target and one for each of its agents for the following three years. It must further set the ceiling on expenditure in the State budget for the following year. This ceiling must include a contingency fund set at 2 percent of total State expenditure to cater for any non-discretionary expenditure requirements not envisaged in the initial budget that may arise in the course of budget execution. In 2003, the first year of application of the Budgetary Stability Law, the State expenditure ceiling and the related contingency fund were set at €114.52 billion and €2.29 billion, respectively. The amount of the fund was in itself highly restrictive, since it represented nearly half the average value of the amendments to budgetary appropriations applied to State expenditure in recent years. As a result, the additions to appropriations were cut back again in 2003 to 0.2 percent of GDP (1 percent of the initial appropriations).

Taxation

Since 1995, the ratio of public revenues to GDP rose by 1.6 percentage points to reach 40 percent of GDP in 2003. One of the most striking features about this period is the increase in tax receipts (by 2.0 percentage points of GDP). This offsets the fall in non-tax revenues (by 1.1 percentage point of GDP). The rise in tax receipts is explained primarily by the sharp increase in the tax bases, in line with employment developments, social security affiliation and a positive evolution of consumption, the housing market and corporate earnings. Discretionary decision-making was essentially limited to the reduction in the personal income tax rates, already mentioned, which was partly offset by the decision not to deflate tax schedules; the allocation of sizeable bonus payments to social security contributions, the increase in certain excise duties and the creation of new indirect and direct taxes, the gradual unification of the maximum bases of the different social security regimes, and a number of changes to the corporation tax aimed at reducing, inter alia, taxation of small and medium-sized enterprises.

The increase in tax receipts was mainly driven by the rise in indirect taxation (by 1.6 percentage points of GDP), which was a result of positive developments in VAT collection (1 percentage point of GDP) and, to a lesser extent, the increase of certain excise duties and the creation of new taxes and rates (insurance premiums, electricity and hydrocarbons). It is also worth noting that the increase in other transfers receivable (by 0.3 percentage point of GDP) is closely related to the rise in housing prices during that period.

By contrast, disregarding the temporary effect on corporation tax collections in 2002, direct taxation increased its share of GDP by just 0.4 percentage points. The corporate income tax behaved in a very different way as compared to personal income tax. The personal income tax collected fell by 1.1 percentage point of GDP following the implementation of the reforms previously mentioned, and the lowering of capital tax revenues, which can be explained both by the reduction in tax rates applied to the yields of financial assets and capital gains and the fall in interest rates during that period. Revenues from corporation tax increased by over 1.4 percentage point of GDP due to increases in corporate earnings during the expansion of the economy. Finally, the ratio of social contributions to GDP increased by 0.7 percentage point of GDP, in line with the rise in employment. However, if the bonus payments to promote employment had been taken into account, the increase in the ratio of the contributions to GDP would only have increased by 0.3 percentage point.

Other non-tax income fell by 0.8 percentage point of GDP mainly as a result of the lower levels of income transferred by the Banco de España (0.7 percentage point of GDP) and a certain reduction in the funds received from the European Union.

The Benefits of the Consolidation Process

The maintenance of sound public finances in combination with a monetary policy that is oriented towards ensuring price stability are considered necessary conditions to increase macro-economic stability and thereby encourage sustained and balanced economic growth. The Spanish case during the last decades is a clear example of this statement. A very basic regression analysis confirms that, between 1980 and 2003, a negative link could be identified between the public balance and real interest rates (see Figure 4.5). In particular, this manifested itself in Spain during the 1990s, when it was observed that the fall in real interest rates paralleled the reduction in the public deficit. From this perspective, the fiscal consolidation process followed in Spain since 1995 has to be considered a key element for the economic expansion observed in that period.

Against this assessment, it could be argued that following the standard macroeconomic models, a reduction in the government deficit has negative effects in the short term on the level of economic activity and employment. The most recent empirical studies, however, put forward the idea that large and sustained fiscal consolidation efforts, as the one followed in Spain in recent years, may have positive effects on demand and output in the economy, offsetting the negative direct effects of fiscal correction. In fact, in situations of high public deficit, its correction can have positive effects on private consumption in that the actors perceive it as an indication of further corrections down the road or even as a means of countering the risks of financial crisis. In this scenario, the credibility of the fiscal consolidation process is essential; the fiscal adjustment must be perceived by economic agents as permanent. Therefore there is a higher likelihood that fiscal consolidation will have such positive effects, where the initial situation is characterised by high levels of government debt and there are large reductions in the deficit. Similarly, the composition of the fiscal adjustment may also be relevant in prompting the above-mentioned positive effects of consolidation on growth in the short term. Adjustments which focus on reducing public expenditure and, in particular, current transfers and compensation of employees, but without increasing taxes on capital and maintaining levels of public investment, could have positive effects on supply, particularly through the decrease in labour costs and the increase in productivity. In this case, the positive response of economic growth to fiscal adjustment could be explained by an increase in private investment.

From this perspective, empirical evidence gathered by the European Commission (2003) suggests that almost half of the fiscal consolidation efforts implemented in the Member States of the European Union have been followed by an immediate burst of economic growth. In Spain's case, the nature of the fiscal adjustment process makes it likely that the effects were in that direction. The main features of the adjustment were the following: (a) the initial levels of public deficit and debt were very high and there was a high risk that Spain would not fulfil the convergence criteria laid down in the Treaty; (b) the size of the adjustment was very large in the first two years, leading to a reduction in the deficit by 3.5 percentage points between 1995 and 1997, as well as in the first four years, with a reduction in the deficit by 5.5 percentage points between 1995 and 1999; (c) as shown above, the adjustment consisted of a decrease in public expenditure, in particular relating to the compensation of employees, while the personal income tax was also reduced.

Moreover, the experience of OECD countries in recent decades shows that the persistence of fiscal imbalances reduces the possibility of fiscal policy acting as a stabilising force; indeed, it makes it necessary to apply tight fiscal policies during downturns so as to avoid excessive budget deficit slippage. The behaviour of fiscal policy in Spain in recent decades again illustrates this assessment. Comparison of the economy's cyclical position, measured by the output gap, and the fiscal policy stance, proxied by the change in the primary structural deficit, reveals that Spanish fiscal policy maintained a clearly pro-cyclical bias in the 1980–1997 period. As a result, the economic expansion of the 1988–1991 period was accompanied by an expansionary fiscal policy that made it necessary to concentrate the fiscal adjustment during the phase of lower economic growth (1993–1997). The behaviour of fiscal policy in Spain over the latest upturn (1998–2001), in which a restrictive stance was maintained on average, is therefore in sharp contrast to what occurred in previous economic expansions. Not surprisingly, the virtually balanced budget position at the outset of 2002 enabled the authorities to let the automatic stabilisers operate, thereby contributing to economic stabilisation without jeopardising budgetary stability (Hernández de Cos, 2004).

Figure 4.5 Real ex-post interest rates and public deficit in Spain

Source: NIE, Banco de España and own calculations.

THE CHALLENGES AHEAD

Anchoring Fiscal Consolidation: The Stability Law

As mentioned earlier, Spain as a member of the EU is subject to all the rules of the Maastricht Treaty and the Stability and Growth Pact. In addition, Spain approved, in 2002, its Budgetary Stability Law, which entered into force in 2003, setting stricter limits on expenditure and even more stringent balance or surplus objectives. In particular, the law targets a balanced budget for the overall general government sector and each of its related agents (Central Government, including Central Administration and Social Security, regional governments and local governments) and sets a spending ceiling for the State and, hereunder, a reserve fund, equivalent to 2 percent of the ceiling, so as to meet unforeseen non-discretionary spending requirements.

What is the rationale for this law? Although, in the light of the budgetary results described earlier, there would seem to be no compelling risk of running up an excessive deficit in the next few years, maintaining budgetary discipline in the longer term will require greater effort for several reasons: consolidation fatigue, the budgetary policy of neighbouring countries, exceptionally high fiscal decentralisation and persisting structural problems reflected in public expenditure which introduce a bias running counter to medium-term sustainability (González-Páramo, 2001).

Consolidation fatigue has been apparent since 1999. This flagging of momentum is evident in most EMU member countries. The structural deficit balance worsened between 1999 and 2003 by 1.3 percentage points of GDP. In this respect, Von Hagen et al. (2001) emphasised that it is important, for continuing domestic consolidation, that fiscal policies pursued by other countries be restrictive in tone. Spain has clearly fared better; the structural balance and primary structural balance have continued to improve. However, the improvement has been small compared with those recorded in previous years. Another sign of this fatigue is provided by the composition of credit adjustments: amendments to appropriations continued to be largely implemented via those mechanisms less subject to parliamentary scrutiny (extended and residual appropriations as opposed to extraordinary and supplementary appropriations). Moreover, some expenditure items, for example purchases of goods and services, have continued to show very high deviations which, in terms of the initially approved appropriation, amounted to 22.9 percent on average in the period 1997–2003.

In addition, Spain has undoubtedly become a very highly decentralised country, in particular in terms of public expenditure. The need to reconcile this element with the need to maintain sound public finances highlights the usefulness of developing rules of fiscal discipline that bind together the different levels of government. In this context, a domestic Stability Pact, as the one defined by the Spanish Stability Law, can be seen as a necessary instrument to make sub-central levels of government also responsible for the maintenance of sound public finances.

Finally, as regards the persisting structural problems, the consequences of ageing and the potential loss of the EU funds represent the main dangers for fiscal sustainability in the future. These two latter issues are analysed further in the following sections.

The Consequences of Ageing

The size and structure of the EU population by age group will change significantly in the coming decades. The combination of a fertility rate that is below the birth rate (2.1 children per woman), the increase in life expectancy and the gradual climb of the baby-boom generation through the population pyramid is leading to the gradual ageing of the population. Forecasts show that the dependency rate in Spain (i.e. the percentage of the population over the age of 65 compared with that of the population aged between 15 and 64 years) will increase moderately until approximately 2020, when it will accelerate to reach a maximum of 56.4 percent in 2048 (compared with 25 percent in 2000).

The characteristics of many of the public expenditure programmes in developed countries imply that the phenomenon of population ageing represents a risk to the sustainability of public finances in the future. In Spain's case, government expenditure on pensions and healthcare, which are the components that will be most affected by population ageing, amounted to 14.3 percent of GDP in 2000 and accounted for over 35 percent of total government expenditure. In the case of the public pension system, according to the forecasts of the European Commission and the OECD, the system will enjoy a surplus until the middle of the next decade, thanks to continuing growth in affiliations. The sudden end to this trend in 2020 and the escalation in the number of pensioners from 2015 onwards will give rise to a growing deficit, reaching its peak in 2040 with an accumulated increase in expenditure from 6 percentage points to 8 percentage points of GDP (European Commission, 2001; OECD 2001). The cost of health care will also be affected by the greater consumption of services and medicines associated with elderly citizens. From the current level of just under 8 percent of GDP, forecasts point to an increase in ageing-related expenditure on health care in the order of 1 or 2 percentage points over the next four decades.

Although, as mentioned previously, some reform measures have been adopted in recent years, more far-reaching endeavours are clearly needed. In this respect, a multidimensional strategy should be pursued consisting of maintaining a balance or in surplus budget that will allow a progressive reduction of the debt ratio, improving the labour market performance by fostering participation rates and reducing early retirement incentives, and reforming the pension system itself by revising the system's parameters so as to make it more actuarially neutral.

The Consequences of EU Enlargement

In May 2004, the 'new' Member States from Central and Eastern Europe and the Mediterranean, that were already receiving financial pre-accession aid through the framework of the Financial Perspectives 2000–2006, entered the European Union. As full members, they have started to be beneficiaries of the structural funds and the agricultural policy funds through the EU budget. For the following financial perspectives, the EU enlargement will cause an inevitable reduction in Community funds granted to Spain, if there is not a considerable increase of the amount of the EU budget devoted to these structural and agricultural policies.

Three main reasons are behind these expected losses of funds:

(1) Real convergence during the current period of Financial Perspectives 2000–2006: as a consequence of the real convergence, and independently of the accession process, some Spanish regions will exceed the limits set for being considered as regions under objective 1 (GDP per capita below 75 percent of the EU average);
(2) Regional statistical effect: the entry of 10 new members will reduce the EU per capita income by around 18 percent in 2007 and, therefore, some Spanish regions currently receiving structural funds will automatically have an average per capita income above 75 percent of the EU-25 average;
(3) National statistical effect: enlargement will move Spanish per capita income above 90 percent of the EU-25 average, thus above the existing threshold to receive Cohesion Funds.

The effects of (1) and (2) will amount to around 0.2 and 0.3 percent of GDP in a seven year period, respectively (Martín y Sanz, 2003). The effect of (3) would amount to an additional loss of 0.3 percent of GDP. In addition, apart from this permanent reduction in structural aid from 2007 onwards, enlargement will have very complex effects—opposite in sign and both temporary and permanent in nature—on the Spanish economy. The combined order of magnitude of these shocks has been estimated by Martín et al. (2002) to represent a reduction in GDP, in terms of the level that would have been recorded without enlargement, of 0.4 percent in the short term, in 2004, reaching a maximum of 1.8 percent in 2008, before falling to 1 percent in 2014.

What is the appropriate response of Spanish fiscal policy in view of these severe changes? Using the deficit elasticities in relation to the output gap as a reference (European Commission, 2002), the deficit would record an automatic maximum increase of 0.7 percent of GDP in the period 2004–08, which would fall to 0.4 percent in 2013. The amount appears to be small and acceptable, given that the shocks are asymmetric, and an expansionary response by the European Central Bank is not in the cards for country-specific shocks. The size of the shock could even be considered to justify a transitory discretionary expansionary reaction by budgetary policy. It can be argued, however, that neither discretionary expansion, nor probably the automatic drift of the deficit by more than 0.5 percent of GDP, is justified. The appropriate reaction to a permanent negative supply-side shock is a reduction (increase) in the structural deficit (surplus) of the budget to compensate for the effect of the automatic stabilisers. In fact, the automatic response of the budgetary balance to permanent changes in aggregate supply tends to be destabilising, since it delays structural adjustment and prolongs inflationary pressures (Artis and Buti, 2000; Buti et al., 2001; Corsetti et al., 2002).

The adjustment required to the structural balance of the budget could be avoided, however, provided that measures are adopted to restructure public expenditure and revenue, with the aim of attaining greater budgetary efficiency as part of a package of reforms that seeks to introduce greater flexibility on the supply side, along the lines spelt out in the following section.

The Efficiency and Quality of Public Expenditure

The process of real convergence followed by the Spanish economy since the middle of the 90s has been mainly based on the growth of the rate of employment, while the productivity gap with the European countries has not been reduced. To ensure the long-term sustainability of economic growth, it is therefore important to boost productivity. Moreover, as mentioned above, EU enlargement will bring additional competitive pressures to bear, thus posing new challenges for the Spanish economy as a whole.

The role of the public sector could be crucial in helping stimulate the necessary productivity increases. For this purpose, the aim should be to improve the quality of public finances, in terms of the composition of both expenses and revenues, and of the efficiency of the public sector as a whole.

In the case of expenditure, although the relation between infrastructures and productivity is not necessarily the same in all countries (Aschauer, 1989; Ford and Poret, 1991; Berndt and Hansson, 1992; Holtz-Eakin, 1992), in the case of Spain all the empirical evidence identifies a positive association between both variables: the capital accumulated by the public sector makes a very significant contribution to the productivity growth of the private sector, and especially so when it takes material form in infrastructures. The relative position of Spain as regards this variable, measured by the per capita public capital stock was, however, in 2003 still below (87 percent) the EU average, although the convergence effort during the last 15 years has been considerable with growth rates of public investment systematically higher than those of the EU average countries. Thus, the public capital gap has been reduced by more than 25 percentage points since the beginning of the 90s. Given the existing gap, however, it would seem that greater competitiveness could only be attained through a sustained and lasting effort in this area.

As regards other public expenditure components of particular relevance to the efficiency and productivity of the economy, education and R&D are the most prominent. The stock of human capital was around 85 percent of the EU average in 2003, although again the improvements in education have been quite dramatic in the last decades, as shown by the fact that in 2004 the percentage of people with secondary or tertiary education was 30 percent among the population between 45 and 64, while it was already 56 percent for the population between 25 and 54. In any case, during these decades the level of public expenditure has been relatively low, with little improvement in comparison with EU average standards. As regards the technological capital stock, the relative position in 2003 was only 45.3 percent compared to the EU level, although there have been also some improvements, in particular as regards the technological public capital stock.

Just as important for growth as an adequate composition of public spending, is the maintenance of an efficient public management. In this sense, the dynamics of public expenditure continue to be excessively influenced by inertia and incrementalism, marked by the 'philosophy of committed expenditure' and the absence of management by objectives. A good indicator of these problems is the growth in public sector employment, which has risen by some 300,000 people since 1996, despite the restrictions imposed by Spain's central government, in part circumvented by increased use of temporary staff. This trend can largely be attributed to expansionary behaviour on the part of local authorities.

The loss of efficiency in the public sector affects all the functions performed by the State, from macroeconomic and redistributive functions to those of resource allocation; but the most important are perhaps the last two. The size of the public sector and the problems found in basic services explain why, in a number of countries around Spain, reforms in public management systems have been tested, with the goal of acceptable levels of efficiency in the performance of public services. These reforms include the gradual introduction of flexibility in contracting and employment, the creation of a competitive environment so that administrative units can test their results against those of other private or public units, the separation of the production and funding of services, the establishment of incentives linked to responsibilities, and in all cases, a more or less visible change of public-service culture (Oxley, 1993).

Towards a More Growth Oriented Tax System

An additional fiscal policy element, crucial for long-term growth perspectives, refers to taxation. The available empirical evidence suggests that the tax burden and the fiscal structure have a significant effect on the competitiveness of the economy, as they may determine medium-term patterns of differential growth between countries (e.g. Plosser, 1992; Dowrick, 1992; Easterly and Rebelo, 1992; Alesina and Perotti, 1995). And the theoretical literature on growth suggests that a country whose objective is to converge with the real income levels of its more developed partners should have less recourse than those others to taxing capital returns during the convergence process (Razin and Yuen, 1993). These factors are of particular relevance in the European context, given that the distorting effects of taxation in the national setting are combined with the risk of flight tax bases.

It is therefore important to identify the differences between the Spanish system and those of other European countries and what reforms of the system might contribute to an improvement in competitiveness. In this respect, it should be stressed that most of the tax reforms applied during the 90s were in the right direction. While the tax reforms until the beginning of the 1990s pursued mainly a modernisation of the Spanish tax system and an increase of the financial resources to cover the increasing demand for public expenditure, the reforms applied in the 90s and the beginning of the new century were certainly aimed at promoting employment, savings, tax neutrality and tax simplification. This is particularly the case for the reforms of the corporate tax in 1995 and of the personal income tax in 1998 and 2003.

Despite these steps in the right direction, there is still some room for improvement. Spain displays a tax take which is below the EU-15 average but remains slightly above the EU-25. Moreover, a bias towards employers' social security contributions still remains, while the tax system continues to favour savings in the form of pension funds, insurance contracts and housing purchases. Therefore, future tax reforms should aim at raising potential output by improving incentives to participate in the labour market and to raise capital formation. Further simplification of the tax system should be pursued with the aim to reduce compliance costs, and efforts to fight against tax evasion should be intensified. Enhanced tax responsibility of territorial governments could also be useful both for bringing the tax administration closer to taxpayers and for increasing the fiscal co-responsibility of the regions.

NOTES

* European Central Bank

1. At the beginning of the 80s the Spanish public enterprise sector was basically spread out in two groups (INI and INH, the latter concentrated on firms included in the liquid fuel sector) and the Directorate General of State Assets.
2. Teneo was created in 1992 as a part of INI to concentrate all firms that were no longer allowed to receive state aids according to the European Community law.

REFERENCES

Alesina, A. and Perotti, R. (1995), 'Taxation and redistribution in an open economy', *European Economic Review*, 39, 961–979.

Argimón, I. and González-Páramo, J.M. (1987a), 'Una medición de la rémora inflacionaria en el IRPF, 1979–1985', *Investigaciones Económicas*, 11.

Artis, M. and M. Buti (2000), 'Close to balance or in surplus, a policy-makers's guide to the implementation of the Stability and Growth Pact', *Journal of Common Market Studies*, 38, 563–592.

Aschauer, D.A. (1989), 'Is public expenditure productive?', *Journal of Monetary Economics*, 23.

Bandrés, E. (1990), 'Los efectos de los gastos sociales sobre la distribución de la renta en España', Monografia 92, Instituto de Estudios Fiscales, Madrid.

Berndt, E.R. and Hansson, B. (1992), 'Measuring the contribution of public infrastructure capital in Sweden', *Scandinavian Journal of Economics*, 94, Supplement.

Buti, M., W. Roeger and J. In't Veld (2001), 'Stabilising output and inflation: Policy conflicts and coordination under a stability pact', *Journal of Common Market Studies*, 39, 801–828.

Comín, F. (1989), 'Las Administraciones Públicas', in J.L. García Delgado (dir.), *España, economía*, Madrid: Espasa-Calpe.

Corrales, A. and Taguas, D. (1991), 'Series macroeconómicas para el período 1954–1989', in C. Molinas y otros (eds.), *La economía española: Una perspectiva macroeconómica*, Madrid: Instituto de Estudios Fiscales-Bosch.

Corsetti, G., J. Flemming, S. Honkapohja, W. Leibfritz, G. Saint-Paul, H.-W. Sinn and X. Vives (2002), *Report of the European Economy 2002*, CESifo, Munich.

De la Dehesa, G. (1993), 'Las privatizaciones en España', *Moneda y Crédito*, 196.

Dominguez Martínez, J.M. (1988), 'El crecimiento del sector público (1970–1986) y la hipótesis Beck', *Papeles de Economía Española*, 37.

Dowrick, S. (1992), 'Estimating the impact of government consumption on growth: Growth accounting and optimising models', mimeo, Australian National University.

Easterly, W. and Rebelo, S. (1992), 'Fiscal policy and economic growth: An empirical investigation', mimeo, CEPR.

Edo, V., De Pablos, L. and Valiño, A. (1988), 'Diferencias entre presupuesto programado y presupuesto ejecutado', *Papeles de Economía Española*, 37.

Edo, V., De Pablos, L. and Valiño, A. (1993), 'El presupuesto como instrumento de control del gasto público', Fundación Banco Bilbao Vizcaya, Programa de Investigaciones del Centro de Estudios sobre Economía Pública, Documentos de Trabajo, mimeo.

Estrada, A., Hernando, I. and López-Salido, D. (2002), 'La medición de la NAIRU en la economía española', *Moneda y Crédito*, 215.

European Commission (2001), 'Budgetary challenges posed by ageing populations', EPC/ECFIN/655/01EN.

European Commission (2002), 'Public finances in EMU-2002', *European Economy*, 3.

European Commission (2003), 'Public finances in EMU-2003', *European Economy*.

Fernández, E. and Gutiérrez, F. (1987), 'La financiación del Tesoro por los bancos centrales en los principales países europeos', *Boletín Económico*, Banco de España.

Fina, L. (1986), 'Evolución de las prestaciones por desempleo en España y en la OCDE', *Papeles de Economía Española*, 26.

Ford, R. and Poret, P. (1991), 'Infrastructure and private-sector productivity', *OECD Economic Studies*, 17.

Fuentes Quintana, E. (dir.) (1976), *Sistema tributario español. Criterios para su reforma*, Madrid: Ministerio de Hacienda.

Fuentes Quintana, E. (dir.) (1988), 'La estrategia presupuestaria española: Entre el drama del déficit y el deterioro de los servicios públicos', *Papeles de Economía Española*, 37.

González-Páramo, J.M. (1989a), 'The role of the public sector in Spain: Structural characteristics and policy adjustment on the road to the EEC Internal Market', mimeo.

González-Páramo, J.M. (1992), '¿En cuánto corregimos la doble imposición sobre los dividendos?', *Hacienda Pública Española*, Monografía, No. 2/1992.

González-Páramo, J.M. (1994a), 'Política pública y convergencia: La modernización del sector público', *Papeles de Economía Española*, 57.

González-Páramo, J.M. (1994b), 'Presupuesto y déficit en 1993: ¿Es España diferente?', España 1993: Un balance, *Economistas*, 58.

González-Páramo, J.M. (2001), *Costes y beneficios de la disciplina fiscal: La Ley de Estabilidad Presupuestaria en perspectiva*, Madrid: Estudios de Hacienda Pública, Instituto de Estudios Fiscales.

González-Páramo, J.M. and Onrubia, J. (1992), 'El gasto público en vivienda en España', Instituto de Estudios Fiscales, *Hacienda Pública Española*, 120–121.

Hernández de Cos, P. (2002), 'The new framework for the Spanish regional (autonomous) governments in Spain', Banco de España, *Economic Bulletin*, July.

Hernández de Cos, P. (2004), 'Empresa pública, privatización y eficiencia', Banco de España, *Estudios Económicos*, 75.

Hernández de Cos, P. (2004), 'La consolidación fiscal en España: un balance', *Presupuesto y Gasto Público*, 35 (2).

Hernández de Cos, P. and García–Vaquero (2003), 'La nueva reforma del IRPF. Principales modificaciones y análisis de sus efectos', Banco de España, *Boletín Económico*, May.

Holtz–Eakin, D. (1992), 'Public sector capital and the productivity puzzle', National Bureau of Economic Research, Working Paper No. 4122.

Lagares, M., Alvarez, R., Raymond, J.L., González–Páramo, J.M. and Encabo, I. (1988), 'Niveles de cobertura del gasto público en España', Fundación FIES–CECA (Monograph).

López Casasnovas, G. (1992), 'Empleo y políticas salariales en el sector público: Una aproximación a su modelización', mimeo, Universidad Pompeu Fabra, Barcelona.

Martín, C. and I. Sanz (2003), 'Las Consecuencias de la Ampliación para la Política Regional Europea: La Perspectiva Española', enero, mimeo, Academia Europea de Ciencias y Artes, Madrid.

Martín, C. and I. Sanz, Herce, J.A., Sosvilla–Rivero, S. and F.J. Velásquez (2002), 'La ampliación de la Unión Europea. Efectos sobre la economía española', Colección Estudios Económicos No. 27, La Caixa, Barcelona.

Martín Aceña, P. and Comín, F. (1991), *INI: 50 años de industrialización en España*, Madrid: Espasa–Calpe.

Mauleón, I. (1986), 'El déficit público y el mercado de trabajo en España: Algunas conexiones e implicaciones', *Investigaciones Económicas*, X.

Mauleón, I. and Pérez, J. (1984), 'Interest rate determinants and macroeconomic performance in Spain', *Documentos de Trabajo,* 8420, Banco de España.

Myro, R. (1988), 'Las empresas públicas', in J.L. García Delgado (dir.), *España, economía*, Madrid: Espasa–Calpe.

OECD (1988), L'enseignement dans les pays de l'OCDE, Paris.

OECD (1993), 'España 1992–1993', *Estudios Económicos de la OCDE*, April, Paris.

OECD (2001), 'Fiscal implications of ageing: projections of age related spending', *Economic Outlook*, 69.

Oxley, H. (1993), 'El sector público en los 80 y experimentos de política pública para los 90', Centro de Estudios sobre Economía Pública (Fundación Banco Bilbao Vizcaya), Documentos de Trabajo, April.

Plosser, C. (1992), 'The search for growth', mimeo, University of Rochester.

Raymond, J.L. and González–Páramo (1988), 'Déficit, impuestos y crecimiento del gasto público', *Papeles de Economía Española*, 37.

Razin, A. and Yuen, C.–Y. (1993), 'Convergence in growth rates: The role of capital mobility and international taxation', CEPR, Discussion Paper Series, 760.

Rodrik, D. (1990), 'Soft budgets, hard minds: Stray thoughts on the integration process in Greece, Portugal and Spain', in C. Bliss y J. Braga de Macedo (eds.), *Unity with diversity in the European economy*, New York: CEPR—Cambridge University Press.

Salas, R. and Jiménez, M. (1992), 'Causas del incremento de la recaudación del IRPF: 1982–1987', Instituto de Estudios Fiscales, Madrid, mimeo.

Saunders, P. and Klau, F. (1985), 'The role of the public sector: Causes and consequences of the growth of government', *OECD Economic Studies*, 4.

Valdés, T., Raymond, J.L. and Argimón, I. (1989), 'Evolución de la recaudación en el IRPF: Determinantes de las causas y estimación de los efectos', *Investigaciones Económicas*, XIII.

Viñals, J. (1985), 'El déficit público y sus efectos macroeconómicos: Algunas reconsideraciones', *Papeles de Economía Española*, 23.

Von Hagen, J., Hallett, A.H. and R. Strauch (2001), 'Budgetary Consolidation in EMU,' European Economy—Economic Papers 148, Commission of the EC, Directorate—General for Economic and Financial Affairs (DG ECFIN).

Zapico Goñi, E. (1988), 'La modernización del gasto público', *Papeles de Economía Española*, 37.

5. Personal Income Taxation: the Cornerstone of the Tax System in a Democracy

Desiderio Romero Jordán * and José Félix Sanz-Sanz**

INTRODUCTION

For reasons of equity, transparency and its revenue raising ability, the personal income tax (PIT) has become the backbone of tax systems in the majority of developed countries. In Spain, however, personal income taxation has a short history since it was only incorporated into the tax system in 1978. Its implementation required many obstacles to be overcome and the complete reform of the Spanish tax framework, which was until then based on commodity taxes. However, despite its short lifetime, the Spanish personal income tax has undergone significant modifications during its 27 years of existence in order to adapt its structure and objectives to the country's economic and social needs. During the almost three decades of its existence, its most significant reforms were undertaken in 1991, 1998 and 2002. There is no doubt that its versatility and ability to adapt to the political, economic and social situation in Spain explain the overwhelming success of the tax since its introduction.

The aim of this chapter is to explain the most significant events during the lifetime of the tax which, since its introduction, has become the form of taxation most widely known by Spanish taxpayers. We will therefore describe its historical origins, analyse its significance within the Spanish tax framework and offer a statistical evaluation of the tax since it came into force. We will also review the three most significant processes of reform since 1978. The first was in 1991 under the Socialist government of Felipe González; the other two were carried out in 1998 and 2002 by José María Aznar's *Partido Popular* government.

HISTORICAL ANTECEDENTS OF THE PERSONAL INCOME TAX IN SPAIN

The Origin of Income Taxation in Spain

The origins of the PIT in Spain can be traced back to 1810 with the *Contribución Extraordinaria de Guerra (CEG).*[1] *CEG* was introduced in response to the need to obtain resources to finance the war against Napoleon's French invaders (Gota, 1971). The levy was subsequently modified to the point where it became akin to a tax on income imposed on the profits of farms, trade, industry and employment. However, the country's economic and social situation, rejection of the tax by taxpayers, and the high amount of fraud condemned it to failure (Aparicio and Álvarez, 2003).

In the 20th century, the first serious attempt to establish a progressive PIT occurred in 1932 during the Second Republic (1931–1936). This tax was named the *Contribución General sobre la Renta (CGR)* [2] and was levied on income obtained by individuals with greater economic wealth (annual income higher than 601 euros—a very high amount at the time). Its schedule was made up of several bands with increasing rates of taxation from 1% to 7.7% for income greater than 6,000 euros at the time. The *CGR* was, without doubt, a milestone in Spanish tax history. Nevertheless, its practical application was once again a failure as the Spanish society was accustomed to commodity taxation and because the tax authority lacked the necessary means to administer it.

During the Franco dictatorship (1939–1975), the steps taken to incorporate progressive income taxation were very timid. Notwithstanding this, at the end of the 1950s the *Tax on Income from Personal Work* and the *Tax on Income from Property* were introduced. A modified combination of these two taxes, called the *General Personal Income Tax,* was introduced in the 1960s. However, this tax was not widely applied, as at its most successful point it only affected three hundred thousand taxpayers in the country as a whole.

The beginning of the 1970s saw a greater fiscal awareness by the country's economic authorities. Therefore, various proposals for tax reform were made in which the main thrust was to tax progressively personal income. This renewed interest in tax matters was led by the Institute for Fiscal Studies. In 1973, under its director Professor Fuentes Quintana, the Institute elaborated a proposal for reform contained in its *Report on the Spanish Tax System*, more popularly known as the *green paper.* This report signalled the need to implement a tax system supported by three basic pillars: a tax on personal income, a tax on company income and a turnover tax. However, in spite of the initial support of the tax authorities, the project was not implemented because of the fragile political health of the country, coinciding with the onset of General Franco's final illness. Nonetheless, years later, this excellent report was the embryo of the 1977 tax reform. By 1977 there was an overwhelming need in the country to prepare an economic plan, without any further delays. This economic plan had, on the one hand, to assist in combating the economic consequences of the 1973 oil crisis and, on the other hand, to lead the nascent political system without Franco on the road towards democracy.

In this respect, the political and social peace necessary for a successful reform was achieved by negotiations between the government and all political parties, leading to the most important political agreement of present-day Spain: the *Moncloa Pacts* signed in October 1977 and analysed in depth by Professor Comín in this book. The tax proposal of this new Global Pact was supported by two basic pillars: reform of the structure and composition of the tax system and reorganisation and boosting of the roles of tax administration and inspection, which had traditionally been regarded as tasks of secondary importance. In terms of the new taxes, the reform introduced three new categories of taxation: *the personal income tax*, *the extraordinary tax on property* and *the corporation tax*. In other words, a progressive personal income tax and a proportional tax on company profits were created. In parallel, the personal income tax was complemented by a general tax on the personal wealth of individuals, which, in addition, aimed to monitor the consistency of the income declared in the PIT.[3] The 1977 reform was so successful that today, almost thirty years later, the Spanish tax system continues to be largely based on these two income taxes. This change in taxation implied the definitive rejection of commodity-based taxation of income and the firm acceptance of a modern tax structure based on direct personal taxation of income. This achievement was, without doubt, assisted by the fact that, in parallel with the formal changes to the tax system, great attention was paid to modernising and improving the tax administration authority itself, involving the reorganisation of the civil service departments dedicated to tax administration and audit.

The Role of the Personal Income Tax in the Spanish Territorial Decentralisation Process [4]

Another of the reform's merits was that it recognised the need for the country's territorial restructuring. The decentralisation of the public sector brought about by the 1978 Constitution allowed the formation of a State of Autonomous Regions, dividing the national territory into seventeen

"Autonomous Communities" and two autonomous cities (Ceuta and Melilla). Territorial public administration required that, in addition to the transfer of public spending competences from central to regional governments, a share of public revenues would also be transferred. In this process, the Constitution recognised two alternative financing systems: the Foral Regime, which was to apply to the Communities of the Basque Country and Navarre, and the Common Regime, which was to govern the remaining Autonomous Communities.[5] These two systems of territorial administration of financial activity had very different structures and ways of operating from the outset. The former was governed by the Covenant and Agreement between the State and the Communities of Navarre and the Basque Country. The Common Regime was regulated by the Organic Act on the Financing of the Autonomous Communities, better known as *LOFCA*.

Unlike the Common Regime, the Foral system from the outset bestowed wide competences on the Foral Communities to manage the vast majority of public expenditure and to establish and regulate their own tax system, with minimal restrictions. Therefore, the Basque Country and Navarre were financed by the so-called agreed or ceded taxes and only customs duties and social security contributions lay outside their remit. As we shall see below, unlike the Common Regime, the Foral Communities acquired wide powers over income taxation.

For the Common Regime Communities, the LOFCA specified that the transfer of powers of expenditure must occur in accordance with the *effective cost method*. This system consisted in evaluating the ability of each regional government to provide the goods and public services transferred, incorporating all of the ongoing costs involved into the analysis. A commitment was also made to review the financial situation of each Community every five years in order to make appropriate changes to ensure the provision of the transferred services in the longer term. The most significant changes to the system were made in 1986, 1992, 1996 and 2001. In 1986 an agreement was reached to replace the effective cost method with a system based on indicators of each Community's expenditure requirements and, in 2001, the five-yearly review ceased to be obligatory.

With regards to the financing system, the LOFCA provided for increasing joint responsibility for public revenues. And so, during the period 1982–1984 the system of state transfers which had been in place until then was replaced by a new system based on the transfer or reassignment of certain taxes and on the sharing of state revenues through what was called the Sufficiency Fund. The objective of this fund was to guarantee the equalisation of the quality of services transferred throughout the national territory. Moreover, in 1997, for the first time, the tax resources of the

Autonomous Communities were greatly increased through the transfer of 30 percent of the personal income tax revenues to the Communities. This transfer required the amendment of the LOFCA to incorporate income tax as one of the potentially transferable taxes since originally this had not been the case. The trend that started in 1997 was significantly reinforced in the 2001 Agreements. The review of the system, which took place that year and entered into force in January 2002, meant an increase both in the number of taxes transferred and the legal powers backing them. Although the income tax was not one of the taxes transferred with greater legal powers, it is clear that the modifications carried out in 2001 greatly increased the potential for using this tax as a tool of regional policy. In 2002, the percentage of income tax revenue transferred increased from 30 to 33 percent. Other taxes transferred included 35 percent of VAT, 40 percent of special taxes on hydrocarbons, tobacco and alcoholic beverages and the total transfer of taxes on electricity and specific modes of transport. Legal competences in relation to taxes already transferred to the Autonomous Communities were also increased. Another important change was that, from 2002, the financial guarantees relating to the income tax destined for the Autonomous Communities were removed. Its increase at a rate equal to nominal GDP growth had, until then, been guaranteed by the central government. The idea was that the elimination of this "guaranteed revenue" would likely strengthen the active role of income tax in the finances of the Autonomous Communities, encouraging them to use their legal powers.

In short, although the Foral Communities already had wide-ranging legal powers over taxation from the outset, the current system of regional financing gave the income tax an important role in the funding of Common Regime Communities. Since January 2002, the Autonomous Communities have had the following specific legal competences with respect to the income tax:

1. To amend the general autonomous tax schedule, while retaining its progressive structure and the same number of bands as the State system.
2. To amend, up to a limit of 50 percent, the rate of general deduction for investment in housing from the deductible share of the autonomous tax base.
3. To introduce deductions for personal and family circumstances and for non-business investments provided that such reductions do not mean a reduction on the effective tax rate of any category of income.

THE PERSONAL INCOME TAX IN FIGURES: THE MOVE FROM COMMODITY TAXATION TO PERSONAL TAXATION

As noted above, with the 1977 reform, a progressive and generally applicable personal income tax was introduced into the Spanish tax system. Table A5.1 in the appendix shows the growing importance of income and wealth taxation on total revenue. Similarly, in the same appendix, Table A5.2 highlights the high impact of income taxation on tax revenues since 1980. It has systematically maintained a level of around 30 percent of the total tax collected, reaching 40 percent of the total revenue from taxation in 1993. Since then, however, personal income taxation has remained relatively stable with a slight fall in recent years. In particular, following the 1999 income tax reform, the relative weight of this tax went from 33.11 percent in 1998 to 30.76 percent in 1999 and 30.36 percent in 2000, with the latter level of revenue being similar to the level at the beginning of the 1980s.

Since its adoption by Congress in 1978, the personal income tax has achieved a high level of social acceptance. Within a few years it became the most accepted form of taxation amongst Spanish taxpayers. Its success was due, in good part, to the deftness of the Government of the day which was able to explain to citizens the new social values which made the tax one of the financial pillars of democratic Spain. As can be seen in Figure 5.1, in a little more than two decades the number of tax returns tripled, increasing from 5 million declarations in 1979 to more than 15.5 million in 2002. This growth in the number of returns filed shows that the tax had become firmly established in social terms. However, there are several reasons for this growth in the number of tax returns. Many of them are linked to circumstantial issues that are not always related to social acceptance of the tax.

We should note several explanatory factors for this growth in the number of returns. The number of taxpayers grew significantly in 1985 and 1986. In large part, this was due to the introduction of the Value Added Tax (VAT hereafter) and to improvements in tax management introduced that year following our entry into the European Economic Community (EEC). Taxes such as the personal income tax and VAT which operate in the same economic environment gave the tax authorities cross-checks on information which assisted the detection of significant instances of tax fraud. In 1986, very probably as a result of VAT being applied, eight hundred thousand more self-employed people filed income tax returns. The sharp increase in the number of returns presented from 1986 onwards was also due to the entry into force of Act 14/85 on the Tax Regime of Certain Financial

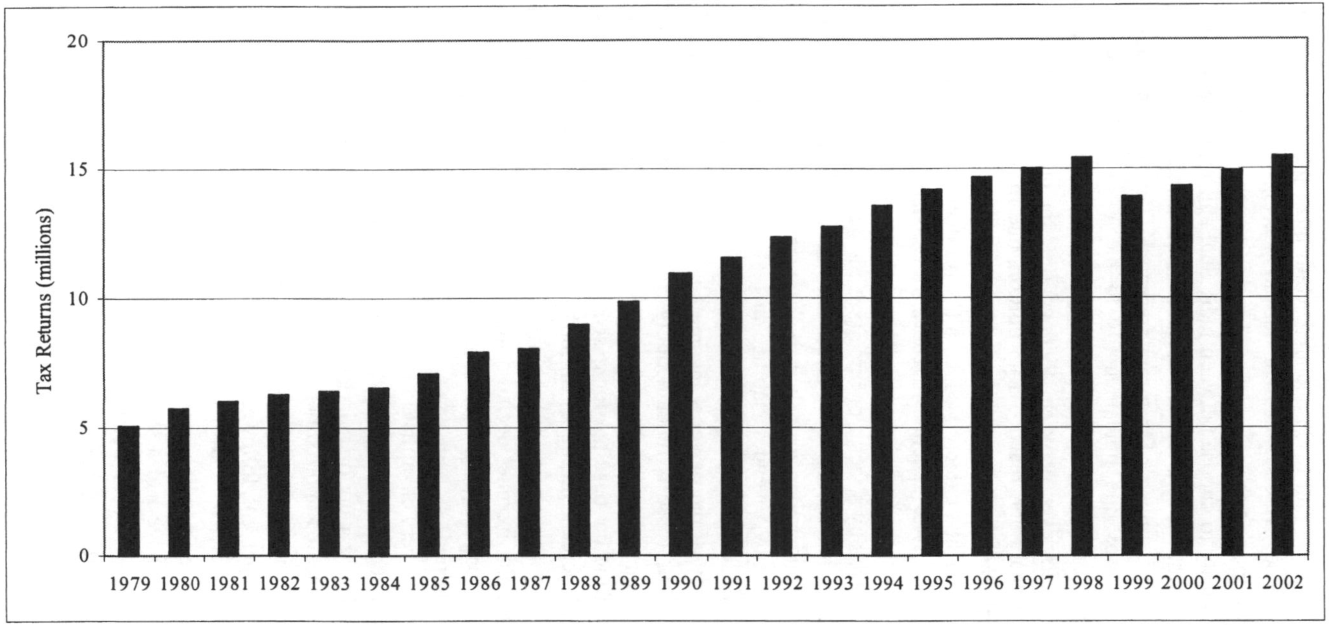

Figure 5.1 Total number of personal income tax returns 1979–2002

Source: a. For 1979: Tax Authority 1980 Annual Report.
b. For 1980 to 2002: BADESPE.

Assets. This Act defined very precisely the way in which the income from different financial assets had to be declared. Until then, the legal vacuum that existed facilitated exercises in financial engineering the sole aim of which was to avoid paying the income tax. In addition, since 1989 married couples had the ability to choose between individual and joint declaration. Thereafter, many joint tax returns were divided into two individual returns, thus increasing the number of returns presented. The fall in returns presented in 1999 was due fundamentally to the 1998 reform, which removed the obligation to file tax returns for individuals with income lower than 21,035 euros. However, between 1999 and 2002 the number of returns began to increase again and reached 15.5 million, due in large part to the large increase in the number of immigrants to Spain during this period.

Another indicator of the extent to which a tax is effectively implemented in a society is its ability to generate revenues. In constant 1980 euros, the revenue generating capacity of the personal income tax between the 1980s and 2002 has increased by a factor of three (see Figure 5.2). Three distinct stages can be identified during this period. The first stage from 1980 to 1991 saw constant and strong growth in real revenues. The second stage from 1992 to 1998 saw revenues stabilise in real terms. Finally, a third stage from 1999 to 2002 saw real revenues again grow strongly.

Another peculiarity of the personal income tax, as shown in Figures 5.3 and 5.4, is that its tax base is fundamentally constituted by ordinary and regular income. Nonetheless, we can also see that the weight of irregular incomes as part of the tax base has increased significantly in recent years, amounting to 6.44 percent in 2000.[6] In 2001 and 2002, the proportion of irregular income has systematically been above 4 percent. This increase in the amount of irregular incomes declared was due, in good part, to the fact that, since 1996, all capital gains were taxed independently of the period in which they were accrued.

Figure 5.5 makes it very clear that in terms of regular income declared, as is the case with other countries with a personal income tax, the Spanish income tax is basically a tax on salaries. On average, since 1980 salaried incomes have represented approximately 80 percent of incomes subject to taxation. In order of importance, company and professional income come next representing 10 percent, followed by investment and property income.

Another important area is that of tax incentives. Here, tax expenditures associated with tax credits, allowances and special treatments allowed since the PIT introduction have had a significant effect on its revenues. Figure 5.6 shows the cost effect of deductions on revenues calculated as the percentage of the total taxable income. As can be seen, up to 1989, deductions reduced potential tax revenues by more than a third. In 1983, this cost was 40 percent.

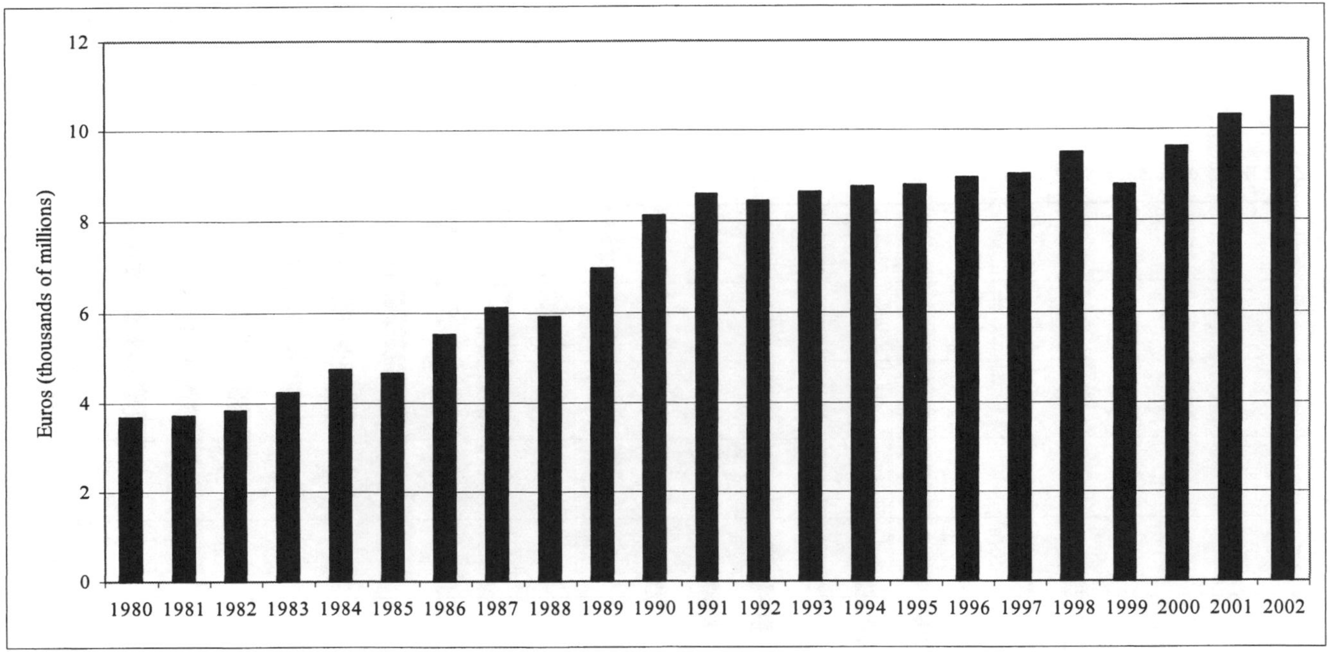

Figure 5.2 Net tax payable 1980–2002 (constant 1980 Euros)

Source: BADESPE.

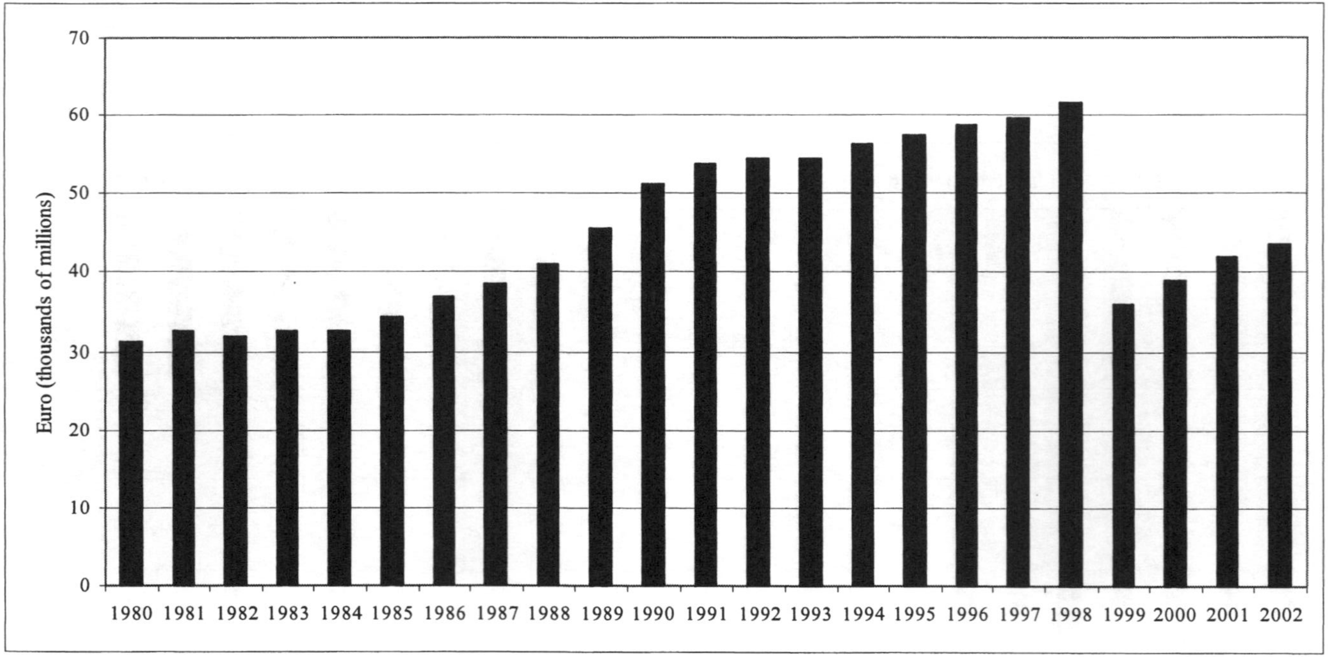

Figure 5.3 Regular taxable base 1980–2002 (constant 1980 Euros)

Source: BADESPE.

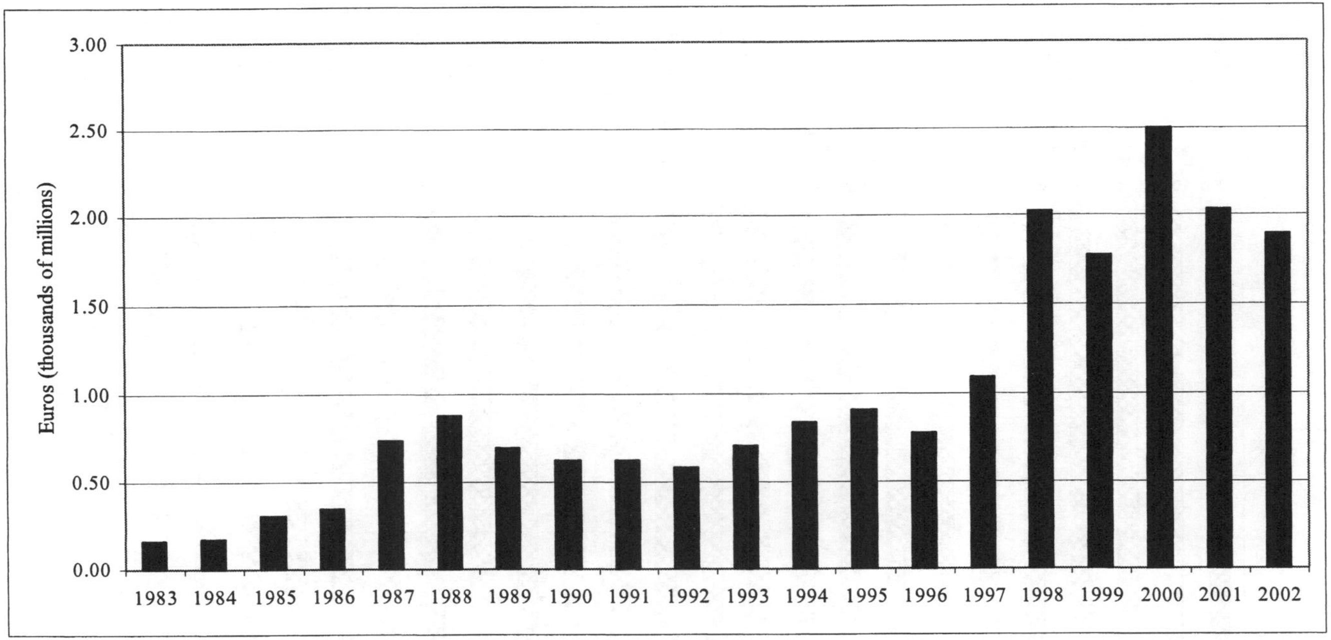

Figure 5.4 Irregular taxable base 1983–2002 (constant 1980 Euros)

Source: BADESPE.

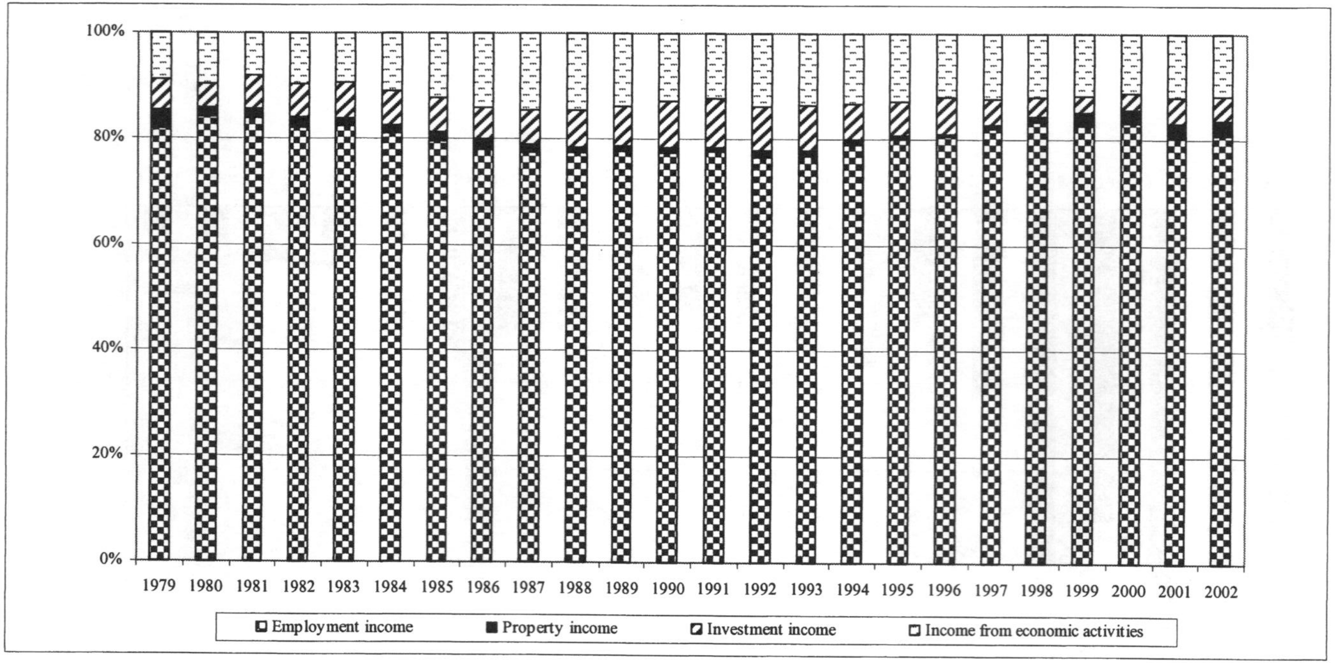

Figure 5.5 Functional distribution of regular income 1979–2002

Source: BADESPE.

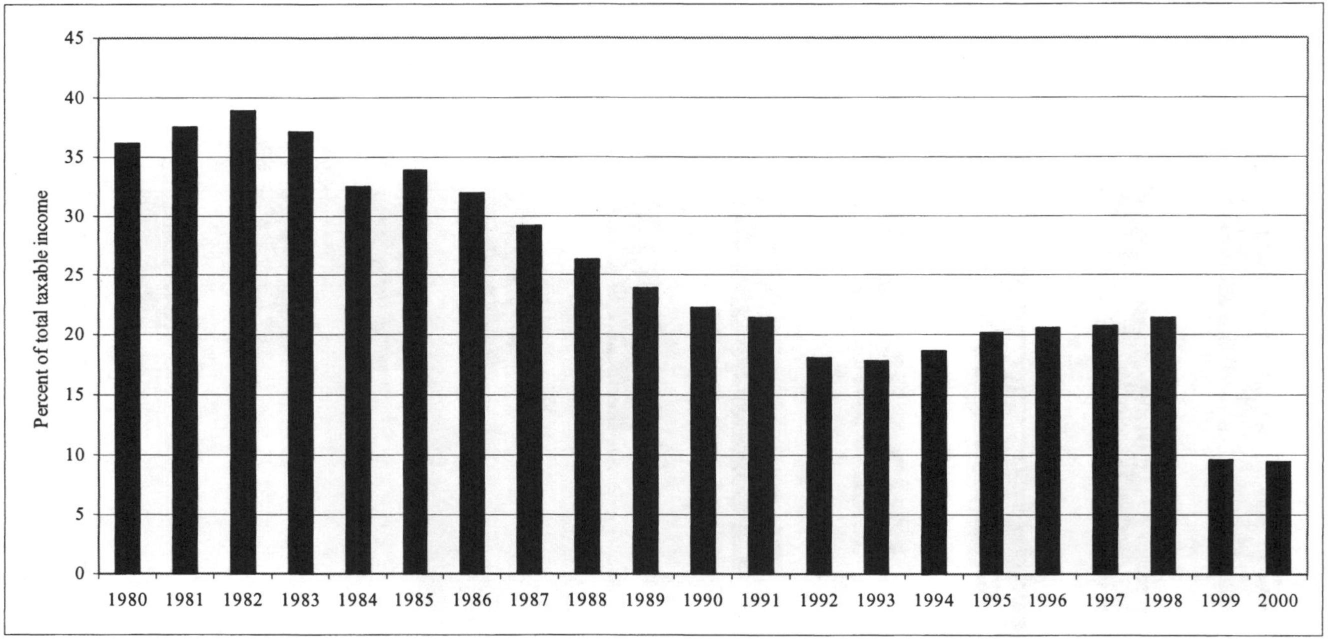

Figure 5.6 Revenue cost of deductions from the tax liability 1983–2002 (constant 1980 Euros)

Source: BADESPE.

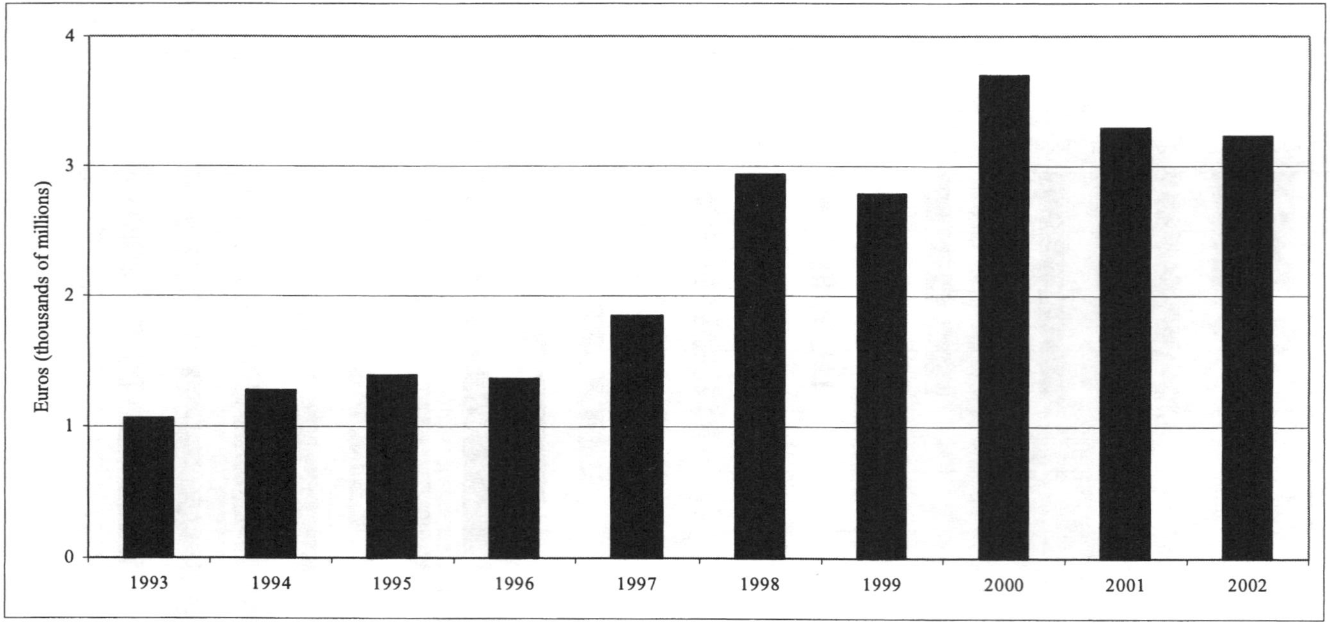

Figure 5.7 Total reductions from the tax base 1992–2002 (constant 1980 Euros)

Source: BADESPE.

Following the 1998 reform, this cost was reduced to approximately 10 percent but this decrease was obviously due to the transfer of deductions from the tax liability (as tax credits) to the tax base (as allowances) which was introduced, as we shall see later, in 1998. As a result, as Figure 5.7 shows, from 1998 the amount of reductions in the tax base increased suddenly and significantly.

A REVIEW OF THE MOST SIGNIFICANT REFORMS TO THE PIT: 1991, 1998 AND 2002

Since 1978, the personal income tax has from time to time been changed and modified. As we stated in the introduction, there were three very significant tax reforms which were implemented in 1991, 1998 and 2002. In addition to these reforms, the Annual Budgets during this almost thirty-year period have introduced small changes in order to update some aspects of the tax, but they did not involve structural changes to the tax. On other occasions, however, the introduction of laws covering financial issues or general economic policy have had consequences for the tax, either by specifying more accurately the tax base, or by describing the terms and conditions for accessing a particular tax benefit in greater detail. The three main fiscal reforms are summarised below.

Principal Features of the 1991 Reform

The first of the three significant tax reforms, carried out during the Socialist government of Felipe González, was largely brought about by a judgement of the Constitutional Court in 1989 which declared that the assessment of the pooled incomes of married couples, established by the 1978 Act on the personal income tax, was illegal on the grounds of discrimination. From its introduction, the personal income tax had required married couples to file jointly. This legal ruling created a serious problem in terms of cumulative earnings, which was particularly prejudicial to couples with two wage-earners and extremely damaging to the horizontal equity of the tax. This aspect of the tax had been widely criticised since it was introduced in 1978. Despite this, no amendments were introduced between 1979 and 1985 to reduce or correct the cumulative assessment of income established by the legislation. In the 1986 and 1987 financial years, the Finance Act introduced a small correction through a deduction based on a polynomic formula applicable to married couples (Act 48/1985 of 7 December), but which only slightly reduced the "marriage penalty".[7]

Nevertheless, it was only in February 1989 that a judgement of the Constitutional Court required that this discrimination be halted forthwith.

Not only did this judgement require the future reform of the personal income tax to stop the penalty on married couples, but it also required it to stop with immediate effect and as a matter of urgency that same year, only three months before the period for filing tax returns for 1988. The Government's chosen solution to rectify this situation was a double tax schedule: one specifically for individuals and one for joint filings. It also granted a deduction for earnings obtained by each member of the family unit.

Besides introducing changes aimed at eliminating discriminatory treatment of married couples, the 1991 reform improved the definition of the tax base. In this context, the most significant improvement was the more accurate and detailed definition of payments in kind and their quantification. This eliminated the use of the latter as a means to avoid paying tax which had been habitual practice at the end of the 1980s. Moreover, important aspects of the tax, which had until then been unclear, were better defined, such as the concepts of habitual residence and the non-residents taxation. Special tax treatments were also established for irregular income and income from long-term savings.

Principal Features of the 1998 Reform

Following the political change in 1996, the *Partido Popular* government took the view that the income tax structure, which had been in force since 1992, was fatigued by the loss of flexibility in tax revenues and its negative impact on employment. Therefore, after its first two years in power, it undertook a reform of the tax with Act 40/1998. The most significant structural change was to define the economic capacities of individuals in accordance with the concept of the "vital minimum". This was based on the idea that tax obligations should only arise for taxpayers once their basic needs had been met. This manner of considering tax obligations meant that the family and personal circumstances of the taxpayer were to be addressed in the tax base instead of in the tax liability.

The structure of the tax schedule was also simplified considerably. The maximum marginal tax rate was reduced from 56 percent to 48 percent, the minimum marginal tax rate was reduced from 20 percent to 18 percent and six tax bands were established. To improve the treatment of the lowest salaried incomes, the tax introduced an earned income allowance which decreased in accordance with the level of the taxpayer's income. In addition, the new legislation removed the obligation to file a tax return from all those tax paying units whose income was lower than 21,035 euros. Previously this limit had been at 7,212 euros. As a result of this significant change in the tax threshold, the 1998 reform exempted more than five and a half million taxpayers from having to file a tax return.

Moreover, in the view of the new Government, the tax had failed to achieve neutrality in its treatment of savings, as evidenced fundamentally by the fact that the opportunity existed to keep capital gains exempt from tax. This capital gains exemption implied moreover a significant loss of the tax's redistributive ability by favouring higher income earners. Therefore, the treatment of capital gains which had been in force since 1991 was reformed in 1996 with further amendments in the income tax reform of 1998. A detailed description of the treatment of capital gains is presented below.

Principal Features of the 2002 Reform

Following the huge change in taxation which the 1998 reform undoubtedly represented, the *Partido Popular* government decided four years later to look at this area in greater depth, leading to a new reform promulgated by Act 46/2002. The change introduced in 2002, which was applied to income obtained in 2003, had neither the depth nor the significance of the 1998 reform, although it did expand on the changes the latter had introduced. Amongst the other changes in this reform, we should highlight the significant reduction in the tax burden for contributing units with the greatest family responsibilities. In particular, the most important modifications introduced by Act 46/2002 can be summarised as follows:

1. It increased personal and family allowances. It also significantly improved the tax treatment of the disabled.
2. It introduced a new deduction for working mothers with children younger than three years.
3. It increased the earned income allowance. In addition, to provide an incentive for extending the working life, this reduction was doubled for workers older than 65 years.
4. It introduced, for the first time, a 50 percent allowance for net income from property for landlords. The objective of this was to encourage rented housing.
5. It reduced the number of tax brackets from six to five and again reduced the highest and lowest marginal tax rates from 48 percent to 45 percent and from 18 percent to 15 percent, respectively.

Following these large-scale tax reforms, the components and structure of the income tax had undergone significant changes. By way of illustration, Table 5.1 shows the process of gradual reduction which the tax has

Table 5.1 Principal features of the personal income tax schedule between 1980 and 2003

Years	Schedule	Marginal rate		Number of bands	Last band of the schedule current euros	Last band of the schedule constant 1980 euros
		Minimum	Maximum			
1980	U	15.00	65.51	28	58,899	58,899
1981	U	14.80	65.09	30	63,707	56,709
1982	U	15.56	68.47	30	63,707	49,927
1983	U	15.72	65.00	34	72,121	50,516
1984	U	16.14	66.00	34	73,323	46,325
1985	U	8.00	66.00	34	73,323	42,657
1986	U	8.00	66.00	34	73,323	38,474
1987	U	8.00	66.00	34	76,989	38,130
1988	U	25.00	56.00	17	48,080	22,478
1989	U	25.00	56.00	16	49,523	21,659
1990	U	25.00	56.00	16	51,999	21,190
1991	U	25.00	56.00	16	54,595	20,804
1992	I	20.00	56.00	17	57,393	20,495
	C	20.00	56.00	16	66,111	23,609
1993	I	20.00	56.00	17	57,393	19,606
	C	20.00	56.00	16	66,111	22,584
1994	I	20.00	56.00	17	57,396	18,875
	C	20.00	56.00	16	66,111	21,741
1995	I	20.00	56.00	18	59,410	18,621
	C	20.00	56.00	17	68,437	21,451
1996	I	20.00	56.00	18	61,435	18,598
	C	20.00	56.00	17	70,859	21,451
1997	I	20.00	56.00	10	63,034	18,650
	C	20.00	56.00	10	72,722	21,516

Table 5.1 Principal features of the personal income tax schedule between 1980 and 2003 (continued)

Years	Schedule	Marginal rate		Number of bands	Last band of the schedule current euros	Last band of the schedule constant 1980 euros
		Minimum	Maximum			
1998	I	20.00	56.00	8	63,106	18,233
	C	20.00	56.00	8	72,938	21,074
1999	U	18.00	48.00	6	66,111	18,570
2000	U	18.00	48.00	6	67,433	18,315
2001	U	18.00	48.00	6	67,433	17,577
2002	U	18.00	48.00	6	67,433	16,836
2003	U	15.00	45.00	5	45,000	10,961

Notes: U refers to the existence of a uniform schedule applicable to all taxpayers, I refers to the schedule for individuals and, finally, C is the joint schedule.

undergone from its creation to the present day. As can be seen, three phases can clearly be distinguished (each is highlighted with a different background in the table). The first of these, running from the introduction of the personal income tax up to 1987, is characterised by a single tax schedule with the number of tax bands varying between twenty-eight and thirty-four, by having maximum marginal tax rates higher than 60 percent and, finally, by minimum marginal tax rates of between 8 percent and 16 percent. The second phase ran from 1988 to 1998. This period coincided with the modifications introduced by the judgement of the Constitutional Court in 1989 (applicable from the 1988 financial year) up to the 1998 income tax reform. During this phase, the double tax schedule was introduced for individual and joint tax returns, the number of tax bands was drastically reduced from thirty-four in 1987 to seventeen in 1988, the maximum marginal tax rate was reduced by ten points to 56 percent and, finally, following the 1991 reform, the minimum marginal tax rate was set at 20 percent. In the third phase, from 1999 to the present day, the process of tax schedule reduction has continued with maximum and minimum marginal tax rates reaching 45 percent and 15 percent following the 2002 reform and the creation of only five tax brackets. Table 5.2, on the other hand, summarises other aspects of the tax such as the taxation of married couples and the main allowances and tax credits over time. As can be seen, before the 1998 reform, the majority of the tax incentives were tax credits instead of deduction allowances. On the other hand, since 1999, tax credits have been restricted in practical terms to the purchase of a habitual residence, for double taxation, and the new deduction for working mothers for the care of children younger than three years old, which was introduced as part of the 2002 reform.

THE ECONOMIC EFFECTS OF THE REFORMS

This section reviews the main economic effects of the reforms described above. Although it is to be expected that the personal income tax has many effects, we will concentrate on the most significant. Firstly, we will evaluate the impact of the tax on employment. Secondly, we will study the tax treatment of habitual residences, a controversial subject because of the high price increases of residential property recently witnessed. Thirdly, we will analyse how the tax treatment of different forms of savings has evolved over time. Finally, we will assess the overall distributive capacity of the tax and its impact on inequality in the distribution of income and on the welfare of taxpayers.

The Tax Treatment of the Labour Factor

Salaried income is easily the source of declared income with the greatest weight in the personal income tax base. This means that any modification to the tax has a particularly significant effect on the operation of the labour market and also on the distribution of employees' income. This proposition is of particular importance in the case of Spain, since it is the European Union country which has maintained the highest rate of unemployment over many years.[8] It is, therefore, not surprising that the objective of encouraging employment has been, without exception, one of the goals set for the three bouts of reform reviewed above. Although there are many factors which determine the level of unemployment, empirical evidence attributes an important role to the tax treatment of labour income (see, for example, European Commission, 2000).

Table 5.2 Principal changes to the structure of the personal income tax following the reforms of 1991, 1998, and 2002

Year	1978	1991	1998	2002
Taxation of married couples	Joint	Individual or joint	Individual or joint	Individua l or joint
Taxation scale	Single schedule	Double schedule	Single schedule	Single schedule
Threshold for declaration of income from employment	1,803 euros	6,010 euros	21,035 euros	22,000 euros
Principal allowances against the base	- Purchase of habitual residence (loan interest) - Contributions to pension plans and supplementary pensions - Reduction for income from employment (5 percent of gross revenue)		- Contributions to pension plans and supplementary pensions Reduction for income from employment (decreasing with income) - Personal minimum - Family minimum (ascendants and offspring) - Minimum for the disabled - Ascendants older than 65. - Offspring - Profits derived from housing rentals(1) - Workers older than 65	
Principal allowances and tax credits	- For income from employment (decreasing with income) - Workers >65 years - The disabled - Ascendants - Offspring - Purchase of habitual residence (loan interest) - Life, death or invalidity insurance - Illness expenses -Housing rental - Donations - Investment in assets with a cultural interest - Double taxation of dividends - Investment incentives for businessmen		- Purchase of habitual residence (principal and loan interest) - Donations - Investment in assets with a cultural interest - Double taxation of dividends - Investment incentives for businessmen - Deduction for mothers with children under 3 years(1)	

Note: (1) From 2003.

A compact measurement of the level of taxation borne by the labour force is the concept of the effective marginal tax rate (EMTR). This tool is useful for evaluating the tax treatment that the labour factor bears at the margin, as well as for quantifying the weight of each of the elements which affect this tax treatment. The generic definition of this measurement is (McKee *et al.*, 1986):

$$EMTR = \left[t_{WE}\left(1 - t_{IS} D_{IS}\right) + \frac{t_C}{1 + t_C} + \frac{T_L}{1 + t_C} \right] \qquad [1]$$

where t_{WE} is the social security contribution rate of the employer, t_{IS} is the rate of corporation tax, D_{IS} is the percentage deduction for employer contributions from the corporation tax, t_C is the average rate of taxation on consumption borne by wage-earners and T_L are the taxes borne by wage-earners (social security contributions of the employee and the personal income tax). The EMTR set out in expression [1] is therefore constructed using the sum of three components: the net cost of employee contributions, taxation on consumption borne by wage-earners and the taxation of wage-earners' income.

Taking a family with two children and a salary equal to that of an average industrial worker, Table 5.3 offers a comparison of computed EMTRs for the period 1983–2001. As can be seen, Spain has a level of effective marginal taxation similar to that of the United Kingdom or Portugal and lower than countries such as Italy, France or Sweden. Moreover, the EMTR trend is decreasing, from values higher than 0.6 in the middle of the 1980s to 0.55 in 2001. In other words, on average, the effective marginal burden of the income tax on the labour factor has been reduced.

The above results are completed with the information set out in Table 5.4 which shows the weighting of the three components of EMTR. As can be seen, in the European countries analysed, approximately 40 percent of the EMTR is comprised of taxes on the income of wage earners while the remaining 60 percent is equally distributed between the other two components of EMTR, employer contributions and consumption taxes. On the other hand, in the United States and Japan the relative weighting of taxes on salary income is 70 percent and 30 percent respectively. The Spanish case is very close to that of other European countries. Although the weight of employer contributions is higher, a lower weighting for consumption taxes makes up for this. It is notable that having experienced higher rates of unemployment than all other countries in Table 5.4, Spain also had the highest weight for employer contributions.

Table 5.3 Effective marginal tax rate (EMTR) on labour use 1980–2001

Year	France	Germany	Italy	Japan	Portugal	Spain	Sweden	UK	USA
1983	0.63	0.54	0.71	0.33	0.40	0.52	0.74	0.52	0.43
1984	0.60	0.54	0.66	0.34	0.42	0.54	0.82	0.53	0.36
1985	0.60	0.53	0.65	0.33	0.40	0.64	0.76	0.53	0.36
1986	0.62	0.54	0.65	0.37	0.44	0.66	0.76	0.53	0.35
1987	0.61	0.54	0.65	0.35	0.44	0.56	0.76	0.51	0.40
1988	0.63	0.54	0.66	0.36	0.45	0.57	0.89	0.51	0.42
1989	0.65	0.55	0.65	0.37	0.54	0.59	0.88	0.48	0.41
1990	0.62	0.56	0.69	0.40	0.53	0.59	0.70	0.48	0.42
1991	0.61	0.57	0.70	0.40	0.52	0.59	0.73	0.48	0.42
1992	0.63	0.56	0.71	0.37	0.54	0.58	0.69	0.49	0.42
1993	0.65	0.56	0.71	0.37	0.53	0.58	0.67	0.48	0.41
1994	0.66	0.60	0.72	0.39	0.54	0.59	0.68	0.49	0.42
1995	0.65	0.59	0.76	0.39	0.54	0.58	0.69	0.51	0.42
1996	0.66	0.64	0.76	0.41	0.53	0.54	0.71	0.48	0.42
1997	0.66	0.65	0.76	0.40	0.54	0.58	0.71	0.48	0.41
1998	0.65	0.65	0.80	0.41	0.54	0.55	0.71	0.48	0.40
1999	0.62	0.66	0.78	0.55	0.54	0.56	0.71	0.49	0.36
2000	0.61	0.65	0.70	0.55	0.55	0.56	0.71	0.48	0.36
2001	0.60	0.70	0.68	0.55	0.55	0.55	0.71	0.48	0.37
Average 1983–85	0.61	0.54	0.67	0.34	0.41	0.57	0.78	0.52	0.38
Average 1986–90	0.63	0.54	0.66	0.37	0.48	0.59	0.80	0.50	0.40
Average 1991–95	0.64	0.57	0.72	0.38	0.53	0.58	0.69	0.49	0.42
Average 1996–2001	0.63	0.66	0.75	0.48	0.54	0.56	0.71	0.48	0.39

Source: Romero and Sanz (2005).

Table 5.4 Breakdown of EMTR (in percentage terms)

Year	Employer contributions			Taxation of the consumption of wage earners			Taxation of the income of wage earners		
	Spain	European countries[1]	Japan-USA	Spain	European countries[1]	Japan-USA	Spain	European countries[1]	Japan-USA
1983	40.9	27.6	13.0	15.8	27.8	18.1	43.3	44.6	68.9
1988	34.9	26.6	13.5	25.4	30.1	17.1	39.7	43.3	69.4
1993	33.9	29.7	16.0	24.6	29.9	16.9	41.4	40.4	67.1
1998	34.1	28.9	15.3	24.4	28.4	16.7	41.5	42.7	68.0
2001	36.8	30.9	16.4	22.7	27.5	17.8	40.5	41.6	65.8
Average									
1983–2001	34.9	29.0	15.3	24.3	29.0	17.1	40.8	42.0	67.6

Notes: (1) Average of the European countries listed in Table 5.3 (excluding Spain).

Source: Romero and Sanz (2005).

One aspect which deserves special attention is the tax treatment of the second *wage-earner* for married couples. As we have already seen, until the 1989 judgement of the Constitutional Court, married couples only had the choice of filing joint returns. This situation created a clear problem of accumulated income which acted as a disincentive for the second wage-earner, normally the wife, to actively seek employment. First, the marginal rate of the personal income tax applied to these workers was higher than the rate which would have been applied if they had filed separate tax returns.[9] Second, the available empirical evidence suggests that the supply of labour by these workers was very sensitive to changes in net salary, with estimated labour supply elasticities at the time close to 2 (García *et al.*, 1989). It is therefore not surprising that the elimination of mandatory joint filing should generate significant efficiency gains which, on average, increased gross family income between 0.11 percent and 0.85 percent by encouraging an increase in the participation of married women in employment (García *et al.*, 1989).

The Tax Treatment of Housing

In the 1960s, home ownership represented 67 percent of the total residential property market in Spain. This rose to 78 percent in the 1980s and to 86 percent at the end of the 1990s. Comparatively speaking, Spain has the highest rate of property ownership in the EU which had an average rate of 61 percent in 1999. In parallel, Spain has the lowest rate of social rental housing at 2 percent compared to the EU average of 18 percent (Trilla, 2001). This clear preference for buying as opposed to renting is, in good part, due to the different tax treatment of these two options in terms of the personal income tax. For the purposes of comparison, Table 5.5 shows the most significant features of the tax treatment of housing, both with respect to ownership and renting, since 1978. Between 1978 and 1998, the treatment of the purchase of a habitual residence for income tax purposes was as follows (see Table 5.5 for details):

1. An imputed income valued at 2% of the value of the house (generally, this was the cadastral value of the house).
2. Mortgage loan interest payments were deductible against income. Moreover, an additional tax credit was also allowed for investment in housing for habitual residence. This tax treatment meant that acquiring a habitual residence was one of the investment decisions with the best tax treatment, although there was a clear problem of regressivity due to the fact that interest payments were deductible from the tax base so that tax savings increased with income.

3. Exemption from taxation was granted for a capital gain obtained from the sale of a habitual residence provided that the total amount obtained in the transaction was to purchase another habitual residence.[10] If the reinvestment was partial, only the proportional share of the capital gain was exempted from taxation.

With the 1998 reform, the income imputation of 2 percent of the value of the house used as habitual residence was eliminated. The two deductions referred to in the previous paragraph were also combined into a single tax credit for interest payments and amortisation of the loan capital. As described in Table 5.5, this new tax framework favours the treatment of habitual residences financed with loans compared to those where loans are not involved. This applies especially to those homes whose date of purchase was less than two years ago as they benefit from greater tax credits. The changes introduced in 1998, which are currently still in force, have meant a significant increase in marginal tax savings for people with low and medium incomes (Onrubia y Sanz, 1999).[11]

Table 5.5 Personal income tax treatment of housing

Item		1978	1991	1998	2002
Investment in habitual residence	Taxation of income	2 % of the value of the home(1)	2 % of the value of the home(1)	-----	-----
	Taxation of expenses	IBI(2)	IBI(2)	-----	-----
	Loan interest	4,808 / 9,616 euros(3)	4,808 / 6,010 euros(4)	-----	-----
	Loan capital	15 %	15 %(5)	-----	-----
	Total expense (own financing)	-----	-----	15% 9,015 euros limit	15% 9,015 euros limit

Table 5.5 Personal income tax treatment of housing (continued)

Item	1978	1991	1998	2002
Total expense (borrowed financing)	-----	-----	First two years(5) (7): 25% / 15% Remainder (5) (8): 20% / 15%	First two years(5) (7): 25% / 15% Remainder (5) (8): 20% / 15%
Housing saving accounts	-----	15%(5)	15%(5)	15% (5)
Exemption for reinvestment	Yes	Yes	Yes	Yes
Rental of habitual residence	-----	15%(6) 450.75 euros limit	-----	-----
Purchase of other homes	-----	10%(5)	-----	-----

Notes: (1) On the cadastral value or by default on the value of the residence for the purposes of other taxes or the price used in the sales transaction (the higher of these values is used). (2) IBI is a local real estate tax on the ownership of residential property and commercial premises. (3) For married couples the limit was 9,616 euros while for other cases the limit was 4,808 euros. (4) For individual and joint tax returns, respectively. (5) Limit: 30% of the net tax base (6) Only for taxpayers with a tax base lower than 12,000 euros and whose expenditure on renting is greater than 10% of net revenue. Between 1995 and 1998 the limit rose to 601.01 euros. (7) Tax credit applicable to the first 4,507.59 euros (on the sum of the total loan capital and interest). (8) Tax credit applicable to the excess up to 9,015.18 euros (on the sum of the total loan capital and interest).

Table 5.6 Tax credit for investment in a habitual residence in the 2002 personal income tax statistics

Income bands (thousands of euros)	Number of beneficiaries	Percentage of beneficiaries	Average allowance (in euros)
1. Zero	1,724	0.03	1,035
2. Up to 1.5	7,149	0.14	996
3. From 1.5 to 6	288,924	5.64	628
4. From 6 to 12	1,493,613	29.17	695
5. From 12 to 21	1,739,010	33.96	808
6. From 21 to 30	837,133	16.35	909
7. From 30 to 60	613,068	11.97	1,045
8. From 60 to 150	127,100	2.48	1,224
9. From 150 to 601	12,353	0.24	1,377
10. Greater than 601	590	0.01	1,460
Totals	5,120,664	100.00	822

Source: Agency for Tax Administration.

With regards to renting, the tax incentives have been, qualitatively and quantitatively, much smaller.[12] Incentives for renting homes only existed between 1992 and 1998. Quantitatively, the tax savings of the renting allowance were much less than those granted for purchasing a home. For example, between 1992 and 1995, the rental tax credit amounted to 15 percent of the rent paid and could not exceed an absolute limit of 7,000 pesetas per tax year (approximately 450 euros).[13]

The spectacular growth of housing prices in Spain, the result of the property boom which began in 1998 (and which is still continuing in 2005), has revived the debate about the need to reform the tax rules on housing for income tax purposes. By way of illustration, between 1997 and 2002 alone, housing prices increased by 78 percent. One of the fundamental factors which appears to be driving the Spanish property market, is the preferential tax treatment given to home purchases. In this respect, recent studies seem to confirm that these tax incentives may be capitalised in the form of higher prices, not by taxpayers but by other economic agents involved in the property market such as builders, developers and financiers. Using this hypothesis, recent modelling of the Spanish situation indicates that the elimination of house purchase tax incentives would reduce prices between 16 percent and 30 percent (see López, 2001). With this outlook, it is not surprising that the reduction and even elimination of tax incentives for

Table 5.7 Estimation of the tax credit for habitual residences

Results	Effects of the Reform
1. Variation in progressivity (Kakwani index)	-3.47%
2. Variation in redistribution (Reynolds-Smolensky index)	3.59%
3. Variation in the average effective rate	6.82%

Source: Authors' analysis.

house purchases is on the politicians' agenda. The effects of the hypothetical elimination of this income tax credit in 2004 are modelled in Table 5.7. As we can see, the removal of incentives would increase tax revenues (by 6.82 percent) as well as the redistributive power of the tax, although its progressivity would be reduced.[14]

Neutrality with Respect to Savings

Differences in the tax treatment of financial assets lead to changes in investment behaviour through arbitrage processes. These processes are characterised by changes in the composition of the portfolio of savers seeking to maximise the net-of-tax returns. In other words, the tax system distorts taxpayers' decisions about saving when it introduces different tax treatments for different assets. For this reason, neutral treatment of savings has become one of the preferred assessment guidelines for all tax reform processes. During the last two decades, six large-scale modifications of the tax treatment of savings have taken place, in 1985, 1991, 1996, 1998, 2000, and 2002. This section analyses the impact of these changes in terms of neutrality. To this end, we describe the tax treatment applied to the most significant financial assets: bank deposits, shares, fixed income instruments, insurance, pension plans and investment funds.

Tax treatment of bank deposits

Bank deposits have traditionally been treated as regular income from investments. The withholding rate has varied considerably, from 25 percent at the outset of the tax reforms in 1978 to the current rate of 15 percent. Apart from changes to the withholding rate, the tax treatment of deposits has seen significant changes since 1978. The 1991 reform introduced a minimum exempt level for investment income. This exemption remained in force from 1992 to 1998 and its amount was successively increased from

150.25 euros in its first year to 174.29 euros in its last year. The 1998 reform allowed deposits to generate irregular income. This income enjoyed a tax reduction provided that it was accrued in more than 2 years. The reduction coefficient applied following the 1998 reform was 30 percent, rising to 40 percent following the income tax reform in 2002.

Tax treatment of shares

Shareholders may be remunerated by dividends and/or capital gains. Dividends are considered to be investment income in the financial year they are received while the sale of shares is taxed as a capital gain at the time of sale. The tax treatment of dividends has had the following specific features:

1. Until the 1991 reform of the personal income tax, different allowances were given for the purchase of stocks and shares. Thus, up to 1987 there was a tax credit which varied between 10 and 17 percent for the purchase of stocks and shares. Similarly, between 1983 and 1987, a tax credit was granted for the purchase of shares by workers in their own company, with the allowances also varying between 10 and 17 percent. Finally, up to the 1991 reform, interest from loans used in the purchase of any kind of fixed or variable income stocks and shares was considered deductible.
2. To avoid the double taxation of dividends, between 1978 and 1994 the tax had a correction system based on tax credits. The percentage deductions were 15 percent up to 1983 and, subsequently, 10 percent up to 1994. Since 1995, the correction system changed to an imputation system with imputation credit equal to 40%.

With regards to capital gains, the personal income tax has traditionally distinguished between short and long-term gains. In general, short term gains mean those generated in a period less than or equal to one year, with the exception of gains generated between 1996 and 2000 when this definition was applied to a two-year period. This distinction is important because the progressive tax schedule is applied to short-term capital gains whereas capital gains classified as long-term are taxed at a reduced rate. This more generous treatment has not been the same over time: up to 1996, a reduced average rate was applied and was obtained by using a capital gains annualisation mechanism, while from 1996 a reduced fixed tax rate was applied. This reduced tax rate has been reduced from 20 percent in the 1996–1999 period to 18 percent in 2000–2002 and to the 15 percent rate in force from 2003. Exceptionally, for tax years 1992–1998, annual small capital gains with a transfer value less than or equal to 3,000 euros were exempt from taxation. In addition to this, a general allowance for saving income valued at 1,202 euros was applicable for financial years 1996, 1997 and 1998.

One of the most significant modifications, and most controversial, to the treatment of capital gains, was the introduction of reduction coefficients in the 1991 reform. As a result, between 1991 and 1996, reduction coefficients were applied to capital gains. Specifically, these percentage reductions, applicable from the second year onward, varied in accordance with the nature of the asset and the number of years of ownership. For quoted shares the reduction coefficient was 5.26 percent. For property, the reduction coefficient was 11.11 percent while for other assets the rate of reduction was 7.14 percent. From 1996, the application of these reduction coefficients was abolished although a transitional regime was put in place for assets acquired before 9 June 1996. Even today, in 2005, this transitional regime leaves substantial capital gains completely exempt from the income tax. Another peculiarity of capital gains is that, traditionally, they were never subject to retentions. This general rule was broken by the 1998 reform which made it mandatory to impose a withholding on capital gains arising from holdings in collective investment institutions (FIM, FIAMM). Other capital gains remain exempt from withholdings.

Tax treatment of fixed income instruments

The returns generated by any fixed rate instruments have been taxed since 1978 as investment income and therefore charged at the marginal tax rate. However, the tax treatment of the amortisation of these instruments—and by extension, their redemption or conversion—has depended on the form in which they are issued. Specifically, the amortisation of instruments issued at a discount (with and without a coupon) was taxed between 1975 and 1984 as a capital gain. To a large extent, this was due to the fact that the legislation governing the personal income tax was a legal vacuum as it did not explicitly include this type of income (called implicit income) in the definition of investment income. Taxpayers therefore declared them as capital gains since these had a more generous tax treatment. Additionally, the coupons were subject to the appropriate withholding tax while no withholding was applied to the amortisation of the instruments. In fact, the absence of a withholding tax made these instruments, especially those issued at a discount and without a coupon, into opaque assets for tax purposes since the tax authority was deprived of the means of identifying their owners.

This situation was remedied by Act 14/85 on the Tax Regime of Certain Financial Assets, which clearly defined the tax treatment of implicit income and imposed a withholding obligation on financial assets issues at a discount, with the exception of discharged Treasury bills.

The 1991 income tax reform basically followed the provisions of the above-mentioned Act 14/85 although it did introduce some important changes. The most significant was the loss of opacity of the Treasury bills and the AFROS. The latter were financial assets subject to a high withholding (55%), which was much higher than the general rate, in exchange for which the issuer was not obliged to identify the owner of the asset. The holders of bills and AFROS were offered the opportunity to choose between keeping them until they were amortised in accordance with the initial terms of issue or to exchange them for Special Public Debt instruments whose amortisation date was set in 1997. In practice, this procedure was a controversial tax amnesty offering advantages both to the owners of the instruments and the government itself. Holders who accepted the exchange for Special Public debt continued to enjoy the opacity of the instruments while the income obtained was not subject to income and wealth taxes. This also gave government a transitional means of financing the public deficit at very low cost as the nominal interest rate offered for the instruments was 2 percent while the nominal market interest rate was over 14 percent.

Accompanying this important change, the 1991 reform also introduced a general exemption for investment income and a new category of income described as mixed. Therefore, from January 1992, investment income arising from capital transfers to third parties has been classified in three categories: implicit, explicit and mixed income. Table 5.9 presents the definition of each of these together with some additional examples.

The 1998 and 2002 reforms retained the treatment of fixed income instruments. However, as previously stated, the 1998 reform introduced a reduction coefficient of 30 percent on income from capital (consequently affecting coupons from fixed income instruments) generated in a period of more than two years. This increased to 40 percent following the 2002 reform.

Tax treatment of insurance

Significant changes have been made to the tax treatment of life and disability insurance since 1978. Until the 1998 reform, incomes generated by these financial assets were considered in general terms to be capital gains. The value of the capital gain was assessed as the difference between the benefit received by the insured party and the value of premiums paid. The amounts arising from capitalisation operations, which were treated as investment income, were the exception to this rule. The 1991 reform

Table 5.8 The treatment of capital gain arising from the sale of financial assets

	1978	**1991**	**1996**	**1998**	**2000**	**2002**
Exempt	----	Annual amount lower than 3,000 euros(4)	Annual amount lower than 3,000 euros(4)	No	No	No
Updating of the purchase value	Yes	No	Yes	No	No	No
Reduction coefficients for capital gains(1) (2)	Equal for all property (since 1983)	7.14% general 11.11% shares 5.26% property	No	No	No	No
Compensa - tion of capital gains with ordinary income	Total	No	No	Yes. For capital gains less than 2 years (10% limit)	Yes. For capital gains less than 2 years (10% limit)	Yes. For capital gains less than 2 years (10% limit)
Taxation of short term capital gains	According to schedule (≤ 1 year)	According to schedule (≤ 1 year)	Reduced average rate (≤ 2 years)	According to schedule (≤ 2 years)	According to schedule (≤ 1 year)	According to schedule (≤ 1 year)
Taxation of long term capital gains	Reduced average rate (> 1 year)	Reduced average rate (> 1 year)	20% Minimum exemption 1,202 euros (> 2 years)	20% (> 2 years)	18% (> 1 year)	15% (> 1 year)

Table 5.8 The treatment of capital gain arising from the sale of financial assets (continued)

	1978	1991	1996	1998	2000	2002
Capital gains retention(3)	No	No	No	20%	18%	15%

Notes: (1) For each year over two years in the taxpayer's wealth. (2) The transitional regime is retained for the reduction coefficients in the 1991 reform. (3) Retention for sale of shares and holdings in collective investment institutions. (4) This applies to the sales value and not to the capital gain.

Source: Authors' analysis from González-Páramo (1991), González-Páramo and Badenes (1999, 2000a, 2000b, 2003) and Rodrigo (2002).

Table 5.9 Investment income arising from capital transfers

Income	Examples	Tax treatment
Implicit	- Bills - Note without coupon - Any financial asset issued at a discount	- The income is calculated as: Purchase value—Amortisation value
Explicit	- Periodic interest from current accounts, loans, fixed income instruments, etc. - Any non-implicit consideration	- Assessed according to their total value including the retention
Mixed	- Notes with issue or amortisation premium.	Treated as explicit or implicit income as appropriate: - If the explicit income fixed in the issue conditions is greater than or equal to the reference interest rate(1), then all income is considered explicit for tax purposes. - If this is not the case, all income is considered to be implicit for tax purposes.

improved the tax treatment of this income, introducing significant reduction according to the age of the person living off the income. In addition, up to 1998 the premiums paid enjoyed a deduction from the tax liability with a percentage allowance of 15 percent until 1986 and henceforth 10 percent (with a limit of 30 percent of the tax base). Apart from the elimination of this deduction, the 1998 reform introduced big changes in the treatment of insurance bought individually.

1. All income is considered as investment income irrespective of whether it is received as capital or income (whether for life or temporary). The sole exception is collective insurance taken out by companies and which fulfils a similar function to social security. In this case, the benefits received are taxed as income from work and receive very favourable tax treatment when they are received in the form of capital. A summary of the reductions applicable to this kind of income is set out in Table 5.10. As this table shows, collective retirement insurance and benefits for total invalidity are among the lowest taxed benefits.
2. The tax treatment for income tax purposes of individual life and disability insurance depends on the form in which payment is received. As Table 5.11 shows, if it is obtained in a capital form (one single payment), reduction coefficients are applied which reward the age of the insurance. On the other hand, when the award is as income, its treatment depends on whether it is for life or temporary. If the income is life-long, the amount subject to taxation is smaller the older the age of the recipient, while if it is temporary, the amount subject to tax is larger the longer the number of years that the benefit is received. Finally, there are specific rules for deferred income, whether for life or temporary, and for those cases where the insurance is redeemed before the contingency occurs.

To conclude, we should point out that some financial products based on insurance operations have been launched in recent years. One of the most popular with investors is unit linked funds because of their tax treatment. A unit linked fund is a life insurance policy linked to a basket of investment funds where the insurance holder invests in accordance with their income-risk preferences. Although contributions to unit linked funds are not tax deductible, the benefits enjoy the reduction coefficients of collective insurance schemes.

Table 5.10 Reduction coefficients applied to collective insurance taken out by companies since the 1998 reform

Form of benefit	Income	Period of generation	Reduction
Capital	Pensions and passive investments Public benefits for retirement, incapacity, accident, infirmity or being an orphan. Benefits from general mutual societies for civil servants or orphanages Benefits from social provision mutual societies. Retirement benefits from company collective insurance schemes.	> 2 years	40%
Capital	Invalidity benefits from social provision mutual societies and collective insurance which meet pension commitments entered into by companies.	----------	40%
Capital	Collective retirement insurance schemes	> 2 years > 5 years > 8 years	40% 65% 75%
Capital	Total invalidity or high invalidity benefits received under collective insurance agreements which meet pension commitments entered into by companies.		65%
Capital	Total invalidity or high invalidity benefits received under collective insurance agreements which meet pension commitments entered into by companies, when a period of more than 12 years has elapsed since the payment of the first premium and other premiums have been paid regularly and correctly		75%

Source: Álvarez and Romero (2005).

Table 5.11 Treatment of life insurance following the 1998 reform

Capital	**Calculation of net income (NI)**	
	NI (Capital received—premiums paid)* (1-reduction coefficient)	
	Reduction coefficients (1)	
	Retirement or survival benefit	**Invalidity**
	• More than 2 years old 40% • More than 5 years old 75% According to the time when the first premium was paid	• 75% if the invalidity is ≥ 65% • 40% for other cases
Immediate income	**Calculation of net income (NI)**	
	NI = Annuity * percentage for calculating net income	
	Percentage for calculating net income	
	Life-long	Temporary
	• Less than 40 years 45% • Between 40 and 49: 40% • Between 50 and 59: 35% • Between 60 and 69: 25% • More than 69: 20% According to the age of the investor at the time the income begins	• Greater than or equal to 5 years: 15% • Greater than 5 and less than or equal to 10 years: 25% • Greater than 10 and less than or equal to 15: 35% • More than 15: 42% According to the duration of the income
Deferred income, life-long and temporary	**Retirement and invalidity benefits**	
	Included in the tax base from the moment they exceed premiums paid or the actual value of income at the time they start to be paid.	
Termination because of redemption of temporary or life-long income	Amount received from the redemption + Income received up to the point of redemption - Value of premiums paid - Amounts taxed as investment income up to that date	

Notes: (1) A reduction coefficient of 75% may be applied in both cases for insurance taken out before 1994 in specific cases.

Precautionary savings: pension plans and alternative schemes

Pension plans are precautionary schemes complementing the social security system which became operational in Spain in 1987.[15] They are, therefore, savings schemes whose purpose is to accumulate long-term capital which, except in the case of serious illness or unemployment of long duration, may only be accessed at the end of an employee's working life. The amounts contributed annually to this savings scheme reduce the tax base with an annual deductible limit which, between 1988 and 1991, was the lesser of two amounts: a fixed amount of 3,000 euros or 15 percent of total income from employment and/or economic activities. During the initial years, when the annual contribution exceeded the limit deductible from the tax base, an additional tax credit of 15 percent of any surplus not deducted from the tax base was allowed. This deduction was subject to a relatively small limit which in the 1991 financial year was 225.37 euros.

Generally speaking, the 1991 reform retained the tax treatment of pension plans although the tax credit was removed. Since 1992, the general absolute and relative contribution limits have been successively increased although in 2003 the relative limit was abolished and a single absolute limit of 8,000 euros per year was established. In recent years, however, two exceptions to the general rule have been introduced. Firstly, from 2000, additional contributions are permitted for disabled dependents or a spouse if he/she has no or very low income. Secondly, from 2003, additional contributions are allowed for employees older than 52 years of age. Therefore, for example, a 65-year old employee could make deductible contributions of up to 24,450 euros.

Table 5.12 Reduction limit for contributions to pension plans

Year of reform	Annual contribution limits	Additional contributions
1988	€3,000 or 15% employment income (1) (2) (3)	-----
1991	€4,507 or 15% employment income(1) (2)	-----
1995	€6,010 or 15% employment income(1) (2)	-----
1997	€6,611 or 20% employment income(1) (2)	-----
1998	€6,611 or 20% employment income(1) (2)	-----

Table 5.12 Reduction limit for contributions to pension plans (continued)

Year of reform	Annual contribution limits	Additional contributions
2000	€7,212 or 25% employment income(1) (2)	- Taxpayer whose spouse does not receive net income from employment or economic activities, or obtains less than €7,212 per year : contributions to spouse's plans: €1,803 per year. - Participants or mutual society members >52 years old: additional 601 euros for each year of age up to a maximum limit of 15,025 euros for 65 years or older
2003	€8,000	- Taxpayer whose spouse is without income to include in the tax base or income lower than €8,000 per year can deduct from their taxable base contributions to the spouse's pension plan up to a maximum limit of €2,000 per year. -Participants >52 years: additional €1,250 for each year of age up to a maximum limit of €24,250 (65 years or older) -Contributions to pensions plans for individuals with a level of invalidity greater than or equal to 65%: €8,000 per year.

Notes: (1) The percentage limit is calculated against the sum of net incomes from employment and self-employment. (2) Applies to the lower of the two limits (3) When the limit is lower than the contribution, the excess not applied to the tax base will be deductible up to a limit of 15% of the liability.

Source: Álvarez and Romero (2005).

With respect to the tax treatment of benefits derived from pension plans, these have traditionally been considered as employment income taxed at the marginal tax rate. However, following the 1998 reform, if a capital benefit was chosen, this would be taxed as irregular employment income and therefore subject to a 40 percent reduction.

In addition to pension plans, there are other precautionary saving schemes which receive favourable tax treatment: retirement plans and life insurance policies. Retirement plans also provide coverage for contingencies such as death or invalidity. In exchange for regular premiums, the beneficiary receives the insured amount at the termination of the agreement in the event of survival (for example, retirement), or in advance of this date in the case of invalidity or death (in the latter case, the beneficiaries are the heirs). They are completely liquid from the moment the agreement is signed. Secondly, they have a guaranteed minimum income. In contrast, they receive less favourable tax treatment than pension plans as the annual contributions cannot be offset against the personal income tax base. Finally, the benefits received, whether in the form of income or capital, are treated the same as the other life insurance schemes described earlier. In 2003, the so-called insured provision plans were regulated. These cover other contingencies apart from retirement such as total and permanent incapacity and the death of the insured party. The tax treatment of the contributions made to these plans and of the benefits received is similar to those for pension plans.

Tax treatment of investment funds

Dividends received from an investment fund are taxed as investment income, whereas capital gains, or where appropriate, capital losses, which result from the sale of holdings in the fund, are treated as a change in wealth for income tax purposes. The general tax treatment of investment income and capital gains from financial assets has been described in detail in previous sections and so it will not be repeated here. However, some new features have been introduced in recent years which specifically affect investment funds. From January 1, 1999, capital gains arising from the sale of holdings in investment funds are subject to a withholding. The initial rate of retention was 20%, which was reduced to 18% in 2000 and further to 15% in January 2003. On the other hand, in 2002, the tax arising when a taxpayer sells his holding in one investment fund in order to reinvest it in a different fund was abolished.

Neutrality in the tax treatment of savings

The huge number of rules affecting the tax treatment of savings makes it difficult to assess its overall impact. However, the effective marginal tax rate concept is a tool which makes it possible to assess the aggregate effect of the tax system on the neutral tax treatment of different savings instruments. The generic definition of this measurement for the specific case of financial assets is:

$$tm_{ei} = \frac{r_{bi} - r_{ni}}{r_{bi}} \qquad [2]$$

where r_{bi} represents a gross financial income generated by the asset i and r_{ni} is the net income finally received by the saver after paying for taxes. In other words, tm_{ei} quantifies the proportion of financial income generated by an asset i which is paid by way of tax. Following this definition, Tables A5.3, A5.4 and A5.5 in the appendix offer a summary of how effective marginal rates have changed following the above-mentioned reform processes. Using this information, Table 5.13 summarises the impact of reforms in Spain on the tax treatment of different savings instruments. In general terms, the effective taxation of financial assets has been reduced by the various reforms. However, in the process, the dispersion of effective marginal tax rates has increased and, as a result, the neutrality of the tax system has deteriorated. There are only two exceptions where neutrality has improved: the treatment of certain assets whose income is deferred for a long time and gains obtained from certain precautionary savings instruments.

Table 5.13 Tax treatment and neutrality of savings

Effects of the reforms		1991	1998	2002
Tax treatment	Ordinary short-term savings (<2 years)	Increased	-For <1 year reduced -Between 1 and 2 years reduced only for low incomes	Reduced
	Ordinary medium and long-term savings	Increased	Reduced for bank deposits Increased for sales of shares and investment funds	Reduced

Table 5.13 Tax treatment and neutrality of savings (continued)

Effects of the reforms		1991	1998	2002
Tax treatment	Precautionary savings	-Reduced pension plan provisions for high incomes	-Reduced pension plan provisions for high incomes	Reduced
Neutrality	Ordinary short-term savings (<2 years)	Worse	Worse	Worse
	Ordinary medium and long-term savings	Worse	-Better for savings >20 years	-Better for savings >8 years
	Precautionary savings	Worse	Moderate improvement	Moderate improvement

Source: Authors' analysis based on González-Páramo (1991) and González-Páramo and Badenes (1999, 2000a, 2000b, 2003).

Horizontal Equity, Progressivity, Regressivity and Welfare

This section reviews the concepts and measurements usually used to quantify horizontal equity, redistributive capacity, and the effects on welfare of the reforms of the personal income tax. In addition, Table 5.16 summarises the results of the three large-scale reforms carried out in Spain in terms of revenues, progressivity, redistribution and employment.

Horizontal equity

Horizontal equity is a concept of fairness related to the equality of tax treatment of taxpayers who are similar in all relevant economic and personal aspects. It is therefore one of the pillars used in the design of personal income taxes. However, the impact of income tax reforms on horizontal equity has received little attention in the case of Spain. The available evidence seems to indicate that the 1991 reform improved the personal income tax horizontal equity (Perrote, 2003), while the 1998 reform may have worsened it by substituting tax credits with deductions from the tax base (Álvarez and Prieto, 2003).

Progressivity and redistributive capacity

A progressive tax structure is concerned with distributing liabilities in accordance with the level of taxpayers' incomes. Therefore, the more progressive personal income tax is, the greater the proportion of total tax revenues borne by higher income individuals (Jakobsson, 1976; Kakwani, 1977a). Progressivity is customarily measured using the Kakwani index (Π^K) defined as

$$\Pi^K = C_T - G_X \qquad [3]$$

where C_T is the concentration index of tax liabilities and G_X is the Gini index of income before taxes. Similarly, the redistributive capacity of a tax is defined as the proportion of total net income which, through the progressive nature of the tax, is transferred from the high part of the income distribution to the low part of this distribution. The redistributive capacity of taxes is usually measured using the Reynolds-Smolensky (1977) redistribution index (Π^{RS}) defined as:

$$\Pi^{RS} = G_X - G_{X-T} \qquad [4]$$

where G_{X-T} is the Gini index of income after taxes, and as before, G_X is the Gini index of income before taxes. The concepts of progressivity and redistribution are tightly linked as a breakdown of the Reynolds-Smolensky index demonstrates.

$$\Pi^{RS} = \frac{t}{1-t}\Pi^K - D \qquad [5]$$

Equation [5] shows that the redistributive capacity of a particular tax structure is determined by the interaction of three factors: its progressivity, its revenue raising ability, and the possible re-ranking effect (D), which may arise as a result of socioeconomic factors other than income.

Table 5.14 summarises the effects on progressivity and redistribution caused by the tax reforms of 1991, 1998 and 2002. The three reforms have reduced the redistributive capacity of income tax by between 5% and 9%. Progressivity increased by 10% with the 1991 reform, by 15% with the 1998 reform and by another 10% in 2002. However these increases in progressivity were not sufficient to compensate for the high tax revenue costs which have oscillated around 15% in all cases. The revenue impact of these reforms is directly related to the increases in net income from which households have benefited. Specifically, the 1998 reform increased the net income of households by an average of between 2.6% and 3.5% while the 2002 reform led to an increase of around 2%.

The 1998 and 2002 reforms had a particularly beneficial effect on income from salaried employment, people receiving unemployment benefits, and families with children younger than 16 years of age. Single person households and those of couples without dependent children received the least favourable treatment.

Excess burdens and effects on welfare

Taxation reforms change the net wage received by salaried workers. This change in salary may affect both the decision to work and the number of hours worked. One of the measurements customarily used to analyse gains or losses in welfare associated with tax reforms is the concept of Equivalent Variation (EV) proposed by Hicks (1939). This measurement quantifies the monetary value of the changes in utility which a reform causes for the taxpayer. Given the cost function, $e(w,v)$, for a salary ω and a reference level of utility V, we get:

$$EV = e(w^0, v^1) - e(w^1, v^1) + (m^1 - m^0) = EV(w) + EV(m) \quad [6]$$

where the superscript numbers 0 and 1 refer to the pre- and post-reform situation and *m* covers any income that is not from wages. From [6] it is possible to determine the variation in the deadweight loss associated with a reform. This is expressed below with R being revenue from the personal income tax:

$$VEG = -\sum_j EV_j(w) - \sum_j (R_j^1 - R_j^0) \quad [7]$$

Table 5.14 Summary of the effects of the three large-scale income tax reforms on progressivity, redistribution and welfare

	Reforms		
Effects	**1991**	**1998**	**2002**
1. Revenue	Reduced (13.99%)	Reduced (15%–17%)	Reduced (14%)
2. Progressivity (a)	Increased (9.19%)	Increased (15.77%)	Increased (9.77%)
3. Redistribution (b)	Reduced (9.19%%)	Reduced (6.06%)	Reduced (5.23%)
4. Individual welfare per household and year (c)	---	Increased by 922.0 euros	Increased by 571.0 euros
5. Percentage of winners, neutrals and losers in welfare terms	---	78.4% winners 18.0% neutrals 3.5% losers	77.4% winners 22.3% neutrals 0.2% losers
6. Net income	---	Increased (2.6%–3.5%)	Increased (1.8%)
7. Type of income most favoured	---	Unemployment, salaries and pensions	Salaries, unemployment and investment income
8. Households most favoured	---	Households with children less than 16 years old	Households with children less than 16 years old

Table 5.14 Summary of the effects of the three large-scale income tax reforms on progressivity, redistribution and welfare (continued)

	Reforms		
Effects	**1991**	**1998**	**2002**
9. Households least favoured	---	Single person <30 years old and >64 years-Single parent families with children <16 years	Couples < 65 years without children
10. Average reduction in deadweight loss	---	587 euros per year	380 euros per year
11. Impact on supply of work	---	Increased by 88,000 FTE posts (d)	Increased by 24,812 FTE posts (d)
12. Value of λ	---		
with inequality aversion parameter equals 0		1,067	1,027
with inequality aversion parameter equals 0.5		1,118	1,039
with inequality aversion parameter equals 1		1,206	1,062

Notes: (a) Kakwani index (b) Reynolds-Smolensky index (c) Equivalent Variation (d) FTE = full time equivalent.

Source: Castañer *et al.* (1999, 2001), Onrubia (2001) and Sanz, Castañer and Romero (2004).

Quantifying the *social value* of a reform is also very useful. One of the measures customarily used is the proportional increment of original equivalent income (λ), derived from the Atkinson's inequality index A, and defined as:

$$\lambda = \frac{\overline{Y}_e^1 \left(1 - A^1\right)}{\overline{Y}_e^0 \left(1 - A^0\right)} \qquad [8]$$

where $\overline{Y}_e$ expresses the average equivalent income and the subscripts 0 and 1 represent the values for pre-reform and post-reform tax scenarios. Values of λ above 1 indicate welfare enhancing tax reforms. The results in Table 5.16 indicate that the 1998 and 2002 reforms increased the welfare of households. The first of these reforms generated an average annual increase of 922 euros per household while the increase in welfare generated by the 2002 reform was on average 571 euros. These gains have affected the majority of the population as may be observed from the fact that more than 75% of households gained in terms of welfare compared to a much lower number who lost out in that reform (0.2%). In terms of whether the reform acted as an incentive or disincentive on the supply of work, the results indicate that the 1998 reform increased the supply of work by 88,000 employment posts to which should be added 24,812 more induced by the 2002 reform. In effect, these increases in the supply of labour generated efficiency gains quantified at 587 euros per year per salaried employee for the 1998 reform and 305 euros for the 2002 reform.

Prospective Reforms of the Spanish Personal Income Tax, Intrinsic Restrictions and Environmental Influences

The nature of the personal income tax approved in 1978 was influenced no doubt by the values on equity and distributive fairness that existed back in the 1970s. By the middle of the 1980s, however, a majority of developed countries had embarked on root and branch reforms of their personal income tax systems. The most common features of these reforms, led by the United States and Great Britain, were the widening of the tax base and the reduction of the formal progressivity of tax schedules. As a result of these reform processes, income taxes in the 1990s were characterised by more widely defined taxable events, lower marginal tax rates and a lower number of tax bands. These modifications were consolidated in the successive reforms of the Spanish tax, leading to a more neutral and simpler tax than the one initially approved in 1978.

In recent years, environmental objectives and the creation of employment have been added to the objectives of neutrality and efficiency (Gago and Labaudeira, 2002). This new tendency in taxation in the 21st century will also affect the future development of the Spanish personal income tax. Amongst the new philosophies of taxation, those which stand out the most are the proposals for linear and dual taxation. The first of these models has basically been applied in certain Eastern European countries such as Russia, Ukraine, and the Baltic Countries. The dual taxation model, which arose as a result of what has become known in the literature as the green tax reform, has been applied for some time in countries such as Denmark (since 1987), Sweden (since 1991) and Norway (since 1992). The justification for moving taxation away from income and towards activities that degrade the environment, which is implicit in the green tax reform, is that in so doing society obtains a double dividend: firstly, from the reduction of polluting activities and, secondly, from increased allocative efficiency arising from more neutral income taxes.

It is to be hoped that in coming years Spain will move its personal income tax towards an even simpler and more neutral structure than it currently has, particularly with regards to the treatment of savings. It is very likely that this linearisation of the tax, which was already present in the spirit of the 1991, 1998 and 2002 reforms, will be maintained in the immediate future, particularly if we bear in mind that the Socialist party, in government since March 2004, defended linear taxation in an unprecedented manner when it was in the opposition. However, it is highly unlikely that Spain will introduce a pure linear income tax. This is fundamentally not because it does not make sense, but rather because the structure of the current personal income tax, albeit much more immune from the privileged treatments bestowed by earlier versions of the tax, still retains special treatment for certain interest groups, who will do everything possible to avoid losing their privileged positions. Nonetheless, although this is not acknowledged by the tax authorities, Spain has been following a pseudo-dual income tax since the beginning of the 1990s, whereby capital income is taxed separately from other income at a much lower average rate. For this reason, it would be desirable that if this linearisation-dualisation is to be continued, it should be done in a more transparent and explicit manner than is currently the case.

Another aspect where change may be desirable is the way personal income taxation is used by the Autonomous Communities, as an instrument of joint fiscal responsibility with the central government. Since 1997, the Autonomous Communities have enjoyed legal powers which, until now, they have only used very selectively, with an insignificant distributive and revenue raising impact. The quality and soundness of fiscal decentralisation in Spain may be improved significantly if, in the coming years, the Autonomous Communities make greater use of this power than has been the case up to the present time. On the other hand, the economic rationality of tax decentralisation would suggest that Spain should embark upon what has become known as "the second decentralisation" in the immediate future. This process, which is currently being debated, would require powers of expenditure and financing abilities to be transferred from the Autonomous Communities to local tax authorities. Without a doubt, if the second decentralisation process were to be carried out, part of the personal income tax revenue currently in the hands of the Autonomous Communities should go into the municipal coffers and would probably require the management and administration processes of this important tax to be amended.

APPENDIX

Table 5A.1 Relative weight of current revenues in the period 1975–2001 (percentage)

Year	Taxes on production and imports	Taxes on income and wealth	Taxes on capital	Social contributions	Interest, dividends and other income	Various current transfers
1975	27.29	17.85	1.00	41.93	5.14	6.79
1976	26.08	18.40	0.84	43.22	4.72	6.75
1977	25.09	18.34	0.75	44.36	4.80	6.66
1978	22.63	20.22	0.70	46.00	4.17	6.28
1979	21.98	21.18	0.64	45.81	3.73	6.65
1980	22.19	23.28	0.62	43.79	3.35	6.78
1981	23.32	22.91	0.66	42.66	4.18	6.27
1982	24.67	21.60	0.53	42.32	4.68	6.19
1983	25.43	23.39	0.46	40.88	4.11	5.74
1984	27.06	24.84	0.54	39.10	3.00	5.46
1985	27.82	24.62	0.60	37.76	3.36	5.84
1986	30.00	23.42	0.53	36.52	3.14	6.38
1987	28.50	27.99	0.55	34.87	2.18	5.91
1988	28.37	28.61	0.67	34.28	2.13	5.94
1989	26.98	31.46	0.61	33.37	2.29	5.29
1990	26.03	31.48	0.61	34.19	2.54	5.15

Table 5A.1 Relative weight of current revenues in the period 1975–2001 (percentage) (continued)

Year	Taxes on production and imports	Taxes on income and wealth	Taxes on capital	Social contributions	Interest, dividends and other income	Various current transfers
1991	25.38	31.03	0.50	34.10	3.39	5.60
1992	25.23	30.41	0.53	35.66	3.16	5.02
1993	23.35	29.10	0.60	36.36	5.34	5.25
1994	25.46	28.73	0.73	36.59	3.40	5.10
1995	28.08	28.03	0.92	35.87	4.54	2.55
1996	27.83	28.01	0.95	35.95	4.65	2.61
1997	28.45	28.38	0.98	35.55	3.84	2.80
1998	30.08	27.56	1.00	35.27	3.36	2.73
1999	31.07	27.26	1.02	34.88	3.18	2.59
2000	31.02	27.78	1.06	35.29	2.80	2.06
2001	30.13	27.64	1.04	35.86	3.31	2.02

Source: Spanish National Accounts Office (various years).

Table 5A.2 Relative weight of taxes in the period 1980–2000 (percentage)

Year	Corporation tax	Income tax	Wealth tax	Inheritance tax	VAT	Taxes on Property sale
1980	5.96	31.65	0.86	0.91	----	0.00
1981	7.88	31.52	0.52	0.88	----	5.36
1982	8.23	28.20	0.47	0.70	----	4.30
1983	8.22	29.95	0.36	0.64	----	3.82
1984	7.71	30.82	0.20	0.76	----	3.58
1985	8.26	29.17	0.19	0.73	----	3.47
1986	9.20	28.50	0.54	0.73	22.94	3.37
1987	11.03	33.55	0.59	0.73	24.39	3.32
1988	10.49	34.13	0.68	0.90	24.17	3.78
1989	13.50	35.25	0.35	0.76	23.92	3.91
1990	14.26	34.55	0.87	0.76	22.37	3.95

Table 5A.2 Relative weight of taxes in the period 1980–2000 (percentage) (continued)

Year	Corporation tax	Income tax	Wealth tax	Inheritance tax	VAT	Taxes on Property sale
1991	12.37	37.21	0.64	0.66	22.21	3.67
1992	10.53	38.54	0.65	0.74	23.17	3.46
1993	9.79	39.32	0.73	0.94	21.45	3.48
1994	8.24	38.44	0.78	1.06	23.29	3.71
1995	9.32	38.13	0.70	0.95	23.39	3.54
1996	9.88	37.75	0.68	0.99	23.64	3.43
1997	12.94	34.50	0.73	1.02	23.65	3.76
1998	12.11	33.11	0.79	0.94	24.16	3.98
1999	13.35	30.76	0.82	0.93	25.74	4.26
2000	14.15	30.36	0.87	1.02	25.82	4.44

Source: Spanish National Accounts Office (various years).

Table 5A.3 Summary of the effects of the 1991 reform on savings effective marginal rates (1)

Financial asset	Average income (2)		High income (3)	
	1991	1993	1991	1993
Bank deposits	40.9	37.0	74.8	67.0
Treasury letter	35.3	31.7	65.9	58.8
Commercial paper	40.2	36.7	70.8	63.2
Treasury bill	68.7	112.5	68.7	112.5
Tax-exempt bond	9.5	5.6	43.4	35.6
Share: dividend (4)	66.4	64.0	88.3	88.2
Share: capital gain at 5 years	71.0	67.2	90.9	83.5
at 10 years	66.8	50.6	83.0	52.7
at 20 years	60.7	48.1	71.5	48.1
Investment fund at 5 years (5)	28.3	24.1	51.6	43.4
at 10 years	23.7	11.2	43.0	19.9
at 20 years	17.3	1.4	31.2	1.4

Table 5A.3 Summary of the effects of the 1991 reform on savings effective marginal rates (1) (continued)

Financial asset	Average income (2)		High income (3)	
	1991	1993	1991	1993
Pension plans: capital (6)	-1.0	-1.1	4.9	-1.9
income (7)	-5.8	-7.1	-4.3	-12.0
Life insurance: capital (6)	6.7	0.0	16.4	0.0
income (7)	4.0	6.1	11.0	10.9

Notes: (1) Assumes nominal profitability of 11% and a 3% inflation rate. (2) 23,138 euros (3) 57,396 euros. (4) Shares officially quoted on the stock exchange. (5) The income is obtained as a capital gain. (6) The income is obtained entirely at the retirement date. (7) The return is received as an income in the 15 years following retirement.

Source: González-Páramo (1991).

Table 5A.4 Summary of the effects of the 1998 reform on savings effective marginal rates (1)

Financial asset	**Average income (2)**		**High income (3)**	
	1998	**1999**	**1998**	**1999**
Bank deposit at 1 year	43.7	38.5	75.9	64.9
at 3 years	32.2	25.6	56.7	43.1
at 5 years	28.9	24.3	50.9	40.9
Treasury bills	42.8	37.9	75.0	64.3
Treasury bonds and notes (coupon)	43.7	38.5	75.9	64.9
Tax-exempt bond	12.4	7.4	44.5	33.8
Share: dividend (4)	52.9	48.3	82.1	72.4
Share: capital gain at 1 year	76.0	72.7	96.8	89.9
at 5 years	58.4	63.2	58.4	63.2
at 10 years	56.5	60.8	56.5	60.8
at 20 years	54.2	57.1	54.2	57.1
Investment fund at 1 year (5)	43.8	39.6	75.6	65.7
at 5 years	20.4	25.9	20.4	25.9
at 10 years	18.1	23.0	18.1	23.0
at 20 years	15.1	18.4	15.1	18.4

Table 5A.4 Summary of the effects of the 1998 reform on savings effective marginal rates (1) (continued)

Financial asset	**Average income (2)**		**High income (3)**	
	1998	**1999**	**1998**	**1999**
Life insurance and unit-linked funds at 1 year	42.8	38.8	75.0	65.2
at 5 years	19.3	24.5	19.3	41.1
at 10 years	17.0	9.2	17.0	15.5
at 20 years	1.8	7.3	1.8	12.3
Pension plans: one-off capital bonus (6)	-11.4	-9.7	-18.1	-18.4
solely income bonus (6) (7)	-3.4	2.3	-0.2	0.7
Alternative schemes to pension plans				
one-off capital bonus (6)	4.8	6.6	26.9	10.4
solely income bonus (6) (7)	10.8	21.9	40.1	34.8
Life-retirement insurance one-off capital bonus (6)	3.1	6.6	12.8	10.4
solely income bonus (6) (7)	1.5	8.9	21.1	14.1

Notes: (1) Assumes nominal profitability of 5.5% and a 1.5% inflation rate. (2) Shares officially quoted on the stock exchange. (3) 21,035 euros. (4) 72,121 euros. (5) For Property Investment Funds (6) For an individual saving for 40 years and making contributions of 5% of his annual income until retirement. The investor hopes to obtain income for 25 years following retirement. The income obtained when he retires falls by 20% of income during his working life. (7) The return is received as an income for 15 years following retirement.

Source: González-Páramo and Badenes (1999).

Table 5A.5 Summary of the effects of the 2002 reform on savings effective marginal rates (1)

Financial asset	Average income (2)		High income (3)	
	2002	2003	2002	2003
Bank deposit at 1 year	42.0	41.4	70.7	66.2
at 3 years	27.8	23.1	46.7	37.2
at 5 years	26.3	21.9	44.2	35.1
Treasury letter	44.2	40.8	69.9	65.6
Treasury bonds and notes (coupon)	42.0	41.4	70.7	66.2

Table 5A.5 Summary of the effects of the 2002 reform on savings effective marginal rates (1) (continued)

Financial asset	Average income (2)		High income (3)	
	2002	2003	2002	2003
Tax-exempt bond	8.1	1.8	36.8	32.4
Share: dividend (4)	52.8	52.2	79.0	74.7
Share: capital gain at 1 year	79.3	79.0	98.0	95.1
at 5 years	65.1	62.6	65.1	62.6
at 10 years	60.1	58.1	60.1	58.1
Investment fund at 1 year (5)	43.2	36.8	71.6	67.0
at 5 years	25.3	21.7	25.3	21.7
at 10 years	22.3	18.8	22.3	18.8
Life insurance and unit-linked funds at 1 year	42.3	41.4	71.0	66.2
at 5 years	26.4	22.2	19.1	35.5
at 10 years	8.2	8.1	13.8	12.9
Pension plans: one-off capital bonus (6)	-9.7	-9.5	-16.6	-15.3
solely income bonus (6) (7):	2.5	2.1	4.3	4.0
Alternative schemes to pension plans				
one-off capital bonus (6)	8.1	5.7	13.7	9.1
solely income bonus (6) (7)	22.8	22.6	12.2	36.3
Life-retirement insurance one-off capital bonus (6)	6.8	5.6	11.5	9.0
solely income bonus (6) (7)	25.2	24.8	39.8	39.7

Notes: (1) Assumes a real return of 4%. (2) Shares officially quoted on the stock exchange. (3) 23,000 euros. (4) 80,000 euros. (5) For Property Investment Funds. (6) For an individual saving for 40 years and making contributions of 5% of his annual income until retirement. The investor hopes to obtain income for 25 years following retirement. The income obtained when he retires falls by 20% of income during his working life. (7) The return is received as an income for 15 years following retirement.

Source: González-Páramo and Badenes (2003).

NOTES

* Department of Applied Economics, Universidad Rey Juan Carlos

** Department of Applied Economics, Universidad Complutense de Madrid

1. Extraordinary War Levy.
2. General Levy on Income.
3. Reform of indirect taxation was more staggered: excise duties on specific consumption were introduced in 1979 and VAT in 1986.
4. For an in-depth study of the financing and expenditure transfer system in the Autonomous Regional Governments, see the chapter in this book by López Laborda and Monasterio.
5. Special arrangements apply to the cities of Ceuta and Melilla and the Autonomous Regional Government of the Canary Islands, although they can be considered as part of the Common Regime.
6. Irregular income is any type of income generated in a period longer than a year. However, the length of time to be considered irregular income depends on the specific Act in force and it changes from time to time. This type of income is normally taxed following special rules.
7. Nonetheless, some people—both in the academic world and in government—have always argued that married couples' income should be taxed jointly. Their case is based on the scale in consumption arising from a couple living together. However, these advocates ignored that a couple living together outside of marriage was becoming more common in Spain. This meant that the tax would in effect penalise married couples over unmarried ones.
8. By way of illustration, the unemployment rate in Spain just after the 1998 reform was 15.7%. However, in March 2004, this rate was reduced to 11.1%. This rate was still higher than the 8.8% average in the euro zone and much higher than countries such as Luxemburg (4.1%), Ireland and Austria (4.5%), the Netherlands (4.7%) or the United Kingdom (4.7%). However, during recent years this differential has reduced significantly and unemployment rates are far removed from the levels of 1995, for example, when the unemployment rose above 25%.
9. In addition, joint tax returns generated clear problems of horizontal equity. The reason is that two women with the same gross salary would have a different net salary depending on the husband's level of income.
10. Additionally, between 1991 and 1998, capital gains from the sale of a habitual residence by people older than 65 years of age were exempt provided that the consideration received by these people was a life-long income.
11. A transitional system, which is still in existence, was introduced for homes bought before this date. This transitional system is more regressive than the tax treatment of housing before 1998 (Onrubia, Romero and Sanz, 2004).
12. Royal Decree-Act 2/1985, of 30 April, on Economic Policy Measures.
13. This deduction has again been introduced in some Autonomous Communities. For example, in the Community of Madrid for taxpayers younger than 30 years of age.
14. This simulation was performed using the personal income tax micro-simulator developed by Sanz et al. (2004).
15. Act 8/1987, of 8 June, on the Regulation of Pension Plans and Funds.

REFERENCES

Agencia Estatal de la Administración Tributaria (several years), *Memoria de la Administración Tributaria*, Madrid: Ministerio de Economía y Hacienda.

Álvarez, S. and Prieto, J. (2003), 'Tributación de la familia y la equidad horizontal en el Impuesto sobre la Renta de las Personas Físicas. Una aplicación a las reformas de 1999 y 2003', in Onrubia, J. and Sanz, J.F. (dir), *Redistribución y bienestar a través de la imposición sobre la renta persona*, Madrid: Instituto de Estudios Fiscales, pp. 151–176.

Álvarez, S. and Romero, D. (2005), Rasgos Básicos de los principales activos financieros y su tributación en la imposición en la renta de las personas físicas en España, Mimeo.

Aparicio, A. and Álvarez, S. (2003), 'El impuesto sobre la renta de las personas físicas: una síntesis de 25 años de historia', *Revista Asturiana de Jurisprudencia*, 27, 19–42.

Castañer, J.M., Onrubia, J. and Paredes, R. (1999), 'Análisis de los efectos recaudatorios y redistributivos de la reforma del IRPF por Comunidades Autónomas', *Hacienda Pública Española*, 150, 79–108.

Castañer, J.M., Onrubia, J. and Paredes, R. (2001), 'Efectos distributivos y sobre el bienestar social de la reforma del IRPF', *Hacienda Pública Española*, 159, 85–113.

European Comission (2000), *Public Finance in EMU*, European Union.

Gago, A. and Labandeira, X. (2000), 'Towards a Green Tax Reform Model', *Journal of Environmental Policy and Planning*, 2, 25-38.

García, J., González-Páramo, J.M. and Zabalza, A. (1989), 'Una aproximación al coste de eficiencia de la tributación familiar en España', *Moneda y Crédito*, 204, 97–104.

González-Páramo, J.M. (1991). 'Imposición personal e incentivos fiscales al ahorro en España', *Banco de España, Estudios Económicos*, 46.

González-Páramo, J.M. and Badenes, N. (1999), 'La fiscalidad del ahorro financiero y el principio de neutralidad: efectos de la reforma de IRPF de 1999', *Cuadernos de Información Económica*, 151, 39–50.

González-Páramo, J.M. and Badenes, N. (2000a), 'Los impuestos y las decisiones de ahorro e inversión de las familias', Fundación de las Cajas de Ahorro, Estudios de la Fundación, 8.

González-Páramo, J.M. and Badenes, N. (2000b), 'Las medidas fiscales de estímulo al ahorro contenidas en el Real Decreto Ley 3/2000: análisis de sus efectos a través del tipo marginal efectivo', Instituto de Estudios Fiscales, Papel de Trabajo, 6/00.

González-Páramo, J.M. and Badenes, N. (2003), 'La fiscalidad efectiva de los productos de ahorro en Europa y Estados Unidos y el principio de neutralidad. Análisis comparado y evaluación de la reforma del IRPF de 2003', Fundación de las Cajas de Ahorro, Estudios de la Fundación, 13.

González-Páramo, J.M. and Onrubia, J. (1992), 'El gasto pública en vivienda en España', *Hacienda Pública Española*, 120/121, 189–227.

Gota, A. (1971), *Tratado del Impuesto sobre la Renta*, Madrid: Editorial de Derecho Financiero.

Hicks, J.R. (1939), *Value and capital*, Oxford: Clarendon Press.

Instituto de Estudios Fiscales (several years), 'Base de Datos del Sector Público (BADESPE)', http://www.estadief.minhac.es/

Instituto de Estudios Fiscales (1998), *Informe para la reforma del Impuesto sobre la Renta de las Personas Físicas*. Madrid: Instituto de Estudios Fiscales.

Jakobsson, U. (1976), 'On the measurement of the degree of progression', *Journal of Public Economics*, 5, 161–168.

Kakwani, N.C. (1977a), 'Measurement of tax progressivity: an international comparison', *Economic Journal*, 87, 71–80.

Kakwani, N.C. (1977b), 'Application of Lorenz curves in economic analysis', *Econometrica*, 45, 719–727.

King, M.A. and Fullerton, D., eds. (1984), *The Taxation of Income from Capital. A Comparative Study of the United States, the United Kingdom, Sweden, and West Germany*, Chicago and London: The University of Chicago Press.

López, M.A. (2001), *Política impositiva, precios y stock de vivienda*, Madrid: Instituto de Estudios Fiscales.

McKee, M.J., Visser, J., and Saunders, P. (1986), 'Marginal tax rates on the use of labour and capital in OECD countries', *OECD Economic Studies*, 7, 45–101.

Naredo, J.M. (2004), 'Perspectivas de la vivienda', *Información Comercial Española*, 815, 143–154.

Onrubia, J. (2001), 'Equidad en la imposición: redistribución y bienestar social', *Papeles de Economía Española*, 87, 128–143.

Onrubia, J., Romero, D., and Sanz, J.F. (2004), 'La compensación de incentivos a la adquisición de vivienda habitual tras la reforma de IRPF de 1999', *Revista de Economía Aplicada*, 35, 105–124.

Onrubia, J. and Sanz, J.F. (1999), 'Análisis de los incentivos a la adquisición de vivienda habitual en el nuevo IRPF a través del concepto de ahorro fiscal marginal', *Hacienda Pública Española*, 148, 227–241.

Perrote, I. (2003), 'Medición de la inequidad horizontal: una aplicación al IRPF', in Onrubia, J. y Sanz, J.F. (dir), *Redistribución y bienestar a través de la imposición sobre la renta personal,* Madrid, Instituto de Estudios Fiscales, pp. 177–192.

Reynolds, M. and Smolensky, E. (1977), *Public Expenditures, Taxes, and the Distribution of Income: The United States. 1950, 1961, 1970*, New York: Academic Press.

Rodrigo, F. (2002), 'La tributación de las ganancias de capital en el IRPF: de dónde venimos y hacia dónde vamos', Instituto de Estudios Fiscales, Papel de Trabajo 2/02.

Romero, D. and Sanz, J.F. (2005), 'An international comparison of marginal effective tax rates on labour use', *Australian Tax Forum*, 20, 1.

Sanz, J.F., Castañer, J.M., and Romero, D. (2004), 'La reforma de la imposición personal sobre la renta. Una evaluación de la reciente experiencia española 1998–2003', Estudios de la Fundación, 18. Madrid: Fundación de las Cajas de Ahorro.

Sanz, J.F., Castañer, J.M., Romero, D., Prieto, J. and Fernández, F.J. (2004), *Microsimulación y comportamiento laboral en las reformas de la imposición sobre la renta personal. El Simulador del Impuesto sobre la Renta Personal del Instituto de Estudios Fiscales (SIRPIEF)*, Madrid: Instituto de Estudios Fiscales.

Trilla, C. (2001), 'La política de vivienda en una perspectiva europea', Colección Estudios Sociales, 9. Fundación La Caixa.

6. The Evolving Role of the Corporate Income Tax

Raquel Paredes Gómez*

INTRODUCTION

The Spanish Corporate Income Tax[1] was born in 1978 after the fiscal reforms associated with the political transition to Democracy. A tax on company's net income, in addition to the personal income tax, was largely influenced by the experience of other European countries within this area of taxation.

Although in many ways it has performed well, in its 25 years history since the 1978 reform, the CIT has suffered from various technical problems and from a general lack of coordination with Accounting and Mercantile Laws. Furthermore, Economic and Monetary Union membership, along with the growing internationalisation of the Spanish economy, has presented new challenges and responsibilities to tax policy makers. In this context, it is not surprising that during this period corporate taxation in Spain has been subjected to continuous evolution, as reflected in numerous reforms. The main amendments to the CIT were introduced in 1995 with the approval of the new CIT Law. Thereafter, reform has carried on at a slower pace, with partial modifications registered in Budget Laws and in the reforms relating to the Personal Income Tax.

The aim of this chapter is to analyse the structure and performance of the Corporate Income Tax in Spain over the last 25 years. We will study the reasons, principles and objectives of the reforms undertaken and will examine the context of these amendments through the evolution of the basic components of the tax. Besides, we will study the performance of the CIT from a revenue viewpoint and we will describe the principal results of the empirical studies that analyse the neutrality and competitiveness of the Spanish CIT. Finally, we will discuss some aspects of the reform which are still pending.

THE 1978 FISCAL REFORM: ORIGIN OF THE CURRENT CORPORATE INCOME TAX

One of the main characteristics of the 1978 Fiscal Reform was the personalisation of taxation on income with the establishment of two taxes: Personal Income Tax and CIT.

As in other countries, the CIT has always been a controversial tax in Spain, so much so that it has been discussed several times over the past whether it should be within the Tax System or not.[2] However, the 1978 Fiscal Reform introduced the CIT in addition to the Personal Income Tax. The main reasons to explain this decision are:

(a) CIT is a control tool on the individual's income inside a company. It helps improve compliance with other taxes, especially Personal Income Tax.
(b) It taxes the undistributed profit of the companies, avoiding the postponement of taxation until the moment of realisation of capital gains.
(c) It is a withholding tax on the non-resident shareholders' incomes. This is an important reason due to the difficulty of controlling these shareholders and their higher possibilities of tax avoidance, plus the fact that eliminating the CIT in Spain would not reduce the tax burden of non-residents subject to universal taxation with foreign tax credits.
(d) Corporate Tax is an economic policy tool, which can be used to control company savings and quality and composition of investments, and therefore to implement macroeconomic stabilisation policies.
(e) There was already a tax on corporate income in Spain[3] and in the Western economies that were trade partners with Spain. It was not a primary source of revenue but it was not insignificant either.[4]

Following the experience of other Western countries and Spain's own experience, the reformers of 1978 opted for a tax on company's net income. Other options were rejected like a tax on the pure profit or a cash flow tax.[5] Company's net income is defined as:

Net Income = Ordinary incomes + Capital Gains and Losses – Ordinary Purchases – Labour costs – Interests of loans – Amortisation – Negative taxable income of previous years.

Regarding the coordination between Personal Income Tax and CIT, a partial integration system was chosen. This system tries to correct for economic double taxation through fiscal credits at the shareholder level.

THE PRINCIPLES BEHIND THE REFORMS

As we pointed out above, the tax born in 1978 was over the years subject to multiple reforms. But none of them, not even the integral reform of the tax in 1995, involved a radical transformation of the basic tax adopted in 1978. We might think that there have been a series of shared principles in all these reforms, though in each of them, some principles have been promoted more than others. These principles are:

- Neutrality.
- Competitiveness.
- International Tax Coordination.
- Transparency of the tax law.
- Coordination with financial accounting rules.
- Coordination with the Personal Income Tax.

In a context of open economies, the reform of corporate taxation should put more emphasis on the first three principles mentioned above. In the case of Spain, the process of increasing openness of its economy throughout past years, shows that the principle of competitiveness should have been the main base of the reform of the CIT. Even the other two relevant principles in a context of economic globalisation (neutrality and international coordination) have found their justification in terms of competitiveness.

Below, we analyse the six mentioned principles and examine the type of reform measures that are justified on the basis of fulfilling those objectives.

Competitiveness

Competitiveness can be defined as the capacity of the companies to keep and expand their participation in the domestic and foreign markets in a continuous way. Its achievement guarantees sustained growth in production and employment.

There are multiple determining factors of enterprise competitiveness. In the first place, it is very important to create a stable macroeconomic framework that guarantees the control of the public sector deficit, price stability and moderate interest rates. But besides this, it is necessary to apply specific policies to foster competitiveness. Regarding the CIT, some authors argue that its biggest contribution to enterprise competitiveness is to increase its neutrality, so that the governing criterion for investment decisions is productivity and not taxation. However, to the extent that all sorts of market failures exist, the CIT can be used as a tool for promotion and enhancement of overall competitiveness in the economy through actions (some more attractive than others) such as:

- Incentives to R&D activities.
- Incentives to employee training.
- Promotion of the internationalisation of Spanish companies.
- Stimulus to exporting activities.
- To facilitate company restructuring and alliances between companies.
- Measures to support small and medium-sized companies, correcting for their financial restrictions.

In addition, the tax bill for the CIT, being a cost component of the company, can be a factor of determining competitiveness. In this sense it is important to analyse the configuration of some basic elements of CIT (nominal tax rate, calculation of taxable income, incentives) and the effective rate of taxation that they represent, and then compare these effective rates with those of other (country) competitors (see the principle of international tax coordination).

International Tax Coordination

The 1978 Law was designed for a closed economy. On the other hand, throughout the years a process of internationalisation of the Spanish economy has taken place. This process has been accelerated by the integration of Spain into the European Union in 1986 and the establishment of the Internal (Common European) Market in 1993.

The principle of free movement of capital associated with the Internal Market allows for capital to move freely among the countries of the European Union, so that its allocation is in response to the criteria of economic efficiency, maximising production and welfare. But, if there are tax distortions that induce capital to be located in response to tax factors rather than efficiency criteria, the freedom of capital movement will not produce the expected benefits in terms of maximisation of production and welfare in the Union. In this context, the harmonisation of capital taxation is seen as an instrument to prevent taxes from becoming an element of distortion, so that the advantages associated with the Internal Market should be realised.

However, the analysis of the harmonisation rules for company taxation shows a low level of development, except for very concrete aspects related to the cross-border cooperation of companies.[6] In its place, a process of tax competition has been developed. In this context, international tax coordination requires to take into consideration the reform trends in the surrounding countries so that no country is placed in a bad position in the competitive race. Besides, we should consider the proposals of several recent reports that have analysed the diversity of company taxation among EU countries and its effects.[7]

The evolution of the CIT in the EU in recent years shows the development of three general simultaneous trends. The first one has consisted of the extension of the taxable income through a decrease of the incentives to investment, particularly those that have a general and permanent nature. The second one has been the reduction of nominal tax rates that has been combined with a reduction of their dispersion among countries. Finally, the third observed trend has been the maintenance or creation of new specific incentives with a dual goal: to help regional politics, in the sense of achieving a balanced development of the different areas, and to promote certain activities considered to be of high economic profitability.

It seems that the net effect of these trends is a progressive reduction of the effective taxation of the European average company and also a decrease in the dispersion of effective company taxation among countries.

As for the reports on company taxation, the proposal with the most significant impact on European Community institutions was the call for the necessary actions to be taken so that companies can take advantage of the Internal Market, eliminating tax obstacles that obstruct the relations among countries. (From this perspective, some measures, such as promoting outbound investments or helping international company reorganisations might be justified.

In addition, it would be necessary to correct two problems of a fiscal nature caused by the process of internationalisation in the presence of tax differences between countries. One of them is international double taxation. It is necessary to apply methods for the correction of both juridical and economic double taxation in the international context. The second problem is international tax avoidance, which justifies measures against the thin-capitalisation of companies, as well as measures against the use of tax havens and transfer prices as mechanisms of tax avoidance.

Neutrality

Neutrality is a basic tax principle that has been a mainstay of fiscal reforms, in general, and corporate taxation reform in particular. A neutral tax is one that does not modify the behaviour of economic agents. In a corporate environment, in general, fiscal considerations should not affect decision-making on the sources of finance, the grade and composition of the investment, location, inputs combinations, the legal status, nor the size of the firm.

a. Financial Neutrality.
This type of neutrality demands the total removal of double taxation of dividends so as not to favour debt financing against issue of new shares. Furthermore, it requires avoiding the application of lower tax rates to retained earnings (for whatever reason, including the goal of encouraging self-financing.)

b. Investment Neutrality.
Investment neutrality is achieved when the effective tax rates applicable to different investment projects are equal whatever the integrant assets. For investment neutrality to hold the definition of taxable income should closely approximate true economic profit. The main policy measures to be applied here include the following:

- Tax amortisation has to be defined in close agreement with the real economic depreciation.
- Capital gains need to be taxed like normal profits without exemption or deferral.
- To allow the full offset of losses.
- The adjustment for inflation in taxable income components, like amortisation, capital gains, stock valuation, taxable and deductible interest and offsetting losses.
- Removing the incentives to investment which favour some assets against others.
- Locational Neutrality.

Location choice should be determined by economic efficiency factors instead of fiscal ones. With this aim, at the national level, incentives to invest in certain regions should be prevented. At the international level, methods for correcting international double taxation should be applied. These methods should bring closer together the fiscal treatment in the following three investment activities: domestic, outbound and inbound investment. Thus, capital export and capital import neutrality could be actively pursued.

c. Neutrality in input combination.
Despite the fact that the economic incidence of the CIT is not known with any certainty, if we consider that the burden of the tax is born by shareholders, then the CIT would discriminate against the use of capital vis-

à-vis other inputs. To prevent this, it has been proposed to tax only the true economic profit, which can be attributed to all inputs as a whole. On the other hand, tax incentives for investments should be avoided because they can favour the use of *capital-intensive* techniques against labour and other inputs.

d. Neutrality in the choice of legal status.
Every company should receive the same fiscal treatment, regardless of its legal form. Thus, special tax regimes to certain entities, like general partnership and cooperatives, should be avoided. In addition, the fiscal treatment for non-corporate and incorporated enterprises should be quite similar.

e. Neutrality in regard to firm size.
Firm size should be based on the optimum size to produce and provide goods and services from an economic point of view. It should not be affected by fiscal reasons.

In spite of being an important principle of fiscal reform, just about every country has introduced exceptions to the principle of Neutrality. Special treatments and exceptions are justified when they try to rectify different forms of market failure. From the point of view of resource allocation, the existence of positive externalities could justify granting incentives to investment in certain activities, for example, R&D or employee training expenses. Others have justified special treatment in cases of certain geographical areas with low investment levels and that are economically depressed, or the special treatment given to certain clusters of enterprises, such as small and medium sized companies, which may be disadvantaged because of the lack of access to credit markets and other forms of financial restrictions. An exception toward neutrality may also be granted for stabilisation policy purposes, whereby fiscal incentives are used on a temporary basis for anti-cyclical purposes.

Anyway, deviations from the neutrality principle through granting different types of tax incentives should include the following terms:

- To follow rigorous and pre-established criteria.
- To choose the incentive techniques to get the objective. Some of these techniques include: accelerated depreciation, exemption or deferral of capital gains, deductions from taxable income or from tax due, or decreases in the nominal tax rate.

- To assess the collection/administration costs of the incentive in relation to the rate of achievement of the objective.
- To avoid too much complexity in the tax law.

International Neutrality

In the context of economic globalisation the meaning of the location neutrality principle turns out to be particularly relevant. This is the concept of neutrality in the international allocation of capital. This means that taxes on capital do not modify the location of the new investments across countries, but rather that the location decision is the same as the one that would take place without taxes. There are two different ways of understanding international neutrality: capital import neutrality (CIN) and capital export neutrality (CEN). The first, CIN, occurs when the importing country taxes domestic and foreign suppliers of capital in the same way. It will be attained with exemption of the outbound income to the exporting country[8] provided that the importing country[9]does not practice tax discrimination between domestic and foreign investors. The second, CEN, prevails when the tax system of the exporting country provides no incentive to invest at home rather than abroad to resident investors, or vice versa. It is achieved when investors are taxed on accrued worldwide income without deferral and receive full credit against the domestic tax liability for all taxes paid abroad.[10]

Both types of neutrality, CIN and CEN could be achieved simultaneously if effective tax rates were identical across countries. The difficulty of achieving such an advanced level of fiscal harmonisation requires giving priority to one of the two concepts. In this context, the CIT reform, in accordance with the international tax neutrality principle, demands correcting for international double taxation, which may better contribute to the achievement of the concept of neutrality that is most desired. Providing support for CIN would imply the use of exemption methods; and providing support for CEN would require the use of credit methods.

Transparency of the Tax Law

The CIT is a complex tax due to the complexity of the object of taxation, a company's business reality, and also because of the legislators' desire (for equity reasons among others) to adapt the tax laws to the true individual taxpaying capacity of the firm. This natural complexity is often reinforced by a feature which regularly has accompanied this tax: the dispersion of the tax law in different legal texts. There are several reasons for this dispersion, including the proliferation of partial reforms and the use of this tax as an economic policy tool via the granting of tax incentives.

All things considered, the 1978 Law was subject to several changes which were dispersed in different legal texts. In these circumstances, a common objective of CIT reform is to increase the transparency of the tax law. This requires avoiding the dispersion of the tax laws. In addition, it requires that taxation rules are certain and clear to the taxpayer. The results of increased transparency are a higher level of certainty for the taxpayer and the reduction of administrative costs for the tax authorities and compliance costs for the taxpayers.

Coordination with Financial Accounting Rules

The tax base of the CIT is the amount of the income generated by the firm during the fiscal year. For the majority of taxpayers, this income is calculated as the balance on the profit and loss account regulated by the Commercial Code, the Corporation Law and the General Accounting Plan.

However, income calculated by accounting principles may not be the same as that defined as the tax base of the CIT. This divergence is generally due to the different objectives of the accounting and fiscal legislation. Nevertheless, one of the objectives of CIT reform has been the better coordination of the tax laws with accounting rules. This has meant the acceptance of accounting principles as a tool for taxation, and in more practical terms, working out the concept of taxable income from an accounting result corrected by clear and exact adjustments. These adjustments have been limited to a minimum so as to achieve the parallelism between accounting and fiscal definitions. This proximity between tax and book profit enhances compliance by taxpayers, providing them with greater certainty and reducing conflict with the Tax Administration.

Among the measures to pursue these objectives, we highlight:

- Book profit needs to be the starting point for the calculation of the tax base.
- Differences between book profit and tax base have to be regulated clearly and exactly whenever a discrepancy between both of them can be justified. Exhaustive and over-detailed regulations of every component of the tax base (incomes, expenses, valuation criteria or timely criteria) should be avoided.
- Fiscal rules should avoid controlling purely accounting aspects.

Coordination with the Personal Income Tax

The CIT in essence is a withholding tax on the capital income that individuals obtain through their participation in legal entities. For this reason, any type of reform of the Personal Income Tax necessitates adaptation of the reforms to the CIT in order to maintain the unity and coherence of personal taxation on income. The need to choose the appropriate method of correcting for the double taxation of dividends and capital gains points us to the types of actions necessary for proper coordination between the CIT and the Personal Income Tax. Other measures needed for the proper coordination of these two taxes include the following:

- Regulation of the facts which affect both taxes following unitary criteria. For example:
    - Taxable event definition
    - Regulation of shareholder-firm operations
    - Taxation of non residents
    - Definitions of capital incomes and withholding obligations.
- Discouragement of tax arbitrage with measures like:
    - Avoiding a significant difference between the CIT rate and the highest marginal tax rate of Personal Income Tax.
    - Approximation of the fiscal treatments of non-corporate and corporate enterprises.

THE CONTENT OF THE REFORMS

The aim of this section is to describe the essential features of the reforms of the CIT in Spain over the last 25 years by analyzing the principal elements of the tax. The discussion will focus on those elements that have a major influence on the effective rate of taxation of corporate income. For reasons of space we will make only reference to the most representative reforms.

Nominal Tax Rate

The Corporate Income Tax, born in 1978, was designed as a proportional tax with only one tax rate, whatever the destination of the profit. This principle was fundamentally respected in the later reforms and it agrees with the experience of most of the countries of the European Union.

The general rate, initially established at 33 percent, was increased to 35 percent in 1983 and it has been kept at that level since then. Besides, there has been special tax rates applied to certain types of companies.[11]

Measuring the Tax Base

This is the most complex of all steps in levying the CIT. For clarity of exposition we decompose this issue into several themes.

Relation to accounting profit

One of the main criticisms directed to the establishment of the CIT in 1978 and to its later developments was its lack of coordination with general accounting rules. One of the problems was that the Regulations on the CIT produced a proliferation of new "accounting" rules and in such a way that, in practice, they took precedence over the non-fiscal rules.

In this context, one of the main innovations of the 1995 reform was the calculation of the tax base from the general accounting results adapted for fiscal purposes with clear, precise and a limited number of adjustments. These adjustments answer, for example, to accounting expenses that are not tax deductible (fines and penalties, interest incurred on share capital, corporate income tax); or to accounting income not taxed, as some foreign incomes that are exempt to correct for international double taxation. Besides, the adjustments can be caused by differences in the time criteria, as accounting provisions and amortisations higher than the tax limits, or tax amortisations higher than the accounting ones because of the application of tax incentives as the accelerated depreciation.

Amortisation

The amortisation methods contained in the 1978 Law continue to be in force at present. The general system is the straight-line method based on official tables, which consists of writing off every asset according to a percentage included between the maximum and the minimum indicated in the tables. Besides, the declining-balance method and the sum of the years digits method are applied with certain conditions. In general, these methods are more favourable to taxpayers than the straight-line method, because they allow advancing the tax amortisation and to postpone the tax due. However, they can not be applied to buildings, furniture and tools.

The most important criticism directed to the CIT in the area of the amortisation, was the high degree of obsolescence of the official tables, which basically dated back to 1965. As a response to this criticism, new tables of amortisation were approved in 1993; these tables continue to be in force at present. Though the new tables offered higher maximum rates for some assets, the most general characteristic, applicable in all the cases, was the expansion of depreciation brackets. So, for a certain maximum rate, the maximum number of years was increased, and thus, reducing the minimum rate and extending the bracket of depreciation rates allowed.

Until 1995, there was no minimum unit cost below which assets might be written off in the year in which they were acquired. This rule was introduced in the 1995 reform, but only for small and medium-sized companies. Another innovation in the 1995 reform was the amortisation of intangible assets. The 1995 reform allowed the amortisation of goodwill and other intangible assets, provided that they had been acquired from non related parties. A straight-line method was established over a maximum period of 10 years, though from 2002 onward, the annual maximum rate for the goodwill has been lowered to 5 percent.

Loss offset

The 1978 reform established a five-year limit on the carry-forward of loss offset against profits. With the passage of time, this term came to be considered as very limiting, not only for equity and neutrality reasons, but also because of the progressive amplification of the loss offset in countries in Spain's economic environment. For this reason, the 1995 reform extended the term of offsetting losses to 7 years, and later reforms extended it to 10 years (from 1999) and to 15 years (from 2002).[12] In no case has the Spanish Corporate Tax allowed carry-back provision, despite the fact that this possibility has been incorporated, though in limited ways, in the tax codes of some other countries.

Adjustment to inflation

Because the CIT is a proportional tax, the inflation affects mainly the calculation of the taxable base. With a tax base calculated on the basis of nominal values, inflation can lead to a monetary profit, which does not reflect the true income or taxpaying capacity of the firm. Levying the tax on nominal profits tends to reduce the horizontal equity and economic neutrality of the tax. This effect seems to be confirmed, in the Spanish case, by several empirical studies.

The basic components of the taxable income which are affected by inflation are amortisation, capital gains, stock valuation, and the taxable and deductible interests. We now proceed to review the responses of the Spanish Corporate Tax to these matters.

a. Amortisation.

The Spanish CIT defines the depreciable base as the historical cost of acquisition or production. In times of inflation this method generates tax liability on monetary profits, which in real terms do not reflect the true individual taxpaying capacity of the firm.

Neither the 1978 Law, nor the later reforms, not even the 1995 reform, applied a formula to adjust the calculation of depreciation in line with inflation with general and regular character. Instead, the possibility of revaluation of assets has been used as a technique for partial adjustment. Specifically, for the fiscal years 1979–1981, 1983 and 1996 the revaluation of fixed assets was allowed according to legally established coefficients. The accounting surplus generated with these revaluations was not taxed.

b. Capital gains.

The 1978 Law made capital gains taxable at the moment of their realisation. In general, the taxable capital gain was the amount by which the proceeds from the sale of the asset exceeded the cost of acquisition. In some years, the revaluation of assets mentioned in the previous paragraph was allowed as the only technique to correct for inflation.

The 1995 reform introduced a mechanism of monetary correction of capital gains. Interestingly this was done in spite of the fact that there were very few other countries that were trying to correct this problem. The correction mechanism was applicable in the transmissions, both onerous and lucrative, of tangible and intangible assets. In the calculation of the taxed capital gain, the financial structure of the company was borne in mind in the sense of reducing the degree of inflation correction as the company was increasingly financed with debt. This type of monetary correction of capital gains was eliminated in 1999 and at present, it is only applied in the case of transfer of immovable property.

c. Stock (inventory) valuation.

The Corporate Income Tax introduced in the 1978 reform allowed stock valuation according to the average cost and the FIFO methods. Nevertheless, it prohibited the application of the LIFO method and of any other one based on the replacement cost. In the presence of inflation these rules generated artificial profits and an unfair burden of taxation.

The 1995 reform extended the number of methods allowed for inventory or stock valuation for tax purposes. This was one of the aspects of the reform in which there was a high degree of agreement between theoretical principles and findings in empirical studies. These studies routinely showed a higher rate of effective taxation associated with inventories vis-à-vis other company assets. Besides these changes were also justified by the recent evolution of the fiscal systems of countries in Spain's economic environment.

In fact, the 1995 Law did not include any specific rule regulating inventory valuation. However, in view of the new model of relating the book profit and taxable income in the 1995 reform, a company may use, for tax purposes, any of the valuation methods which it has applied in its commercial balance sheet, included the LIFO method.

d. Taxable and deductible interest.

The Spanish CIT allows, as a deductible expense, the nominal amount of interest paid on loans, and requires the inclusion as income interest payments received also for its nominal amount. A process of inflation increases the volume of nominal interests paid and received, creating opposing effects on both sides of the balance sheet and in lenders and borrowers. There is an increase in the tax due by creditors because their taxable base increases; and there is a decrease in the tax due by debtors because their deductible expenses as financial charges increase.

This effect of inflation has not been corrected for in the Spanish CIT, according to the international experience with this issue. However, as we pointed out above, currently the CIT takes into account the financial structure of the firm in the calculation of capital gains. This can be considered as a method, though partial and imperfect, of taking into account the advantages of debt financing of assets in inflationary periods.

Incentives to Investment and Employment

The 1978 reform established different instruments within the CIT with the purpose of stimulating private investment. Some of these instruments were to act through a reduction in the taxable base, such as in the case of the exemption of capital gains or accelerated depreciation provisions; others, such as in the case of investment credits, were to work by directly reducing the tax liability.

This scheme of incentives was one of the aspects of the Spanish CIT that received most direct criticism. Its shortcomings were apparent in terms of lack of effectiveness and neutrality, administrative complexity and high collection costs. The same shortcomings had been detected in other countries and had led to fiscal reforms characterised by a reduction in general incentives and keeping or even promoting specific incentives to certain areas or activities.

Spain was not isolated from these reform trends, even before the 1995 Law. As examples we can mention the suppression of tax credit for securities in 1982; the progressive reduction of the percentage of tax credit for new tangible assets;[13] the elimination, except for handicapped personnel, of the tax credit for employment; and the creation or improvement of deductions such as the ones related to exporting activities, employee training or R&D activities.

The 1995 reform introduced, as a principal innovation, the elimination of the tax credit for new tangible assets as a permanent fiscal incentive, though the Budget Laws should be able to restore it on a temporary basis for economic stabilisation purposes. This power was only used in 1996.

Accelerated depreciation survives but with a very selective application. For example, under certain conditions, mining assets, the assets of Labour Companies and certain expenses and assets used in R&D activities can be freely amortised.

The 1995 Law maintained the incentive to reinvest profits with important innovations. The most remarkable one was the substitution of the exemption formula for the deferral of capital gain according to the recommendations offered in the Ruding Report[14] and the experiences of other countries in this regard, so that, the non-taxed capital gain in a given period had to be included in the taxable income in future years. Another innovation was that the transferred assets and those in which the proceeds had been reinvested could be not only tangible and intangible assets, but also shares or other participations provided that they formed a holding of at least 5 percent in any entity.

The deferral regime was removed in 2002 and replaced by a fiscal credit for reinvestment. The general percentage of deduction at present is 20 percent. So, in the case of reinvestment, capital gains, instead of the general rate of 35 percent, pay an effective tax rate of 15 percent, which is the same rate that is applicable in the Personal Income Tax to the capital gains generated in periods exceeding one year.

As we have already indicated, a characteristic of CIT reform in Spain has been the improvement of the specific incentives. These incentives have the goal of correcting market failures and they must have a selective and permanent nature. This fact justifies their incorporation in the CIT Law. In Spain these incentives are driven mainly through credits (deductions from tax liability) and they include the following:

a. Research, development and innovation activities.
b. Exporting activities
c. Investments in cultural assets, new film productions and new books.
d. Investment for environmental protection.
e. Expenses in training personnel
f. Handicapped personnel employment.

Some of these deductions have been introduced after the reform of 1995, but others (a, b, c and e) existed even before this date. The analysis of the evolution of the latter deductions shows the improvement of the incentives with an increase in its generosity. This effect is particularly intense in the fiscal credit for R&D and innovation. To be emphasised also is the recent introduction of a measure with a specific objective of promoting outbound investment. This is a deduction from the taxable base with deferral to stimulate the establishment of companies abroad.

To conclude, the establishment of a special regime for small and medium-sized companies needed to be outlined in the 1995 reform. Since then, the concept of "Small and medium-sized company" has been an object of multiple reforms. All of them have tended to extend the area of application of the special regime in order to have more companies enjoying the incentives provided to this type of company.[15] Among these incentives stand out especially diverse modalities of accelerated depreciation and the application of a reduced tax rate of 30 percent.[16] Besides, a tax credit exists for new data processing technologies.[17]

Relief from Economic Double Taxation

The 1978 Law corrected the double taxation of dividends through a mechanism of partial integration at the shareholder level. In particular, a variant of the credit system was applied. The shareholder was including in his taxable income the dividend received, and was deducting from the tax liability an amount that in no way was directly related to the corporate tax paid by the company distributing the profits. Concretely, the individual shareholder was deducting 15 percent of the dividend received and the corporate shareholder was deducting 50 percent of the proportional part of his quota derived from the dividend. However, where there was a parent-subsidiary relationship (shareholdings of at least 25 percent), dividends received from national subsidiaries were usually tax exempt.

The criticism addressed to the weak mitigation of the double taxation that this system was providing, gave rise, paradoxically, in 1985, to a reduction of the deduction in the case of an individual shareholder from 15 to 10 percent.

The 1995 reform increased the degree of correction for economic double taxation. A variant of the credit system continued to be applied. To the corporate shareholder, the most prominent innovation was the amplification of the full correction for double taxation to a holding of at least 5%, and the correction for double taxation of capital gains with certain conditions. On the other hand, the "estimated imputation system" was chosen for the individual shareholder. This method consists of adding, to the taxable base of the Personal Income Tax, the sum of the dividend received plus an estimation of the CIT in relation to the dividend. This estimated CIT is deducted from the tax liability. In general, the CIT is estimated at 40 percent of the received dividend. The correction for double taxation would be full if the effective tax rate in the CIT were 28.57 percent.[18]

Another system that, from the theoretical point of view, is useful to correct the economic double taxation is the "tax transparency", according to which the profits generated in certain corporations, both distributed and retained, are taxed as part of the shareholder's income tax.

This regime was introduced in the Spanish tax system by the reform of 1978 under two modalities: voluntary and compulsory. Only the voluntary tax transparency, applicable to certain small and medium-sized companies, had the purpose of removing the double taxation problem. On the contrary, the compulsory tax transparency, applicable to certain portfolio and fixed investment companies and to professional companies, had the purpose of preventing tax avoidance through the creation of conduit companies. In that time in Spain, there was a difference of more than 20 points between the corporate tax rate and the highest marginal tax rate for Personal Income Tax. This fact was clearly inciting the creation of conduit companies for tax avoidance purposes, since the dividends distributed to corporations were paying a lower tax rate than those distributed to individual shareholders with high income levels. The regime of compulsory tax transparency was justified as a method of avoiding this type of behaviour.

After the fiscal reform of 1985, the voluntary tax transparency was eliminated, despite the criticism from most of the studies on this subject. On the other hand, the compulsory regime was kept, but only positive taxable bases were imputed. The negative taxable bases were compensated in the transparent company according to the general criteria of the CIT. Thus, tax transparency turned into a sanctioning regime for these companies.

The 1995 Law keeps the compulsory character of the transparency regime, but with important innovations. The most important one is that the transparent companies are subjected to the general tax rate in the CIT. On the other hand, shareholders continue to include, in their taxable income, their share in the positive taxable base of the company. In the recent past, the transparency regime has been subjected to a barrage of criticisms of a diverse nature. The regime has turned out to be excessively complex for the Administration and the taxpayers and it has not always managed to avoid the evasive use of conduit companies. The regime could have also reduced the attraction to the corporate legal status, which is the preferred juridical form in a market economy. Besides, the approximation of the corporate tax rate and the maximum marginal tax rate of Personal Income Tax reduces attraction to the interposition of conduit companies.

All these criticisms have caused the removal of the tax transparency regime in 2003. The professional companies are now taxed according to the general regime of the CIT; and the portfolio entities and the fixed investment companies are taxed with the new "State Companies Regime". In this regime the taxable income of the company is divided, in accordance with the regulation of the Personal Income Tax, in two parts. The general part is taxed at a rate of 40 percent, which is five points over the general corporate tax rate to prevent the use by individuals of the state companies without business activity. The special part pays 15 percent and it applies to long term capital gains.

International Aspects

There are two problems of a fiscal kind caused by the economic internationalisation process in the presence of tax differences between countries. They are international double taxation and international tax avoidance.

Relief from international double taxation

The topic of relief from international double taxation is among those that have generated most changes in the regulations of the CIT in the recent past. These legal changes can also be read as the position taken by the Spanish authorities in the discussion of what is the best method to address international double taxation: exemption or credit?

The 1995 Law, in clear continuity of some previous rules, chose the credit method with limitation to correct both juridical and economic double taxation. The credit method allows for the deduction of taxes paid abroad from the tax due in Spain, if such amount is lower than the tax paid in the Spanish CIT for the foreign income. This method survives with some change in the current regulations and practice, but as we will explain immediately below as a residual or default method.

A chief reason for having chosen this option has been the desire to achieve capital export neutrality. Actually, with an imputation system, two domestic residents with the same worldwide income would pay the same taxes whether that income comes from domestic or from foreign sources. Nevertheless, this advantage might be invalidated if a limitation to tax credit is established. Concretely, if the tax rate in the source (importing) country is higher than the tax rate in the resident (exporting) country, the whole tax paid abroad will not be allowed as a credit, so that the international double taxation will not be fully corrected. The resident investor will be subjected to the effective tax rates of the source country, and therefore, capital export neutrality will not be achieved.

If the limitation to tax credit does not take effect because the source rate is lower than the residence rate, the main problem remaining with the credit method is the loss of competitiveness of the residents who compete in the foreign markets. Actually, the resident investor would be subjected to the tax rate in the residence (exporting) country that would be higher than the rate of the competitors in the source (importing) country.

In 1996 the exemption method was introduced in the Spanish CIT. This method is, under certain conditions, applied to dividends and capital gains generated in foreign subsidiaries and to the income obtained through permanent establishments located abroad. If there is a limitation to the tax credit, the exemption method is equal or better from the view point of the taxpayer than the imputation method. So, although at present both methods coexist, the credit is a residual regime applicable when the requirements to exemption are not fulfilled.

This more recent change of trend in the Spanish tax system in favour of the exemption method is due to the legislators' goal of supporting the internationalisation of the Spanish companies. The exemption method, which supposes the exclusive burden of the income in the source country, allows the companies to compete in the same conditions (for tax effects) in international markets. There are, therefore, reasons of international tax competition that explain the current preference for this method to correct for international double taxation. Besides, it is easier than the credit method. Finally, as we pointed out before, the exemption method achieves capital import neutrality but not capital export neutrality.[19]

Methods of reducing international tax avoidance

The CIT law and the Spanish Tax Administration have adopted different methods to try to prevent international tax avoidance schemes. For example, on transfer prices, the CIT law demands to value the operations between related companies in accordance with the arm's length principle, without admitting opposite proof. Nevertheless, in order to increase the certainty to the taxpayer, the reform of 1995 took into consideration the possibility that the taxpayer carries out a proposal for the valuation of related transactions before their realisation. On the other hand, the reform of 1995 established a thin capitalisation rule in order to avoid the abuse of the debt between related entities, in such a way that the interest payments considered excessive will be considered as dividends for tax purposes, and therefore will not be a deductible expense.

International Tax Transparency is another anti-tax avoidance method used by the Spanish CIT since 1994. This consists of including some positive incomes obtained by non-resident entities in the taxable base of the resident entities. Its aim is to prevent the advantages of using conduit companies in foreign territories with low taxation to avoid or to postpone the payment of the Spanish tax.

Besides the mentioned measures, we might consider the fact that the CIT Law is sprinkled with articles in which cautions are established with regard to tax heavens. On the other hand, the extension and improvement of the bilateral tax treaties signed by Spain must be labelled not only as a mechanism to correct international double taxation, but, also, as a way of tax coordination with other countries to prevent incomes avoidance practices.

THE PERFORMANCE OF THE SPANISH CORPORATE INCOME TAX IN TERMS OF TAX REVENUE, NEUTRALITY AND COMPETITIVENESS

Tax Revenue

This section reviews the revenue performance of the CIT in Spain vis-à-vis other countries in the OECD.

Tables 6.1 and 6.2 show the quantitative importance of the Corporate Income Tax during the period 1965–2001 using two indicators—Corporate Tax as percentage of GDP (CT/GDP) and Corporate Tax as percentage of total taxation (CT/ TT). Three areas are analysed: OECD, European Union (15) and Spain.

The Corporate Income Tax evolution during the analysed period finds its main explanation in the economic environment evolution, although we have to consider legal changes, which can explain the figures in certain periods. For example, tax revenue increases in 1983 and 1985 can be explained by the increment of the nominal tax rates and the reduction of incentives, respectively.

CT/GDP index (Table 6.1) is, in general, lower in Spain than the average of the OECD and EU (15). Until the late eighties the weight of the Corporate Tax in GDP in Spain is approximately 60% of the other two areas analysed. However, since 1987 the figure has been getting closer, and in the nineties the percentage gets to around 80% of the levels in the other two areas analysed in this section.

CT/TT index (Table 6.2) is, in general, lower in Spain than the OECD average. Comparison with EU (15) shows, with some exceptions, that the CT/TT index is higher in Spain in the period before 1978 reform and lower in the period after the reform.

Neutrality and Competitiveness

This section shows the main results of the empirical studies on effective taxation, which analyse the degree of fulfilment of the neutrality and competitiveness principles of the Spanish CIT.

a. Internal neutrality of the Spanish CIT

The studies that have analysed the internal neutrality of the Spanish CIT have quantified the effective tax rates of different investment projects, deducing the presence or absence of neutrality from the analysis of the dispersion among the tax rates. Though there have also been studies that calculate effective average tax rates, most of the studies have calculated effective marginal tax rates applying the King and Fullerton methodology (King and Fullerton, 1983).[20] Among the latter works, there are important methodological differences. For example:

- Period to which the results refer.
- Variables of classification of the results: assets, source of finance, activity sector, firm size, legal status or location area.
- Specific methodological assumptions for the calculation of the different variables.
- Effective taxation indicator: effective marginal tax rate, cost of capital and tax wedge.

Nevertheless, in spite of these methodological differences, it is possible to summarise the principal conclusions of these works.

Espitia et al. (1989) and Paredes Gómez (1992) quantify effective tax rates on the marginal investment for types of assets, taking into account, exclusively, the influence of the CIT. These studies differ in the assumption about the source of finance of the marginal investment. The first study considers a combination of internal and external financing; and the second considers exclusively internal financing. Though they refer to different periods,[21] they agree in their findings about the scant neutrality of the Spanish CIT with the relative treatment of the different assets. The buildings and, especially, the stock are the assets with the highest effective tax rates, whereas the investment in machinery and vehicles is subjected often to negative effective tax rates that show that these assets receive a

Table 6.1 Corporate tax as percentage of GDP

	1965	1970	1975	1980	1985	1990	1995	1996	1997	1998	1999	2000	2001
OECD	2.2	2.4	2.2	2.4	2.7	2.7	2.9	3.0	3.2	3.3	3.3	3.6	3.5
European Union (15)	1.9	2.1	2.1	2.1	2.6	2.6	2.7	3.1	3.4	3.5	3.5	3.8	3.6
Spain	1.4	1.3	1.3	1.2	1.5	2.9	1.8	1.9	2.6	2.5	2.8	3.0	2.8

Source: OECD (2004), Statistical Compendium.

Table 6.2 Corporate tax as percentage of total taxation

	1965	1970	1975	1980	1985	1990	1995	1996	1997	1998	1999	2000	2001
OECD	8.8	8.8	7.5	7.6	8.0	7.9	8.0	8.3	8.8	8.9	8.8	9.7	9.6
European Union (15)	6.7	6.9	6.0	5.8	6.4	6.8	6.9	7.7	8.5	8.7	8.7	9.2	8.6
Spain	9.2	8.2	6.9	5.1	5.2	8.8	5.4	5.8	7.8	7.3	8.0	8.6	8.1

Source: OECD (2004), Statistical Compendium.

marginal subsidy to the investment. Besides, in a historical analysis, Espitia et al. conclude that the introduction of the CIT in 1979 supposed a general reduction of the effective tax rates, due to the establishment of tax incentives for investment, and a great dispersion of the marginal effective tax rates applicable to the different assets.

More recently, Paredes Gómez (2002) has compared the effective tax rates by type of asset in 1989 and 2001. The results show an increase of the effective tax rates for all the assets with the exception of stock. The increase is such that machinery and vehicles reach positive effective tax rates due to the elimination of the general tax credits for the investment. The effective tax rate for stock is reduced due to the admission of the LIFO system for inventory valuation. The buildings are the assets most penalised fiscally. Besides, there is an observed reduction in the dispersion of effective tax rates among assets between 1989 and 2001. This reduction shows a substantial improvement in the neutrality of the Spanish CIT in the relative treatment of the different assets during the last decade.

Other studies, also related to the Spanish case, analyse the joint effect of the company and individual income taxes. The results refer to, not only assets, but also sectors, source of finance, firm size, location area or legal status of the firm.[22] Though methodological differences exist among them and they refer to different periods,[23] we might emphasise some general conclusions:

(a) The combination of the CIT and of the Personal Income Tax generates a tax structure that imposes burdens, of very unequal form, on the capital income of different investment projects.
(b) For type of asset, stock is the asset most penalised fiscally, while machinery and vehicles receive the most favourable treatment.[24]
(c) From the financial perspective, the debt receives the best tax treatment. Inside the internal financing, the retained earnings have a comparative advantage relative to the issue of new shares.
(d) In the sectoral field, a dispersion among sectors is observed.[25]
(e) The calculations for the firm size show that big companies face lower effective taxation than small and medium sized ones.

An interesting question is what influence inflation has had on the effective taxation on the Spanish companies. From a theoretical point of view, it is not possible to draw firm conclusions on this matter. There are different factors that can act in opposite directions. For example, the over-taxation of a fixed asset whose amortisation is calculated from the historical cost can be compensated if this investment is financed by debt, due to the possibility of deducting the nominal interest. For all this, the empirical analysis is necessary.

The empirical studies done on the Spanish case[26]conclude that, in general, inflation increases effective tax rates of all investment projects.[27] Besides, the sensitivity to price inflation is very different among the different projects, which worsens the lack of internal neutrality of the Spanish CIT.

b. International tax competitiveness.

As we have already indicated, the CIT, as a cost component of the company, can be a factor in determining competitiveness. Actually, if a resident company in Spain was subjected to an effective tax that is higher than for resident companies in other countries, the Spanish company would be at a competitive disadvantage relative to foreign companies with which it has to compete on the international market. For this reason it is important to know the level of effective taxation in Spain and to compare it with the levels in the surrounding countries, particularly in the European Union.

There are numerous studies that calculate indicators of effective taxation in different countries.[28] Studies that do calculations for countries of the European Union refer to different periods and offer methodological differences. As such, they are not always comparable. Nevertheless, they seem to show that Spanish companies are more taxed than the average European company. This conclusion is independent of the indicator of effective taxation used, and is a common one, though with some exceptions, in the analyses for the type of asset and for the source of finance. As an example, we can mention, for its major current importance and for its methodological contributions, the report "Company Taxation in the Internal Market" (European Commission, 2001).[29] This report concludes that in Spain, the cost of capital, the effective marginal tax rate and the effective average tax rate, are higher than the average of the European Union[30]. In an ascending order of tax rates, Spain is in the twelfth position in regard to the marginal tax rate; and in the ninth position in regard to the average tax rate. This major value of the indicator of effective taxation is produced for all the assets and sources of finance with the sole exception of stock in the case of the average tax rate, and of the stock and machinery, in the case of the marginal rate and the cost of capital.

On the other hand, it would be interesting to know how the effective taxation of the CIT in the countries of the European Union has evolved during the past years and how the relative position of Spain has changed. Work by Paredes Gómez (2002), which calculates effective marginal tax rates for CIT for type of asset in the years 1989 and 2001, can shed some light on this matter. The results show a reduction in the effective marginal tax rate of the average European company, and a reduction of the dispersion of the tax rates among countries.

Spain, departing from an effective tax rate higher than the European one in 1989, has experienced a lower reduction. This shows the loss of competitiveness by the Spanish companies in the framework of the European Union during the nineties if we isolate the influence of the CIT. This deterioration of the competitiveness of the Spanish position in the European Union holds for all the assets with the exception of stock.

c. International tax neutrality

An empirical analysis of international tax neutrality needs to calculate the effective taxation, not of the domestic investment, but of the transnational investment. It is a question of knowing the tax treatment of the investments located in a country, and realised by residents in other countries. There are numerous studies that have made this type of calculation.[31] We can point out, again, the report "Company Taxation in the Internal Market" (European Commission, 2001).[32] We are interested in knowing the results of this report for the Spanish transnational investment for two reasons:

(a) To know the tax treatment of Spanish investment in different countries in the European Union and the degree of capital export neutrality.
(b) To know the tax treatment of foreign investment in Spain and the degree of capital import neutrality.

The analysis of the degree of CEN from the Spanish perspective shows that the Spanish tax system does not achieve the CEN. On average, domestic investment in Spain is more taxed than Spanish investment abroad. This result occurs when the subsidiary is financed, exclusively, by retained earnings or new equity. Nevertheless, in the case of debt finance, domestic investment receives a more favourable tax treatment.

As for the countries in which, from a tax point of view, it is more appealing to establish subsidiaries of a Spanish parent, it is observed that it turns out to be particularly profitable to locate a subsidiary in Ireland. Other attractive destinations include Sweden, Finland and the United Kingdom. On the other hand, subsidiaries in Germany and France would be the most taxed in relation to the Spanish domestic investment. In this analysis of the relative position of the countries, an extraordinary parallelism has been observed by the arrangement obtained for domestic investment. There is a proximity, which in some cases is converted into exactness, in the values of the cost of capital (or effective average tax rate) for both types of investment—domestic investment in the countries of the European Union, and transnational investment of a Spanish parent in the same countries. All this seems to indicate that the tax system in the country of location of the subsidiary is the main determining factor of the effective taxation imposed on the investment of the Spanish parent in European Union countries.

The analysis of the degree of CIN from the Spanish perspective shows that the Spanish tax system does not achieve the CIN. On average, foreign investment in Spain is more taxed than domestic investment. For source of finance of the subsidiary, the previous result holds for debt finance. Nevertheless, the lack of CIN occurs in the opposite direction when the subsidiary uses the other two sources of finance (retained earnings and new equity) as the domestic investment turns out to be more taxed.

In an analysis of countries, it is observed that the parent companies from different countries of the European Union that have a subsidiary in Spain will not be subjected to the same effective tax. Different results are obtained for different indicators of effective taxation. The results for the cost of capital show that the Spanish tax system achieves the CIN for ten of the fourteen countries of the European Union, which include Austria, Holland, Luxembourg and Greece, the countries in which parent companies find it less attractive to invest in a Spanish subsidiary. On the other hand, the effective average tax rate shows that in the case of Germany the constitution of the parent leads to a lower tax burden, opposite to the case for Greece, Holland and Austria. Besides, it seems to be the case, Germany being the principal exception, that there is an association between countries with low nominal tax rates in the CIT and countries with effective average tax rates below the average.

In short, the results of the Report of the European Commission show that the Spanish CIT does not achieve neutrality in the international allocation of capital, but provides a different tax treatment for domestic investment, for Spanish investment abroad and for foreign investment in Spain.

CONCLUSIONS AND FINAL REMARKS

Although the modern Spanish CIT introduced in 1978 represented an important step at the time, it rapidly faced criticism that put pressure on policymakers to reform it. The major reform of the CIT came in the 1995 Law, but before and after this major reform several partial changes of the tax took place. So, we can say that the CIT reform in Spain has been a constant process of adjustment, in an attempt by the legislators to "get it right", but also as a response to the changing circumstances of the Spanish economy, especially the opening of the Spanish economy, and the inevitable internationalisation of Spanish companies.

In this reform process, there have not been radical changes, meaning a transformation of the structure of the CIT established in 1978. Fortunately, the continuous reform process of the CIT has been generally informed by a common set of principles, although in each stage of the reform process some of them have been heeded more than others. These principles included: neutrality, competitiveness, international tax coordination, transparency of the tax law, coordination with financial accounting rules, and coordination with the Personal Income Tax.

In the context of open economies, the reform of corporate taxation should put more emphasis on the first three principles mentioned above. In the case of Spain, the process of increasing the openness of its economy in more recent years explains that the principle of competitiveness should have been the main basis for the reform of the CIT. Even the other two relevant principles in the context of economic globalisation (neutrality and international coordination), have found their justification in terms of competitiveness.

In the third section of the paper, we examined the principles that the reform of the CIT should have followed, especially the ones with an international perspective, and the reforming measures that were justified in trying to fulfil these objectives.

Although the principle of economic neutrality has been increasingly respected in CIT reform, insofar as market failures exist, the CIT has been used in Spain to promote particular activities including R&D, employee training incentives, actions to support small and medium sized companies, promotion of the internationalisation of Spanish companies, and helping company restructurings.

The last two mentioned measures also might be justified according to the international reports of company taxation[33] that propose to apply the necessary actions in order that the companies can take advantage of the Internal (Common European) Market. The Spanish authorities have put considerable effort in achieving the international coordination principle, as shown in the reforms and work dedicated to address the two problems of a fiscal nature that originated in the process of economic internationalisation in the presence of tax differences between countries. These are the problems of international double taxation and international tax avoidance. Besides, in the international field, the international neutrality principle demands the application of correcting methods of international double taxation which serve to achieve the concept of neutrality that is considered a priority. The CEN support would imply credit methods; and the CIN support would imply exemption methods. In Spain, although at present both methods coexist, the credit is a residual regime applicable when the requirements to exemption are not fulfilled. There are reasons of international tax competition that explain the current preference for the exemption method.

The essential features of the most representative reforms of the CIT in Spain over the last 25 years were described in the fourth section. The main elements that have a major influence in the effective taxation have been analysed. The fifth section shows the main results of the empirical studies on effective taxation which analyse the degree of fulfilment of the principles of neutrality and competitiveness of the Spanish CIT. These studies coincide with the scanty neutrality of the CIT with the relative treatment of the different investment projects. Nevertheless, during the nineties, there has been a substantial improvement in the neutrality of the Spanish CIT in the relative treatment of the different assets.

The studies on international tax competitiveness seem to show that the Spanish company is more taxed than the average European company and they show a loss of competitiveness during the last decade. Finally, the Spanish CIT does not achieve the neutrality in international allocation of capital.

The fact that the CIT falls on such a changing entity as the company makes us foresee that the reform process will continue in the future. The agenda for reform in the future includes a greater effort to advance the approximation of the tax base to the concept of book profit. This, no doubt, will entail a major reconsideration of what are tax deductible expenses. For example, concerning provisions, it would be a question of accepting, in fiscal terms, what has been already accepted in the accounting field. In the area of amortisations, it has been proposed that the maximum amortisation rates be increased to adapt them to the new managerial reality in which the assets have less and less useful life. Other proposed measures have been: extending the assets to which regressive methods can be applied; and generalising the possibility of immediate amortisation of small value assets.

On the other hand, the importance of going deeply into the reform of the international aspects of the CIT has to be outlined. Though methods can be adapted to unilateral level, the most effective action in this matter is the fiscal coordination with other countries, especially EU countries. Measures like the expansion of the area of application of the mergers and parent-subsidiary directives; the agreements about transfer prices or the signing of a multilateral tax treaty, are justified from this point of view.

We are going to finish with a final reflection on the process of fiscal competition in the European Union regarding CIT and its implications for Spain. This process, that has led to a moderate decline of the CIT in EU countries, demands the consideration of the reform trends in the surrounding countries so that Spain is not placed in an unfavourable competitive position.

The relatively high effective taxation that the Spanish company carries in the European context, showed by some empirical studies, should make us think about reforms that tend to reduce the tax burden on the Spanish company. Though there are many elements which determine the effective tax rate, empirical work has demonstrated that the nominal tax rate is a particularly influential factor. So, a moderated reduction of the nominal rate would have a direct influence upon the reduction of the effective tax rate to ensure that it approaches the average of the European Union.

Besides the described one, there are other reasons that might support a reduction of the nominal tax rate of the CIT. The Spanish general rate of 35 percent, invariable since 1983, though it was quite low at the end of the eighties in the European context, is at present above the average in Europe. This, together with the psychological effect that it might have on the managerial decisions, seems to justify a reduction of the general tax rate by not less than two points.

NOTES

* Dpto. de Hacienda Pública y Sistema Fiscal, Universidad Complutense de Madrid

1. Hereafter CIT.
2. From an economic point of view, only individuals are capable of paying taxes. Corporate entities are only a way to transfer income to individual shareholders.
3. It is considered that the first regulation of CIT in Spain was in 1900 with the Fernández Villaverde Fiscal Reform. After multiple reforms, in 1978 the modernisation of this tax integrated it together with the Personal Income Tax into the Spanish Tax System.
4. See first section.
5. Pure profits of a corporation is the net income over remuneration of all production factors, including capital. This must allow a deduction for an ordinary rate of return on corporate equity from the corporate income tax base. Cash-flow tax would levy the net cash flow from the corporate transactions. The taxable income would be worked out as the difference between the total corporate income (coming from goods and services profits), minus corporate goods and services purchases, including current and capital accounts.
6. Directive 90/434/EEC relative to the common tax regime applicable to mergers, spin-offs, asset contributions and share exchanges between companies in different member States; Directive 90/435/EEC relative to the common tax regime applicable to parent companies and subsidiaries in different member States, amended by Directive 20037123/EC; Convention of 23-7-90 relative to the elimination of double taxation when correcting the profits of associated companies.
7. Some of the main reports are: European Commission (1992), OECD (1991) and "Company Taxation in the Internal Market" (European Commission, 2001) .
8. The exporting country is the country of the residence of the investor. Hereafter "Resident country".
9. The importing country is the country of the location of investment where the income originates. Hereafter "Source country".

10. Also it can be achieved with the exemption in the source (importing) country and the payment of taxes exclusively in the residence (exporting) country.
11. Hydrocarbon research and exploitation companies are subject to corporate income tax at a rate of 40 percent. The following reduced rates apply:
    25 percent for mutual insurance companies, rural and cooperative banks and credit cooperatives, non-profit organisations that do not meet the statutory requirements set out in Law 49/2002, professional associations and trade unions.
    20 percent for specifically protected credit cooperatives.
    10 percent for non-profit organisations within the scope of Law 49/2002.
    1 percent for collective investment institutions.
    0 percent for pension institutions and funds.
12. Another innovation in the 1995 reform was the introduction of restrictions on the carry-forward of losses in the case of shares purchased in companies without business activity.
13. Reduction from 15 to 10% in 1987 and to 5% in 1989.
14. European Commission (1992)
15. From 2004 the maximum amount of sales turnover to which this regime is applicable is 6 million euros.
16. This reduced tax rate was established in 1997 and it is applicable to the first 90.151,81 € of taxable income.
17. Until 1998, reinvested capital gains were exempted.
18. See calculation in Albi, E. (2001) and in the chapter in this book written by E. Albi..
19. The debate on the preference for CEN and the use of credit methods, or CIN and the use of exemption methods, is not closed. There are arguments in favour and against each of these two options. For more details of this topic, see OECD (1991). The main conclusions of the empirical studies that analysed CEN and CIN from the Spanish viewpoint are in the second section.
20. For an analysis of the advantages and disadvantages of the average and marginal effective tax rates, see Bradford, D.F. and Fullerton, D. (1981) and Fullerton, D. (1983).
21. Espitia, M. et al. (1989) quantify effective marginal tax rates in Spain for the period 1965–1987, whereas Paredes Gómez. (1992) quantifies the same tax rates, both in Spain and in the twelve community countries, for the year 1989.
22. Among these works we can emphasise: Cuervo-Arango, C. and Trujillo, J.A. (1986); Sanz, J.F. (1994); Domínguez, F. and López, J. (1997 and 1999) and Romero, D. (1999).
23. For example, Cuervo-Arango, C. and Trujillo, J.A. (1986) refer to 1985; Sanz-Sanz (1994) to the period 1991–1993, Domínguez, F. and López, J. (1997) to 1996; Romero, D. (1999) to the period 1991–1994; and Domínguez, F. and López, J. (1999) to 1998 and 1999.
24. The higher effective taxation for the stock is common to all the studies that relate the results to periods before the CIT Law of 1995.
25. The different works that use sectorial analysis are not directly comparable because they use different sectorial classifications. As example, we can mention Cuervo-Arango, C. and Trujillo, J.A. (1986) that emphasises that the manufacturing sector is the one that supports a higher effective tax rate; and Sanz-Sanz (1994) that indicates the food sector as the most marginally taxed.
26. See, for example, Cuervo-Arango, C. and Trujillo, J.A. (1986); Espitia, M. et al. (1989); Paredes, R. (1992) and Sanz, J.F. (1994).
27. According to Cuervo-Arango, C. and Trujillo, J.A. (1986) the only exception to this general result refers to the debt financed projects. The effective taxation of these projects reduces when inflation increases. This latter relation is not deduced by Sanz,

J.F. (1994), though he concludes that debt is the source of finance least affected by the inflation, whereas the internal financing is the most sensitive to the price evolution.

28. Among these works we can mention: Auerbach and Jorgenson (1980); Boadway, R.W., Bruce, N. and Mintz, J.M. (1982); Auerbach (1983); King, M. and Fullerton, D. (1983); King, M. (1985); McKee et al. (1986); Alworth, J.S. (1987); OECD (1991); European Commission (1992); Paredes, R. (1992); Rodríguez, J.A. (1996); European Commission (2001) and Paredes, R. (2002).
29. This study calculates effective average and marginal tax rates that burden domestic and transnational investments of 15 countries of the European Union in accordance with the tax system in force in 1999. The results are disaggregated for five assets (intangibles, industrial buildings, machinery, financial assets and inventories), and three sources of finance (retained earnings, issue of new equity and debt).
30. 6,5 opposite to 6,33 for the cost of capital; 22,8 percent opposite to 20,18 percent for the effective marginal tax rate; 31 percent opposite to 29,53 percent for the effective average tax rate.
31. Among the works that, from King and Fullerton methodology, obtain effective tax rates for the transnational investment we can mention: Crooks, E. et al. (1989); Devereaux, M. and Pearson, M. (1989); Bovenberg, L. et al. (1989); Frenkel, Razin and Sandka (1991); OECD (1991) and European Commission (2001).
32. In the context of the European Union, this Report supposes a parent company that invests in a foreign country across a subsidiary with a holding of 100 percent. In the same way as in the case of the domestic investment, it is supposed that the subsidiary can invest in five assets and can use three sources of finance. The parent company also can use these three financing sources.
33. Such as European Commission, 1992 and 2001.

REFERENCES

Albi Ibañez, E. (2001), 'Líneas de reforma en el Impuesto sobre Sociedades'. *Hacienda Pública Española.*

Alworth, J.S. (1987), 'Taxation and the cost of capital: A comparison of six European countries', in Cnossen, S. (ed), *Tax Coordination in the European Community*, Series on international Taxation No. 7, Kuwer Law and Taxation Publishers.

Auerbach, A.J. (1983), 'Taxation, Corporate Financial Policy and the Cost of Capital', *Journal of Economic Literature,* XXI.

Auerbach, A.J.and Jorgenson, D.W. (1980), 'Inflation-proof depreciation of assets', *Harvard Business Review,* Sep–Oct.

Boadway, R.W., Bruce, N. and Mintz, J.M. (1982), 'Corporate Taxation and the Cost of Holding Inventories', *Canadian Journal of Economics,* 2.

Bovenberg, L., Anderson, K., Aramaki, K. and Chand, K. (1989), 'Tax Incentives and International Capital Flows: the case of the United States and Japan', in Razin, A. and Slemrod, J. (eds), *Taxation in the Global Economy,* National Bureau of Economic Research, Chicago: The University of Chicago Press.

Bradford, D.F. and Fullerton, D. (1981), 'Pitfalls in the construction and use of Effective Tax Rates', Woodrow Wilson School of Public and International Affairs, Princeton University, Discussion Papers in Economics.

Cnossen, S. (ed.) (1987), *Tax Coordination in the European Community*, Series on international Taxation No. 7, Kluwer Law and Taxation Publishers.

Corona Ramon, J.F. (1987), 'La reforma del Impuesto sobre Sociedades', *Papeles de Economía Española,* 30–31.

Corona Ramon, J.F. and Paredes Gómez, R. (1996), *La reforma de la imposición empresarial en España*, Instituto de Estudios Económicos, colección Estudios.

Crooks, E., Devereux, M., Pearson, M. and Wokey, Ch. (1989), ' Trasnational taxation and incentives to invest', The Institute for Fiscal Studies, Working Paper No. 89/9.

Cuervo-Arango, C. and Trujillo, J.A. (1986), *Estructura fiscal e incentivos a la inversión*, F.E.D.E.A.

Devereaux, M. and Pearson, M. (1989), 'Corporate tax harmonisation and economic efficiency', The Institute for Fiscal Studies, Report Series, No. 35.

Domínguez Barrero, F. and López Laborda, J. (1997), 'Incentivos a la Inversión para las Empresas de Reducida Dimensión en el Impuesto de Sociedades', *Hacienda Pública Española*, 141/142.

Domínguez Barrero, F. and López Laborda, J. (1999), 'Efectos de la reforma del IRPF sobre las decisiones de financiación e inversión societaria y sobre la elección de la forma de la empresa, Instituto de Estudios Fiscales, Papeles de Trabajo, No. 6/99.

Espitia, M., Huerta, E., Lecha, G. and Salas, V. (1989), 'Estímulos fiscales a la inversión a través del Impuesto de Sociedades', monografía nº 69, Instituto de Estudios Fiscales.

European Commission (1992), 'Report of the Committee of Independent Experts on company taxation (Ruding Report)'.

European Commission (2001), 'Company Taxation in the Internal Market', Commission Staff Working Paper, SEC (2001), 1681.

Frenkel, J.A., Razin, A. and Sadka, E. (1991), *International Taxation in an integrated world*, Massachusetts Institute of Technology.

Fullerton, D. (1983), 'Which Effective Tax Rate?', National Bureau of Economic Research, INC, Working Paper, No. 1.123.

Fundación De Estudios De Economica Aplicada (FEDEA) (1988), *La Fiscalidad de la Empresa.*

Gonzalez-Paramo, J.M. (1990), 'La fiscalidad empresarial en España: evolución, efectos y tendencias', *La Hacienda Pública en la democracia*, Ariel Economía.

Hacienda Publica Española (1992), 'Impuesto sobre Sociedades', No. 2/1992, Instituto de Estudios Fiscales.

Hacienda Publica Española (2001), 'Tendencias de reforma fisal', Monografía 2001, Instituto de Estudios Fiscales.

King, M. (1985), 'Capital tax reform', *Economic Policy,* November.

King, M. and Fullerton, D. (1983), 'The Taxation of Income from Capital: A comparative study of the US, UK, Sweden and West Germany', National Bureau of Economic Research, INC, Working Paper, No. 1.073.

López Laborda, J. and Romero Jordan, D. (2001), 'Eficacia de los incentivos fiscales a la inversión: aspectos teóricos y aplicados', *Hacienda Pública Española.*

McKee, M.J., Visser, J.C. and Saunders, P.G. (1986), 'Marginal tax rates on labour and capital in OECD countries', *OECD Economic Studies*, 7, Autumn.

Ministerio De Hacienda (1994), *Informe para la reforma del Impuesto sobre Sociedades.*

Montoro Romero, C. (1990), 'La imposición empresarial: Sugerencias para una reforma ineludible', *Revista de Economía Pública,* 8.

OECD (1991), *Taxing Profits in a Global Economy: Domestic and international issues*, Paris, 1991.

OECD (2004), *Statistical Compendium.*

Paredes Gómez, R. (1992), 'Criterios para la reforma del Impuesto de Sociedades en España: Aspectos técnicos y condicionantes comunitarios', Investigaciones No. 1, Instituto de Estudios Fiscales.

Paredes Gómez, R. (2002), *Evolución del Impuesto de Sociedades en la Unión Europea: Contrastación de la hipótesis de la convergencia a través del análisis de los tipos marginales efectivos (1989–2001),* Instituto de Estudios Fiscales.

Razin, A. and Slemrod, J. (1989), *Taxation in the Global Economy*, National Bureau of Economic Research, Chicago: The University of Chicago Press.

Revista del Instituto de Estudios Económicos (2002), *La reforma del Impuesto sobre Sociedades*, No. 1 and 2.

Rodríguez Ondarza, J.A. (1996), 'Fiscalidad de la inversión societaria: un estudio comparado para la Unión Europea', *Hacienda Pública Española,* 136.

Romero Jordan, D. (1999), 'El crédito fiscal a la inversión en presencia de restricciones financieras: Análisis de su impacto a partir de microdatos tributarios', Tesis Doctoral, Universidad Complutense de Madrid.

Sanz Gadea, E. (2003), 'Historia del Impuesto sobre Sociedades. Perspectiva de evolución', *Manual del Impuesto sobre Sociedades*, Instituto de Estudios Fiscales.

Sanz-Sanz, J.F. (1994), 'Un análisis de las distorsiones impositivas sobre las rentas del capital en España a través del concepto de tipo impositivo efectivo', Investigaciones No. 3, Instituto de Estudios Fiscales.

Zubiri Oria, I. (2001), 'Las reformas fiscales en los países de la Unión Europea: causas y efectos', *Hacienda Pública Española.*

7. Personal Wealth Taxes: the Inheritance and Gift Taxes and the Net Wealth Tax

Laura de Pablos Escobar*

INTRODUCTION

Spain's Tax Reform, initiated in 1977, constitutes one of the most important factors in understanding the main political, social and economic changes in the country over the last 25 years. Even though the change in the Spanish political system that came with Franco's death was the catalyst for the reform process, the success of these reforms depended critically on the agreement reached among the different political and social forces in the country at the time.

As one of the main authors of the tax reform put it (Fuentes Quintana, 1983): "What happened in 1977 was really amazing for many people, because the offer of taxation reform created its own demand. This peculiar and extraordinary occurrence of Say's Law seemed to control our Public Finances: the demands for Tax Reform coincided with what had been recommended in the reform studies and proposals made some years ago." In more concrete terms, the election programmes of the political parties participating in the first (post-Franco era) democratic elections in 1977 all agreed that the tax reform was necessary and the political moment made it practically inevitable. But what was more unusual was the fact that there was a high level of social and political consensus regarding the contents of this reform.

This general agreement favoured a sense of urgency in its implementation. Thus, even before the main tax package got approved, some measures were implemented with the main goal of increasing tax collections. For example, the Law Decree of September 7th, 1977 created a special group of financial and taxation Inspectors that unified separate and uncoordinated groups of tax inspectors.

Just a few months later, and in accordance with the decisions in the Moncloa Agreements, the process of Spanish tax reform began with the promulgation of the Law for Urgent Measures on Fiscal Reform (14 November 1977). This Law had four main objectives.

The first objective was to improve voluntary compliance among taxpayers by creating an environment of sincerity and openness between the authorities and taxpayers. The actions taken in this direction included:

- Allowing individuals and juridical persons to regulate voluntarily their fiscal situation.
- Implementing an Extraordinary Tax on Personal Net Wealth with the objective of improving the enforcement and audit of income and net wealth.
- Eliminating the principle of banking secrecy in order to enhance and regulate the collaboration between financial entities and the tax administration authorities.
- Introducing specific tax offences in the Criminal Code.

The second objective was to strengthen public revenue collections. To this end the following steps were taken:

- The introduction of the Extraordinary Tax on Personal Net Wealth, which besides serving as a control instrument for income tax enforcement, would also contribute to increasing overall revenues.
- The rates for some taxes involving the consumption of luxury products were increased.
- The extension for an additional year of the existing surtax on top of the corporation income tax.

The third objective was to improve the distribution of income. This was supported by the introduction of the net wealth tax and also by a surtax applied to certain types of labour incomes[1] and increasing the minimum exemption for labour income.

From the perspective of this chapter, it is particularly important to emphasise the essential role played by the net wealth tax from the very beginning of the tax reform process. Spain's tax structure had never before had a tax levied on personal aggregate net wealth on an annual basis. There existed great expectations at the start of the reform about what this tax would be able to accomplish, in particular in the areas of the fight against tax evasion and avoidance, and as an instrument to achieve a more equitable distribution of income. Given the lack of a historical precedent, it was quite exceptional that the introduction of this tax was surrounded by very little controversy and taxpayer resistance.

However, historically, in Spain this type of tax had been the subject of a fairly strong controversy, with implacable detractors of this kind of taxation having many passionate supporters. Internationally, controversies with similar arguments for and against net wealth taxes would appear to have been the cause of very few adoptions of this type of tax in national tax systems. In fact, at present, there appears to be little interest in the net wealth tax. In recent years this tax has been practically excluded from any discussion or doctrinal debate on tax reforms, and over time has fallen into disfavour. In the nineties, countries such as Germany[2] and Denmark[3] abolished their net wealth taxes. More recently the Netherlands abolished its net wealth tax on 1 January 2001. Fuentes Quintana (1987) pointed out several reasons for the limited interest in this type of tax, including limited collections, the priority given to efficiency versus equity issues, and overall low political interest. Quite likely capital market liberalisation has contributed to its demise.

In any case, actual revenue collections from the net wealth tax in Spain always remained modest. This basic fact hints that the impact of the net wealth tax was more of an indirect nature, for example how it helped in the enforcement of the personal income tax or its impact on income distribution.

Let us now turn to the other type of wealth tax to be studied in this chapter. The General Inheritance Tax has had a long tradition in Spain, with a history much earlier than the start of the tax reforms in 1977. Interestingly, this tax was not reformed until Law 29/1987 of December 18th on the implementation of the inheritance and gift taxes. The long tradition of the inheritance tax in the Spanish tax system, as elsewhere, is due to its potential as an income and wealth redistributing tool.

However, in recent years, in Spain and many other countries, we have witnessed an important debate with regard to the desirability and convenience of its continuance. In Spain the debate has been more political than academic but it has had specific effects on the structure of the tax. As in the case of the net wealth tax, the inheritance tax in Spain has been gradually transferred (reassigned) to the Autonomous regions since the beginning of the 1980s. And most Autonomous regions have used their normative discretion over the structure of the tax to significantly reduce overall tax liabilities. Nowadays, from a collections viewpoint, the inheritance tax is a trivial tax with a light collection weight. However, academic and political controversies are still alive in other countries.[4]

The rest of this chapter is organised as follows. First, we examine the debate surrounding this type of taxation, summarising the main economic arguments that have been used for and against these taxes. Second, we review the basic features of the personal net wealth tax and the inheritance and gift tax in Spain and some other OECD countries. Third, we study the effectiveness of the net wealth tax since the early reforms of 1977 to today in achieving its initial objectives: improving the distributions of income and wealth and supporting the enforcement of the income tax. Fourth, we analyse the economic incidence of the inheritance and gift tax. Finally, we provide summary conclusions, and list some proposals regarding the future role of these taxes in tax systems.

ARGUMENTS FOR AND AGAINST PERSONAL WEALTH TAXES

The topic of personal wealth taxation has been hotly debated through much of modern history. Because of the longer tradition of the debate over inheritance taxes, we start the review with these taxes and then we move on to examine the essence of the more recent debate concerning the net wealth tax.

Arguments For and Against the Inheritance and Gift Taxes

Let us start with the arguments that have been used in support of these taxes.

The first type of arguments has involved fundamental notions of equity. In this sense, the use of inheritance taxes has been justified as the means of greatly increasing the progressivity of tax systems. For example, Gale and Slemrod (2001) maintain that the equity argument remains absolutely valid in the twenty-first century. Independently of the merits of the argument, the reality is that the distribution of income and wealth has become more unequal in many countries over the last two decades.[5] These worsening trends tend to buttress the equity argument (Slemrod and Bakija, 1999).

However, the overall progressivity of this tax depends much more on its incidence than in the formal structure of the rate schedule and so on. A study at the end of the nineties from the Treasury Department of the United States concluded that, assuming the incidence of the inheritance tax falls on decedents, this tax was more progressive than the personal income tax. Households in the top 1 percent income bracket bore 64 percent of the inheritance tax, while bearing only 25 percent of the income tax (Cronin, 1999).

Against this previous argument on the progressivity of inheritance taxes, it has been argued that the tax is actually imposed on the potential heirs or legatees and that there is no reason to expect that they would have such

Table 7.1 Gifts and inheritance distribution in Spain, 1998 (equivalent net total income in Pesetas)

Deciles	Equivalent Income	Households with Inheritance or Donations	Households without Inheritance or Donations	% Households with Inheritance or Donations	% Households without Inheritance or Donations
1st	416227.9	5.5	481	9%	9%
2nd.	584705.8	4	587	6%	11%
3rd.	719676.8	6	530	9%	10%
4th	822268	4.6	570	7%	11%
5th	940000	2.6	540	4%	10%
6th	1089227	4.2	540	7%	10%
7th	1292093	6	548	9%	10%
8th	1632295	10.6	547	17%	10%
9th	2095535	11.4	507	18%	9%
10th	More 2095535	9	507	14%	9%
		64	5357	100%	100%

Source: Phogue (1998) (author's calculations).

high incomes. However, as some recent studies show (e.g., Slemrod, 2000) the existing data reaffirm the conclusion of the progressivity of the tax. Recipients of large inheritances are richer than the rest of population. The average income of heirs in the United States in the Slemrod (2000) study was 47,433 dollars. But the average income of heirs with inheritances between 2.5 and 10 million dollars was 123,000 dollars and of the ones who receive inheritances above 10 million dollars was 271,000 dollars. For the case of Spain, the income distribution of heirs for 1998 is shown in Table 7.1.

In Spain the average equivalent income declared by households during the survey was less than a million pesetas. However, this type of survey tends to provide income figures that are biased downward. Anyway, it seems that households with higher incomes get more gifts and inheritances than the others.

To continue with the typical discourse on the inheritance tax, the argument is made that if progressivity is the main reason for the existence of inheritance and gift taxes, that is not a strong or valid enough argument.

The question could be asked as to why we do not get the desirable level of progressivity through the income tax. Of course, the extent of progressivity of the income tax is limited. For example, typically capital gains are taxed on a preferential way, and, of course, only in the case they are realised. From this perspective, the inheritance tax would have two roles: first, to tax capital gains that have escaped taxation during the lifetime of the deceased, and second, to increase the tax level on capital income (Poterba and Scott, 2000).

Other less substantial arguments have been used for and against inheritance taxes from an equity viewpoint. For example, it has been argued that there is a need for taxing the advantages provided by the fact of inheriting itself.[6] On the other hand, others have argued that taking advantage of death in order to tax an individual is unpleasant.

Let us now turn to the arguments that have been used against inheritance taxes. The opponents of this tax also have powerful reasons. Bartlett (1997) summarises them as follows.

First, inheritance and gift taxes are usually discredited because, despite the scarce revenue collection they represent, they can reduce the incentive to accumulate wealth in two ways: reducing the incentive to work, and increasing the incentives to consume more (and to save and invest less). Bartlett (1997) actually derides the thinking that the impact of the inheritance tax on economic growth is negative and significant, on the basis of the existing empirical evidence (e.g., McCaffery, 1994, Gale and Scholz, 1994). According to this view, one of the main incentives parents have for working and saving is to leave an inheritance to their children.[7]. Another negative economic effect attributed to inheritance taxes is that on small business enterprises, encouraging their sale and absorption by big companies (Kotlikoff and Summers (1998), Poterba (1998), Maydew (1995), Hausman (1998), and Bosland, 1963).

Certainly, from an efficiency viewpoint, the theory of the optimal taxation does not advise tax inheritances in any special way. However, a good part of the existing theoretical work on this issue seems inclined to the idea that the Inheritance Tax's effects depend critically on the nature of the reasons behind the bequest motive.

In the first hypothesis it is assumed that one person leaves an inheritance because he dies before he expected to and thus did not manage to consume all his wealth. The heirs did not expect the inheritance and did not change their behaviour. In this case, the inheritance tax can be considered as a lump sum tax.

In the second hypothesis bequests may be interpreted as payments for services provided by the potential inheritors. That is to say that the donor tries to manipulate the inheritors in order to get certain services. In this case, the inheritance tax could be considered as an excise tax on purchases of certain services and should be handled as such.

In real altruistic models, it is presumed that a person leaves an inheritance to his children with the purpose of increasing their welfare at the expense of lowering his. From an intuitive stand, there would appear to be no reason to believe that social welfare would be altered. However, it is possible that children who expect to inherit could have incentives to overconsume instead of saving (The Samaritan's Dilemma). In this case, the inheritance tax would be a good tool to reduce this form of distortion.

The multiplicity of possible transfer motives, the significant differences in optimal taxation, and the inability of empirical literature to distinguish very clearly between the motives, imply that conclusions about optimal taxation must be drawn very cautiously.

There is almost no empirical evidence to support claims either way on the effects of inheritance taxes. Some of the empirical studies have attempted to corroborate the intuitive appraisals of bequest motives. It is not our intention in this chapter to provide an exhaustive review of empirical literature. There is a wide variety of good models that clearly illustrate the existing difficulties in providing conclusive results. The model developed by Kopczuck and Slemrod (2000) provides a good example of this. The conclusion reached by these authors, after a careful analysis, is that the effect of the inheritance tax on wealth accumulation depends on the age of a person. At the beginning, consumption falls but it later recovers if a person lives a long time. The effects are not visible until many years after the tax reform. In any case, the final effects will depend on the behavioural response that tax reform causes on labour demand and supply. This result is in line with other empirical studies, which show no conclusive negative effects of the inheritance tax on capital accumulation (Joulfaian, 1998b; Kopczuk and Slemrod, 2000).

In reality, the evidence of the progressivity of inheritance taxes is lacking. Eller (1997) provide findings showing the regressivity of the tax for the highest wealth levels in the United States (Table 7.2).

There are several reasons why the effective tax rate may vary significantly. At the lowest level, inheritances below 1 million dollars in the United States may be exempt, which will tend to make the tax more progressive. On the other hand, those with higher inheritances and subject to higher nominal rates have a higher incentive to employ a variety of methods to reduce the tax burden, for example through different methods of establishing trusts. Clearly, these practices can make rates effectively regressive. In fact, there are so many possibilities for tax avoidance and evasion[8] that some authors have called the inheritance tax in the United States a voluntary tax.[9]

Table 7.2 Effective rates—inheritance tax in USA, 1995

Inheritance Amount (Dollars)	Tax *	Percentage
600,000–1,000,000	651.2	2.3
1,000,000–2,500,000	2999.8	8.3
2,500,000–5,000,000	2748.2	15.2
5,000,000–10,000,000	2053.4	17.6
10,000,000–20,000,000	1384.8	17.6
20,000,000	2003.8	12.9

Notes: * Millions of Dollars.

Source: Eller (1997).

To close this discussion on the inheritance tax, we must add that opponents often deride this tax as inefficient, inequitable (Smith, 1995) and with high administration costs and a high evasion possibility. In reality, it is hard to establish what is fact and what is fictional creation convenient for political design. There is some evidence, however, that the administration costs of this tax tend to be a bit higher than average. In a recent estimation carried out in the United States, administration costs of this tax seem to be around 7 percent of collected funds (Smith, 1995). In Spain, these costs seem to be around 3 percent of collected revenues.[10]

Arguments For and Against the Net Wealth Tax

The lack of interest over the past decade in this type of tax, as already mentioned, has meant that little has been recently written in the literature about it. The traditional arguments in support of the Net Wealth Tax can be classified into four categories (Sanford, 1983, de Pablos Escobar, 1998):

First, from an equity viewpoint, in one way, there is the belief that the net wealth is a good indicator of economic capability and as such, it should be taxed. In addition, this tax can contribute to increased progressivity of the system, raising the effective rates of tax on certain types of capital gains. Following the trend of all EU countries, at present Spain has an income tax which treats income differently depending on the source, and in general capital gains receive a better treatment than labour income. If a net wealth tax can contribute to increasing the effective taxation on certain assets, as seems to be the case,[11] this would enhance the overall equity of the tax system, thus becoming a basic reason justifying the application of the tax.

Second, the net wealth tax can be a good complement of an income tax that does not tax unrealised capital gains. Not taxing unrealised capital gains may cause a "locked in" effect, but it also turns out to be scarcely equitable. The contribution of a net wealth tax would be to tax capital gains annually and independently from the timing of when they arise.

Third, the supporters of this tax frequently have emphasised its capability for improving income and wealth distribution. In some cases it has been argued that the net wealth tax may be a better tool for achieving those goals than an inheritance tax (Lagares,1972, p.25). Some favourable features of the net wealth tax include its annual incidence and the larger revenue potential. However, there are many more authors who have pronounced the inheritance and gift tax a superior instrument (Atkinson, 1972; Albi Ibáñez, 1974 and 1986; Breña, 1982). In this view, the inheritance tax is a tax on capital, while net wealth tax is only nominally a tax on capital but effectively taxes income. As such, a main reason for inequality is wealth transfers, which can also be considered unfair and uncertain.[12] This controversy does not imply that the two taxes are actually incompatible. With proper management and regulations, the two taxes can be perfectly combined and useful as tools for improving the distribution of income and wealth.

Fourth, the use of the net wealth tax has been justified because of its possible use for controlling and managing the enforcement of the personal income tax and the inheritance and donations tax. In particular,

- the net wealth tax helps the verification of income. Net wealth elements will show revenues derived from them that have been hidden and reciprocally the different revenue entries will demonstrate the capital assets that are used as support and have not been declared. In addition, the net wealth tax allows controlling capital gains because their presence should imply changes in the taxpayer's net wealth. But from the enforcement angle, the most important contribution of the tax is to provide information on the net wealth value that a taxpayer has at the beginning and at the end of each fiscal year. This is really important information for auditing income flows.
- annual net wealth reports are useful in reconstructing the value of inheritances when someone dies.

Several arguments have been used to detract the net wealth tax. The disqualification of this tax is most frequently based on the chance that its implementation would affect savings negatively. However, theoretical studies have produced indeterminate results on this issue and there are only a few empirical studies that have found evidence of the negative effects on savings. It is more likely that the tax has led to modifications in the patterns of the net wealth composition due to the great heterogeneity of valuation criteria that are applied in Spain at the moment of calculating the tax base.

Likewise, it has been argued that the net wealth tax can be a disincentive for foreign investment, mainly because not all countries, and from Spain's perspective not all EU countries, have a tax of this nature. This argument needs to be taken into account.

The problems associated with the management and administration of the net wealth tax have also been used as arguments against its use. These problems are of different kinds. There are many difficulties with acquiring information on the assets in taxpayers' hands, legal ownership of the same, and their valuation. The existence of legal entities and other organisations, to which wealth may be attributable, is a well-known and common problem in income taxation. The difficulty associated with arriving at the proper value of each one of the assets has been the most mentioned reason by detractors of this tax. The choice of criteria and procedures should be carefully considered; also many factors should be taken into account in their selection, such as administrative and management costs.

BASIC CHARACTERISTICS OF THE NET WEALTH TAX: SPAIN AND OTHER COUNTRIES

The net wealth tax has never played an important role in advanced tax systems, and year after year, its importance has continuously declined. As we already mentioned in the introduction, countries such as Germany and Denmark abolished their net wealth taxes in the 1990s. The Netherlands abolished its net wealth tax in January 2001. The reasons offered during those countries' reforms were centred on the fact that the net wealth tax has had more problems than advantages. The presence of this type of taxation in other countries' tax systems has been dependent on political changes.[13] Nowadays, the net wealth tax is only implemented in six European tax systems (Finland, France, Sweden, Norway, Luxembourg and Spain).[14]

The main characteristics of the Spanish net wealth tax include:

- Resident individuals are subject to the net wealth tax. Spouses must file individual separate returns. If the taxpayers are married under a joint property regime, the assets are attributed to the spouses on a 50/50 basis, unless another method of apportionment can be substantiated. If they are married under a separate property regime, the assets are attributed to the appropriate owner. The tax is levied on the net wealth. Debts and liabilities that decrease the net wealth value are deductible from the base.

- The net wealth tax is assigned to the Autonomous regions: all revenue collections generated in the region's territory accrue to the Autonomous regional government. The usual residence of the taxpayer is taken into account. The regional governments have discretion to regulate the level of the minimum exempt, any deductions, and the rate structure of the tax.[15]
- Taxpayers residing in Spain pay the tax on their worldwide wealth, while non-residents pay the tax only for the assets located in Spain. However, non-residents do not have a full reductions right; they are just able to deduct those debts that decrease the value of properties located in Spain. The value of different assets is calculated on the basis of rules established in the tax law. Most of these value rules are very specific to the asset, leaving the use of the fair market value as a residual criterion. Examples: immovable properties are often valued on the basis of administrative values; shares from (stock market) unquoted companies on the basis of accounting values, and the shares from (stock market) quoted companies on their fair market value. The result of the application of these appraisal rules is that values are really different for each asset. These regulations made the net wealth tax very inequitable and this became one of its main problems.
- Assets of businesses and professional shares are exempt. It is required that the activity be exercised by the taxpayer in a usual, personal and direct way and become his main source of income. It is considered that this requirement has been fulfilled when at least 50 percent of taxable personal income liability is derived from profits of business and professional activities.
- Works of art and antiquities are exempt as long as they achieve certain requirements. The same applies to properties of historical artistic value, patents and copyrights, and consolidated pensions' rights.
- The rates are progressive and range from 0.2 percent to 2.5 percent.
- The aggregated burden of income tax and the net wealth tax due by a resident taxpayer may not exceed 60 percent of his total regular (annual) taxable income. If it exceeds that amount, the taxpayer may reduce his net wealth tax liability by the excess amount to a maximum of 80 percent of the net wealth tax liability.
- The principal residence of the taxpayer has remained exempt due to the measures approved and considered under Law 6/2000. (The maximum amount was 150,253 euros in 2003).

- Resident taxpayers have a minimum exemption on net wealth of 108,182.18 euros. This minimum exemption works like a deduction.
- Residents in Spain should always file this tax if net wealth is over 108,182.18 euros or if the gross value of the property subjected to taxation is over 601,012.10 euros.[16]

The net wealth tax applied in other European countries tends to be simpler than the Spanish case. For example, the property of spouses and children is taxed jointly; generally, the value of net wealth is fair market value; there are fewer exemptions than in Spain; personal allowances are lower; and the tax rates are also lower, usually less than 1 percent and the top rate is 1.8 percent. Some of the exemptions applied in Spain are unusual in other European countries, e.g. assets of business and professional shares. See Table 7.3 for a description by country.

Table 7.3 European net wealth tax

FINLAND

Taxable persons
Resident individuals are subject to national net wealth tax. The property of spouses and children is taxed jointly.

Taxable Base
Property subject to taxation includes all assets owned by the taxpayer. The value, generally, is the fair market value. However several exceptions are applied. Examples: values of assets used in a business are taken at their book value. Securities, including shares, employee stock options and various derivative instruments are valued at 70 percent.

Deductions on the taxable base
Residents: debts may be deducted according to rules for corresponding assets. Taxpayers who are non resident only deduct debts attributable to assets subject to tax in Finland.
Resident married taxpayers are allowed deductions of EUR 2,000 for each dependent child under 17.

Rates: EUR 80 on the net wealth of EUR 185,000 and 0.9 percent on the amount over it.

LUXEMBOURG

Taxable persons
Resident individuals and companies are subject to the net wealth tax. The property of spouses and children is taxed jointly.

Table 7.3 European net wealth tax (continued)

LUXEMBOURG (continued) **Taxable base** It is worldwide net wealth: the value of the assets less liabilities. Usually the assets are valued at the fair market value. However, some elements are subjected to specific valuation. **Exemptions** EUR 75,000 (double for married couples) for bank deposits. EUR 75,000 for insurance contracts (double for married couples). EUR 25,000 for art collections. Resident individuals have a reduction of EUR 2,500. **Rate**: 0.5 percent
FRANCE **Taxable persons** Resident individuals are subject to an annual net wealth tax. **Taxable Base** Fair market value of assets owned, minus liabilities. **Exemptions** Tax is levied if the net wealth value exceeds EUR 720,000. **Rates**: are progressive and vary from 0.55 to 1.80 percent.
NORWAY **Taxable persons** Resident individuals are subject to national and municipal net wealth taxes. The property of spouses and children are taxed jointly if they are living together. **Taxable Base** The net wealth taxes are levied on the net tax value of the assets. The property of spouses and children is taxed jointly. Unquoted companies are valued at 65 percent of the company's net tax value. Shares in unquoted non resident companies are valued at 65 percent.

Table 7.3 European net wealth tax (continued)

<u>NORWAY</u> (continued) **Exemptions** The value of personal property up to NOK 100,000 is exempt. **Rates** The national net wealth tax is levied at progressive rates on net wealth in excess of NOK 120,000. There are only two rates: 0.2 and 0.4 percent. The municipal net wealth tax is also levied only on net wealth in excess of NOK 120,000 and it has only one rate that may vary between municipalities from 0.7 to 0.4 percent.
<u>SWEDEN</u> **Taxable persons** Resident individuals are subject to a national net wealth tax. However, foreigners temporarily residing in Sweden for a maximum of 3 years are deemed not to be resident for net wealth tax purposes. The property of spouses and children under 18 is taxed jointly if they are living together. **Taxable base** The tax is levied on worldwide capital owned: the value of all assets less liabilities. **Exemptions** Tax is only levied if the taxpayer net wealth exceeds SEK 1.5 million for single taxpayers and SEK 2 million for those taxed jointly. **Rate:** 1.5 percent

Source: Adapted from Kesti (2004),

BASIC STRUCTURAL ASPECTS OF THE INHERITANCE AND GIFT TAXES IN SPAIN AND OTHER COUNTRIES

The General Inheritance Tax was part of the Spanish Tax System from the beginning of the Fiscal Reform of 1977. The General Inheritance Tax contained four taxable bases:

- Acquisitions *mortis causa*.
- Gifts *inter vivos* and *mortis causa*.
- Complementary levy on acquisitions *mortis causa* and on gifts.
- Tax on properties of corporate entities.

The tax on inheritance or acquisitions *mortis causa* fell on inheritance shares received by heirs or legatees. The tax rate depended on the relationship between the heirs and the deceased. It was very progressive and could reach 84 percent, if the inheritance share was higher than 100 million pesetas and the relationship was more distant than the fourth degree.

The gift tax was applied on whatever kind of gifts. The structure of this tax was similar to the one previously mentioned in respect to the inheritance tax and the rates were also the same.

The complementary tax on acquisitions *mortis causa* and gifts was imposed on the whole of the individual acquisitions and on gifts over 10 million pesetas. The minimum and maximum rates were 7 and 18 percent, respectively. The top rate was applied if the inheritance share or the gift's amount exceeded 100 million pesetas and if the relationship between deceased or donor and heirs or beneficiary was more distant than the fourth degree.

The Property Tax for Corporations was an old tax, and its origins lie in 1795. In 1964 the Reform Law of the Spanish Fiscal System decided to continue application of this tax. The Property Tax for Corporations was levied on properties that could not be transferred as inheritance. The rate was 0.5 percent.

The General Inheritance Tax was abolished on December 31st 1987 and replaced in 1988 by the inheritance and gift tax. Below we will describe this latter tax, and how radically different it is from the tax which it replaced.

The main structural features of the inheritance and gift tax are:

- This tax is levied on behalf of the 17 Autonomous regions on property passing to individuals by way of gift or on death. Free transfers to corporate recipients are not subject to this tax but are subject to the corporate income tax.
- The tax is applied on inheritance and gift shares received by heirs or legatees and amounts obtained by the beneficiaries of life insurances when the contractor is a different person from the beneficiary.
- A recipient who is a resident in Spain is liable to this tax with regard to property in Spain or abroad, acquired through free transfer.
- Non-resident recipients are subject to this tax only on assets located in Spain.
- In general, the value of these properties is calculated net of debts and liabilities by their fair market value. Some asset values are estimated by specific criteria. Household, furniture and effects value is estimated at 3 percent of the whole inheritance value. When the value of the

household, furniture and effects is higher than this value, it is estimated according to its fair market value.

- In the exemptions chapter, as is the case in other countries such as the United States, Ireland or England, important reductions are contemplated for agrarian and forestry exploitations and for family enterprises. In relation to agrarian and forestry exploitations, and to promote their modernisation, Law 19/1995 introduced some reductions. The transfer of a family firm, a professional business or companies' shares in favour of spouses, descendants or adopted children, receives a reduction of 95 percent of the value of the property transfers. This reduction will be applicable as long as the acquisition is maintained during the ten years following the death of the deceased. Likewise, the acquirer may not sell the firm or get involved in transactions that alter in a substantial way the value of the firm. This and many other reductions are regulated in a different manner by the Autonomous regions. (See Annex Table A7.1)
- As in other countries, the donations accumulation from the same donor is regulated to avoid fragments of the patrimonial transfers that reduce the progressiveness of the rates. In this sense, the donation accumulation is also established to the donor's inheritance. In the first case, gift transfers by the donor to a same recipient will be accumulated for over three years. The years taken as reference for the case of donation accumulation to the inheritance will be the five years previous to the death of the donor.
- Some anti-avoidance measures attribute certain assets to the deceased to include them in his inheritance and apportion to the beneficiaries for inheritance tax purposes.
- The rates are progressive and depend on the relationship between the deceased/donor and the heir/recipient, the value of the property received, and the amount of the previous net wealth of the heirs and recipients. This last aspect truly differentiates the Spanish treatment from that in other European inheritance and gift taxes. (See Table 7.4.) In particular, it significantly increases the effective rates of this tax in Spain. The top rate may be as high as 81.6 percent. This is the highest rate of all EU inheritance and gift taxes. The general rates vary from 7.65 percent to 34 percent. The correction of rates in relation to the pre-existing net wealth of the heirs is performed by multiplying coefficients regulated in the following manner by groups:[17]

    - In groups I and II, they vary from 1 to 1.2 percent.
    - In group III from 1.5882 to 1.9059 percent.
    - In group IV from 2 to 2.4 percent.

The maximum rate would be 34 percent, which, multiplied by 2.4, yields the above mentioned top rate of 81.6 percent.

The information in Table 7.4 shows that individuals (heirs and legatees) are most commonly the taxable person, but sometimes companies are also taxable. The tax falls typically on the share of inheritance and gifts received. In some countries, such as the US and Denmark, the inheritance duty is imposed on the net value of the estate of the deceased person. The inheritance and gift tax is generally levied at progressive rates. The progression depends on two factors: the relationship between the deceased/donor and the heir/recipient and the value of the property received. The rates vary, in the European countries, from 2 percent to 65 percent. In Spain, as we saw, the top tax rate may be 81.6 percent. In some countries (e.g., Denmark, France, Luxembourg and Belgium) there are differences in tax treatment of property depending on whether it is acquired by inheritance or gift.

The most usual exemptions include: reductions of the value of business and agricultural properties; reductions of the value of any transfers between spouses or to beneficiaries who are mentally or physically handicapped; and reductions for gifts and inheritance to charity.

In this international context, we must note that the inheritance and gift tax in Spain has the highest maximum rate but it could also be the one with the lowest effective rate for all the countries reviewed in Table 7.4. In general the tax is Spain is very inequitable and the total burden depends on individual property circumstances. The enormous disparity in how different assets are treated and valued, for example between family businesses and others, is not logical. This situation has worsened since the Autonomous regions were granted normative power on rates and deductions. The situations can be very different, as in Andalucia and Murcia; in the latter there are no special reductions, while in Andalucia there is a general reduction of EUR 500,000 for descendants and spouses. Andalucia also has a reduction of 99.99 per cent on the principal residence of the diseased. In the Autonomous Community of Baleares, gifts to children to buy the first main residence are exempted (see Annex Table A7.1 for more detail on the variations of treatment across the autonomous communities).

Table 7.4 Inheritance and gift taxes in EU countries and the US

AUSTRIA

Taxable persons. Inheritance and gift tax is imposed when property is transferred free of charge. Individuals and companies are taxable if they are resident in Austria.

Taxable base. Worldwide assets are subject to the tax. There are some exemptions: domestic assets of an agricultural or forestry enterprise; immovables located in Austria; property used by a non-resident enterprise with some permanent representation and trade marks registered or exploited in Austria.

Personal Allowances
EUR 2,200 for categories I and II.
EUR 440 for categories III and IV, and
EUR 110 for category V.

Rates. Inheritance and gift tax is levied at progressive rates. The progression depends on two factors: the relationship between the deceased/donor and the heir/recipient and the value of the property received. The rates range from 2 percent to 60 percent.

Double taxation relief
Unless there are treaty provisions to the contrary, there is neither a credit for foreign tax nor exemption for foreign property. However, foreign inheritance and gift taxes can be deducted as expenses from the Austrian tax base.

BELGIUM

There are differences if the property is acquired by inheritance or gift.

Taxable persons. The heir and legatees, resident and non-resident. The liability is incurred at the time of death of the deceased.

Taxable base. Resident: worldwide assets are subject to the tax. The tax is computed on the fair market value less amount of debts of these properties. Special valuation rules are applied to certain property (quoted shares). Non resident: can't deduct debt; the tax is levied only on the properties situated in Belgium.

Rates. Inheritance and gift tax is levied at progressive rates. The progression depends on two factors: the relationship between the deceased and the heir and the value of the property received. The rates change between regions. Example: Brussels: the spouse and relatives in the direct line of ascent or descent of the deceased are entitled to a tax allowance of EUR 50,000 each. The rates vary between 20 percent and 65 percent.

Table 7.4 Inheritance and gift taxes in EU countries and the US (continued)

BELGIUM (continued)

Double taxation relief. Any foreign inheritance tax levied immovable property may be deducted from Belgian tax.

Gift Tax. Gift tax is imposed on the registration in Belgium of a written document in which a gift is granted. The recipient is liable to pay the tax and the rate depends also on the relationship between the donor and the recipient and the value of the property received.

DENMARK

There are differences if the property is acquired by inheritance or gift.

Taxable persons
Inheritance tax comprises an inheritance duty imposed on net value of the estate of the deceased person, coupled with an additional tax on property passing to certain close relatives.

Exempt
The close relatives who are not subject are: children/stepchildren and their descendants; spouse of children/stepchildren and parent.

Taxable base
Residents: worldwide assets are subject to the tax. The tax is computed on the fair market value less amount of debts on these properties. Non residents: only immovable property sited in Denmark, fixtures pertaining to such property and the assets of permanent establishments in Denmark are subject to tax. Deductions are limited to liabilities that are attributable to the taxable part of the inheritance.

Rates
The inheritance duty is imposed to the inheritance net value of a deceased person. The rate is 15 percent. An additional inheritance tax is imposed to transfer of property and the rate is 25 percent.

Gift tax. Gift tax is payable by the recipient, but the donor liable for the tax, and is levied on the fair market value. The rates are different and dependent on the relationship between donor and recipient. Example: from step parents and grandparents the rate is 36.25 percent.

Table 7.4 Inheritance and gift taxes in EU countries ann the US (continued)

FINLAND

Taxable persons. The beneficiary or recipient is liable for the inheritance and gift taxes.

Taxable base. Residents: worldwide assets are subject to the tax. The values are determined according to fair market value. All gifts received by the beneficiary from the same donor within 3 years prior to the date of death are added to taxable inheritance of that beneficiary. Gifts received from the same donor receive the same treatment.

Exemptions
Household furniture and appliances, up to an amount of EUR 3,400, any other gift worth less than EUR 3,300.
The surviving spouse may deduct EUR 6,800 from the inheritance. Any lineal descendant under 18 years of age may deduct EUR 3,400.

Rates. Inheritance and gift taxes are determined on two factors: the relationship between the donor and the recipient and the value of the property received. The top rate is 16 percent.

Double taxation relief. Foreign inheritance tax levied on immovable property may be deducted from Finnish tax with some limitations.

FRANCE

There are differences if the property is acquired by inheritance or gift.

Taxable persons. Inheritance and gift tax is not imposed on the inheritance of the deceased or donor but on each beneficiary in respect of his share.

Taxable base. Net value is calculated less liabilities. In the case of gifts liabilities are not deductible. In most cases, the tax is imposed on the fair market value of the assets. Some assets are valued on specific criteria. Example: jewellery, and art collections must be declared by their estimated value, but not below their insured value. Net value is calculated less liabilities. In the case of gifts liabilities are not deductible.

Table 7.4 Inheritance and gift taxes in EU countries and the US (continued)

FRANCE (continued)

Exemptions. Historical monuments, woodlands, 20 percent of the value of a principal residence, 50 percent of the value of shares in companies and assets in businesses.
Exemption of EUR 46,000 for direct descendents or beneficiaries that are mentally or physically handicapped.
For donations made in full title between 25 September 2003 and 30 June 2005, the taxable base is reduced by 50 percent.

Rates. Rates are determined on two factors: the relationship between the deceased/donor and the beneficiary/recipient and the value of the property received. Between spouses the rate changes from 5 percent to 40 percent.

Double taxation relief. Foreign inheritance tax levied on property may be deducted from French tax with some limitations.

GERMANY

Inheritance and gift tax is imposed:

On acquisitions by way of inheritance and gift;
On donation encumbered with a charge for a particular purpose;
Once in every 30 year period on the property of family foundation.
Gifts and inheritance are treated in the same manner.

Taxable person. Tax is levied on each beneficiary or recipient

Taxable base. Residents: worldwide assets are subject to the tax. For non residents the tax is levied on the following: German-situs property, agricultural and forestry property, land and buildings; shares in a resident company; business property let to a business in Germany.

Exemptions
The first EUR 225,000 of business acquired by inheritances is exempt; and only 65 percent of any excess is taxable.
For inheritance and gifts between spouses EUR 307,000 and to children and stepchildren EUR 205,000.

Rates. These are progressive and range from 7 per cent to 50 percent depending the relationship between the deceased/donor and the beneficiary/recipient and the value of the property received.

Table 7.4 Inheritance and gift taxes in EU countries (continued)

GERMANY (continued)

Double taxation relief. Foreign inheritance tax levied property may be deducted from German tax with some limitations.

UNITED KINGDOM

Taxable persons. Inheritance tax is charged on the transfer of all property passing on death. No general gift tax exists, but to avoid too obvious avoidance an inheritance tax is also levied on certain gifts made within the 7 years before death of a person. Also certain transfers inter vivos are taxed at the moment of the transfer (lifetime transfer).

The liability to pay tax falls on the donor in the case of lifetime transferral though the recipient may elect to pay the tax. In the case of death transfer the liability falls on the executor. In the case where the passing of trust property gives rise to an inheritance tax charge, the trustees of a trust are liable.

Taxable base. Domiciled individuals and trusts are subject to tax on worldwide property. Non-domiciled are liable to tax only on assets situated in the UK except holdings in certain UK collective investment schemes.

Exemptions. Transfer of property between spouses. If the transferee is not domiciled in the UK the exemption is limited to GBP 55,000.

Regular gifts (year by year) which represent normal household expenditure.

Donations to charity and political parties.

For some business transfers 50 percent.

Rates. A nil rate applies up to GBP 255,000 (from 6 April 2003). Above this amount the rate is 40 percent for chargeable transfers and 2 percent for chargeable lifetime transfers.

Foreign inheritance tax levied on property may be deducted (tax-credit).

UNITED STATES

The United States uses a combination of an inheritance tax and a gift tax system that applies to the cumulative total value of all transfers made by an individual during life and at the time of death.

Inheritance tax

Table 7.4 Inheritance and gift taxes in EU countries and the US (continued)

<u>**UNITED STATES**</u> (continued)

Taxpayer. Inheritance tax is imposed on the value of property owned at the time of death. The tax is imposed and paid out of the inheritance of the decedent rather than on the persons who receive property as an inheritance.

Taxable base. Citizens and foreign nationals who are residents in USA must pay for worldwide asstes, and non-domiciles only on property that is deemed to have a US situs. Property is valued at fair market value on the date of death. An alternative valuation may be elected under which property is valued on the date 6 months after taxpayer's death. The value of the gross inheritance is reduced by expenses, losses, mortgages, debts, certain taxes and bequests to qualified charities.

Exemptions. Transfer of property between spouses. For non domiciled this exemption is limited for property situated in the United States.

Rate. The unified inheritance and gift rate tax is progressive from 18 percent to 50 percent. Under the 2001 Tax Act the inheritance tax is phased out between 2002 and 2009, and fully repealed in 2010. The phase-out is implemented by a combination of gradual reductions in the maximum tax rate (from 50 percent to 45 percent) and the exclusion from the taxable base of different (from USD 1 million to 3.5).

Gift tax

Taxable persons. The taxpayer is the donor. It is applied to all US citizens and residents. Non-residents are subject to the gift tax only on property that is deemed to have a US situs.

Exemptions.
Each recipient, each year has an exclusion amount of taxation, which was USD 11,000 for 2004.
An unlimited deduction is applied to gifts made by a married person to his or her spouse. If the spouse is not a US citizen the annual deduction is limited (USD 11,400 for 2004).

Source: Adapted from Kesti (2004),

ANALYSIS OF THE EFFICACY OF NET WEALTH TAX REFORMS TO DATE

As we discussed above, the introduction of the net wealth tax in Spain had been justified on the basis of an explicit set of criteria and objectives. This section of the chapter takes a look at how close the net wealth tax in Spain got to what it set out to accomplish.

The Net Wealth Tax as an Instrument of Control and Redistribution of Income and Wealth

In studying the effects of the Spanish net wealth tax, it is possible to distinguish three well differentiated phases:

1. (1978–1988): from its introduction up to its adaptation to the Constitutional Court ruling on 23 February 1989.
2. (1989–1991): from the adaptation to the Constitutional Court ruling until the implementation of the actual Net Wealth Tax by Law 19/1991.
3. (1992–2001): from the instrumentation of the new Tax to date.

In the first phase, very few normative changes were introduced to the then Extraordinary Tax on the Physical Persons Net Wealth.[18] Not even quantitative limits changed in relation to the minimum exempt. This meant a constant increase in the number of the net wealth tax returns from 1978 until 1988, each time the number of positive declarations being more important. In that period the expected role of the tax was to improve income and wealth distribution and work as a good tax enforcement control instrument. Both functions stumbled on serious problems. First, with the transfer of the tax to the Autonomous regions,[19] the role of the tax as a control instrument became much more difficult. The co-ordination between different tax administrations was all the more complex for enforcement purposes, while its effectiveness in achieving redistributive objectives was severely handicapped. This is shown in the Reynolds-Smolesky Index data offered in Table 7.5. This is not to imply that the tax was not progressive. In fact, it was. But its incidence impact was very limited and did not cause changes in wealth distribution.

In the second phase (1989–1991), the net wealth tax was subjected to several normative changes. The Spanish Constitutional Court declared unconstitutional (Ruling of 20 February 1989) the obligatory joint taxation system of spouses, which up to then had been so regulated. Based on this sentence, Law 20/1989 adapted several precepts of the net wealth tax, eliminating the possibility of joint tax returns. From there on, the assets and rights were attributed to each spouse separately and spouses needed to file individual returns. If they are married under a community property regime, the assets are attributed to the spouses on a 50/50 basis, unless another method of apportionment can be applicable. If they are married under a separate property regime, the assets are attributed to the appropriate owner. That modification has important consequences, of which we would like to mention three:

- The division of net wealth among members of a family caused an immediate decrease in the number of fiscal declarations during the first taxable year it took effect: 1988. There were probably two effects here: the number of declarations should have gone up because two (separate) declarations were needed for each couple instead of one (joint) declaration. Second, with the split of assets, more taxpayers fell under the minimum exempt. This latter was more important. With the passage of time, the number of declarations slowly recuperated.
- The adaptation of the income tax to the Constitutional Court's sentence did not follow the same rules. For the income tax it was possible, and it is still possible, to choose between filing individual or joint returns. This discrepancy between the two taxes makes the control role of the net wealth tax extremely difficult. The taxpayers of both taxes don't have to be the same and, therefore, the data review is complex. As we indicated, all the relevant magnitudes of the tax decreased considerably as a consequence of the mentioned adaptation, although it was not only the adaptation that motivated these declines. Some of the decline was attributed to the increase of the reductions for children.
- The two objectives for this tax pursued by the tax authorities in that period were, first, to use the net wealth tax as a census instrument and as a control instrument for the income tax, and second, to use it as surtax on the income tax. [20] We have just mentioned the difficulties of obligatory individual return filing of the net wealth tax as a control instrument. In relation to its function as a re-distributing instrument, during this second phase the Gini indexes of the taxable base, net base, and the concentration index of the net liability, did not change significantly. These indexes remained around 0.53, 0.67 and 0.77, respectively. The concentration degrees are truly elevated, above all in the case of net base and net liability. The Suits index measures the degree of concentration of the net liability in relation to the taxable base. It is often used to measure the degree of tax progressiveness. Positive values indicate that the tax is progressive. The Kakwani index corroborates this result (see Table 7.7). In this second phase, again we have to repeat the same conclusion: the tax was progressive but its

incidence was so small that it did not change wealth distribution in any practical sense.

In the third phase, the new net wealth tax was applied on 1 January 1992, and it meant the end of the exceptional and transitory character that the Extraordinary Tax on the Physical Person Net Wealth had until this time. As we briefly saw above, some of the most important changes of this period are:

- Assets of business and professional shares are exempt. It is required that the activity be exercised by the taxpayers on a usual, personal and direct way and become his main source of income.
- The aggregate burden of the income tax and the net wealth tax on a resident taxpayer may not exceed 60 percent of his total regular taxable income.[21] If it exceeds that amount, the taxpayer may reduce his net wealth tax liability by the excess amount to a maximum of 80 percent of the net wealth tax liability, as originally calculated. That means that the taxpayer must pay at least 20 percent of net wealth tax liability.
- Works of art and antiquities are exempt as long as they achieve certain requirements. The same applies with properties of historical artistic value, patents and copyrights, and consolidated pensions' rights.
- The principal residence has remained exempt due to the measures approved and considered under the Law 6/2000. (The maximum amount is EUR 150,253 in 2003).
- The tax rates are progressive and range from 0.2 percent to 2.5 percent.

Without forgetting its census role, the objectives that are attributed to net wealth tax in its current form put more emphasis on its performance in regard to a more productive utilisation of wealth and as a supplement to the income tax. In addition, there is still potential in this tax as a redistributive tool for income and wealth.

During this phase, the number of tax declarations did not recover the level reached in 1990. In reality, the number of declarations fell in 2001, possibly due to the exemption of the principal residence. Although the taxable base increased significantly, that increase did not translate into a superior effective tax. The degree of progressivity remains more or less as in previous phases, although in general, the concentration degrees of the tax's main magnitudes decreased in a significant manner, pointing at a more equal distribution of bases and liabilities. The Reynolds-Smolensky Index in 1992 indicates a significant re-distributive effect of the net wealth tax. This effect is fairly neutralised in subsequent exercises, although we note again the decreases in the Gini and Concentration Indexes for all of the

Table 7.5 Evolution of reductions in the net wealth tax

Pesetas	**1980–1987**	**1988–1990**	**1991**	**1992–1994**	**1995–1997**	**1999**	**2003**
Minimum Exempt	6,000,000	9,000,000	10,000,000	15,000,000	17,000,000	17,300,000	€ 108,182,18
Matrimony	2,000,000	–	–	7,000,000[(1)]	–	–	–
Deduction Children	500,000	1,500,000	1,500,000	–	–	–	–
Disabled or Handicapped Children	–	–	–	–	–	–	–
With Deduction	1,000,000	3,000,000	3,000,000	–	–	–	–

Notes: (1) Only for 1994, and for reviewed administration values.

Source: Records of the Tax Office (author's computations).

Table 7.6 Evolution of main magnitudes of the net wealth tax

	1986	1990	1992	1994	1997	1999	2001
TAXABLE BASE							
Nº of declarations	779,964	973,789	862,940	809,339	892,214	980,956	873,812
Total amount in millions of pesetas	16,863,937	27,954,109	29,686,352	34,392,835	48,851,930	55,286,189	52,465,381
Average amount in millions of pesetas	21.62	28.71	34.40	42.49	51.39	56.3	60.04
TAXABLE BASE LESS REDUCTION							
Nº of declarations	778,335	912,691	831,585	781,463	891,297	980,167	871,963
Total amount in millions of pesetas	10,343,101	19,920,026	19,889,580	23,038,357	31,240,575	38,892,775	37,329,294
Average amount in millions of pesetas	13.29	21.83	23.918	29.48	35.05	39.6	42.8
GROSS LIABILITY							
Nº of declarations	523,781	902,405	829,842	780,830	876,527	968,632	853,075
Total amount in millions of pesetas	42,378	70,559	83173	118,826	129,357	171,159	167,748
Average amount in millions of pesetas	0.081	0.078	0.1	0.119	0.15	0.176	0.196
EFFECTIVE RATES							
On liquidating base	0.41%	0.35%	0.42%	0.40%	0.41%	0.44	0.44

Source: Records of the Tax Office (author's computations).

Table 7.7 Gini and connection indexes for the net wealth tax

	1985	1987	1989	1991	1992	1994	1997	1999
Taxable Base	0.5678	0.568	0.546	0.5287	0.4223	0.4233	0.3873	0.4484
Liquidating base	0.881	0.8827	0.6779	0.6609	0.6536	ND	0.5491	0.6063
Quota to be entered	0.8792	0.8873	0.7987	0.7802	0.7791	0.745	0.7119	0.7794
CONCENT. INDEX BI –CI	0.568	0.567	0.5456	0.5281	0.3674	0.4227	0.3872	0.4493
Other Indexes	1985	1987	1989	1991	1992	1994	1997	1999
Suits	0.5228	0.5067	0.4096	0.3741	0.4355	0.4079	0.44	0.42
Reynolds-Smolensky	-0.001	0.001	-0.001	+0.0006	+0.0549	+0.0006	+0.0001	-0.001
Kakwani	0.3114	0.3193	0.2527	0.2515	0.3568	0.3217	0.3246	0.3260

Source: Records of the Tax Office (author's computations).

main magnitudes of the Tax. However, this tendency practically stops in 1999 (See Table 7.7).

The Role of the Net Wealth Tax as a Complement of the Income Tax

One of the highest theoretical objectives attributed to net wealth tax is its possible contribution as surtax on personal capital income. This possible role finds greater justification when we observe the very favourable income tax treatment of capital gains in most of the EU countries.

A way to verify if the net wealth tax has been able to tax incomes from capital sources is to calculate the effective burden represented by that Tax with respect to the different income presumably obtained from different assets. The purpose is to know the effective burden supported by determinate assets, attributable exclusively to the net wealth tax.

Simplifying a bit, we could summarise our methodology into the following steps. In the first place, we are interested in isolating exclusively the taxable burden derived from the net wealth tax. In the second place, this tax is nominal on the capital, so we have to calculate the decrease in the gross wealth of the taxpayer attributed to this tax. And last but not least, although it is a nominal levy on capital, it is presumed to be an effective levy on the income, so the tax liability calculated on the taxpayers' net wealth has to be effective on the profitability of each kind of asset. In short, the tax liability is calculated exclusively following the net wealth tax regulation and applying exclusively this tax, while the effective burden is calculated as the ratio of this liability to the income that presumably each asset yielded to its owner. Those rental incomes, contrary to what is presumed in the effective rate literature, are not deemed equal for all the assets, but different for each asset.

The computations are done for the years 1990, 1992 and 2000. This selection corresponds to the tax's effect period during which it was affirmed that it would act as an income tax complement; besides, some important normative changes occurred during this period.

The assets that have a more specific weight on the declared net wealth are:

- Real estate inheritance, mainly urban property.
- Participation in entities, although during these last years shares quoted in the stock exchange market have acquired more weight than the ones not quoted.
- Bank deposits.

From all these assets we calculated the effective rates on real estate assets, quoted shares, and bank deposits.

In each one of the referenced years, the net wealth tax rules are applied in relation to the analysed assets. Accordingly, we calculated the net taxable base in terms of the specific weight of the asset in the taxpayer's gross wealth composition, the minimum exemption established for the tax, and the debts which would supposedly affect the taxpayer. This latter information is taken from the information published by the Tax Administration Agency. From those data, we calculated the marginal rate and the tax liability that correspond to each assumed taxpayer. This work is performed for five different scenarios and for each asset.[22]

The five scenarios of assumed taxpayers are:

- Taxpayers with 35 million ptas of gross wealth.
- Taxpayers with 100 million ptas of gross wealth.
- Taxpayers with 500 million ptas of gross wealth.
- Taxpayers with 1,500 million ptas of gross wealth.
- Taxpayers with 4,000 million ptas of gross wealth.

The results obtained are presented in Annex Tables A7.2, A7.3, and A7.4. They are in nominal terms and can be summarised in a synthetic manner as follows: unoccupied houses are the ones that support greater nominal burdens. In fact, during the year 2000, for values near the fair market price and patrimonies greater than 500 million pesetas, the effective rate could be 100 percent or more of the rental income. In general, it can be affirmed that the effective marginal burden supported by the ownership of houses is high and increasing through time, and depends, above all, on the value criterion that the taxpayer must use for computing the house value and the net wealth amount.

In relation to the burden imposed on quoted shares, it depends on the quoting value and the gross wealth amount of the taxpayer. The year 2000, given the evolution followed by the Stock Exchange, presents truly high rates (see Table A7.3 in the Annex).

Bank deposits paid lesser taxes during the year 1999. But during 2000, large patrimonies were paid for these types of assets, mainly the total amount of the investment yield.

In general, we can say that the net wealth tax works like surtax for the income tax especially if the taxpayer possesses a net wealth over 100 million. Besides, the net wealth tax has become harder as the taxation of capital gains has been reduced. Obviously, its role as a complement to the income tax is only for persons who are subject to net wealth tax. These taxpayers represent about 10 percent of the total income tax returns. In addition we must remember that the aggregate burden of the income tax and the net wealth tax due by a resident taxpayer may not exceed 60 percent of his total regular taxable income. This limitation means that we must be cautious with the results of our investigation.

THE INCIDENCE OF THE INHERITANCE AND GIFT TAXES

The incidence analysis of inheritance and gift tax gets complicated because the data provided by the Tax Agency are few and discontinuous. In particular, the same information is not offered every year; even in some recent years there is no information at all. These information difficulties have been, very possibly, augmented by assigning the tax to the Autonomous regions. In the case of inheritance and gift tax, the Autonomous regions not only have responsibility for collections, but also have normative power to decide reductions, tax rates, and deductions. This fact has led to some notable differences in the tax regulations among different Autonomous regions. For example: in the Basque Country and Navarra, inheritances and gifts transferred in a direct relationship line and between spouses, are exempt.[23] Nowadays, most of the Autonomous regions have their own different reductions and deductions (see Annex Table A7.1).

Besides the potential inequities these differences create across Autonomous regions, the common regulations of the tax present other important problems. Some of these problems include:

- Different treatment of gifts and inheritance taxes, in favour of the latter. Besides, gifts are also encumbered by income tax.
- The application of exemptions that leave transferences mortis causa out of the tax system, without sufficient justification from the point of view of economic efficiency, and which also produce very serious inequities. We also have to mention favourable fiscal treatment given to family firms. This privilege is usually justified as a way to help family businesses. However, this privilege and others associated with this tax, go against reducing wealth inequalities and also produce an unequal application of the tax.
- Generally the closest family members have lower taxes than other heirs or recipients. This is common in the European tax practice, but if excessive, could go against the inheritance and gift tax objectives.
- The common normative applicable for computing the value of the net wealth to tax produces situations of great juridical uncertainty for the

taxpayer. In general property must be valued at its real value on the date of death, but it is difficult to know which one is the real value: fair value, accounting value, administrative value, etc.

- The application of the tariff jointly with the corrections for the previous net wealth of the heir or recipient, produces an excessively progressive tax (higher than the European taxes) and it penalises savings. Also it produces "step type rates errors".[24] All these factors, together, do not provide an incentive for a high degree of tax compliance (González and Cabrillo, 2001).
- In relation to the incidence of the inheritance and gift tax, we have some data provided by the Tax Agency, based on a sample of the inheritance tax returns presented at the Madrid tax offices for the years 1988, 1989, 1990, 1991 and 1992.[25] In general terms, referring in first place to the inheritance tax, more than 50 percent of the persons who presented their inheritance tax returns belong to the low and medium levels of the taxable base and to Group II (descendants older than 21, ascendants, spouses and adopted persons.) Besides, they consign a pre-existing net wealth lower than 50 million pesetas. In all the analysed years, one can observe a very similar behaviour: approximately 57 percent of the persons who filed an inheritance tax return had a taxable base of around 4 million pesetas; 97.96 percent of these taxpayers declared less than 50 million pesetas of pre-existing net wealth. In spite of this, the collection tends to be concentrated at the higher levels of taxpayers' wealth. In 1990, 0.9 percent of the analysed inheritance tax returns belonged to taxpayers with a taxable base higher than 50 million pesetas, and generated almost 18 percent of the net base and 30 percent of the net liability. This fact shows the progressive character of the tax.
- Donations show very similar characteristics. Approximately 77 percent of the analysed gifts belong to taxable levels under 4 million pesetas. Also, 77 percent corresponded to a relationship degree of Group II and nearly 99 percent have a pre-existing net wealth below 50 million. The bulk of the collected revenues basically come from the highest levels of wealth. During this same year, 9 percent of the persons who presented fiscal declarations for gifts, generated 31.6 percent of the net tax liability. The average rates are located around 12 and 18 percent, respectively. Since 1989, the effective rate is always lower than the average. The analysed data shows the same for inheritance and gift taxes, except that the effective rates are at the same level as the average.
- One of the arguments often used against the inheritance and gift tax is the lack of tributary fulfilment, due to fiscal evasion. We have tried to

estimate, through the number of homes that have received inheritances and gifts, the approximate number of potential tax filers. For example, during 1995,[26] from a sample of 6,522 homes, 95 answered that they received inheritances or gifts for an amount less than 1,275,000 pesetas; 55 received amounts between 1,275,000 and 6,500,000 and 12 received inheritances over 6,500,000. In total, the number of persons who received some amount of the said transfers is 162, which is 2.4 percent of the sample taken from homes. As was the case with the inheritance tax returns sample taken by the tax office, it also happens that the bigger part of the surveyed persons have a taxable base below four million. Pursuant to the samples provided by the Tax Office, and without great inter-annual variations, the majority of the inheritances are produced between parents and children, or descendants, and between spouses. Concretely, more than 50 percent of the inheritances and donations occur in favour of descendants over 21 years of age. Inheritances in those cases are subject to reductions that would leave all the heirs out of the effective tax margin. But if an heir is under 21 years of age, there would be much higher reductions, and for this reason, it is probable that some of the surveyed persons were exempt persons. Of the 162 surveyed persons that revealed having received inheritances in 1995, very possibly more than 60 percent, according to our results, are not subject to the inheritance and gift tax. In surveys, there are always problems with revealing real income, and the results of the PHOGUE analysis during the 1994–1998 period shows this problem clearly. In 1998, of the 5,427 surveyed households, 64 revealed having received inheritances or gifts—very few persons to be the potential taxpayers for this tax.

- Finally, we have tried to study the economic characteristics of homes that are beneficiaries of inheritances and gifts. This study has already been shown in this chapter in Table 7.1. Even though the results need to be taken cautiously, they seem to indicate that the homes with higher income are the main beneficiaries. In fact, the distribution of homes by deciles of equivalent income is much more equitable when we refer to non beneficiaries of inheritances or gifts. Those results corroborate the idea that wealth transfer is the best predictor of the economic status of an individual (Bowles and Gintis, 2002).

CONCLUSIONS AND RECOMMENDATIONS FOR REFORM

The hypothetical role given to the net wealth tax at the beginning of the 1977 Fiscal Reform was essential. Great achievements were expected from it, mainly in the struggle against fiscal evasion and avoidance, in complementing income tax progressivity, and in obtaining a more equitable income distribution. The inheritance and gift tax was reformed years later, but already existed in 1977. Also, this tax was expected to improve income and wealth distribution.

In general the personal wealth taxes are justified because they may greatly increase the system's equity and progressivity. On the other hand, they are usually discredited because, despite the meagre collections, they can reduce the incentive to accumulate wealth in two ways: reducing the incentive to work, and by increasing the incentives to consume (less savings and investment). The existing theoretical and empirical studies are not conclusive on the negative effects on capital accumulation, depending on the predominant effect, income or substitution, and on the importance and probability of evading this tax. Certainly, both taxes, traditionally, have been associated with strong controversies. Over time we can find implacable detractors of this kind of taxation facing not less passionate supporters.

In Spain these taxes have had an unsuccessful experience since the 1977 Fiscal Reform to date.

The main problems faced by the net wealth tax in achieving its proclaimed objectives are:

- The tax was re-assigned to the Autonomous regions in the early 1980s. This new situation made its effectiveness as a control instrument very difficult. The co-ordination between different tax administrations was complex. Also its adaptation to the Constitutional Court ruling meant the elimination of joint tax returns. Spouses, or each member of a family, must file individual returns. The adaptation of income tax to the Constitutional Court ruling did not follow the same rules. For the income tax it is possible to choose filing individual or joint returns. This discrepancy between the two taxes makes the net wealth tax control role even more difficult. Taxpayers of the two taxes do not have to be the same person and, therefore, the data review is complex.
- We have also found that even though the tax is progressive, its incidence is so small that it does not change wealth distribution.
- There are enormous disparities in how different assets are treated and valued; for example, family firms are almost exempt, immovable

properties are valued, in most of the cases, at administrative values, quoted share by fair market value, unquoted shares by accounting values etc. This situation made this tax very unequal, and the situation is very similar with the inheritance and gift tax. The European net wealth taxes are simpler than the Spanish tax. There are fewer exemptions; tax rates are lower than in Spain; and there are fewer personal allowances.

One of the most serious problems with the inheritance and gift tax is the favourable fiscal treatment given to family firms. This privilege is usually justified as a way of helping family businesses. However, this privilege, and others, associated with this tax go against reducing wealth inequalities and also produce an unequal application of the tax. Other problems with this tax include:

- The normative applicable for computing the value of the net wealth to tax, produces situations of great juridical uncertainty for the taxpayer.
- The application of the tariff jointly with the corrections for the previous net wealth of the heir or recipient, produces an excessive degree of progressivity and "step type rates errors".
- The inheritance and gift tax in Spain can be at the same time the highest and the lowest of all the reviewed inheritance taxes. The effective rate depends on individuals' property circumstances. This renders the Spanish tax very inequitable.

The problems of the net wealth tax and the inheritance and gift tax identified in this chapter are often serious. However, this does not mean that either of these taxes should be abolished. It is really necessary to continue the political and academic debates on the desirable reform of these taxes. In this debate we must particularly rethink the role of personal wealth taxes.

In my opinion, personal wealth taxes are necessary in the actual tax systems in general, and in particular, in the Spanish tax system. One of the principal reasons used for justifying these taxes is that they may greatly increase the system's progressivity. This argument remains absolutely valid in the twenty-first century. Moreover, some recent estimates of changes in the income and wealth distributions in the last twenty years show that the concentration of both has increased. Another interesting objective that can be associated with the personal wealth tax is its possible contribution as a surtax on personal capital income, especially in the presence of the very favourable treatment that income tax gives to capital gains.

Some of the main items that must be reconsidered in the reform of these taxes are:

- These taxes should be applicable to more citizens. The use of exemptions that leave wealth out of the tax system, without sufficient justification, leads to severe inequities. These exemptions must be carefully reconsidered.
- The value of the different assets should be calculated on the basis of fair market value. The fewer exceptions to the fair market value principle, the better.
- The inheritance and gift tax is levied at progressive rates. Actually, in Spain, the degree of progressivity depends on the wealth of the heir or recipient previous to the donation and inheritance. These rules push up the applicable rates too high. In Spain, the top tax rate is 81.6 percent. In other European countries tax rates range from 2 to 65 percent. Thus rates in Spain could be lower to approximate to those in other European countries.
- The rates of net wealth tax should be lower, around 1 percent to make them comparable to those in other European countries.
- The tax administration authorities need to improve the management and enforcement tools in relation to personal wealth taxes.

The immediate future of the Spanish net wealth tax and inheritance and gift tax is quite uncertain. It is urgent to initiate a debate around their reform. In my opinion, these taxes should be given a chance because they are still necessary if we care about equity objectives.

ANNEX

Table A7.1 Some examples of the main reductions in inheritance and gift tax implemented by Autonomous regional governments

ANDALUCIA

- 99.99% reduction for the acquisition mortis causa of the principal residence of the deceased.
- 100% reduction for acquisitions mortis causa by the acquirer of Groups I and II (or collated) when the amount of net wealth is not larger than 500,000 euros, with determined requirements.

Table A7.1 Some examples of the main reductions in inheritance and gift tax implemented by Autonomous regional governments (continued)

BALEARIC ISLANDS

Mortis causa acquisitions

- 100% reduction for acquisition of deceased's principal residence, as long as the successor is spouse, ascendants, descendants and collateral over 65 years of age, that have lived with the decreased.
- Reduction of 300,000 euros for acquisitions by handicapped taxpayers

Mortis causa bonification
85% in mortis causa acquisition by descendants or adopted persons under 21 years.
Inter vivos deductions
99% deduction for monetary gift from parents to children under 36 years for the acquisition of their first principal residence.

CANTABRIA

Mortis causa

- From 50,000 to 200,000 Euros of reduction for handicapped persons.
- 100% reduction for amounts received by beneficiaries of insurance contracts.
- 98% reduction for acquisition of companies or enterprises, professional business or company shares.
- 98% reduction for deceased's principal residence
- 95% reduction for historical or cultural wealth assets
- 100% reduction for the assets that have been the object of two or more transfers during a maximum period of 10 years

Inter vivos:

- 95% reduction for acquisition of individual enterprises or companies, professional business or company shares.
- 95% reduction in assumed acquisition of historical or cultural wealth assets

CASTILLA-LEON

Reductions

Mortis causa

- From 125,000 Euros to 225,000 Euros reduction for acquisitions for handicapped persons
- 6,000 Euros additional reduction for acquisitions for descendants and adopted persons under 21 years of age.

Table A7.1 Some examples of the main reductions in inheritance and gift tax implemented by Autonomous regional governments (continued)

CASTILLA-LEON (continued)

- 99% reduction for acquisitions of agrarian enterprises.
- 99 % reduction for individual enterprises or companies, professional business or company shares.
- 99% reduction for indemnifications due to a toxic syndrome or terrorist acts.
- 99% reduction for acquisitions of historical artistic wealth, as long as they are transferred to museums, with determined requirements.

Inter vivos
99% reduction for monetary donations to descendants under 35 years of age for acquisition of their first principal residence.

Mortis causa reduction
99% for acquisitions of descendants or adopted persons under 21 years of age

CATALONIA

Mortis causa reductions

- Variable reductions depending on relationship degree
- From 245,000 to 570,000 Euros reduction for disabled persons
- 100% reduction for amounts received by beneficiaries of insurance contracts
- 95% reduction for acquisition of individual enterprise or company, business
- 95% reduction for acquisition of principal residence
- 95% reduction for acquisition of rustic farms dedicated to forestry
- 95% reduction for acquisition of historical wealth assets
- Reduction assuming that the same assets have been the object of two or more transfers during a maximum period of 10 years

Inter vivos deductions
80% deduction on donations to descendants under 32 years of age for acquisition of their first principal residence

MADRID

Mortis causa reductions

- Variable reductions depending on relationship degree.
- From 47,000 to 153,000 Euros reduction for handicapped persons.

Table A7.1 Some examples of the main reductions in inheritance and gift tax implemented by Autonomous regional governments (continued)

MADRID (continued)

- 100% reduction for amounts received by beneficiaries of life insurance contracts.
- 95% reduction for acquisition of individual enterprises or companies, professional business or company shares.
- 95% reduction for deceased's principal residence.
- 95% reduction for acquisition of historical wealth assets.
- 99% reduction for indemnification of heirs of persons affected by the exposure to toxic substances or Terrorism.

Source: Records of the Tax Office.

Table A7.2 Effective marginal burden

NET WEALTH TAX %

	NOMINAL								
OWN HOUSE	OWN HOUSE			RENTED HOUSE			UNOCCUPIED HOUSE		
	1990	1992	2000	1990	1992	2000	1990	1992	2000
Gross Wealth: 35 mill.									
IPN Value									
0.33	0.84	1.01	1.57	0.34	0.41	1.62	1.3	1.76	4.55
0.5	1.21	1.53	2.38	0.52	0.63	2.46	1.98	2.66	6.89
0.7	1.79	2.15	3.33	0.73	0.88	3.45	2.72	3.73	9.65
1	2.54	3.07	4.76	1.04	1.26	4.93	3.96	5.33	13.79
Gross Wealth: 100 mill.									
IPN Value									
0.33	1.26	2.53	1.65	0.51	1.04	4.07	1.96	4.44	11.37
0.5	1.92	3.84	5.95	0.78	1.58	6.17	2.97	6.66	17.24
0.7	2.69	5.38	8.33	1.09	2.22	8.64	4.15	9.33	24.13
1	3.84	7.69	11.9	1.56	3.17	12.34	5.94	13.33	34.48
Gross Wealth: 500 mill.									
IPN Value									
0.33	2.75	8.63	13.35	1.12	3.56	13.28	4.24	14.96	38.68
0.5	4.16	13.07	20.23	1.69	5.39	20.98	6.43	22.66	58.62

Table A7.2 Effective marginal burden (continued)

NET WEALTH TAX %									
	NOMINAL								
OWN HOUSE	OWN HOUSE			RENTED HOUSE			UNOCCUPIED HOUSE		
	1990	1992	2000	1990	1992	2000	1990	1992	2000
Gross Wealth: 500 mill.									
IPN Value									
0.7	5.83	18.3	28.33	2.37	7.55	29.38	9	31.73	80.68
1	8.31	26.5	40.47	3.39	10.79	41.97	12.87	45.33	117.24
Gross Wealth: 1500 mill.									
IPN Value									
0.33	4.65	10.66	16.5	1.89	4.44	17.11	7.18	18.48	47.79
0.5	7.05	16.15	25	2.87	6.66	25.92	10.89	28	72.41
0.7	9.87	22.61	35	4.02	9.33	36.29	15.24	39.2	101.37
1	14.1	32.3	50	5.74	13.33	51.85	21.78	56	144.82
Gross Wealth: 4000 mill.									
IPN Value									
0.33	8.46	12.69	19.64	3.44	5.23	20.3	13.06	22	56.89
0.5	12.82	19.2	29.76	5.22	7.93	30.86	19.8	33.33	86.2
0.7	17.94	26.92	41.66	7.31	11.11	43.2	27.72	46.66	120.6
1	25.64	38.46	59.52	10.44	15.87	61.72	39.6	66.66	172.41

Source: Records of the Tax Office (author's computations).

Table A7.3 Marginal effective burden (%): shares

SHARES			
	NOMINAL		
	1990	1992	2000
Gross Wealth: 35 millions			
IPN Value			
General Index	0.17	1.45	9.07
Bank and Financial Companies	0.16	0.14	8.46
Electricity	0.2	1.18	8.46
Food	0.18	1.3	6.15
Construction	0.18	1.2	6.53
Portfolio and Investment	0.18	0.93	8.61
Metal-mechanics	0.13	1.33	8.3
Oil and chemicals	0.16	1.59	10.38
Communications	0.18	1.76	12.3
Other industries and services	0.14	1.25	7.38
Gross wealth: 100 millions			
IPN Value			
General Index	2.76	3.62	22.69
Bank and financing companies	2.6	3.5	21.15
Electricity	3.34	4.5	21.15
Food	2.92	3.41	15.38
Construction	2.14	3	16.34
Portfolio and investment	3.02	2.33	21.53
Metal-mechanics	2.15	3.33	20.76
Oil and chemicals	2.57	3.95	25.96
Communications	2.89	4.41	30.76
Other industries and services	2.28	3.12	18.48
Gross wealth: 500 millions			
IPN Value			
General Index	5.22	12.32	77.15
Bank and financing companies	4.91	11.9	71.92
Electricity	6.31	15.3	71.92
Food	5.52	11.61	52.3
Construction	5.64	10.02	55.57
Portfolio and Investment	5.7	7.93	73.23
Metal-mechanics	4.06	11.33	70.61
Oil and chemicals	4.85	13.45	88.26
Communications	5.46	15.01	104.61
Other industries and services	4.31	10.61	62.21

Table A7.3 Marginal effective burden (%): shares (continued)

SHARES			
	NOMINAL		
	1990	1992	2000
Gross wealth: 1500 millions			
General Index	8.29	15.22	95.3
Bank and financing companies	7.81	14.7	88.84
Electricity	10.02	18.9	88.84
Food	8.77	14.35	64.61
Construction	8.96	12.6	68.65
Portfolio and Investment	9.06	9.8	90.46
Metal-mechanics	6.46	14	87.23
Oil and chemicals	7.71	16.62	109.38
Communications	8.67	18.55	129.23
Other industries and services	6.84	13.12	77.53
Gross wealth: 4000 millions			
General Index	12.28	18.12	113.46
Bank and finance companies	11.57	17.5	105.76
Electricity	14.85	22.5	105.76
Food	13	17.08	76.92
Construction	13.28	15	81.73
Portfolio and investment	13.42	11.6	107.69
Metal-mechanics	9.57	16.6	103.84
Oil and chemicals	11.42	19.79	129.8
Communications	12.85	22.08	153.84
Other industries and services	10.14	15.62	92.3

Source: Records of the Tax Office (author's computations).

Table A7.4 Marginal effective burden (%): bank deposits

BANK DEPOSITS			
	NOMINAL		
	1990	1992	2000
Gross wealth: 35 millions			
IPN Value			
0.8	1.14	1.33	6.15
1	1.42	1.66	7.69
Gross wealth: 100 millions			
IPN Value			
0.8	1.71	3.33	15.38
1	2.14	4.16	19.23
Gross wealth: 500 millions			
IPN Value			
0.8	3.71	11.33	52.2
1	4.64	14.16	65.38
Gross wealth: 1500 millions			
IPN Value			
0.8	6.28	14	64.61
1	7.85	17.5	80.76
Gross wealth: 4000 millions			
IPN Value			
0.8	11.42	16.66	76.92
1	14.28	20.83	96.15

Source: Records of the Tax Office (author's computations).

NOTES

* Universidad Complutense Madrid

1. We are talking of personal wages.
2. See Juhani Kesti (2004), Amsterdam 2004.
3. The Danish measure became effective on January 1st 1999.
4. For example, the United States has witnessed in recent years an interesting controversy regarding the existence of the inheritance and gift tax. In 1999, the Republican majority voted for the abolition of the inheritance tax for a period of 10 years. Recent studies on this subject, such as Bartlett (1997) and Slemrod (2000), also demonstrate that the academic debate is alive and well.
5. See, for example, Atkinson (2003), and De Ferranti, et al. (2003).
6. Galbraith (1962)
7. There are many reasons why parents save and bequeath. For a review see Carroll (2000).
8. Evasion is one of the main problems of the inheritance tax. However, not even on this point does consensus exist. Poterba (2000) on a recent estimation concludes that the declared facts differ a lot from the actual facts.

9. Cooper (1979), mentioned in Bartllett (1997, p106).
10. See Esteller-Mora (2003).
11. See González-Páramo and Badenes (2000) who calculate effective marginal rates of taxation on several assets.
12. Authors like Bowles and Gintis (2002) come to the conclusion that inheritances received are the best predictors of economic status of people during lifetime.
13. This seems to be the case of the French "tax on large fortunes."
14. Some countries of Latin America apply a tax similar to the net wealth tax. Examples: Uruguay, Ecuador and Costa Rica have a tax that is levied on net value of assets with rates not too high. In Costa Rica, the taxes on net worth consist of a tax on education and culture, a tax on vehicle property and a tax on firms' assets (the latter apply a rate of 1 per cent).
15. Applying this regulation authority, Catalonia has regulated a general minimum exemption of 108,200 Euros and a special one for disabled people of 216,400 Euros.
16. Some of these amounts differ by Autonomous region.
17. Group I: descendants under 21 years of age.
    Group II: Descendants older than 21 and spouses.
    Group III: siblings, aunts, uncles, nephews, nieces.
    Group IV: 4th degree collaterals, first degree cousins, sons and daughters of nephews and nieces, degrees more distant and strangers.
18. See De Pablos Escobar L. (1990): "Una valoración del Impuesto sobre el patrimonio neto". Monographs N° 80, Institute of Fiscal Studies. In this paper a truly meticulous analysis of the tax is offered, and the few changes that the tax suffered during its first 10 years of life can be studied in detail.
19. In 1982, the tax was transferred to Catalonia, in 1984 to Andalucía, Aragón, Canaries, Cantabria, Valenciana Community, Extremadura and Galicia; in 1985 to Castilla-La Mancha and Castilla-León and in 1986 to Asturias, Baleares, Murcia and La Rioja. In Madrid this transfer happened much later, in 2003.
20. See Records of the Tax Agency, 1989, pp. 121 and subsequent.
21. The limit since 2003 is 60 percent of regular taxable base; before it was 70 percent of total taxable base.
22. The exact methodology used in each case can be consulted in De Pablos Escobar (2003)
23. In the Basque provinces of Vizcaya and Guipúzcoa, this exemption applies only to the inheritance tax and in the case of insurance payments.
24. "Step type rates errors" are produced when the rate tax i is applied by steps. Then, a little increase in the taxable base generates an increase in the liability bigger than the increase in the taxable base.
25. See Records of Tributary Administration 1988 to 1992.
26. See de Pablos Escobar (1989) for a complete description of the survey characteristics and analyses of the data for other years.

REFERENCES

Aaron, H. and Munnell, H.A. (1992), 'Reassessing the Role for Wealth Transfer Taxes', *National Tax Journal*, 45 (2), 138.

Abel, A. (1985), 'Precautionary Saving and Accidental Bequest', *American Economic Review*, 75 (4), 777–791.

Albi Ibánez, E. (1974), 'Las transferencias intergeneracionales y la distribución de la renta y el patrimonio', Hacienda Pública Española, No. 28. Instituto de Estudios Fiscales, 153 y ss.

Albi Ibánez, E. (1986), 'Las nuevas orientaciones de la teoría de la imposición y la política tributaria', Hacienda Pública Española, No. 100, 185–204.

Andreoti, J. (1989), 'Giving with Impure Altruism: Application to Charity and Ricardian Equivalence', *Journal of Public Economics*, 59(1), 55–68.

Atkinson, A.B. (1972), *Unequal Shares*, London: Allen Lane, The Peguin Press.

Atkinson, A.B. (2003), 'Income Inequality in OECD countries. Data and Explanations', *CESifo Economics Studies*, 49 (4), 479–513.

Auten, G. and Joulfain, D. (1996), 'Charitable Contributions and Intergenerational Transfers', *Journal of Public Economy*, 58 (1), 55–68.

Bartlett, B. (1997), 'The end of State Tax? Special Report', *Tax Notes*, July, 7, 105–110.

Behrman, J.R., Pollak, R. and Taubman, P. (1981), 'Parental Preferences and Provision for progeny', *Journal of Political Economy*, 90 (1), 52–73.

Blundell, R. and MaCurdy, T.T., (1999), 'Labour Supply: A Review of Alternative Approaches', in Orley Ashenfelter and David Card (eds), *A Handbook of Labour Economics*, vol.3, Amsterdam, New York: North Holland.

Boadway, Bruce and Mintz (1984), 'Taxation, inflation and the effective marginal tax rate on capital', *Canadian Journal of Economics*, 17, 62–79.

Bosland, C.C. (1963), 'Has Estate Taxation Induced Recent Mergers', *National Tax Journal*, 16 (2), 159–168.

Bowles, S. and Gintis, H. (2002), 'The Inheritance of Inequality', *Journal of Economic Perspectives*, 16 (3), 3–30.

Breña Cruz, F. (1982), Impuesto Extraordinario sobre el Patrimonio de las Personas Físicas, Ministerio de Hacienda, Secretaría General Técnica, Madrid.

Carroll, Cristopher D. (2000), 'Why Do the Rich Save so Much?', in Selemrod (ed.): *Does Atlas Shrug? The Economic consequences of taxing Rich*, New York: Harvard University Press and Russell Sage Foundation.

Chapman, K., Govind, H. and L. Southwick (1996), 'Estate Taxes and Asset Accumulation', *Family Business Review*, 9 (3) , 253–268.

Cooper, G. (1979), A Voluntary Tax?. New Perspectives on Sophisticated Estate Tax Avoidance, Washington: Brookings Institution.

Cronin, J.A. (1999), U.S. Treasury Distribution Analysis's Methodology. Office of Tax Analysis, Working Paper 85, Department of the Treasury.

De Ferranti, D. et al. (2003), i: 'Desigualdad en América Latina y el Caribe: ¿ruptura con la historia?', Estudios del Banco Mundial en América Latina y el Caribe'.

De Pablos Escobar, L. (1985), 'El Impuesto sobre Sucesiones y Donaciones en España y en la Comunidad Económica Europea', *Hacienda Pública Española*, 96, 201–229.

De Pablos Escobar, L. (1985), 'Los Impuestos sobre Transmisiones Patrimoniales y Actos Jurídicos Documentados en España y los Derechos de Registro e Hipoteca en la C.E.E', *Hacienda Pública Española*, 96, 229–257.
De Pablos Escobar, L. (1988), *El Impuesto sobre el Patrimonio Neto*, Universidad Complutense de Madrid.
De Pablos Escobar, L. (1989), 'La incidencia del Impuesto sobre el Patrimonio Neto y su funcionalidad real (I)', *Actualidad Financiera*, 11, 763–792.
De Pablos Escobar, L. (1989), 'Un comentario acerca de los nuevos valores catastrales', *Actualidad financiera*, 6, 421–440.
De Pablos Escobar, L. (1989), 'La funcionalidad del Impuesto Extraordinario sobre el Patrimonio de las Personas Físicas y la valoración de su base imponible', *Actualidad financiera*, 1, 1–47.
De Pablos Escobar, L. (1989), 'La Incidencia del Impuesto sobre el Patrimonio Neto y su funcionalidad real (II)', *Actualidad Financiera*, 11, 763–792.
De Pablos Escobar, L. (1990), 'Una Valoración del Impuesto sobre el Patrimonio Neto', Monograph No. 80, Instituto de Estudios Fiscales, Madrid.
De Pablos Escobar, L. (2001), 'La imposición personal sobre la riqueza: su papel en los sistemas tributarios actuales', *Hacienda Pública Española*, Monographic.
De Pablos Escobar, L. (2002), La imposición personal sobre la Riqueza. Su papel en los sistemas tributarios actuales, Investigación IEF, Mimeo.
De Pablos Escobar, L. (2003), El impuesto sobre el Patrimonio como complemento del IRPF, Public finance Congress, 2003.
Domínguez Barrero, F. (1995), 'Los planes de pensiones como una fórmula de ahorro previsión. Una valoración desde la perspectiva de la planificación fiscal', *Hacienda Pública Española*, 133, 33–61.
Domínguez Barrero, F. (1999), 'Fiscalidad del ahorro en la nueva ley del IRPF: ¿Un paso hacia la neutralidad?', *Papeles de trabajo*, 1/99, Instituto de Estudios Fiscales, Madrid.
Domínguez Barrero, F. and Lopez Laborda, J. (1998), 'Elegir con impuestos. Una introducción a la planificación fiscal', *Cuadernos Económicos 'Escuela y Despensa' No. 5*, Facultad de Ciencias Económicas y Empresariales. Universidad de Zaragoza.
Domínguez Barrero, F. and Lopez Laborda, J. (2001), *Planificación fiscal,* Ariel Económica.
Eller, M.B. (1997), 'Federal Taxation of Wealth Transfers, 1992–1995', *Statistics of Income Bulletin*, 16 (3), 43–46.
Erikson, R. and Goldthorpe, J. (2002), 'Intergenerational inequality. A sociological Perspective', *Journal of Economic Perspectives*, 16 (3), 31–44.
Esteller Mora, A. (2003), 'La Eficiencia en la Administración de los Tributos Cedidos. Un análisis Explicativo', *Papeles de Economía Española*, 9, 320–335.
Eurostate: Phogue (1998), Panel de Hogares Europeo.
Fuentes Quintana, E. (1983), Hacienda Democrática y Reforma Fiscal. Notas para un balance de la reciente experiencia española. Alianza Universal Madrid.
Fuentes Quintana, E. (1987), 'Opciones Fiscales de los Ochenta', *Papeles de Economía Española*, 30/31, 175–193.
Galbraith (1962), *The Affuent Society*, Penguin Books.
Gale, W.G. and Scholz, J.K. (1994), 'Intergenerational Transfers and the Accumulation of Wealth', *Journal of Economic Perspectives*, 8.
Gale, W. G. and J.B. Slemrod (2001), 'Policy Watch. Death Watch for Estate Tax?', *Journal of Economic Perspectives*, 15 (1), 205–218.

González-Páramo, J.M. and Badenes, N. (2000), *Los Impuestos y las decisiones de ahorro e inversión de las familias*, Colección estudios de la Fundación. FUNCAS.

González De Aguilar, C. and F. Cabrillo (2001), *Distribution of Wealth and Inheritance Tax*, IUDEM, Working Document 2001–1.

Hausman, I. (1998), 'Family Limited Partnerships', *Tax Notes Today*, May.

Instituto De Estudios Económicos (1982), *El Impuesto sobre el Patrimonio*, No. 1.

Johnson, B. (1994), 'Compendium of Federal Estate Tax and Personal Wealth Studies', Department of Treasury, Internal Review Service, Pubb.1773, 4–94.

Joulfaian, D. (1998), 'The Federal Estate and Gift Tax: Description, Profile of Taxpayer and Economic Consequences', Office of Tax Analysis Paper 80, U.S. Department of Treasury.

Kesti, Juhani (ed.) (2004), *European Tax Handbook*, Amsterdam: International Bureau of Fiscal Documentation.

King, M. and Fullerton, D. (eds) (1984), *The Taxation of Income from Capital: A Comparative Study of the U.S., U.K. Sweden and West Germany*, Chicago: University of Chicago Press.

Kopczuk, W. and Slemrod, J. (2000), 'The Impact of the Estate Tax on the wealth Accumulation and avoidance behaviour of donors', Working Paper Series, Working paper No. 7960, National Bureau of Economic Research.

Kotlikoff, L. and Summers, L. (1981), 'The Role of Intergenerational Transfers in Aggregate Capital Accumulation', *Journal of Political Economy*, 90, 706–732.

Kotlikoff, L. and Summers, L. (1998), 'The Contribution of Intergenerational Transfers to Total Wealth: A Reply', in Kessler and Masson (eds), *Modelling the Accumulation and Distribution of Wealth,* Oxford, England: Clarendon Press, 53–76.

Lagares Calvo, M.J. (1972), *El Impuesto sobre el Patrimonio*, Características y funciones en un sistema tributario, Libro de Bolsillo del Instituto de Estudios Fiscales.

Maydew, G.L. (1995), 'How to Convey a family Business without Raising a Bumper Crop of Inheritance taxes', *National Public Accountant*, April.

McCaffery (1994), 'The Uneasy Case for Wealth Transfer Taxation', *Yale Law Journal*, 104 (2), 319–321.

OCDE (1979), The Taxation of Net Wealth, capital gains of individuals, Comite de Fiscal Affairs.

OCDE (1994), Taxation of household savings, Paris.

OCDE (2003), OECD Revenue statistics, Paris

Paredes, R. (1992), Criterios para la reforma del impuesto sobre Sociedades en España. Aspectos técnicos y condicionantes comunitarios, UCM. Collection investigations No. 1, Instituto de Estudios Fiscales.

Peacock, A. (1972), 'Las ventajas Económicas de un Impuesto Británico sobre el Patrimonio Neto', *En Libro de bolsillo*, 11, Instituto de Estudios Fiscales.

Poterba, J.M. (1998), The State Tax and After-Tax Investment Returns, Working Paper 98–11, Office of Tax Policy Research, University of Michigan, December, 17, 40.

Poterba, J.M. (2000), 'The State Tax and After-Tax Investment Returns', in Slemrod J., *Does Atlas Shrug? The Economic Consequences of Taxing the Rich*, New York: Harvard University Press and Russell Sage Foundation.

Poterba, J.M. and W. Scott (2000), 'The Distributional Burden of Taxing Estates and Unrealised Capital Gains ay the Time of Death', in Gale, W.G., Hines J.R., and J. Selemrod (eds), *Rethinking the State and Gift Taxation*, Washington, D.C.: Brookings Institution Press.

Ruiz-Huertas, J., Sastre, M., Martinez, R., Ayala, L. and A. Vaquero (1999), Distribución de la Renta y Mercado de Trabajo en la OCDE. III Simposio sobre Igualdad y Distribución de la Renta y la Riqueza, Fundación Argentaria.

Sandmo, A. (1985), *The effects of taxation on saving and risk taking in Handbook of Public Economics*, Vol. 1, (ed.) Alan Auerbach and Martin Feldstein, North Holland. Amsterdam, pp. 265–309.

Sanford, A. (1983), 'Capital Taxes—Past, Present and Future', *Lloyds Bank Review*, October, 34–49.

Sanford, C. (1984), *Economic Public Finance*, Third edition, Oxford: Oxford Pergamon Press.

Scholews and Wolfson (1992), *Taxes and business strategy. A planning approach*, Englewood Cliffs, New Jersey: Prentice Hall.

Slemrod, J. (ed.) (2000), *Does Atlas Shrug? The Economic Consequences of Taxing the Rich*, New York: Harvard University Press and Russell Sage Foundation.

Slemrod, J. and Bakija, J. (1999), Does Growing Inequality reduce Tax Progressivity? Should It?, Office of Tax Policy Research Working Paper No. 99–3, University of Michigan.

Smith, J.P. (1995), *Unequal Wealth and Incentives to Save*, Santa Mónica, CA: Rand Corporation.

8. The Reform of Indirect Taxation: VAT and Excises

José Sánchez Maldonado and J. Salvador Gómez Sala*

INTRODUCTION

The role of indirect taxation in the Spanish tax system has a long tradition, as reflected perhaps by the fact that Spain was the home of the alcabala, the most ancient general form of indirect taxation[1]. By the 1970s, indirect taxes accounted for around 65 percent of total tax revenue, in large part due to the continued delays and failed attempts to put into place a modern personal income tax. However, after successive modifications to tax legislation (see Box 1) since the restoration of democracy, the share of indirect taxes fell to 55 percent of total tax revenue in 1986 and to 45 percent at the beginning of the present decade.

In this chapter we analyse the reform and evolution of consumption taxes in Spain over recent decades, paying particular attention to the new developments stemming from the introduction of the VAT in 1986 and the modifications carried out to excise taxes in order to bring the Spanish tax system into line with European Community legislation. In the second section we proceed to review the situation of consumption taxation in Spain in the years previous to the democracy's fiscal reform. The third section deals with a basic description of the before mentioned reform and includes an analysis of its main economic effects. It ends with the consideration of the role of indirect taxation in the financing of the territorial governments. The fourth section describes the evolution of the consumption taxation pattern in Spain in relation to other OECD countries, beginning in the year 1965. The fifth section analyses the process of fiscal harmonisation of the VAT and of excise taxes in the European Union. The incidence of indirect taxation in Spain is studied in the sixth section from a personal and territorial perspective, given the implications of the latter in the finance of regional and local governments (Comunidades Autónomas y Corporaciones Locales). In the seventh section, we consider the main pending issues as well as a variety of future reform options. The last section of the paper offers some concluding thoughts.

Box 1: Important Tax Legislation Modifications

Law of Emergency Measures (Law 50/1977)—The public was first introduced to the idea of a total reform of the tax system.

General Law of the Indirect Tax Regime (1979)—Laid the groundwork for the VAT.

The Excise Tax Law 39/1979—Dealt with the issue of modernising these taxes.

Law 30/1985 on VAT and Law 45/1985 on Excise Taxes—The reforms of the VAT and excise tax laws in 1993 were made necessary by the introduction of the Single Market.

THE CONSUMPTION TAX SYSTEM BEFORE THE 1977 TAX REFORM

The consumption tax system before the fiscal reform of 1977 had been in force since 1964 and revolved around three main components: the general tax on "company trading" (sales), the tax on luxury goods, and excise taxes. These were complemented by other taxes of lesser importance, such as taxes on the income from the petrol and tobacco monopolies, advertising, radio and television duties and customs duties.

Within this fiscal framework, the General Tax on Company Trading (*Impuesto General sobre el Tráfico de las Empresas*, IGTE) was by far the most important in quantitative terms. This tax was basically a Spanish version of the multiple general sales tax which had been used in other European tax systems and whose earliest precedent can be found in the old Spanish alcabala tax. It has long been recognised that this form of taxation suffers from many problems, arising from both the type of sales tax chosen as well as the specific formulation of the tax. Thus, the accumulative multi-phase or "cascading" nature of the general tax on company trading gave rise to a series of problems: there was a severe lack of neutrality, which promoted the integration of firms; the tax burden was not uniformly distributed with respect to the value of the different goods; investment goods suffered from double taxation, on the one hand from their sale and on the other from the sale of final products whose price included the amortisation of the investment goods; it gave rise to the well-known pyramidisation effect on prices and gave rise to non-neutral tax adjustments at the borders for export and import activities. Moreover, the IGTE did not tax the whole production and distribution process up to the final acquisition by the consumer because retail trade was not subject to the tax. Finally, the tax benefits conceded were very costly in fiscal terms and there were administrative problems which proved to be an obstacle to the efficient management of the tax.

To summarise, the multi-phase IGTE taxed all the phases or stages of the production and distribution processes from fabrication to final consumption (attempting, at the same time, to avoid levying the tax at the final retail stage) in such a way that at each stage the tax applied to the accumulated value including the tax paid in the previous stages, thus levying a tax on tax and leading to the pyramidisation of the tax. Again, the results were the arbitrary creation of para-fiscal benefits, incentives for vertical integration, and in some instances export dumping.[2]

The tax on luxury goods, on the other hand, was comprised of a large number of taxes on a list of goods and services which were classified as luxury commodities. On a first principle basis the existence of this tax was made compatible with other indirect taxes because of its specialised pursuit of the equity objective. However, from an efficiency perspective the tax on luxury commodities had important negative effects since it was levied on the production or distribution of certain goods and services which had previously been subject to other indirect consumption taxes, in particular the IGTE. This thereby accentuated the double taxation effects and the lack of uniformity with which the burden of the general tax on company trading was distributed across sectors. Moreover, because the tax on luxuries was comprised of numerous charges which were applied at various rates, the result was a further departure from neutrality for the entire set of consumption taxes.

The remaining component of consumption taxation in pre-reform Spain was formed by the excise taxes, which were taxes on specific goods which supposedly existed in their own right (*sustantividad propia*) and their tax treatment at that time was independent of the treatment other goods. In particular, excise taxes and the IGTE were mutually exclusive. Excises applied to the fabrication of certain goods and the supply of particular services. In total, there were six excise taxes: tax on liquor, tax on sugar, tax on chicory, tax on beer and soft drinks, tax on petrol, and tax on telephone use. Different rates were applied for each, which again aggravated the lack of neutrality of indirect consumption taxes. Of course, some of the non-neutrality was intentional and in some cases, for example liquor or petrol, was justified because of the externalities the consumption of those commodities imposed on others. Nevertheless, the different effective indirect tax rates on commodities were arbitrary and hardly justifiable. The malfunctions of the consumption tax system grew to a crisis stage making clear the need for deep reform.

The principles underlying the future reforms of consumption taxes in Spain are documented in two comprehensive studies: The first, the "Report on the Spanish Tax System" (I.E.F., 1973), also known as the "Green Book", and the second, "Spanish Tax System: Criteria for Reform" (I.E.F. 1976), known as the "White Book". After undertaking serious critical analyses of the existing regime, these studies proposed a new configuration for consumption taxation in the country built around two main levies, the Value Added Tax and (the new) Excise Taxes.

THE REFORM AND MODERNISATION OF CONSUMPTION TAXES

The process of modernising the consumption tax system in Spain began with the 1978 fiscal reform and was consolidated with the entry into the Common Market at the beginning of 1986. The initial stage covering the years 1978–85 was a transition period with some partial reforms of the consumption tax system.

The 1977 Reform

The tax system in place at the beginning of 1977 had two basic characteristics. On the one hand, fiscal pressure was at a level well below that of the average for EEC members. Total tax receipts amounted to 21.6 percent of GDP, 13.1 points below the average for the European Community (excluding Spain) and representing half of the fiscal pressure of the country with the highest taxes in that year (the Netherlands). Only Greece, Portugal and Italy had comparable fiscal pressure indices. On the other hand, the structural characteristics of the tax system converted it into an obstacle to the process of economic modernisation which was to come.

At that time, half of the government's revenue (from coercive sources, that is) came from Social Security contributions, close to 30 percent corresponded to indirect taxation, and just under 20 percent came from personal income and profit taxes. Prominent among the indirect taxes was the IGTE, a "cascading" tax which plagued interior transactions with distortions and was not neutral with respect to international trade as it gave rise to the need for complex frontier adjustments which, as already mentioned, facilitated protectionist practices.

Coinciding with the change in political regime, the urgent need to meet increasing social pressure in favor of increases in public expenditure made radical reform of the tax system necessary, and this became a priority in the political agenda. All political and social forces were in agreement over the need to tackle a profound reform of the tax system. This consensus took shape in an agreement called the Programme for Economic Overhaul and Reform, and known as the Moncloa Pacts, signed on the 25th of October, 1977.

The starting point of the 1977 reform goes back to a year earlier when the government approved on November 14th, 1977, Law 50/77 of Urgent Tax Reform Measures. This law had a major social impact and informed public opinion of the idea of the needed changes in the tax system. This first step was aimed above all at securing the objective of reforming the tax system and strengthening a new ethic of tax compliance (tax amnesty, abolition of bank secrecy, creation of a special patrimony tax and the introduction of criminal sanctions for fiscal offences).

Within this framework, the Transitory Indirect Tax Regime Law (*Ley de Régimen Transitorio de la Imposición Indirecta*) was passed in 1979 with the primary aim of preparing the way for the Value Added Tax which would inevitably come into force at a future stage. In the following years the IGTE tax rate was gradually increased to levels close to that of the future VAT so that excessive distortions were avoided; property transfers by companies and company income from property rental were subjected to tax; and taxes on the exportation and purchase of natural products were eliminated.[3] Also in preparation for deeper reforms in excise taxation, the government passed Law 6/79, changing various aspects of the Luxuries Tax, including the modification and elimination of taxable events, and the simplification of tax rates.

In January 1980, the new Excise Tax Law (*Ley de los Impuestos Especiales*) came into force, representing the first major change in the area of excise taxes. This reform had the aim of modernising these taxes and was spurred on by two basic, concurrent needs: firstly, the need to adapt the structure of these taxes to the ideas prevailing at the time in the European Economic Community (EEC) with an eye to the eventual incorporation of Spain into the European Community; and secondly, the need to coordinate these taxes with the future Value Added Tax in such a way that they would together constitute the basic pillars of indirect taxation. As a consequence of the above, the excise taxes on sugar and chicory were eliminated and those on soft drinks and telephone usage were maintained conditional on the coming into force of the VAT.

Furthermore, there was a notable rise in tax rates, fundamentally on the Ethyl Alcohol and Alcoholic Drinks Tax. The same occurred with the Tax on Petroleum, Derivatives, and Similar Products, where the tax concept "Monopoly Income" (*Renta del Monopolio*) was replaced by the concept "Excise Tax".[4]

Finally, the Tax on Manufactured Tobacco was given Excise Tax status. The effective introduction of this tax was also linked to that of the VAT, so in the meantime manufactured tobacco continued to be charged in accordance with the Luxuries Tax Law (*Texto Refundido del Impuesto sobre el Lujo*).[5]

Thus, in this initial stage of tax reform the foundations were laid for the future, definitive, introduction of VAT and the modernisation, technification and systematisation of the excise taxes.

The 1985 Reform

The second stage of tax reform covered the years 1985 and 1986. The highlight of the reform was the adaptation of Spain's consumption taxes to meet the demands for entry into the European Common Market.

The VAT was introduced into the Spanish tax system in Law 30/1985.[6] After countless studies and three legal bills, the VAT came into force on January 1st, 1986, in a climate of distrust. Business taxpayers were concerned with its practical implementation while the public was afraid of the possible effects on consumer prices.

The Spanish VAT model followed the sixth Community Directive, whose philosophy is to tax economic fact, meaning the generation of value by firms which in turn determines the value of final consumption, rather than legal entities. VAT is, above all, a tax based on economic rationale whose operational features are carried out in an accounting context. In keeping with this, the main characteristics of Spanish VAT are the following:

- It is a consumption-type VAT, that is, an immediate deduction is permitted for the VAT associated with investment activity carried out during the period when the goods were acquired.
- It is applied using the tax credit method, that is, the VAT to be paid or returned is determined by the difference between VAT receipts and payments.
- Certain activities are exempt from VAT charges. Among these are the public postal service, medical services (except hospitalisation in private clinics with no price controls), social work, education, insurance, gambling, leasing of real estate, services of plastic artists, writers, musicians, etc. These exempted activities only have the right to deductions for VAT paid, which means that this is just another cost for

those companies which sell these types of goods and these will try to incorporate this into the sales price.

- Goods and services which are exported are also exempt from VAT charges in the country of origin. In this case, however, the exporter can deduct VAT paid. On arrival at the frontier of the exporting country, VAT payments which have been made by the exporter are returned to him, so the product crosses the frontier of the importing country free of indirect taxes. At the frontier, the products are charged with the VAT of the destination country. This assures that all the products in a given market compete on the same conditions, thereby preserving efficiency with regard to the decisions of the consumer.
- In principle, three rates were contemplated: a general rate of 12 percent; a reduced rate of 6 percent for necessity goods; and a higher rate of 33 percent for luxury goods. At present, the general tax rate is 16 percent, and two reduced rates, one of 6 percent and another of 3 percent. The 6 percent rate is applied to food products; health material; housing; passenger transport; certain types of hotel and restaurant services; cinema, theatre and other cultural services; rubbish collection; waste treatment; and funeral services. The lower reduced rate of 3 percent is applied to certain foods; books, magazines and newspapers; certain pharmaceuticals; cars and prostheses for the handicapped; and social housing.
- VAT paid on purchases can only be deducted when the goods acquired correspond to activities on which the tax is placed. This means that if a company carries out different activities, some exempt and others not, a pro-rata rule must be applied so that VAT is only deducted for purchases which correspond to taxed activities. There are a series of purchases for which deductions are not allowed for VAT payments made. The objective of this restriction is to prevent personal expenditure and expenditures which are not directly related with professional or firm activity from being converted into firm expenditure. Thus, there is no right to VAT deductions for, among other things, the purchase or hire of vehicles, travel costs and expenses which are considered remuneration as far as personal income tax is concerned, and expenditure on jewellery.
- There is no limit on the deduction for VAT paid on purchases. Thus, if in a given fiscal year the VAT paid on purchases was greater than that received on sales, the excess can be deducted in later fiscal years or the Treasury will reimburse the company.
- Special regimes exist for agriculture, small firms, used goods, antiquities and valuable objects, travel agencies, and retail trade. The equivalent surcharge regime deserves a special mention. This consists

of a surcharge applied by manufacturers or wholesalers to certain retailers in lieu of the VAT which should be charged. Merchants are not obliged to do the accounting needed to settle the difference between VAT payments and receipts. The dues which should be paid in are charged by the suppliers through the application of a surcharge to the sales price ranging from 0.5 percent to 4 percent depending on the type of good.

To summarise, it can be stated that Spanish VAT is a tax which is borne by the consumer, rather than the businessman or professional. Strictly speaking, it does not fall on value added, and its magnitude does not depend on the number of phases of transformation or distribution through which a good passes. Finally, the typical form of collection is the application of a rate of tax to the sale price to the final consumer.

Many taxes were absorbed by the Value Added Tax, including the General Tax on Company Trading (IGTE), the luxuries tax, certain excise taxes (those charged on soft drinks and telephone usage) and the compensatory scheme for internal charges. Similarly, when the VAT came into force the tax deductions on exports were abolished.

The Royal Decree-Law 6/85 adapted indirect taxation in the Canary Islands, Ceuta and Melilla. VAT is not applied in these Spanish territories and they maintained the IGTE along with special provincial levies (*Arbitrios*). Afterwards, Law 10/1991 regulated the special position of the Canaries. As is well known, the treaty covering Spanish accession to the European Community, signed in 1985, excluded the Canary Islands from the VAT regime, under a commitment to introduce taxes which would compensate for this exemption. When the transition period came to an end, the Canary Island General Indirect Tax (IGIC) was created, as were the Dock Dues (Arbitrio) on Production and Exports. These are taxes which come under State law, and are usually modified on an annual basis through State budget legislation. This occurred through Article 11 of Law 24/2001 (December 27th) on fiscal, administrative and social order measures, which replaced the original excise tax with a new one called Dock Dues on Imports and Delivery of Merchandise to the Canary Islands (AIEMIC-Arbitrio sobre importaciones y Entregas de Mercancías en las Islas Canarias), that has been in force since the 1st of January, 2002.

In very simple terms, the IGIC is an indirect tax on sales which is somewhat similar to VAT but which has lower tax rates and is applied to fewer goods than VAT. The AIEMIC is an indirect tax on which each good is charged a specific tax rate in accordance with the structure of the European Community's customs tariffs. The regulation of the formal obligations surrounding the IGIC, the setting, within a predetermined band, of the tax rates applicable, and the administration, settlement, collection and inspection of the tax all correspond to the Autonomous Community. With regard to the AIEMIC, however, the Autonomous Community is only responsible for the tasks of administration, settlement, collection and inspection.

On the other hand, Law 8/1991 (25th March), through which the Dock Dues on Production and Exports was passed for Melilla and Ceuta,[7] adapted the local tax regime of these cities to the second Protocol of the Accession treaty. Article 25 of this Treaty covers the conditions under which the provisions of the EEC and ECSC Treaties regarding the free movement of goods are to be applied, as well as the acts of the Community institutions in relation to customs' legislation and trade policy in the Canaries and Ceuta and Melilla. This tax is basically an indirect tax of municipal character, which is charged on the production, manufacture and import of all types of movable goods, services provisions and the supply of immovable property situated in the cities of Ceuta and Melilla.

The second part of the 1985 reform also consisted of the adaptation of excise taxation to EEC standards. This was achieved in the same year through Law 45/85 on Excise Taxes, which was introduced due to the need to restructure indirect taxation. Excise tax reform is justified on several grounds. In the first place, there is coexistence with VAT generated problems of both compatibility and double taxation which had to be addressed. Similarly, the process of tax harmonisation, which we refer to later, is a problem that needed to be resolved. In the third place, the very nature of the excise tax system gave rise to a series of deficiencies, including a lack of neutrality due to the different tax percentages applied to the final price of each product and the distortions arising from the use of excise taxes rates.

Different options for reform were possible which included: the elimination of the excise tax with its corresponding integration into the VAT; independent conservation of excise taxes, where these would have the characteristics of a tax on specific consumption goods; or making all consumption goods subject to VAT while at the same establishing an excise tax on certain categories of consumption goods. The second of these options was adopted, in line, as we will see later, with the majority of developed countries.

After the approval of Law 38/1992 and subsequent partial reforms, Spanish excise taxes were organised as follows:

(a) As a single stage tax on manufacturers in the following cases.
- taxes on alcoholic beverages:
    - tax on beer

- tax on wine and fermented beverages
- tax on intermediate products[8]
- tax on alcohol and derived drinks

- tax on hydrocarbons
- tax on retail sale of certain hydrocarbons
- tax on manufactured tobacco
- tax on electricity
- tax on insurance premia

(b) As a single stage tax at the retail stage in the case of the excise tax on certain means of transport

In the new regime Excise Taxes coexisted with the VAT in the sense that excisable commodities pay the excise tax first and on top of that they pay the VAT (on a price that includes the excise tax). This is a common international practice and is justified through the negative externalities argument: the consumption of certain goods (the excisable goods) is in some way detrimental to society in that it generates social costs which are not included in the private costs or price of the goods. These additional social costs are "internalised" through a specific tax on the consumption of these products which provides disincentives to consumption as well as compensates for those social costs to the community at large generated by such consumption. Thus, these specific taxes serve not only to raise funds for the exchequer but also as policy tools in the areas of health, energy, environment, and so on.

Principal Economic Effects of the Reform

The aforementioned fiscal changes, especially the introduction of VAT, had important economic effects both with regard to the personal and sectoral incidence of indirect taxes as well as the modifications it implied to the mechanism for fiscal adjustments at borders. Regarding the consequences for the volume of the tax revenues, the political aim of the reform was to make it revenue neutral, leaving the tax burden unchanged in such a way that VAT would provide the same tax intake as the taxes which it replaced. In particular, the choice of the three tax rates of 6, 12, and 33 percent had this objective in mind. It can be checked that the elasticity of consumption tax revenue with respect to GDP rose as a consequence of these modifications. Concretely, using OECD data ("Revenue Statistics of OECD Member Countries") we estimate that the elasticity in relation to consumption taxes as a whole was around 1.0054 for the period 1965–1985, rising to 1.051 for the period 1986–2001. If we consider general consumption taxes only, the introduction of the VAT in 1986 significantly raised the elasticity with respect to GDP—we estimate it was 0.994 during the period 1965–1985, rising to 1.195 in 1986.

Castellano and Raymond (1985) analysed the economic consequences of the introduction of the VAT in January 1986. Using Input-Output tables, these authors argued that the introduction of the VAT would add between 2 and 4 percentage points to the private consumption deflator, based on the downward rigidity of prices and the different distribution across sectors of the tax burdens from the Tax on Company Trading (ITE) and the VAT. Later, Burgos *et al.* (1992) analysed the effects on the main macroeconomic variables, especially inflation, of the reforms introduced in January 1992 on the VAT, hydrocarbons taxation, and tobacco taxation. They found that these taxes added 1 percent to the inflation rate.

González Calbert and Rey del Castillo (1998) analysed the consequences of the changes to indirect taxation for prices. These authors found that reductions in VAT rates translated into an immediate and integral fall in prices, whereas the rises in prices when VAT rates were raised were either not maintained over time or were not integral. Among the various increases in VAT rates, they estimate that the rise which took place in January 1992 produced a practically integral rise in prices. In August 1992 and January 1995, on the other hand, they estimate that the inflationary impact was lower than that which would have been produced had there been an integral price rise. Their explanation for such asymmetry is the incidence of the cyclical position of the economy. Whereas in January 1992 national demand was still rising at rates of over 3 percent, in the summer of the same year there was a considerable weakening which led to a deep recession. The authors believe that in certain periods companies were unable to pass some of the tax increases onto prices, with the consequence that profit margins suffered during what were particularly difficult times.

Izquierdo, Melguizo and Taguas (2001) analysed the effects on the evolution of the Consumer Price Index (CPI) of the introduction of the VAT and subsequent legislative changes to this tax, as well as the effects of changes in the three most important excise taxes—alcohol, tobacco and hydrocarbons—over the period from January 1983 to December 2000. The main methodological contributions of this study are that it employs a level of disaggregation beyond the five classical components of the CPI, which permits a more detailed analysis of the results, and that the sample period used covers all the modern reforms to indirect taxation in Spain. These authors estimate that the introduction of the VAT in 1986 caused an increase of two points in consumer prices. They also estimate that the three point increase in the normal rate in 1992 together with the reduction in the higher rate from 33 percent to 28 percent provoked a further increase of 1.3 points in consumer prices; the creation of the super-reduced rate of 3 percent in 1993 reduced prices by 0.3 points; the general one point rate rise in 1995 increased prices by 0.5 points; the reduction of vehicle registration tax in 1996 caused a reduction of 0.1 points; and, finally, the reduction of VAT on butane from 16 percent to 7 percent in 1999 reduced prices by 0.05 points.

Izquierdo, Melguizo and Taguas (2001) also obtain consumer price series for tobacco, hydrocarbons and electricity for which the variations due to changes in indirect taxes have been eliminated. Aggregating these results with the effects of changes to the VAT, they find that the consumer price level in the year 2000 was 5.6 percent greater than what it would have been in the absence of the legislative changes. This implies that the rate of accumulated inflation from 1983 to 2001, 142.6 percent, would have been 13 percentage points less than that observed.

With the introduction of the VAT in 1986, associated with accession to the European Community, a debate arose surrounding the possibility of substituting social contributions with the VAT in an attempt to favor employment and exports (Benelbas et al., 1987, Servén, 1988 and Zabalza, 1988). The argument used was the potential positive effect of the VAT on external trade in comparison with social contributions which were not "frontier-adjustable". As Spanish producers have tended to be labour-intensive, the incorporation of social contributions into prices would damage the competitive position of companies. Thus, a policy of reducing these contributions, balanced by increases in VAT, would favor employment. According to Izquierdo, Melguizo and Taguas (2001), however, if the structure of the tax wedge is not important, and its level does not vary, the positive effect on employment and the potential benefits to the external sector would be eroded under the present provisional VAT regime and the large volume of intra-Community transactions.

Finally, the complex workings of the IGTE with cascading effects on prices made it impossible to determine the correct rates which should have been applied to compensate for internal tax payments and to tax deductions on exports.[9] Under the IGTE, the result, depending on the case at hand, was that imports were either penalised or subject to deductions and exports. These imports were either given hidden subsidies or compensated insufficiently since no one knew with certainty how much tax had been paid in the case of the exports and what was the right equivalent tax for the case of imports. This situation changed radically with the introduction of the VAT. One great advantage of the VAT is its external neutrality: precise calculations could be made of the needed tax adjustments which had to be made at borders in order to apply the principle of charging the tax in the country of destination. This is the standard treatment of indirect taxes in international relations, in general, and in the European Communities in particular.

Thus, the introduction of the VAT did away with a set of fiscal adjustments which particularly affected export sectors. Therefore, the change in the tax scheme would affect primarily the economy export sector through the alteration of border tax adjustments (Soto Guinda. 1982, p 132). If these adjustments, alongside the substitution of the VAT for the IGTE, would mean a relatively higher burden for imports and a lower burden for exports, the implement action of the VAT would bring an advantage for the commercial balance, and vice versa. According to the *Memoria* which accompanied the first *Proyecto de Ley de IVA* (bill on the VAT; published on the *Diario de las Cortes* from 14-9-1981), the most numerous group of exporters (concretely, around 75 percent, who took on more than the 60 percent of the total exports) was going to be favored by the implementation of the VAT, due to the neutrality and clarity of its border adjustments. On the other hand, the rest of exporters would experience a comparative loss from this perspective.

Indirect Taxation and the Financing of Autonomous Communities

The reform of the system of financing of the Autonomous Communities, stemming from Law 7/2001, granted for the first time a certain role for consumption tax as a financing tool for the regional governments. The previous lack of a such a role for indirect taxation was in sharp contrast with the reality in the majority of countries with decentralised tax systems, where taxation on consumption, and in particular tax applied at the retail stage, is widely used by intermediate levels of government.

Most studies which have addressed the issue of using indirect taxation in the financing of territorial entities have cast serious doubts on the advisability using the VAT as a decentralised tax. However, the experience of dual VAT use in Canada and certain recent proposals (McLure, 2000a) have significantly modified the possibilities for decentralising the VAT.

Three forms of VAT which are capable of use in tax decentralisation can be identified. Firstly, we highlight the experience of Quebec, known as dual VAT, where a central VAT coexists with a subcentral VAT which is employed for interprovincial operations along the lines of the transitory regime of the European Union. Exports from Quebec to other provinces (and abroad) carry a zero subcentral VAT rate, while imports to Quebec from other provinces (and from abroad) follow the deferred tax procedure.[10]

Secondly, we can point to the compensating VAT (CVAT). This form was originally suggested by Varsano (1995, 2000) and adapted by McLure

(2000a). The basic idea is to protect, in interjurisdictional sales, the zero rate/deferred tax of the subcentral VAT by introducing the CVAT alongside the centralised VAT. In McLure's version, the CVAT would be applied in interjurisdictional sales to both the payer of the tax (Varsano's proposal) as well as to the final consumers. However, whereas the CVAT is deductible, in interjurisdictional acquisitions, for the agent paying the tax (the same as for any VAT), for the final consumer it functions as a substitute for the subcentral VAT. The idea of the compensating VAT appears to be particularly appropriate for protecting interjurisdictional sales revenue in cases where a highly professional tax administration does not exist at all levels, as is the situation in developing countries. According to some experts in the field (Bird, 2000), the CVAT may become one of the main innovations in taxation techniques this century, in the way that pay-as-you-earn income tax or indeed VAT itself were important innovations in the past.

Finally, there is the proposal of Keen and Smith (1996), who suggested a new scheme known as Viable Integrated VAT (VIVAT). This is an attempt to address the situation in the European Union where a centralised VAT is not available. The proposal of Keen and Smith consists of a single-rate VAT to be applied to payers of tax (intermediate transactions) within the EU and a tax to be applied to sales to final consumers, where the form of the latter would be a question for each State to decide. This scheme can be interpreted in two alternative ways (Keen, 2000, 418–419):

(a) a centralised VAT (in theory) with a uniform rate plus a series of subcentral taxes on retailers at rates equal to the difference between these subcentral taxes and the centralised VAT;
(b) a common tax at an intermediate rate (which is charged and deducted at each phase without generating revenues) plus a tax on the final sales to consumers at the rate of the destination country.

As Pedraja and Salinas (2001) argue, formulas such as the CVAT and the VIVAT strengthen the possibilities of decentralising VAT and of placing such a decentralisation on the agenda for future tax reform. Both revolve around the role of consumption in decentralised financing and focus on the VAT, whose technical superiority makes it by far the most relevant sales tax in force nowadays and the use of which permits subcentral tax authorities to have control over what is considered the most strategic variable in the exercise of the principle of autonomy, namely the capacity to modify tax rates.[11]

In the Spanish case, the retail phase does not come under the VAT. However, professionals and businessmen which are legal entities are not subject to the special regime of equivalent surcharge. Instead, VAT at the retail stage applies.

In the most recent reforms of 2002 the actual model for indirect taxation at the subnational level chosen in Spain, for the most part, has been revenue sharing with the regions of the collections of the central VAT and excise taxes.[12] The model of revenue sharing is applied to the financing of both Autonomous Communities (or regional governments) as well as local governments. On the other hand, the central government has also granted the Autonomous Communities some degree of tax autonomy with indirect taxes in the form of the Tax on Certain Means of Transport (*Impuesto sobre Determinados Medios de Transporte*). This tax gives the Autonomous Communities the possibility of increasing the tax on the retail sale of hydrocarbons (an option used up to now by very few Autonomous Communities, among which are Catalonia and Madrid).

More specifically, the current arrangements for revenue sharing of central government indirect taxes with the Autonomous Communities are as follows:

(i) A share of 35 percent of VAT revenues, distributed among the Autonomous Communities according to the index of territorial consumption elaborated by the National Statistics Institute (INE).

(ii) A share of 40 percent of revenues from the tax on beer, the tax on wine and fermented drinks, the tax on intermediate goods, the tax on alcohol and derived drinks distributed among the Autonomous Communities according to the indexes of territorial consumption elaborated by the National Statistics Institute.[13]

(iii) A share of 40 percent of the revenues from the tax on hydrocarbons, distributed among the Communities according to the territorial index of deliveries of gasoline, diesel and fuel oils elaborated by the Ministry of Economics.

(iv) A share of 40 percent of revenues from the tax on manufacturd tobacco, distributed among the Communities according to the territorial index of sales to tobacconists, elaborated by the Tobacco Market Commission.

(v) A share of 100 percent of revenues from the tax on electricity, distributed among the Communities according to the territorial index of net electric energy consumption elaborated by the Ministry of Science and Technology.

Regarding the revenue sharing for local governments with these taxes, the latest reform of the system of local finance in 2002 established that these bodies were entitled to a share of the collections from both the VAT and excise taxes.[14] Local corporations had a share of VAT and excise tax revenue with the percentages that follow:

(i) 1.0538% of the net VAT revenues.
(ii) 1.2044% of the net revenues from the Excise Taxes on Beer, Wine and Fermented Drinks, Intermediate Goods, Alcohol and Derived Drinks, Hydrocarbons, and Manufactured Tobacco.

These percentages are not applied to the total intake from these taxes, but rather to the part which corresponds to the State once the shares of the Autonomous Communities have been deducted.[15]

The sharing of these indirect taxes with local governments can be a complex task. For the sharing of VAT revenues, local entities are entitled to a portion of these revenues which will be determined through the application of the index of territorial consumption of the Autonomous Community that each local government belongs to. This index is weighted according to the shares of population represented by each local government (in this case a province) within the Autonomous Community. The weighting is carried out as follows:

$$PVAT_t^p = 0{,}010538 \times NIVAT_t \times IC_t^i \times (P_t^p / P_t^i) \qquad [1]$$

where:

- $PVAT_t^p$ is the VAT return to province p in year t.
- $NIVAT_t$ is the net VAT revenues to the State in year t, excluding those shared with the Autonomous Communities.
- IC_t^i is the index of territorial consumption for the year t elaborated by the National Statistics Institute with the aim of allocating VAT among the Autonomous Communities, where i represents the Autonomous Community to which province p belongs.
- P_t^p and P_t^i are the legal populations of province p and Autonomous Community i respectively, in accordance with the updated municipal register in force on the 31st of December of year t.

For the sharing of excise tax revenues (Excise Taxes on Beer, Wine and Fermented Drinks, Intermediate Goods, and Alcohol and Derived Drinks) with local governments, a similar approach is followed. The share is determined by weighting the net revenues of the State for each of these taxes according to the index of territorial consumption of the Autonomous Community to which the province belongs, with the result again being weighted by the population share of each province in its respective Autonomous Community. The calculation is carried out as follows:

$$PIIEE(h)_t^P = 0.012044 \times RLIIEE(h)_t \times IC_t^i (h) \times (P_t^P / P_t^i) \qquad [2]$$

where:

- $PIIEE(h)_t^P$ is the amount of Excise Tax h handed over to province p in year t.
- $RLIIEE(h)_t$ is the net revenues from Excise Tax h corresponding to the State in year t which excludes those shared with the Autonomous Communities.
- IC_t^i (h) is the index of territorial consumption, elaborated by the National Statistics Institute to allocate Excise Tax h to the Autonomous Communities, of the Autonomous Community i to which province p belongs.
- P_t^P and P_t^i are the legal populations of province p and Autonomous Community i respectively, in accordance with the updated municipal register in force on the 31st of December of year t.

For the Hydrocarbons Tax, transfers to local governments are calculated using the index of deliveries of gasoline, diesel and fuel oils corresponding to that territory, using data from the Ministry of Economics, weighted by the corresponding tax rates. The same basic approach is used for determining revenue sharing for the Tax on Manufactured Tobacco. In this case, the calculation is carried out using the index of sales to tobacconists in that territory, according to data from the Tobacco Market Commission, weighted by the corresponding tax rates.

CONSUMPTION TAXES IN SPAIN AND THE OECD COUNTRIES SINCE 1965

This section reviews the evolution of the consumption taxes take in Spain, using OECD data. As a percentage of GDP, consumption taxes as a whole rose from 6 percent to 10.2 percent over the period 1965 to 2001 (Table 8.1), with taxes of a general nature rising from 3.3 percent to 6 percent of GDP and excise taxes rising less, from 2.7 percent to 3.3 percent. From Figure 8.1 it can be seen that three stages can be identified in the evolution of the two types of taxes. From 1965 to 1980, the share of both types in terms of GDP remained relatively stable, with a tendency towards convergence. From 1980 up to 1986, which was the last large reform of

Table 8.1 Consumption tax revenues as a percentage of GDP: Spain 1965–2001

	Goods and services	**Production and sales**	**General**	**VAT**	**Excise taxes**	**Use**
1965	6.0	6.0	3.3	–	2.7	–
1966	6.1	6.1	3.3	–	2.8	–
1967	6.0	6.0	3.3	–	2.7	–
1968	5.7	5.6	3.1	–	2.5	–
1969	5.9	5.9	3.3	–	2.7	–
1970	5.8	5.8	3.3	–	2.5	–
1971	5.4	5.4	3.1	–	2.3	–
1972	5.5	5.5	3.1	–	2.4	–
1973	5.7	5.7	3.2	–	2.4	–
1974	4.7	4.7	3.1	–	1.6	–
1975	4.5	4.5	2.9	–	1.6	–
1976	4.7	4.7	2.9	–	1.8	–
1977	4.7	4.6	2.8	–	1.8	–
1978	4.7	4.7	3.0	–	1.6	–
1979	4.7	4.7	3.0	–	1.7	–
1980	4.8	4.8	2.3	–	2.4	–
1981	5.3	5.3	2.5	–	2.8	–
1982	5.4	5.4	3.0	–	2.4	–
1983	6.4	6.4	3.3	–	3.1	–
1984	7.1	7.1	3.9	–	3.3	–
1985	8.0	7.7	4.1	–	3.6	0.2
1986	9.8	9.4	5.3	4.4	4.2	0.2
1987	9.6	9.2	5.3	5.0	3.9	0.4
1988	9.7	9.3	5.4	5.2	3.9	0.4
1989	9.6	9.1	5.6	5.4	3.6	0.5
1990	9.4	8.8	5.3	5.2	3.5	0.6
1991	9.5	8.8	5.3	5.2	3.5	0.7
1992	9.8	9.0	5.7	5.6	3.4	0.7
1993	9.0	8.2	4.9	4.9	3.3	0.7
1994	9.5	8.7	5.3	5.3	3.4	0.7
1995	9.4	8.6	5.2	5.2	3.4	0.8
1996	9.4	8.6	5.3	5.3	3.3	0.8
1997	9.7	8.9	5.5	5.5	3.4	0.8
1998	10.0	9.2	5.6	5.6	3.6	0.8
1999	10.5	9.6	6.1	6.1	3.5	0.8
2000	10.5	9.6	6.2	6.2	3.4	0.8
2001	10.2	9.3	6.0	6.0	3.3	0.8

Source: OECD.

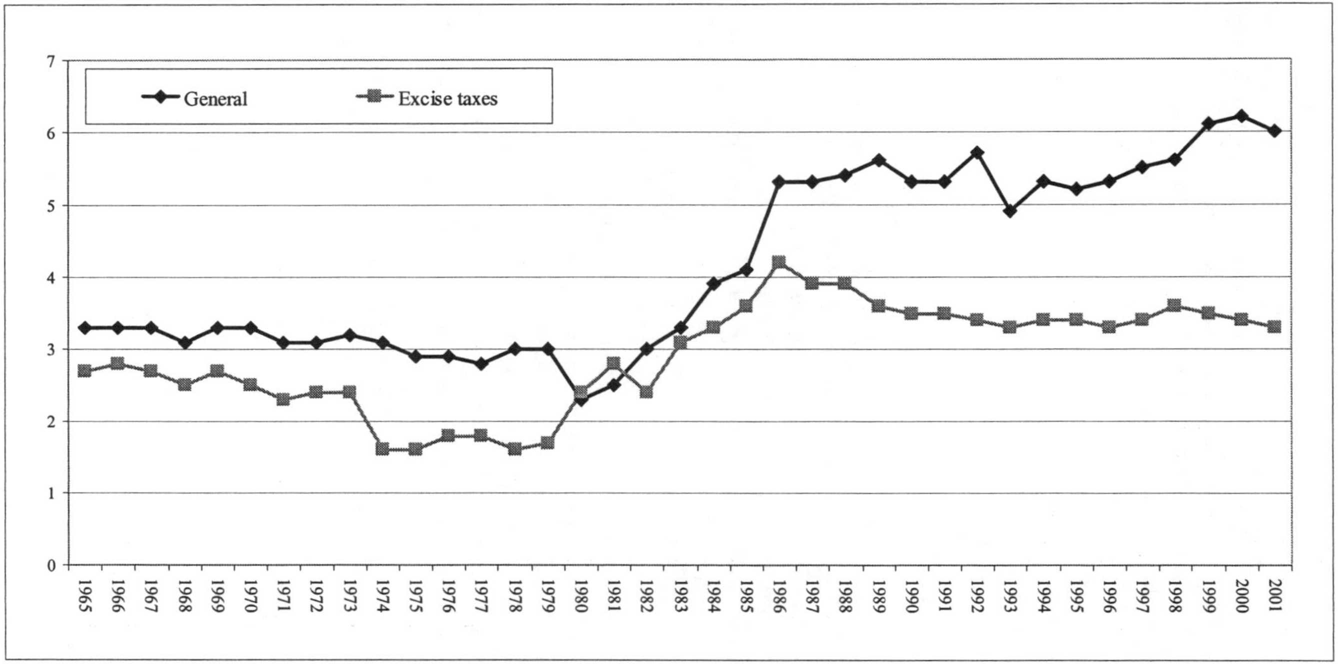

Figure 8.1 Consumption tax revenues as a percentage of GDP: Spain 1965–2001

indirect taxation in Spain, both groups of taxes rose strongly (as happened with other taxes), but with general taxes rising faster (from 2.3 percent to 5.3 percent of GDP). From 1986 on, the two groups diverged, although not sharply, as happened in other developed economies. Thus, the take from general taxes, after the introduction of the VAT, rose from 5.3 percent to 6 percent of GDP, whereas the take from excise taxes fell from 4.2 percent to 3.3 percent. This differentiated behavior can be explained by the fact that the VAT replaced the old tax on sumptuary consumptions and other figures smaller than the special taxes.

Despite this, consumption taxes as a share of total tax revenues have fallen, due to the fact that other public earnings have risen much faster as a percentage of GDP. As can be seen in Table 8.2 and Figure 8.2, taxes on goods and services went from representing 40 percent of total revenues in 1965 to 20 percent in 1980. The share of taxes of a general nature (the IGTE was still in existence) fell by almost 12 percentage points over this period (from 22.21 percent to 10.16 percent of the total intake) while that of excise taxes fell by more than 11 percentage points (from 18.42 percent to 7.38 percent in 1979). Since the beginning of the 1980s, the share of total revenues corresponding to excise taxes has remained fairly stable at around 10 percent while that of taxes of a general nature has risen strongly since 1981, especially after the introduction of the VAT.

From an international perspective, effective burdens from indirect taxation in Spain have been in the middle of the road. At the beginning of the 2000s, consumption tax burdens were lower for the non-European OECD countries (see Table 8.3 and Figure 8.3). In terms of the share of these taxes in GDP, the average for the European zone (at 12.1 percent of GDP in 2001) was higher than that of the American and Pacific zone (both barely up from 9 percent). However, if we consider the percentage that consumption taxes represent of the total tax revenues (Table 8.4 and Figure 8.4), we can observe that this share is higher for the non-European countries. This result is due mainly to the weight given to consumption tax in Mexico and Korea (53.1 percent and 39.6 percent, respectively, of total tax revenues corresponds to consumption taxes in those two countries). On the other hand, Japan, the United States and Switzerland are the countries where consumption tax is of lesser importance (in terms of both their share of GDP and the percentage of total tax revenues).

Table 8.2 Consumption tax revenues as a percentage of tax revenue: Spain 1965–2001

	Goods and services	Production and sales	General	VAT	Excise taxes	Use
1965	40.84	40.63	22.21	–	18.42	0.21
1966	45.02	44.96	24.14	–	20.82	0.06
1967	35.65	35.59	19.42	–	16.17	0.06
1968	35.17	35.11	19.22	–	15.89	0.06
1969	36.14	36.07	19.76	–	16.30	0.07
1970	35.87	35.77	20.29	–	15.48	0.10
1971	32.85	32.73	18.59	–	14.15	0.11
1972	31.50	31.36	17.63	–	13.74	0.13
1973	31.50	31.37	17.96	–	13.41	0.13
1974	26.92	26.78	17.73	–	9.05	0.14
1975	24.16	24.02	15.30	–	8.72	0.14
1976	24.92	24.79	15.12	–	9.67	0.13
1977	22.49	22.39	13.62	–	8.77	0.10
1978	21.39	21.30	13.90	–	7.39	0.09
1979	20.98	20.91	13.53	–	7.38	0.07
1980	20.69	20.69	10.16	–	10.53	0.01
1981	21.93	21.92	10.28	–	11.64	0.01
1982	22.07	22.06	12.40	–	9.67	0.01
1983	23.96	23.95	12.28	–	11.67	0.01
1984	25.51	25.51	13.86	–	11.65	–
1985	28.71	27.68	14.67	–	13.02	0.62
1986	33.21	31.94	17.73	14.76	14.21	0.81
1987	30.59	29.28	16.90	16.03	12.38	1.24
1988	30.83	29.42	17.15	16.42	12.27	1.36
1989	28.81	27.35	16.68	16.29	10.67	1.41
1990	28.39	26.53	16.03	15.73	10.50	1.79
1991	28.36	26.34	15.89	15.59	10.45	1.93
1992	28.36	26.19	16.45	16.19	9.73	2.07
1993	26.87	24.51	14.72	14.65	9.79	2.22
1994	28.28	25.99	15.80	15.74	10.19	2.12
1995	28.62	26.14	15.87	15.85	10.27	2.32
1996	29.00	26.49	16.23	16.21	10.25	2.36
1997	28.88	26.50	16.34	16.34	10.15	2.25
1998	29.54	27.09	16.57	16.57	10.52	2.33
1999	30.03	27.51	17.42	17.42	10.09	2.41
2000	29.83	27.37	17.60	17.60	9.77	2.37
2001	28.83	26.35	17.06	17.06	9.29	2.39

Source: OECD.

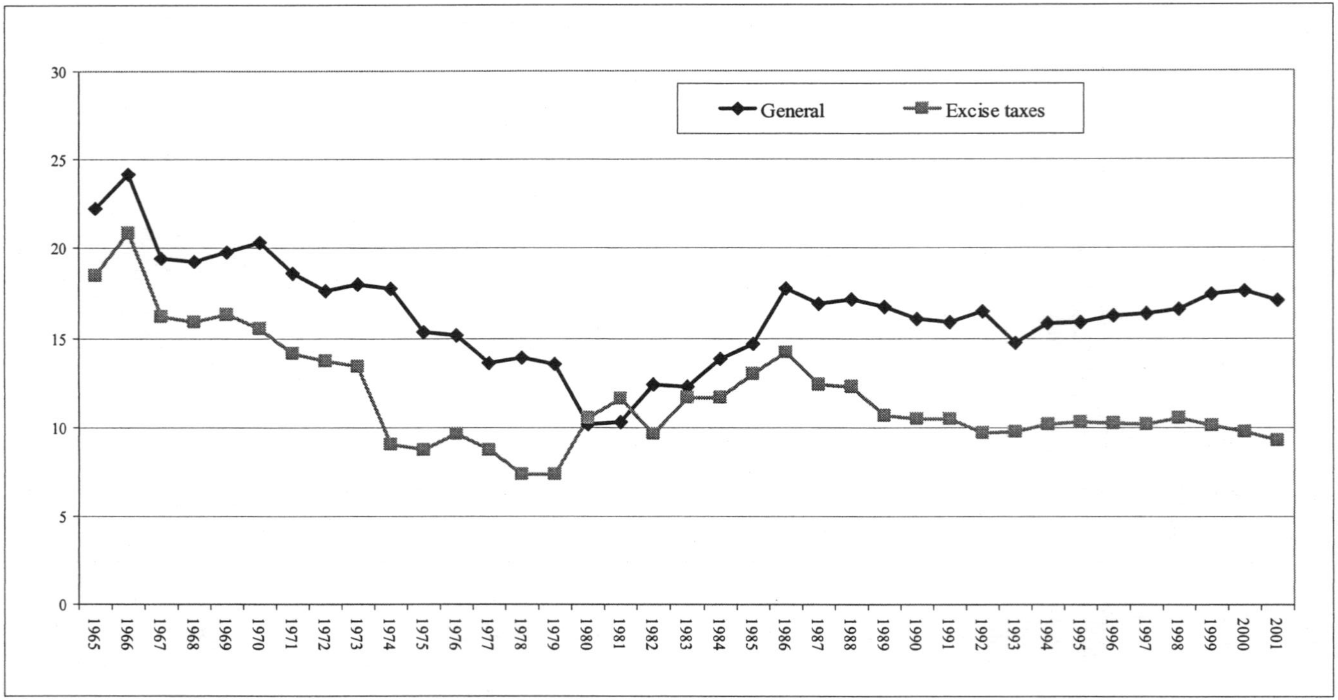

Figure 8.2 Consumption tax revenues as a percentage of tax revenue: Spain 1965–2001

Table 8.3 Consumption taxes as a percentage of GDP

	1965	1970	1975	1980	1985	1995	2001	Variation
OECD Total	9.7	10.0	9.7	10.1	10.9	11.4	11.5	1.8
OECD Europe	10.3	10.8	10.4	10.9	11.8	12.4	12.1	1.8
European Union (15)	10.4	10.8	10.2	11.0	12.0	12.2	11.9	1.5
OECD America	8.0	7.6	7.7	7.7	8.8	7.7	9.2	1.2
OECD Pacific	6.4	6.3	7.0	7.7	7.8	8.5	9.1	2.7
GERMANY	10.4	10.3	9.5	10.2	9.5	10.7	10.6	0.2
FRANCE	13.3	13.0	11.9	12.4	13.0	12.1	11.4	-1.9
ITALY	10.1	10.1	7.7	8.1	8.7	11.2	11.0	0.9
NETHERLANDS	9.4	9.9	10.1	11.0	10.9	11.4	12.3	2.9
BELGIUM	11.6	12.6	11.0	11.6	11.6	11.5	11.2	-0.4
LUXEMBOURG	6.8	3.6	7.9	8.4	10.8	11.2	11.4	4.6
UNITED KINGDOM	10.1	10.7	8.8	10.3	11.9	12.3	11.7	1.6
IRELAND	13.1	15.1	13.5	13.7	15.6	13.3	10.3	-2.8
DENMARK	12.2	15.2	13.5	16.4	16.2	15.9	15.8	3.6
SPAIN	6.0	5.8	4.5	4.8	8.0	9.4	10.2	4.2
GREECE	9.8	10.8	10.2	10.0	12.2	13.3	13.9	4.1
PORTUGAL	7.0	8.6	8.5	10.8	11.4	14.1	13.8	6.8
UNITED STATES	5.6	5.5	5.3	4.8	4.9	4.9	4.7	-0.9
MEXICO	–	–	–	8.3	11.0	9.0	9.7	–
CANADA	10.4	9.8	10.2	10.0	10.4	9.1	8.8	-1.6
KOREA	–	–	9.3	11.1	10.1	8.8	10.9	–
JAPAN	4.8	4.5	3.7	4.1	3.8	4.2	3.9	-0.9
AUSTRALIA	7.6	7.2	7.8	8.5	9.6	8.6	8.7	1.1
NORWAY	12.2	14.8	14.8	15.1	16.3	16.0	14.1	1.9
NEW ZEALAND	6.9	7.3	7.4	7.2	7.6	12.5	12.4	5.5

Table 8.3 Consumption taxes as a percentage of GDP (continued)

	1965	**1970**	**1975**	**1980**	**1985**	**1995**	**2001**	**Variation**
SWEDEN	10.9	10.9	10.3	11.4	12.9	11.5	11.1	0.2
FINLAND	12.9	12.6	11.9	12.9	13.6	13.3	13.6	0.7
ICELAND	16.4	16.5	18.5	17.4	17.3	15.4	14.8	-1.6
SWITZERLAND	6.0	6.1	5.6	5.9	5.8	6.3	7.1	1.1
AUSTRIA	12.7	12.9	12.9	12.6	13.6	11.5	12.4	-0.3
TURKEY	5.7	6.2	6.6	4.6	5.6	8.5	13.9	8.2
CZECH REPUBLIC	–	–	–	–	–	13.2	11.9	–
SLOVAKIA	–	–	–	–	–	–	11.0	–
HUNGARY	–	–	–	–	–	17.2	14.9	–
POLAND	–	–	–	–	–	14.0	12.5	–

Notes: The last data entry for Portugal, the United States, Australia, Iceland and Poland corresponds to the year 2000.

Source: OECD.

Table 8.4 Consumption taxes as a percentage of total tax revenue

	1965	1970	1975	1980	1985	1995	2001	Variation
OECD Total	38.05	35.61	32.63	32.34	33.54	32.31	31.84	-6.2
OECD Europe	40.05	37.98	33.28	31.95	33.01	32.68	30.34	-9.7
European Union (15)	38.18	36.08	31.36	31.05	31.55	31.1	28.7	-9.5
OECD America	31.62	25.81	25.78	33.81	38.47	32.48	39.01	7.4
OECD Pacific	29.63	27.19	32.98	33.1	32.37	30.13	37.52	7.9
GERMANY	32.97	31.81	26.9	27.11	25.65	27.98	29.28	-3.7
FRANCE	38.41	38.13	33.29	30.42	29.67	27.44	25.18	-13.2
ITALY	39.47	38.69	29.36	26.46	25.38	27.29	26.24	-13.2
NETHERLANDS	28.64	27.78	24.17	25.25	25.65	27.16	30.77	2.1
BELGIUM	37.17	36.47	27.44	27.24	25.33	25.75	24.7	-12.5
LUXEMBOURG	24.74	14.33	21.12	20.93	24.1	26.69	26.74	2.0
UNITED KINGDOM	33.07	28.78	25.02	29.2	31.53	35.42	31.24	-1.8
IRELAND	52.64	52.42	46.51	43.71	44.42	40.75	35.25	-17.4
DENMARK	40.62	38.8	33.63	37.39	34.18	32.21	32.24	-8.4
SPAIN	40.84	35.87	24.16	20.69	28.71	28.62	28.83	-12.0
GREECE	48.84	48.18	46.8	41.24	42.72	42.13	33.96	-14.9
PORTUGAL	44.24	44.63	40.75	44.88	42.79	43.46	39.93	-4.3
UNITED STATES	22.76	19.95	19.55	17.63	18.82	17.87	15.72	-7.0
MEXICO	–	–	–	51.23	64.8	54.15	53.06	–
CANADA	40.49	31.68	32.01	32.58	31.81	25.43	24.96	-15.5
KOREA	–	–	61.07	62.65	59.48	43.07	39.64	–
JAPAN	26.25	22.36	17.31	16.34	14.02	15.17	18.87	-7.4
AUSTRALIA	34.71	31.97	29.33	31.1	32.85	29.02	27.52	-7.2
NORWAY	41.16	42.81	37.66	35.4	37.61	38.61	31.29	-9.9
NEW ZEALAND	27.93	27.23	24.22	22.3	23.14	33.26	35.66	7.7

Table 8.4 Consumption taxes as a percentage of total tax revenue (continued)

	1965	1970	1975	1980	1985	1995	2001	Variation
SWEDEN	31.18	28.25	24.35	24.01	26.6	24.23	20.79	-10.4
FINLAND	42.46	39.64	32.37	35.66	33.92	29.62	29.37	-13.1
ICELAND	62.73	61.25	62.98	59.9	61.06	48.79	42.52	-20.2
SWITZERLAND	30.48	26.94	19.96	20.52	19.29	18.84	20.47	-10.0
AUSTRIA	37.38	37.36	34.52	31.52	32.57	27.69	27.18	-10.2
TURKEY	53.93	49.37	41.29	25.61	36.02	37.57	38.74	-15.2
CZECH REPUBLIC	–	–	–	–	–	32.93	30.55	–
SLOVAKIA	–	–	–	–	–	–	33.17	–
HUNGARY	–	–	–	–	–	40.63	38.62	–
POLAND	–	–	–	–	–	35.23	36.62	–

Notes: In all tables the last data entry for Portugal, the United States, Australia, Iceland and Poland corresponds to the year 2000.

Source: OECD.

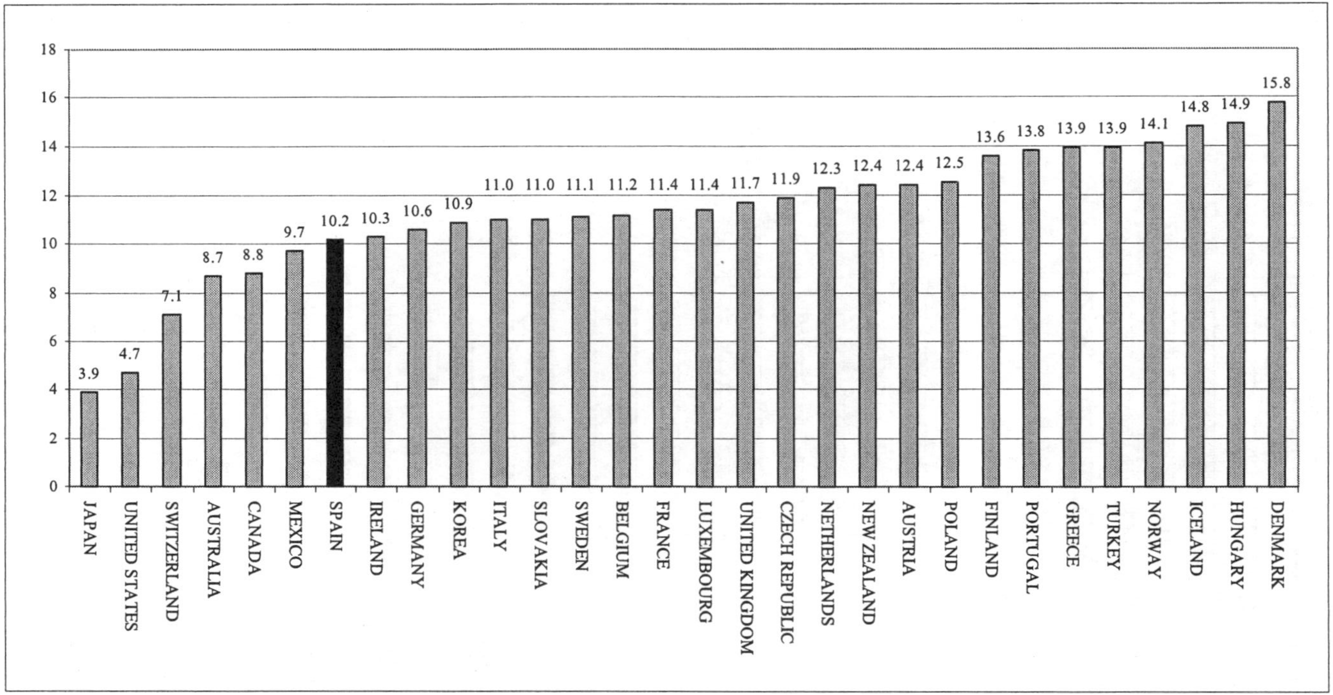

Figure 8.3 Consumption taxes as a percentage of GDP 2001

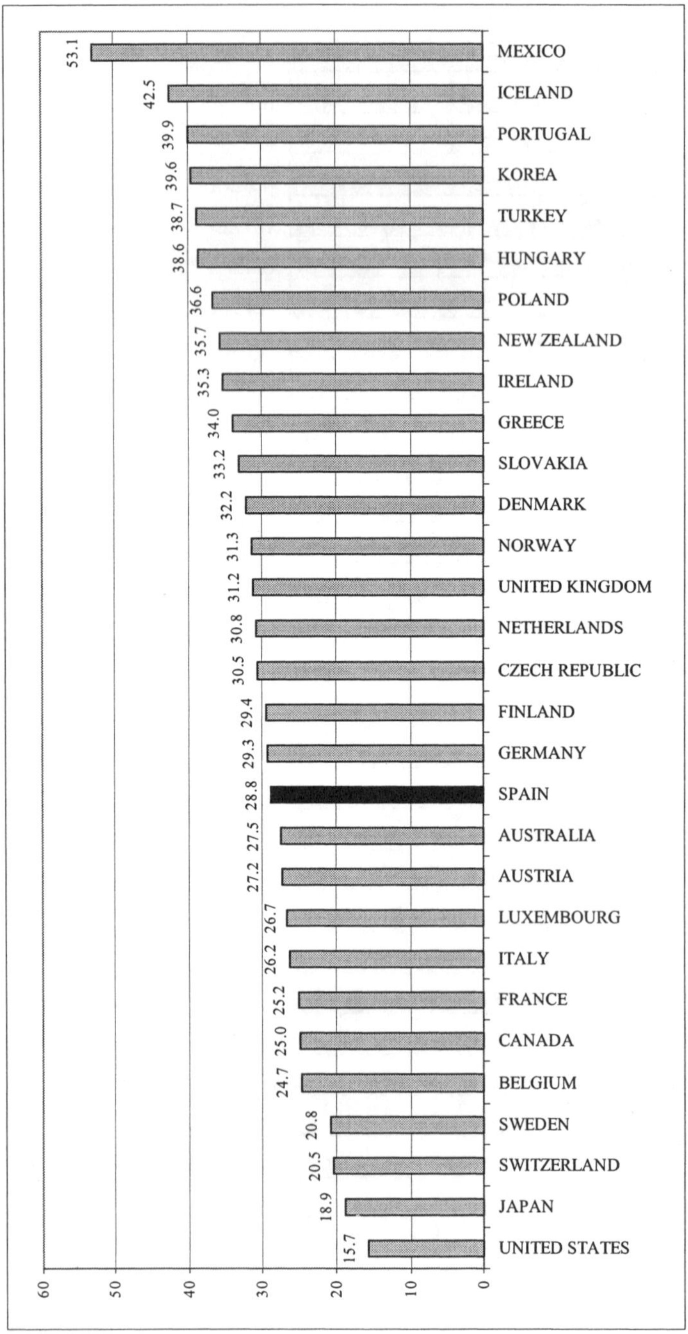

Figure 8.4 Consumption taxes as a percentage of total tax revenue 2001

In terms of the current weight of consumption taxes in total revenues (Figure 8.4) as opposed to fiscal pressure, Spain, for which these taxes contribute 28.8 percent of public revenue, is closer to the average than the other European countries.

If we focus on excise taxation, we can observe that as a percentage of GDP Spain has converged towards its peers (Table 8.5 and Figure 8.5). The figure for Spain rose from 2.7 percent of GDP in 1965 to 3.3 percent in 2001 whereas the OECD average fell from 5.8 percent to 4 percent over the same period. There has also been a convergence in terms of the share these taxes represent of the total public revenue, due primarily to a substantial reduction in the figure for all countries (Table 8.6 and Figure 8.6). Despite this, in the year 2001 Spain occupied the twenty-fourth position out of the thirty two OECD countries under consideration in terms of the specific fiscal pressure of excise taxes, and was twentieth in terms of their contribution to the total tax revenues.

With regard to consumption taxes of a general nature (Tables 8.7 and 8.8, Figures 8.7 and 8.8), the distance of Spain from the developed countries has been substantially reduced, though a gap still persists. Whereas the average fiscal pressure for OECD-Europe rose from 3.7 percent to 7.4 percent of GDP between 1965 and 2001, the corresponding rise for Spain was from 3.3 percent to 6 percent. Spain is considerably closer to the other countries considered when it comes to the share these taxes represent of fiscal resources as a whole.

The appearance and the increase in importance of the VAT in those OECD countries where this tax exists, namely all except the USA, is detailed in Tables 8.9 and 8.10. The generalisation of the VAT goes a long way towards explaining the rise observed over recent decades in the intake derived from consumption taxes. Australia introduced a Goods and Services Tax in 2000; Greece, Spain and Portugal introduced the VAT in the 1980s as a consequence of joining the EU; Iceland, Japan and New Zealand introduced the VAT around the same period; and Switzerland did the same at the end of that decade. The economies of the former Soviet bloc have also introduced theVAT as an important source of tax revenue in most cases starting with the beginning of the transition to a market economy.

In the European countries, VAT represented some 7 percent of GDP in 2001, while the figure for Spain was about 6 percent, though VAT as a percentage of total tax revenue was similar at over 17 percent.

Interestingly, countries tend to apply quite different VAT rate structures (Table 8.12):[16] Denmark has a single rate; there are two rates in Germany, Holland and the UK; and structures with multiple rates in Greece, France, Italy, Ireland, Spain, Austria, Portugal, Finland and Sweden. Nominal rates also vary widely: Sweden and Denmark have rates of 25 percent and

Iceland has a rate of 24.5 percent, Canada has a rate of 7 percent and Switzerland a rate of 7.5 percent. For the EU countries as a whole the standard tax rate fluctuates between 15 percent and 25 percent, while for the OECD it fluctuates from 5 percent (Japan) to the aforementioned 25 percent in Sweden and Denmark. Moreover, in the last twenty years all countries have raised their standard nominal rates, such that the EU average has risen from 17.5 percent to 19.4 percent.

There is also significant variation in effective rates. Table 8.11 and Figure 8.10 show the effective rates derived from the application of VAT (column 5). To calculate these rates we have divided the revenue from this tax by family expenditure on final consumption, which is used as measure of the potential base of the VAT for each country.

In the final column of Table 8.11 (column 6) we present calculations of the consequences arising from the existence of exemptions, minimum allowances and reduced rates by country, thereby relating the aforementioned effective rates with the standard nominal rate for each country. It can be seen that for Luxembourg, Switzerland, Japan and Norway the effective rates are quite similar to the nominal rates; in most cases, however, the effective rates range from 60 percent to 80 percent of the nominal rates. For Spain, the efficacy of the tax in this regard is quite low (see Figure 8.10), since the estimated effective rate of the IVA is 10.58 percent, by comparison to the 16 percent statutory rate. Thus, the productivity of the VAT in Spain is 66.1 percent of the statutory rate.

In the ambit of the EU, the lack of neutrality between countries which is reflected in the large differences between effective and nominal rates highlights the need to make advances in the area of reducing distortions which affect competition within states, e-commerce and cross-border purchases.

The consequences of the different VAT regulations and the different degrees of compliance for tax-collection are reflected in the productivity of VAT by country (column 4 of Table 8.11; Figure 8.9). VAT productivity has been calculated by dividing the specific fiscal pressure of VAT for each country by the standard nominal rate in place that country. The values for Switzerland, Turkey, Portugal, Korea and Greece are high but those of the remaining countries vary from 30 percent to 40 percent (Figure 8.9).

Table 8.5 Excise taxes as a percentage of GDP

	1965	1970	1975	1980	1985	1995	2000	2001	Variation
OECD Total	5.8	5.5	4.8	4.8	4.9	4.5	4.2	4	-1.8
OECD Europe	6.2	5.8	5	4.9	4.9	4.8	4.3	4	-2.2
European Union (15)	6	5.6	4.6	4.6	4.9	4.6	4.2	3.9	-2.1
OECD America	4	3.7	3.5	3.9	4.9	3.9	3.7	4.5	0.5
OECD Pacific	4.7	4.5	4.9	5.1	4.9	3.5	3.6	3.3	-1.4
GERMANY	4.6	4.2	3.8	3.5	3.3	3.6	3.3	3.5	-1.1
FRANCE	4.9	4	3.2	3.4	3.8	4	3.7	3.5	-1.4
ITALY	6.2	6	3.6	3	3.1	4.6	4.2	3.8	-2.4
NETHERLANDS	4.8	4.1	3.4	3.2	3.1	3.8	3.7	3.6	-1.2
BELGIUM	4	4.3	3.7	3.7	3.7	3.8	3.2	3.2	-0.8
LUXEMBOURG	3.1	2.3	3.1	3.9	5	5.1	5.3	4.8	1.7
UNITED KINGDOM	7.7	7.4	5.2	4.7	5.2	5.1	4.7	4.4	-3.3
IRELAND	10.8	10.5	8.6	8.9	7.7	5.7	4.4	3.5	-7.3
DENMARK	8.7	7	5.9	5.9	6.2	5.7	5.5	5.4	-3.3
SPAIN	2.7	2.5	1.6	2.4	3.6	3.4	3.4	3.3	0.6
GREECE	6.8	6.1	5.2	6.1	6	5.3	4.4	4.3	-2.5
PORTUGAL	6.6	6.5	5.6	6.6	7.6	6.3	5.2	5.2	-1.4
UNITED STATES	3.7	3.3	2.7	2.2	2.2	2.1	1.9	1.9	-1.8
MEXICO	–	–	–	5.6	8.2	6	6.2	5.9	0.3
CANADA	4.3	4.1	4.3	4	4.2	3.5	3	3.1	-1.2
KOREA	–	–	7.2	7	6.3	4.5	5.1	5.8	-1.4

Table 8.5 Excise taxes as a percentage of GDP (continued)

	1965	1970	1975	1980	1985	1995	2000	2001	Variation
JAPAN	4.6	4.2	3.2	3.5	3.3	2.2	2.1	1.6	-3
AUSTRALIA	5	4.6	5.1	6.2	6	4.3	4.4	4.4	-0.6
NORWAY	5.5	6.2	6.3	6.9	7.9	6.7	5.3	5.2	-0.3
NEW ZEALAND	4.6	4.6	4.2	3.6	3.8	3.2	2.6	2.6	-2
SWEDEN	6.7	6.3	4.5	4.4	5.6	4.2	3.6	3.6	-3.1
FINLAND	7.1	6.3	5.6	6	5.6	5.2	4.9	4.8	-2.3
ICELAND	11.8	10.2	9.9	8.7	7.5	4.4	4.6	4.6	-7.2
SWITZERLAND	3.7	3.9	3	2.8	2.5	2.4	2.5	2.5	-1.2
AUSTRIA	6.1	6.2	5.2	4	4.2	3.3	3.4	3.4	-2.7
TURKEY	5.7	6.1	6.5	4.5	1.9	1.4	5.3	5.4	-0.3
CZECH REPUBLIC	–	–	–	–	–	5.4	4.3	4	–
SLOVAKIA	–	–	–	–	–	–	4.8	3.4	–
HUNGARY	–	–	–	–	–	8.8	5.4	4.7	–
POLAND	–	–	–	–	–	7	4.8	4.8	–

Notes: In all tables the last data entry for Portugal, the United States, Australia, Iceland and Poland corresponds to the year 2000.

Source: OECD.

Table 8.6 Excise taxes as a percentage of total tax revenue

	1965	1970	1975	1980	1985	1995	2000	2001	Variation
OECD Total	24.07	20.46	17.54	16.57	16.05	13.08	11.78	11.4	-12.67
OECD Europe	25.24	21.46	16.82	15.14	13.97	12.4	11.13	9.99	-15.25
European Union (15)	22.92	19.07	14.55	13.78	13.33	11.84	10.33	9.5	-13.42
OECD America	15.99	12.5	11.81	18.56	23.31	17.85	16.07	20.47	4.48
OECD Pacific	22.07	19.49	23.84	21.85	20.46	13.21	12.24	14.69	-7.38
GERMANY	14.62	12.89	10.8	9.27	8.75	9.49	8.81	9.61	-5.01
FRANCE	14.28	11.63	9	8.38	8.75	9.14	8.18	7.81	-6.47
ITALY	24.11	23.16	13.97	9.74	9.12	11.1	10.04	9.11	-15
NETHERLANDS	14.73	11.57	8.11	7.32	7.24	8.98	8.85	9.12	-5.61
BELGIUM	12.96	12.59	9.26	8.63	8.1	8.6	7.08	7	-5.96
LUXEMBOURG	11.1	9.32	8.43	9.69	11.1	12.07	12.65	11.4	0.3
UNITED KINGDOM	25.21	19.92	14.82	13.28	13.85	14.58	12.44	11.76	-13.45
IRELAND	43.38	36.37	29.68	28.26	21.99	17.51	14.12	11.92	-31.46
DENMARK	29.17	17.86	14.68	13.4	12.97	11.48	11.28	10.96	-18.21
SPAIN	18.42	15.48	8.72	10.53	13.02	10.27	9.77	9.29	-9.13
GREECE	33.8	27.37	23.87	25.08	20.87	16.65	11.74	15.17	-18.63
PORTUGAL	41.45	33.83	26.98	27.2	28.75	19.48	15.17	15.17	-26.28
UNITED STATES	15.14	11.74	10.03	8.28	8.4	7.66	6.32	6.32	-8.82
MEXICO	–	–	–	34.37	48.56	35.99	33.37	32.21	-2.16
CANADA	16.84	13.27	13.58	13.02	12.97	9.89	8.51	8.72	-8.12

Table 8.6 Excise taxes as a percentage of total tax revenue (continued)

	1965	1970	1975	1980	1985	1995	2000	2001	Variation
KOREA	–	–	47.3	39.53	37.39	21.92	19.66	21.09	-26.21
JAPAN	25.02	20.95	15.09	14.13	12.08	7.98	7.79	15.45	-9.57
AUSTRALIA	22.65	20.35	19.15	22.56	20.69	14.45	13.99	13.99	-8.66
NORWAY	18.39	17.84	16.11	16.21	18.25	16.2	13.27	11.63	-6.76
NEW ZEALAND	18.53	17.17	13.81	11.17	11.67	8.49	7.52	7.55	-10.98
SWEDEN	19.15	16.29	10.71	9.19	11.57	8.73	6.72	6.8	-12.35
FINLAND	23.4	19.81	15.3	16.63	13.95	11.58	10.4	10.25	-13.15
ICELAND	44.99	37.9	33.57	29.8	26.47	14.05	12.44	12.44	-32.55
SWITZERLAND	18.97	17.1	10.64	9.77	8.36	7.25	6.99	7.36	-11.61
AUSTRIA	17.96	17.98	13.98	10.07	9.94	7.9	7.73	7.43	-10.53
TURKEY	53.44	48.77	40.94	25.22	12.39	6	16.04	15.12	-38.32
CZECH REPUBLIC	–	–	–	–	–	13.42	10.96	10.33	–
SLOVAKIA	–	–	–	–	–	–	13.4	10.13	–
HUNGARY	–	–	–	–	–	20.86	13.85	12.27	–
POLAND	–	–	–	–	–	17.54	14.15	14.15	–

Notes: In all tables the last data entry for Portugal, the United States, Australia, Iceland and Poland corresponds to the year 2000.

Source: OECD.

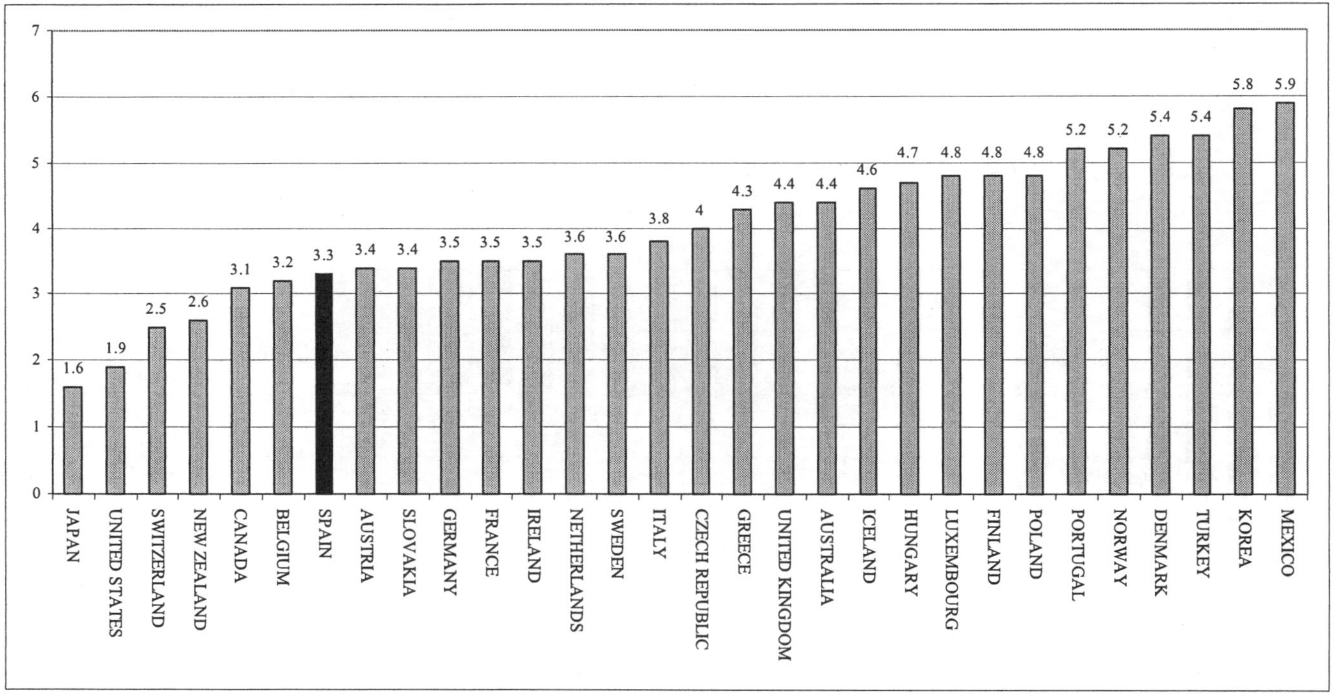

Figure 8.5 Excise taxes as a percentage of total tax revenue 2001

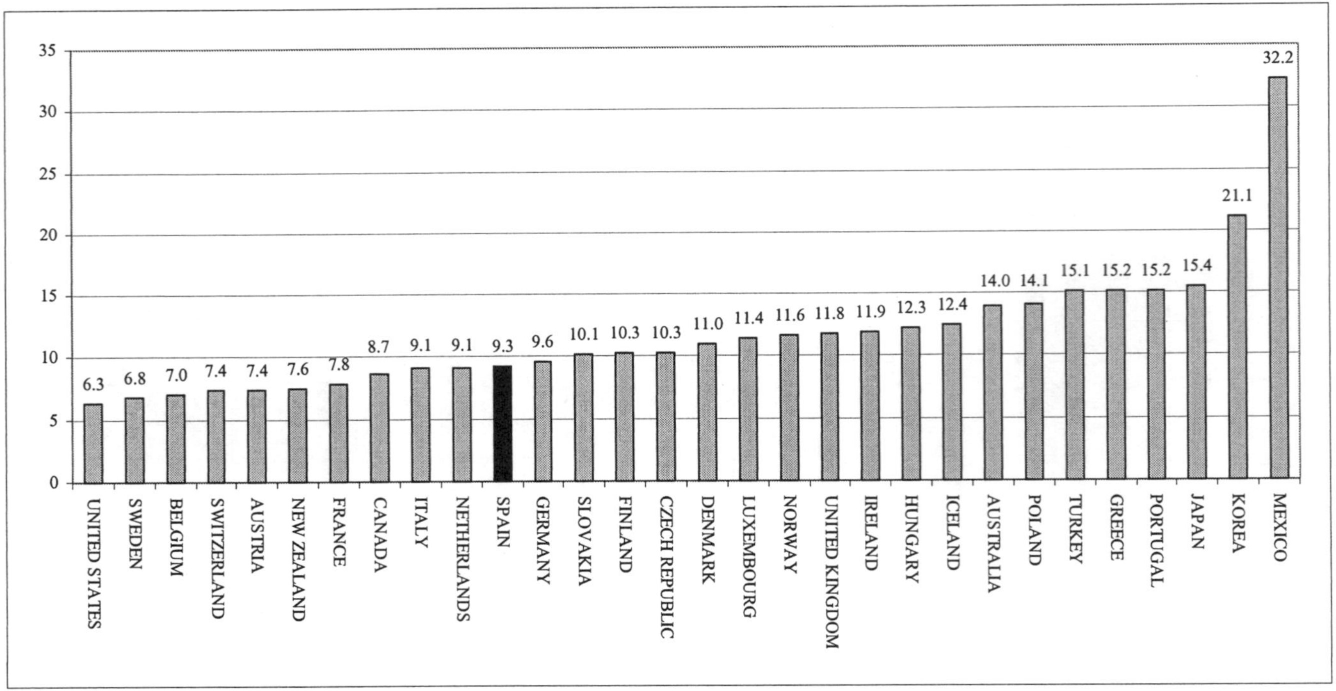

Figure 8.6 Excise taxes as a percentage of total tax revenue 2001

Table 8.7 General consumer taxes as a percentage of GNP

	1965	1970	1975	1980	1985	1995	2000	2001	Variation
OECD Total	3.3	4	4.3	4.8	5.4	6.3	6.9	6.9	3.6
OECD Europe	3.7	4.5	5	5.6	6.4	7.1	7.7	7.4	3.7
European Union (15)	3.8	4.6	5.1	5.9	6.5	7	7.5	7.3	3.5
OECD America	2.9	3	2.9	2.7	3	3.3	3.6	4.4	1.5
OECD Pacific	1.2	1.3	1.6	2.2	2.3	4.1	4.8	5.3	4.1
GERMANY	5.2	5.5	5.2	6.2	5.9	6.7	7	6.7	1.5
FRANCE	8	8.7	8.4	8.6	8.7	7.6	7.7	7.6	-0.4
ITALY	3.3	3.4	3.7	4.8	5	5.7	6.6	5.9	2.6
NETHERLANDS	4.1	5.2	6	6.9	6.9	6.5	7.2	7.5	3.4
BELGIUM	6.6	7.4	6.5	7.3	7.2	6.8	7.4	7.1	0.5
LUXEMBOURG	3.4	–	4.5	4.3	5.6	6	6	6.4	3
UNITED KINGDOM	1.8	2.5	3.1	5.2	6	6.6	6.9	6.8	5
IRELAND	1.4	3.8	4.3	4.6	7.2	7	6.7	6.4	5
DENMARK	2.7	7.4	6.8	9.8	9.5	9.5	9.6	9.6	6.9
SPAIN	3.3	3.3	2.9	2.3	4.1	5.2	6.2	6	2.7
GREECE	2	3.8	4	3.2	4.9	7.3	8.6	8.5	6.5
PORTUGAL	–	1.6	2.3	3.9	3.3	7.6	8.3	8.3	6.7
UNITED STATES	1.2	1.6	1.9	1.9	2	2.2	2.2	2.2	1
MEXICO	–	–	–	2.5	2.7	2.8	3.5	3.6	1.1
CANADA	4.6	4.5	4	3.5	4.3	5	5.2	5.2	0.6
KOREA	–	–	1.9	3.9	3.6	3.9	4.5	4.7	-1.9
JAPAN	–	–	–	–	–	1.4	2.4	2	2
AUSTRALIA	1.6	1.7	1.8	1.4	2.3	2.6	3.9	3.9	2.3

Table 8.7 General consumer taxes as a percentage of GNP (continued)

	1965	1970	1975	1980	1985	1995	2000	2001	Variation
NORWAY	6.4	8.2	8.1	7.8	7.9	8.8	8	8.2	1.8
NEW ZEALAND	1.9	2.1	2.8	3.3	3.4	8.5	8.7	9	7.1
SWEDEN	3.6	4	5.1	6.3	6.8	7.1	7.3	7.1	3.5
FINLAND	5.6	6.2	6.2	6.8	7.8	7.8	8.5	8.5	2.9
ICELAND	4.4	5.9	8.4	8.4	9.3	10	11	11	6.6
SWITZERLAND	1.9	1.8	2.2	2.6	2.9	3.4	4.1	4.1	2.2
AUSTRIA	6.3	6.4	7.4	8	8.8	7.6	8.3	8.2	1.9
TURKEY	–	–	–	–	3.6	7	7.8	8	8
CZECH REPUBLIC	–	–	–	–	–	6.9	7.5	7	–
SLOVAKIA	–	–	–	–	–	–	8	7.6	–
HUNGARY	–	–	–	–	–	8.2	10.2	10	–
POLAND	–	–	–	–	–	6.8	7.6	7.6	–

Notes: In all tables the last data entry for Portugal, the United States, Australia, Iceland and Poland corresponds to the year 2000.

Source: OECD.

Table 8.8 General consumer taxes as a percentage of total tax revenue

	1965	1970	1975	1980	1985	1995	2000	2001	Variation
OECD Total	11.85	13.06	13.34	14.17	15.79	17.54	18.34	18.51	6.66
OECD Europe	12.99	14.62	15.03	15.61	17.59	18.83	19.42	18.27	5.28
European Union (15)	13.28	14.95	15.25	16.02	16.68	17.75	18.22	17.58	4.3
OECD America	11.31	10.14	9.75	11.42	12.33	13	13.54	17.27	5.96
OECD Pacific	5.01	5.14	7.09	9.37	9.84	13.87	15.72	20.9	15.89
GERMANY	16.49	17.14	14.63	16.63	15.81	17.44	18.37	18.52	2.03
FRANCE	23.26	25.51	23.4	21.14	19.95	17.34	16.92	16.66	-6.6
ITALY	12.89	13.15	14.31	15.62	14.5	13.82	15.76	14.13	1.24
NETHERLANDS	12.37	14.61	14.36	15.83	16.18	15.6	17.34	18.81	6.44
BELGIUM	21.11	21.51	16.29	17.1	15.72	15.33	16.25	15.64	-5.47
LUXEMBOURG	12.35	–	11.93	10.68	12.52	14.22	14.29	15.02	2.67
UNITED KINGDOM	5.91	6.83	8.91	14.66	15.88	19.08	18.37	18.25	12.34
IRELAND	5.68	13.1	14.68	14.76	20.59	21.25	21.49	21.78	16.1
DENMARK	9.11	18.77	16.9	22.25	20.12	19.32	19.58	19.53	10.42
SPAIN	22.21	20.29	15.3	10.16	14.67	15.87	17.6	17.06	-5.15
GREECE	10.26	16.82	18.32	13.16	17.16	23.11	22.66	20.93	10.67
PORTUGAL	–	8.38	11.16	16.16	12.58	23.39	24.21	24.21	15.83
UNITED STATES	4.8	5.85	7.04	7.02	7.88	8	7.45	7.45	2.65
MEXICO	–	–	–	15.69	15.95	17.01	18.72	19.75	4.06
CANADA	17.82	14.43	12.46	11.54	13.16	13.99	14.45	14.78	-3.04
KOREA	–	–	12.66	22	21.07	18.88	17.02	17.25	-12.66

Table 8.8 General consumer taxes as a percentage of total tax revenue (continued)

	1965	**1970**	**1975**	**1980**	**1985**	**1995**	**2000**	**2001**	**Variation**
JAPAN	–	–	–	–	–	5.21	8.89	19.6	19.6
AUSTRALIA	7.36	7.44	6.67	5.27	7.93	8.69	12.25	12.25	4.89
NORWAY	21.51	23.75	20.49	18.22	18.19	21.21	19.74	18.34	-3.17
NEW ZEALAND	7.65	7.99	9.02	10.21	10.36	22.72	24.71	25.85	18.2
SWEDEN	10.37	10.26	11.98	13.36	13.96	15	13.38	13.38	3.01
FINLAND	18.46	19.31	16.79	18.66	19.54	17.32	18.03	18.39	-0.07
ICELAND	16.71	21.98	28.59	28.92	33.05	31.75	29.38	29.38	12.67
SWITZERLAND	9.45	7.82	7.76	9.16	9.46	10.32	11.49	11.84	2.39
AUSTRIA	18.68	18.53	19.84	20.11	20.99	18.23	19.04	18.01	-0.67
TURKEY	–	–	–	–	23.29	31.07	23.3	22.23	22.23
CZECH REPUBLIC	–	–	–	–	–	17.16	18.89	18.05	–
SLOVAKIA	–	–	–	–	–	–	22.25	23.05	–
HUNGARY	–	–	–	–	–	19.43	26.08	25.82	–
POLAND	–	–	–	–	–	17.06	22.19	22.19	–

Notes: In all tables the last data entry for Portugal, the United States, Australia, Iceland and Poland corresponds to the year 2000.

Source: OECD.

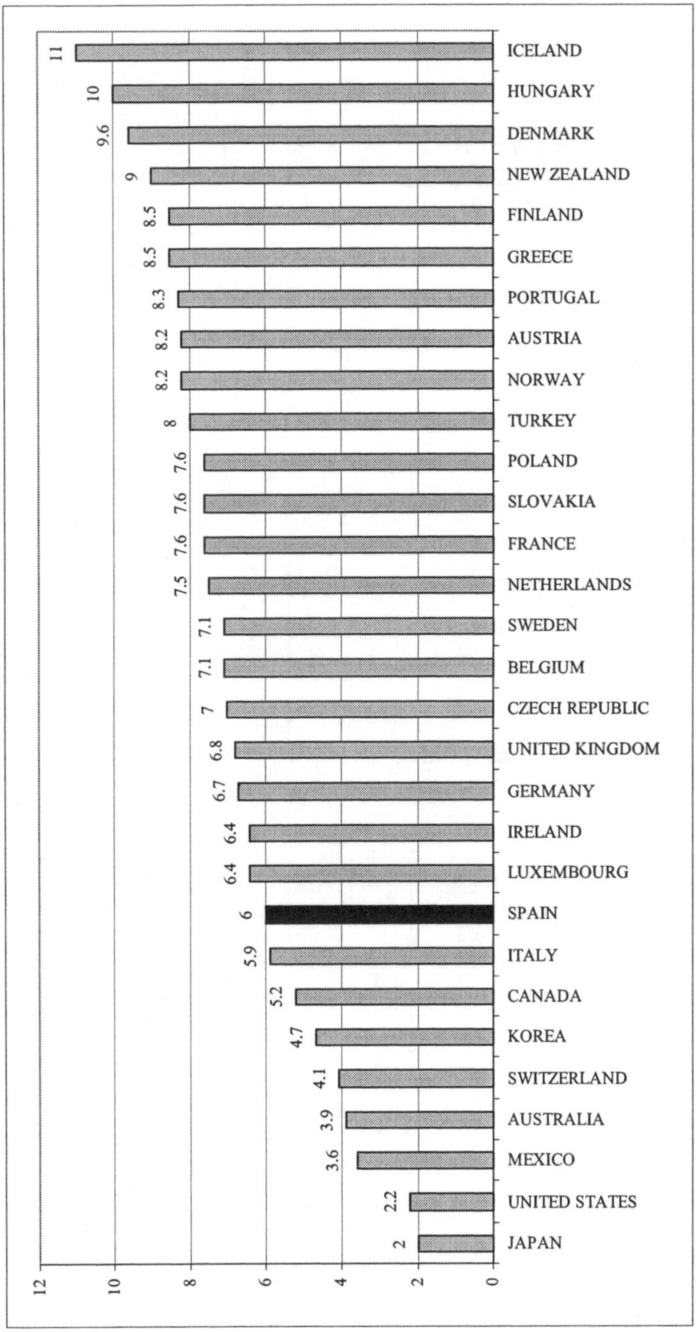

Figure 8.7 General consumer taxes as a percentage of GNP 2001

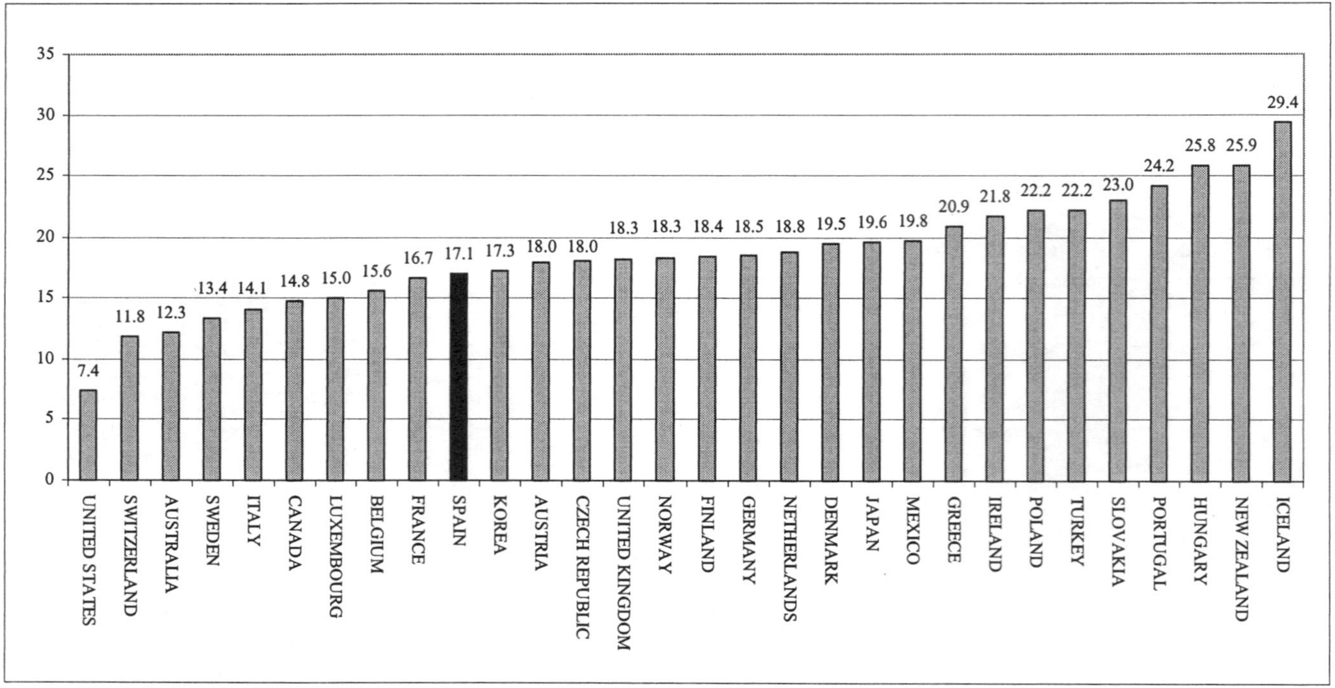

Figure 8.8 General consumer taxes as a percentage of total tax revenue 2001

Table 8.9 VAT as percentage of GDP

	1965	1970	1975	1980	1985	1995	2000	2001	Variation
OECD Total	0.5	2	3	3.5	3.9	5.9	6.6	6.5	6
OECD Europe	0.7	2.6	3.9	4.5	5	6.9	7.5	7	6.3
European Union (15)	0.8	2.7	4.4	5.2	5.6	6.9	7.4	6.8	6
OECD America	–	–	–	0.8	0.9	1.7	2	3.1	3.1
OECD Pacific	–	–	–	1	0.9	3.5	4.8	5.3	5.3
GERMANY	–	5.5	5.2	6.2	5.9	6.7	7	6.7	6.7
FRANCE	6.9	8.7	8.3	8.5	8.6	7.5	7.5	7.3	0.4
ITALY	–	–	3.6	4.8	5	5.7	6.6	5.9	5.9
NETHERLANDS	–	5.2	6	6.9	6.9	6.5	7.2	7.5	7.5
BELGIUM	–	3.9	6.5	7.3	7.2	6.8	7.4	7.1	7.1
LUXEMBOURG	–	–	4.5	3.9	4.8	5.1	5.5	6	6
UNITED KINGDOM	–	–	3.1	5.2	6	6.6	6.9	6.8	6.8
IRELAND	–	–	4.3	4.6	7.2	7	6.7	6.7	6.7
DENMARK	–	7.4	6.8	9.8	9.5	9.5	9.6	9.6	9.6
SPAIN	–	–	–	–	–	5.2	6.2	6	6
GREECE	–	–	–	–	–	7.1	8.3	8.2	8.2
PORTUGAL	–	–	–	–	–	7.6	8.3	8.3	8.3
MEXICO	–	–	–	2.5	2.7	2.8	3.5	3.6	3.6
CANADA	–	–	–	–	–	2.4	2.6	2.6	2.6
KOREA	–	–	–	3.9	3.6	3.9	4.5	4.7	4.7
JAPAN	–	–	–	–	–	1.4	2.4	2	2
AUSTRALIA	–	–	–	–	–	–	3.6	3.6	–
NORWAY	–	8.2	8.1	7.8	7.9	8.8	8	8.2	8.2

Table 8.9 VAT as percentage of GDP (continued)

	1965	1970	1975	1980	1985	1995	2000	2001	Variation
NEW ZEALAND	–	–	–	–	–	8.5	8.7	9	9
SWEDEN	–	4	5.1	6.3	6.8	7.1	7.2	7.1	7.1
FINLAND	5.6	6	5.8	6.3	7.3	7.4	8.1	8.2	2.6
ICELAND	–	–	–	–	–	9.5	10.3	9.3	9.3
SWITZERLAND	–	–	–	–	–	2.4	4.1	4.1	4.1
AUSTRIA	–	–	7.4	8	8.8	7.6	8.3	8.2	8.2
TURKEY	–	–	–	–	3.5	5.5	7.8	8	8
CZECH REPUBLIC	–	–	–	–	–	6.9	7.5	7	–
SLOVAKIA	–	–	–	–	–	–	8	7.6	–
HUNGARY	–	–	–	–	–	7.5	8.8	8.7	–
POLAND	–	–	–	–	–	6.7	7.6	7.6	–

Notes: In all tables the last data entry for Portugal, the United States, Australia, Iceland and Poland corresponds to the year 2000.

Source: OECD.

Table 8.10 VAT as a percentage of total tax revenue

	1965	1970	1975	1980	1985	1995	2000	2001	Variation
OECD Total	1.61	5.84	8.1	9.77	10.77	16.12	17.54	17.46	15.85
OECD Europe	2.03	7.38	10.66	11.39	12.79	18.05	19.05	17.34	15.31
European Union (15)	2.57	7.77	12.13	13.22	13.5	17.48	18.02	15.81	13.24
OECD America	–	–	–	5.19	5.31	7.88	8.65	13.56	13.56
OECD Pacific	–	–	–	5.5	5.27	11.7	15.48	20.9	20.9
GERMANY	–	17.14	14.63	16.63	15.81	17.44	18.37	18.52	18.52
FRANCE	20.07	25.46	23.1	20.88	19.68	16.99	16.49	16.2	-3.87
ITALY	–	–	13.68	15.62	14.5	13.82	15.76	14.13	14.13
NETHERLANDS	–	14.61	14.36	15.83	16.18	15.6	17.34	18.81	18.81
BELGIUM	–	11.28	16.29	17.1	15.72	15.29	16.14	15.57	15.57
LUXEMBOURG	–	–	11.93	9.71	10.78	12.25	13.28	14.12	14.12
UNITED KINGDOM	–	–	8.91	14.66	15.88	19	18.37	18.25	18.25
IRELAND	–	–	14.68	14.76	20.59	21.25	21.49	21.49	21.49
DENMARK	–	18.77	16.9	22.25	20.12	19.32	19.58	19.53	19.53
SPAIN	–	–	–	–	–	15.85	17.6	17.06	17.06
GREECE	–	–	–	–	–	22.49	21.96	20.2	20.2
PORTUGAL	–	–	–	–	–	23.39	24.21	24.21	24.21
MEXICO	–	–	–	15.56	15.94	17.01	18.72	19.75	19.75
CANADA	–	–	–	–	–	6.62	7.24	7.37	7.37
KOREA	–	–	–	22	21.07	18.88	17.02	17.25	17.25
JAPAN	–	–	–	–	–	5.21	8.89	19.6	–
AUSTRALIA	–	–	–	–	–	–	11.31	11.31	11.31
NORWAY	–	23.75	20.49	18.22	18.19	21.21	19.74	18.34	18.34

Table 8.10 VAT as a percentage of total tax revenue (continued)

	1965	1970	1975	1980	1985	1995	2000	2001	Variation
NEW ZEALAND	–	–	–	–	–	22.72	24.71	25.85	25.85
SWEDEN	–	10.26	11.98	13.36	13.96	15	13.29	13.28	13.28
FINLAND	18.46	18.96	15.72	17.33	18.32	16.35	17.35	17.67	-0.79
ICELAND	–	–	–	–	–	30.07	27.67	26.79	26.79
SWITZERLAND	–	–	–	–	–	7.35	11.49	11.84	11.84
AUSTRIA	–	–	19.84	20.11	20.99	18.23	19.04	18.01	18.01
TURKEY	–	–	–	–	22.34	24.32	23.3	22.23	22.23
CZECH REPUBLIC	–	–	–	–	–	17.13	18.89	18.05	18.05
SLOVAKIA	–	–	–	–	–	–	22.25	23.05	–
HUNGARY	–	–	–	–	–	17.82	22.45	22.48	–
POLAND	–	–	–	–	–	17.02	22.19	22.19	–

Notes: In all tables the last data entry for Portugal, the United States, Australia, Iceland and Poland corresponds to the year 2000.

Source: OECD.

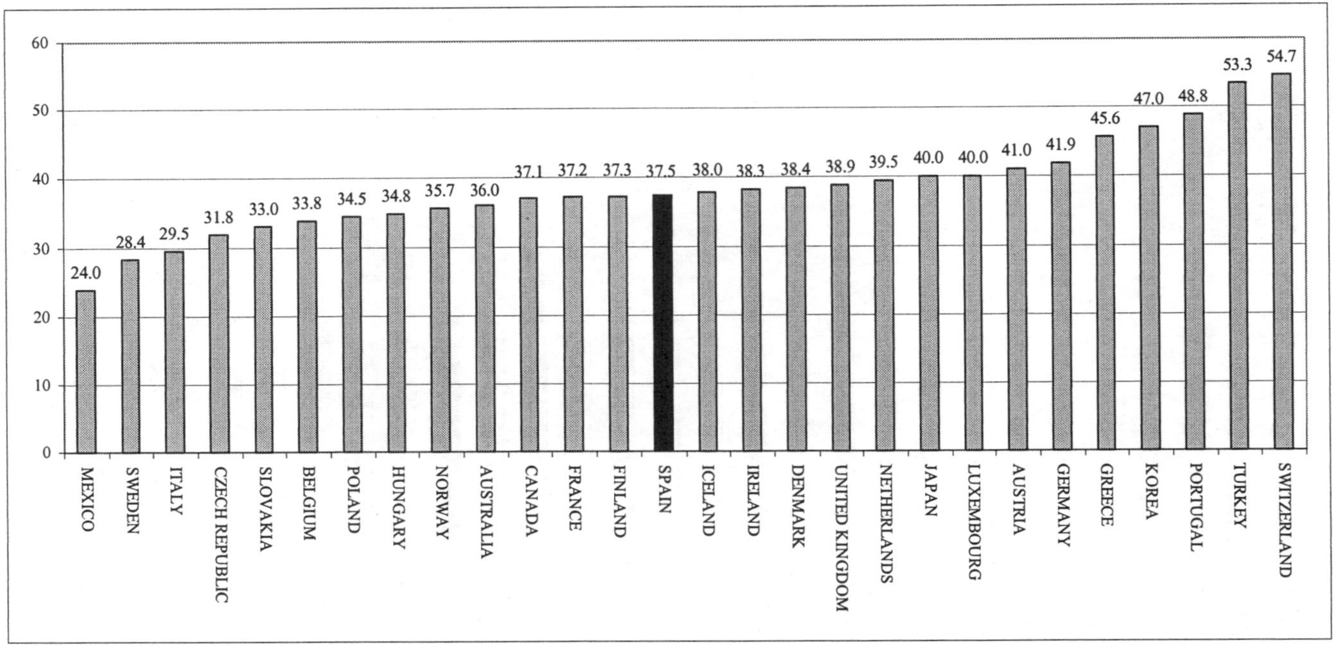

Figure 8.9 VAT productivity 2001

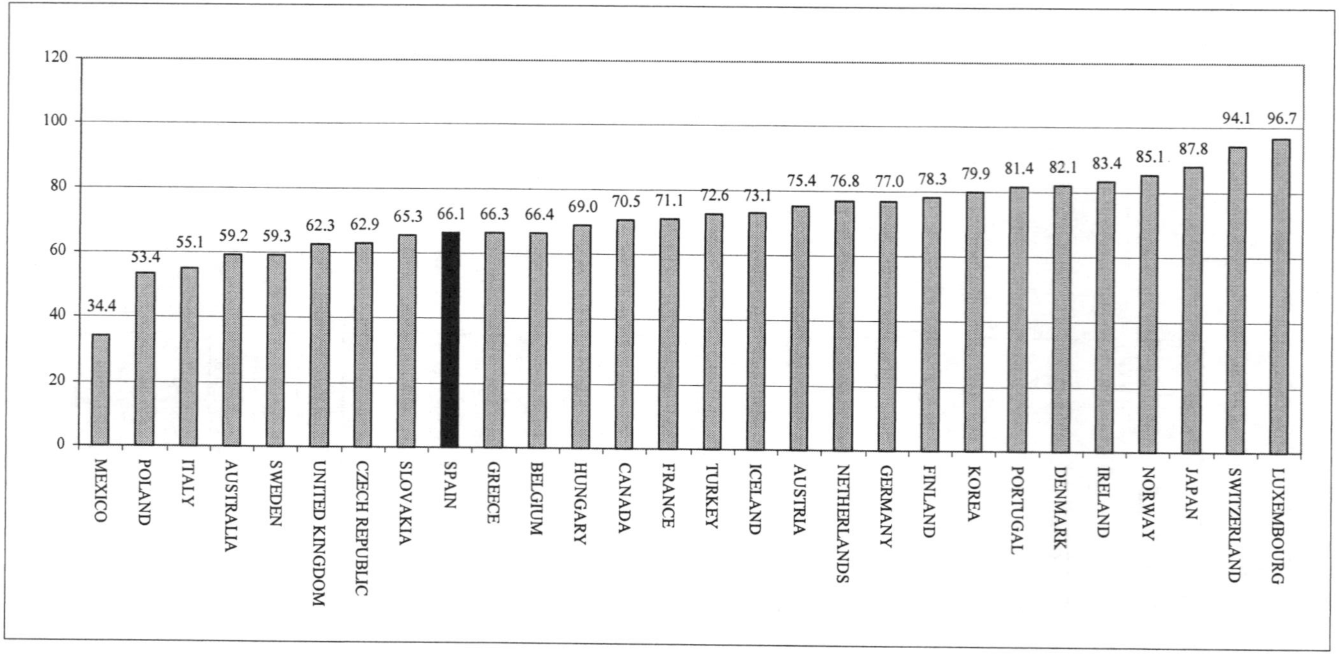

Figure 8.10 Effective VAT rate as percentage of nominal VAT rate 2000

Table 8.11 VAT: Productivity and effective tax rates

	Revenue		**Nominal rate**	**Productivity**	**Effective rates**	
	% GNP 2000	**% share of public revenue 2000**	**2000**	**2000**	**2000**	**% of nominal**
	(1)	**(2)**	**(3)**	**(4) = (1)/(3)**	**(5)**	**(6) = (3)/(5)**
GERMANY	6.7	18.52	16	41.9	12.31	77.0
FRANCE	7.3	16.2	19.6	37.2	13.93	71.1
ITALY	5.9	14.13	20	29.5	11.02	55.1
NETHERLANDS	7.5	18.81	19	39.5	14.60	76.8
BELGIUM	7.1	15.57	21	33.8	13.94	66.4
LUXEMBOURG	6	14.12	15	40.0	14.50	96.7
UNITED KINGDOM	6.8	18.25	17.5	38.9	10.91	62.3
IRELAND	6.7	21.49	17.5	38.3	14.60	83.4
DENMARK	9.6	19.53	25	38.4	20.53	82.1
SPAIN	6	17.06	16	37.5	10.58	66.1
GREECE	8.2	20.2	18	45.6	11.94	66.3
PORTUGAL	8.3	24.21	17	48.8	13.84	81.4
MEXICO	3.6	19.75	15	24.0	5.16	34.4
CANADA	2.6	7.37	7	37.1	4.93	70.5
KOREA	4.7	17.25	10	47.0	7.99	79.9
JAPAN	2	19.6	5	40.0	4.39	87.8

Table 8.11 VAT: Productivity and effective tax rates (continued)

	Revenue		Nominal rate	Productivity	Effective rates	
	% GNP 2000	% share of public revenue 2000	2000	2000	2000	% of nominal
	(1)	(2)	(3)	(4) = (1)/(3)	(5)	(6) = (3)/(5)
AUSTRALIA	3.6	11.31	10	36.0	5.92	59.2
NORWAY	8.2	18.34	23	35.7	19.58	85.1
SWEDEN	7.1	13.28	25	28.4	14.82	59.3
FINLAND	8.2	17.67	22	37.3	17.24	78.3
ICELAND	9.3	26.79	24.5	38.0	17.90	73.1
SWITZERLAND	4.1	11.84	7.5	54.7	7.06	94.1
AUSTRIA	8.2	18.01	20	41.0	15.08	75.4
TURKEY	8	22.23	15	53.3	10.88	72.6
CZECH REPUBLIC	7	18.05	22	31.8	13.85	62.9
SLOVAKIA	7.6	23.05	23	33.0	15.03	65.3
HUNGARY	8.7	22.48	25	34.8	17.25	69.0
POLAND	7.6	22.19	22	34.5	11.74	53.4

Notes: Productivity: collection of the VAT in percentage of the GDP divided by nominal type.
Effective rates: Collection of the VAT in percentage of the expense in final consumption of the families.

Source: OECD and own elaboration.

Table 8.12 VAT rates in the EU (15) (as of May 2002)

	Super Reduced	Reduced	Standard	Rate Parking
GERMANY	–	7	16	–
FRANCE	2.1	5.5	19.6	–
ITALY	4	10	20	–
NETHERLANDS	–	6	19	–
BELGIUM (*)	–	6	21	12
LUXEMBOURG	3	6	15	12
UNITED KINGDOM (*)	–	5	17.5	–
IRELAND (*)	4.3	12.5	21	12.5
DENMARK (*)	–	–	25	–
SPAIN	4	7	16	–
GREECE	4	8	18	–
PORTUGAL	–	5/12	17	–
SWEDEN (*)	–	6/12	25	–
FINLAND (*)	–	8/17	22	–
AUSTRIA	–	10/12	20	–
Evolution in Spain				
	Super Reduced	**Reduced**	**Standard**	**Rate Parking**
1/1/1986	–	6	12	33
1/1/1992	–	6	13	28
8/1/1992	–	6	15	28
1/1/1993	3	6	15	–
1/1/1995	4	7	16	–

Note: (*) Countries that use the zero tax rate.

Source: European Commission (2003).

THE PROCESS OF HARMONISATION OF VAT AND EXCISE DUTIES WITHIN THE EUROPEAN UNION

Since its origins, the European Common Market has progressed with the ultimate objective of achieving free circulation of goods and services. With this aim, tariffs were eliminated among the participant states and the neutrality of indirect taxes was declared a fundamental goal. In this regard, Articles 95 and 96 of the Treaty of the European Economic Community embody two principles which must be respected in all cases: the principle of equal treatment of goods, and the principle of no discrimination. Article 99, on the other hand, explicitly contemplates the harmonisation of indirect taxes.

After the elimination of tariffs, the European Community began to harmonise the structure of sales taxes and their rates. In 1967 the Council decided to substitute the taxes on company trading with a VAT on consumption applicable on a destination principle, partly to prevent the manipulation of adjustments at frontiers aimed at favouring national exports or substituting imports, which are practices that are incompatible with the objectives of the Common Market. Since then there have been over twenty directives on harmonisation, of which the most important was the Sixth, in 1977, which provided a large step towards greater uniformity of the tax base and was partly driven by the decision to convert VAT into a tool for financing the European Community budget.

VAT Harmonisation

It is well known that the establishment of a common market implies, among other things, that fiscal frontiers and border controls should be eliminated for intra-community transactions. That is, goods should circulate between two community countries with the same freedom with which they circulate between two locations in the same country. In common with standard practice in international trade, VAT was subject to the destination country criterion in Europe and the administration of this was carried out at the physical borders between community countries (indeed, this still occurs for trade with the rest of the world). Thus, the fiscal adjustment occurs at the border. The exporter has the right to a VAT credit and the importer is charged the VAT of the destination country.

The elimination of fiscal frontiers within the European Community meant that the system had to change so that intra-Community operations occur in the same way as those carried out within individual member states. One possibility in this respect would be to apply origin-destination VAT within the Community. In other words, the agent acquiring the good in the importing country is charged the VAT of the exporting country, and the importer has the right to deduct the payments made to the origin country at the standard rate.

This solution gives rise to serious difficulties, the most fundamental being that the VAT intake does not correspond to the level of final consumption within each country. Under origin-destination VAT, the exporting country receives a return which the agent acquiring the good in the importing country uses as a deduction; the countries within the Community which export more, increase their VAT intake at the expense of the countries which import more, and these see their VAT intake reduced. However, VAT intake should basically depend on a country's consumption. This problem thus requires the creation of a compensation mechanism between member states which would permit the destination country to be compensated for the VAT received by the origin country and deducted by the destination country.

Since January 1st, 1993, the European Union opted to provisionally maintain the destination principle despite the elimination of VAT controls at intra-Community borders. This provisional regime was developed in Directive 91/680/EEC (16th of December), which regulates the legal framework of intra-Community trade and which modified the Sixth Directive of 1977; in Regulation 92/218/EEC (27th of January) on administrative cooperation in the field of indirect taxation; and in the agreements reached on the harmonisation of tax rates. As a technical solution, the taxable event of acquisition of intra-Community goods was created. This permitted the elimination of customs procedures (formally, imports and exports do not exist between member states), with verification of VAT payments now being performed through company accounting. Under the taxable event of intra-Community acquisition of goods, each intra-Community transaction is divided into two operations: a delivery, exempt from tax, but with the right to a VAT deduction for the person making the delivery; and an acquisition, subject to tax, whose VAT is borne by the acquirer who in turn deducts it, initiating the VAT chain in the destination country.

As the European Council has not made any declaration on this subject, the provisional system has been automatically extended and remains in force at present. As already mentioned, this system was laid out in Directive 91/680/EEC, Regulation 92/680/EEC, and the agreements reached on the harmonisation of tax rates. The contents of these agreements can be summarised as follows: the standard rate of VAT cannot be lower than 15 percent; one or two reduced rates may be applied, provided they are no lower than 5 percent; higher VAT rates may not be applied. However, there are some exceptions: Spain and Luxembourg can apply a special reduced rate no lower than 3 percent; the UK and Ireland can maintain their traditional zero-rates; and the rights of States which had been applying rates below 5 percent are generally respected.

In summary, the system is too complex, excessively combining the origin and destination principles. This leads to insecurities and uncertainties with regard to fiscal responsibility and increases the administrative burden. This situation makes it advisable to move from the provisional regime to a more definitive regime, and it is in this direction that the European Comission has focused much of its harmonisation effort in recent times. For this transition, a series of fundamental measures must be made regarding two issues: (a) the general application of the taxation principle of destination or origin, and (b) greater or lesser harmonisation of tax rates.

Recent Commission proposals aimed at achieving the establishment of a definitive VAT system based on the origin principle include:

- the elimination of the present distinction between interior and intra-Community operations and, as a consequence, the elimination of the taxable event of intra-Community acquisition of goods and the exemption applied to deliveries of goods whose destinations are other member states.
- the possibility to deduct certain VAT instalments on goods used for both company and personal activity, such as, for example, cars.
- VAT revenues collected by member states where taxpayers have their fiscal residence will be entirely redistributed between member states in function of the consumption of goods and services subject to the tax which has taken place in their respective territories, as determined by statistical data.[17]
- regarding the harmonisation of the rules regulating the structural elements of the tax, it will be necessary to establish a single standard VAT rate band (between 15 percent and 25 percent) as a preliminary step, with a view to reducing the width of this band. At present, the only obligation is to respect the minimum of 15 percent for the standard rate. The number of reduced rates should be limited to the minimum, and if possible to only one, with a band as narrow as that envisaged for the standard rate.
- each member state should be responsible for the management, collection and control of tax corresponding to taxpayers whose fiscal residence is in the territory of that State and to that due for imports of goods into that territory. States who, due to a lack of diligence, endanger VAT receipts may be obliged to redress the corresponding losses.
- the establishment of standard methods to ensure more efficient control and collection. This will determine the need to create new instruments and methods of cooperation and to perfect the present system of information exchange.
- a study is due on the legal instrument (directive or regulation) which will be used, and a modification of Article 99 of the Treaty to substitute the principle of unanimity now required to adopt such measures with that of a qualified majority.

In June 2000, the Commission presented a Communication in which it set out its strategic programme to improve the workings of the VAT regime within the framework of the internal market. The programme proposed a series of pragmatic measures centred around four main objectives: the simplification and modernisation of existing rules, a more uniform application of existing regulations, and cooperation at administrative level. This strategy was based on the observation that it was unlikely, given the reluctance of the member states, that significant advances would be made in the near future on the establishment of a common VAT regime based on the origin principle.

The main objective of the strategy was to provide a new impulse to the European Council with the aim of achieving concrete and necessary improvements to the existing tax regime in the short run, without calling into question the long-run objective of a definitive regime based on taxing in the origin member state. Since the new strategy was put into place almost three years ago, the Council has put forward several proposals on the issue of the VAT. However, as pointed out by the Commission (European Commission, 2003a) the maintenance, in an enlarged Union, of the principle of unanimity when taking decisions on taxation represents a serious threat to this incipient progress. If future work is carried out within the framework of Article 93 of the Treaty, the member states will more than ever have to show flexibility at negotiations in order for progress to continue. This flexibility will be even more necessary when it comes to measures aimed at a key element of the VAT system, namely the determination of where operations should be taxed.

A more extended and better use of electronic means of communication between operators and the tax administration, as well as between the tax administrations of different member states, would allow the VAT regime to be simplified for operators, safeguarding and even extending control measures. In effect, through the creation of a one-stop-shop mechanism, an operator established in the European Union can contact the Administration of the member state in which he is established in order to comply with his obligations regarding tax declarations and payment. The introduction of this mechanism greatly facilitates procedures in cases where an operator carries out taxable transactions for which he appears as a debtor in other member states where he is not established. The use of this mechanism would reaffirm the principle of taxing in the place of consumption (the destination principle), without generating administrative burdens for Community operators or hindering the workings of the internal market. Moreover, taxing in the place of consumption, at the VAT rate which is applicable in the member state where consumption has taken place, guarantees the correct functioning of the internal market while at the same time permitting that the member states preserve certain sovereignty when it comes to setting the VAT rates to be applied in their territory.

On the other hand, the Commission is continuing with efforts to modernise the present regime and to guarantee its more uniform application. In particular, the proposals towards providing legal substance to the debates of the VAT Commission[18] as well as the planned initiative aimed at introducing a mechanism for managing individual cases should contribute to settling cases of double taxation, a practice which has no place in an authentic internal market.

The observation that the present regime has defects which can give rise to fraud is not a new one. Carousel fraud exploits these defects inherent to the basic principles which constitute the foundations of the present regime.

As is known, in the present provisional VAT regime of the European Union transactions involving deliveries of goods between companies of different EU member states are subject to VAT through the application of a system under which transactions are exempt in the origin member state. VAT fraud on intercommunity transactions occurs in many varieties but basically functions somewhat as follows. A company, which we call Firm 1, registered in an EU member state which we call State X, carries out an inter-Community delivery of goods to Firm 2 located in another State Y. Firm 2 acquires these goods free of VAT and immediately carries out a delivery to another firm, Firm 3, in the same state as itself, State 2. Firm 2 (the "missing trader", which is the name commonly given to these types of fraudulent operators) charges the VAT from the previous delivery to Firm 3, but does not lodge it and after a short while disappears. Firm 3 ("broker") deducts the VAT it has paid on its acquisitions from 2 and sells the goods in the internal market of State Y, charging VAT. The loss in VAT revenue is equal to the payment made by Firm 3 to Firm 2, which the latter has not lodged. At times, and with the objective of obscuring the relationship between Firm 2 (missing trader) and Firm 3 (broker), the goods are supplied from one to the other through one or more intermediary companies ("buffers").

The scheme just outlined turns into "carousel fraud" when, instead of selling the goods in the internal market of State Y, Firm 3 carries out an inter-Community tax-exempt delivery to a company in the origin state, State X. Once in this State, the operation can be repeated indefinitely. The fraud is therefore manifest in the application for a VAT return made by Firm 3. In the so-called "document" carousel fraud, the merchandise does not even exist and there is only a circulation of invoices. However, the Commission is of the opinion that an ever-increasing collaboration between the member states, with the support of the Commission, should make it possible to keep fraud within acceptable limits.[19] If in spite of the efforts of the authorities carousel fraud becomes so intense as to affect the normal functioning of the economic market, causing unacceptable distortions to competition for honest operators, a need will arise for a debate at Community level on the future common VAT regime.

With regard to the future path of VAT harmonisation, attention should be drawn to the stagnation into which the definitive VAT regime has fallen, with the consequent major slowdown in the process of tax harmonisation in Europe that this has caused. The uncertainties which hang over the existence, conditions and terms of the origin system are generating an impasse even with regard to the changes which are needed to maintain the present provisional system. Spain, in its position as a net importer within the EU, is comfortably positioned within the great majority of member states against change, given that a significant share of tax revenue would be lost in a macroeconomic "clearing" with uncertain results. The large differences in opinion between member states with regard to the need to carry out serious progress in the field of tax harmonisation combined with the requirement of unanimity in the Council to adopt proposals in this area make it unlikely that the so-called definitive regime will be put in place in the next few years.

The Commission itself recognises the incoherence of some of its proposals in relation to the objective, more and more theoretical as time goes by, of taxing in the State of origin which should have been complied with on the 31st of December, 1996. Taxation in the state of origin only pins down the territory in which the taxpayer has to pay the tax, and only a system of reallocation would guarantee that each member state would receive the revenue corresponding to it, given the distortions which could arise from the fact that the taxpayer belongs to one state whereas final consumption takes place in another. The problem is that this would require the differences between tax rates to be reduced, practically to the extent they were unified. The main obstacle is not technical, but political, so that as long as States are unwilling to abandon the principle of taxing in the destination country, any improvements in the common VAT regime can only be aimed at guaranteeing strict compliance with the present structure. This is manifest in the almost definitive confirmation that the future of tax harmonisation is going to be centred on technical modifications to the Sixth Directive (with a large impulse given to inter-administrative cooperation), and that there are two steps which are not going be taken in the medium term: the transition from the destination principle to the origin principle, on one hand, and the unification of tax rates on the other. This opinion is reinforced not only by the pessimism of the Commission itself but also by the fact that this pessimism arose in a Union with 15 member states, leading us to the conclusion that it will only get worse with a Union of twenty-five members and with the amplified Union from 2007 on.

Finally, motivated by the year 2002 financing reform of the Autonomous Communities, the central government put forward the alternative of a partial ceding of VAT, in particular the retail phase. To this end the European Commission was consulted for its opinion on this possibility.

The position of the Commission can be summarised as follows. With regard to handing over part of VAT revenue, no restrictions are placed by the EU on member states. The member states are sovereign, and can distribute their tax revenue according to their needs provided that this does not have any affect on its own resources derived from VAT.

On the other hand, Community VAT provisions currently in place do not permit the Autonomous Communities to fix differential VAT rates. Article 12, Paragraph 3a, of the Sixth Directive stipulates that a single normal rate be set for each member state. Member states can then apply one or two reduced rates. Moreover, the possibility that the Autonomous Communities charge a supplementary tax which would act as a tax on the volume of business is not allowed either given the provisions of Article 33 of the Sixth Directive. In light of the above, it can be asserted that the possibilities for future changes will be restricted to the percentage share in the tax intake.

Excise Taxes

Regarding excise taxes, the trend towards maintaining the destination based principle of taxation is likely to continue, as has been mentioned above. This brings with it a need for harmonisation of the tax rates in force in the member states as well as a minimum harmonisation of the structures (taxable events, systems of collection, tax exemptions, etc.) if fiscal frontiers are to be effectively eliminated. Over the years, the Commission has put forward many proposals, mainly related to the harmonisation of tax *structures* rather than tax *rates*. However, progress has been slow, primarily due to the budgetary impact.

Community norms on the harmonisation of excise taxes regulate the structure of these taxes and establish the minimum rates applicable for each product category. This has permitted the member states to maintain large differences in tax rates. Up to now these differences have not generated unbearable distortions because it is only on sales to private agents (for the satisfaction of their needs and transported by them) that the principle that the tax be received in the country where the goods are acquired and at the rates applicable in that country applies. Otherwise, the tax is generated and paid in the destination country.

The delay in bringing minimum excise tax rates up to date is damaging the process of harmonisation of excise duties on hydrocarbons—tainted by the controversy over the CO^2 tax—and alcohol and tobacco. The story of the "CO^2 tax" begins in 1992 when the Commission proposed the creation of a harmonised tax on energy consumption in order to comply with the Community commitment to reduce CO^2 emissions. Two years later, and faced with the impossibility of arriving at an agreement on the obligatory establishment of an "ecotax" (which some defended on environmental grounds while others were opposed on grounds of competitiveness), the Essen summit seemed to have abandoned the project, although it did establish the setting of some common parameters so that states who wished to introduce taxes of this nature could do so without distorting the functioning of the Single Market.

The Commission has not presented proposals corresponding to the revision of excise duties on alcohol and tobacco either. These have been blocked by the full body of the Commission due to the eternal disagreements surrounding the taxation of these goods. There is a division between the states which produce cheap manufacturing tobacco, who defend ad valorem rates, and those who produce expensive tobacco, who defend a lump-sum tax. There are also divisions between wine-producing states, who defend the present zero rate and limited control, and non-producers, who wish to tax wine the same way as other alcohol products.

On the other hand, the member states have created non-harmonised excise duties to get around the limitations imposed by the harmonisation of VAT and to take advantage of its shortcomings. In some cases, these excise duties have compensated the obligatory elimination of higher VAT rates, such as the Spanish vehicle registration tax. In other cases consumption tax was extended beyond the straitjacket of VAT to certain sectors for which Community directives permitted exemptions. An example of this is the tax on insurance premia recently introduced in Spain and which had already been introduced in the majority of member states.

The changes which can be expected in the coming years and which can be gathered from the proposals awaiting approval presented by the Commission are not particularly important, and will not achieve (nor is it their aim) the unification of rates of taxes on specific consumption goods nor even the establishment of tax bands. It will thus remain the norm that large differences exist among member states with regard to the tax burden borne by products subject to the regime of taxes on specific consumption goods.

With regard to the use of excise taxes in the financing of the Autonomous Communities, the future could be marked by the creation of new national taxes under certain conditions, which include: (i) that the objective pursued be not primarily budgetary; and (ii) that the tax be claimed only at the point of consumption. These taxes could then be handed over to the territorial governments, as has happened with the excise tax on fuels.

The current solution of imposing excise duty on manufacturing in the country where consumption takes place, in force since the 1st of January, 1993, is likely to be maintained in the medium term. Excise taxes are subject to what has come to be known as a "suspension system", which is defined in the Spanish Excise Tax Law (*Ley Española de Impuestos Especiales*) as the "regime applicable to the manufacture, transformation, holding, and circulation of products subject to excise taxes for which the taxable event has occurred but the tax has not accrued, and hence the tax is not demandable".

At present, therefore, under the "destination-based principle of taxation" the circulation of goods in EU territory is carried out freely under duty suspension arrangements up until they arrive at the tax warehouses (*depósitos fiscales*) in the destination country, where the excise tax is paid (at the tax rates in force) at the moment the product is consumed. This is the same as before with the difference that there have been no controls at internal frontiers since January 1st, 1993. Despite its problems, the system does not seem to be in need of radical reform.

In summary, we note that there are serious defects in the provisional VAT regime still in place. We believe it will not be long before there is an origin-destination system in place in the Community where the repercussions of the VAT will not interrupt transactions between business people and professionals of the member states. As we have commented, however, it is unlikely that the definitive origin country regime will be adopted in the medium term.

A reduction of the dispersion of existing tax rates is also possible. On the other hand, the present structure of excise taxes can be maintained, and perhaps extended to an environmental tax.

INCIDENCE OF INDIRECT TAXATION

As predicted by theoretical analysis, Spanish indirect taxes on the whole are markedly regressive in nature. From a personal point of view, the fact that these taxes basically fall on consumption suggests that this is indeed the case. This conjecture has been confirmed by numerous empirical studies which have been carried out for Spain on the distribution of indirect tax burdens across income levels. Both the studies carried out before the introduction of VAT[20] and those carried out after its introduction[21] conclude in all cases that indirect taxation is regressive. This is so, in spite of the radical changes carried out to the structure of this class of taxes, the constant evolution of Spanish consumption patterns, and the changes in income distribution over this long period.

The comparison of the results in Avellaneda (1998), for the year 1991 for the set of all consumption taxes, with those in Argimón, González-Páramo and Salas (1987) for the year 1980 also for the whole set of indirect taxes, allows us to calculate the variation of effective average tax rates over the decade. Thus, over this period the average rates as a percentage of expenditure rose from 7.34 percent to 8.805 percent and as a percentage of income from 8.43 percent to 11.293 percent.[22] Though the tax structures corresponding to both years are quite different, the comparison is reasonable due to the fact that consumption taxes accounted for practically all indirect taxation in 1991.

If we focus exclusively on VAT, the rates found by Avellaneda (1998) for 1991 are lower than those found by González-Páramo and Salas (1991) for 1986. As a percentage of expenditure, the rate fell from 7.88 percent in 1986 to 6.571 percent in 1991, while as a percentage of income the rate fell from 9.02 percent in 1986 to 8.558 percent in 1991. The changes in the VAT rates[23] brought about a rise in fiscal pressure from 1993, with the average rate as a percentage of expenditure rising 0.615 points from 8.805 percent to 9.420 percent and the average rate as a percentage of income rising by 0.801 points from 11.923 percent to 12.094 percent. While taxes increased across the board, excise taxes increased much more than VAT as a consequence of the elimination of the higher VAT rates and the introduction of the new Vehicle Registration Tax.

Although consumption taxes as a whole are regressive, VAT is somewhat less so than excise taxes. However, two excise taxes, namely the fuel and vehicle registration taxes, seem to be progressive. This is a consequence of the fact that the consumption of these goods is highly conditioned on income levels. The high prices of motor vehicles, the possession of which determines the consumption of oil-based fuels, imply that families with higher incomes are the ones buying them. Alcohol and tobacco duties, on the other hand, are extremely regressive. The consumption of these goods, which are accessible to people at all income levels, given that their prices are low, is determined above all by cultural factors. However, it is likely that those sectors of the population which are better-informed will consume less of these products given the prejudicial effects they have on health. As there is a high correlation between information levels and income, low-income families tend to consume more of these products and thus contribute more than high-income families to this tax (Avellaneda and Sánchez Maldonado, 1999).

Serrano (2003, p.80 and thereafter) examines the redistributive impact of the present VAT arrangements in Spain. With regard to VAT payments, the present system is characterised by the fact that the tax burden is not spread proportionally across income distribution. The concentration index is 0.2268, whereas the Gini index is higher (0.2964). In other words, the tax payments concentration curve lies above the Lorenz curve of pre-tax income, for every percentile, which implies that indirect taxes are globally regressive. The negative value of the Kakwani index (-0.0696) confirms the regressiveness of VAT, again from a global point of view. As an illustration, the poorest 30 percent of the population has 14.59 percent of income but pays 20 percent of the VAT burden. The richest 10 percent of the population, on the other hand, receives 23.47 percent of the income but only pays 17.06 percent of the VAT. The reduction of the average effective rate as income rises is another indicator of the regressiveness of the present VAT regime in Spain.

The studies by Avellaneda and Sánchez Maldonado (1999) and Sánchez Maldonado, Gómez Sala and Avellaneda (1999) analyse the distribution of the fiscal burden from consumption taxes across individuals according to the Autonomous Community of residence as well as income. The comparative analysis of the rates of the different taxes in the different regions for two different years allows us to compare the relative incidence of each tax in each region and to measure the impact of the 1993 reform on each region. These studies show that regional tax rates are far from homogeneous. There is a significant variation of rates as a percentage of expenditure as well as income, with the dispersion in income terms being higher, and there are also variations across the individual taxes. The increase in tax as a result of the 1993 reform also affected different regions quite differently. Their expected conclusion is that the taxes are regressive on the whole, and that the effective rate of taxation is higher in lower-income regions than in higher-income regions. Again, this result is to be expected if we extend the finding that consumption taxes are regressive at the level of household income to the territorial level.

Another relevant fact is that if we take the composition of households into account then the taxes are even more regressive in terms of their territorial distribution. The extent of this is such that the only two progressive taxes, namely fuel and vehicle registration taxes, become regressive. This is an important factor when it comes to analyzing the equity of the indirect tax system because for a given income level a household with more members has less capacity to pay such taxes. Finally, the 1993 reform slightly reduced territorial regressiveness for the taxes as a whole as well as for each individual tax with the exception of the tax on alcoholic drinks, which became much more regressive than before.

SOME OUTSTANDING PROBLEMS AND OPTIONS FOR REFORM

As has been stated (Cnossen, 1998), the introduction of Value Added Tax (VAT) on an almost universal level should be considered as the most important event of the second half of the twentieth century as far as the evolution of tax systems is concerned. Since the end of the nineteen-sixties, VAT has become the main consumption tax in 123 industrialised and developing countries. At present, the most notable absences from the list of countries where VAT exists are the USA and India. For different reasons, in these jurisdictions traditional consumption taxes have been relied upon. The motive for adopting VAT varies from one given country to another, though the main reason in all cases has been the realisation that a correctly designed value added tax is capable of generating greater public revenues than any other broad-based general consumption tax, and with lower economic and administrative costs.

However, a large number of problems persist with regard to VAT in many of the countries where it has been introduced (Cnossen, 1998a, 2001; Ebrill et al. 2001). Among these, the following can be highlighted. Firstly, on many occasions, and as happens in the Spanish case, VAT does not extend to the retail consumption stage. Secondly, it has been noted that many countries generalise the practice of exempting certain services, ignoring the costs of doing so in terms of economic distortions and administration problems. Noteworthy in this regard is the treatment given to public services (postal services, telecommunications, public transport), which often remain exempt without any theoretical or practical justification. The same occurs with a large portion of cultural services (books, DVDs, etc) and the activities of education and health.

Thirdly, many countries find it difficult to tax real estate, financial services, agricultural activity and small enterprises.[24] In the case of real estate, subjection to tax is clearly preferable to exemption. No clear solution to the treatment of financial services appears in sight,[25] while different ad hoc systems are used to tax the agricultural sector.

Fourthly, there is the problem of the number of tax rates. In high-income countries the establishment of a reduced VAT rate for basic products is not a good system of aid for the underprivileged due to the convergence produced in consumption patterns—it is better to apply a single rate. In low-income countries, on the other hand, where administrative capability is more limited, the existence of reduced rates and exemptions on basic foods does contribute to mitigating the regressiveness of VAT. However, the equity gains which can be achieved through differentiated VAT rates depend on the level of other instruments available. For example, excise duties on goods with inelastic demands can destroy the main equity gains achieved through differentiated VAT rates. The greater the restraints on the redistributive role of other government taxes and expenditure, the stronger the justifications for differentiated VAT rates on the grounds of equity. Obviously, these justifications will be weaker when an effective income tax can be used. While the benefits from differentiated VAT rates can be large in developing countries, it is also true that the administrative and compliance costs associated with a differentiated structure can be high. In any case, the existence of a heterogeneous tax scale complicates the management of and compliance with VAT. However, as Ebrill et al. (2001) state, the importance of differentiated rates seems to have been exaggerated on many occasions. Even leaving aside other instruments, there are aspects of the VAT structure, such as exemptions, which can generate much more damaging effects than having a variety of rates.

Fifthly, the interjurisdictional aspects mentioned earlier are becoming more and more important, especially in the case of countries that are growing or part of an economic union.

Finally, and as mentioned above, in the case of common markets where no customs controls exist, the adjustments which were previously carried out at the frontier are substituted by the control of agents' accounting, through a system of deferred payments, which seems to be working well in the EU. Cross-border control is possible thanks to a system of information exchange. Dual VATs, such as in Canada, are probably more effective, but would require a supranational VAT in the EU which is at odds with the fiscal subsidiarity of the member states. In the Commonwealth of Independent States, exports are taxed and a tax credit is given on imports. However, this system appears unstable unless accompanied by a well-functioning compensation mechanism.

Various proposals have been made by the European institutions as well as scholars of this issue to address interjurisdictional problems of trade adjustments and overcoming the provisional regime (Table 8.13), of which the following can be highlighted:[26]

(a) Draft directives 1987/1989

These attempts by the Commission to produce a new model of VAT, which like the 1996 proposal were rejected, tried to get around the problems of breaking the VAT chain and the asymmetric treatment of Community trade by taxing sales according to the rates in the country of origin. In this framework, taxpayers in the destination country have the right to deduct VAT paid on their purchases. To ensure that the VAT collected on these inter-Community transactions flows to the destination country, that is, to the administration in whose territory the consumption of taxed goods takes

Table 8.13 Comparison of VAT proposals for the EU single market

	National VAT rate autonomy	**Incentive compatibility**	**Avoidance of break in VAT chain (VAT rate on intra-community supply)**	**Compliance symmetry**	**Clearing requirement (*) characterisation of clearing regime**
Draft directives 1987/89	Yes	No	Yes (country of supply rate)	Yes	High (micro-or macro-clearing)
1996 VAT proposal (Commission 1996)	No	No	Yes (uniform rate)	Yes	High (VAT revenue sharing)
VIVAT (Keen and Smith)	Yes	Yes	Yes (uniform Euro-VAT rate)	Yes	Low (multilateral intra-Community trade imbalances)
CVAT (McLure)	Yes	No	Yes (uniform CVAT, zero national rate)	No	Low (multilateral intra-Community trade imbalances)
Dual VAT (Bird and Gendron)	Yes	Yes	No (zero rate)	No	Low (special regimes)
Prepaid destination VAT (Vanistendael)	Yes	No	Yes (country of acquisition rate)	No	High (bilateral VAT-transfers to destination states)

Notes: (*) National VAT revenue is allocated in line with national consumption, apart from tolerable cross-border purchases.

Source: Genser (2003).

place, the administration of the origin country would be obliged to compensate the administration of the destination country for the quantity of VAT charged by its companies.

The most glaring drawback of this system is the creation of adverse incentives for the administrations in destination countries or importers with regard to the examination of VAT payments which can be deducted, as these will be reimbursed by the administration of the origin country or exporters who, at the end of the day, are the ones that suffer the consequences of any fraudulent deductions that may occur. Consequently, the introduction of such a system requires the reinforcement of the control and harmonisation of the collection systems.

With regard to the system of compensation between countries, in 1987 it was proposed that this be based on the invoices of the different transactions, whereas in 1989 it was proposed that this compensation be also based on aggregate EU trade and consumption data.

(b) 1996 Commission proposal

This proposal broadly coincides with the previous ones. Now, however, a greater uniformity of the bases and the rates of the tax throughout the different EU countries is advocated in order to achieve a symmetric treatment for trade and to facilitate the compensation mechanism. This mechanism would include a clearing house which would centralise VAT collection and from which the redistribution would be made in accordance with aggregate data on national consumption. One of the requirements of this proposal is the intensification of cooperation between administrations and the harmonisation of norms of control and collection.

The main drawback of this proposal, apart from the adverse incentives explained in relation to the above proposals, is that the requirement of uniform tax rates, aimed at avoiding distortions when the origin principle is applied, comes at the expense of the degree of fiscal autonomy provided to the national administrations up to this point by VAT regulation.

The introduction of any of the Commission proposals implies a greater harmonisation of VAT throughout the EU. In particular, it is necessary to harmonise the VAT base in order to extend the system of invoices to inter-Community transactions, as well as harmonise the tax rates in order to simplify the compensation mechanism.

(c) VIVAT

The proposal of Keen and Smith (1996, 2000) requires a simpler compensation mechanism due to the fact that the common or supranational VAT is the same for the set of EU countries. It is sufficient to have a multilateral compensation to compensate for possible collection deficits caused by intra-Community transactions, which are taxed at the same rate at all times.

(d) CVAT

The proposal by McLure (2000a) also consists of a dual VAT, where the present heterogeneity of tax rates can be maintained for domestic operations, while intra-Community sales would be subject to a common CVAT for all EU countries.

(e) Dual VAT

Bird and Gendron (1998, 2000 and 2001) propose a system similar to that of the Canadian province of Quebec: a central VAT which allows a certain degree of fiscal autonomy to this regional autonomy. The system operates in a similar way to the present provisional regime (and does not overcome the drawbacks associated with the interruption of the tax chain). Its advantage is that the common supranational VAT would act as a mechanism for controlling fraud in intra-Community transactions, as well as that associated with each country's own VAT.

(f) Prepaid destination VAT

Vanistendael (1995) proposes that buyers in intra-Community transactions be taxed according to the tax rates prevailing in their country of residence. It follows that the tax authorities in each country would be obliged to immediately transfer the revenue collected from these transactions to the administrations of the countries of residence of the buyers.

Genser (2003) carries out a comparison of the six proposals above with the present provisional regime in terms of five objectives which he considers the new EU VAT regime should aim towards achieving (Table 8.14):

(1) it should permit a certain degree of fiscal autonomy at national level with regard to the establishment of tax rates.
(2) it should incorporate incentives for efficient tax management in the control of invoices on the part of the administrations involved.
(3) it should avoid breaking the tax chain in the internal market.
(4) it should bring with it a symmetric treatment of trade in the whole of EU territory, such that transactions between different EU countries should be treated identically to those carried out within a single country.
(5) the revenue collected should be allocated on the basis of consumption made in each country.

Table 8.14 Coordination requirement of VAT proposals in the EU single market

	Harmonised VAT base	**Harmonised VAT rate(s)**	**Harmonised revenue-sharing mechanism**	**Harmonised VAT control**
Transitional VAT regime (since 1993)	No	No	No	Yes (zero-rating, tax fraud)
Draft directives 1987/89	Yes	No	Yes	Yes (undersupply of control effort)
1996 VAT proposal (Commission 1996)	Yes	Yes	Yes	Yes (undersupply of control effort)
VIVAT (Keen and Smith)	Yes	Partial (supra national VAT rate)	Low	Low (small clearing volume)
CVAT (McLure)	Yes	Partial (VAT on cross border trade)	Low	Yes (undersupply of control effort)
Dual VAT (Bird and Gendron)	No	Partial (supra national VAT rate)	No	Yes (zero-rating, tax fraud)
Prepaid destination VAT (Vanistendael)	Yes	No	Yes	Yes (undersupply of control effort)

Source: Genser (2003).

Genser (2003), while recognising that any evaluation of these alternatives depends on the relative importance attributed to the objectives, notes that VIVAT scores comparatively higher than the other options.

The second comparison made by Genser (2003) is aimed at evaluating the various alternatives on the basis of the degree of coordination or harmonisation of national policies their introduction would require. Greater coordination and harmonisation of national policies amounts to a loss of fiscal autonomy for member states. The harmonisation of the VAT base is a requirement of all the proposals except Dual VAT, where national VAT bases may be different from the common or supranational VAT.

Regarding the harmonisation of rates, this is necessary only for the supranational VAT in the cases of VIVAT, Dual VAT and CVAT.

As far as collection and compensation mechanisms are concerned, the coordination and administration needs corresponding to each alternative are directly proportional to the volume of tax revenue which has to be redistributed. The requirements of VIVAT and CVAT in this sense are limited as bilateral disequilibria tend to offset each other to a large extent, while any remaining collection deficits are compensated on a multilateral basis.

In short, the provisional regime, as Genser (2003) states, has obvious virtues but is capable of improvement. However, it will always have the essential characteristics of a zero rate for intra-Community transactions and asymmetry. Therefore, either the Commission should revise its goals (and abandon symmetry and the abolition of a zero rate in order to implement in a credible manner a reform of the provisional regime) or it should continue supporting both elements. If it chooses the latter, VIVAT will probably be backed at the expense of the provisional regime, until a form of VAT superior to VIVAT appears.

In regard to excise taxes it is to be expected that we will see a growing interest. Cnossen (2005)[27] observes a greater academic attention paid to this issue lately, which might have been brought about for three reasons. In the first place, the greater awareness about environmental problems, such as the greenhouse effect of gas emissions or acid rain, has developed an expanding literature on the economic mechanisms, such as excises, that help to internalise the externalities caused by polluting activities. In the second place, the recognition of the health problems caused by smoking has prompted worldwide campaigns against tobacco consumption, which include an increase in tobacco excises. In the third place, this author calls attention to the difficulties arising in the taxation of capital income due to greater capital mobility, as well as to the disincentive effects of high taxes on labour supply and demand, which has led governments to make a wider use of excise taxes to raise more revenues.

CONCLUSIONS

The 1978 Fiscal Reform and the later introduction of the VAT in 1986 completely transformed indirect taxation in Spain. In a short space of time indirect taxation in Spain went from having a traditional structure to a modern one more in line with its European peers. This transformation basically came about through the introduction of a modern VAT and the substitution of traditional "fiscal monopolies" by modern excise taxes.

The future role of indirect taxation in Spain will be conditioned by the process of tax harmonisation within the single market within the EU, as well as by the way in which it will be used in financing regional and local authorities (Autonomous Communities and Local Corporations). In this context, it is worth highlighting that VAT is applied in a very complex fashion in the majority of European countries and that it has been the object of a multitude of special schemes.[28] This situation, along with the successive extensions of the provisional regime, is a serious obstacle to tax harmonisation and for the implementation of the origin-country principle. At this point it should also be noted that any advances in the area of indirect taxation with regard to the harmonisation of national legislation and/or tax rates will entail, at minimum, a rise in the fiscal pressure of these taxes in Spain.

VIVAT appears to be one of the plausible alternatives for a radical future change in the VAT structure in the hypothetical situation of surpassing the provisional regime. In the longer term, and if the present provisional regime is consolidated in the European Union, the introduction of some of the VAT alternatives such as Dual VAT, CVAT or VIVAT could be considered.

With regard to the financing of regional and local authorities, it would appear likely that any future legislative changes will bring about, on one hand, an elevation of the tax rates or an increment of the participation percentages in the collection of the indirect taxation and, on the other, the creation of new specific taxes on the consumption of alcohol and tobacco, and the likelihood of tax retailers having to pay on the sales of hydrocarbons.

In relation to the incidence of this type of taxation, Spain is no different at present from its peers. Consumption tax as a whole maintains its predictably regressive character, although VAT, as a result of the application of the differentiated tax rates, is considerably less so than excise taxes as a whole.

In terms of their share of GDP, the relative importance of consumption taxes in Spain has risen from 6 percent to 10.2 percent over the period 1965–2001. Consumption taxes of a general nature rose from 3.3 percent to 6 percent of GDP, whereas excise taxes rose from 2.7 percent to only 3.3 percent. From 1965 to 1980, the share of GDP of both these tax categories remained relatively stable with a tendency towards convergence. From 1980 up to the last major reform of indirect taxation in 1986, the contribution of both groups rose strongly (as occurred with the other taxes), especially that of taxes of a general character (which rose from 2.3 percent to 5.3 percent of GDP over this period). From 1986, and in line with what occurred in the other developed countries, the contribution of these tax groups diverged somewhat. Revenues from the general taxes rose from 5.3 percent to 6 percent of GDP as a result of the introduction of VAT, while excise tax revenues fell from 4.25 percent to 3.3 percent of GDP.

Despite the above, and as a consequence of the fact that the share of GDP of the remainder of public revenue grew much faster than that of consumption taxes, the share of the latter in tax revenue as a whole fell significantly. Goods and services taxes fell from representing 40 percent of public revenue in 1965 to 20 percent in 1980; those of a general character fell by almost twelve percentage points in these terms over this period (22.21 percent to 10.61 percent) while excise taxes fell by over eleven points (from 18.42 percent to 7.38 percent in 1979). Since the beginning of the 1980s, the relative share represented by excise taxes has stabilised around 10 percent, whereas that of the general tax has risen strongly, especially since the introduction of the VAT.

At present, and with the exception of Switzerland, Spain is the European member of the OECD for which the share of GDP of this set of taxes is the lowest, although the distance from other members has been reduced significantly over the last twenty-five years. With respect to the share of these taxes in total tax revenue, the Spanish figure of 28.8 percent is now close to the European average. More specifically, regarding VAT, the average contribution of this tax in European OECD countries was 7 percent of GDP in 2001, whereas the figure for Spain was 6 percent. The share the VAT represents in total public revenue in Spain, at over 17 percent, is similar to the current European average. For Luxembourg, Switzerland, Japan and Norway, the estimated effective VAT rates are close to the nominal rates, although in most cases the range varies from 60 percent to 80 percent. For Spain, the efficacy of the tax in these terms is not very high.

If we focus on excise taxation as a percentage of GDP, we can observe that Spain has converged towards its peers: the figure for Spain rose from 2.7 percent of GDP in 1965 to 3.3 percent in 2001 whereas the OECD average fell from 5.8 percent to 4 percent over the same period.

APPENDIX: VAT AND THE STRUCTURE OF EXCISE TAXES SINCE 1986

In the following tables and figures we detail the evolution of consumption taxes in Spain since the introduction of VAT and accession to the EC in relation to tax revenues net of Social Security returns.

We consider the tax-take as the sum of revenues corresponding to Chapters I and II of the State Budget (*Presupuestos Generales del Estado*) with the exception of Social Security payments for basic pensions. With regard to excise taxes, we distinguish, from 1993 on, between excise duties on manufacturing and the Excise Tax on Certain Means of Transport. We provide individual information for each tax, with the exception of the Intermediate Products Tax: this became a tax in its own right from 1993 but is still collected jointly with the Tax on Alcohol and Derived Drinks, so we do not treat it separately in the interest of maintaining the homogeneity of our comparisons.

With this same aim of making comparisons between homogeneous values, the tax-take from the Hydrocarbons Tax and the Petroleum Monopoly Income are reported jointly. The Hydrocarbons Tax had been gradually replacing the Monopoly Income up until June 1990. In that month, the State stopped selling petroleum products which came under the Monopoly and hence such tax revenue was no longer generated (with the exception of quantities pending from previous years). The table includes the revenues from Monopoly Income imputable to each year.

Tables A8.1 and A8.2 show that from 1986 to the beginning of the present decade indirect taxes have decreased from 56 percent to 45 percent as a share of the total public revenues under consideration. It can be seen in Figure A8.1 that VAT shows an upward trend, except for the decreases in 1993 and 2001–2002, and accounts for 31 percent of total revenue. The decreasing weight of indirect taxes as a whole can be basically explained by the decline in the tax-take relating to external trade (which fell from 5 percent of the total to less than 1 percent) and general decline in excise taxes (which went from over 16 percent during the 1990s to less than 13 percent at present).

The Hydrocarbons Tax has traditionally been the most important of the excise taxes, and the decline in the importance of this tax goes a long towards explaining the reduced importance of Excise Taxes as a whole. The Hydrocarbons Tax accounted for 7.59 percent of the total tax-take in 2003, whereas it accounted for over 13 percent in 1986. Second in importance among the excise taxes is the Tax on Manufactured Tobacco, whose share rose steadily up to 1998 when it reached its maximum of 4.26

percent of total tax revenue compared with a percentage of only 1.81 percent in 1988.

The Tax on Certain Means of Transport is third among the excise taxes with revenues corresponding to almost 1 percent of the total in 2002. The revenue from Alcohol and Derived Drinks and Intermediate Products represents 0.65 percent of the total over recent years. Finally, the revenue from the Electricity Tax, which was incorporated into the excise taxes in 1998, represented 0.59 percent of the total in 2003, well above that obtained by the Beer Tax, which holds last place among the excise taxes.

Table A8.3 offers a breakdown of the State tax-take from VAT from 1999. This permits us to differentiate between revenues corresponding to internal transactions, on one hand, and those relating to imports and transactions assimilated under imports on the other, as well as to identify the volume of refunds and the discrepancies with respect to the budgeted figures.

It can be seen that VAT on imports and assimilated transactions, which accounted for 26 percent of VAT returns during the 1990s, has risen since the year 2000 to account for over 30 percent of VAT. The VAT on transactions assimilated to imports, for which disaggregated data are available only from 1996, reached 5,083.7 million euros in 2001, representing 47.5 percent of import tax revenue and 14.7 percent of the total net VAT take compared with figures of 40.8 percent and 10.2 percent respectively in 1996.

With regard to possible discrepancies between the actual and budgeted VAT takes, it has generally been the case that the former has been higher than the latter, as occurred in 1999 and 2003, although in the years 2000 and 2002 the tax-take was below the budgeted amount.With the information provided by the annual VAT declarations, the State Tax Collection Agency (*Agencia Estatal de Administración Tributaria*, AEAT) publishes statistics on this tax on its web-page (AEAT, 2003). The data available from 1997 to 2002 indicate that the weighted-average effective rate calculated from tax declarations fell from 11.4 percent in 1997 to 10.7 percent in 2002. Over this period, the average rate rose in only one year, and fell in the rest, implying that there was an average annual reduction of 1.3 percent. This source also indicates that the aggregate tax base of VAT rose by an average of 9.5 percent.

In a recent study, González-Calbert and Frutos-Vivar (2004) attempt to explain the reasons why VAT revenue rose at an annual rate of 9.1 percent over the period 1995–2003, which was much higher than the 6.8 percent average growth of GDP. As changes in tax regulations do not appear to explain this growth, attention is focused on the aggregate tax base of VAT from a macroeconomic point of view. In particular, they consider this base to comprise three fundamental components: household expenditure on final internal consumption, expenditure on the purchase of housing, and expenditure by public administrations.

From the analysis carried out, the authors highlight the important role played by housing in explaining the growth in the tax-take, given that expenditure on new housing multiplied by a factor of 3.4 over the eight-year period considered whereas expenditure on internal consumption rose by a factor of 1.6. They estimate that 35 percent of the growth of VAT fiscal pressure can be explained by the relative growth of the prices of housing compared to those of GDP as a whole. The authors also argue that the growth in the effective rate of VAT, an average of 1.4 percent, can be explained by the fact that the tax base and the tax-take from VAT are pro-cyclical in nature, so that there exists a crowding-out effect whereby consumption of necessity goods (which are generally taxed at reduced rates) is displaced by consumption of goods taxed at standard rates. This crowding-out effect is intensified in periods of high economic growth. Data on consumption, disaggregated by products, from the National Accounts confirm this phenomenon, showing that in the latter half of the 1990s there was a significant shift in consumption from food products to other goods and services such as automobiles and telephone services.

Tables A8.4 and A8.5 show a breakdown of the recent evolution in the census of VAT declarers, obtained from the aforementioned source[29] (AEAT, 2003). In 2002, 2,815,770 declarations were made by companies and organisations from all economic sectors. This represented an increase of almost 86,000 from the previous year and continues the trend from the years before. The most numerous group of declarers comprises those under the general deduction scheme (52.23 percent of the total, Table A8.4), although its relative weight has been declining due to the growing importance of those subject to reduced rates. By economic sectors, the greatest number of declarers come from construction and property services (34.75 percent of the total), followed by the retail trade sector (15.72 percent), with the first of these being by far the most dynamic. On a territorial basis, and excluding taxpayers who declare exclusively to the territorial administrations of the Basque Country and Navarra, the greatest number of declarers are from Catalonia (21.7 percent), Andalusia (15.5 percent) and Madrid (15.1 percent).

Table A8.1 Evolution of tax revenues in Spain (millions of euros)

	1986	1988	1990	1991	1992	1993	1994	1995	1996
DIRECT TAXES	12,780.2	20,861.3	29,631.8	32,882.2	35,538.3	35,429.4	36,107.8	39,047.2	40,067.3
INDIRECT TAXES	16,720.30	25,872.70	26,898.50	25,930.80	29,141.80	27,118.50	30,907.90	32,838.30	35,191.80
- VAT (*)	9,728.90	12,642.40	15,129.10	16,255.70	18,872.40	16,670.50	19,201.50	20,308.00	21,899.10
- Excise Taxes	4,825.30	10,311.90	9,189.60	7,975.60	8,715.50	9,566.20	10,810.40	11,502.60	12,404.40
Hydrocarbons (1)	3,868.20	8,979.60	7,498.10	6,225.00	6,673.20	6,719.60	7,293.50	7,745.40	8,216.20
Manufactured Tobacco (2)	713	844.3	1,122.70	1,189.10	1,447.20	1,591.50	2,048.00	2,292.30	2,687.70
Alcohol and Derived Drinks (3)	197.4	411.3	481.5	476.1	510.7	416.8	529.4	546.9	624.4
Beer	46.7	76.7	87.3	85.4	84.4	140.5	179.8	190.3	199
Electricity	–	–	–	–	–	–	–	–	–
Tax on Certain Means of Transport	–	–	–	–	–	697.8	759.7	727.7	677.1
- Foreign Trade	1,311.30	2,308.00	2,020.30	1,741.20	1,254.00	594.5	566.5	730.7	581
- Other Indirect Taxes	854.80	610.4	559.5	-41.7	299.9	287.3	329.5	297	307.3
TAX REVENUE	29,500.50	46,734.00	56,530.30	58,813.00	64,680.10	62,547.90	67,015.70	71,885.50	75,259.10

Table A8.1 Evolution of tax revenues in Spain (millions of euros) (continued)

	1997	1998	1999	2000	2001	2002	2003	2004(*)
DIRECT TAXES	46,770.4	44,229.7	46,350.0	50,757.0	54,598.0	67,173.0	69,367.0	75,384.0
INDIRECT TAXES	37,601.40	42,154.00	47,776.20	51,267.30	53,187.90	56,204.00	59,602.00	62,982.00
- VAT (1)	24,052.6	26,253.7	30,733.8	33,394.5	34,697.9	36,913.0	40,579.0	42,874.0
- Excise Taxes	12,439.60	14,380.8	15,428.9	16,056.9	16,611.3	17,330.0	16,854.0	17,758.0
Hydrocarbons (2)	7,922.7	8,399.9	8,946.8	9,077.8	9,243.9	9,505.0	9,790.0	10,164.0
Manufactured Tobacco (3)	3,014.3	3,679.7	3,811.5	4,186.2	4,513.2	4,919.0	5,243.0	5,672.0
Alcohol and Derived Drinks (4)	582.6	710.0	734.9	771.7	795.2	817.0	833.0	887.0
Beer	163.6	177.7	181.1	193.1	197.4	208.0	229.0	228.0
Electricity	–	505.3	598.4	648.9	657.9	692.0	759.0	807.0
Tax on Certain Means of Transport	756.4	908.2	1,156.20	1,179.20	1,203.70	1,189	–	–
- Foreign Trade	660.3	800.1	865.7	967.2	956.8	923.0	1,020.0	–
- Other Indirect Taxes	448.9	719.4	747.8	848.7	921.9	1,038.0	1,149.0	2,350.0
TAX REVENUE	84,371.80	86,383.70	94,126.20	102,024.30	107,785.90	123,377.00	128,969.00	138,366.00

Notes:
(*) Budgeted figures.
(1) Includes the former General Tax on Company Trading (I.G.Tráfico Empresas) and the Luxuries Tax (Impuesto sobre el Lujo).
(2) Includes the Petroleum Monopoly Income.
(3) Includes 44.054 million euro from Tobacco Tax in 1986.
(4) From 1993, this includes payments corresponding to the Tax on Intermediate Products (Impuesto sobre Productos Intermedios).

Source: AEAT (2002, 2004).

Table A8.2 Evolution of tax revenue in Spain (percentage of total tax)

	1986	**1988**	**1990**	**1991**	**1992**	**1993**	**1994**	**1995**	**1996**
DIRECT TAXES	43.32	44.64	52.42	55.91	54.94	56.64	53.88	54.32	53.24
INDIRECT TAXES	56.68	55.36	47.58	44.09	45.06	43.36	46.12	45.68	46.76
- VAT (*)	32.98	27.05	26.76	27.64	29.18	26.65	28.65	28.25	29.10
- Excise Taxes	16.36	22.07	16.26	13.56	13.47	15.29	16.13	16.00	16.48
Hydrocarbons (1)	13.11	19.21	13.26	10.58	10.32	10.74	10.88	10.77	10.92
Manufactured Tobacco (2)	2.42	1.81	1.99	2.02	2.24	2.54	3.06	3.19	3.57
Alcohol and Derived Drinks (3)	0.67	0.88	0.85	0.81	0.79	0.67	0.79	0.76	0.83
Beer	0.16	0.16	0.15	0.15	0.13	0.22	0.27	0.26	0.26
Electricity	–	–	–	–	–	–	–	–	–
Tax on Certain Means of Transport	–	–	–	–	–	1.12	1.13	1.01	0.90
- Foreign Trade	4.45	4.94	3.57	2.96	1.94	0.95	0.85	1.02	0.77
- Other Indirect Taxes	2.90	1.31	0.99	-0.07	0.46	0.46	0.49	0.41	0.41
TAX REVENUE	100.00	100.00	100.00	100.00	100.00	100.00	100.00	100.00	100.00

Table A8.2 Evolution of tax revenue in Spain (percentage of total tax) (continued)

	1997	1998	1999	2000	2001	2002	2003	2004(*)
DIRECT TAXES	55.43	51.20	49.24	49.75	50.65	54.45	53.79	54.48
INDIRECT TAXES	44.57	48.80	50.76	50.25	49.35	45.55	46.21	45.52
- VAT (*)	28.51	30.39	32.65	32.73	32.19	29.92	31.46	30.99
- Excise Taxes	14.74	16.65	16.39	15.74	15.41	14.05	13.07	12.83
Hydrocarbons (1)	9.39	9.72	9.51	8.90	8.58	7.70	7.59	7.35
Manufactured Tobacco (2)	3.57	4.26	4.05	4.10	4.19	3.99	4.07	4.10
Alcohol and Derived Drinks (3)	0.69	0.82	0.78	0.76	0.74	0.66	0.65	0.64
Beer	0.19	0.21	0.19	0.19	0.18	0.17	0.18	0.16
Electricity	–	0.58	0.64	0.64	0.61	0.56	0.59	0.58
Tax on Certain Means of Transport	0.90	1.05	1.23	1.16	1.12	0.96	–	–
- Foreign Trade	0.78	0.93	0.92	0.95	0.89	0.75	0.79	0.00
- Other Indirect Taxes	0.53	0.83	0.79	0.83	0.86	0.84	0.89	1.70
TAX REVENUE	100.00	100.00	100.00	100.00	100.00	100.00	100.00	100.00

Notes: (*) Budgeted figures.

Table A8.3 VAT: Evolution of revenues (millions of euros)

	1999	2000	2001	2002	2003
Budgeted	28,890	33,987	36,194	37,017	39,181
Tax revenues	30,735	33,389	34,673	36,913	40,579
Imports	7,972	10,196	10,683	10,724	11,594
Internal transactions	22,763	23,193	23,990	26,189	28,985
Returns	9,693	12,437	14,701	16,004	18,537
Gross revenue	40,427	45,826	49,374	52,917	59,117
Departure from Budget	1,845	-598	-1,521	-104	1,398
Percentage of budget execution (%)	106.4	98.2	95.8	99.7	103.6

Source: AEAT.

Table A8.4 Number of VAT declarers, 1999–2002

	Simplified scheme	Reduced rates	Special deduction	General deduction	Total
1999	362,109	693,253	25,933	1,484,049	2,565,344
2000	360,102	762,867	27,941	1,491,453	2,642,363
2001	365,407	808,119	30,694	1,525,625	2,729,845
2002	371,866	940,656	33,239	1,470,009	2,815,770
BIG COMPANIES					
1999	–	6,415	2,076	7,963	16,454
2000	–	7,222	2,288	8,993	18,503
2001	–	8,090	2,416	10,135	20,641
2002	–	8,978	2,616	11,177	22,771
SMALL COMPANIES					
1999	362,109	686,838	23,857	1,476,086	2,548,890
2000	360,102	755,645	25,653	1,482,460	2,623,860
2001	365,407	800,029	28,278	1,515,490	2,709,204
2002	371,866	931,678	30,623	1,458,832	2,792,999

Note: (*) Large enterprises: turnover larger than 6,010,121.04 € (1,000 million pesetas).

Source: AEAT (2003).

Table A8.5 Number of VAT declarers by sector, and region 1999–2002

	1999	2000	2001	2002	%
TOTAL	2,565,344	2,642,363	2,729,845	2,815,770	100.00
ENERGY AND WATER	3,822	4,045	4,211	4,215	0.15
INDUSTRY	227,495	229,551	231,327	231,686	8.23
CONSTRUCTION	860,758	895,219	950,588	978,428	34.75
COMMERCE	416,586	424,661	434,160	442,562	15.72
TRANSPORTATION AND COMMUNICATION	197,039	196,582	197,406	198,754	7.06
HOTEL AND RESTAURANT	241,161	242,797	245,754	249,372	8.86
FINANCIAL	10,592	10,931	11,569	11,901	0.42
SERVICE	232,081	246,372	262,234	275,631	9.79
EDUCATION AND HEALTH CARE	30,413	31,916	30,367	31,728	1.13
OTHERS	345,397	360,289	362,229	391,493	13.90
Number of VAT declarers by CCAA. 1999–2002					
TOTAL	2,565,344	2,642,363	2,729,845	2,815,770	100.0
ANDALUCIA	385,900	401,102	417,792	435,681	15.5
ARAGÓN	100,023	101,242	103,433	105,675	3.8
BALEARES	83,525	87,115	90,764	93,509	3.3
CANTABRIA	35,051	35,996	37,013	38,247	1.4
CASTILLA - LA MANCHA	109,334	112,701	116,030	120,130	4.3
CASTILLA Y LEÓN	173,770	176,969	179,267	181,785	6.5

Table A8.5 Number of VAT declarers by sector and region, 1999-2002 (continued)

	1999	**2000**	**2001**	**2002**	**%**
CATALUÑA	559,899	575,093	593,822	611,988	21.7
EXTREMADURA	56,817	58,789	60,317	62,067	2.2
GALICIA	188,778	193,716	196,887	200,734	7.1
LA RIOJA	22,963	23,491	24,156	24,850	0.9
MADRID	382,131	393,615	410,778	424,842	15.1
R. MURCIA	72,609	75,794	79,218	82,713	2.9
C. VALENCIANA	320,174	330,665	342,729	355,098	12.6
P. ASTURIAS	71,960	73,572	74,831	75,553	2.7
T. FORALES	700	707	749	755	0.0
RESTO	1,710	1,796	2,059	2,143	0.1

Source: AEAT (2003).

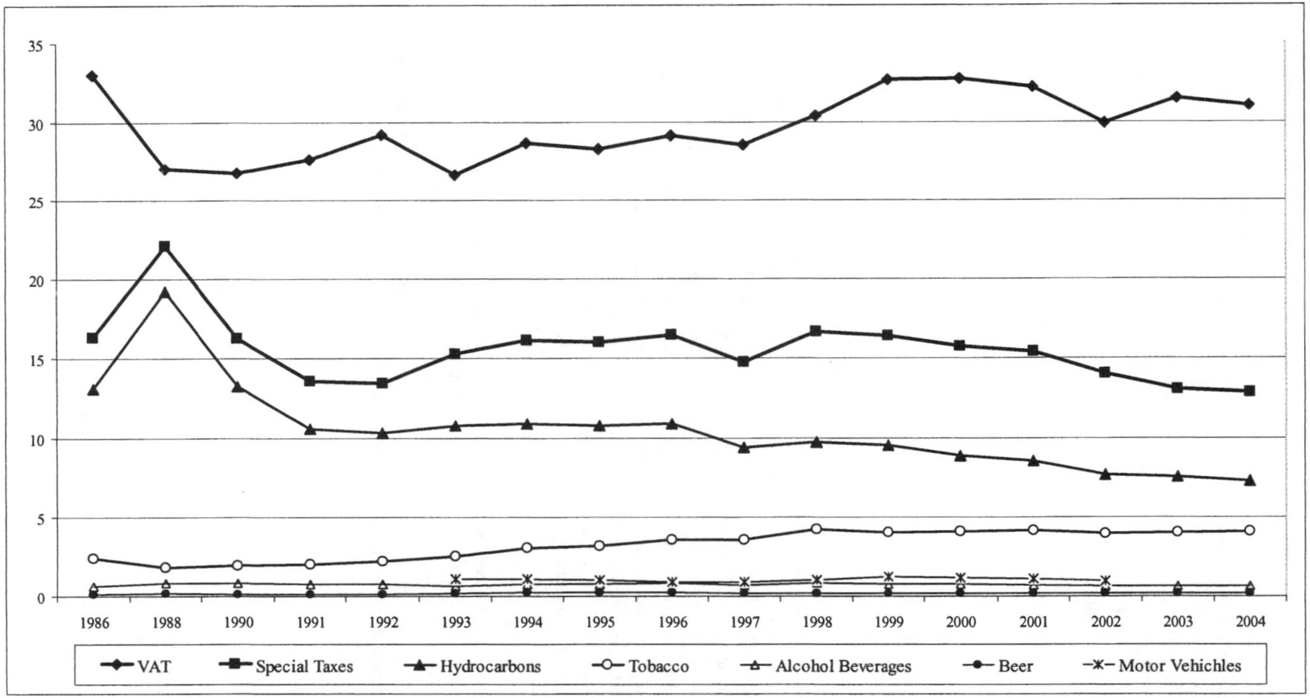

Figure A8.1 Evolution of tax revenues in Spain (percentage of total tax)

NOTES

* Universidad de Málaga

1. This was the name given to the tax which was charged on the value of all movable goods and real estate which were sold or exchanged. The alcabala appeared during the middle ages (there are references which date back to the reign of Alfonse X) as a local tax. It was generalised during the epoch of Alfonse XI (1342), although it was of a temporary character and limited to 5%. During the time of the Trastámara dynasty (1369) it became permanent and was raised to 10% of the value of merchandise, although the Crown was unable to prevent the nobility from appropriating it in many of the feudal estates. The Court of Cádiz abolished the alcabala along with many other indirect taxes, but it did not disappear completely until the fiscal reform of Mon (1845). In America, the tax was not charged during the early period of the conquest but the needs of the Treasury brought about its gradual imposition. It was first charged in Mexico in 1574, and limited to 2%. In the following years it was extended to New Galicia and Guatemala and in 1591 to the Viceroyalty of Peru. Finally, it should be noted that the Castillian alcabala was not strictly a sales tax in the sense that we understand it today, rather a tax on all sales in that it was applied not only to the exercise of an economic activity (acts of commerce) as we now perceive it but also to incidental and isolated sales (civil acts) and the sale of real estate. Stretching the imagination a little, we thus see the beginnings of future real estate VAT.
2. Given that goods which are inputs in productive processes are taxed under the IGTE both when they are sold as well as when they are incorporated into the final sale price of other goods of which they form part, the IGTE can be considered as a cascading tax on goods until the final stage of consumption. This gives rise to a non-uniform and arbitrary distribution of the tax burden in relation to the price of finished goods and impedes the correct determination of compensating taxes on imports and fiscal reductions on exports. This in turn gave rise to fiscal adjustments at frontiers which were of a non-neutral character. In effect, the compensating tax rates applied were generally higher than the tax burden suffered by equivalent national goods, while the fiscal deductions on exports were generally higher than the tax burden implicit from the price of goods which were exported. Thus, the frontier tax adjustments made in Spain were incorrect and the compensating tax could be considered to some extent as a tariff while the tax deductions on exports could be partly considered as a subsidy to exporting sectors.
3. These two measures had the objective of preparing the way for the introduction of VAT, where exports were exempt and where a special regime was foreseen for the purchase of natural resource products.
4. The resources obtained from petroleum products were channelled through three concepts: the gains from the Petroleum Monopoly Income; excise taxes on petroleum products (excise tax on petroleum and derivative products, created by the law of March 17th, 1932) and luxury taxes on high-grade fuel gasoline and the gains from shares of the State-owned company CAMPSA. The gains from Petroleum Monopoly Income were included in the excise taxes, thereby increasing fiscal transparency and preparing the way for the future elimination of this monopoly.
5. While in the case of tobacco a monopoly existed, the tax was entirely articulated through the luxuries tax.
6. The immediate consequence of Law 30/1985 was the repeal of the IGTE and the Luxuries Tax.

7. Later to become the Tax on Production, Services and Imports (Impuesto sobre la Producción, los servicios y la importación) from 1997 on due to Law 13/1996.
8. Intermediate products are those with an alcoholic degree over 1,2° and under 22°, and not subject to tax on beer or tax on wine and fermented beverages.
9. The system previous to the implementation of VAT used the country of destination principle by means of the *Desgravación Fiscal a la Exportación* (DFE; tax credit for exports) and the *Impuesto de Compensación de Gravámenes* (ICGI; compensation of inner levies tax). In general and for each item in the tariff of customs, the compensation rate established the amount to pay for the imports so that they carried the same fiscal burden as the goods and services produced internally. On the other hand, the rate of the tax credit to the exports sought to alleviate the internal fiscal burden incorporated in their price. This system implied the coincidence between the rates of the tax credit for exports and the compensation of inner levies tax. Nevertheless, there were a fair amount of exceptions to the rule, which responded to political economy reasons. So, the different rates of the tax credit might be considered as mean values for each economic sector. In some cases the rate of the tax credit could be higher than that resulting from the cascade turnover tax, which meant an implicit subsidy to the exports and a penalisation of the imports.
10. See Bird and Gendron (1998, 2000 and 2001).
11. Piffano (2003), after analyzing the advantages and disadvantages of the various forms of VAT which can be used in a multi-level government context, recommends the option of combining a national VAT with another decentralised VAT applicable to retail sales.
12. For a more detailed analysis of the role that consumption taxes could play in regional financing in Spain, see Sánchez Maldonado and Gómez Sala (1995, 1996a, 1996b and 1999).
13. A different index is elaborated for each of the taxes according to the territorial distribution of respective consumption.
14. Law 51/2002 and Legislative Royal Decree 2/2004, 5th March, which passed the recast text (*texto refundido*) of the Law on the Regulation of Local Finance.
15. The Central Government has not explicitly revealed how these respective percentage shares are calculated.
16. Of the fifteen considered countries seven apply the type zero instead of the exemptions, to allow the deduction of the VAT supported in the acquisitions. See European Commission (2003).
17. The Commission is aware that this demands major efforts and progress to be made on the issue of coordinating statistics.
18. The VAT Committee debates issues related to the application of the common VAT regime. Normally the results of these debates are put together to form guidelines. However, the VAT Committee is not empowered to make these guidelines binding. In this setting, in 1977 the Commission presented a proposal to modify the statute of the VAT Committee. However, the Council did not come to an agreement on this matter and it is unlikely that significant progress will be made in the near future. Indeed, the adoption of application measures in the area of taxation, in accordance with established procedure, remains the main obstacle to the adoption of this proposal. A modification of the Treaty is the only way a new impulse could be given to this subject.
19. See European Commission (2003) and (2004).
20. Among these are Perona (1972), Pérez Morales (1974) and Lagares (1975). See also Argimón, González-Páramo and Salas (1987).
21. See González-Páramo and Salas (1991), Avellaneda (1998), Briones, Estrada and Hernando (1993), Mayo (1995) and Serrano Mancilla (2003).

22. The apparently contradictory fact that the rates estimated for expenditure are lower than those for income is due to the fact that in the Family Budget Survey (EPF—*Encuesta de Presupuestos Familiares*) many social groups tend to underdeclare their income but have no such problems when it comes to declaring their expenditure. According to Ruiz-Castillo and Sastre (1998), over 60% of households report higher expenditures than revenues. This agrees with the work of Sanz (1996) on the 1990–91 EPF according to which EPF incomes are undervalued by some 40% when aggregate incomes are compared with the comparable total from the National Accounts.
23. In 1992 the normal VAT rate rose from 12% to 13% (Law 31/1991) and in August of that same year (Royal Decree 5/1992 and Law 28/1992) to 15%. From 1995 it was 16%. On the other hand, the higher VAT rate, which was 33% from 1986 to 1991 and 28% in 1992, disappeared in 1993 (Law 37/1992), and the Tax on Certain Means of Transport was introduced so that vehicles were now taxed by VAT at the normal rate and by the new tax (Law 38/1992 on Excise taxes). The super-reduced rate came into force on the 1st of January, 1993. In 1993 and 1994 it was 3%, and from the 1st of January of 1995 it was 4%. The reduced rate was 6% from 1986 to 1994 and 7% from the 1st of January 1995.
24. In the case of small enterprises, it seems clear that size alone does not appear to be a relevant issue with regard to the appropriateness or not of being subject to VAT, except in those cases where the smaller average size of taxed firms would lead to a situation where collection costs would be higher than those generated by other types of tax.
25. On this issue see Huizinga (2002).
26. We base this section on the work of Genser (2003).
27. Cnossen (ed.) (2005) examines carefully the characteristics and particularities of modern excise taxes on tobacco, drinking, gamling, pollution and driving.
28. In Spain, apart from the general regime there are seven special value added tax regimes: 1. Simplified regime. 2. Special regime for agriculture, livestock and fisheries. 3. Special regime for used goods, objects of art, antiquities and collectors' items. 4. Special regime applicable to operations with investment gold. 5. Special regime for travel agencies. 6. Special regime for the equivalent surcharge.

    The simplified regime is applied under certain conditions to physical persons and entities who are attributed as rent earners under the regime of the Income Tax on Physical Persons (IRPF). Its objective is to determine the amount of VAT to be paid or the equivalent surcharge. Thus, it does not follow the general criterion of collecting the difference between VAT charged and paid.

    The special regime for agriculture, livestock and fisheries applies to the owners of holdings in these categories, unless they opt to remain outside the regime, provided they comply with certain requirements. It functions in a different way from the general regime as the taxpayers are reimbursed by the Treasury at the standard rate (for operations outside the territory where VAT is applied) or by the receiver of the goods or services.

    The special regime for used goods, objects of art, antiquities and collectors' items is applied on a voluntary basis to resellers of these goods. Regarding the special regime for travel agencies, this is obligatory for operations carried out by the travel agencies when they act in their name with respect to travellers and use goods or services of other firms or professionals in the operation of the trip.

    Finally, the special regime of the equivalent surcharge is obligatory and is applied to firms dedicated to retail trade. The taxpayers subject to this regime charge VAT at the corresponding rate, and make VAT payments that they are charged plus a special surcharge. Thus they do not make VAT declarations, except in very particular cases, as it is supposed that the VAT quota they should pay is precisely the special surcharge which their supplier has charged them. The administrative burden on these firms is therefore reduced.

29. The transactions of subjects who declare exclusively to the Territorial Administrations of the Basque Country and Navarra are not included. Similarly, it should be noted that although VAT regulations exclude taxable persons under certain special schemes (Special Scheme for Agriculture and Fisheries and the Special Compensatory Charge Scheme) from the obligation of declaring and settling taxes, this does not imply that the transactions carried out by these collectives are excluded from the VAT statistics elaborated by the AEAT in relation to these collectives. On the contrary, the transactions carried out within the ambit of the Special Scheme for Agriculture and Fisheries are incorporated in the statistics through the compensations carried out by those who acquire the products corresponding to this scheme. The activities of retail traders carried out under the Special Compensatory Charge Scheme are incorporated through the increments and VAT instalments arising from the delivery of goods by taxable wholesalers to those taxable persons covered by the Special Scheme. These are declared in their annual reports along with any other transactions.

REFERENCES

AEAT (2002), *Estudio sobre los Impuestos Especiales. 2001.*

AEAT (2003), 'Estadísticas tributarias: Resultados económicos y Tributarios en el I.V.A.Estadística del año 2002 (99/02)', http://www.aeat.es/estad/iva/home.htm.

AEAT (2004), *Informe anual de recaudación tributaria 2003.*

Argimón, González-Páramo, J.M., and Salas, R. (1987), '¿Quién pagaba los impuestos indirectos en España? Un ejercicio de reparto de la carga impositiva indirecta en 1980', *Hacienda Pública*, 104, 99–127.

Avellaneda, P.A. (1998), 'Incidencia personal y territorial de la imposición sobre el consumo en España. 1991–1993', Tesis doctoral. Universidad de Málaga.

Avellaneda, P.A. and Sánchez Maldonado, J. (1999), 'Incidencia territorial de la imposición sobre el consumo en España. 1991–1993', *Hacienda Pública Española*, 150.

Benelbas, L., L. Sastre, and D. Taguas (1987), 'Efecto sobre la demanda de empleo de la sustitución cuotas empresariales a la Seguridad Social por IVA', *Información Comercial Española*, 647, 7–23.

Bird, R.M. (2000), 'Rethinking subnational taxes: A new look at tax assignment', *Tax Notes International*, 20, 2069–96.

Bird, R.M. and Gendron, P.P. (1998), 'Dual VATs and cross-border trade: Two problems: One solution?', *International Tax and Public Finance*, 5, 429–442.

Bird, R.M. and Gendron, P.P. (2000), 'CVAT, VIVAT and Dual VAT: Vertical Sharing and International Trade,' *International Tax and Public Finance*, 7, 753–761.

Bird, R.M. and Gendron, P.P. (2001), 'VATs in Federal States: International Experiences and Emerging Possibilities,' *Bulletin for International Fiscal Documentation*, 55, 293–309.

Briones, J., Estrada, A. and Hernando, Y. (1993), 'Evaluación de los efectos de reformas en la imposición indirecta', *Documento de Trabajo*, 9306. Banco de España.

Burgos, J., H. Ruiz, and D. Taguas (1992), 'Una evaluación del impacto económico de la modificación de los tipos de la imposición indirecta', *Boletín Económico de Información Comercial Española*, 2327, 1741–1744.

Calonse, S. and Manresa, A. (1997), 'Redistribución y estado de bienestar', *Moneda y Crédito*, Fundación Central-Hispano, 204.

Carey, D. and H. Tchilinguirian (2000), 'Average effective tax rates on capital, labour and consumption', OECD Economics Department Working Papers, No. 258.

Castellano, F. and J.L. Raymond (1985), 'Efectos económicos de la implantación del IVA en España', *Papeles de Economía Española*, 23, 337–342.

Cnossen, S. (1998a), 'Global trends and issues in Value Added Taxation', *International Tax and Public Finance*, 5, 399–428.

Cnossen, S. (1998b), 'Tax policy in the European Union. A review of issues and options', *FinanzArchiv*, 58, 466–558.

Cnossen, S. (2005), 'Economics and politics of Excise taxation', in Cnossen, S. (ed.) (2005), *Theory and Practice of Excise Taxation. Smoking, Drinking, Gambling, Polluting, and Driving*, New York: Oxford University Press, pp. 1–19.

Cnossen, S. (ed.) (2005), *Theory and Practice of Excise Taxation. Smoking, Drinking, Gambling, Polluting, and Driving*, New York: Oxford University Press.

Creedy, J. (1997a), 'Marginal indirect tax reform in Australia', Research paper No. 568, Department of Economics, The University of Melbourne.

Creedy, J. (1997b), 'Are consumption taxes regressive?', Working Paper Series No. 20/97, Melbourne Institute of Applied Economic and Social Research.

Creedy, J. (2001), 'Indirect tax reform and the role of exemptions', *Fiscal Studies*, 22 (4), 457–486.

Decoster, A. and Van Camp, G. (2001), 'Redistributive effects of the Shift from Personal Income taxes to Indirect taxes: Belgium 1988–1993', *Fiscal Studies*, 22 (1), 79–106.

Decoster, A., Schokkaert, E. and Van Camp, G. (1996), 'Horizontal Neutrality and Vertical redistribution with Indirect Taxes', in S. Zandvakili (ed.) (1997), *Taxation and Inequality*, JAI Press.

Dolado, J.J., González-Páramo, J.M., and Roldán (1994), 'Convergencia económica entre las provincias españolas: Evidencia empírica', *Documento de Trabajo*, 9406. Banco de España.

Ebrill, L., Keen, M., Bodin, J., and Summers, V. (2001), 'The modern VAT', International Monetary Fund, Washington D.C.

European Commission (1999), 'Harmonization of turnover taxes. Indirect taxes and e-commerce', Working paper, Working party, 1, June, Brussels.

European Commission (2000), 'A strategy to improve the operation of the VAT system within the context of the internal market', Communication from the Commission to the Council and the European Parliament, COM (2000) 348 final, Brussels.

European Commission (2003), 'VAT rates applied in the member states of the European. Situation at 1st May 2002', DOC/2908/2002 – EN, Brussels.

European Commission (2003a), 'Review and update of VAT strategy priorities', Communication from the Commission to the Council, the European Parliament and the European Economic and Social Committee, COM (2003) 614 final, Brussels.

European Commission (2004), 'Report from the Commission to the council and the European Parliament on use of the administrative cooperation arrangements in the fight against VAT fraud', Doc. Com. 260 final, Brussels.

Genser, B. (2003), 'Coordinating VATS between EU member Statues', *International Tax and Public Finance*, 10, 735–752.

González Calbert, L. and Rey del Castillo, P. (1998), 'Efecto en los precios de las alteraciones en los impuestos indirectos', *Papeles de Trabajo*, 16/98, IEF.

González Calbert, L. and Frutos Vivar, R. (2004), '¿Por qué creció tanto la recaudación por IVA entre 1995 y 2003?', *Cuadernos de Información Económica*, 180, 23–33.

González-Páramo, J. M. and Salas, R. (1991), 'Incidencia redistributiva del IVA', *Hacienda Pública Española*, 119.

Huizinga, H. (2002), 'A European VAT on financial services?', *Economic Policy*, 17 (35), 497–534.

Instituto De Estudio Fiscales (1973), *Informe sobre el sistema tributario español.* Madrid.

Instituto De Estudio Fiscales (1976), *Sistema tributario español. Criterios para su reforma*. Madrid.

Instituto De Estudio Fiscales (1982), *Introducción del Impuesto sobre el Valor Añadido en España*, Ministerio de Hacienda.

Izquierdo, J.F., Melguizo, A., and Taguas, D. (2001), 'Imposición y precios de consumo', *Documentos de trabajo*, No. 1/01, Servicio de Estudios BBVA.

Joumard, I. and A. Varoudakis (2000), 'Options for reforming the Spanish tax system', Working Papers No. 249, OECD Economics Department.

Keen, M. (2000), 'VIVAT, CVAT and All That: New Forms of Value-Added Tax for Federal Systems', *Canadian Tax Journal*, 48, 409–424.

Keen, M. and Smith, S. (1996), 'The future value-added tax in the European Union', *Economic Policy*, 23, 375–411.

Keen, M. and Smith, S. (2000). 'Viva VIVAT!', *International Tax and Public Finance*, 7, 741–751.

Kehoe, T.J., Manresa, A., Polo, C., and Sancho, F. (1989), 'Un análisis de equilibrio general del sistema impositivo indirecto en España', *Documento de Trabajo'*, 8903. Fundación Empresa Pública.

Lagares, M. (1975), 'La distribución de la carga tributaria en España: Algunos aspectos de interés para la política fiscal', *Hacienda Pública Española*, 33.

Lasheras, M.A., Radabán, I., and Salas, R. (1994), 'Efectos redistributivos entre CC.AA.', *Hacienda Pública Española*, 129–2.

Mayo, R. (1995), 'Análisis redistributivo del IVA: Incidencia de los tipos impositivos', *Hacienda Pública Española*, 132, 153–187.

Mayo, R. and Salas, R. (1994), 'Incidencia redistributiva del IVA Tipos efectivos declarados (1989)', *Hacienda Pública Española*, 128, 133–173.

McLure, C.E. Jr. (2000a), 'Implementing subnational Value Added Taxes on Internal Trade: The compensating VAT (CVAT)', *International Tax and Public Finance*, 7 (6), 723–740.

McLure, C.E. Jr. (2000b), 'Tax assignment and subnational autonomy', *Bulletin for International Fiscal Documentation*, 54 (12), 626–635.

Moreno Valero, P.A. (2001), 'La armonización del IVA comunitario: un proceso inacabado', Consejo Económico y Social. Madrid.

Pedraja, F. and Salinas, J. (2001), 'La descentralización del IVA: Propuestas, experiencias y enseñanzas para la financiación de las Comunidades Autónomas', *Hacienda Pública Española,* Monografías, 343–357.

Pena, B., Callealta, J., Casas, J. M., Merediz, A., and Núñez, J. (1996), *Distribución Personal de la renta en España. Ediciones Pirámide*, Madrid.

Pérez Morales, L. (1974), 'Distribución de la carga tributaria por escalones de renta', *Hacienda Pública Española*, 27.

Perona, D. (1972), 'Estimación estadística de la carga tributaria por escalones de renta. Aplicación al caso de España', Instituto de Estudios Fiscales. Ministerio de Hacienda. Madrid.

Piffano (2003), 'Reconsiderando la pregunta: ¿Es el IVA Subnacional la alternativa preferible?', http://www.depeco.econo.unlp.edu.ar/federalismo.

Radabán, I. and Salas, R. (1996), 'Convergencia y redistribución interterritorial en España: Efecto de los impuestos directos, cotizaciones sociales y transferencias', Centro de Estudios de Economía sobre el Sector Público. Fundación BBV.

Ruiz-Castillo, J. and Sastre, M. (1998), 'Desigualdad y bienestar en España en términos reales', Documentos de Trabajo, Documento No. 9808, Facultad de Ciencias Económicas y Empresariales, UCM, Madrid.

Sánchez Maldonado, J. and Gómez Sala, J.S. (1995), 'La imposición sobre el consumo y la financiación de las Comunidades Autónomas a la luz de la teoría de la hacienda y del derecho comparado: Especial referencia al IVA', Mimeo, Consejería de Economía y Hacienda, Junta de Andalucía y Universidad de Málaga.

Sánchez Maldonado, J. and Gómez Sala, J.S. (1996a), 'La imposición sobre el consumo y la financiación autonómica', *Papeles de Economía Española*, 69, 212–226.

Sánchez Maldonado, J. and Gómez Sala, J.S. (1996b), 'El impuesto sobre el valor añadido como tributo descentralizado: análisis del caso español', *Revista de Estudios Regionales*, 45, 2ª época, 43–88.

Sánchez Maldonado, J. and Gómez Sala, J.S. (1999), 'El papel de la imposición sobre el consumo como instrumento de financiación autonómica: una estimación de su incidencia territorial', Boletín Económico de Andalucía, Consejería de Economía y Hacienda, Junta de Andalucía, 27, 49–78.

Sánchez Maldonado, J., Gómez Sala, J.S., and Avellaneda, P.A. (1999), 'El papel de la imposición sobre el consumo en la financiación autonómica: Una estimación de su incidencia territorial', *Boletín Económico de Andalucía*, 27.

Sánchez Maldonado, J., Gómez Sala, J.S., and Avellaneda, P.A. (2000), 'La imposición sobre el consumo y la financiación autonómica', en 'Economía Pública Regional e Local. Actas do 1º Encontro Ibérico APDR – AECR', Associação Portuguesa para o Desenvolvimento Regional, Coimbra, Portugal, 229–267.

Sanz, B. (1996), 'La articulación micro-macro en el sector hogares: de la Encuesta de Presupuestos Familiares a la Contabilidad Nacional', en 'La desigualdad de recursos. Segundo Simposio sobre la distribución de la renta y la riqueza', Fundación Argentaria, Colección Igualdad. Volumen VI, 45–86

Sanz Sanz, J.F. , Romero Jordán, D., Castañar Carrasco, J.M., Prieto Rodríguez, J., and Fernández Díaz, F. J. (2003), 'Microsimulación y comportamiento económico en el análisis de la imposición indirecta. El simulador de imposición indirecta del Instituto de Estudios Fiscales', IEF, Madrid.

Serrano Mancilla, A. (2003), 'Reforma del impuesto sobre el valor añadido: Evaluación del impacto redistributivo, pobreza y bienestar social', Tesis Doctoral, Departament d'Economia Aplicada, Universitat Autonoma de Barcelona.

Servén, L. (1988), 'La sustitución de cotizaciones sociales por IVA: Una evaluación', documento de trabajo 88-06 (marzo), fundación de estudios de economía aplicada (FEDEA).

Smart, M. (2002), 'Reforming the Direct-Indirect Tax Mix', *International Tax and Public Finance*, 9, 143–155.

Solana, F., Arana, R., Barrio, J., Fernández, R., Fernández, P., and López, M. (1989), 'Efectos económicos de los Impuestos Especiales', Instituto de Estudios Fiscales.

Soto Guinda, J. (1982), 'Efectos económicos de la introducción del IVA en España', Instituto de Estudios Fiscales, op. cit., 125–136.

Vanistendael, F. (1995) 'A proposal for a definitive VAT system: Taxation in the country of origin at the rate of the country of destination without clearing', *EC Tax Review*, 1, 45–53.

Varsano, R. (1995), 'A tributacao de comercio interstadual: ICMS versus ICMS partilhado', *Texto par discussao*, 382, Instituto de Pesquisa Economica Aplicade, Brasilia.

Varsano, R. (2000), 'Subnational taxation and the treatment of interstate trade in Brazil: Problems and a solution', in S.J. Burki and G. Perry (eds), *Decentralization and accountability of the public sector,* Annual World Bank Conference on Development in Latin America and Caribbean 1999, The World Bank, Washington.

Zabalza, A. (1988), 'Efectos económicos de las cotizaciones a la Seguridad Social', En Fundación de Estudios de Economía Aplicada, FEDEA (1988): La fiscalidad de la empresa, 49–73.

9. Social Protection and Social Security Contributions in Spain

Ignacio Zubiri*

INTRODUCTION

In the last thirty years Spain has undergone a radical political, economic and social change. Dictatorship has been transformed into democracy, a closed, overprotected and underproductive economy has given rise to a modern and highly competitive economy, and a country with low social expenditure has been turned into a very generous welfare state.

One of the most important changes has been the development of an ample social protection safety net. At present, the Spanish pension system is one of the most generous in the world (in terms of replacement rate), healthcare is free for everyone (in practice even for illegal immigrants) and unemployment benefits are substantial. This social protection is financed by both Social Security contributions and general taxes.

These changes in the social protection safety net, however, have taken place in an economic context that has not been always favourable. On the one hand, just after the so called *transition* (from dictatorship to democracy) there was a long period of sluggish growth.[1] On the other hand, during the last 30 years Spain has had one of the highest levels of unemployment among OECD countries. Only in the last 10 years has unemployment decreased significantly and it is still high in comparison with other countries.

The purpose of this paper is to analyse social protection in Spain and its financing, paying special attention to the possible relationship between social protection and unemployment. I will first describe the evolution of the social insurance system in Spain and compare it with that of other countries. The third section describes the evolution of unemployment in Spain and explores its causes. In the next section, I analyse Social Security contributions and their possible impact on unemployment. The final section contains the conclusions.

SOCIAL INSURANCE IN SPAIN

Social insurance programmes in Spain date back to the beginning of the 20th century. For instance, the first old-age programme was established in 1921. The Constitution approved in 1931 recognised the right of all workers to old-age pensions, health coverage, unemployment benefits, invalidity and illness pensions, and so on. In any case, the actual insurance programmes have a more recent origin, because they were started after the Spanish civil war (1936–39). The old age programme was created in 1940, the health insurance programme in 1942 and unemployment insurance in 1961.

The two main contingencies covered by the present system of social insurance are old age and unemployment. The insurance system also covers many other contingencies such as illness, invalidity, survivors, wages unpaid by firms (because of a bankruptcy), etc. Health coverage was part of the National Social Insurance Programme until 1986. This changed in 1986 with the approval of the *General Health Law* which, among other things, established that healthcare would be provided free to the entire population, and would be financed exclusively by general taxes in the medium term. The General Health Law of 1986, therefore, transformed the existing social insurance system of public healthcare (healthcare was financed by contributions and restricted to contributors) into a National Health System (healthcare is financed by taxes and free for the entire population). Following the enactment of the Health Law of 1986, the amount of Social Security contributions used to finance healthcare services started to decrease. This transition process ended in 2000, and all healthcare expenditures of the National Health System since this time have been financed exclusively by taxes.[2]

Expenditure

Expenditures on social protection depend on both the generosity of the benefits and the number of beneficiaries. The two main insurance programmes—pensions and unemployment[3]—offer quite generous benefits, at least in comparison to other countries of the European Union and the United States.

In the case of pensions, benefits increase from the early seventies to the nineties and have remained basically stable afterwards. In this process, the replacement rate[4] of pensions increased from less than 50 percent in 1969 to almost 100 percent in 1989, where it has remained to the present. As a result Spain has become the country with one of the most generous public pension systems (in terms of replacement rate) of the OECD. As Table 9.1 shows, the replacement rate (net of taxes) in Spain is much higher than the replacement rate in the United States or even in France or Germany. This does not mean, however, that all pensioners in Spain receive high pensions. In fact, during the last 25 years unemployment has been very high, and as a result of this many retirees could not contribute all the years required to receive a full pension.[5] Many were not even able to contribute the minimum years of service[6] and, therefore, received only assistance pensions. In addition, survivor pensions have been quite low.

Table 9.1 Net replacement rates[a] of old age pensions

Country	Net Replacement Rate
France	87
Germany	77
Italy	80
United Kingdom	40
Average EU–4	**71**
Spain	**101**
United States	**58**

Notes: [a] Replacement rates (pension as percentage of last wage) for an average production worker net of taxes and contributions.

Sources: Casey et al. (2003).

As for unemployment, Table 9.2 shows the evolution of unemployment benefits in Spain and other countries. In the case of Spain, despite the high level of unemployment or perhaps because of it, unemployment benefits have increased from a replacement rate[7] of 20 percent in the mid-seventies to 30 percent in the nineties. The current rate remains around 30 percent. This replacement rate is similar to that of Germany and Italy, but is 50 percent less than the rate of the French unemployment system. As in the case of pensions, the benefits of the unemployment systems of the United States and the UK are significantly smaller. For instance, the Spanish system offers close to twice the amount of benefits compared to the United States or the UK.

Table 9.2 The OECD summary measure of unemployment benefits[a]

	1971	1975	1981	1991	2001
France	24	26	31	38	44
Germany	29	29	29	29	28
Italy	2	2	1	3	34
United Kingdom	25	22	24	18	17
EU–4	**20**	**20**	**21**	**22**	**30**
Spain	**12**	**21**	**28**	**34**	**31**
United States	**11**	**12**	**15**	**11**	**14**

Notes: [a] The OECD summary measure is defined as the average of the gross unemployment benefit replacement rates for two earnings levels, three family situations and three durations of unemployment.

Source: OECD (2004).

As in the case of pensions, the fact that unemployment benefits in Spain are high does not imply that most of the unemployed are well protected. On the contrary, many long-term unemployed citizens have exhausted their unemployment benefits and only receive minimal unemployment assistance or do not even meet the contribution requirements to receive unemployment benefits in the first place.

In summary, even though the benefits of the Spanish social insurance system are reasonably high, only a fraction of the population has historically received full benefits. In the future, however, most of the population will have full coverage.

Figure 9.1 compares the evolution of Social Insurance expenditure in Spain, the United States and the EU–4 in the period 1980–2001. As already mentioned this expenditure is the result of generosity (of the system) and need (number of beneficiaries). As Figure 9.1 shows, during the eighties and beginning of the nineties social expenditure in Spain rose steadily from 15.2 percent of the GDP (in 1980) to a maximum of 21 percent (in 1993). During this period the expenditure in Spain increased at a similar pace to that of the main European countries (EU–4). Afterwards, social expenditure in Spain decreased while the expenditure of the EU–4 remained basically constant. As a result the expenditure gap between Spain and the EU–4 increased substantially. This should, however, not be interpreted as a reduction of social protection in Spain (in comparison to EU–4) as most of the reduction of expenditure is due to the improvement of economic

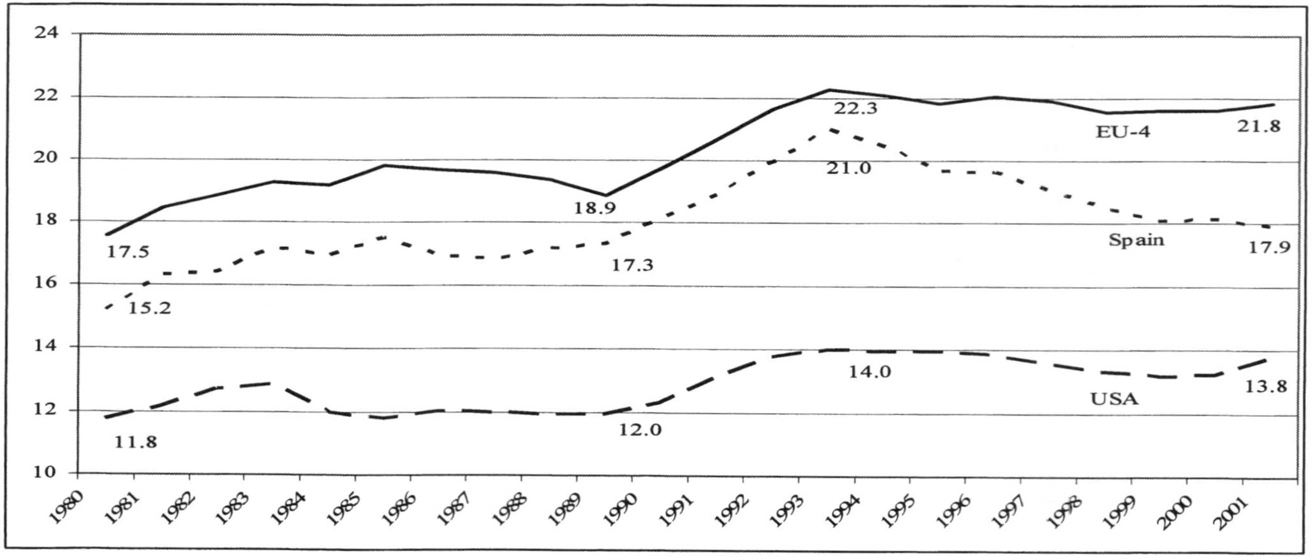

Figure 9.1 Social insurance expenditure[a] 1980–2001

Notes: [a] Pensions, unemployment and health.
EU–4 =Average of Germany, France, Italy and UK.

Source: OECD Social Expenditure Database.

conditions (high increase of GDP, reduction of unemployment, slowing of the ageing of population, and so on.)

As for the comparison with the United States, the social insurance expenditure in Spain has always been much higher. At the beginning of the nineties, Spain spent 50 percent (as a percentage of GDP) more than the United States on social insurance. Even after the decrease of the expenditure in the last couple of years, Spain still spends almost 30 percent more in terms of GDP than the United States on social insurance.

Financing

Traditionally, social expenditures have been financed by both Social Security contributions and revenue from general taxes. As already mentioned, after the 1986 General Health Law, the Health system became a National Health system and, as a result, after a transition period, it became financed exclusively by taxes. Social Security contributions are primarily used to finance pensions and unemployment benefits.[8] Table 9.3 summarises the relative importance of Social Security contributions and other revenues (mainly general taxes) in the financing of social expenditure.

As Table 9.3 shows, social expenditure (as a percentage of GDP) increased between 1980 and 1993 and decreased thereafter, while Social Security contributions have remained basically constant.[9] As a result, the share of social expenditures financed by contributions has been decreasing up to the mid-nineties, and increasing afterwards. In any case, Social Security contributions have always financed less than 75 percent of social expenditures and, at times, they did not even cover 60 percent of the expenditure. At present they finance about 70 percent of social expenditure.

UNEMPLOYMENT

Without any doubt, unemployment has been the basic economic problem of Spain during the last 25 years. Figure 9.2 shows the evolution of the unemployment rate in Spain, the EU–4 and the United States between 1970 and 2003. At its peak in 1995, the unemployment rate in Spain reached 23.9 percent.[10] In contrast, the unemployment rate was 10.3 percent in the EU–4 and only 6 percent in the United States. Even at the present time, after a substantial reduction, the unemployment rate in Spain (11.3 percent) is well above the EU–4 rate (8.1 percent) and the United States rate (6.0 percent).

Table 9.3 Financing of social protection expenditure in Spain (1980–2001)

	Social Protection Expenditure[a] (A)	Social Security Contributions[a] (B)	A–B	(A–B)/A
1980	15.2	11.2	4.0	73.8
1981	16.3	11.6	4.7	71.2
1982	16.4	11.5	4.9	70.2
1983	17.2	12.0	5.2	69.9
1984	16.9	11.5	5.4	67.9
1985	17.5	11.5	6.0	65.7
1986	17.0	11.3	5.7	66.6
1987	16.8	11.4	5.4	67.7
1988	17.2	11.2	6.0	65.1
1989	17.3	11.6	5.7	67.1
1990	18.2	11.8	6.4	65.0
1991	18.9	11.9	7.0	62.9
1992	20.0	12.6	7.4	63.1
1993	21.0	12.7	8.3	60.5
1994	20.5	12.5	8.0	61.1
1995	19.7	11.9	7.8	60.4
1996	19.6	11.7	7.9	59.5
1997	19.1	11.8	7.3	61.9
1998	18.5	11.9	6.6	64.3
1999	18.1	12.2	5.9	67.4
2000	18.2	12.3	5.9	67.7
2001	17.9	12.5	5.4	69.8

Notes: [a] As a percentage of GDP.

Source: OECD Social Expenditure database and OECD Statistical Compendium.

In the seventies Spain had a very low unemployment rate compared with other countries. For instance, in 1975 the unemployment rate was 4.5 percent, while it was 4.3 percent in the EU–4 and 8.3 percent in the United States. At the time of the transition, unemployment started to mount, and almost 2 million jobs were lost in just ten years (see Figure 9.3). This,

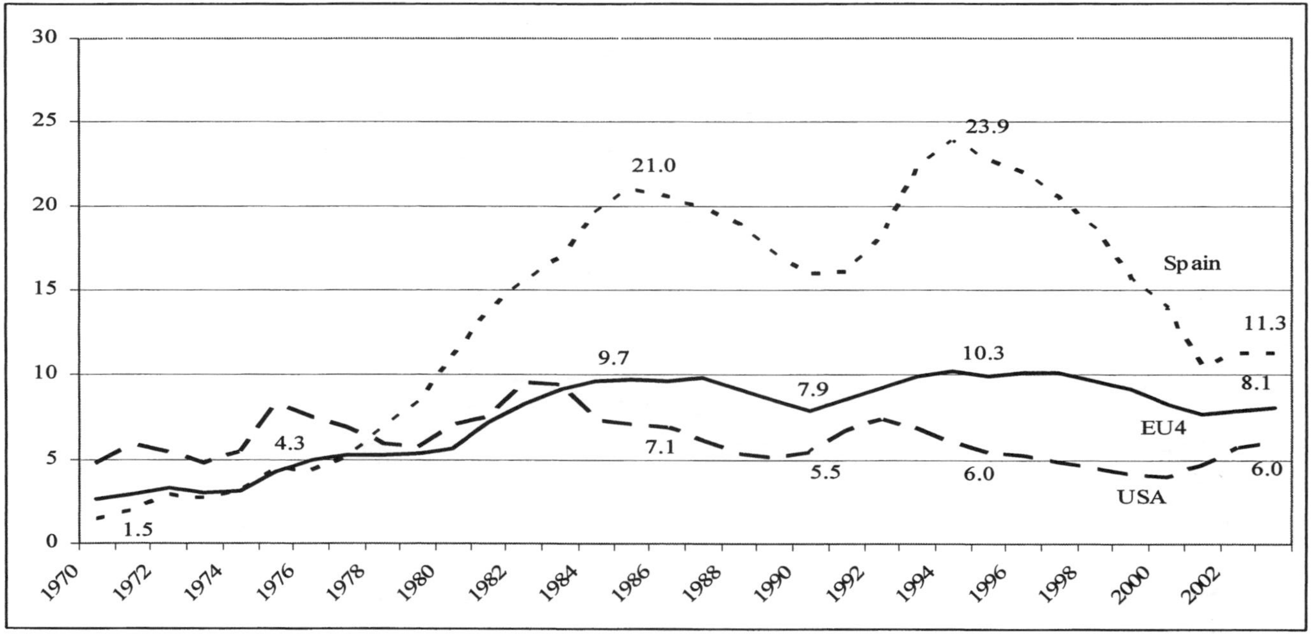

Figure 9.2 Unemployment rate in Spain 1970–2003

Source: Economic Outlook, OECD.

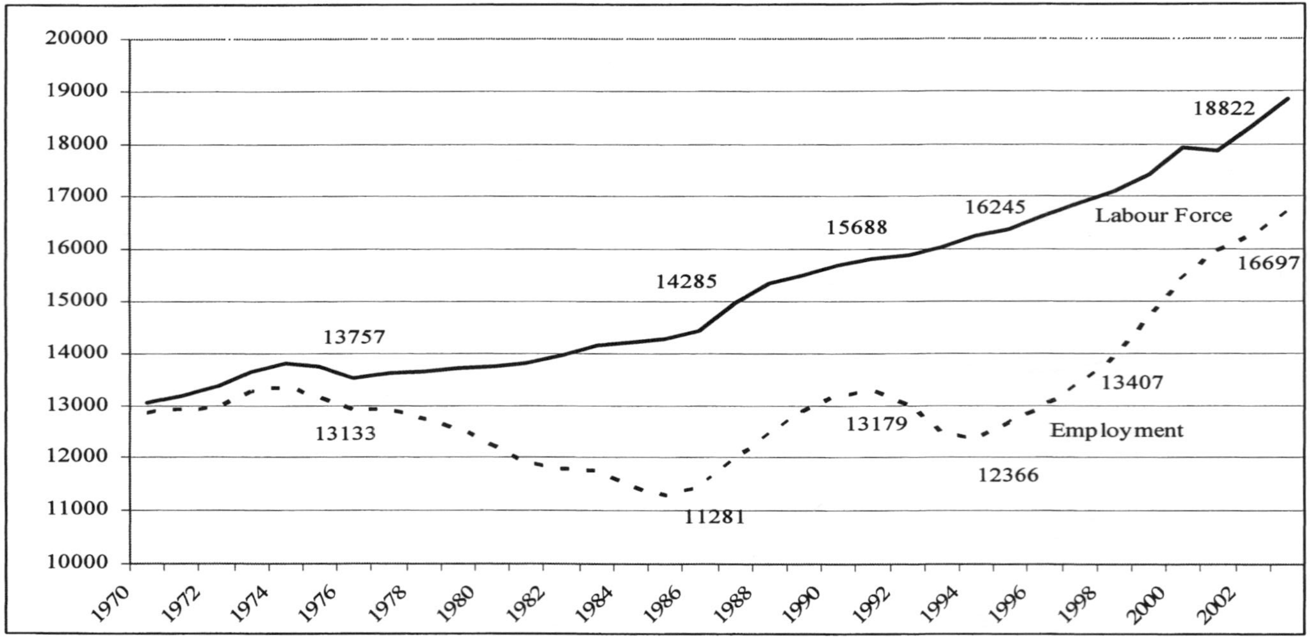

Figure 9.3 Labour force and employment in Spain 1970–2003 (in thousands)

Source: OECD Statistical Compendium.

along with a moderate increase in the size of the labour force, led to the unemployment of 3 million people in 1985, which was equivalent to an unemployment rate of 21 percent. Certainly, the decade 1975–85 was a period of economic crisis in most advanced economies due to the oil crises of 1973 and 1979. The increase in unemployment in Spain was, however, much higher than in any other European country. For instance, between 1975 and 1985 the unemployment in Spain increased by 14 percentage points, while the increase was only of 5.7 percentage points in the EU–4. This suggests that, beyond a general world oil crisis, there were factors specific to Spain that amplified the unemployment effects of the economic crisis.

There are several reasons that explain why unemployment grew in Spain so much more than in other European countries. The more important reasons were the inflexibility of the labour market, the lack of mobility of workers,[11] the high proportion of people still working in agriculture in the seventies and even eighties,[12] the poor education of the population, the existence of many inefficient producers protected by tariffs and export subsidies and, as mentioned, a moderate increase in the labour force. The adverse effects that these factors had on employment were amplified by the fact that Spain was in transition in the late seventies [13] from a dictatorship to democracy.[14] It is worth mentioning that, even during this period of increasing unemployment, GDP grew slowly. Therefore, there was a substantial increase in lag productivity.

In 1985 the unemployment rate reached an historical maximum of 21 percent for this time period. The following year, however, the Spanish economy started to grow at a high rate[15] and five years later in 1990, the 2 million jobs lost in the previous decade were recovered. The general growth of the world economy and the stimulus provided by the accession to the European Community in 1986 were some of the factors behind the Spanish economic expansion in that period. However, despite the increase in the number of jobs, the unemployment rate dropped only to 16 percent (well above the 7.9 percent of the EU–4) because the labour force increased substantially (by almost 1.5 million people).

The period from 1991–94 brought a sizeable loss of employment. More than 800,000 jobs were lost in just a couple of years. The main reasons were a world economic crisis combined with an overvalued Spanish currency. Furthermore, the labour force increased by almost 600,000 people. As a result the unemployment rate skyrocketed to an historical high of almost 24 percent.

The year 1995 was a turning point for unemployment in Spain. Employment started to grow at a very high rate and in a few years the unemployment rate dropped to 11.3 percent, where it stands now. Such a low level (by Spanish standards) of unemployment had not been seen in Spain since the early eighties. Some of the causes behind this fall in unemployment were the buoyancy of the world economy, the moderation of prices and wages, the consolidation of public finances (due to the requirements of the stability and growth pact) and the reforms of the labour market regulations (e.g. a reduction of firing costs).

SOCIAL SECURITY CONTRIBUTIONS

As pointed out above, Social Security contributions cover pensions, unemployment benefits and other contingencies (for instance, unpaid wages in bankruptcies). Until 2000 some of the proceeds from Social Security contributions were used to finance the Healthcare system. Table 9.4 shows the evolution of Social Security tax rates between 1978 and 2005. Table 9.5 compares the tax rates in Spain with those of other countries.

As shown in Table 9.4, despite the increase in social expenditure, Social Security tax rates have remained remarkably stable during the last 30 years (between 36 percent and 39 percent). This simply means that a good deal of the social protection has been paid with taxes instead of with Social Security contributions. For instance, as Table 9.3 above shows, Social Security contributions financed more than 70 percent of social protection in the early eighties, but by the mid nineties the percentage had decreased to 60 percent.

Table 9.4 also shows that even though the total Social Security tax rate contributions have not changed, due to the increases in unemployment, about 5 points of the rate has been shifted from common contingencies to unemployment protection.

Even though the total tax rate for Social Security contributions has not changed dramatically, due to the high level of unemployment, there have been always a large number of different reductions in the tax rate for employers hiring workers (and offering indefinite jobs) belonging to groups with special difficulties in finding jobs. Most of the reductions are temporary (generally for one or two years) and have been applied to groups such as the long term unemployed, women over 45, or workers finding their first job.

Since 2002, the Social Security System has been utilised to induce workers to stay in the labour market after they have reached the age of 65. To this end, workers of 65 years or more are exempted from Social Security contributions.[16] They also receive a 2 percent increase of their pension for every year worked after 65.[17] The objective of these measures is, obviously, to reduce the cost of the system of pensions.[18]

Table 9.5 compares the rate of Social Security contributions in Spain with those of other countries. The tax rate in Spain is 35 percent lower than in France and about 10 percent lower than in Germany and Italy. On the other hand, it more than doubles that of the UK and the United States. In general, Social Security contributions in almost all the EU countries are substantially higher than in the United States. The trivial observation that these non wage labour costs are much higher in the EU, and that the unemployment rate is much lower in the United States, is the basis of the EU Commission recommendation to reduce the Social Security contributions in the member countries.[19]

Figure 9.4 shows that the revenue from Social Security contributions has remained stable since 1980 at around 11.5 percent of the GDP. This is a result of the constancy of tax rates combined with the incapacity of the Spanish economy to create employment. Only in recent years (and in the early nineties) when employment has risen sharply have Social Security contributions grown above 12 percent of the GDP. At present they stand at 12.7 percent which is basically the same as in the EU–4[20] and 80 percent higher than in the United States.

Table 9.4 Social security tax rates in Spain (1978–2005)[a]

	1978	**1980**	**1990**	**2000**	**2005**
Common contingencies	34.3	34.05	28.8	28.3	28.3
employer	29.15	28.55	24	23.6	23.6
employee	5.15	5.5	4.8	4.7	4.7
Unemployment	2.7	4.0	6.3	7.8	7.55
employer	2.35	3.48	5.2	6.2	6.0
employee	0.35	0.52	1.1	1.6	1.55
Other	1.1	1.1	1.2	1.1	1.1
TOTAL	**38.1**	**39.15**	**36.3**	**37.2**	**36.95**

Notes: [a] Old Age, survivors, sickness, invalidity and up to the year 2000, health.

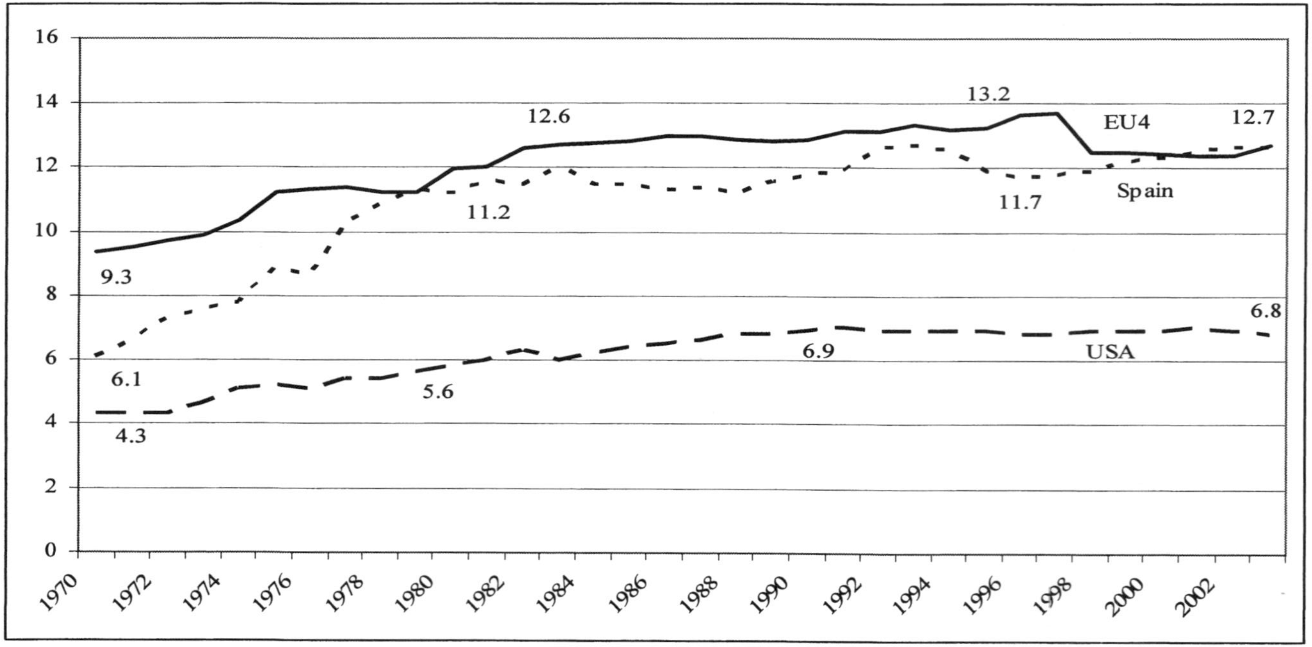

Figure 9.4 Social security contributions 1970–2003 (as % of the GDP)

Source: OECD Statistical Compendium.

Table 9.5 Social security rates[a] distribution (2003)

	Total Rate	Share of Employee	Share of Employer
France	55.18	24.65	75.35
Germany	42.10	50	50
Italy	42.27	21.7	78.26
United Kingdom	18.37	46.22	53.78
EU–4	**39.48**	**33.14**	**66.86**
Spain	36.95	17.19	82.81
United States	15.30	50	50

Notes: [a] For the average paid worker.

Source: Taxing Wages (2004), OECD.

THE EFFECTS OF SOCIAL SECURITY CONTRIBUTIONS ON EMPLOYMENT

Social expenditure has grown quite rapidly in Spain. At the same time unemployment has been very high, at least in comparison with other advanced economies.[21] A natural question to ask is if, to some extent, the financing of social protection is responsible for some of the unemployment. In other words, have Social Security contributions (or other wage taxes) resulted in high labour costs that have in turn caused some unemployment?

Theory

On theoretical grounds, the effects of Social Security contributions on labour costs and employment are indeterminate and, to a large extent, depend on factors such as the structure of the labour market, the bargaining power of trade unions, the elasticities of supply and demand of labour, and so on.

If there is perfect competition and either the labour supply is perfectly inelastic or the workers are fully aware of the future benefits they will receive for the present contributions,[22] the Social Security contributions will be borne entirely by the workers in the form of lower wages and the distribution of the total contribution between employer and employee will be irrelevant. This general result has, however, two qualifications. First, it only holds true in the long run. Therefore, even under the assumptions of perfect competition and inelastic labour supply (or full awareness of benefits), an increase in the employer's Social Security contribution will be borne by the employer, at least in the short and medium run.[23] The second qualification is that when a country has minimum wage laws, the employers cannot shift their Social Security contributions to workers earning this minimum wage or close to it. That is one of the reasons why it is usually assumed that Social Security contributions are especially harmful for low skilled workers.

On the other hand, when markets are competitive but labour supply is not inelastic or workers do not realise the future benefits of increased contributions today, both employers and employees will share the burden of the tax. The share of each will depend on the elasticities of supply and demand.

When labour markets are not competitive, the incidence of Social Security contributions is much less clear and, basically, anything can happen. The bargaining power of trade unions, the degree of centralisation in bargaining,[24] the reservation wage[25] (which will depend, among other things, on the tax treatment of income sources such as unemployment benefits, and of the extent of the underground economy), market imperfections and the use of wages as incentives for productivity (efficiency wage models[26]) are some of the factors that determine the incidence of the Social Security contributions and may change the full shifting result obtained in the standard competitive model with inelastic labour supply.

Empirical Evidence

Theory cannot determine the effect of Social Security contributions on wages and employment. Unfortunately, the empirical evidence cannot resolve this ambiguity either. A widely held view is that the competitive model holds (with inelastic labour supply) and as a result Social Security contributions are borne by workers and have no effects on employment, at least in the long run. Many empirical estimations support this view and show that the effect of taxes on employment, if any, is small. For instance, Blanchard and Wolfers (2000), Gruber (1997) and Nickell and Bell (1996) find that payroll taxes do not have any effect on employment. Elmeskov et al. (1998), Nickell and Layard (1999), and Nickell (2004) find a moderate impact of labour taxes on unemployment. Nickell (2004), for instance, estimates that a 10 percentage point rise in the tax wedge will reduce overall labour input provided via the market by around 2 percent of the population of working age.

There are also studies suggesting a strong effect of taxes on employment. Daveri and Tabellini (2000), for instance, argue that taxes are responsible for a substantial part of unemployment in Europe.[27] Even though their estimations have been seriously questioned[28] their results support many of the assertions of the negative effects of taxes on employment.

On the other hand, many studies suggest that institutions matter. For instance, Everaert and Heylen (2002) argue that, except in the case of strong, union bargaining at intermediate levels, there is a full shifting of Social Security contributions to workers.

In the case of Spain most of the empirical studies conclude that Social Security contributions are fully shifted to workers[29] and that, as a result, they have little effect on labour costs, competitiveness and employment.

Taking everything into account, the least that can be said is that there is not strong evidence that payroll taxes have a significant effect on labour costs and, therefore, on employment. It is not surprising, therefore, that most studies on incidence assume that Social Security taxes (both the employer and employee part of the tax) are borne by the worker.[30]

Taxes and Unemployment in Spain

Tax rates and the collection of Social Security contributions have remained basically constant since 1980 in Spain (see Tables 9.3 and 9.4). It is, therefore, obvious that Social Security contributions could not have had any effect on either the increase of unemployment that occurred up to 1995 or the decrease in the last years. As for other taxes, as Table 9.6 shows, the personal income tax has increased steadily up to the mid nineties and then has experienced a moderate decrease. Total taxation, however, has been almost constantly increasing in the last 30 years.[31] In fact, the highest level of taxation took place between 1995 and 2003, precisely when unemployment experienced the steepest decrease. All this suggests that taxes have little (or nothing) to do with the reduction of unemployment in Spain that started in 1995 simply because taxes, if anything, increased during that period.

This does not mean, however, that a reduction in taxes would not decrease unemployment further. Nevertheless, most of the studies about the causes of unemployment in Spain do not consider taxes as a prominent factor.[32] Some studies, however, consider that the reduction of wage taxes is important to reduce unemployment. For instance, Bentolila and Jimeno (2003) estimate that the structural unemployment rate (as measured by the NAIRU) decreased 7.2 percentage points between 1995 and 2001, and that almost 50 percent of this decrease (3.6 percentage points) was due to the reduction of wage taxes. This result is somewhat surprising. First, the reduction of wage taxes, if any, was small, certainly too small to cause a reduction of 3.6 percentage points in the unemployment rate. Second, in the same paper these authors estimate that of the 17 percentage point increase of the unemployment rate between 1970–74 and 1995–99, the (substantial) increase in taxes was responsible for less than 1.1 percentage points.[33] Given this information, it is surprising how a small decrease in wage taxes could reduce the structural unemployment so much during the period 1995–2001.

Table 9.6 Taxes in Spain, 1975–2003 (as a percentage of the GDP)

	1975	1980	1995	2000	2003
Personal Income Tax	2.7	4.7	7.7	6.6	6.8
Social Security Contributions	8.9	11.2	11.9	12.3	12.6
Total Taxation	18.8	23.1	32.8	35.2	35,8

Source: OECD Statistical Compendium.

What are the reasons for this increase, and then later decline of unemployment in Spain? As mentioned in the third section, there are several potential causes that led to the increase of unemployment leading up to 1995: inflexibility of the labour market, lack of regional mobility of workers, high proportion of people still working in agriculture in the early eighties, poor education of the population, producers protected by tariffs and export subsidies, a moderate increase in the labour force, the political transition, and two world oil crises. In other words, the causes of the reduction of unemployment that started in 1995 are not all that clear. Nevertheless, some of the factors that have contributed to the reduction of unemployment are economic growth, wage moderation, reduction of firing costs, and, probably, a more efficient economy.

CONCLUSIONS

This paper has analysed the development of social protection in Spain in the last 30 years. During that period, social protection has grown considerably and now Spain has one of the more generous social protection systems of the world. Healthcare is free for the entire population, pensions (as a percentage of the last wage) are among the highest in the world and unemployment benefits are generous. The result of these improvements is that social protection expenditures in Spain have risen considerably.

The expenditure in social protection is financed by taxes and Social Security contributions. The system has always introduced incentives (via temporary reduction of the tax rates) to hire workers with special difficulties to find a job and, since 2002, to workers over 65 (through the exemption of Social Security contributions and a 2 percent increase of pension for every year worked over 65). Despite these incentives, both the general tax rate and the collection of Social Security contributions have remained remarkably constant since 1980. The bulk of the increase in social expenditure has, thus, been financed by general taxes in the last 30 years. Depending on the year, taxes have financed between 60 percent and 70 percent of social protection.

The basic economic problem of Spain has been, and to a certain extent still is, unemployment. Since 1980 the unemployment rate has been well above that of any developed country. At its peak, the unemployment rate in Spain reached almost 24 percent and until 1995 it did not start to decrease significantly. Now it remains a little above 11 percent. This is somewhat higher than in most advanced countries, but it is also the lowest rate in the last 20 years.

There is little evidence that Social Security contributions (or other taxes) had any influence in the level or evolution of unemployment. Rather than taxes, the high unemployment is related to factors such as the inflexibility of the labour market and others already mentioned. On the other hand, the reduction in the unemployment rate started in 1995 is likely due to a variety of reasons including economic growth, wage moderation, reduction of firing costs, and probably, a more efficient economy.

NOTES

* University of the Basque Country

1. According to OECD data, between 1975 and 1983, GDP per capita in Spain decreased from 61.1 percent of the average of EU15, to 52.9 percent. Afterwards it started to recover. Now it stands at 75 percent (almost 90 percent if adjusted by purchase power parities).
2. In the process, the Social Security contribution rate was not decreased. This increased the resources available for pensions and unemployment.
3. Healthcare is provided to the entire population free of charge. Prescriptions, however, have a 40 percent copayment (pensioners and those suffering from a chronic illness are not required to pay for prescriptions)
4. This is the percentage of the wage previous to retirement that is replaced by the pension (for a worker receiving a full pension).
5. To receive full benefits a worker should have contributed for 45 years.
6. To receive some pension a worker has to contribute a minimum of 15 years.
7. Unemployment benefits as a percentage of the wages lost.

8. The rest of expenditure is financed by taxes. Also, if Social Security contributions cannot cover all the cost of pensions and unemployment benefits the "deficit" is financed by central government transfers; that is, by taxes.
9. See the fourth section for further details.
10. It should be noted that unemployment has varied considerably across regions, age groups and according to gender.
11. In Spain there have always been tremendous differences in the unemployment rate of regions. These differences, however, didn't give rise to significant migrations within the country. These differences persist today. For instance, in December 2004 the unemployment rate in the region of Navarre was 4.6 percent, while in Andalusia it was 19.2 percent.
12. In 1975, 22.1 percent of the workers were in the agricultural sector. By 1994 the share of workers in agriculture had decreased to 9.9 percent and in 2003 is 5.6 percent. In fact, according to some studies the main cause that explains the much higher unemployment in Spain (as compared to other European countries) is the importance of agriculture. Simply, agriculture lost more than a million and a half jobs and other sectors couldn't absorb such a large labour force (see for instance, Marimón (1997) and Marimón y Zilibotti (1998)).
13. The *Transition* is the name of the years that followed the death of the dictator Franco and turned Spain into a democracy. It should be recalled that Franco died in 1975 and the existing Constitution was approved in 1978 (the first Spanish constitution dates back to 1812)
14. The political instability and the climate of social unrest made difficult to take certain policy measures.
15. In 1986 Spain's GDP growth rate was 3.3 percent. In 1987 it increased to 5.5 percent. The growth rates of 1988 and 1989 were, respectively, 3.8 percent and 3.5 percent.
16. As long as previously they have contributed to the system at least 35 years.
17. Also, to discourage early retirement, the reduction of the pension for every year of retirement before the age of 65, was increased to 8 percent.
18. For an analysis of the Spanish pension system, see Zubiri (2003).
19. See, for instance, the Broad Economic Policy Guidelines 2000 and 2001.
20. This average is however misleading because the Social Security contributions in the UK, 6.4 percent, are very low relative to the other countries (France, 16.7 percent, Germany 14.7 percent, Italy 12.9 percent).
21. One of the surprising things about Spanish unemployment is that Portugal, which suffered shocks similar to those of Spain (including a political transition to democracy), always had very low unemployment rates. So far there is not a generally accepted explanation for this difference.
22. This simply means that they realise that paying more contributions today will entail receiving more benefits (pensions, unemployment benefits, etc) in the future.
23. One of the reasons is that the shift of the tax from employers to employees will be done, not by reducing today's wage, but by increasing less (even below inflation) future wages. This way, the shifting takes time.
24. Calmfors and Driffill (1988).
25. Pissarides (1998); Nickell and Layard (1999); Daveri and Tabellini (2000).
26. Shapiro and Stiglitz (1984), Akerlof (1984).
27. According to their estimates, the rise of 14 percentage points in labour taxes between 1965 and 1995 in the EU could account for a rise in EU unemployment of roughly 4 percentage points and a growth slowdown of about 0.4 percentage points per year.
28. See, for instance, Everaert and Heylen (2002) and the references therein.

29. See, for instance, Argimón and González Páramo (1987), Escobedo (1991) and Herce (1996).
30. See, for instance, Mitrusi and Poterba (2000) or Pechman (1985). Pechman, however, considers also the possibility that half of the Social Security contributions (the employer share in the USA) are shifted to consumers.
31. To be precise, taxation in Spain increased sharply between 1976 and 1988 (1 point of GDP per year) and moderately between 1988 and 1993 (0.4 points a year). After a small decrease (due to the economic slowdown) of 3 years, in 1997 total taxation started to increase again very slowly.
32. See for instance Marimón (1997), Dolado and Jimenez (1997) and Toharia (1999)
33. They impute 1.1 points of the increase of unemployment to both wage taxes and active employment policies.

REFERENCES

Akerlof, G. (1984), 'Gift Exchange and Efficiency Wage Theory: Four Views', *American Economic Review*, 74, 79–93.

Argimón, I. and González Páramo, J.M. (1987), 'Traslación e incidencia de las Cotizaciones Sociales por niveles de renta en España, 1980–1984', *Fundación Fondo para La Investigación Económica y Social,* D.T.#1.

Bentolila, S. and Jimeno, J. F. (2003), 'Spanish Unemployment: The End of the Wild Ride?', *FEDEA, Documento de Trabajo 2003–10.*

Blanchard, O.J. and Wolfers, J. (2000), 'The role of shocks and institutions in the rise of European unemployment: the aggregate evidence', *Economic Journal,* 462, 1–33.

Calmfors, L. and Driffill, J. (1988), 'Centralisation of wage bargaining and macroeconomic performance', *Economic Policy,* 6, 13–61.

Casey, B., Oxley, H., Whitehouse, E., Antolin, P., Duval, R. and Leibfritz, W. (2003). 'Policies for an Ageing Society: Recent Measures and Areas for Further Reform', *OECD Economics Department Working Papers*, 369.

Daveri, F. and Tabellini, G. (2000), 'Unemployment and taxes: do taxes affect the rate of unemployment?', *Economic Policy*, 30, 47–88.

Dolado, J. and Jiménez, J.F. (1997), 'The causes of Spanish Unemployment: A Structural VAR Approach', *European Economic Review,* 41 (7), 1281–1307.

Duval, R. (2003), 'The Retirement Effects of Old-Age Pension and Early Retirement Schemes in OECD Countries', Working papers No.370, OECD Economics Department.

Elmeskov, J., Martin, J.P. and Scarpetta, S. (1998), 'Key lessons for labor market reforms: evidence from OECD countries' experiences', *Swedish Economic Policy Review* 5, 205–252.

Escobedo, I. (1991), 'Un análisis empírico de los efectos finales producidos sobre el empleo industrial por el sistema de financiación de la seguridad social: 1975–1983', *Investigaciones Económicas*, 15, 169–192.

Everaert, G. and Heylen, F. (2002), 'Labor Taxes and Unemployment in the OECD A Nonstationary Panel Data Analysis', mimeo, http:\\www.sherppa.be

Gruber, J. (1997), 'The incidence of payroll taxation: evidence from Chile', *Journal of Labor Economics*, 15, 72–101.

Herce, J.A. (1996), 'Protección social y competitividad: el caso español', *Fundación BBV.*

Kugler, A. and Kugler, M. (2003), 'The Labor Market Effects of Payroll Taxes in a Middle Income country: Evidence from Colombia', Discussion Papers in Economics and Econometrics no 0306, University of Southampton.

Layard, R. and Nickell, S. (1986), 'Unemployment in Britain', *Economica*, 53: 121–169.

Marimón, R. (1997), 'Reconsidering Spanish Unemployment', *Els Opuscles del CREI*, n. 1, http://www.econ.upf.es/crei/research/opuscles/op1ang.pdf

Marimón, R. and Ziliubotti, F. (1998), 'Actual vs. Virtual Employment in Europe. Is Spain different?', *European Economic Review*, 42, 123–153.

Mitrusi, A. and Poterba, J. (2000), 'The Distribution of Payroll and Income Tax Burdens, 1979–99', in James M. Poterba (ed.), *The Economic Effects of Taxation*, National Tax Journal, Volume LIII, No. 3, Part 2.

Nickell, S. (2004), 'Employment and Taxes', CEP Discussion Paper No. 634.

Nickell, S. and R. Layard. (1999), 'Labor market institutions and economic performance', in O. Ashenfelter and D. Card (eds), *Handbook of Labor Economics*, Vol. 3 (North Holland, Amsterdam), pp. 3029–3084.

Nickell, S. and Bell, B. (1996), 'Would Cutting Payroll Taxes on the Unskilled Have a Significant Impact on Unemployment?', in Denis Snower and Guillermo de laDehesa (eds), *Unemployment Policy: Government Options for the Labor Market*, pp. 296–332.

OECD (2004), *Benefits and Wages: OECD Indicators*, Paris.

Pechman, J.A. (1985), *Who Paid the Taxes, 1966–1985?*, Washington, DC: The Brookings Institution.

Pissarides, C.A.(1998), 'The impact of employment tax cuts on unemployment and wages: The unemployment benefits and tax structure', *European Economic Review*, 42, 155–183.

Schneider, F. and Klinglmair, R. (2004), 'Shadow Economies around the World:What Do We Know?', *IZA DP* No. 1043, http://opus.zbw-kiel.de/volltexte/2004/1708/pdf/dp1043.pdf

Shapiro, Carl and Stiglitz, J.E. (1984), 'Equilibrium Unemployment as a Worker Discipline Device', *American Economic Review*, 75, 433–44.

Toharia, L. (1999), 'Los factores Determinantes de la Tasa de Paro en España', www2.uah.es/ltoharia/L3b.pdf

Zubiri, I. (2003), *El Futuro del Sistema de Pensiones en España*, Madrid: Instituto de Estudios Fiscales.

10. Environmental Taxes in Spain: A Missed Opportunity

Alberto Gago, Xavier Labandeira, Fidel Picos and Miguel Rodríguez*[1]

INTRODUCTION

In recent decades several European countries have instituted taxes on the emission of polluting substances into the different natural environments. The reasons for doing so include the aggravation of environmental problems, or the appearance of new ones, with varying spatial scope (local, regional and global) and by the cost-efficient properties of this alternative as compared to other regulatory options. Essentially, an environmental tax succeeds in internalising negative external effects at a minimal cost (static efficiency) and constitutes a continuous incentive for the adoption of conducts that are beneficial from an environmental perspective (dynamic efficiency).

However, the introduction of environmental taxes in fiscal systems does pose certain problems. When they form part of general measures (e.g. a series of policies designed to fight climate change) their implications in terms of efficiency and equity are very relevant, since they affect all types of agents and sectors. In addition, the design process is complex and requires a careful preparation of the fiscal architecture in which such taxes will be implemented. This has occurred in various Northern European countries, which since the beginning of the 1990s have applied different variations of the model known as the Green Tax Reform (hereinafter GTR). The essence of a GTR strategy is to exchange taxation on income and social contributions for environmental taxation, with the aim of obtaining an additional dividend in terms of welfare.

However, Spain has remained relatively distant from the use of these instruments and from this widespread process of fiscal innovation. In fact, successive Spanish governments have put into practice a defensive strategy, making use of the unanimity requirements existing within the European Union in the area of fiscal harmonisation. Such behavior undoubtedly reflects the belief that environmental taxes may hamper economic growth in a country still below most EU average economic indicators.

This does not mean that environmental taxation is unknown in Spain, as the fiscal systems of the regional governments have been using these instruments at an increasing pace. Here Spain has witnessed a very interesting federal experience, albeit a poorly coordinated one that has been plagued with institutional tension, mainly as the result of the fiscal restrictions to which the regional governments are subject by the central authorities.

The aim of this chapter is to analyse and assess the experience of Spain's fiscal system with environmental taxes in the context of the tax reform process that started in the late 1970s. The chapter is organised into six sections, including this introduction. The next section will provide the context, with a brief review of the foundations of environmental taxation and GTRs. The third section describes how the Spanish central government and the municipalities have reacted to the growth of this alternative environmental and fiscal policy. In the fourth section we review and explain the wide range of regional applications given to these instruments.

All these considerations allow us to extract lessons that can be used to predict the future of environmental taxation in the Spanish tax system, and this is the subject of the fifth section. We believe that the absence of a consistent environmental strategy guiding the regional experience has led to a poor design/use of these measures and it explains why we describe the Spanish experience as a missed opportunity and the cause of numerous current problems. The future holds a reduced role for taxation within European environmental policies, although we should expect intense fiscal actions in the areas of solid waste, transport and tourism. It is in these areas where the regional administrations can and should play a relevant role, putting to good use the new opportunity that is arising. Finally, section six summarises the main conclusions of the chapter.

THE ENVIRONMENTAL AND TAX CONTEXT

The greater regulatory effectiveness of the so-called economic instruments of environmental policy (mainly taxes and tradable emission rights) is well known.[2] Compared with conventional regulations, these mechanisms are more flexible and decentralised, putting decisions regarding how and how much to pollute into the hands of the polluters. In a context characterised by asymmetric information and a large number of involved agents, two factors which hinder conventional regulatory design and functioning, economic instruments have the advantage of emulating market behavior in their features and effects. In particular, taxes function as a price paid for polluting, which leads polluters to equalise their marginal pollution abatement costs and thus to achieve the new pollution level at a minimum total (social) cost. Such static efficiency is accompanied by dynamic efficiency, since polluters have continual incentives to reduce their emissions and thus avoid payments (Labandeira, 1996).

The relevance of environmental taxes has been clearly heightened by the appearance or worsening of multiple environmental problems, something which has become especially evident in the second half of the past century worldwide. Specifically, the serious harm linked to climate change requires that immediate and effective action be taken to reduce the emissions causing this phenomenon. Since the magnitude of the allocative and distributional effects associated with any control policy is quite evident, market instruments should be made to play a predominant role.

Moreover, since the United States and the United Kingdom put into effect intense reform processes in the first half of the 1980s, practically all developed countries have modified their fiscal systems along these lines. In general, these changes have followed a uniform model characterised by a compensatory scheme in which the reduction of rates and brackets in direct taxation are countered by the broadening of bases, the elimination of preferential treatment and a change in the tax mix in favor of indirect taxation (OECD, 1993; Messere, 1993; Messere, 2002). This reformist model, based on reasons of efficiency and simplicity, has continued since that time, with different elements comprising the compensatory scheme. In fact, in the middle of the 90s environmental taxes started to play the role of broadening tax bases and increasing VAT rates, with the aim of further leveling the scales of direct taxation (Majocchi, 2000; Hoerner and Bosquet, 2001; Joumand, 2001).

Environmental taxes, in addition to being coherent with prevailing fiscal principles (indirect taxation applied to products and consumption, without concern for vertical equity and having a relatively simple application), could generate further benefits in exchange for direct taxation. This is because, in addition to the gains in efficiency derived from the reduction of maximum rates (fiscal dividend), we must consider the gains of a strictly environmental type, derived from their dissuasive-corrective nature of environmental taxes. All of the foregoing gave rise to what is called the Green Tax Reform model, in which environmental taxation becomes the main actor in fiscal modifications (Gago and Labandeira, 2000). This is only possible with environmental taxes that are powerful and stable from the point of view of revenue collection, and for this reason energy taxes on

Table 10.1 Principal features of the GTRs applied in Europe

Country	**Year**	**Taxes reduced or eliminated**	**Environmental taxes and fiscal changes adopted**
Germany	1999	Social Contributions	- Increase of excise duties on gasoline, heating and natural gas - Tax on electricity
Austria	2000	Social Contributions	- Energy Tax (CO_2)
Denmark	1994	PIT, Corporate Tax and Social Contributions	- Energy Tax (CO_2) - SO_2 Tax - Landfill Tax - Adaptation of energy excise duties
Finland	1990/ 1997	PIT and Social Contributions	- Energy Tax (CO_2) - Landfill Tax
Italy	1999	Social Contributions	- Increase of energy excise duties
Netherlands	1996	PIT, Corporate Tax and Social Contributions	- Energy Tax (CO_2) - Landfill Tax
Norway	1992/ 1999	PIT	- Energy Tax (CO_2) - SO_2 Tax - Taxes on fertilisers and pesticides
Sweden	1991	PIT and Corporate Tax	- Energy Tax (CO_2) - SO_2 Tax - Taxes on fertilisers and pesticides
United Kingdom	1996 2001	Social Contributions	- Landfill Tax - Climate Change Levy

Source: Gago and Labandeira (2002).

gases contributing to climate change are made the central axis of GTRs. Table 10.1 shows that the applied experience with GTRs has grown in both diffusion and diversity.

CENTRAL AND LOCAL ENVIRONMENTAL TAXES IN SPAIN

At the end of the 1980s, the OECD documented the existence of almost 100 taxes with environmental objectives and this figure has only grown since that time (OECD, 2003). However, these initial experiences were not part of an overall scheme involving fiscal change and thus the environmental taxes remained mere appendices added on to fiscal systems; at the same time, policymakers responsible for the fiscal systems remained very skeptical as to their possible fiscal and regulatory advantages. The change in the role of environmental taxes occurred a few years later, as mentioned above, owing to urgent needs for correction and the fiscal potential connected with the problem of climate change.

In such a context, it could be expected that the environmental and fiscal responsibilities would be distributed among the various levels of government existing in Spain in accordance with the usual principles and theory of fiscal federalism (Peltzman and Tideman, 1972). Thus environmental problems of a global type and subsequent tax-related solutions should be referred to the central administration, while the regional and local administrations should deal with problems corresponding to their territorial scope. Basically this would leave the most powerful environmental taxes in the hands of the central government, while the majority of the specific measures would be implemented by the subcentral governments.

However, in Spain so far, both the central and the local governments have chosen to ignore this regulatory and fiscal option. Local governments tended to ignore this option because of their inability to create and/or manage this type of measure, although the field for action in the local sphere is quite large. Even more astounding has been the attitude of the central government, which has not only avoided the creation of environmental taxes and the reform of existing energy taxes, to say nothing of the implementation of a GTR, but has actually gone so far as to torpedo the attempts of the European Commission (EC) to act along these lines.

At the beginning of the 1990s, the EC proposed the creation of a mixed tax on carbon content and (non-renewable) energy, its harmonised application throughout the EU and fiscal revenues for member states, with the recommendation that such receipts be used to reduce pre-existing taxes. However, the response of some EU members (Spain among them) was to block this initiative, which required unanimous approval under the rules established for fiscal matters in the EU Treaty. Their posture centred expressly on disagreement with the relinquishment of part of the fiscal sovereignty of member states in favor of the fiscal power of the EU, but also on the potential negative effects that such a tax could have on economic growth. Spain was unwilling and for the first time set forth arguments related to its development differences with other EU countries and the incompatibility of economic growth and environmental control.

This failure prompted the EC to change its strategy regarding the use of energy-environmental taxes. Maintaining the objectives of reducing emissions, it directed its political initiative towards a harmonised increase of excise duties paid on the consumption of fossil fuels. For Spain, such a proposal would have implied substantial increments in excise taxes on the consumption of electricity, gasoline and gas oil, as well as the introduction of new excise duties on carbon and natural gas, as illustrated in Figure 10.1.

Once again Spain chose to oppose the new proposal of the Commission, but this time the argument was based much more explicitly on the growth differential issue. Establishing harmonised minimums in excise duties on energy is aimed mainly at avoiding fiscal competition among member states and moving forward with the consolidation into a single market. However, with such a high degree of fiscal diversity as the starting point, the road leading in this direction would, for countries with less intense taxation such as Spain, be very long indeed.

In 2002 Spain finally accepted the directive to harmonise excise duties on energy proposed by the Commission, but it did so in a much broader negotiating framework, consenting to a much less demanding proposal that gave member states more room to maneuver. This sheltered much better the competitive position of less developed countries, albeit at the cost of delaying national programmes for environmental protection and, especially, programmes designed to fight climate change. In fact, this explains why Spanish greenhouse gas emissions by the year 2000 had already far exceeded the limits set for compliance with the Kyoto Protocol in 2010.

Thus, the attitude of the Spanish fiscal authorities has been a very cautious one with regard to new taxes of an environmental type. Without the pressure of a demanding environmental policy and with the braking effect of the arguments for economic convergence in Europe, Spanish tax policy has not had sufficient independence and strength to promote and impose the GTR criteria. In addition, other environmental actions that could have been developed through fiscal mechanisms implemented by the central government, such as the reduction of certain types of waste, the discharge of liquid waste into general hydrological areas, etc. have not been considered and the application of taxes already existing in the legal system has even been avoided.

Furthermore, the existing Spanish tax system has not made room for mechanisms awarding positive environmental conduct. In fact, it has neither eliminated certain fiscal provisions in the personal and corporate income

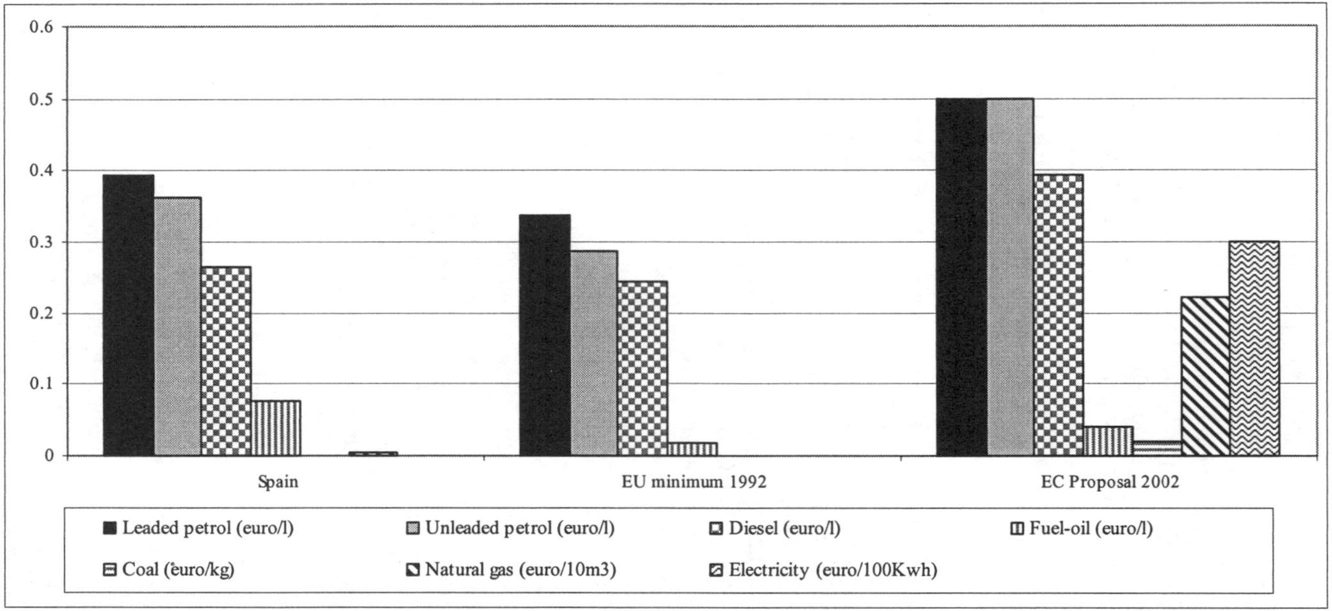

Figure 10.1 Excise duties on fossil fuels in Spain, in relation to the EU minimum and the proposal of the European Commission

Source: Gago and Labandeira (2002).

tax codes which are contrary to the environmental argument (e.g. deductibility of private transport expenses by self-employers), nor incorporated tax credit systems to bring visibility to the principle of receiving benefits for pollution abatement.

This attitude has brought with it another important consequence: Spain has not enacted general laws regulating the energy and tax systems which are capable of setting general guidelines for the definition and use of environmental taxes. This absence is what has made it possible for the tax systems of the autonomous regions (or second level systems) to take action on this type of tax initiatives, although they have had only relative success, as we will see below.

Actually, the only recognisable strategy of the central government has been that of deferral, in the interest of extending the time available to maintain competitiveness in production costs and relaxed institutional requirements, in search of a differential growth path and economic convergence within the EU. Such an approach is clearly questionable given the serious environmental problems that have been generated in 20 years of significant economic growth, to say nothing of the doubtful relationship between lax environmental regulations and economic progress. In fact, in previous papers (e.g. Labandeira and Labeaga, 1999) on the simulated effects of a GTR in Spain, we concluded that these policies have very positive environmental and energy effects, at a low economic and distributional cost.

A GENUINELY REGIONAL EXPERIENCE

We have already mentioned that the use of environmental taxes has become relatively generalised in the developed world, with experiences in practically all the jurisdictional levels of government. On this subject, the OECD (2003) points to the existence of up to 38 environmental measures of a sub-central nature and 14 countries in which this practice is frequent, with applications in the fields of energy, private transport and the discharge of liquid waste being the most relevant.

In the case of Spain, public finance bodies at the regional level contrast with the practically nonexistent interest shown in these instruments by the other levels of government. Thus, since the beginning of the 1980s, almost all the autonomous regions have approved and put into effect various measures with some environmental objective. The intense action on the part of the autonomous regional governments in this area probably has to do with their financial needs, reduced visibility and good political marketing of these taxes. It is also likely that the tight legislative restrictions on their ability to tax, the non-exportability of the tax burden and, especially, the no duplication with other levels of government, have had some influence in their behavior. In any case, it constitutes an interesting and not very well known experience, to which we will devote special attention by describing the main actions undertaken.

Table 10.2 shows the different environmental taxes existing in the various autonomous regions. Most of the environmental taxation at the regional level (and the first chronologically) is related to the emissions of liquid waste. These were followed by taxes on facilities having an environmental impact, the measures implemented being of a revenue-raising nature and zero environmental value, and also plagued by serious legal problems. Some autonomous regions now assess taxes on polluting emissions of an energy origin (based on the design developed in Galicia in 1995). These taxes have a more solid environmental foundation and today represent the most popular form of environmental tax. Finally, taxes on energy products and processes have been developed and, most recently, some which tax the deposit of different types of solid waste.

Figure 10.2 shows the per capita receipts of the environmental taxes in each autonomous region for the year 2004. The high receipts obtained by the regions of Catalonia and the Balearic Islands contrast with the limited receipts of Navarre, Aragon and Andalusia. The differences in the revenue collection capacity of the sanitation charges result from the variable tax rates and the various industrial sectors (i.e. wastes) existing in each autonomous region. The revenue derived from such charges makes up the largest part by far (82 percent) of the income generated from all the environmental taxes. In any event, the revenue obtained from all the environmental taxes is of little significance in relation to the total tax receipts in each autonomous region (given the high degree of devolution of central taxes to the autonomous regions), although it is very relevant within the taxes corresponding to the autonomous region itself (over which these levels of government have total autonomy).

Sanitation and Water Charges

Sanitation charges constitute the most representative environmental tax measure in the Spanish autonomous regions, as they are used by more than two thirds of these governments. Their objective is two-fold: to regulate the discharge of sewage and in general to fund expenditures in the investment and exploitation of the infrastructures necessary for sewage treatment. Thus it is a tax in which the revenue collected is earmarked.

The administrative processing of the sanitation charges is usually carried out by autonomous bodies which could generically be called water

Table 10.2 Environment taxes of the autonomous regions of Spain

	Sanitation/ Water Charge	Liquid Waste Charge	Tax on Air Emissions	Tax on Facilities	Tax on Energy Products	Waste Charge	Tax in Deposit of Hazardous Waste
Andalusia	–	1994	2003	–	–	–	2003
Aragon	1997	–	–	–	–	–	–
Asturias	1994	–	–	–	–	–	–
Basque Country	–	–	–	–	–	–	–
Balearic Islands	1991	–	–	1991[i]	–	–	–
Canary Islands	–	1987*	–	–	1986	–	–
Cantabria	2002*	–	–	–	–	–	–
Castilla y León	–	–	–	–	–	–	–
Castilla-La Mancha	2002*	–	2000	–	2000	–	2000
Catalonia	1981	–	–	–	–	2003	–
Extremadura	–	–	–	1997	–	–	–
Galicia	1993	–	1995	–	–	–	–
La Rioja	1994	–	–	–	–	–	–
Madrid	1984	–	–	–	–	2003	–
Murcia	2000	1995*	1995*	–	–	1995*	–
Navarre	1989	–	–	–	–	–	–
Valencia	1992	–	–	–	–	–	–

Note: * Approved but not applied.
[i] Declared unconstitutional.

Source: Gago and Labandeira (2002).

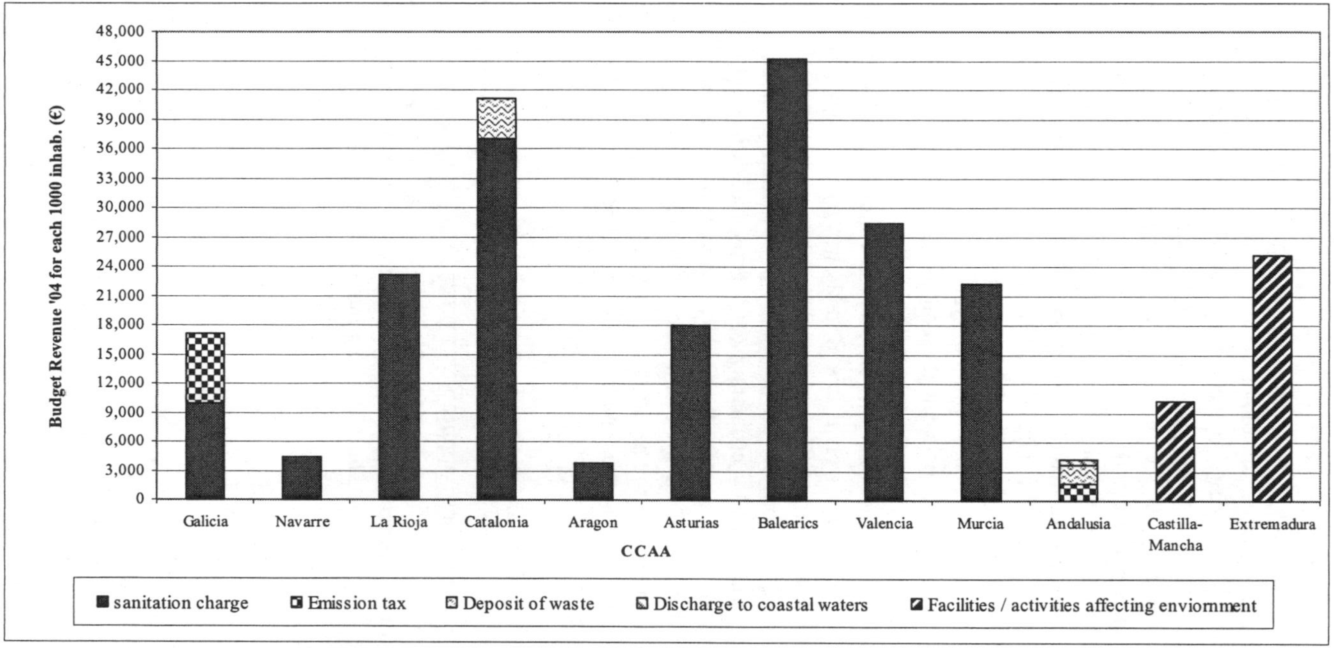

Figure10.2 Revenue from environmental taxes at regional level in 2004

Source: Authors' computations.

agencies. These bodies implement the policies on the sanitation of sewage in each autonomous region and, in general, perform all activities related to hydrological planning. The companies or utilities (whether public or private) that supply water are obligated to invoice and transfer the revenue from the sanitation charge to these bodies, acting as substitutes for the taxpayers and thus facilitating the processing of the tax.

The taxable event is the discharge of sewage into the environment, whether it takes place directly or through the sewage networks. A definition like this one brings with it significant problems of an administrative nature due to the technical difficulties of measuring the discharge and the high management cost of the tax. It is therefore common for the public administration not to tax the discharge directly but rather to do so indirectly, by taxing the consumption of water from any source. Thus there is assumed to be a link between the consumption of water and sewage discharge.

The tax base is constituted, generally, by the volume of water consumed, measured in cubic meters or, if this is unknown, by the volume of water estimated by means of different indicators or signs. In addition, most autonomous regions consider the possibility of determining the base of the tax for industrial uses by estimating or directly measuring the pollution load. Determining the tax base in this way allows two important objectives to be met: (i) it adjusts the tax base to the environmental damage produced or, where appropriate, to the costs of treatment and purification of the substances discharged, thus putting into practice the "polluter pays" principle, and (ii) it provides incentives for the reduction of polluting emissions.

There are various alternatives in the design of the tax rates, the most common practice being to differentiate between the rates applicable to domestic uses and those applicable to other uses. In some cases the tax breaks down into a fixed component and a variable component which depends on the volume of water consumed. In addition, the variable part of the tax liability can be modulated taking into account different factors, such as the pollution load, the population of the municipality, monthly water consumption, etc.

The first conclusion we can draw from the sanitation charges collected by the autonomous regions is that direct incentives aimed at the reduction of polluting emissions are limited. This is due, in the first place, to the flaw in the aforementioned concept linking the consumption of water to the production of waste. And, secondly, it is also due to the ineffectiveness associated with the low elasticity of consumption of water, which requires very high rates to be able to significantly affect consumption and the discharges.

The second conclusion is that the sanitation charges are principally a tax instrument for funding public sewage treatment services. The design of the tax reveals that greater weight has been given to taxation management principles, such as simplicity and efficiency, than to principles such as environmental effectiveness. In fact, the earmarking of the revenue collected for certain purposes is a good indication of the true objectives of the tax.

Taxes on Atmospheric Pollution

In 1995 the regional government of Galicia approved a tax on atmospheric pollution which at the time constituted the most environmentally-based tax measure applied in Spain. For several years it was the only tax of its type, although recently very similar taxes have been created in Castilla-La Mancha (2000) and Andalusia (2003). It is interesting to note that these regions are among the less developed and those with comparatively larger emissions in Spain, which probably explains their leading role in the issue. The Galician tax is levied on emissions of sulfur oxides and nitrogen oxides, pollutants related to the burning of fossil fuels and a primary cause of acid rain. Its appearance probably has to do with the great significance of the emissions localised in the periphery of Spain, where many large contaminating facilities are found. It uses a tax rate that varies according to the level of emission (progressive) and calculates the assessment base through either direct control or indirect estimation systems, while maintaining low administrative costs. The revenue collected is partially earmarked for a contingency fund for environmental catastrophes.

The taxes levied by the autonomous regions on atmospheric pollution share quite a few features, but they also have important differences. Although all of them have a clear environmental purpose, the scope of the tax in Andalusia is considerably greater, in that: (i) it is applied to a high number of industrial facilities, regardless of the volume of emissions, while the other two have very high tax-exemption minimums (in the case of Galicia this means that only six large polluting firms have to pay taxes on their emissions); (ii) it also taxes carbon dioxide emissions; (iii) its tax rates are notably higher, each additional ton being taxed at a higher rate, and it thus approaches the real environmental damage caused by the contaminating emissions.

In short, it can be said that the Andalusian tax represents a modernisation and a correction of the main problems of the taxes implemented in Galicia and Castilla-La Mancha. Nonetheless, all three taxes can be criticised from the perspective of jurisdictional allocation of responsibility, since the scope of the damage they hope to avoid transcends the territories in which they are applied, especially in the case of carbon dioxide emissions. Their effectiveness is debatable, as the tax rates are relatively low and, furthermore, the internalisation process is hampered by the institutional arrangements existing in the Spanish energy sector.[3]

Other Taxes

Starting at the beginning of the 1990s several fiscal measures were approved in Spain to tax, either directly or indirectly, the production and transport of energy (see Table 10.2). This is the case of the Balearic Islands (the tax was in effect from 1991 to 2000, the year in which it was repealed by the Constitutional Court because it was considered a case of duplication in taxable matters) and Extremadura (in effect since 1997), with slight variations on the Balearic design but also challenged by the central government in the Constitutional Court.

Unlike the taxes on emissions, these measures represent options which are much more dubious from a theoretical point of view. Here the legislative body apparently assumes the objective of recovering environmental costs generated by certain activities, but the narrow definition of the taxable events and the uncertain environmental connection of some of them cast doubt on this intention. In particular, the taxes in the Balearic Islands and Extremadura use asset-related information for the calculation of the environmental tax base, which makes one wonder about their true environmental nature. On the other hand, the Castillian tax on the production of nuclear energy (in effect since 2000) generates no type of environmental incentive, since nuclear-fired generators are continuously in operation due to the extremely large costs associated with switching them on and off.

Finally, several recently-created regional taxes are levied on the deposit or storage of certain solid wastes (radioactive in the case of Andalusia and Castilla-La Mancha, and ordinary solid waste in Madrid and Catalonia). As is the case with the emissions taxes, the environmental connection of these measures is quite clear, since they directly tax the sources of pollution. In any case, an appropriate definition of the tax rates would make it possible to recover the social costs derived from the production and recovery of the waste, which has become a large and growing problem in recent years.

In the light of experiences from around the world, taxes levied on waste offer great potential. Furthermore, they correspond with the jurisdictional profile of the governments of the autonomous regions. Not everything, however, is positive, since the possible reaction by the taxpayers may be quite small due to the limited possibilities of waste reduction, especially in the case of radioactive waste, and the tax may turn into a mere revenue instrument.

THE FUTURE OF ENVIRONMENTAL TAXATION IN SPAIN

The considerations set forth above make it clear that the Spanish experience with environmental taxation contains both high points and low points. Beginning with the positive features, there are interesting applications which are technically correct and innovative in the field. In these cases, an efficient alternative has been put in place for the internalisation of environmental deterioration and this has been made possible within a fiscal federalism framework.

The low points are also abundant, however. For example, the central government has maintained a contrary attitude and there have been many difficulties (both legal and practical) in applying these kinds of taxes at the local level. This has brought about a marked environmental deterioration and serious problems in fulfilling the international agreements related to climate change. Additionally, the lack of coordination is evident, since environmental taxes vary considerably from territory to territory and they generally do not correspond to the environmental responsibilities that can be allocated to a sub-central government.

In this context, our reflections and recommendations for the future can be organised into four large areas: (i) coordination; (ii) actions in energy taxation; (iii) the possibility of GTRs; (iv) other potential fields.

As for coordination, in the first place we think that a more efficient jurisdictional allocation would be advisable. Thus, taxes on global problems should be allocated to the central government, while the sub-central governments are put in charge of taxes pertaining to a more reduced spatial area. Secondly, a certain territorial harmonisation appears to be called for, perhaps in the form of a law on territorial powers that gives a great deal of autonomy to sub-central units, so that the conflict currently existing between the different levels of government is limited. Thirdly, it is necessary to avoid excess of fiscal and environmental regulation on certain sectors which already withstand considerable control measures (e.g. through the emissions trade market recently created in the EU).

The role of conventional energy taxation must also be considered, firstly, because of the high correlation between the consumption of these products and contemporary environmental problems; and secondly, because of the relatively low level of such taxes as compared to those existing in countries around Spain, which makes immediate action necessary. In addition, these are taxes in which the territorial governments have quite a lot of say, as they are the object of partial devolution and various taxes of this type are already assessed by some autonomous regions. In general, the environmental argument should be incorporated as an assessment criterion in these measures, their rates should be raised considerably, and a jurisdictional allocation should be implemented which gives partial autonomy to the subcentral units and limits the creation of regional taxes which may distort the markets.

And it is precisely the use of stable environmental taxes with powerful revenue capacity (e.g. excise duties on energy or taxes on waste) which allows us to consider the application of GTRs at different jurisdictional levels. We have already indicated that sufficient empirical evidence exists to justify their application in Spain: low inflationary effects, improvements in employment and economic growth, few distributional concerns, etc. Surprisingly, no Spanish government has introduced a compensatory package of this type (more environmental taxes in exchange for fewer income taxes and social contribution obligations), even though there are legal possibilities for its application at both the central and the regional levels.

Lastly we come to the question of the fields for potential action. We have already mentioned the case of solid waste and excise duties on energy, which are very good examples of where environmental taxes can be applied or raised, at practically all the jurisdictional levels. In the case of the latter, greater taxation on transport would be of special interest, since transport causes a very large part of the constant increase in Spanish emissions of greenhouse gases. Also, the Spanish tourism industry causes (and is in turn affected by) serious environmental deterioration, and therefore constitutes a preferential area of action. However, it is important to avoid looking for a mere exportation of the fiscal burden to nonresidents. Efforts should instead be aimed at correcting environmental problems through public revenue, without discrimination among the agents involved.

Another wide-open field is the necessary reform of the conventional taxes belonging to all the public administrations. This should take place through the incorporation of new environmental incentive mechanisms, mainly to clean up the old structure of key taxes such as the personal income or profit taxes, but also to introduce new specific fiscal benefits in other cases.

CONCLUSIONS

In this chapter we have described the developments observed in environmental taxation in recent decades in Spain. In general, we have seen how the Spanish fiscal system as a whole appears to be an island within the tendencies prevailing in modern fiscal systems with regard to environmental taxation. The absence of GTR processes and the lack of interest on the part of the central and local governments in these matters explain our choice of the phrase "missed opportunity" in the title. This passive, and even negative, attitude of a large part of the public sector has given rise to accelerating environmental deterioration and an energy sector which is inefficient at best (as well as very dependent on imports).

A certain interest in the use of these mechanisms has been observed only in the regional governments. We have indicated that this has much more to do with financial concerns and the difficulties these governments face in imposing taxes of their own, and much less to do with environmental objectives. This situation has led to rather erratic actions, with measures that are often technically defective, and to considerable territorial variability within the country. Especially worrying is the lack of correspondence between certain taxes and the jurisdictional scope of these governments, something very evident in the case of climate change and acid rain.

Standing out among the experiences in environmental taxation at the level of Spain's autonomous regions are the generalisation and revenue-collection capacity of sanitation charges. These generally constitute taxes on the consumption of water (as an indicator of the level of emissions) and are earmarked for sanitation activities. Also important are taxes on emissions into the air of certain pollutants, generally caused by the burning of fossil fuels.

Doing a bit of forecasting, we would say that in the future, environmental taxes on transport, tourism and solid waste will take on a certain importance. First, this is so because the need for intervention is becoming more and more acute due to the negative evolution of these emissions in recent years. Also, these sectors are relatively free of environmental regulation through market instruments and the existing levels of taxation are very low in EU terms. Finally, these are sectors that can be regulated by practically all the jurisdictional levels and they represent a possible source of stable and significant income.

In this context, it is to be hoped that the various levels of the Spanish government do not let these opportunities go by once again, and instead apply credible fiscal policies which contribute to the very necessary efforts made in environmental protection. The central government will probably have to renounce the ability to introduce taxes against climate change, since there is a European emissions trade system, but it can make its conventional taxes more environmentally friendly and increase energy taxes. The subcentral governments also have quite a few possibilities for action, although they must work to avoid the problems currently plaguing this field. A neutral introduction of these taxes, within the framework of a GTR process, could further reduce the economic problems often associated with these measures and therefore constitute a worthwhile pursuit for all levels of the Spanish government.

NOTES

* REDE and Department of Applied Economics (Universidade de Vigo)

1. We acknowledge financial support from the Spanish Ministry for Science and Technology and ERDF (Project SEC200203095), and the Galician government (Project PGIDIT03PXIC30008PN).

2. See e.g. Bovenberg and Goulder (2002) for a theoretical and comprehensive perspective and European Environment Agency (2000) for a summary of actual applications.
3. Nowadays the price of energy for large consumers is set by the marginal generator, which means that this tax is likely to have no effects at all unless it particularly affects this unit.

REFERENCES

Bovenberg, A. and Goulder, L. (2002), 'Environmental Taxation and Regulation', in Auerbach, A. J. and Feldstein, M. (eds) *Handbook of Public Economics*, vol. 3, North-Holland, Amsterdam.

European Environment Agency (2000), 'Environmental Taxes: Recent Developments in Tools for Integration', EEA Environmental Issues Series, 18. Copenhagen.

Gago, A. and Labandeira, X. (2000), 'Towards a Green Tax Reform Model', *Journal of Environmental Policy and Planning*, 2, 25–38.

Gago, A. and Labandeira, X. (Dir) (2002), 'Energía, Fiscalidad y Medio Ambiente', Instituto de Estudios Fiscales, Madrid.

Hoerner, A. and Bosquet. B. (2001), 'Environmental Tax Reform: the European Experience', Center for Sustainable Economy, Washington D.C.

Joumand, I. (2001), 'Tax Systems in European Union Countries', OECD Economics Department WP 301.

Labandeira, X. (1996), 'Market Instruments and the Control of Acid Rain Damage. Effects of a Sulphur Tax on the Spanish Electricity Generating Industry', *Energy Policy*, 24, 841–854.

Labandeira, X. and Labeaga, J. M. (1999), 'Combining Input-Output Analysis and Microsimulation to Assess the Effects of Carbon Taxation on Spanish Households', *Fiscal Studies*, 20, 303–318.

Majocchi, A. (2000), 'Greening Tax Mixes in OECD Countries: a Preliminary Assessment', Com/Env/Epoc/Daffe/Cfa (99), 112/Final, Paris.

Messere, K. (1993), *Tax Policy in OECD Countries: Choices and Conflicts*, Amsterdam: IBFD.

Messere, K. (2002), *The Tax System in Industrialized Countries*, Oxford: Oxford University Press.

OECD (1993), *Taxation in OECD Countries*, Paris.

OECD (2003), Database on Environmentally Related Taxes, OECD, Paris., www.oecd.org /env/policies/taxes.

Peltzman, S. and Tideman, T. (1972), 'Local Versus National Pollution Control: Note', *American Economic Review*, 62, 959–963.

11. Regional Governments: Vertical Imbalances and Revenue Assignments

Julio López Laborda* and Carlos Monasterio Escudero[1]**

INTRODUCTION

This chapter provides an overview of the key issues in public economics arising from the process of territorial decentralisation that has taken place in Spain since the restoration of democracy and the Constitution of 1978, and which resulted in the emergence of the "Autonomic State".

The first section focuses on the assignment of competencies between central and regional levels of government and explains in some detail the methodology used to quantify the "effective cost" of the services devolved to the Autonomous Communities (hereinafter ACs). We have paid special attention to health services, which is the most significant item for regional budgets in quantitative terms.

The second section deals with revenue assignment, transfers and borrowing, and describes the two systems established to finance regional expenditure. These are the "common system" (*régimen común*) applied in the majority of the ACs and the "charter system" (*régimen foral*), which is based on the historical rights accorded to the Basque Country and Navarre.

The last section appraises the decentralisation process and notes some emerging issues of debate.

ASSIGNMENTS OF COMPETENCIES TO THE AUTONOMOUS COMMUNITIES

Initial Assignment of Competencies

The decentralisation of the public sector in Spain began with the democratic Constitution of 1978, which recognises the right of the Autonomous Communities to regional self-government.

This process resulted in the emergence of the "Autonomic State", which is essentially similar to a federal State, with which it shares a number of common features (Aja, 1999: 31–39):

1. The fundamental division of competencies between central and regional government is settled at the constitutional level.
2. Legislative and executive offices in the Autonomous Communities (Parliament and President) are elective and officeholders are accountable to the regional electorate alone.
3. Disputes between central and regional government are handled by the Constitutional Court.

The Autonomic State is formed by seventeen Autonomous Communities, in addition to the Autonomous Cities of Ceuta and Melilla (see Figure 11.1), which are highly diverse in terms of size, population and other factors. Table 11.1 provides a summary of population, area, income levels, number of local jurisdictions (provinces and municipalities[2]), the year the Statute of Autonomy (a sort of regional Constitution for each AC) was enacted, the level of devolution at the time each AC was founded, and the applicable financing system. We shall return to the latter two features later on in this chapter.

The design of Spanish devolution allots the distribution of competencies between the central and the regional level of government to the Constitution, which nevertheless sets out only general principles in the matter of revenue assignment.

Over time, the ACs have taken on responsibility for the provision of a wide range of regional public goods and services which specifically impact the well-being of people living within their territory. These include town and country planning, housing, public works, regional transport and infrastructure, farming, environment, culture, tourism, sport and so on, as well as health and education, the two basic public services provided by the Welfare State. Originally, and for historical reasons, only a small group of ACs were granted powers in education and health matters. This led to a distinction between "high level Communities" (i.e. those with a high level

Figure 11.1 The Spanish autonomous communities

of devolved competencies) and "low level Communities". Though certain minor differences persist (e.g. only some Communities have powers for the administration of the prison system and the police), it may fairly be said that all of the ACs nowadays have substantially the same competencies.

The competencies assigned to the central government, meanwhile, are related to economic stability, income and wealth redistribution and the provision of national public goods and services, that is, those that affect all of the citizens of Spain equally, such as international relations, defence, customs and tariffs, foreign trade, the currency system, basic regulation of the financial, banking and insurance systems, the bases and coordination of general economic planning, public finances and debt, basic Social Security legislation and funding, national public works, infrastructure and transport, and so on.

Central government is currently responsible for approximately 50 percent of total public expenditure, the ACs some 35 percent and local government institutions around 15 percent. Regional public employment represents more than 50 percent of general government employment.

The ACs do not exercise their powers within a framework of complete freedom. While they have exclusive competencies in some areas (such as regional public works, infrastructure and transport) without intervention

Table 11.1 Key characteristics of the autonomous communities

AUTONOMOUS COMMUNITY	POPULATION		AREA (1)		GDP 2004 (1)		Per capita GDP 2004 (1)	
	Population	%	Km.²	%	Thousands of €	%	€	Index Average = 100
Andalusia	7,687,518	17.80%	87,597	17.31%	110,404,080	13.84%	14,361	77.75%
Aragon	1,249,548	2.89%	47,720	9.43%	24,568,098	3.08%	19,662	106.45%
Asturias	1,073,761	2.49%	10,604	2.10%	17,339,025	2.17%	16,148	87.42%
Balearic Islands	955,045	2.21%	4,992	0.99%	19,708,718	2.47%	20,636	111.73%
Canary Islands	1,915,540	4.43%	7,447	1.47%	32,743,304	4.10%	17,094	92.54%
Cantabria	554,784	1.28%	5,321	1.05%	10,191,284	1.28%	18,370	99.45%
Castile-La Mancha	1,848,881	4.28%	79,463	15.70%	27,042,295	3.39%	14,626	79.19%
Castile and León	2,493,918	5.77%	94,223	18.62%	44,517,892	5.58%	17,851	96.64%
Catalonia	6,813,319	15.77%	32,114	6.35%	146,598,797	18.37%	21,517	116.49%
Valencia	4,543,304	10.52%	23,255	4.60%	77,481,394	9.71%	17,054	92.33%
Extremadura	1,075,286	2.49%	41,634	8.23%	13,996,176	1.75%	13,016	70.47%
Galicia	2,750,985	6.37%	29,574	5.84%	42,421,254	5.32%	15,420	83.49%
Madrid	5,804,829	13.44%	8,028	1.59%	138,670,768	17.38%	23,889	129.33%
Murcia	1,294,694	3.00%	11,313	2.24%	19,778,993	2.48%	15,277	82.71%
Navarre	584,734	1.35%	10,391	2.05%	13,544,294	1.70%	23,163	125.41%
Basque Country	2,115,279	4.90%	7,234	1.43%	50,485,864	6.33%	23,867	129.22%
La Rioja	293.553	0.68%	5,045	1.00%	5,961,985	0.75%	20,310	109.96%
Ceuta	74,654	0.17%	19	0.00%	1,297,009	0.16%	17,374	94.06%
Melilla	68,016	0.16%	13	0.00%	1,138,894	0.14%	16,745	90.65%
TOTAL	43,197,648	100.00%	505,987	100.00%	797,890,124	100.00%	18,741	100.00%

Table 11.1 Key characteristics of the autonomous communities (continued)

AUTONOMOUS COMMUNITY	PROVINCES	MUNICIPALITIES (2)	APPROVAL OF STATUE	INITIAL LEVEL OF COMPETENCIES	FINANCING SYSTEM
Andalusia	8	769	1981	HIGH	LOFCA
Aragon	3	730	1982	LOW	LOFCA
Asturias	1	78	1981	LOW	LOFCA
Balearic Islands	1	67	1983	LOW	LOFCA
Canary Islands	2	87	1982	HIGH	LOFCA
Cantabria	1	102	1981	LOW	LOFCA
Castile-La Mancha	5	916	1982	LOW	LOFCA
Castile and León	9	2,247	1983	LOW	LOFCA
Catalonia	4	945	1979	HIGH	LOFCA
Valencia	3	541	1982	HIGH	LOFCA
Extremadura	2	382	1983	LOW	LOFCA
Galicia	4	315	1981	HIGH	LOFCA
Madrid	1	179	1983	LOW	LOFCA
Murcia	1	45	1982	LOW	LOFCA
Navarre	1	272	1982	HIGH	CHARTER
Basque Country	6	250	1979	HIGH	CHARTER
La Rioja	1	174	1982	LOW	LOFCA
Ceuta	0	1	1995	–	–
Melilla	0	1	1995	–	–
TOTAL	50	8,101	–	–	–

Note: LOFCA—*Ley Orgánica de Financiación de las Comunidades Autónomas.*

Source: Instituto Nacional de Estadística (1), *Ministerio de Administraciones Públicas* (2), and author's computations.

from any other tier, their actions in others are subject to restrictions of differing intensity.

In some cases, such as environmental and farm policy, EU Directives determine minimum environmental quality standards and the kinds of crops that may be grown. The most significant limitations, however, refer to services such as healthcare and education. Although managed by the ACs, these are shared competencies and the central government establishes the basic conditions for the provision of the service, the rules governing access by users and other matters that cannot be altered by regional governments. These restrictions are intended to ensure that the conditions of the service remain essentially the same nationwide. Within this framework, the ACs have the power to enact specific regional laws applicable within their territory, manage the service and improve the conditions under which it is provided. They cannot, however, lower basic standards.

It is important to note here that all of the competencies assigned to the ACs, with the sole exception of the institutions of self-government (regional government and parliament) which represent a minimal part of total AC expenditure, are devolved from services that were formerly provided out of central government budgets and were transferred to regional budgets after decentralisation. Consequently, the cost of the services transferred is a key issue, which we shall consider immediately.

Valuation of Competencies and Effective Cost Method

Decentralisation of the public sector involves rather more than simply demarcating the competencies transferred to the new regional governments. It also requires an accurate assessment of the cost of each service and the allocation of the relevant financial resources to the Autonomous Community concerned to ensure provision is properly funded.

The cost of devolved services was calculated in Spain using the "Effective Cost Method", which is based on the following criteria:

1. Users of public services should not suffer changes in the level of provision due to the devolution of competencies from central to regional governments. This requires transferring all the human and material resources used and required for the provision of the service from central to regional governments.
2. The financial sufficiency of both tiers of government (the level devolving the service and the level assuming the new competency) must be assured (the vertical fiscal balance) and increments in public spending avoided. This requires removing the expenditure item from the central government budget in an amount equal to the funding received by the Community concerned.

The volume of spending associated with the competencies transferred was quantified by valuation commissions formed by representatives of central government and of the AC concerned. These "Mixed Transfer Commissions" *(Comisiones Mixtas de Transferencias)* agreed to the value of the devolved competencies mainly on the basis of budget data. Competencies cannot be devolved unless the AC is in conformity with this valuation.

The importance of the effective cost method to the structure of AC finance can hardly be overstated, since the application of the method determines the total volume of resources funded. Consequently, any discussion of ACs' finances and respect for the principle of sufficiency will always be tantamount to a debate over the appropriateness of the effective cost method.

In essence, the effective cost method seeks to establish the monetary value of each competency by identifying all costs that will be incurred by the AC affected as a result of the devolution of the service. This is the key figure if the AC is to continue the service at the same level of provision as central government prior to the transfer.

Table 11.2 shows how the effective cost of a competency *j* for an Autonomous Community *i* (*ECij*) is calculated on the basis of the sum of costs, less fees charged to users of the service.

As Table 11.2 reflects, the method involves the calculation of the *net effective cost*, because fees charged to partially fund the service transferred (*Fij*) are deducted from the total cost of provision. This procedure seems appropriate because the logic of the benefit principle requires that the provider of the service decide the level of fees charged. Thus, the transfer of services also implies the transfer of revenues where these arise from the application of the benefit principle.

The effective cost comprises only current and capital expenditure, excluding financial charges in respect of public debt servicing (interest and repayment) and transfers.

The exclusion of financial charges associated with public debt is absolutely logical because in devolving the competency for a service, the central government also transfers the stock of public capital required for provision, but retains the stock of public debt issued to fund the same. It would therefore be inappropriate to include the effective cost of interest charges or debt repayments.

Transfers, meanwhile, are excluded because the logic of the effective cost method requires that those associated with redistribution should remain the competency of central government.

Table 11.2 Quantification of the effective cost of devolved services

ECij = DCij + ICij + RIij + NIij –Fij
DCij: Direct costs incurred in the provision of the service. These comprise wages and salaries, and current purchases of goods and services by the agencies directly providing the service.
ICij: Indirect costs. These comprise wages and salaries, and current purchases of goods and services by agencies that do not directly provide the service to end users but are responsible for support functions, planning and coordination.
RIij: Replacement investment. Capital expenditure required to maintain the stock of public assets transferred under the same conditions of use.
NIij: New investment. Capital expenditure intended to increase the stock of public assets (this component was not included in the calculation of the effective cost until 1995)
Fij: Fees charged to users of the service in accordance with the benefit principle

Source: Author's computations.

This criterion, however, ignores the crucial distinction between public provision (public funding for a service which is made available to the consumer without charge per unit consumed) and public production (public funding for a service directly produced by the public sector, contracting the necessary inputs).

Public production in fact seems to be the only alternative considered in the effective cost method. If this were not the case, transfers to private sector providers of public services would have to be considered in the calculation of the cost of the services transferred.[3]

The methodology used to calculate the effective cost of services suffers from certain problems, including the following:

1. The absence of a reliable source of data for the application of the methodology. This is due to the lack of public sector cost accounting and the fact that budget accounting methods are designed for expenditure control rather than the measurement of the cost of services. Thus, the effective cost method results in a *negotiated cost* rather than

an *assessed cost* of services. Central government enters the negotiations leading to the quantification of the effective cost with a certain advantage due to the asymmetry of information available to the parties, because it has prior management experience and data. The process of devolution and valuation of services may be viewed as a recurring game where the ACs have gradually acquired experience in successive rounds of negotiations, starting from an initial situation in which central government had a clear information advantage.

As we have explained, the effective cost of the service depends on central government expenditures immediately prior to devolution. In these circumstances, there is a clear temptation to adjust budgets downward in the year prior to the transfer. Such underbudgeting certainly creates problems for central government in its last year providing the service, but it offers the advantage of lowering the transfer of funds that must be made to the ACs in subsequent years, which amply offsets any such difficulties.

The attractions of such a manoeuvre only increase where overall devolution of a major competency (such as education or health) is concerned.

2. The effective cost refers to the moment of devolution, and the expense associated with central government provision of the service is calculated at the level prevailing *in each region* at that time. As a result, two similar ACs could simultaneously obtain the devolution of (say) education but each be assigned differing, possibly even widely diverging, effective cost.
3. Given that regional finances were carved out from the existing national exchequer, it would seem reasonable for this process to have covered both the assets and liabilities of central government. Since the carve-out concerns *what there is* and not *what there should be* in the central government exchequer, the effective cost could have included a share of the deficit (a part of the stock of debt) in respect of the competencies devolved, but it did not. A part of the accumulated central government debt would thus have been allocated to the improvement of the services devolved to the ACs, and the question therefore arises whether a portion of this outstanding debt should not also be decentralised together with the services. Placing the public assets associated with the services transferred in the hands of the ACs without simultaneously transferring that part of the stock of debt that might rationally be associated with such assets is not without its consequences. In the first place, the debt burden came to represent an increasing share of the central government budget, which at the same time shrank as a result of the transfers. The other outcome was that the

ACs maintained their borrowing capacity intact with the full course left to run up to the established ceilings. This, of course, provided a certain incentive to borrow further.

Despite these criticisms, it must be recognised overall that the effective cost method did provide an effective basis for the orderly devolution of a significant volume of competencies from central government to the ACs without causing excessive budgetary tensions. Based on an analysis of the decentralisation process in terms of the available alternatives, it must be allowed that it would have been far from easy to proceed in any other way given the weaknesses inherent in the original accounting data.

The Devolution of Health Services

In Spain, as in the majority of federal countries, the decentralisation of health services has been rather limited (Banting and Corbett, 2002: 16–25) and to a great extent the goal has been to ensure territorial equality in the quality of healthcare.

This is, then, a shared competency, where the level of healthcare coverage (universal in the case of Spain), the list of guaranteed medical services and general funding are decided at the central government level. The regional governments, on the other hand, are responsible for the delivery of healthcare to the citizen within their own territory and the distribution of health funding among hospitals and clinics. At the same time, they have the power to expand the list of guaranteed services, though they must seek additional financing from the regional taxpayer.

There are two reasons for the special treatment of health services within the range of competencies devolved to the ACs. In the first place, health is by some way the largest of the ACs' expenditure programmes, normally representing between 40 and 50 percent of total spending (Table 11.3). In addition, the rate of growth in health expenditure exceeds that of GDP growth and the outlook is for strong upward pressure in the future due to the aging of the population.

Secondly, health services were fully devolved to all of the ACs only very recently (2002) and were funded through a system of conditional grants that lay outside the general financing system.[4] Health competencies in fact continue to display certain peculiarities even after 2002, insofar as the ACs are required to guarantee a minimum increase in spending.

Table 11.3 Autonomous community health expenditure indicators, 2002 (€ '000 and %)

Autonomous Community	1. Total spending – all competencies	2. Total health spending	% Health spending (2/1)	Devolution of health services (Year)
Andalusia	12,918,377.92	5,401,165.42	41.81	1984
Aragon	2,306,090.03	986,297.47	42.77	2002
Asturias	1,992,620.35	901,628.36	45.25	2002
Balearic Islands	1,332,388.68	612,060.14	46.28	2002
Canary Islands	3,195,461.64	1,274,100.67	39.87	1994
Cantabria	1,114,478.55	492,407.07	44.18	2002
Castile-La Mancha	3,254,504.96	1,339,768.18	41.17	2002
Castile and Leon	4,783,475.14	1,941,595.28	40.59	2002
Catalonia	11,230,690.90	4,860,026.70	43.27	1981
Valencia	6,778,431.90	3,045,965.02	44.94	1988
Extremadura	2,172,560.12	839,507.47	38.64	2002
Galicia	5,172,261.91	2,100,252.67	40.61	1991
Madrid	8,675,745.43	3,788,044.69	43.66	2002
Murcia	1,897,040.16	835,604.27	44.05	2002
La Rioja	555,480.49	244,485.05	44.01	2002
Total ACs (common regime)	**67,369,608.19**	**28,662,909.46**	**42.55**	–

Source: Ministry of Finance (2004) and author's computations.

Until the general devolution of health competencies to all of the ACs, funding was provided through a separate system of specific grants, so that the amount received by each region represented a part of the total health budget in proportion to the regional population entitled to receive healthcare (Monasterio, 2002: 165–166). Unlike other competencies, then, the effective cost method was not used for health service finance, which was assessed rather on the basis of an explicit criterion of equity in the allocation of resources, i.e., equality in terms of *per capita* spending.

Over time, one of the main problems for the financing of the healthcare system has been the growth in spending, which in most years outstrips GDP growth. Expanding pharmaceutical expenditure has been a cause of particular concern, because it represents a higher percentage of total health expenditure in Spain than in other countries of the European Union or in the USA.

Nevertheless, it cannot be denied that health indicators are good in Spain, with long life expectancy, a reasonable hospital network and a more or less universal public health system reaching 99.4 percent of the population in 2000 (European Observatory on Health Care Systems, 2000).

In view of the high level of health coverage, concerns about rising health spending in the future are based mainly on the aging of the population (which raises *per capita* use of the health services) and the higher cost of care resulting from the introduction of new medical technologies and medicines, which are not only more effective but also more expensive.

For this reason, special guarantees have been established for healthcare funding, even though these services have formed part of the general "common regime" AC financing model since 2002. These include:

1. Guaranteed increases in healthcare funding at least equal to percentage GDP growth. This guarantee resulted in additional expenditure of € 209 million in 2002, and € 224 million in 2003.
2. Healthcare is defined as a basic public service and funding will be reviewed in those ACs where the annual increase in public system users exceeds 3 percent of the increase in national average. Where applicable, these ACs may receive specific purpose grants to improve regional healthcare services, the so-called "Basic Public Services Equalisation Grants" *(Asignaciones de Nivelación de Servicios Públicos Fundamentales)*. A similar guarantee is also applied to the education service.

In addition, the collection of the hydrocarbons retail sales tax, which is levied at the regional level, is tied to health (or environmental) spending.

The final goal pursued through the above measures is to ensure adequate funding for an expenditure item that absorbs almost half of regional budgets and is a basic public service for the Welfare State. This funding must be sufficient to guarantee the national list of health services nationwide and to provide the ACs with a margin to improve the service. The ACs are supposed to obtain additional resources by raising those taxes over which they have control. To date, however, only few ACs have availed themselves of the chance to raise the hydrocarbons retail sales tax for this purpose. These groundbreakers are Madrid (in 2002), Asturias, Galicia, Catalonia (2004), and Castile-La Mancha and Valencia (2006).

REVENUE ASSIGNMENT, TRANSFERS AND BORROWING[5]

Having quantified the cost of the services devolved to the ACs, the next step is to assign them their own resources to finance expenditure needs. The Constitution of 1978 establishes two basic systems for the funding of the ACs, the "common" system applicable to all of the ACs except the Basque Country and Navarre, and the "special" or "charter" system applicable to the latter based on their regional charters.[6] These systems differ widely both in terms of structure and outcomes, and we therefore discuss each separately.

The Common System

The design of the common system was originally established by the Autonomous Communities Financing Act, 1980 (*Ley Orgánica de Financiación de los Comunidades Autónomas—LOFCA*), which was comprehensively reformed in 2001. Consequently, the common system is also referred to as the LOFCA system. The Act establishes the basic principles of the system, while specific applications are settled by the Autonomous Communities Fiscal and Financial Policy Council (*Consejo de Política Fiscal y Financiera de las Comunidades Autónomas, CPFF*), the bi-partite body responsible for the coordination of financing at the central and regional levels. The CPFF assesses the evolution of regional finances on a regular basis (in principle once every five years) and makes any necessary changes. The most significant reviews took place in 1986, 1992, 1996 and 2001.

Initially (end of the 1970s and early 1980s) the common financing system worked in the following manner. The net effective cost of the j devolved competencies was calculated for each Autonomous Community i:

$$EC_i = \sum_{j=1}^{n} EC_{ij} \quad i = 1,...,15 \qquad [1]$$

This cost was financed by way of lump-sum general grants. Hence, the total funding received by the AC was:

$$R_i = EC_i \qquad [2]$$

This model had two main weaknesses. In the first place, the effective cost method failed to ensure that the ACs would be able to provide the devolved services on a roughly equal basis, allowing them rather to continue the former central level provision. This level, however, may differ widely from provision in other ACs.

The second weakness is that the funding system was based exclusively on grants, thwarting the effective action of two basic criteria for decentralisation: the principle of financial autonomy, which requires that a jurisdiction should be in a position to decide the level and structure of its revenues and spending; and the principle of accountability, in accordance with which the cost of providing regional public goods and services should be directly borne by the beneficiaries for reasons of efficiency.

Both central government and the ACs were aware of these two problems, and the subsequent evolution of the common financing system has consisted of gradual efforts to correct the resulting weaknesses, using the tools that the LOFCA anticipated.

It was first agreed as early as 1986 to replace the effective cost method with a quantification of regional spending based on indicators that would more accurately reflect the *expenditure needs* of each AC, in other words the costs incurred by each AC in order to provide the same level of public goods and services as other ACs. The indicators currently applied and their relative weightings are shown in Table 11.4. These cover three blocks of competencies: health, social and other services (including education). Population is the indicator with the highest weighting.

Despite this use of indicators in the quantification of regional spending, however, effective cost remains decisive for the determination of the ACs' expenditure needs. This is because all of the regional financing reviews approved by the CPFF included the condition that no AC would be assigned lower revenues than it had hitherto received.

The financing instruments used for regional spending have also changed. The system of funding based exclusively on general purpose grants was soon abandoned and replaced (1982–1984) with "ceded taxes" (*tributos cedidos*) and the "sufficiency fund" (*fondo de suficiencia*, referred to as "sharing in State revenues", *participación en los ingresos del Estado*, until 2002), two revenue sources that were more in line with theoretical recommendations and the experience of other federal countries.

Ceded taxes are established and regulated at the central level, which assigns certain competencies to the ACs. Until 1997 these competencies comprised only collection and administration of the tax. The ACs were not given any powers to regulate the taxes ceded, and the system should

Table11.4 Criteria applied in the quantification of common system Autonomous Communities' expenditure needs (since 2002)

CRITERION	OTHER SERVICES	HEALTH	SOCIAL SERVICES
Population	94%	–	–
Area	4.2%	–	–
Dispersion	1.2%	–	–
Island territory	0.6%	0.5%	–
Protected population	–	75%	–
Population > 65	–	24.5%	100%
Total	100%	100%	100%

Source: Author's computations.

therefore properly be described as a tax sharing arrangement rather than own taxes. Since 1997 certain regulatory competencies have been devolved for certain ceded taxes, allowing the Autonomous Community in question to set the tax rate and establish tax credits and allowances. In line with the literature (see, for example, Bird, 1993) these may be defined as own regional taxes, as long as the AC concerned has discretion to set the tax rate.

Table 11.5 enumerates the taxes ceded to date with a description of the competencies assigned to the ACs with regard to tax collection, administration and regulation. The last column of the table classifies these taxes from an economic standpoint as own taxes or tax sharing arrangements. Central government retains all powers over the collection, administration and regulation of corporate income tax, the tax on insurance premiums, import duties, payroll taxes and non-resident taxes.

Concerning the personal income tax, the tax schedule is divided into a central and a regional tax schedule. The central government schedule, which is equal to 67 percent of the total tax, is allocated at the central level, while the regional schedule, equal to 33 percent, is allocated to each AC. The ACs may maintain this tax schedule, in which case they will receive 33 percent of the total tax take, or they may increase or reduce the rate (as well as establishing their own tax credits) in which case the take would be either higher or lower than 33 percent.

Table 11.5 Taxes ceded to Autonomous Communities under the common system

TAX	COLLECTION	ADMINISTRATION	REGULATION	CLASSIFICATION
Personal Income Tax	33%	NO	Tax schedule and tax credits	Own tax
Tax on Net Wealth	100%	YES	Threshold, tax schedule and tax credits	Own tax
Inheritance and Gift Tax	100%	YES	Allowances, tax schedule, tax credits, administration and collection	Own tax
Capital Transfer Tax, Taxes on the raising of capital, and Stamp Duties	100%	YES	Tax rates, tax credits, administration and collection	Own tax
Gaming Taxes	100%	YES	Allowances, taxable base, tax rates, administration, collection and inspection	Own tax
Vehicles Excise (registration)	100%	YES	Tax rates	Own tax
Hydrocarbons Retail Sales Tax	100%	YES	Tax rates, administration, collection and inspection	Own tax
Value Added Tax, VAT	35%	NO	NO	Tax sharing
Excise Duties (alcoholic beverages, tobacco and petrol)	40%	NO	NO	Tax sharing
Electricity Tax	100%	NO	NO	Tax sharing

Source: López-Laborda (2004).

The tax yield that each AC should obtain by making the same tax effort as the others (the "standard tax yield") is calculated for each tax ceded. To the extent that this yield may be insufficient to meet expenditure needs, the system guarantees a genuine equalisation grant (the sufficiency fund) to cover the difference between expenditure needs and fiscal capacity. The sufficiency fund is a lump-sum unconditional grant.

Let us now consider how the sufficiency fund is determined. The CPFF establishes a "base" year for the system and calculates the expenditure needs of each Autonomous Community, E_{i0} and the standard yield for the ceded taxes, T^*_{i0}. The sufficiency fund, SF_{i0}, is calculated as the difference between expenditure and taxes:

$$SF_{i0} = E_{i0} - T^*_{i0} \qquad [3]$$

In some Autonomous Communities (e.g. the Balearic Islands and Madrid) the standard tax yields may exceed their expenditure needs. In such cases, the grant is negative and the amount is redirected from the AC to central government.

The sufficiency fund is not determined annually. For any year t subsequent to the base year, the amount is calculated by applying to the base year fund the rate of growth in State taxes equivalent to those ceded to the ACs (*Ingresos Tributarios del Estado, ITE*):

$$SF_{it} = SF_{i0} \cdot \frac{ITE_t}{ITE_0} \qquad [4]$$

Consequently, the revenues that Autonomous Community I would receive in year t would be the sum of the sufficiency fund and the actual yield from the taxes ceded (not the standard yield, which is used only to calculate the sufficiency fund in the base year):

$$R_{it} = SF_{it} + T_{it} = SF_{i0} \cdot \frac{ITE_t}{ITE_0} + T_{it} \qquad [5]$$

Based on the above, it may fairly be said that the common system of regional financing guarantees that all of the ACs will receive in the base year the funds they require to finance the services devolved at a reasonably equal level. However, it is no less true that the equalisation procedure may gradually be weakened over time, insofar as the sufficiency fund evolves at the same rate for all ACs, while the expenditure needs and the standard tax yield are likely to evolve at different rates. This is, in fact, what actually occurred in the early years of the application of the prevailing system, when population growth was unevenly spread across the Autonomous Communities.[7]

The ceded taxes and the sufficiency fund make up what might be called the "basic financing model". However, the ACs also have certain additional resources that can be used to provide more or better services than would be affordable through this basic model.

For example, they may establish genuine regional taxes and surcharges (or "truly" regional taxes, according to Bird, 1993: 213). In contrast to the ceded taxes, the ACs have full powers of collection, administration and regulation in such cases. There are, however, strict bounds to this power. Suffice to say that the Autonomous Communities Financing Act (LOFCA) prevents the ACs from trespassing on the terrain already occupied by central government and municipal taxes. This limitation explains why the ACs have established so few regional taxes (basically environmental and gaming taxes), and why the tax yield is so small.

The ACs also receive conditional grants intended to foster regional development, with the goal of reducing differences in income and wealth. Examples of this type of grant are the Interterritorial Compensation Funds (*Fondos de Compensación Interterritorial, FCI*) and certain revenues obtained from the European Union budget, such as the European Regional Development Fund (ERDF).

Table 11.6 shows the structure of ACs' non-financial revenues in 2004. Own revenues (comprising ceded and genuine regional taxes) represent 34 percent of regional non-financial revenues. If tax sharing formulas (which are based on the derivation principle and, so, are closer to own revenues than transfers) are included, this share rises to almost 55 percent. Conditional grants, meanwhile, represent some 20 percent of Autonomous Communities' non-financial revenues.

Finally, the ACs may run deficits and borrow. This source of financing is, however, subject to certain restrictions. In the first place, debt may only be used for investment purposes. Secondly, annual repayments of principal and interest may not exceed 25 percent of the AC's current revenues. Thirdly, all AC borrowing is coordinated with central government borrowing, and certain operations (foreign credit and regional public debt) are subject to central government approval.

Table 11.6 Percentage structure of common regime Autonomous Communities' non-financial revenues per 2004 budgets

OWN REVENUES		**34.01**
Regional taxes, surcharges, fees, charges, public prices and others		5.25
Personal Income Tax	14.18	
Net Wealth Tax	1.08	
Inheritance and Gift Tax	1.62	
Capital Transfer Tax, Taxes on the raising of capital, and Stamp Duties	9.58	
Gaming Taxes	0.14	
Vehicle Excise	1.24	
Hydrocarbons Retail Sales Tax	0.92	28.76
TAX SHARING AND GRANTS		**65.99**
Tax sharing		20.87
Value Added Tax, VAT	13.84	
Excise Duties	7.03	
General purpose grants		24.07
Sufficiency fund	24.07	
Specific purpose grants		21.04
Interterritorial Compensation Funds	0.94	
Other central and other agents grants	12.10	
European Union transfers	8.00	

Source: Author's computations.

As shown in Figure 11.2, the ACs have made increasing use of debt since the late 1980s and early 1990s. Many reasons have been advanced to explain this behaviour, such as the insufficiency of the revenues generated by the "basic model", the limited scope for genuine regional taxes and surcharges to play a role in the improvement of services, and the familiar phenomenon of the "fiscal illusion" associated with debt financing. As explained in the first section of this chapter, a certain incentive for regional indebtedness was built into the system because the ACs were not assigned a part of the deficit related with devolved competencies.

In 1992 central government and common and charter regime ACs recognised the need for coordination to achieve the fiscal convergence objectives established in the Maastricht Treaty. The resulting agreement

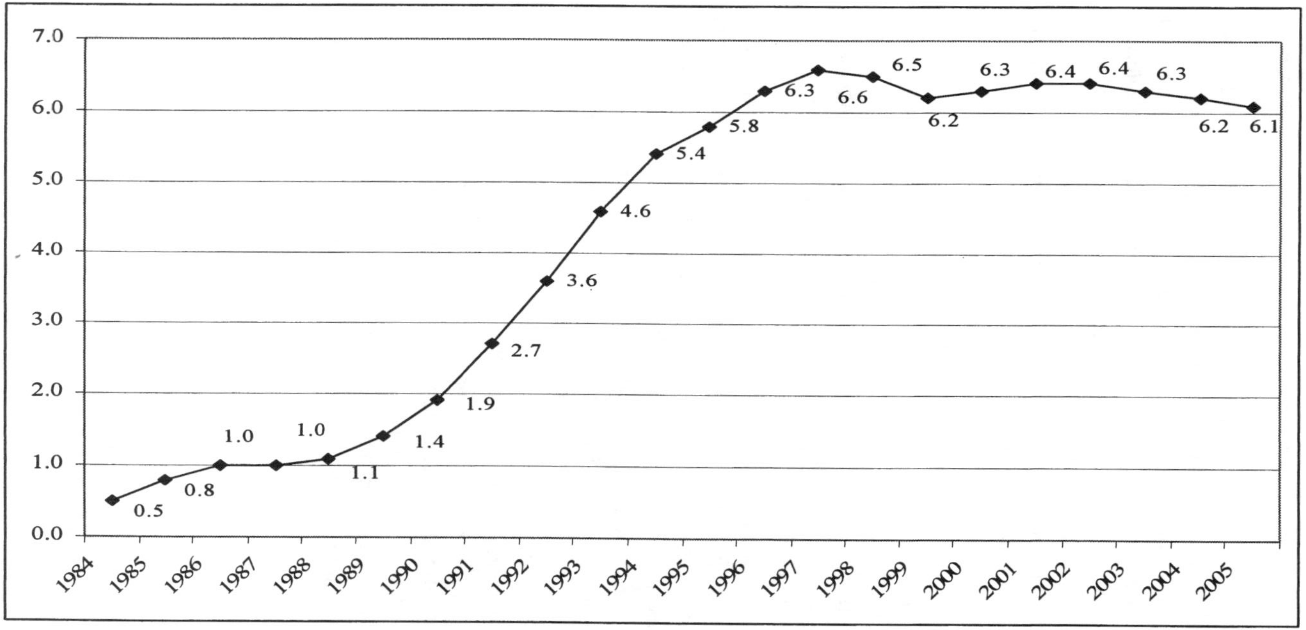

Figure 11.2 Evolution of the common and charter regime Autonomous Communities' stock of debt in relation to GDP (%)

Source: Bank of Spain, *Statistical Reports*.

gave rise to the Budgetary Consolidation Scenarios (*Escenarios de Consolidación Presupuestaria, ECP*), which set annual limits on the deficit and debt of each AC.

Compliance with the Budgetary Consolidation Scenarios has been uneven, with some ACs observing and others repeatedly breaching their terms. The greatest virtue of these arrangements has certainly been their contribution to restraining the growth of regional debt in aggregate terms. As Figure 11.2 clearly shows, the growth rate slowed after 1992, and since 1997 the debt/GDP ratio has even fallen.

Since 2003 the Budgetary Stability Act has created a new scenario in which the Spanish public sector as a whole is required to maintain a balanced budget or achieve budget surpluses, which implies that indebtedness must be kept stable or reduced.

In this new context, central government sets budgetary stability targets for the ACs as a whole over a three-year period, subject to a report from the CPFF. The CPFF is also responsible for establishing the stability targets for each individual AC, and if agreement proves impossible, every AC is required to pass and implement a balanced or surplus budget.

If any Community breaches these rules in the approval or settlement of its budget, it is required to prepare a medium term economic and financial correction plan.[8] In such cases, central government approval is required for all regional borrowing operations. Finally, if breaches by any AC result in or contribute to non-compliance by Spain with its obligations under the European Union Stability and Growth Pact, the AC is required to assume the attributable part of any liability that may arise.

Undoubtedly, budgetary stability legislation represents a challenge for the ACs. It limits their access to borrowing and they may be forced to improve the management of public spending, reduce the level of services provided to their citizens, or raise taxes, with the risk of adopting pro-cyclical policy measures. ACs could also circumvent fiscal rules using off-budget financing and other "creative techniques".[9] There is some evidence about the use of this kind of instruments: the debt issued by regional-owned companies has risen from 0.6 percent of the GDP in 1995 to 1.3 in 2003.

The Spanish Parliament is currently debating the amendment of the Budgetary Stability Act with a view to making the legislation more flexible.[10]

The Charter System

The charter financing system applies to Navarre and the Basque Country. Specifically, it is called the *Convenio* in Navarre and the *Concierto* in the Basque Country, both terms referring to the regional financing arrangements currently governed by the "Economic Agreement between the State and Charter Community of Navarre Act", 2003 (*Ley del Convenio Económico entre el Estado y la Comunidad Foral de Navarra)* and the "Economic Agreement with the Autonomous Community of the Basque Country Act", 2002 (*Ley del Concierto Económico con la Comunidad Autónoma del País Vasco).*

In contrast to the common financing system, the charter system is not based on the assignment of specific revenues to fund a given level of spending. The chief feature of the charter system is that it provides the regions concerned with close to the maximum fiscal autonomy. Both the *Convenio* and the *Concierto* basically recognise the capacity of the charter regions to establish and regulate their own fiscal system provided that the free movement and establishment of persons, and the free movement of goods, services and capital is ensured.

In essence the charter regions are financed exclusively through tax revenues called "agreed taxes" (*tributos convenidos* in Navarre and *tributos concertados* in the Basque Country). The charter regions (more precisely the provinces or "Historical Territories" of Álava, Guipúzcoa and Vizcaya in the Basque Country) have wide powers over these revenues, which are in general considerably greater than the powers of the common regime ACs for "ceded taxes". Table 11.7 details the taxes concerned using the same structure as Table 11.5. The only taxes currently outside the charter regime are import duties and payroll taxes.

In contrast to the common regime regions, then, the charter regime ACs have full powers over all personal and corporate income taxes. The regional finance departments also control the main indirect taxes, comprising VAT and excise duties,[11] although only to the extent of administering the tax without regulatory powers. This is mainly due to the restrictions established by European rules governing the harmonisation of indirect taxes.

In practice, the charter ACs have made wide use of their regulatory powers in tax matters, generally to reduce the tax burden. For example, corporate income tax depreciation allowances are more generous than in the common regime ACs and tax credits for investment and job creation are higher, while tax rates in general are lower.[12]

In light of Table 11.7, and given the level of incomes in the Basque Country and Navarre (Table 11.1), it is evident that the charter regime ACs do not require additional grants to finance their expenditure needs, which are adequately covered by their tax revenues. Indeed, these ACs actually make annual transfers to the central government, the Basque "quota" (*cupo*) and the Navarre "contribution" (*aportación*), to help fund the cost of national public goods or, to put it another way, those matters over which central government retains competencies (citizens under the common regime ACs help to finance the cost of national competencies through non-ceded taxes: 67 percent in the personal income tax, 100 percent in the corporate income tax, 65 percent in the VAT, and so on). Basically, the quota (for the purposes of simplicity we shall apply this term both to the Basque quota and to the contribution made by Navarre) is calculated as follows.

The share in the cost of national public goods, *G*, attributable to each charter territory is based on the "imputation index", which is basically a relative income function. The imputation index is 1.6 percent for Navarre and 6.24 percent for the Basque Country.

Since the State collects certain revenues in the charter regions (non-agreed taxes and non-tax revenues) and a part of central government expenditure is financed through the deficit, a distinction is made between the Gross Quota, *GQ*, and the Net Quota, *NQ*, calculated as the gross quota less all revenues obtained by the national exchequer in the charter AC. The amount of the Gross Quota in the "base" year for charter Autonomous Community *f* is as follows:

$$GQ_{f0} = i_f \cdot G_0 \quad , f = \textit{Navarre, Basque Country} \qquad [6]$$

where i_f is the imputation index for charter Autonomous Community *f*, and G_0 represents national public goods in the "base" year. Let us call revenues not covered by the financing agreements *TN* and the deficit *D* (a surplus would operate in the opposite direction). We may now calculate the value of the Net Quota, which is the amount actually transferred by the regional finance departments to the central Finance Ministry as follows:

$$NQ_{f0} = i_f \cdot G_0 - i_f \cdot TN_0 - i_f \cdot D_0 = i_f \cdot \left[G_0 - (TN_0 + D_0)\right] \qquad [7]$$

The quota is not calculated on an annual basis. The calculation methodology is reviewed every five years. For any year *t* subsequent to the base year, the amount is calculated by applying to the base year value the rate of growth in State taxes equivalent to agreed taxes, *IE*:

$$NQ_{ft} = NQ_{f0} \cdot \frac{IE_t}{IE_0} \qquad [8]$$

Table 11.7 Agreed taxes assigned to the charter regime regions

TAX	COLLECTION	ADMINISTRATION	REGULATION	CLASSIFICATION
Personal Income Tax	100%	YES	Full	Own tax
Tax on Net Wealth	100%	YES	Full	Own tax
Inheritance and Gift Tax	100%	YES	Full	Own tax
Corporate Income Tax	100%	YES	Full	Own tax
Non-Resident Taxes	100%	YES	Full for permanent establishments	Own tax
Capital Transfer Tax, Taxes on the raising of capital, and Stamp Duties	100%	YES	Full, with some exceptions	Own tax
Gaming Taxes	100%	YES	Full, with some exceptions	Own tax
Vehicles Excise (registration)	100%	YES	Tax rates, declaration and payment forms and payment periods	Own tax

Table 11.7 Agreed taxes assigned to the charter regime regions (continued)

TAX	COLLECTION	ADMINISTRATION	REGULATION	CLASSIFICATION
Hydrocarbons Retail Sales Tax	100%	YES	Tax rates, declaration and payment forms and payment periods	Own tax
Value Added Tax, VAT	100%	YES	Tax declaration and payment forms and payment periods	Tax sharing
Excise Duties (alcoholic beverages, tobacco and petrol)	100%	YES	Tax declaration and payment forms and payment periods	Tax sharing
Electricity Tax	100%	YES	Tax declaration and payment forms and payment periods	Tax sharing
Tax on Insurance Premiums	100%	YES	Tax declaration and payment forms and payment periods	Tax sharing

Source: López-Laborda (2004).

Hence, the revenues received by Autonomous Community *f* in year *t* will represent the difference between the tax yield actually obtained from agreed taxes, T_f, and the amount of the quota:

$$R_{ft} = T_{ft} - NQ_{ft} = T_{ft} - NQ_{f0} \cdot \frac{IE_t}{IE_0} \qquad [9]$$

As in the common financing system, the above outline represents only the "basic model" for charter AC funding. The Basque Country and Navarre also have other sources of revenues with which to fund their competencies, such as taxes, surcharges, borrowing, etc.

There can be no doubt that the charter system scores highly from the standpoint of the principles of financial autonomy and accountability. The charter ACs finance all expenditure out of their own revenues, in contrast to the common regime ACs, and this brings them closer to the situation in the world's most fiscally decentralised countries, such as the United States, Switzerland and Canada.

Other issues, however, do not come out so well. In the first place, the greater financial autonomy of the charter ACs provides an incentive for asymmetric tax competition between these regions and the common regime ACs. For example, if a charter AC decides to implement tax measures to attract firms from other regions, the common regime ACs are unable to react, because they do not have regulatory powers over corporate income tax.

Secondly, comparison of the structure of the common and charter financing systems shows that an equal level of tax effort will provide the charter regime ACs with higher revenues than the common regime ACs to finance the same competencies. To put it another way, the common regime ACs have to levy higher tax rates on their constituents to provide the same standard of regional-type public services.

An explanation for this difference is that the charter system is so designed that citizens resident in these ACs fund the cost of regional public goods and the respective share of national public goods out of their taxes. The citizens of the common regime ACs on the other hand *also* finance equalisation grants (the sufficiency fund) allowing those ACs with low fiscal capacity or high expenditure needs to provide the same level of regional public goods and services as the other ACs.

AN APPRAISAL: WHAT DOES THE FUTURE HOLD?[13]

To conclude, let us reflect on the key features of the decentralisation process that has taken place in Spain since the end of the 1970s and consider some emerging areas of debate:

1. The view that Spain has undergone a very fast and intense process of public expenditure decentralisation is widely held, but none the less true for that. The ACs currently handle 35 percent of total public spending and participate in the provision of the public goods and services that are closest to the lives of citizens and most affect their well-being. The level of decentralisation is similar to that found in the classic federal states, and it is therefore an error to continue to include Spain among the centralised or unitary States, as is generally the case in the literature. From both the institutional and the financial standpoint, Spain is a genuinely federal country.

   Local government in Spain has less weight than in other decentralised states. To some degree, this could be explained by the fact that in those countries (e.g. the United States, Canada and Switzerland) education is devolved down to the local level, while in Spain it remains at the regional level. Nevertheless, there is considerable insistence on the need to strengthen local competencies and financing in a "second decentralisation" process following the successful consolidation of regional government.

   Probably the sharpest criticism of the Spanish decentralisation process comes from those who believe that the autonomy achieved by the ACs is of poor quality, wide though it may be (Viver, 2003). Central government intervention in all areas of the Autonomous Communities' competencies is intense (even in matters reserved exclusively for the ACs), and in practice this substantially reduces their ability to adopt their own policies. According to these authors, the resulting system is closer to an administrative than to an authentically political autonomy. If this is the case, a key task for the immediate future will be to *guarantee that ACs are allowed to exercise their competencies without undue interference from the central government.*
2. In every review of the common financing model, the ACs have complained that the system does not assure them sufficient funding, and that central government should assign additional resources. On the one hand, it should be remembered here that all of the competencies held by the ACs were devolved after they had accepted the effective cost appraisal in the "Mixed Transfer Commissions". On the other, it has not been proved that the evolution of central and autonomous

government revenues has resulted in any vertical tax imbalance to the detriment of the ACs.

There are various reasons for these demands. On the one hand, an element of strategic calculation pervades the conduct of the ACs, which have sought to push the cost of their spending decisions over to all of the citizens of the country rather than accepting the political cost of increasing the taxes paid by those resident in their own territory (the classic "common pool problem"). However, it is also true that the central government sometimes takes decisions that have a significant impact on the revenues of the ACs, such as changes in the tax system that reduce the yield of the taxes ceded, or the requirement that the ACs undertake certain expenditure programmes.

The satisfactory development of any federal state such as Spain requires that *all levels of government act in accordance with the principle of federal or constitutional loyalty* derived from the Constitution and expressly enshrined in the LOFCA. Consequently, the ACs cannot shift the financial consequences derived from the exercise of their powers either to central government or to other ACs, nor can central government ignore the impact of its actions for regional finances.

3. The decentralisation of public revenues has lagged considerably behind expenditure. However, own revenues currently form a significant part of Autonomous Community finance, representing 100 percent in the charter regime Communities and between 35 and 55 percent in the common regime ACs.

   Any further efforts to strengthen autonomy and accountability will mean *expanding the scope of common regime ACs' own revenues, and at the same time reducing dependence on grants from the central government.* There are few options open, however. The expansion of the percentage allocation of certain ceded taxes might be considered, for example, or the devolution of regulatory powers over certain indirect taxes such as excise duties or even at some later date Value Added Tax. Another possibility would be to strengthen environmental taxes at the regional level, where the ACs have already established an incipient though scattered presence. Greater involvement of the ACs in tax collection and management is another avenue that must be explored.
4. The financing system guarantees a reasonable level of equalisation between the common regime ACs. Thus, if two Autonomous Communities require the same tax effort from their citizens, the system ensures that both will also be in a position to provide a reasonably

similar level of devolved public goods and services should they so wish.

The appropriate degree of equalisation is a matter of permanent debate in Spain and will certainly continue to be so in future, hotting up if anything. The ACs that are the beneficiaries of the grant system support a high level of equalisation on the grounds of solidarity, pointing to Germany, Australia and Canada by way of example. However, those ACs with the highest fiscal capacity have come to demand a system based on the resources generated in each region and a lowering of equalisation between territories, appealing to the principle of efficiency (as in the United States and Switzerland).

5. The Constitution permits the existence of two financing systems with very different structures. The common regime is based on taxes ceded by central government and grants from the sufficiency fund, while the charter regime is based on a regional tax system with bottom-up grants.

   What the Constitution does not permit, however, is that the results of the two systems should differ, so that ACs with the same competencies provide different regional public goods and services depending on whether they receive funding under the common or charter regime.

   This is an emerging issue in the debate over the evolution of the Spanish regional State. On one side are *those who favour the extension or generalisation of the charter regime* to the common system ACs. On the other, are the supporters of *measures aimed at bringing the results of the charter regime into line with those of the common regime* without changing its special nature. The solution to this dilemma is highly related to the one of the debate concerning equalisation.

6. The expansion of the European Union to include ten new member States from Central and Eastern Europe also raises issues for regional financing.

   The first and most important of these will be the loss of European Structural Funds and especially those aimed at regional development, which currently benefit more than a few of the Autonomous Communities of Spain. Given the low income levels of the new member States and the decision to freeze the EU budget at 1.24 percent of the Union's GDP, regional aid will be switched toward the countries of the East from 2006.

   The loss of such regional development funds, as well as the need to constrain borrowing and deficits in accordance with European rules governing public finance and the Spanish Budgetary Stability Act, could jeopardise investment and the improvement of regional public capital stock. The effect is important because the ACs are the main

Spanish public sector investors, currently making around 40 percent of total public investment.

As explained above, these restrictions represent a challenge for regional governments, which will either have to improve their management of spending or raise taxes on their constituents.

NOTES

* Universidad de Zaragoza
** Universidad de Oviedo

1. This paper is associated with research project SRJ 2004-08253/ECON, which has received research funding from the Spanish Ministry of Education and Science.
2. In Spain, the term "province" refers to a tier of local government grouping a number of municipalities within certain geographical boundaries. Its main purpose is thus to assist the municipalities with the performance of their functions.
3. In recognition of this, funds associated with grant maintained private educational establishments were included in the 1992 reform of the regional finance system.
4. This was the case for the common regime ACs but not for the charter regime ACs, where health financing is included in the special arrangements we describe in the next section.
5. For a more detailed analysis see Monasterio and Suárez-Pandiello (1998).
6. The Autonomous Community of the Canary Islands includes certain special features due to its geographical location, although it forms part of the "common" system. The two North African cities of Ceuta and Melilla also have a special status, which is halfway between the position of a municipality and an Autonomous Community.
7. The system provides two instruments to correct this problem, although neither has so far been applied. As explained in Section 1.3, an AC may in the first place receive a "Basic Public Service Equalisation Grant" when the annual increase in education or healthcare services users exceeds 3 percent of the increase in the national average. Should this grant be allocated again to the same AC in a period shorter than five years, then the sufficiency fund must be adjusted to reflect the substantial change in the AC's expenditure needs. Secondly, the law requires analysis of the impact of demographic changes in the ACs on their expenditure needs.
8. To date, Catalonia, Galicia, Valencia (2004), Balearic Islands, the Canary Islands, Castile-La Mancha and Castile and León (2005) have found themselves obliged to present correction plans.
9. The purchase of financial assets is not included in the calculation of the deficit.
10. See Joumard and Giorno (2005: 27).
11. The case of VAT and excise duties is highly complex, because the tax yield collected by the AC (which depends on regional value added in the case of VAT) has to be adjusted to obtain the yield finally corresponding to the regional government, which is based on consumption by the residents of the AC (see Zubiri, 2000: 39–40).
12. Some of these measures have been challenged by the European Court and by the Spanish Supreme Court, which has viewed them as regional public aid distorting competition (Zubiri, 2000: 212–225).
13. For a complementary viewpoint, see Joumard and Giorno (2005).

REFERENCES

Aja, E. (1999), El Estado Autonómico. Federalismo y hechos diferenciales, Madrid: Alianza.

Banting, K. and S. Corbett (2002), *Health Policy and Federalism. A comparative Perspective of Multi-Level Governance*, London: Institute of Intergovernmental Relations.

Bird R. (1993), 'Threading the fiscal labyrinth: some issues in fiscal decentralization', *National Tax Journal*, 46, 207–227

Docteur, E. and H. Oxley (2003), 'Health-Care Systems: Lessons from the Reform Experience', OECD Health Working Papers, 9. Paris: OECD.

European Observatory on Health Care Systems (2000), *Health Care Systems in Transition. Spain*, WHO Regional Office for Europe.

Joumard, I. and C. Giorno (2005), 'Getting the most out of public sector decentralisation in Spain', OECD Economics Department Working Paper, 436, Paris: OECD.

López-Laborda, J. (2004), 'Financiación y gasto público en un Estado descentralizado, *Economía Aragonesa*, 24, 63–82.

Ministerio de Economía y Hacienda (Ministry of Finance) (2004), 'Financiación de las Comunidades Autónomas por los impuestos cedidos (IRPF, IVA e Impuestos Especiales) Fondo de Suficiencia y garantías de financiación de los servicios de asistencia sanitaria en el año 2002 y liquidación definitiva de dicho ejercicio', www.minhac.es

Monasterio, C. (2002), 'El laberinto de la financiación autonómica', *Hacienda Pública Española*, 163, 157–185.

Monasterio, C. and J. Suárez-Pandiello (1998), *Manual de Hacienda Autónomica y Local*, Barcelona: Ariel.

Viver Pi-Sunyer, C. (2003), 'Finalmente, una amplia autonomía de baja calidad', *El País*, 6 de septiembre de 2003.

Zubiri, I. (2000), El Sistema de Concierto Económico en el contexto de la Unión Europea, Bilbao: Círculo de Empresarios Vascos.

12. Financing Local Governments: The Spanish Experience

Francisco Pedraja-Chaparro*, Javier Salinas-Jiménez, and Javier Suárez-Pandiello*****

INTRODUCTION

Summarising twenty five years of Spanish local public finance is not an easy task. In 1978, the new democratic Constitution completely changed the face of public administration in Spain. Until then, and apart from some minor, unsuccessful attempts at decentralisation during the Second Republic in the early thirties of the last century, the model of governance was based on a pure version of Napoleonic centralism.

Nevertheless, the decentralisation process initiated by the Constitution gave the regional governments (that is, created *ex novo*) a leading role. The aim of this process was to provide the regions with growing competences and responsibilities in relation to expenditure assignments, and to a lesser extent, in revenue assignments. This new tier of government received major political and administrative support while local jurisdictions remained in the background from which they are, however, presently showing signs of emerging.

In 1978, Spanish local authorities managed around 13 percent of total public expenditure while, currently, this figure is scarcely 15 percent. Thus, little would seem to have happened during a period of almost three decades. Given the intensity of regional decentralisation during this period,[1] these percentages would seem to point to stagnation in local governments. However, this is not quite the case. Actually, the relative importance of the public sector in the Spanish economy has increased considerably since the restoration of democracy to the extent that a welfare state, which already existed in neighboring countries, needed to be created from scratch. In fact, the ratio of total local government expenditure to GDP increased from 5.02

Table 12.1 Some data on Spanish local finance

	1980		1990		2000	
	% GDP	% PAs*	% GDP	% PAs	% GDP	% PAs
Ordinary Expenditure	2.18	7.88	4.66	9.70	4.98	14.16
Investment Expenditure	2.84	68.16	1.60	22.07	1.17	23.21
Total Non-Financial Expenditure	5.02	14.30	6.26	11.32	6.15	15.30

Note: * PAs stands for Public Administrations (or Total Government Expenditures).

Source: Gago and Labandeira (2002).

percent in 1980 to 6.15 percent in 2000, which shows that even if the relative weight of total local government expenditure in total government expenditure has not changed, the volume of local expenditure has significantly increased, since GDP has grown from €91,161 million in 1980 to €610,541 million in 2000 (see Table 12.1).

Financing the increasing expenditure has often been controversial and led to conflicts between local governments and the central government, as the latter is constitutionally responsible for guaranteeing the economic sufficiency of local governments. Although the search for an efficient and equitable financial system for local governments is still ongoing, the process to date has been shaped by six significant milestones.

1. Devolution of the old Production Factor Taxes (PFT) (1979). The first major action in the field of local finance in democratic Spain was the devolution, to local authorities, of some of the old PFT eliminated by the central administration when it introduced a personal income tax[2]. At that time, local governments were able to collect (but not to regulate) taxes on income arising from rural or urban properties and occupational taxes on commercial, industrial, professional, and artistic activities. The former category of taxes would develop, over time, into a property tax and the latter category into a business tax. These levies became the centrepiece of local finance and joined a whole range of small taxes with limited revenue-raising capacity, which were already available to the local authorities. These taxes were, however, rather revenue inelastic and incapable of responding to increasing pressure from citizens who, following the restoration of local democracy, were demanding more and better local public services. At the beginning, it was objectively very difficult to meet local residents' demands, given that the new democratic local administrations were reborn in difficult financial circumstances and overwhelmed by excessive expectations. Moreover, local governments were poorly equipped both in terms of their legal bases and qualified employees, to meet these new demands. If we also take into account the fact that assistance from the central government via transfers was limited, due to the need to modernise the Spanish economy and the building of a welfare state, it is understandable that local governments began to incur debts as their own resources and state subsidies were insufficient to meet new expenditure needs. Compounding the problem was the fact that the newly elected local authorities were unwilling to frustrate citizens' expectations during a period of intense political and economic change.

In the face of an impending financial crisis, the central government reacted by adopting a series of extraordinary measures which culminated in the 1983 *Ley de Medidas Urgentes de Saneamiento y Regulación de las Haciendas Locales* (Act on Urgent Measures to Reorganise and Regulate Local Public Finance—hereafter, the AUM).

2. Act on Urgent Measures to Reorganise and Regulate Local Public Finance (1983). The objectives of the AUM were twofold. On the one hand, public finance was to be rationalised, implicitly acknowledging that the poor financial situation of local authorities was caused by the structural deficiencies of the local finance system. Therefore, the AUM honored debts and made the State responsible for "actual debts" (as confirmed by audits of the town councils which availed themselves of the law). On the other hand, in order to avoid a repetition of financial difficulties in the future, the AUM tried to strengthen local taxation by conferring greater autonomy on local councils in the area of revenue collections, in particular enabling local governments to establish freely the rate of the property tax in urban areas, and by assigning, as a new local tax, the option of establishing a piggyback local income tax: a surtax (with a tax rate chosen by local councils) on the net tax liability of the state personal income tax.

The response to the AUM was different among town councils and adoption of the new financial tools was particularly uneven. Thus, at the end of 1986 local indebtedness was in overall terms greater than it had been prior to the AUM, reaching worrying levels in some municipalities and demonstrating the limited success of the law. In any case, the AUM was given the coup de grace by two decisions of the Constitutional Court which invalidated the section of the law which allowed local authorities to set the rate of the urban property tax and the surtax on the personal income tax without any limitation. This was resolved later for the property tax by establishing a range of minimum and maximum rates. Nevertheless, the autonomy in setting the rate on the surtax on the personal income tax was never restored.[3]

3. *Accession to the EEC, Implementation of VAT, Abolition of the General Tax on Business Transactions (GTBT) and Changes in the Sumptuary Tax and Provincial Finance (1985).* Before joining the European Economic Community, the core of indirect taxation in Spain was the GTBT, a multiphase sales tax, which was charged on the total value of sales (not value added) in each phase. This tax was technically very imperfect, because it created adverse differences in the taxation of goods and services according to the chain of production and distribution (the number of phases from the origin to the final consumer). Because of that, all countries interested in being part of the EEC were required to adopt the VAT as the only general indirect tax, and Spain was no exception. At the local level, the substitution of GTBT by VAT had significant consequences. Firstly, because Provincial governments were financed by a surcharge on GTBT and also collected another indirect tax (Canon sobre la Producción de Energía—Energy Production Tax), both of which were abolished. Secondly, there was a municipal tax on luxury expenditures (Impuesto sobre Gastos Suntuarios) that also was notably capped. In both cases, there was a compensation for lost tax receipts with general grants.

4. *Local Government Finance Act (1988).* The enactment of the *Ley Reguladora de las Haciendas Locales* (law regulating local finance—hereafter the LGFA) initially represented significant progress in the area of local financing. From a qualitative point of view it meant the end of the existing dependence-based model, whereas from a quantitative point of view, it brought new resources into the system to satisfy the needs identified on a daily basis. Later in this chapter, we set out a more detailed analysis. For the moment, let us simply point out that the LGFA finally introduced revenue autonomy for local governments as it allowed them to establish the rates of local taxes (within some maximum and minimum bounds), which were simplified as they were reduced in number from ten to five. As far as transfers were concerned, the system was formula-based, establishing the total amount to be distributed among local governments which would be updated on an annual basis according to objective criteria. The transfer model has been revised since then every five years, both in terms of its amount and distribution criteria. This enabled local governments to calculate available external resources very accurately in spite of the highly critical judgments it received concerning the equity aspects of the model.[4] Lastly, the LGFA also allowed local governments to

take on debt albeit within certain limits set in order to allow central government to coordinate macroeconomic policies.

5. General Act on Budgetary Stability (2001). The practical implementation of the LGFA gradually led to the establishment of a "tax culture" and joint fiscal responsibility in the local sphere which were almost unheard of at the time. Authorities now turned directly to citizens for the resources required for their spending programmes rather than "begging" for subsidies from other Public Administrations. However, all of the Spanish Public Administrations had to overcome many problems in order to comply with the macroeconomic targets imposed at the European Union level (such as the convergence of deficit, debt, interest rates and inflation rates) with a view to creating a Monetary Union where every national currency would be replaced by the new "euro". These difficulties led the central government to introduce the so-called *Ley General de Estabilidad Presupuestaria* (General Act on Budgetary Stability—hereafter GABS). The explicit objective of this law was to increase budgetary restraints at every level of government, in particular severely restricting access to credit so as to balance the public accounts on an annual basis where possible. To the extent that public debt had been mainly used to finance capital expenditure and that local governments are, above all, investing institutions (see Table 12.1), the adoption of this law in 2001 was a matter of concern for local managers because they were compelled to use alternative finance sources to maintain the desired levels of investment. The practical consequence of this was an increase in the tax burden (with associated political costs) or resorting to financial engineering and accounting tools in order to get around this new legislation. In the end, this decreased the transparency of public management.[5] In addition to the controversy raised by the introduction of the budgetary stability criteria, at that time the central government announced its intention, in the context of a wider reform of the LGFA, to eliminate the business tax—the second most important local tax in terms of its revenue raising power. This decision together with the *fait accompli* that local authorities were gradually assuming new competences (demanded by citizens) without any financial support exacerbated the uncertainty about local public finances.

6. Act Reforming the LGFA (2002). Finally, in 2002 the LGFA was reformed and the amended Act forms the basis for the current legal framework on local public finance which we will describe and assess in the rest of this chapter. For the time being, it should suffice to say that the new legislation dramatically affected each of the main sources of income for local councils.

Therefore, the next section examines the local tax system in depth in the context of the current Spanish framework. The third section reviews the model or rather the models for intergovernmental transfers, while the fourth section considers debt recourse. In all cases we will describe the regulatory aspects from the perspective of the theoretical principles of fiscal federalism. Finally, the fifth sction will include some concluding remarks and loose ends to be considered in the very near future.

LOCAL TAXATION

At the present time, following the last local government finance reform examined in the previous section, the Spanish local tax system has the same number of taxes as established by the LGFA in 1988, but the main taxes have undergone substantial change. Specifically, Spanish local authorities levy five taxes: property tax (PT), business tax (BT), vehicles tax (VT), tax on buildings and tax on land value increase in urban areas. The first three are compulsory taxes to be collected by all local councils, whereas the other two are optional. In all cases local authorities are free to set tax rates within a legal range of maximum and minimum rates. However, together with these local taxes, municipalities may also collect fees and user charges (fees levied on the use of certain public services). These revenue instruments have grown in importance over the recent years. Table 12.2 shows the relative importance of these taxes within a period of five years, in 1998 and 2003, before and after the time of the last reform.[6] We will examine each of these taxes separately.

Table 12.2 Municipal fiscal revenue structure

	1998		2003	
	Thousands of €	**%**	**Thousands of €**	**%**
Property Tax (PT)	4,000.33	33.83	5,368.61	34.12
Vehicle Tax (VT)	1,265.56	10.70	1,802.73	11.46
Tax on Land Value Increase	667.55	5.65	1,053.70	6.70
Business Tax (BT)	1,640.45	13.88	1,241.87	7.89
Tax on Building	946.00	8.00	1,547.13	9.83
User Charges	3,303.79	27.94	4,720.75	30.00
Fiscal Revenue (*)	**11,823.68**	**100,00**	**15,734.79**	**100.00**

Note: (*) Excluding collection of extinguished taxes.

Source: Directorate General of Community Funds and Territorial Funding.

The Property Tax (PT)

In accordance with the most conventional tax federalism theories, the property tax appears to be one of the most suitable taxes to provide a basis for local own source finance. In particular, it is argued that the location of the taxpayer is especially relevant: we are dealing with a tax with a non movable tax base unlikely to be affected by emigration in the event the tax burden is high. The inability to export the tax burden beyond the boundaries of the beneficiary[7] jurisdiction provides cost internalisation under the benefit principle. In spite of this, there has been no shortage of controversy in the literature regarding the global effects of this tax on efficiency and equity. In particular, one of its most controversial aspects is its economic incidence: who bears the tax burden arising from this tax. There has been no agreement on this issue in the empirical literature. [8]

Following these guidelines, and as may be seen in table 12.2, the property tax seems to be the centrepiece of Spanish local taxation, contributing to one third of total tax revenues. In terms of its structure, the Spanish local property tax is mostly a standard property tax which falls on the administratively assessed gross value of immovable property in rural or urban areas.[9] So revenues depend critically on the assessment of immovable property and consequently on the swiftness with which price increases in immovable property (including new buildings) are recorded in the local tax registers in order to establish the appropriate tax base. In Spain "cadastral management" (the administrative process consisting of an initial valuation and further revisions updating the assessed values of properties) falls outside the jurisdiction of local authorities. Actually, the Central Government is responsible for all cadastral management. This situation has given rise to continuous disagreements and disputes between administrations. Thus, local councils (especially the biggest) have been claiming the right to be involved in the cadastral management of this tax, given that they have as much at stake as the Central Government in the census update. Furthermore they believe that, as they are closer to the ground, they are in a better position to understand the key components of the process (in particular the trends in property values). The Central Government, on the other hand, believes it cannot cease to set common valuation criteria for Spain as a whole and, consequently, the application of global rules can only be achieved if its own administrative bodies conduct all cadastral management.

A second controversial issue over this period is in relation to the alleged need to personalise the tax. This is a well known subject in the tax literature, according to which a pure tax on property turns out to be inequitable insofar as it is based on gross value without deducting debts and charges. This is a tax with a corporeal nature which does not allow for aspects such as family conditions, the health conditions of those liable to pay, or income level.[10] In the Spanish case, this issue was dealt with in the recent amendment of the LGFA, by devolving competences to local governments enabling them to introduce new family-related tax relief (for instance, benefiting large families) or a surtax where dwellings are kept empty, in the pursuit of the non-fiscal objective of helping to mobilise these idle resources through their sale or rental. Nevertheless, some observers see these changes in the legislation as making the tax more complex with questionable effectiveness. These same observers have suggested that this type of actions should be better channeled through expenditure policies, leaving the property tax exclusively as a revenue tool.[11]

Beyond such controversies the local property tax seems to be a fully consolidated tax at the local level in Spain, and will undoubtedly continue to represent the main source of revenue to local governments.

The Local Business Tax (BT)

The second tax in order of magnitude was, until recently, the local business tax (around 14% of local tax revenues in 1998) as shown in Table 12.2.

From a theoretical point of view, the local business tax was originally based on the benefit principle of taxation, presuming that there is a link on a proportional basis between the public services consumed by business and their productive activity.

However, in its practical implementation it may be carried out in several ways. International practice provided three approaches to taxation of economic activity at the local level, and each has different outcomes from the perspectives of equity and efficiency. The three bases are: (i) *consumption,* taxing sales carried out within the municipality; (ii) *income,* taxing income attributable exclusively to business profits in the area or all incomes received by citizens in the area; and (iii) *use of production factors*, which could be made through differentiated tax rates in a hypothetical *property tax* on the business premises engaged in this activity or through *payroll taxation* (use of the labour factor) or through an index which weights the *various factors* used, meaning that the business would be taxed according to its use of the factors. The third criterion is the most difficult to design, as it is necessary to include labour and all fixed assets. This must be achieved according to rules that comply with the targets to be met, which may on the other hand hinder the application of the economic efficiency principle. In any case, the effective incidence of this approach may be questionable. It would also be expected that the economic actors will try to shift the burden of taxation forward through higher selling prices of their production (goods or services) or backward through lower real wages for example, which shifts the tax burden onto one or more factor suppliers depending on market conditions (supply and demand elasticities of outputs and inputs). In addition in some cases the tax burden may be exported, or shifted outwards, to taxpayers outside the boundaries of the tax collecting jurisdiction.

The Spanish local business tax fits into the third option. It was defined in the 1988 LGFA as "...a direct tax with a non-personal nature and on the following taxable event: businesses, professional or artistic activities carried out in the Spanish territory whether or not in specific premises, whether or not classified in the tax schedule".

In real practice, the taxation of Spanish businesses by means of objective indicators, which do not always take into account taxable capacity, and with no regard to their income or profits, has made the business tax a particularly controversial tax. This tax has been strongly criticised by professional associations and politicians. It would seem that the extensive modifications to the way the tax is applied in the 2002 Act on Reform of the LGFA was a direct consequence of the business tax's unpopularity, magnified by purely political interests, as well as pressure from specific interest groups.[12] As a consequence of these changes, the new local business tax is only levied on organisations with an annual turnover higher than one million euros. In practice, this reform means that, in addition to a large number of previous taxpayers falling outside the scope of the tax (about 90% of those who paid the local business tax previously are now exempt), numerous Spanish local councils have been deprived of their previous business tax revenue. After the reform, the Central Government has been forced to compensate those local governments with a new non-conditional transfer.[13]

However, the new regulations have not put an end to the controversy surrounding the business tax. Some authors still criticise it because it is unfair, as major groups of professionals and businessmen with a significant economic capacity no longer pay the tax. Others criticise its poor legal structure. In fact, various appeals have been lodged at the Spanish Constitutional Court on the basis that the current regulation discriminates against enterprises that still pay the tax. Consequently, and in spite of a 25 percent increase in the business tax rate, and beyond any changes to the new framework that may be decided by the courts, it seems obvious that the business tax is no longer a key component of Spanish local finances.

Other Taxes

The other Spanish local taxes have not been the subject of as much controversy as the previous two. In fact, the vehicle tax (the third compulsory tax) is a longstanding local tax that is annually charged on the administrative value of cars and other vehicles. From time to time there has been a move to integrate it with the other taxes levied on cars (taxes collected by the regional governments or Autonomous Communities) with a view to reduce its compliance and administration costs.[14]

As far as the non compulsory (for local government use) taxes are concerned, the tax on building and the tax on land value increases in urban areas are taxes which aim to share with local councils the income derived from construction activities in general and urban development in particular. This has constituted a dynamic and important sector in the Spanish economy over the past several decades. Indeed, although in theory the revenues from these taxes tend to be erratic and less stable than the taxes described above, in practice they have brought in major complementary resources basically to large town councils and to those with higher growth levels, particularly local authorities of regional capitals and tourist resorts.

Moreover, in light of forthcoming tighter restrictions introduced by the law on budgetary stability, there is likely to be a tendency to revive other taxes with a long tradition in the Spanish local government system such as special taxes which apply the profit principle to the funding of public investment. In practice these charges try to internalise a portion of the increase in the value of identified private properties produced as a consequence of the realisation of public works in their proximity.

User Charges

Finally, it is important to note a growing trend in recent years where municipalities charge users directly for publicly provided goods and services they consume. In fact, as economic theory states, where service users are fully identifiable (as services are divisible) and such services have no redistribution bias, the most efficient way to finance such services is to charge the users for the full cost of the service. Since a substantial volume of services supplied by Spanish municipalities meet these two characteristics, it is not surprising that fees and user charges have reached the level shown in table 12.2 (more than a quarter of tax revenue).

GENERAL TRANSFERS TO LOCAL GOVERNMENTS

A Description of the Present System

Municipalities' sharing in central taxes (MSCT) is the main transfer of central public finances to local governments. It represents around a fourth of total non-financial local revenue though there are notable differences in relative importance depending on the size of the municipality. The MSCT is a non-conditional transfer with a global amount which is revised every five years. It changes within each five-year period according to the change in nominal GDP, with a guaranteed minimum annual increase equal to the increase in the consumer price index (CPI). Once the funding of "special municipalities" (Madrid and Barcelona amongst others) are deducted from the general Fund,[15] the remainder is distributed among the different local governments according to a range of variables which include factors reflecting expenditure needs, revenue raising capacity and tax effort.

In fact, for the period 1999–2003 the MSCT was distributed according to the following criteria and weights:

- Need variables:

1. 75 percent according to weighted population taking into account municipality size, using the following coefficients:

Number of inhabitants	Coefficient
More than 500.000	2.85
From 100.001 to 500.000	1.47
From 50.001 to 100.000	1.32
From 20.001 to 50.000	1.30
From 10.001 to 20.000	1.17
From 5.001 to 10.000	1.15
No more than 5.000	1.00

2. 2.5 percent according to the number of school units whose building maintenance is a charge for municipal governments.

- 8.5 percent according to the (inverse) *revenue raising capacity* calculated by municipal taxes and charges.
- 14 percent according to the tax effort calculated as a ratio of current to potential revenue of the most important municipal taxes (PT, BT, VT and TLVI).[16]

In any case, a general minimum amount equal to that received during the last year of the previous five year period and additional funding consisting of a minimum grant (of approximately €100 per inhabitant) for municipalities with less than 5,000 inhabitants is guaranteed. This transfer complements municipal tax resources with a view to improving revenue sufficiency without an explicit equalisation objective.

As indicated in the introduction, the 2002 Act reforming the LGFA changed the MSCT significantly. From a single general transfer system with all its nuances, there was a shift to a dual system which established a new model for calculating general transfers for the 1999–2003 quinquennium according (basically) to the size of the municipality. However, the new scheme is considered permanent because the five year revisions which characterised it have been removed. This parallels the new finance system arrangements for regional governments, which are also supposed to be permanent.[17]

A new scheme for municipalities with a *de jure* population equal to or higher than 75,000 inhabitants, and for some small local governments for administrative reasons (being the capital city of a province or of an autonomous regional community) identified as "*large municipalities*" has been introduced. This new scheme has been added to the distribution formula with multiple factors, which was in force in the previous quinquennium and which is still being applied to municipalities with small populations ("*small municipalities").*

In the case of *"large municipalities*", the general grant for each of them in the base year (2004) is made up of two components: on the one hand, "territorialised" shares in several central government taxes and, on the other, a Complementary Fund, which we describe below.

- The "territorialised" shares are specific percentages of revenue from central government taxes not transferred to the autonomous regional communities such as: the personal income tax (1.6875%), VAT (1.7897%) and EU harmonised excise taxes (2.0454%). With regard to personal income tax, the allocation of local revenue is on a derivation basis assessed according to the net tax liability of residents in the municipality. The allocation of revenue from consumption taxes (general consumption tax and excises) follows a highly indirect procedure: firstly, it is related to the share of the consumption of the autonomous regional community (to which a municipality belongs) in the context of national consumption; and, secondly, according to the importance of the *de jure* population in relation to that in the autonomous regional community the locality belongs to.

- The second component, the Complementary Fund, is calculated (in the first year) for each one of the municipalities as the difference between the grant they received previously and the territorialised shares discussed above.

From a dynamic perspective, territorialised shares will develop in line with the collection of shared taxes—either the municipality's tax revenue in the case of personal income tax and excise taxes on oil and tobacco or the general tax revenue of the nation in the case of VAT and all other excise taxes. They will also evolve according to dynamics of the autonomous community (to which the municipality belongs) compared to the national dynamics. The Complementary Fund will develop in line with the evolution of *National Tax Revenues* (NTR) minus revenues liable to be transferred to the autonomous regional communities, derived from personal income tax, VAT, and harmonised excise taxes.

For the other municipalities (*small municipalities*) the current distributive formula explained above is still applied but with some changes in relation to the previous five-year period (1999–2003). The pool of funds of the general grant is updated according to the NTR which replaces nominal GDP. The CPI is abolished as the basis for a guaranteed minimum increase. The provision of a minimum grant for municipalities with less than 5,000 inhabitants is also removed.

Once the pool of funds for the general grant has been determined, it is shared out according to a formula containing a range of variables which, as explained, try to include municipal differences in expenditure needs, fiscal capacities and revenue effort.

One of the two variables related to needs (school units) is removed in such a way that population is the only variable, with the same 75 percent. Once the higher population strata—to which the new transfer system is applied (*"large municipalities*")—have been excluded, the others are adjusted under the LGFA demanding more competences for them. Some of them will have their weights increased. (See table).

Number of inhabitants	Coefficient (previous)
From 50,001 to less than 75,000	1.40 (1.32)
From 20,001 to 50,000	1.30 (1.30)
From 10,001 to 20,000	1.17 (1.17)
From 5,001 to 10,000	1.17 (1.15)
No more than 5,000	1.00 (1.00)

The *revenue raising capacity* variable now called *tax capacity* carries greater weight in the distributional formula (increasing from 8.5% to 12.5%) while the weighting of tax *effort* is reduced to the weight for revenue raising capacity (decreasing from 14% to 12.5%). The Act defines neither the tax capacity nor the tax effort, a task entrusted to future Finance Acts. In the next section, we will explain and assess the definition of these variables in the last Finance Act.

There is a third system of transfers specifically for those municipalities within the group of "*small municipalities*" that are considered to be tourist destinations. This is basically a hybrid system combining the "*small municipalities*" regime and the regime introduced for "*large municipalities*".[18]

Assessment of General Transfers in the Light of Theory and Comparative Experience

The purpose of this section is to assess the experience of local government in Spain in regard to the design of the transfer system. The theoretical precepts of fiscal federalism and comparative[19] experience will provide the basis for assessing both progress and ways of improving the system of financing.

In fact, one of the main achievements of the implementation of the 1988 LGFA was undoubtedly the shift from a yearly assessment of the grant amount (which was therefore subordinate to other, more urgent, objectives of the Ministry of Finance) to a formula approach linking the pool of funds for transfers, subject to quinquennial revisions, to the change in the level of resources available to the Ministry of Finance, as in the case of the autonomous regional communities. Complying with the objective of a vertical rebalancing, some decisions such as a move to dynamic indices on magnitudes liable to be monitored by the central public finance[20] or to indices assessed on fewer resources,[21] and the abolition of quinquennial revisions should be criticised due to the uncertainty of results of the new system.

Not only do transfers play a role in achieving a vertical rebalancing, they also have an impact on the horizontal dimension. Thus, they must attempt to bridge the gap between expenditure needs and tax capacities among town councils. In addition to the "non-conditional" character of the transfer, it seems appropriate to require clear objectives for the system which is expected to result in equilibrium between expenditure and fiscal capacities. It is difficult to deduce clear objectives for a dual (large and small municipalities) or even trinitarian (when there are touristic municipalities among the small ones) transfer system. As we have shown in another paper,[22] the design of the multiple-factor distributional scheme that is being implemented does not ensure financial equalisation among municipalities. This means that there is a possibility for future reform which, given the changes in funding involved and the need to adjust to them, would require (if implemented) a transitional period. However, leaving structural elements such as tax capacity and effort unresolved and to be addressed in subsequent finance Acts will introduce uncertainty in this important piece of intergovernmental finance.

Among the factors which must be in a scheme distributing the general grant fund, there are two that are essential—those dealing with expenditure needs and with fiscal capacity. A third one reflecting the tax effort of the jurisdiction is debatable. In any case, in order to increase the transparency of the distributional scheme, the number of factors representing the dimensions above should be reduced to the minimum. Below we will examine each of them in the Spanish formula.

In terms of the factors used to measure local *expenditure needs*, the most important advances are in the representativeness and simplicity of the new methodology. Given the large number of Spanish municipalities (more than 8,000) and their heterogeneity, it seemed appropriate to move towards the highest degree of simplification (a single factor). In this context, population was the unquestionable candidate on the grounds of its (spatial and competence) representativeness, its relative easiness to calculate, and the difficulty of manipulating these data. The definitive removal of the second factor (schools), whose weighting was halved in the previous quinquennium, is appropriate not only on simplification grounds but also because, nowadays, it is not relevant in terms of local expenditure responsibility (currently, the autonomous regional communities are responsible for them) and municipalities are in charge of a very small portion of expenditure (cleaning and surveillance).

But the essential issue when using the population as a variable representing local needs lies in the coefficients used to give different weights to municipalities according to size; especially the existing difference between the coefficients for the two strata with larger population (a coefficient of 2.85 for municipalities with more than 500,000 inhabitants is just about double the coefficient of 1.47 allocated to the stratum of municipalities with 100,000–500,000 inhabitants). It must be taken into account that the population variable represented 70 percent of the general transfer (during the 1994–1998 quinquennium). For this reason its financial consequences are important.[23] The differences between these coefficients are not justified by greater expenditure responsibilities (in particular, there is no legal obligation to assign more competences to municipalities with more than 50,000 inhabitants). In addition, there is a lack of empirical basis to support the different coefficients; the sparse evidence in Spain does not support it.[24] Moreover, they are exaggerated from a comparative perspective. For example, the increase in the weighting of an inhabitant in a locality with 510,000 inhabitants compared to one with 120,000 inhabitants does not amount to 5 percent in Germany, while in Spain it is more than 90 percent. All other countries do not make any distinction by size, since population size already is the automatic adjustment. If there are no differences in expenditure responsibilities by size, then the only fact that would justify a higher weight coefficient for large municipalities would be the presence of increasing costs or diseconomies of scale. But the international evidence of the cost functions for public services is that unit costs for many services get pretty flat after a sharp decline reflecting increasing returns to scale up to 25,000–50,000 residents.

Firstly, the traditional lack of factors including the *tax capacity* as a distributive element of the allocation scheme is surprising. As explained above, an element of capacity index was introduced in the five year period 1999–2003 but was incorrectly implemented for several reasons. The main problem was that it identified fiscal capacity with actual revenues collected, thus introducing perverse incentives in the distribution formula (because there was the possibility of increasing the size of the transfers by decreasing tax rates and therefore tax collection, even though tax capacity had not changed at all). Other shortcomings lie in the fact that discretionary taxes for municipalities are included in the measure of fiscal capacity only for those municipalities that decide to make use of them. Consequently perverse signals are introduced again in the transfer system (by increasing the measure of tax capacity only for those municipalities levying optional taxes). The faulty design of the distribution formula is more evident when we focus on the clear contradiction of trying to reward tax effort of municipalities through the introduction of an independent factor for this end in the formula, and at the same time penalise, via a higher reading of fiscal capacity, those municipalities that have decided in favor of the implementation of optional taxes. Finally, income from user charges and other fees are included in tax revenue and fiscal capacity. However, the amount of this revenue is biased by the new ways of managing public services on a cost recovery basis similar to what is done in the private sector. From this perspective, these revenues (fees and charges) should not be included in the calculation of fiscal capacity.

Finally, the Finance Act for the 2004 financial year, which makes use of the authorisation granted by the new LGFA, correctly defines fiscal capacity as the average tax base per inhabitant of the municipality in relation to its population stratum. However, several points need to be made about this definition. With regard to its scope, the Act falls short as it only makes reference to the Property Tax, while incorrectly omitting the other two compulsory taxes (business tax and tax on vehicles).[25] Moreover, the discretion of the municipalities to change the structure of these levies (beyond the tax rates) as provided by the 2004 reform must be taken into account when tax capacity is calculated.

As regards the *tax effort*, its use as an explicit variable of the distribution formula for general transfers is much more questionable. To start with, the transfer system should not discourage tax effort, and that will be accomplished with the proper definition and quantification of fiscal capacity. But, in the second place, there is no good fundamental reason why the transfer formula should stimulate effort. How much to tax should be left to the municipalities' collective decisions; there is nothing inherently superior to higher tax effort.

Another important issue is the calculation of the effort itself. In Spain, we start from a weighted sum of four taxes (the three compulsory taxes and the tax on land value increase in urban areas) bearing in mind actual revenues in relation to the maximum possible. The idea is clever, but the calculation has many deficiencies which have gotten worse following the last reform of the LGFA. In any case, the results obtained should reflect the concept we wish to measure—the tax effort. This is not easy to judge for the following reasons.

- There are no available data for every tax; therefore the maximum value of effort is always allocated to all municipalities with respect to vehicle tax and tax on land value increase.
- The result should not be susceptible to manipulation. Unfortunately, this is the case as long as the weightings in the calculation are internal (relevance in terms of revenue of each tax with respect to total revenue in the municipality).
- The last reform removes the Business Tax from some small municipalities (it should be remembered that big municipalities are excluded from the distributional scheme). In addition, its incidence is marginal in many others where it is still in force, which weakens the very concept of effort.

Updated data must be used, but data prior to the 2002 reform have been used to calculate municipal grants in 2004 in order to avoid some of the difficulties already mentioned. Thus, the variable does not seem to produce results in line with the concept which we are trying to measure. The final proof is that the formula itself contains specific limits on the value of the tax effort of the different municipalities.

All in all, we think that the justification for a tax effort variable in a distribution scheme makes sense when levying taxes or exercising legal capacity that have not been long standing, and in any case its use should be temporary. From this perspective, this factor could be justified when establishing a new tax system derived from the 1988 LGFA but the passing of time and a significant and generalised exercise of legal capacity by Spanish municipalities makes it groundless in the distribution scheme. Its removal, which is advisable, would also mean a step towards higher simplicity and transparency of the grant system.

Let us now evaluate the grant applicable to the "large municipalities." From 2004 onwards following the last LGFA reform, this grant is composed of territorialised shares plus a Complementary Fund. Two main points can be raised.

From a static perspective, if larger municipalities' transfers are accepted as a starting point, we also accept the exaggerated weight coefficients applied to the largest municipalities. The approach raises an obvious problem present in territorialising any consumption taxes (both general as the VAT and specific taxes, such as the excises). This problem is that it is impossible to use the traditional approach for apportioning part of the tax revenue according to relative consumption in the related territory because of the difficulty in assessing local consumption. In any case, territorialised shares continue to be transferred revenues and, as a consequence, they do not entail an improvement in autonomous principles.

On the other hand, from a dynamic perspective, the following considerations must be taken into account. Assuming the initial situation is correct (which is most unlikely), differences in funding from transferred incomes will arise insofar as one of the following two conditions among municipalities are met (actually both are likely to be met): the relative importance of each element (the various territorialised shares and the Complementary Fund) in the initial transfer is different and the dynamics of these elements are also different across municipalities. These differences, which could become significant through time, cannot be justified by assuming new expenditure responsibilities or by different tax effort among municipalities as these are simple transferred revenues. This situation will be particularly serious if we consider that the new MSCT will not be revised every five years as mentioned before.

In spite of the improvements in MSCT in the last few years, its current design presents a series of flaws that should be corrected. Introducing territorialised shares will increase differences in financing between municipalities which will be added to the ones existing as a consequence of the exaggerated weights given to population in the largest municipalities. This may be considered a problem since the system is not designed to achieve horizontal equity among municipalities. Besides, there is no provision for the system to be revised every five years as before. The introduction of a true fiscal capacity index (restricted to PT) should be completed by including the rest of the compulsory municipal taxes. Finally, the tax effort index should be eliminated taking into account its inconsistent results and the consolidation of the municipal tax system, which will help to simplify an excessively complex transfer system.

MUNICIPAL DEBT

Although local governments in Spain are basically suppliers of public goods and services, the need to make long term investments has often meant they have had to resort to borrowing to finance local projects. From a theoretical point of view, financing investments can be accomplished in two ways:

- Using money saved in each tax year—dedicating a share of tax revenues from one period to finance investment projects they wish to undertake ahead of time. This is sometimes known as the "pay-as-you-go" system (PAYG).
- Borrowing so that financing is spread over a period of time and financial obligations arising are met by the stream of profits from the investments made. This is known as the "pay-as-you-use" system (PAYU).

Debate is focused especially on the issue of intertemporal equity. Defenders of the PAYG system, and therefore critics of borrowing argue that, given that it is the current residents who decided to spend, it would be unfair to transfer the cost to future generations who have had no involvement in the decision. In effect, while the choice between saving and borrowing is taken by individuals in the private sphere, in the sense that the costs assumed are internalised by the individuals themselves, the choice of governments generates external effects on future generations. In fact, the current generation has an incentive to try and avoid, via government borrowing, the costs arising from the public spending programme. The probable result of this attitude would be an over-expansion of public spending beyond what would be optimal.

Nevertheless, there are also solid arguments in favor of the PAYU system from the viewpoint of intertemporal equity. Principally these are:

- Borrowing allows the payment of the costs of a project to be made at the same time as its benefits are reaped.
- The postponement of financing means that the cost per capita is reduced as the number of people benefiting from and paying for the service increases.
- Moreover, when there is inflation, greater income per capita in nominal terms would also produce a reduction in the charge per capita.
- Finally, and in entirely pragmatic and operational terms, the burden of financing arising from the PAYG system is excessively high, except for the case of small investment projects, making it impossible to finance most of the projects that are needed.

The issue of intertemporal equity causes an additional problem which arises from the possible transfer of the burden to future generations because of a decrease in capital formation. So, if we assume that there is full employment, increasing public services through borrowing, involves "crowding out", i.e. transferring resources from the private sector to the public sector (funds loaned to the Administration are no longer available for the private sector) and this can be done either by reducing private consumption or reducing private investment. In the first case, the outcome will be a reduction in the welfare of the current generation but in the second case, the welfare of future generations is reduced, as they inherit a lower stock of capital, although this reduction can be (more than) compensated by the increase in public capital.

These arguments based on criteria of intertemporal equity are not exclusively applicable to subcentral government tiers, but are equally valid for analyzing central debt. However, some problems of *intratemporal* equity are specific to the local sphere. These may arise as a consequence of inter-jurisdictional mobility as a response to borrowing policies. Actually, while central debt is mainly internal debt which is serviced basically by a country's residents, greater market opening in the local sphere means that a good part of the debt is external, in the sense that the holders of this debt are residents in other jurisdictions and, therefore, in the future transfers of income will be required between residents and non-residents. As a result, the existence of local public debt means that current residents have an incentive to emigrate in order to avoid facing future fiscal commitments to pay financial charges associated with this debt. The lower the costs of moving are, the greater this incentive will be. However, in the absence of asymmetries of information, with perfect mobility and if we assume free access to capital markets at a single rate of interest, it will be difficult to take such refuge. The reason for this is that fiscal obligations would be expected to be capitalised in property values such that any hypothetical purchaser who is aware that he is acquiring the property with an associated tax commitment which is expected to increase, would discount the current value of these taxes from the maximum he would be willing to pay for the property. As a consequence, if the potential emigrant attempts to sell his property, he would not be able to shift this cost onto the purchaser and would therefore bear the tax burden reducing his present and/or future consumption and providing a strong disincentive to inter-jurisdictional mobility. At the same time, capitalisation also affects profits arising from debt financed investments, which would operate in the opposite sense. The final outcome would therefore be that, according to the hypothetical situation above (perfect information, free movement, no access cost to capital markets and a single interest rate), PAYU and PAYG finance would be equivalent and there would be no incentive to emigrate. Less strict hypothetical criteria could lead to different conclusions as they would introduce arbitration factors which would alter inter-territorial equity.

In practice, the Spanish local government legislation has allowed recourse to credit, although the restrictions on this have varied over time.[26] Historically speaking there have been three types:

- *Restrictions on intended use*, such that a local government may only borrow *to carry out investment projects* (the so called golden rule) or to cover *temporary cash imbalances* (or bridge financing).
- *Restrictions on implementation* such that contracting external debt or the issuing of public debt instruments require central government authorisation.
- *Restrictions on amounts*, the reference criteria for this have been the most variable.

Focusing on the last of these restrictions, the objectives of quantitative limits on debt have been to safeguard the financial solvency of local governments and prevent undesirable uses of public credit. Alarm mechanisms have been established for this purpose together with the requirement for authorisation by central government. Thus, the 1988 LGFA took as a reference the level of debt service or the *financial charges* arising from current debt (interests plus repayments of the principal) in relation to the local government's current revenues, so that when this indicator reached a value of 25 percent, the local government required authorisation to carry out new credit operations. The 25 percent level was therefore the "alarm level" for financial insolvency. Similarly, the LGFA prevented treasury operations for liquidity purposes and the like from being carried out when the amount exceeded 35 percent (subsequently lowered to 30 percent) of current revenues assessed in the previous financial year. This meant that in these cases borrowing was being used inappropriately in contravention of the restriction on intended use mentioned earlier.

Although the philosophy of quantitative restrictions was maintained for a long period of time, this has not been true for its implementation in practical terms. Therefore, the 1998 Act substantially amended the LGFA frames of reference, such that the relevant indicators became the existence of net negative savings and the fact that the current debt of the local government exceeded 110 percent of current revenues received. In the event that one of the cases described should arise, in addition to the requirement for central government authorisation, local governments are required to present a financial restructuring plan to restore their position to less worrying levels and, in any event, lower than the levels which caused the alarms. In addition, municipalities with more than 200,000 inhabitants are allowed to substitute the authorisation regime with a Budget Consolidation Plan approved by the Ministry of Finance or by the Regional Government which has, if appropriate, competence in this area, following a report from the aforementioned Ministry.

Finally, as we indicated in a previous section of this chapter, the introduction in 2001 of the legislation on budgetary stability had a serious impact on the ability of local governments to resort to credit as it obliged all Public Administrations to balance their budgets.

The legislation on budgetary stability which was adopted involved establishing a regulatory framework directed at ensuring budgetary discipline in order to comply with macroeconomic objectives. This internal legislation on budgetary stability established the credibility of Spain's fiscal policy as is attested by the positive outcomes from the restructuring of public finances. Although, as Kopits (2001) indicates, it is not a panacea, the adoption of legislation on budgetary stability (fiscal rules) should offer mechanisms enabling a reputation for fiscal discipline to be earned. As seen earlier, such a reputation has a high economic value, is difficult to achieve, and is easily lost.

An unavoidable initial assumption in developing the legislation on budgetary stability was the acknowledgment of the genuinely multi-jurisdictional character of Spain's public finances, a factor of great complexity with far-reaching consequences for fiscal discipline. This leads to considering the legal framework of budgetary stability as an "internal stability settlement," in line with the experience of certain countries with highly decentralised public sectors.

The General Act on Budgetary Stability (GABS, 2001) establishes the principles which should govern budgetary policy in Spain. The first of these, *budgetary stability*, is identified with a balanced budget or, where appropriate, a budget surplus, calculated on a national basis. The second principle involved is that of *multi-annual planning* which aims to achieve the realistic planning of public sector budgets, although it must always be compatible with the traditional annual budgetary principle which governs the approval and execution phases. The third principle, which is extremely important for the effectiveness of disciplinary mechanisms contained in the GABS, is *transparency*. This requires that the information which is important for verifying compliance with the principle of budgetary stability is adequate and correct as well as publicly available. The last principle contemplated in the GABS is *efficiency in the allocation and use of public resources*. This principle recognises the importance of accounting for macroeconomic aspects of budgetary stability and the microeconomic aspects of public management which impose an obligation, in a context of scarce resources, to manage according to standards of efficiency, quality and effectiveness. In our opinion, this acknowledgement fully justifies budgetary stability which has at times been deliberately derided as being simply "a numbers exercise".

The measures in GABS make it mandatory for all agents involved in the state, regional and local government public sector budget process to include, in their budget and public spending rules, all the instruments and procedures that are necessary to achieve the objective of budgetary stability. To this end, the GABS legislation makes this a responsibility of the national government. Failure to comply with this objective, owing to exceptional situations of a deficit, is considered by the legislation but all such cases will require an explanation to be given as to their causes and proposed corrective measures. This is one of the Act's incentive mechanisms reinforced by the principle of transparency—the threat of the deficit being made public knowledge.

The coordination of the budgetary activities at all levels of government is a responsibility of the national government. Before 31 March each year, the latter must set the budgetary stability target on a multi-annual basis covering the next three financial years on a rolling basis. The setting of multi-annual budgetary targets must be carried out in conjunction with the development, for the same time period, of a macroeconomic scenario in the Stability Programme required by the European Commission. These targets, approved by the Spanish Parliament, will be assessed annually at the end of the financial year in a report made to the government before September 1st each year by the national audit commission.

With regard to the budget preparation process, the legislation on budgetary stability foresees a series of reform measures of different scope according to the competences assigned to each administration. In the sphere of concern here—that of local government—the measures foreseen in the GABS are:

A. The setting by the government, following a proposal from the Ministry of Finance, of the overall target for budgetary stability for local governments as a whole. The GABS assigns, to an organisation called the National Local Government Commission, the role of the coordinating body which must be informed of these budget stability related activities. The Ministry of Finance is responsible for supervising and monitoring these budgetary activities and may demand any information necessary for this purpose.
B. Local governments which do not comply with the budget stability target that has been set are obliged to prepare a medium term financial plan to correct the imbalance. This plan must be submitted to the Ministry of Finance as the supervisory body.

As a result, the laws on Budgetary Stability establish the basis for satisfying the principles of budgetary stability arising from the Stability and Growth Pact Settlement agreed at the EU Amsterdam Council of July 1997 for the different levels of government, therefore allowing the challenges facing our economy in the medium and long term to be met.

There has been no shortage of voices, both from the world of management and from the more strictly academic, questioning the need to apply this legislation strictly to local bodies.[27] So, on the one hand, some people have stated that there is no need for it. This is on the grounds that the deficit and debt figures for local governments prior to the introduction of the law indicated that the overall behavior of these authorities was characterised in general by relative austerity and responsible conduct with respect to the large macroeconomic targets arising from Spain's agreements with the European Union. In fact Table 12.3 makes clear that there have been budget surpluses and financial charges were far below the figure of 25 percent of current revenue, a limit which had at one time been set as an indicator of the risk of insolvency.

On the other hand, the proliferation of organisations created to implement the new forms of public management (autonomous bodies, municipal companies, consortia, etc.) may forewarn of the possible appearance of "creative" accounting mechanisms which tend to undermine the objective of transparency in financial management. To the extent that identifying budgetary stability with an absence of a deficit in practice implies a quantitative limit on the recourse to new credit operations with a ceiling marked by the repayment of existing debt, governments needing new resources to finance large investment projects may be tempted to use these methods. This would mock the spirit of the budgetary stability legislation and, more importantly, in our opinion, would obviate one of its principal virtues, which is the search for transparency of information. In the

Table 12.3 Deficit (€ millions) and local financial charges (% costs/current revenue)

		1995	1996	1997	1998
Municipalities	Non-financial Deficit (-) or Surplus (+)	410.18	877.35	1,392.57	1,006.50
	Primary Deficit (-) or Surplus (+)	1,744.03	2,202.95	2,528.93	1,937.03
	Financial charges	17.22	17.26	17.25	12.25
Other Local Governments	Non-financial Deficit (-) or Surplus (+)	109.85	588.12	355.99	544.61
	Primary Deficit (-) or Surplus (+)	540.16	1,003.95	710.74	812.01
	Financial charges	–	–	–	–
Total Local Authorities	***Non-financial Deficit (-) or Surplus (+)***	***520.03***	***1,465.47***	***1,748.56***	***1,551.12***
	Primary Deficit (-) or Surplus (+)	***2,284.19***	***3,206.90***	***3,239.67***	***2,749.04***
	Financial charges	***14.77***	***14.87***	***14.38***	***11.12***

Source: Ministry of Finance.

event that this occurs generally, and it is still too early to verify this given the short time the Act has been in force, then the results of this well-intentioned legislation may be questionable.

CONCLUDING REMARKS

We began this chapter by highlighting the difficulty of summarising 25 years of democratic local government in Spain in a few pages. Along the way we have described the successive reforms of the financing model and how they have affected local taxation, inter-governmental transfers and the opportunities for debt recourse, as the principal instruments used to finance an ever greater number of goods and services, while citizens make ever greater demands with respect to their quality.

Having reached this point, we would like to point out by way of a closing note one last aspect which presents an ongoing challenge to the process of decentralisation. We are referring to what has come to be known as "second wave decentralisation". In this context, we should remember that, at the outset of the process following the adoption of the Constitution of 1978, the objective under discussion was that, at its conclusion, Central Government would manage only 50 percent of public spending, leaving 25 percent in the hands of the regional governments (the "Autonomous Communities") with 25 percent being managed by local governments. Compared to our neighboring countries, achieving these objectives would have placed Spain in the group of the most decentralised federal countries, even though it was clear from the beginning that the 50-25-25 target appeared to be inspired more by the magic of round numbers than reasoned economic and administrative analysis.

In fact, as the decentralisation process has evolved, the management ability of the Autonomous Regional Communities has increased significantly and its volume of expenditure now easily exceeds 25 percent of total public expenditure, whereas local spending has not changed significantly from the target that was implicitly set (50-25-25).

Seen in this way, it would appear that the significant decentralisation process that followed the approval of the 1978 Constitution has stalled at the regional government level and has not reached or had a strong effect on the level of government nearest to the people. In this sense, there are some important nuances which should be taken into account both in the area of the structure of local government and in the broadening of its areas of responsibility.

In fact a simple analysis of the official competences reveals, without much effort, that there are several fields of activity where regional and local governments operate simultaneously. This is the case, for example, for cultural, tourism or urban planning activities. It is often said that an overlap of competences produces inefficiencies in the management of services, either because it causes unnecessary cost duplications or because this overlap prevents either administration from acting effectively as a consequence of a lack of coordination between them. These problems would apparently be solved if there were a clearer definition of competences so that the responsible authorities were identified explicitly and, in this respect, applying the *subsidiarity principle*, such that the more remote authority does not do what could be done by the closest, has been selected as the basic rule for action.

However, there is a risk that this type of analysis may be over-simplistic. In fact, there are many areas of activity where overlapping competences, far from having an adverse effect, actually improve performance. Examples of these are in the areas of infrastructure policies related to local development or the economies of scale which may be generated by regional coordination of public transport in metropolitan areas.

All in all, up to now, in addition to concurrent competences which have not always resulted in the development of cooperation mechanisms for managing public services for the benefit of citizens, local authorities have complained on many occasions about having to perform works which theoretically, in terms of the current legislation on local matters, do not fall within their remit. In spite of this, citizen pressure on the closest levels of government has meant that these governments have become more and more involved in performing certain tasks where regional governments were observed to be deficient, particularly with respect to activities related to social services and local development. This has occurred with no additional financing and has forced local governments to reduce the quantity or quality of their own services or, more often, to increase their level of debt.

The need to reallocate competences between the subcentral government tiers underlies the long list of grievances expounded in the Spanish Federation of Municipalities and Provinces and is behind the so-called *Local Agreement*. The *Local Agreement* results from a political commitment to decentralisation from the regional government's management and powers to the municipalities. Such entities are closer to the citizens' interests. It is aimed at enabling municipalities to have more management competences and avoiding the overlap of authorities in a jurisdiction. The *Local Agreement* is based on the subsidiarity principle; this implies that the administration which is closer to the citizens must be responsible for provision of services, more effective and less expensive in terms of public expenditure. Although it is true that in recent years certain legislative measures have been adopted in this regard—for example, expanding the sphere of responsibility of local governments in areas such as movement of traffic (traffic and road safety), public transport (both in terms of collective urban transport and taxis), the use, planning and management of sporting facilities and activities, training and employment policies, the fields of provision for young people, environment, women, civil protection, social services, tourism or urban planning—these measures have not been accompanied by substantial increases in ordinary financing.

In any event, even in this upper range of competences it will, in practice, be difficult for activities managed by local governments to increase to 25 percent of public expenditure. Spain's neighboring countries, whose local authorities have achieved this ratio of expenditure and even higher have, as a common denominator, the fact that local authorities have responsibility for primary education. In practice, it therefore seems difficult for Spanish local governments to reach these levels unless their competences expand in this direction. Objectively speaking, this is very difficult unless an ambitious reorganisation of the municipal sphere is undertaken to achieve minimum population groupings which take advantage of the economies of scale necessary to manage such an important service. Given the current fragmentation at the local level, the generalised decentralisation of this type of competence would not make sense. Of course, it could be possible to have asymmetric assignments to the municipalities depending on their size and capacity, but a lot of political problems would arise in determining which municipalities might get additional competences.

At the present time, the current legislation gives the Autonomous Communities the power, albeit via a complex legislative procedure, to modify municipal boundaries and the creation and suppression of municipalities. As a result, a task which so far has not been undertaken, but which seems necessary if it is considered desirable to complete the decentralisation process on the basis of the efficient provision of public goods and services, is to realign the territory and redefine the municipal map. However, this involves overcoming inertias and local resistance which are for the most part unjustified from an economic point of view.

One way of advancing the process would be to initiate the transfer of competences to the most populated municipalities and the recently approved *Act on Measures to Modernise Local Government* has established the legal basis by providing for new forms of government for the most populous cities. Although we have a certain degree of skepticism about the effectiveness of some of the measures included in this law, known popularly as the *Big Cities Act*.[28] we believe that introducing new forms of management for the most populated areas will facilitate legal access to competences such as civic safety, active employment policies, family policies, education or social services. In fact, it is likely that the progress of municipalism and the policies of proximity within the Welfare State may be considered as the principal objective of public management in future years. The assessment that citizens make about the way the decentralisation process is developing will depend critically on the response to this challenge, while not forgetting, of course, the finance issue.

NOTES

* Universidad de Extremadura

** Instituto de Estudios Fiscales, Universidad de Extremadura

*** Universidad de Oviedo

1. See López Laborda and Monasterio (in this volume).
2. In the preconstitutional period, the main direct taxes existing in Spain were some *Production Factor Taxes* that charged individually the gross income arising from production factors. Concretely, there was a Tax on Capital Income (*Impuesto sobre las Rentas del Capital—IRC*), a Tax on Labour Income (*Impuesto sobre la Renta del Trabajo Personal—IRTP*), a Tax on Industrial Earning (*Impuesto Industrial—II*), a Tax on Urban Properties Income (*Contribución Territorial Urbana—CTU*) and a Tax on Rural Properties Income (*Contribución Territorial Rústica y Pecuaria—CTRP*). All were collected by central government. IRTP was divided in two parts, an IRTP of dependent workers and an IRTP of independent workers. This last tax and II had two

parts, a fix charge for the license and a variable part falling on earnings. The PFT devolved to local governments were CTU, CTRP, and the fix quotas of IRTP and II.

3. See Monasterio and Suárez-Pandiello (1998) for more details on the AUM, its changes and effects.
4. See Pedraja and Suárez-Pandiello (2003) for an extensive analysis of the model and its development.
5. This would include public works financed and carried out by the private sector, which incurs into debt, converting the charges in recurrent expenditures as opposed to debt repayment. Another example is the translation of several fields of public management out of administrative controls, by transforming public or mixed enterprises which could operate in market conditions, avoiding thus the constraints of GABS.
6. At this time tax income was 45% of the total income of Spanish municipalities (49.97% if we exclude financial income).
7. See for example Oates (1972), Musgrave (1983) and King (1984).
8. See Hirsch and Rufolo (1990). Some recent contributions to this debate can be found in the pages of *National Tax Journal.* See Zodrow (2001), Brueckner and Saavedra (2001) and Fischel (2001).
9. The last reform included a new category of property (the so-called "property of a special nature") including some with a controversial rural or urban assignation such as dams or toll motorways.
10. See, for example, the line of argument in the Layfield Report (1976) on the attempts to reform the British Property Tax. In the United States, many states and local governments have made use of the so called "circuit breakers," which allow reduced assessment and/or rates for owning families with special conditions such as the elderly, low income, etc.
11. See for example Suárez-Pandiello (2003a).
12. See Suárez-Pandiello (2002).
13. We must remember that collections have fallen after reform to only 7.89 per cent.
14. Typically, the *Impuesto sobre Matriculación de Vehículos* that charges only one time the first matriculation or putting in service of vehicles.
15. These municipalities share the same percentage they had in MSCT in 1998; as a consequence, their transfer increases annually at the same rate as the nominal GDP (or CPI).
16. Besides, a limit to the effort is established in such a way that, for no municipality, its value is not greater than five times the least value reached for group of municipalities of the last population stratum.
17. However, flaws in the regional and municipal transfer system will bring about changes in the short run.
18. These municipalities have a share in some of the central government taxes in which "*large municipalities*" take part (excise taxes on oil and tobacco). The system will be favourable (unfavourable) for these municipalities when the revenue from these taxes is higher (lower) than those corresponding to National Tax Revenue. It is controversial that tourist municipalities (those according to 51/2002 Act having a *de jure* population higher than 20,000 inhabitants and where the number of secondary residences is higher than that of first ones) should have a favourable legal treatment. On the one hand, they need a greater factor supply to attend to a higher number of inhabitants in certain periods of the year but, on the other hand, they have a higher fiscal base than the rest of the municipalities. In any case, it seems clear that MSCT is not the appropriate instrument to do this.

19. For a comprehensive study of the major decisions which shall be taken in line with theory and experience, see Martínez-Vázquez and Boex (2000) and Bird and Smart (2002).
20. NTR compared to nominal GDP used in the five year period 1999–2003.
21. Current NTR is a narrower base than the one used in the five year period 1994–1998. The latter also included business taxes and Social Security tax, precisely those taxes with a higher increase in the last few years.
22. See Pedraja and Suárez-Pandiello (2003).
23. See Pedraja and Suárez Pandiello (2002) for information on differences in funding for the 1994–1998 quinquennium.
24. See Solé and Bosch (2003)
25. It must be borne in mind that, subsequent to the business tax reform, there are now more differences (in revenue-raising capacity) between municipalities where this distributional scheme is implemented because the above tax no longer exists in some of them.
26. About the borrowing limits in Spain and other European countries, see Dafflon (2002).
27. See, for example, Suárez Pandiello (2001).
28. See Suárez-Pandiello (2003b).

REFERENCES

Bird, R. M. and Smart, M. (2002), 'Intergovernmental Fiscal Transfers: International Lessons for Developing Countries', *World Development*, 30 (6), 899–912.

Brueckner, J. K. and Saavedra, L. A. (2001), 'Do Local Governments Engage in Strategic Property Tax Competition?', *National Tax Journal*, 54 (2), 203–230.

Dafflon, B. (ed.) (2002), *Local Public Finance in Europe. Balancing the Budget and Controlling Debt*, Northampton: Edward Elgar.

Färber, G. and Otter, N. (eds) (2003), *Reforms of Local Fiscal Equalization in Europe*, Speyer: Speyer Forchungsberichte.

Fischel, W. A. (2001), 'Homevoters, Municipal Corporate Governance, and the Benefit View of the Property Tax', *National Tax Journal*, 54 (1), 157–174.

Gago, A., and Labandeira. X. (eds) (2002) *Energia, Fiscalidad y Medio Ambiente en España* (Energy, Taxation and the Environment in Spain). Instituto de Estudios Fiscales, Madrid.

Hirsch, W. Z. and Rufolo, A. M. (1990), *Public Finance and Expenditure in a Federal System*, New York: Harcourt Brace Jovanovich.

King, D. (1984), *Fiscal Tiers: The Economics of Multi-Level Government*, London: George Allen & Unwin.

Kopits, George (2001), 'Fiscal Rules: Useful Policy Framwork or Unnecessary Ornament?' *IMF working Paper* 01/145

Layfield Report (1976), Local Government Finance: Report of the Committee of Inquiry, London: H.M.S.O.

Martinez-Vazquez, J. and Jameson Boex, L.F. (2000), 'The Design of Equalization Grants: Theory and Applications', World Bank Institute, Andrew Young School of Policy Studies, Georgia State University.

McLure, C.E. (ed.) (1983), *Tax Assignment in Federal Countries*, Canberra: Centre for Research on Federal Financial Relations, ANU.

Monasterio, C. and Suárez-Pandiello, J. (eds) (1998), *Manual de Hacienda Autonómica y Local*, Barcelona: Ariel.

Musgrave, R. A. (1983), 'Who should tax, where and what?', in McLure, *Tax Assignment in Federal Countries*, Canberra: Centre for Research on Federal Financial Relations, ANU, pp. 2–22.

Oates, W. E. (1972), *Fiscal Federalism*, New York: Harcourt Brace Jovanovich.

Pedraja, F. and Suárez Pandiello, J. (2002), 'Subvenciones Generales a los Municipios: Valoración y Propuestas de Reforma', *Papeles de Economía Española*, 92, pp. 120–129.

Pedraja, F. and Suárez-Pandiello, J. (2003), 'Local Fiscal Equalisation in Spain: Some Ideas for a Neccesary Reform', in Färber and Otter (eds), *Reforms of Local Fiscal Equalization in Europe*, Speyer: Speyer Forchungsberichte, pp. 275–295.

Solé, A. and Bosch, N. (2003), 'On the Relationship Between Local Authority Size and Expenditure: Lessons for the Design of Intergovernmental Transfers in Spain: Reforms of Local Fiscal Equalization in Europe', in Färber and Otter (eds), *Reforms of Local Fiscal Equalization in Europe*, Speyer: Speyer Forchungsberichte, pp. 339–376.

Suárez-Pandiello, J. (2001), 'El futuro de la financiación local en el contexto del Estado de las Autonomías', *Hacienda Pública Española*, Monografía, 359–377.

Suárez-Pandiello, J. (2002), 'Impuesto sobre Actividades Económicas: ¿Terapia o eutanasia?', *Papeles de Economía Española*, 92, 240–253.

Suárez-Pandiello, J. (2003a), 'Financiación Local y Corresponsabilidad Fiscal Local: ¿Ganamos con el Nuevo Modelo?', *Revista de Estudios Regionales*, 2ª Época, 66, 115–128.

Suárez-Pandiello, J. (2003b), 'Grandes Ciudades y Modernización del Gobierno Local', *Economistas*, 100, 209–213.

Zodrow, G. R. (2001), 'The Property Tax as a Capital Tax: A Room with Three Views', *National Tax Journal*, 54 (1), 139–156.

13. The Reform of the Tax Administration in Spain

Jorge Onrubia*

INTRODUCTION

It is hard not to agree with Aaron and Slemrod (2004) when they state that tax administration is the dullest of topics and government functions that arouses powerful emotions. A probable explanation for this lies in the wisdom in the following anonymous quote: "It would be nice if we could all pay our taxes with a smile, but normally cash is required. Throughout tax history, in any country, that is how it is and that is all there is to it."

However, we can not ignore the influence over tax compliance that the tax system in every country may have. The tax system and the tax administration charged with enforcing it ought to be consistent. It is not possible for a rudimentary tax administration to manage complex taxes like some currently applied in developed countries. Efficiency in tax administration is not only a matter of administrative costs but also of compliance costs. Modern tax systems which involve complex taxes require high levels of human and capital resources, including information technology, to make them reasonably easy to comply with by taxpayers. The bottom line is clearly expressed in a well-known maxim attributed to the Italian economist and prominent statesman Luigi Einaudi: "Any tax system ends up being largely worth what the tax administration in charge of its management is worth."

In the case of Spain, Einaudi's maxim tends to reflect reality quite perfectly. Like in many other countries, the history of Spanish tax reforms can not be understood without bearing in mind the evolution of the Spanish tax administration through the corresponding time periods. This interdependence in Spain must also be seen through the lenses of the evolving political framework. As we will see in the second section of this chapter, the almost four decades that General Franco's dictatorship lasted, prevented the Spanish tax system from moving in parallel with developments in tax policy and administration in OECD countries. So, Spain kept, until the late seventies, an obsolete tax system, more typical of the beginning of the twentieth century, in which schedular taxes, together with a cumulative multistage general tax on sales, were the main tax figures.

In correspondence with this tax system scenario, at the beginning of the political transition's tax reform in 1977, Spain had a very centralised tax administration with only a few General Directorates, which were incorporated within the formal organisational structure of the Ministry of Finance with fairly limited autonomy. Besides the central tax administration at the centre, town councils had their own tax administrations, although these were rather small services for collecting from and inspecting local business and administering real property taxes and several minor local charges.

The adoption of a modern tax system included a progressive personal income tax and a corporate income tax, and later on the European harmonised Valued Added Tax. This became the backbone of the central government tax revenues and forced the ineluctable transformation of the Spanish Tax Administration. These initial stages in the modernisation of the tax administration culminated, in 1991, in an entirely new organisational arrangement, the State Tax Agency. Since then the great challenges of the State Tax Agency have been the fight against tax evasion, the reduction of both tax administration and tax compliance costs, and the widespread implementation of an effective assistance-to-taxpayers' service. These challenges have largely provided the guidelines for the Agency's human resources policy as well as its technological investment policy. However, this evolution did not involve only the expected management issues, typical of the tax administration in other developed countries. An unknown (to Spain) new element arose in the middle of this process of tax administration reform: the deep political decentralisation process at the regional level. Decentralisation meant a complete change in the assignment of tax powers and, in consequence, forced a redefinition of the global objectives that ought to guide tax administration policy and reform.

This chapter deals with the evolution of tax administration in Spain from the initial stages of the democratic process, way back in the second half of the seventies, up to the present time. Given the relevance of the classical interrelation between the tax reform processes and tax administration reforms, we review the main events and milestones in the last three decades. We analyse the influence that institutional, economic, and political factors have had on both the architecture of the tax administration and its organisational behaviour. Nevertheless, based on what we have just said, the performance of the Spanish tax administration cannot be satisfactorily assessed without explicit reference to the deep decentralisation experienced by the Spanish tax system from the early eighties, and especially since 1994. That is why a considerable part of the chapter is devoted to analysing the role played by the successive reforms of the Autonomous Communities' financing system, and the decisions of the regional governments themselves, in shaping Spain's tax administration.

This chapter is organised as follows. In the next section, we review the main features of the Spanish tax system prior to the first tax reform under democracy in 1977, as well as the situation of the Spanish tax administration in that period. This retrospective look is essential for understanding aright the challenges faced in the building of a modern tax administration system. The third section is devoted to considering the demands imposed on the Spanish tax administration by the new taxes implemented through the 1977–1978 tax reform. In the fourth section, we review the limitations in the organisation of the tax administration revealed at the end of the eighties; our focus is on identifying the factors that drove the central government to turn the State tax administration into a semi-autonomous State Tax Agency in 1991. The creation and development of the State Tax Agency, which lasted until 1996, is considered in the fifth section. The sixth section is devoted to analyzing how tax-sharing arrangements and the devolution of taxing powers to the Autonomous Communities influenced the organisational model of the State Tax Agency starting with 1997. The seventh section examines the effects of the tax reform of 1998 and the consolidation of a new administration paradigm focused on taxpayer services. The eighth section tries to ascertain to what extent the State Tax Agency is an autonomous institution in relation to political power, assessing its successes and failures up to now. The ninth section concludes.

SPANISH TAX ADMINISTRATION BEFORE THE DEMOCRATIC TAX REFORM OF 1977

An adequate understanding of the last three decades of tax administration reforms in Spain requires knowing the realities of the Spanish tax system in the years prior to the transition to a democratic state after General Franco's death. The essential economic reforms, including the opening up of the economy to international trade, taken in the Stabilisation Plan of 1959 as a result of the agreement reached between the International Monetary Fund and the Spanish Government, brought about the beginning of a long period of significant economic growth (so-called "the sixties Spanish economic development").

However, the dictatorial regime preserved an economic model of state intervention characterised by a low level of budgetary activity, with total expenditures barely reaching 25 percent of GDP in 1975. Moreover, from a qualitative point of view, the composition of budgetary expenditures and programmes differed considerably from the ones in more developed European countries, which were immersed at the time in the full building of the Welfare State. Public expenditures in health, education, and social security benefits, including unemployment benefits, were very limited in Spain in comparison to its northern European neighbours. A similar profile existed for public investment. Public revenues, mainly taxes, did not compare well with European standards. Tax burdens in Spain were substantially lower than the average for the developed European countries and the composition of taxes was also quite different. Among the most important taxes were Social Contributions (around 10 percent of GDP) together with indirect taxes (about 7 percent of GDP). Direct taxation contributed to tax revenues was only 6 percent of GDP. Furthermore, most direct taxes (4.5 percent of GDP) were schedular taxes with proportional tax rates, which taxed separately different income sources such as income from labour and returns to financial investments.

Nevertheless, the presence of the public sector in the Spanish economy was very considerable through huge numbers of public enterprises in practically all sectors of the economy, and an extensive regulatory framework of the business sector. During this period, intensive public intervention policies were adopted with little regard for efficiency considerations, and in a large number of cases they were instruments for job creation, mechanisms to transfer income, or simply restrictions to market competition.

The tax system was not only obsolete and short of fundraising power, but it also lacked any ability to redistribute income and wealth. Most taxes in force in that period had proportional statutory rates. After accounting for the high tax evasion levels, mainly among high income citizens, it is quite likely that the tax system was *de facto* regressive.

A far from complete list of deficiencies of the tax system back then would include:

- A much lower tax burden than the average in OECD countries (24 percent against 40 percent in 1977).
- A tax yield insufficient even to finance the reduced public expenditure (around 25 percent of GDP).

- A schedular income tax structure including a payroll tax, an industrial and commercial profit tax, both with proportional rates, and an obsolete presumptive tax that was applied separately to each professional group. Taxation of capital income included proportional taxes on interests and dividends. The payment of these direct taxes was made by tax receipts emitted by the tax administration using information from taxpayers' censuses.
- Although there was a so-called "general personal income tax", this tax was only applied to a very limited percentage of the population (1 percent). The levels of tax avoidance and evasion corresponding to this tax were very high.
- There was a general Corporate Income Tax, with a statutory rate of 32 percent, but its taxable income was beset by exemptions and other discriminatory tax treatments targeted at sheltering important sectors of the economy such as utilities and building enterprises. The deep economic crisis of the seventies and the existing generalised tax avoidance and evasion cut the yield of this tax to a bare 1 percent of GDP.
- The main piece of indirect taxation was a cumulative multistage general tax on sales (*Impuesto General sobre el Tráfico de Empresas, IGTE*). There were also several excise taxes on production, distribution and consumption of alcoholic drinks, tobacco, petrol, and other specific goods. In addition, a luxury tax was imposed on some goods and services.

In regard to the tax system as a whole, it is by no means surprising to find that the tax administration in charge of its implementation was quite modest in terms of size and means. The main features of that Spanish tax administration previous to the democracy tax reform of 1977 were:

- The organisational structure was overly simple, integrated by two General Directorates of the Ministry of Finance. One, the *Dirección General de Inspección* (General Directorate of Tax Audit) was dedicated to the management and enforcement of the general internal taxes. The second one, the *Dirección General de Aduanas e Impuestos Especiales* (General Directorate for Customs and Excise Taxes) was in charge of especial domestic levies and taxes on foreign trade.
- The territorial organisation across the country was very centralised. There was only one tax office, the *Delegación de Hacienda*, in each one of the fifty provinces that integrated Spain, and located in the provincial capital (recall that it was not until the early 1980s that Spain

introduced the current regional level of government, the Autonomous Communities).[1]

- The number of employees in the service of the tax administration was quite reduced. Approximately, in 1977 there were 9,000 public employees (in comparison to 30,000 in 2003.) This fact is quite significant for the effectiveness of the tax administration at the time given that the general approach was a labour-intensive tax administration system. There were several classes of public employees according to specialisation.
- Information technology was practically not available until the second half of the 1980s. The first stage of the general computerisation of the tax management culminated in the year 1986, at the same time that the Value Added Tax was introduced in the Spanish tax system.
- The number of taxpayers in the tax net was proportionally small. The 400,000 taxpayers in the tax books in 1977 have been multiplied by almost 40 (more than 15.5 million taxpayers) in 2003.
- With the exception of the tax payments collected using withholding and through automatic price increase mechanisms, the tax collection was in the hands of private agents devoid of administrative status, especially in the case of collection of overdue tax liabilities.

In conclusion, Spain had a small-sized tax administration only appropriate for the obsolete tax system that it had to manage. In addition, the training of tax officials not in many cases suitable owed, among other things, to the absence of a tax-culture similar to that existing in other European countries at the time. In this regard, we should point out that until the 1980s there did not exist a law regulating the holding of multiple private and public posts applicable to the public employees in the tax administration service and elsewhere in the Spanish public sector.

BUILDING A NEW TAX ADMINISTRATION FOR A MODERN TAX SYSTEM (1978–1987)

The world economic crisis that burst after the first oil shock in 1973 caught Spain in the middle of the transition process towards a democratic regime. The structural problems the Spanish economy had accumulated over the previous stage deepened the effects of the oil crisis. The political situation after the first democratic general elections held in June 1977 did not facilitate the adoption of many necessary and urgent measures to confront the economic crisis.

In the context of the public finance, several structural and relating-to-the-moment factors seriously affected Spanish fiscal sustainability. The clearest sign of the lack of sustainability was the increasing public deficit (Fuentes-Quintana, 2004:175). The meagre provision of public services and public utilities, and the practical absence of a system of social protection -comparable to what other European countries had developed,- pushed public expenditure up exceedingly. The obsolete existing tax system was incapable of bringing in sufficient revenues to a budget which was under severe pressure from demands for social expenditures that had surfaced after many years of an autocratic political regime. Besides the thin revenue-collecting potential aggravated by the 1970s economic recession, the existing taxes were extensively evaded.

The high levels of evasion had several roots. Firstly, a poor tax culture did not encourage tax compliance. Secondly, the important limitations of the tax system with regard to distributive justice, both in terms of horizontal and vertical equity, discouraged tax compliance, especially among the middle class, who felt that they were the only ones paying taxes. Lastly, as we have seen, there were important problems of organisation, resources and adequate legal framework, all of which affected the effectiveness of the tax administration.

The alarming situation of the Spanish economy in the summer of 1977 prompted the then appointed President of Government Adolfo Suarez to commission a programme for putting the economy back on a sound footing, which was given the title of *Programa de Saneamiento y Reforma Económica*. This economic programme was to become the basis for the Moncloa Pacts of October 1977, agreed to after obtaining a broad political consensus with all the political parties with representation in the Parliament. The peremptory need for dealing with the reform of the tax system played a part in the design of these historical political agreements, which among other things established that the tax reform should be initiated before the end of 1977. This reform was to include the following taxes: (a) a personal income tax (*Impuesto sobre la Renta de las Personas Físicas,* hereafter *IRPF*), with a comprehensive tax base and a progressive tax schedule, that should replace the old schedular income taxes that had prevailed until then; (b) a permanent (non transitory) personal net wealth tax, properly harmonised with the IRPF to avoid its confiscatory character, applicable on real wealth bases and with a progressive tax schedule; (c) a corporate income tax, without the discriminatory exemptions for special economic sectors that had been so frequent in the previous tax on corporate income; (d) In relation to indirect taxation, an appeal to the inescapable need to align the Spanish tax system with the taxes applied by the member countries of the European Economic Community. This effectively meant the introduction of the Value Added Tax (hereafter VAT) as the main figure of the general taxation on consumption. However, in this case no time limits were set, in part to avoid possible negative effects on the price level, which at the time was still out of control.

In spite of the political conflict inherent in any tax reform, in so far as it produces alterations in the *status quo* among interest groups, the Spanish tax reform coming out of the Moncloa Pacts had an extensive political acceptance, at least in the first years after its implementation. In the early seventies, still in the last years of the dictatorship, the *Instituto de Estudios Fiscales* (Spanish Institute for Fiscal Studies), the think tank attached to the Ministry of Finance, directed by the famous Professor Fuentes-Quintana, had prepared several reports that included concrete proposals for the reform of the Spanish tax system. Although these proposals were initially sterile due to the absence of political will on the part of the governments of General Franco, with the arrival of democracy, the rigorous studies allowed a considerable acceleration for the parliamentary approval of the tax laws.

It is now common knowledge in the literature on tax reform that any substantial modification of the tax system should take into account the possibilities and limitations of the tax administration in charge of managing and enforcing the new taxes (Bird, 1990, Musgrave, 1969, Slemrod, 1992). But in the case of Spain the tax reform initiated in 1977 played a deeper role than the usual tax reform. In many ways it was conceived like an indispensable social commitment to guarantee the process of political transition towards democracy (Lasheras, 1990). Through the reform, the political class intended to send an unmistakable message to society about the irrevocable will to establish an internationally comparable democratic regime in Spain. Therefore, although there was immediate recognition of the need to reform the tax administration, this task was considered secondary and something to take on after the respective tax acts came into effect. Therefore, the reforms in tax policy jumped ahead of the existing capabilities in tax administration, but with a clear sequence established for the administrative reforms that were to follow.[2]

The tax reform initiated in 1977 was phased in over the next eight years, starting with the first measures in early 1978 and concluding with the last measures in 1985. The tax reform of the new democracy opted for implementing a modern tax system, conforming to the systems in the most developed countries. The aims pursued by the reform of 1977 can be summarised as follows:

- The new tax system should provide enough public revenues for financing the "new public sector." The old taxes proved unable to finance the limited public expenditure in the early seventies. In this respect, Spain's foreseeable integration into the European Economic Community suggested an important increase in public expenditure for the "construction" of the welfare state (increased public health, education, housing, public pensions, and other public subsidies and grants, such as unemployment benefits). In addition, the need to provide public infrastructures comparable with the EEC standards also was expected to significantly contribute to the expansion of the budget. From a social point of view, it must not be overlooked that after four decades under a dictatorial regime, the new democratic regime was expected to stimulate people's demand for public services and social benefits.

- The reduction of inequality in the distribution of income was another main objective of the tax reform. The old pieces of the Spanish direct taxation had not contributed to any noticeable degree of progressivity, since these taxes had proportional tax rates and tax evasion was unusually high among the top income groups. For improving income redistribution, it was necessary to introduce a substantial progressive tax, such as the personal income tax (IRPF). This tax was devised in accordance with the dominant trends in the OECD countries at that time: a comprehensive taxable income base that added almost all income sources, a progressive tax schedule with more than thirty tax brackets, numerous tax credits and allowances (for dependents, age, financial investments in public debt and stocks issued, home buying and so on).
- The IRPF, introduced in 1979, involved a withholding tax system applied to labour and financial investment incomes. For labour income, the withholding was calculated monthly as a percentage of gross wages from an annual wage scale that was adjusted based on the number of children and marital status. Whenever a taxpayer received interest or dividends, a fixed percentage of that income was withheld at source. However, capital gains and rents from property were not subject to withholding. For the self-employed a withholding fixed percentage was deducted on their professional revenues when these were paid by individual entrepreneurs, other professionals, corporations or other institutions. On the other hand if the income came from final consumers the withholding did not apply.
- In accordance with the first Law passed by Parliament initiating the tax reform – Law 50/1977 *de Medidas Urgentes de Reforma Fiscal* (Law of Urgent Measures on Tax Reform) – a personal net wealth tax was introduced in 1978 into the Spanish tax system for the first time in the history of the country. Really, this new tax did not aim at either increasing tax revenue collections or achieving important redistributive

effects. The main justification for this tax was to have information and control of all sources of income. At the time, there was a widely held belief that without this information on taxpayers' financial and real-estate assets, it would become practically impossible to apply the new personal income tax uniformly. Being conscious of the huge tax evasion there was in the pre-democratic Spain, the reform Government coupled the introduction of the wealth tax with a tax amnesty. Under this amnesty, all taxable incomes derived from any asset, or any rights or liabilities, filed in the personal net wealth tax return were exempt up to 31 December 1978. This measure aimed to motivate taxpayers to reveal hidden income sources. This was essential for a successful implementation of the new IRPF. Obviously, from that time on, if tax inspectors found out about any other undeclared source of income, it was to be regularised with the appropriate tax liability and penalties and interest on taxes not paid.[3]

The approval of the personal net wealth tax was complicated and had to be negotiated within the Moncloa Pacts signed in October 1977. In fact, when the Government proposed its inclusion, it led to significant social controversy, with an important protest movement coming from the right political parties and economic powers. The passing of this tax law in Parliament required the inclusion of the qualifying term "temporary" in the name used for the tax: *Impuesto Extraordinario sobre el Patrimonio Neto* (Extraordinary Personal Net Wealth Tax).[4]

Although the new personal and corporation income taxes came into force in 1979, the tax administration essentially remained the same until 1984. As pointed out above, all along, the discussion of the new tax system considered the reform of the tax administration as indispensable. However, the implementation of this plan was tackled in a gradual manner, as a reform that could not be hurried. Up to a point there was a general understanding that the approval of the new legal procedures itself would modernise the tax administration, but the actual changes in tax administration would come later on. Thus, we are indeed faced with a permanent feature of the successive Spanish tax administration reforms: the dissociation between the design of the organisational architecture and the administrative procedures that should govern the application of the different taxes. In fact, this strategy has not been exclusive to the tax administration, but rather it has been present in all the processes of reform of the Spanish public administration.[5]

In order to understand the intricacy of these tax changes, it is necessary to take into account some features of the Spanish tax administration in those days, which determined a particular model of tax relations both from the taxpayer point of view and that of the administration. In this respect, it is worth mentioning two:

(a) Firstly, the changes in the legal tax procedures were rather limited, concerning only those matters directly related to the new taxes. On this point, it must be highlighted that the new taxes, introduced in the 1977 Reform, had to be paid by means of a self-assessment principle. This contrasts with the previous schedular taxes which were levied through receipts prepared by the tax administration or using a simple at-source mechanism and in the absence of annual tax returns. The adoption of self-assessment brought about a complete revolution for the Spanish tax administration. At the time, the tax administration was faced with the need to process several millions of tax returns (8 million for 1979, the first year of the new IRPF, against the 1.5 million the year before, under the previous personal income tax).

    We must also take into account that the *Ley General Tributaria* (Spanish General Tax Law) in charge of governing all tax procedures (procedures on tax management, tax inspection, tax collection, taxpayers' complaints, and tax refunding) dates back to 1963. As an example, this law did not regulate explicitly the self-assessment procedure until 1991 even though it had become absolutely dominant since 1979 in the application of the tax laws. Actually, it was not until the more recent General Tax Law of 2003 that the principle of self-assessment became worthy of the legislators' appropriate attention.

(b) Secondly, the organisational structure of the central tax administration remained almost unchanged after the 1979 reform, with its two General Directorates, one for Tax Inspection, and the other one for Customs and Excise Taxes. The innovation was the *Dirección General de Tributos* (General Directorate for Taxes) with competence for designing tax regulations and establishing the criteria for their enforcement. These three General Directorates were accountable to the *Subsecretario* (Deputy Minister of Finance) and predominantly carried out a political role. But, it should also be noted that during this period, the Data Processing Centre started to receive attention within the organisation. This Centre would play a crucial role over the following years in the computerisation of the tax administration.

The first assessment of the application of the new taxes was done in 1983 when the Socialist party formed a new government after its electoral win in October 1982. The results obtained from the evaluation revealed a general popularity of the new taxes, but also the figures provided by the Ministry of Finance showed the existence of a substantial level of tax evasion. The average taxable income for businessmen and the self-employed was considerably lower than the mean of income declared by employees subject to withholding. Moreover, the worsening of the economic crisis, consequent to the second oil shock, contributed significantly to the slowdown in tax collections. The government could not remain indifferent to this situation. The fight against tax evasion began to grow in importance on the government's agenda. These circumstances led to the inevitable re-organisation of the tax administration, including the need to substantially increase the human resources and capital investment needed for developing powerful information systems.

Let us now focus on another important aspect of the tax administration in the early democratic period. This was the commitment to the modernisation of tax management in the broadest sense. The first step for achieving this objective was to design and implement a new tax management procedure. This was just called the *Nuevo Procedimiento de Gestión Tributaria*, commonly known inside the tax administration as NPGT. Two determining and related factors influenced this decision. On the one hand, the increased use of self-assessment for collecting the main levies of the new tax system. On the other hand, the above mentioned spectacular increase in the number of taxpayers.

The new taxes required not only one tax return form a year, but also a large number of quarterly tax returns for prepayment of income taxes, withholding tax payments, and any other periodic tax payments, such as the VAT payments. Generally, the use of self-assessment principles represents an abandonment of traditional administrative procedures on efficiency and effectiveness grounds, in favour of a more targeted approach to verify the information contained in millions of tax returns.

Since the taxpayers became responsible for calculating the tax liability, it was necessary to redefine the administrative control for all tax returns filled out by any natural person or legal entity. This new view of tax management brought about a new and urgent need on the side of the taxpayers. The tax administration had to provide them with the necessary information in order for them to comply with their tax obligations appropriately. This new role forced the tax administration to allocate a considerable sum of budget resources for creating tax information services and assistance to taxpayers in each tax office.

A key element for the development of the new tax management procedure was the establishment of a unique and permanent taxpayer's personal identification code (Tax Identification Number, *NIF*). From the moment *NIF* was introduced, it became compulsory to use it in all economic transactions with tax implications.

The computerised matching of all taxpayers' returns became a main requirement for proper enforcement of the tax laws. This was going to be the main organisational challenge to deal with in the implementation of the new income taxes and especially the Value Added Tax, following Spain's integration into the EEC as member State in 1986.

The computerisation process of the Spanish state tax administration tackled two main targets in its initial phase. The first one was to take a reliable census of taxpayers. This taxpayer roll had to provide on time accurate information about all the tax liabilities and any other official requirement derived from the management of the state tax system. The delimitation of this set of tax liabilities for each taxpayer or their substitute was made by means of the definition of a tax vector which incorporated all the data with regard to these obligations as a whole. The second target corresponded with the computer processing of all tasks related to recording and supervision of millions of tax returns, monthly, quarterly or yearly, received in each local tax office as a result of the general application of the tax self-assessment mechanism.

The huge volume of interrelations among the annual tax returns and tax payments on account carried out by businessmen, the self-employed, and the withholding by employers, required an efficient computerised system by the Data Processing Centre. Furthermore, most of the annual IRPF returns call for a refund for taxes overpaid, which should be done within the established time of about seven months from the time of tax filing.[6]

The computerisation process was carried out in an all-round way, including both the head offices and the over two hundred branch offices of the state tax administration in Spanish territory, except the Autonomous Communities of the Basque Country and Navarre. These enjoy a particular tax regime, the so-called *Foral* regime, which includes their own tax administration for all taxes collected in their territories.[7] All the computer systems were managed by a central unit - the Data Processing Centre (*CPD*). In addition, local computer units (*ULIs*), provincial units (*UPIs*), and regional computer units (*URIs*) were created, following the territorial organisation of the state tax administration. Its implementation involved a lot of budget resources, as well as a great deal of effort to train a large number of computer experts.

In the initial years, the non-existence of civil servant corps specialised in computing was a serious handicap. Nevertheless, this scarcity was alleviated in part by recruiting non-civil-servant public employees from the private sector, and also thanks to the meritorious effort of many public officials voluntarily involved in the modernisation of the tax administration. All things considered, it can be said that the data processing effort allowed management, with reasonable effectiveness, to process the enormous number of tax returns and tax requests caused by the taxpayers' voluntary compliance. However, the important volume of information accumulated in the system was, for a time, underused in the fight against tax evasion.

With regard to tax audit, its performance was an exclusive task for the tax inspectors who had to be officials belonging to the special corps of State Tax Inspectors. Starting 1980, the administration created a new corps, the State Tax Sub-Inspectors, which, in a few years, was to become the bulk group of tax specialists.

From the mid eighties, the central tax administration began to coordinate the tax inspection actions through the so-called "audit plans", whose main objective was to select efficiently the taxpayers to be audited during the year. The administrative reorganisation of the State Tax Inspection established three different levels to carry out the task of inspecting - one on a nationwide basis, through the National Inspection Office (head unit in charge of inspecting big business), a second one at the regional, and a third at the provincial level.

In addition, the central administration created two specific tax inspection units, one of them devoted to fight organised tax evasion, the *Unidad de Vigilancia y Represión del Fraude Fiscal*, and the other with exclusive competence in international tax matters. Broadly speaking, it can be said that the territorial decentralisation of the tax inspection was less profound than in tax management units. The provincial level of inspection was especially strengthened under economies of scale arguments (not completely confirmed.) Staffing of the new Local Tax Administrations was fundamentally filled by officials of intermediate level (sub-inspectors), who took charge of auditing small businessmen and the self-employed. The main change in the upper organisational structure was to establish a new superior level of decision-making, the *Secretario General de Hacienda* (Secretary General of Finance), who was under the *Subsecretario de Hacienda*. From that moment, all the General Directorates related to taxes had to report to the Secretary General of Finance.

In addition, the central administration created two new General Directorates for improving the implementation of the new taxes, the *Dirección General de Recaudación* (General Directorate for Tax Collection), and the *Dirección General de Gestión Tributaria* (General Directorate for Tax Management). The first directorate would take charge of controlling the tax payments collected in a voluntary way, mostly through financial institutions, as well as responsibility for unpaid tax liabilities. Until this time, this task had been assigned to private tax collectors. The second directorate would be in charge of organising relations with taxpayers deriving from the usual management of taxes, as well as providing taxpayers with information and assistance for preparing their tax returns. From an administrative point of view, the General

Directorate of Tax Management had to keep the taxpayers' census up-to-date and record and verify all the tax self-assessments received. This General Directorate was also in charge of designing all the tax forms to be used by the taxpayers.

In short, the Spanish tax administration's new structure consisted of one directorship, the Secretary General of Finance, who directed and coordinated the four operative General Directorates, namely General Directorate of Tax Inspection, General Directorate for Customs and Excise Taxes, General Directorate for Tax Collection, and the General Directorate for Tax Management. The Data Processing Centre, also hierarchically directly under the Secretary General of Finance, remained the main body responsible for tax data processing. All these General Directorates grew significantly in size in terms of their human resources.

As mentioned above, the territorial deconcentration was the most important change in the organisational reform of the tax administration. In accordance with the new Spanish territorial political organisation, seventeen *Delegaciones Especiales del Ministerio de Hacienda* (Regional Offices of the State Tax Administration) were created, one in each Autonomous Community. From that time, the old *Delegaciones Provinciales de Hacienda* (Provincial Offices of the State Tax Administration) went on to be answerable to these Regional Offices.[8] Nevertheless, the more important fact was the creation of the new Local Tax Offices, simply called *Administraciones de Hacienda*. This represented the establishment, across the country, of more than 200 Local Tax Offices, which sought to forge a closer relationship with the taxpayers. These Local Tax Offices were distributed across the cities and main towns of Spain, as well as in the districts of the big cities.[9] The implementation of the new territorial organisation was put into effect in two years.

The new figure of the Regional Office of the State Tax Administration meant a *de facto* deepening in the decentralisation of the different aspects of tax management and it was quite crucial for the operational effectiveness of Local Tax Offices. In the new territorial model, the Principal Tax Administrator in each Autonomous Community took on the task of organising all the available resources necessary for meeting management, inspection, and collection objectives allotted by the respective central General Directorate. This allowed the reorganisation of the tax administration resources, bringing them closer to the special features of each territory. Nevertheless, there still was inflexibility in human resources management caused by the standardised tradition of the Spanish public administration system. This affected such main features as training, personnel careers, and wage policy.

Between 1982 and 1987, the territorial reform of the state tax administration led to an increase in human resources, practically by a factor of two (from 11,600 to 22,500 employees). At this stage, two new corps of tax government officials were created. The first was the *Cuerpo Especial de Gestión de la Hacienda Pública* (Tax Managers Special Corps) that would later become the biggest, and carried out tax management, inspection and collection activities. The second, the Tax Agents corps, was charged with getting information *in situ* about taxpayers' economic activities and their assets. In the early years of the introduction of the VAT, the function of Tax Agents was crucial, feeding back information on a serious black economy outcrop. Moreover, in 1984, different higher corps of tax government officials (tax inspectors, comptrollers, and other public expenditure officials) who worked for the different Departments in the Ministry of Finance and for the *Dirección General de Presupuestos* (General Directorate of Budgets) were fused, creating a single higher corps of Inspectors of State Finances. However, officials from the previous Tax Inspectors Corps held nearly all the positions in the Tax Inspection units, thus restricting the entrance to members of other corps.

THE LIMITS OF THE FORMER ORGANISATION AND THE DRIVE TOWARDS AN AUTONOMOUS TAX ADMINISTRATION AGENCY (1988–1991)

As we reviewed in the previous section, the Spanish tax administration reforms, established between 1984 and 1987, represented an important transformation in the centralised model that prevailed until then. There is no doubt this change was fundamentally induced by the replacement of the old product tax system for a modern tax system, which included income taxes as a basic mainstay. In this respect, it can be said that the two principal elements that characterised the first phase of the reform were, on the one hand, the adaptation to the critical need to maintain relations with taxpayers, and on the other hand, the close-to-taxpayer policy promoted through territorial reorganisation.

However, in the late eighties, almost ten years after the new income taxes came into effect in 1979 and after four years of the VAT introduction, everyday reality still showed important weaknesses in the operation of the Spanish tax administration. Once the initial effort for computerisation was practically finished and reached an acceptable level of tax system management, some important limitations started to emerge, especially in two areas. On the one hand, the fight against tax evasion did not seem to be effective enough. Spanish society suspected the existence of high levels of tax evasion, something that already had begun to be corroborated in several studies. For example, the *Comisión para el Estudio y Prevención el Fraude Fiscal* (Commission for the Study and Prevention of Tax Evasion), instituted by the Spanish Parliament for evaluating the IRPF compliance, quantified the taxable income concealment for the year 1987 at 43.5 percent of all incomes earned and subject to this tax. Moreover, this Commission admitted that barely 60 percent of the people legally required to submit an IRPF return actually did.

The evolution of IRPF compliance assessed by this Commission during the period 1979–1987 is shown in Table 13.1. From these data, it can bc inferred that although taxpayers and taxable incomes showed a significant increase, it is safe to say that compliance was only acceptable in the slightest among employees (about 70 percent of real taxable incomes). But for all income sources, the concealment of taxable income was very worrying (about 45 percent of real taxable incomes).

Table 13.1 Spanish personal income tax compliance (1979–1986) (as a percentage of magnitudes recorded in all IRPF tax returns on equivalent Spanish macroeconomic data)

Year:	1979	1980	1981	1982	1983	1984	1985	1986
% of Potential Tax Returns	52.20	56.90	56.17	56.10	59.37	58.71	60.95	64.09
% of True Taxable Income	42.90	47.84	48.92	49.57	50.83	50.52	51.95	55.08
% of True Labour Taxable Income	54.00	62.07	63.42	64.76	66.63	66.66	68.88	71.28
% of True Non-Labour Taxable Income	22.34	24.34	24.56	25.20	23.41	24.60	26.15	30.36

Source: Report of Spanish Tax Evasion Commission (1990).

The appraisal of these results aimed in two directions. The first was the important weight that the black market economy had in those years. This was in part the result of the rapid and intense increase of tax burdens from

1979, although their levels still were below the average of OECD countries, but nevertheless a new experience for Spaniards. The second was the limitations in human and capital resources that made it practically impossible to improve tax compliance beyond the withholding of employees' incomes. Spanish society perceived clearly that most of the tax revenues were obtained from wage earners whereas the incomes from financial assets and especially those earned by businessmen and the self-employed enjoyed a much greater laxity of tax compliance. This situation contributed little to improving taxpayers' predisposition to comply with their tax obligations. In addition, the high level of complexity of the Spanish tax regulations made it easier to exploit loopholes for legal tax avoidance.

The fragmentation of the tax management system as a result of the reassignment at the regional level of all wealth taxation (specifically, the Inheritance and Gift Tax, the Net Wealth Tax, and the Net Wealth Transactions Tax) to the Autonomous Communities in the early 1980s brought about an important pitfall for the effectiveness of tax audit activities. The lack of tax information exchanges between the Social Security Administration and the state tax administration also hindered the fight against tax evasion and the black market economy.

From a macroeconomic perspective, and using the currency demand approach, Mauleón and Sardá (1997) estimated the size of Spain's underground economy from 1973 up to 1996 (see Table 13.2). The tax implications of these figures are not simple to assess but reveal the significance of the phenomenon, in harmony with the results reached by the Commission for the Study and Prevention of Tax Evasion.

Recently, Esteller (2005) analysed the determining factors of the IRPF compliance and its level during the period 1993 to 2000, using stochastic frontiers methodology. The paper finds that the average compliance was around 80 percent, although with important differences among provinces.[10] As regards the main relevant factors which explain this tax compliance level, the author points out: (a) the different productive structure in each province, which influences the Agencia Estatal de Administración Tributaria's control plan; (b) "electoral competence", "political cycle", and "budgetary policy"; and (c) Autonomous Communities' level of sharing in the IRPF.

From the point of view of the state tax administration's internal organisation both coordination among units and the starting incentives to foment team work were weakening. This was largely due to the greater mobility experienced by the Spanish public administration after the *Ley de Medidas de Reforma de la Función Pública* (Law of Reform of the Civil Service) introduced in 1984 caused a rapid rate of turnover in staff

Table 13.2 Estimates of Spain's underground economy (1973–1996) (as a percentage of GDP in the National Accounts)

Year	% of GDP	Year	% of GDP
1973	12.3	1985	15.7
1974	12.6	1986	15.5
1975	14.4	1987	15.7
1976	15.3	1988	15.7
1977	16.5	1989	15.9
1978	17.6	1990	16.2
1979	18.5	1991	16.7
1980	17.9	1992	18.0
1981	17.9	1993	18.4
1982	17.1	1994	17.8
1983	17.1	1995	16.4
1984	16.2	1996	16.3

Source: Mauleón and Sardá (1997).

positions.[11] Moreover, two factors influenced the lack of personnel stability over the late eighties. On the one hand, wage policy was too standardised in relation to the rest of the public administration departments which explains the large drain of highly qualified tax specialists to the private sector in those years. On the other hand, there was a lack of a design of careers with the tax administration in the proper sense of the word, which led to constant turnover amongst heterogeneous positions.[12]

In this setting, the professional association of State Tax Inspectors (a true corporate spirit union) lobbied for initiating a very important organisational reform of the state tax administration. They specifically demanded the creation of a self governing public body, which should assume all the functions involved in implementation of the state tax system. Other forces were present to give this idea greater credence and strength.

THE ESTABLISHMENT OF THE STATE TAX AGENCY AND ITS PERFORMANCE UNTIL 1996

The strong economic growth of the Spanish economy in the second half of the 1980s after Spain's admission to the EEC in 1986 brought to the surface many tensions in the tax system. These included the above mentioned perception by taxpayers of the rapid increase in individual tax burdens, and their unfair distribution among taxpayers, in particular the high level of tax compliance among wage earners vis-à-vis the rest. In parallel, the end of the 1980s also saw important operational problems emerging in the state tax administration, many of which had been accumulating after the 1977–1978 tax reform came into effect.

In addition, the late 1980s brought about a complete revolution for personal income taxes as a result of the Constitutional Court ruling, according to which compulsory joint returns for couples applied since 1979 were unconstitutional for horizontal equity reasons (the over-taxation of married taxpayers) and individual privacy. From that time, according to the Court's ruling, it was an inalienable right to be able to file individual IRPF returns for any married or single person. That irrevocable judicial decision, together with the obstinate refusal to include non-discriminatory joint taxation mechanisms (e.g. the income splitting or the familial quotient applied for many years in most developed countries), significantly swelled the number of IRPF returns filed with state tax administration starting in 1988.[13]

Nevertheless, the single most important fact that triggered off the creation of an autonomous body responsible for the management of the state tax system was the pressure from the tax inspectors union. The response to these demands was the modification of the legal status of the units that made up the state tax administration before then. From a legal point of view, the new organisation was going to adopt a legal status that should introduce more flexibility for managing budgetary and human resources.

The creation process of the *Agencia Estatal de Administración Tributaria* (hereafter, AEAT or simply State Tax Agency) formally started in the year 1991. The initial phase can be described as hasty and, in a way, disorderly. It is startling that, in spite of the importance of this organisational reform, the new State Tax Agency did not deserve a specific foundation Act since its legal incorporation was laid out in an Article of the Law 31/1990 of *Presupuestos Generales del Estado para 1991* (State General Budgets for the year 1991). Subsequently, both Law 18/1981 that reformed the IRPF after the Constitutional Court's ruling of 1989 and Law 31/1991 of State General Budgets for 1992 also incorporated some regulations. This legal regulatory dispersion revealed the short planning for such a significant organisational change.

From January 1992, the Spanish State Tax Agency has been responsible for implementing and enforcing the tax and customs systems. As we have seen above, the AEAT was established by the State General Budgets Law of 1991, even though the new organisation did not start its operations until 1992. We can say that at first the tax administration was mainly reformed in response to demands for higher wages for the executive tax personnel. In the Spanish general public administration, payments of all public employees were legally limited by general criteria compulsorily applicable to all employees, such as the civil servant's qualification group and the office held. Let's also remember that in the second half of the 1980s, as a result of the spectacular economic growth and of Spain's incorporation into the EEC, there was an important increase in private demand for skilled tax and finance experts with the consequent effect on the wages offered in the private sector.

From a legal point of view, an easy solution was to modify the organisation's legal status from the traditional departmental hierarchical structure toward an alternative legal organisational framework which allowed it to manage its budget with more flexibility. The chosen legal organisational form was a public entity with full legal capacity within the ambit of both public and private law.[14]

At the beginning, there were reasons to suggest that the organisational change was essentially more formal than it was real, in so far as the Ministry of Finance's priority was to achieve the maximum possible flexibility. In reality, different General Directorates, directly under the General Secretary of Finance, joined to form the new state institution with a specific legal status and with more flexibility in regulating the management of the system. A case could be made that more autonomy granted by the tax administration reform was initially more a response to the need for greater budget flexibility than a planned search for improving organisational efficiency. The fact is that during the early nineties, the organisation charts of the different new AEAT departments remained almost without changes in relation to the former General Directorates. Nevertheless, we should not forget that during the late 1980s, tax administration had been reorganised from the territorial perspective. In this regard, over two hundred local tax administration offices, created between 1984 and 1987, brought tax administration closer to citizens. Moreover, another element to take into account is that until 1994, none of the three main taxes (IRPF, Corporation Income Tax, and VAT) had been transferred or shared out with the Autonomous Communities.

Although we have emphasised the fact that it was the need to increase wages for tax experts that triggered the creation of the new Agency, there is consensus about the role played by the absence of an own human resources policy. Before the creation of the Agency, competence in this matter was fragmented among several General Directorates, some of them belonging to the Ministry of Finance, and others to the Ministry for Public Administration, and there was no professional career for tax specialists. From 1984, the Law for the Reform of the Spanish Civil Service authorised any civil servant to hold any position left vacant in any Department or Ministry, practically without restrictions for higher corps of tax inspectors and customs officers. This fact prompted an important rate of turnover of personnel, and today, twenty years after, this issue is still not resolved.

The law creating the AEAT established it as an administrative organisation responsible for the management of the state tax and customs systems, even though it would act on behalf of the state. In addition, the AEAT would also be in charge of collecting financial resources for other Public Administrations, domestic public institutions or for the European Communities, whose management could be entrusted by means of law or agreement.

According to the State Tax Agency's own regulation, the Agency should carry out all those management, inspection and collection activities which are necessary for an efficient and universal implementation of the State taxes. Although in a vague way, it also established the minimisation of tax compliance costs. Since public finance theory traditionally separates administrative costs and strictly compliance costs, it is reasonable to suppose that the legislator referred to all those costs which the tax administration incurs to collect tax liabilities, including hidden taxation costs incurred by taxpayers such as direct monetary costs, time consuming costs and psychological costs.[15]

From an organisational perspective, the AEAT was the result of joining, into a superstructure, the old General Directorates belonging to the General Secretary of Finance until 1991. In terms of designation, the General Directorates went on to be called Departments, even though their chief executives maintained the rank of General Director. However, this takeover process also involved staffing dimensional changes, since both the new Departments and the General Manager office assumed quite a lot of areas of competence which, before then, were under the General Secretary of Finance and of the *Secretario de Estado de Hacienda* (State Secretary of Finance).

The legal status allowed the State Tax Agency to set up some internal financial and budgetary control units inside the AEAT organisation chart. This task was allotted to the new Internal Auditing Service and the *Oficina*

Delegada de la Intervención General de la Administración del Estado (State General Comptroller Office) which is traditionally the agency in charge of financial control in the Spanish state public sector. The Internal Auditing Service took over the duties of the *Inspección de Servicios del Ministerio de Hacienda* (Ministry of Finance's General Inspectorate of Services) inside the AEAT. In addition to the public employees control, the AEAT's Inspectorate of Services took on management audit tasks including the procedural analysis, all this with the aim of detecting organisational dysfunction and inefficient performance, as well as suggesting measures for improving tax management. The success within this initiative can be judged as rather modest, considering the typical general limitations of the Spanish public administration in this matter.

In addition, the AEAT was provided with its own Legal Service department which took on the responsibility for the legal representation of the state tax administration in all courts of justice lawsuits brought up by taxpayers. This configuration allowed the state's legal defence team to concentrate its efforts on tax matters and to specialise. Until that point, state lawyers were always dispersed among the different legal services required by the entire public administration. It appears that this reorganisation of the state tax administration's legal services achieved greater administrative coordination.

As regards human resources management, these competences were assumed almost completely by the Human Resources and Economic Administration Department. The AEAT took over all responsibilities in both staff design and staffing decisions. Thereafter, the setting of wage scales and the qualifications for each post also became a competence of the AEAT. All these human resources management responsibilities were very important in a labour-intensive organisation. As previously mentioned, this area of competence constituted the biggest strength of the new organisational model.

All the employees of the State Tax Agency are subjected to the general regulations of the Spanish Civil Service. From the outset, selection of officials was based on traditional competitive examinations as in the rest of public administration departments, except for accessory or non permanent positions, for which private contracts for services are accepted. At the beginning, all those public bodies whose officials worked at the tax administration were redeployed to the new AEAT.

Recruitment of new employees continued to abide by the general rules of the Civil Service, in particular with an examination as a precondition. Nevertheless, the State Tax Agency has full capacity to announce separate entrance examinations of its own. With regard to career development inside the AEAT, the patterns are similar to those in the rest of the Spanish public administration, where job seniority remains the main criterion for promotion. The only exception is for executive positions, which generally are filled according to political confidence criteria. The existence of, considerably, above average wages in the AEAT relative to the rest of the public sector was effective in significantly reducing the high mobility of labour, which is still a common phenomenon in the whole of the Spanish public administration.

The new legal status of the AEAT put the procurement of supplies and investment in capital assets within the ambit of the Private Law which meant an important change with regard to the previous situation when the procurement was ruled by the *Ley de Contratos del Estado* (State Public Contracts Law). This new legal framework tried to make all contracting procedures more flexible so as to ease acquisitions and increase their efficiency.

For safeguarding the rule of Law and to coordinate the large number of state-funded purchases, all the powers were centralised in the AEAT's Sub-Directorate of Economic Administration, specifically in the Under-Department of Purchasing and Contracting. For achieving greater efficiency, simplified general procedures as well as purchase approval protocols were established. Similarly, the AEAT established periodical calls for supply tenders.

Since its creation, the AEAT was provided with its own budgetary financing system. According to the statute, the main financial sources of the State Tax Agency are transfers from the State General Budgets and the tax collections, shared yearly at a fixed percentage of all State taxes collected as a result of its actions[16]. Therefore, its funding has two basic components. One is of a budgetary nature (fixed); and other is variable, according to annual collections.

In addition, the AEAT can also get revenues from local and regional public administrations as a result of entering into agreements in regard to the collection of revenues assigned to those administrations. The returns on AEAT real estate are considered minor revenues in the statute. As for borrowing powers, this is only allowed for the case of an improbable liquidity gap.

On the side of expenditure budget, the State Tax Agency also enjoys a very different system vis-à-vis the majority of the Spanish public administration units. Every year, the AEAT draws up its preliminary budget plan which is then submitted to the Government for approval and finally sent to the Spanish Parliament. The expenses contained in this budget are limited in its overall amount, while the internal budget appropriation for different headings is only an estimate. Along with the autonomy as regards human resources management and contracting, this power to redeploy the expenses into the annual budget has contributed quite significantly to a flexible management approach in the state tax agency.

THE ROLE OF THE STATE TAX AGENCY AFTER THE AUTONOMOUS COMMUNITIES BEGAN SHARING THE MAIN CENTRAL TAXES (SINCE 1997)

When the State Tax Agency came into operation in 1992, none of the three large taxes (IRPF, Corporation Tax, and VAT) was shared with the Autonomous Communities. In the early 1980s, regional governments had been assigned a series of minor State levies (among others, the Personal Net Wealth Tax, the Inheritance and Gift Tax, the Tax on Property Transactions, and some betting and gambling duties) with limited revenue potential but with greater importance for the control of income sources. From that date on, the majority of the Autonomous Communities created their own tax administrations, which were initially staffed with personnel from the state tax administration.

The initial AEAT's regulation allowed for the possibility of having the State Tax Agency manage those reassigned taxes transferred to the Autonomous Communities, whenever the proper agreement had been reached with the respective regional government. This was mostly seen as a transitory situation as the Autonomous Communities developed their own tax offices. In view of the perspectives of a deep decentralisation, instruments of coordination and cooperation at regional and local levels were considered (though not specified) in the interest of efficient management of the Spanish tax system in its entirety.[17]

However, the tax decentralisation process soon began to surpass this overall view of the tax system. All the Autonomous Communities created their own tax administration departments which were put in charge of managing both the newly transferred state taxes and their own taxes, although the taxes included in "own taxes" were very few. We must note that the administration and enforcement of all shared state taxes (the IRPF since 1997, and subsequently the VAT and some excises since 2002) remains the exclusive jurisdiction of the AEAT.

The most recent reform of the Autonomous Communities financing system, in force since 2002, modified some aspects of the regulation of the management of the shared State taxes.[18] This reform also redefined the form in which the regional governments (except for the Basque Country and Navarre, which have their own full tax administration) participate in the AEAT's board of directors. On paper, it should be a change of a big magnitude, since the new model of Autonomous Communities' financing granted them a large share of revenues in the IRPF, VAT, and state excise taxes.

Specifically, from 2002, the Autonomous Communities share in the following state taxes (although as we see later, to different extents) : (a) the IRPF; (b) the Personal Net Wealth Tax; (c) the Inheritance and Gift Tax; (d) the Tax on Property Transactions; (e) the Betting and Gambling Duties; (f) the Value Added Tax; (g) the Beer Excise Tax; (h) the Wine and other Fermented Drinks Excise Tax; i) the Excise Tax on Intermediate Products; (j) the Excise Tax on Alcohol and Related Drinks; (k) Excise Tax on Hydrocarbons; (l) Excise Tax on Tobacco; (m) the Excise Tax on Electricity Consumption; (n) the Vehicles Registration Tax; and (o) the Petrol Retail Sales Tax. The Financing Law 21/2001 provides for the possible elimination or reform, by the Central Government, of any one of these state taxes, with the simultaneous abolition or modification of its shared component by the regional governments. The tax sharing is on the principle of "derivation" basis: that is, the Autonomous Community is entitled to the agreed percentage on the tax liabilities collected in its territory. For the territorial delimitation of taxable events, tax connection points have been established to avoid having several regional governments claiming the same tax bases.

Law 21/2001 provides for two types of transferred taxes with different implications as regards their management. For the first kind, the transfer only applies to a percentage of the tax liabilities collected from that tax in the respective territory by the AEAT, which is in charge of carrying out all activities of management, inspection and collection of these taxes. This alternative, generally known as revenue sharing in the literature and called "partial transfer of taxes or shared taxes" in Law 21/2001, applies to the IRPF (33 percent of total tax liabilities collected in the Autonomous territory), VAT (35 percent of VAT revenues linked to the personal consumption expenditure in the autonomous territory), and some Excise Taxes at a sharing rate of 40 percent of their respective revenues, except for the Tax on Electricity Consumption, which is shared at 100 percent.

The second model of transferred taxes involves the transfer of 100 percent of the tax bases and consequently of all its tax liabilities. These taxes are called, in the strict sense of the term, "transferred taxes", and currently include taxes originally transferred in the early eighties such as the Personal Net Wealth Tax, the Inheritance and Gift Tax, the Tax on Property Transactions, the Betting and Gaming Duties, besides the Vehicles Registration Tax, transferred in 2001. The last reform has created an optional tax, the Petrol Retail Sales Tax, whose yield goes to the Autonomous Community that decides to apply it.[19] For all taxes included in this second group, the Financing Law 21/2001 provides that each Autonomous Community, on behalf of Central Government, has to be in charge of carrying out all those activities necessary to manage, collect and inspect the taxes transferred. The management of these transferred taxes should be audited yearly by the *Inspección General de Servicios* (General Inspection of Services), General Directorate (in the Ministry of Finance), which must prepare a management audit report including efficiency and effectiveness aspects of their administration. Insofar as the Spanish Autonomous Communities enjoy a high level of self-government, these audits are rather a formal requirement with hardly any implications for improving the regional tax administrations.

As we have seen, the Autonomous Communities' financing model in force since the year 2002 extended considerably the sharing of state taxes, especially for the IRPF (shared since 1997), and the VAT (first shared in 2002). Moreover, this new model significantly extended the Autonomous Communities' tax regulation powers or competences with regard to some of the transferred state taxes - powers that, for the first time, appeared in the regional financing model for the period 1997–2001. Currently, regional governments can modify some specific elements of the tax structure. In this regard, the Autonomous Governments' competence for modifying the IRPF's marginal tax rates (although on condition that the tax schedule will be progressive and will have the same brackets as the state tax schedule) and the ability to introduce new personal tax credits stand out. However, the competence to modify the tax schedule has not been used by any of the fifteen regional governments involved, whereas the passing of the new tax credits by the regional parliaments has been quite prolific even though their cost in budgetary terms has been rather modest. Since the IRPF' management is performed by the AEAT free of charge, the Autonomous Communities which decide to introduce these own tax credits are responsible for establishing all the requirements and the documentation necessary to be able to verify them successfully.

With respect to the Personal Net Wealth Tax, parliaments of the Autonomous Communities can legislate on the personal minimum allowance, the marginal tax rates included in the tax schedule as well as on tax credits, but on condition that any change has to be compatible with the original state regulation for this tax. The special relation between the IRPF and the Personal Net Wealth Tax for audit and control purposes has led to multiple statements and calls for cooperation between the State Tax Agency and the regional tax administrations. Fulfilling these demands would require setting up bilateral agreements between the State Tax Agency and each regional tax administration. However, until now this coordination has only been achieved in some administrative matters, such as filing seasons and form design. Although the regional tax administrations are responsible for inspecting the taxable events of Personal Net Wealth Tax, the AEAT still maintains full competence for inspecting those taxpayers who are being audited with regards to the IRPF.[20]

The institutional collaboration between the AEAT and the regional tax administrations for exchange of information concerning the administration and enforcement of the Personal Net Wealth Tax is laid down in the law. Nevertheless, the experience so far shows that the joint planning of tax audit activities can be much more effective than the written law.

For the case of the Inheritance and Gift Tax, the Autonomous Communities have discretion to change allowances and exemptions, the tax rate schedule and tax surcharges, as well as the tax credits. Because in the case of this tax it is the Civil Law Code that defines the taxable events, its administration is more complicated than for other taxes. As such, the implementation of the self-assessment by the regional tax administrations is conditional on availability of assistance units that should give advice to taxpayers for filling their tax returns. In any case, it is not a real self-assessment system, in so far as all taxable events are checked at least in their main elements and data declared in the tax returns.

With regard to the Tax on Property Transactions, the regional governments can modify the rates of this tax, and also introduce new tax credits or change existing ones. For the Vehicles Registration Tax, the regulation competence of regional governments only affects the tax rate-fixing. For the Betting and Gambling Duties, this legislative competence is wider, including the regulation of permissions, auditing, and other administrative requirements to be fulfilled by the taxpayers (the organisers). In any case, it should be emphasised that the fact that regional regulation competence powers are not exercised does not mean taxpayers are truly exempt; central government regulation cannot be repealed by the regions. The only exception is for the new Petrol Retail Sales Tax because in this case the central government regulation provided for the possibility of zero tax rates for all taxable categories, which is tantamount to its optional application.

For this group of "fully transferred" taxes, there is also full devolution of tax administration competences, including all the necessary actions to effectively enforce these taxes. In addition to tax management and collections, this also entails taking on the audit function which includes the qualification of tax offences and the imposition of tax penalties, as well as the ruling on appeals lodged against these tax actions. Nevertheless, all these devolved tax activities are under the General Tax Law which regulates all the tax procedures. Moreover, with regard to audit, the Autonomous Communities have to prepare their action plans jointly with the *AEAT*. Each year, they are also obliged to report to the Ministry of Finance and to the Spanish Congress and Senate. In addition, there is a reciprocal obligation to exchange information between the AEAT and each regional tax administration, even though its performance is not operative.

In view of the high degree of decentralisation of the Spanish tax system, the coordination, both vertical (between the AEAT and each regional tax administration) and horizontal (between regional administrations), represents an aspiration which can never be given up if the main aim of the central and regional governments is to fight tax evasion and increase voluntary tax compliance. However, this aim is unlikely to be achieved without a minimum level of efficient coordination among all tax administrations in charge of managing the tax system as a whole. Up to now there is no record of major advances in cooperation between the two levels of tax administration; at the least the experience in previous years does not suggest any significant improvement of the situation.

The last revision of the Autonomous Communities' financing system in 2001 listed a series of basic principles which should be fulfilled to realise this necessary wide institutional coordination. The Financing Law 21/2001 lays down the following coordination requirements: (a) need to realise mutual exchange of information, without exclusion, and at the instance of any tax administration; (b) need to prepare coordinated plans of tax audit for all the transferred taxes, paying particular attention to those taxpayers who change their fiscal residence; and (c) need to reach agreements of cooperation and mutual tax assistance targeted at improving application of some transferred taxes. Moreover, the 2001 Financing Law provides for the possibility of reaching collaboration agreements by which the Autonomous governments may contribute financial and human resources to the State management of the IRPF, Personal Net Wealth Tax, VAT, and the Vehicles Registration Tax. However, all the indications are that it will be difficult to advance institutional coordination this way. The 2001 Financing Law also indicates that the Autonomous Communities can take their taxpayers to court over offences regarding the fully transferred taxes. However, in these cases a mutual information procedure must be followed.

The substantial increase in revenue sharing by regional governments in some of the main state taxes solely managed by the State Tax Agency has brought to the surface increasing demands by the Autonomous Communities to be able to get more involved in the AEAT's management board. In 1994, after the newly agreed first tax-sharing of 15 percent of the IRPF territorial collection, the regional government of Catalonia made a proposal to create a sole tax administration for each Autonomous Community which should have full powers to manage all taxes levied in its territory.[21] After the general election on March 1996, the new Popular Party government needed the support from the *Convergencia i Unió* Party in Parliament, which had been governing in Catalonia since the advent of democracy in 1979. This influenced the appointment of some top executives close to this Catalonian Party to the AEAT board of directors. These appointments happened at the same time as an extensive reform of its organisation chart whose foremost element was the creation of a new *Departamento de Organización, Planificación y Relaciones Institucionales* (Department of Organisation, Planning and Institutional Relations), which was put in charge of relations with the regional tax administrations. But with time it became evident that during 1997–2001 this greater regional involvement experience was not as effective as had been expected, rather it was inoperative.

After a complicated bilateral negotiation process, the passing of the Autonomous Communities Financing Law meant for the first time, regional representation on the AEAT's board of directors. Firstly, Law 21/2001 created the *Consejo Superior de Dirección* (Higher Board of Directors) in which six Autonomous Communities representatives are full members, and one of them holds the position of second Deputy President. The State Secretary of Finance (second in command at the Ministry of Finance) is the *ex officio* President of the Higher Board of Directors, with other members including the General Director of the AEAT (who holds the post of First Deputy President) and other top executives of the AEAT's staff (the heads of Department). The six Autonomous Communities representatives are yearly designated by the *Consejo de Política Fiscal y Financiera* (Council of Fiscal and Financial Policies), which is the highest body for tax and fiscal affairs in the relations between Central Government and Regional Governments.

The powers conferred on the Higher Board of Directors are the following: (a) informing the Annual Objectives Plan before its endorsement; this Plan includes the AEAT Regional General Plan resulting from the aggregation of the individual Plans for every Autonomous Community, as well as the guidelines for the AEAT Tax Audit Plan; (b) assessing annually the results of the Annual Objectives Plan for the previous year, in addition to its periodic follow-up; (c) suggesting the strategic action outlines for the Joint Commission on Tax Management Coordination and for the Tax Management Territorial Steering Committees; (d) advising the President of the AEAT as regards the coordination and cooperation among the Ministry of Finance bodies and the tax administrations of the regional and local governments, as well as for the management of the state tax system in a broad sense.

In this new organisational framework, the bodies in charge of the intergovernmental tax relations are the Joint Commission on Tax

Management Coordination and the Tax Management Territorial Steering Committees. The first takes decisions as voted on by its members' body, where the Central Government has as many votes as the regional governments. However, the approval of guidelines and plans of action related to the management and regulation of the fully transferred and shared taxes have to be supported by a majority vote of the interested Autonomous Communities. The Joint Commission on Tax Management Coordination is presided over by the State Secretary of Finance in his/her capacity as President of the State Tax Agency, and it is made up of the General Director of the AEAT who acts as Deputy President of the Joint Commission, seven AEAT representatives, one representative of the Ministry of Finance's General Inspection of Services, two other representatives of the State Secretary of Finance, and one representative for every Autonomous Community.[22] For carrying out their different duties, the Joint Commission can work in plenary sessions, at least once every six months, or in permanent or temporary working groups, which always have to be composed in a "peer manner" (equal number of votes for the State and the Autonomous Communities). The plenary sessions can be unilaterally convened by the President or when at least three Autonomous Communities ask for it. As a means of permanent communication between all tax administrations, the Financing Law of 2001 has created a Permanent Technical Secretary within the Joint Commission whose top official must belong to the AEAT.

Amongst the functions allotted to the Joint Commission on Tax Management Coordination, Law 21/2001 lists the following: (a) conducting studies to improve tax design and management of transferred state taxes; (b) the assessment of all legal reforms which aim to modify the regulation of transferred or shared taxes; (c) drawing up the political general guidelines of tax management for shared taxes managed by the AEAT; (d) establishing the action criteria as regards tax management coordination and exchange of information between the Autonomous Communities and the AEAT; (e) coordinating the tax assessment criteria; (f) preparing the reports asked for by the Council of Fiscal and Financial Policies, the Ministry of Finance, or the regional finance authorities; (g) evaluating the transferred taxes management outcomes, as well as the performance of the Tax Management Territorial Steering Committees; (h) informing the Arbitration Committee for Tax Conflict Resolution on cases related to transferred state taxes; (i) taking part in the design of inspection plans for shared taxes managed by the AEAT and in the establishment of guidelines to carry out coordinated actions; (j) assessing the AEAT's General Direction annual report on the shared taxes managed by the State Tax Agency; (k) proposing the implementation of the specific systems for telematic exchange of information between the AEAT and the regional tax administrations; (l) promoting tax management activities by means of coordination between two or more tax administrations.

The Tax Management Territorial Steering Committees were created within the organisation chart of the AEAT Provincial Offices, with their main task being to undertake many of the functions entrusted to the Joint Commission. To this end, its norm of creation takes into account the following activities: (a) adopting arrangements and agreements as regards exchange of information between State Tax Agency and the regional tax administrations; (b) carrying out coordination and collaboration tasks of tax management; (c) the design and the planning of the coordinated actions included in the inspection plans; (d) deciding on entrusting tax management proposals; (e) running the AEAT's management for the shared taxes, in accordance with Joint Commission guidelines; (f) assessing the outcomes from the AEAT management for the shared taxes; (g) evaluating and suggesting measures for improving the management of the shared taxes; (h) carrying out specific inspection plans with regard to the shared taxes managed by the AEAT.

There are fifteen Territorial Steering Committees, one in every Autonomous Community subject to the common regime. Each one of them is made of seven members: four representatives of the AEAT including the Special Delegate in the respective Autonomous Community, and three representatives of the corresponding regional tax administration. At least each Committee must hold a quarterly meeting and at the request of either of the two parties. In these meetings, the decisions must be taken by majority although for some matters related to the AEAT's management of the shared state taxes the decisions must be reached by mutual agreement. Amongst others, this consensus is required for the following issues: (a) the supply of information for its incorporation into the annual Inspection Plan; (b) the incorporation, by one regional tax administration, of own specific inspection programmes into the National Inspection Plan; (c) the territorial adaptation of the advertising campaign on information and assistance to taxpayers, as well as to agree on tax application criteria in each territory.

In view of this prolific regulation on tax administration coordination and cooperation, we can say that the strong fragmentation experienced by both the tax system and tax administration in its entirety has been identified as a crucial problem. The process of deep political decentralisation that took place in Spain in the last two decades encouraged the creation of regional tax administrations, which saw the light of day at the same time the state tax administration began its modernisation process. The instability of the regional financing system has confronted regional tax administrations with continued challenges. Moreover, the complex political circumstances of these devolution processes have not facilitated the organisational redesign of the Spanish tax administration, in accordance with the need for correcting the vertical and horizontal externalities that are inherent to a fragmented tax system like this.[23]

The AEAT Reports for the years 2002 and 2003 (AEAT, 2002 and 2003) include an inventory of the actions taken by these Territorial Steering Committees since their creation by Law 21/2001. Although the information provided by the reports is strictly descriptive, the volume of actions registered seems to show a considerable activity which can be appreciated positively, at least in terms of communication among tax administrations. Nevertheless, in this regard, we should point out that this is the view publicised by the State Tax Agency, in other words, by the Central Government, which should be qualified in so far as the majority of these actions are carried out by the AEAT for managing, inspecting, and collecting transferred taxes with the greatest revenue-raising power.

Only a short time elapsed since the current Financing Law 21/2001 incorporated these new organisational instruments of Autonomous Communities' involvement in the AEAT board of strategic and operative management. This does not allow an adequate assessment of their performance. However, as has been said above, we are not optimistic about this organisational structure, at least in the short run, in relation to the efficiency improvement of the tax administration as a whole. Conspicuous is the absence of the necessary incentive mechanisms to promote the coordination actions laid out in the legal framework. This fact is particularly worrying in regard to the bilateral exchange of information. As the economics of organisation suggests, the role of incentives is essential to achieve an efficient coordination between independent organisations, since without them, fulfilling any agreement or commitment of collaboration will be a simple goodwill gesture, although possibly worthwhile for the political strategy of the central government.

THE TAX REFORM OF 1998 AND THE CONSOLIDATION OF A NEW "CLOSE-TO-THE TAXPAYER" MODEL

The creation of the AEAT implied a clear redefinition of the Spanish Government's priorities in relation to the state tax system management. Although it is true that the usual tax evasion-fighting campaigns made a deep impression among the citizens, the main commitment in the long term continued to be improving the assistance and advice to taxpayers with the aim of reducing both administrative and compliance costs. Within this ambit, it can be said that the achievements have been meritorious, even though it is certain that they should also be valued jointly with the tax reforms of these years, which contributed considerably to simplifying the Spanish tax system.

In 1992, an ambitious computerisation plan for the Information and Assistance-to-Taxpayers Services was set in motion, creating units for assistance in filing the IRPF, firstly in the most important provincial AEAT offices, and not long afterwards in the rest of provincial and local tax offices. Likewise, this process led to the creation of Taxpayer's Offices in the provincial AEAT central offices whose function was to give assistance and all-round advice to citizens in all their relations with the State Tax Agency (filing of tax returns, tax certificates, tax refund requests, appeals to the state tax administration, etc.). As Díaz-Yubero (1993) indicates, these Taxpayer's Offices also represented an important information source for the heads of AEAT's departments insofar as they could detect all those points of inefficiency and underperformance in the application of the tax procedures.

An electronic documentary database (called *INFORMA*) was also created for access to frequently asked questions (FAQ) in relation to the main state taxes (IRPF, Corporation Income Tax and Value Added Tax), whose contents have been constantly updated by the central services. *INFORMA* provides tax information based on internal rulings (AEAT and the *Dirección General de Tributos* --General Directorate of Taxes), as well as on administrative rulings on tax appeals and court rulings. The users of this electronic database were mainly taxpayers, but also tax officers used it. Later, the evolution of the system and its online access through the Web have become a useful help-to-taxpayer instrument, and especially essential for IRPF taxpayers.

From the beginning, the State Tax Agency promoted the creation of software for do-it-yourself tax returns. The programme for filling the IRPF tax returns (the *PADRE* programme) has been very widely used for many years. The programme for filing the Corporation Tax has been also widely used, although this was introduced not long ago. The successful implementation of the user-friendly software has made it possible to generalise its utilisation with some very important positive effects on tax administration and compliance costs. On the one hand, all these programmes set up filters and controls that permit detection of the frequently inadvertent or intentional errors which are a common occurrence in a self-assessed tax system. In the *PADRE* case, the design of programme allows the use of information provided by the taxpayers themselves (date of birth, marital status, family kinship, age of relatives, transaction dates, etc.)

to check up on limits or amount of exemptions, deductions, tax credits, or the tax schedule applicable.

To some extent, there is a broad consensus that the greatest achievement of the AEAT since its creation may have been the implementation of an effective assistance-to-taxpayer model which has been implemented in a gradual way. Nevertheless, we need to be aware that there is an important interrelation between this success and the simplification and the quality improvements introduced in the regulation of both taxes and tax procedures by the successive reforms implemented in recent years. In this respect, we must bear in mind what the IRPF reform of 1998, in force from January 1999, involved. The IRPF Law 40/1998 shaped a new model of personal income tax aimed at increasing the elasticity of revenue collections and making it compatible with a significant tax cut aimed at reducing individual tax burdens.[24] Setting aside its political opportunism, there was general agreement on the fact that the IRPF reform of 1998 was certainly unavoidable, since we are indeed faced with a tax which revealed clear symptoms of too much and too frequent change (González–Páramo, 1997).

But over and above that, the Government opted for the simplification of the IRPF, both on its tax structure and relating to its legal regulation. Although the Spanish IRPF came into effect way back in 1979, the legal framework for its enforcement had become more and more complex, which increased both taxpayers' compliance costs and tax avoidance opportunities. Undoubtedly, the huge number of tax matters in litigation, both in the administrative and judicial ambit, originated in the "too ambiguous" regulations. In order to achieve these simplification objectives, the alternative offered by the Government was to combine both the regulatory and the public finance-designing measures of reform. Thus, the new IRPF embodied important changes of structure which broke with previous patterns, such as: (a) the consideration of the personal and family circumstances of the taxpayer through a set of tax allowances, the so-called "personal and family minimum", which replace the previous family tax credits; (b) the reduction of the number of brackets in the tax schedule, including the abolition of the first zero-rate bracket; (c) the disappearance of the special schedule for joint taxation, returning to a system of a single schedule for both individuals and joint declarations; (d) a general reduction of marginal tax rates; and e) capital gains obtained for a time period longer than a year (it was two years up to the year 2000) to be taxed with a proportional tax rate of 18 percent (currently fixed at 15 percent), equal to the lowest marginal tax rate of the progressive schedule.

But, in spite of the initial intentions, the simplification of the legal regulation has been almost imperceptible. The legal process of drafting the bill ruined this aim, which incorporated the traditional casuistry of the previous tax coding again. The regulation on capital incomes or on tax gains in the current IRPF Law or the vast case law established by the General Directorate of Taxes are two good examples of this failure.

As for the AEAT, it attempted new plans in the field of the information technology, whose main objectives were: (a) providing the possibility of filling the tax returns online through the Internet; (b) providing taxpayers with all tax information gathered by the AEAT every year (such as their annual income, withholdings and other deductions for tax purposes) which is necessary to process IRPF annual returns; (c) making IRPF return drafts and sending them to taxpayers, who can sign and file the drafts if they agree. Those challenges could be taken on, thanks to the tax structure simplification introduced by the new IRPF Law since it allowed a reduction in the amount of information needed, and consequently the number of operations to conduct.

From a tax compliance point of view, providing taxpayers with all tax information in the possession of the AEAT can be risky. Taxpayers can be tempted to not include those incomes misreported by withholders which are unknown to the tax administration. This problem will only be diminished if taxpayers are also included in the audit tax plans with a positive probability of being audited. Although it involves an increase in administrative costs in the short term, it will be an efficient solution in the long term.

Moreover, the IRPF reform brought with it a redefinition of the labour income tax withholding system. In the current system, each employer, whether he is a natural person or legal entity, must calculate the average tax rate for each employed worker at the start of the year. The calculation should consider his/her expected gross salary throughout the year, the IRPF-deductible social security payments, as well as those personal and family circumstances considered in the tax allowances. Thus, the withholding rate is applied to all incomes paid by this employer during the year, and will have to be modified if the labour conditions (salary, contract of employment extension or cancellation) or the family circumstances (number of children, marital status) change.

This new withholding tax method for labour incomes has greatly reduced AEAT tax refunds since the difference between the definitive tax liabilities in the annual IRPF returns and the withheld tax amount has been reduced considerably.[25] In addition to this simplification of the withholding tax system, the tax-filing threshold was significantly increased. So, all taxpayers who earn labour incomes below 21,000 euros are not bound to submit an IRPF annual return.[26] The result was a significant reduction in the number of tax returns filed yearly. For those numerous cases in which a tax rebate is due, the AEAT implemented a new system of quick tax rebate. The system involves an application form to be submitted two months before the IRPF annual filling period, beginning the first day of May. For reducing the number of tax refunds, where appropriate, husband and wife can opt to offset between them their positive and negative tax return balances for three years.

The Spanish Ministry of Finance announced in June 2003 that 1.7 million tax returns attributed to the IRPF tax campaign of 2003 had been transmitted to the tax administration through the Internet. This number represented an increase of 50 percent relative to the previous year.[27]

The effects of this IRPF reform on tax compliance relative to the previous design have been investigated in Delgado, Salinas and Sanz (2001). Their conclusions show a favourable assessment, although in a modest way. The reform implied a 28 percent decrease in the indirect burden on the IRPF taxpayers.[28] With regard to monetary costs incurred by taxpayers in order to comply with their tax obligations, costs dropped from 1.8 percent of the tax bill in 1998 to 1.3 percent in 1999. The average time devoted by taxpayers to completing their tax returns has decreased by 1 hour and 25 minutes.[29] In addition, those tax compliance costs of a psychological nature would seem to have been also reduced as the result of a lower degree of uncertainty in relation to the enforcement of the new IRPF Law. Most assuredly, the general availability of the *PADRE* assistance-to-taxpayers programme has influenced this change in the perception of taxpayers.

In this respect, we can say that one of the most important advances in the Spanish tax administration in the last decade is the advent of free software to assist individual and professional taxpayers in computing their tax returns and other tax documents. It is reasonable to assume that this innovation has meant important decreases in compliance costs, fundamentally due to the positive reduction of the taxpayers' material errors in the returns and the less time taken to fill out tax forms. However, this may have had a negative influence on the desirable reduction of tax complexity. Generally, tax software has obviated the desirability of tax simplification, with negative consequences for a group of the tax population - those who do not use tax software. In actual fact, if we observe the tax regulations for the new *IRPF* related to the taxable income from financial assets or from capital gains, we would be hard pressed to admit that there has been any simplification at all. Furthermore, the large number of cases in tax dispute sours, in certain respects, the positive results obtained with regard to the tax administration costs.

In addition to the abovementioned changes introduced by the IRPF reform of 1998, the growing sensitivity to the need to improve taxpayers' legal security led to Law 1/1998 on *Derechos y Garantías del Contribuyente* (Taxpayer's Rights and Guarantees Law). This Law stated the citizen's rights which must be respected in all their relations with the tax administration. To protect these rights, Law 1/1998 created the *Defensor del Contribuyente* (Taxpayer's Counsel), charged with protecting the rights of citizens. The role of the Taxpayer's Counsel is independent of the administrative and judicial legal system and can lodge an appeal against any level of tax administration.

REALLY AN AUTONOMOUS TAX AGENCY? SUCCESSES AND FAILURES OF THIS ORGANISATION MODEL

All the reviewed organisational changes related to Autonomous Communities' involvement in the AEAT board have been introduced at a political decision level, although the chairman maintains his pre-eminent position on the strategic direction of the State Tax Agency (see Figure 13.1).

In fact, the organisational architecture of the AEAT has remained practically unchanged. From an operational point of view, the State Tax Agency is divided into central and territorial services, both directed by its general manager (the *Director General* of the AEAT). The AEAT central services are organised into functional and support areas – tax management, tax inspection, collection, customs and excises, organisation and planning and institutional relations, information technology, and human resources and economic administration. The territorial services follow the same scheme by areas, but on a territory-by-territory basis (see Figure 13.2). Currently, there are 17 Regional State Tax Offices (one in each Autonomous Community) and 56 Provincial State Offices, containing 240 Local State Tax Offices, 37 of which are Customs Offices.

From the viewpoint of organisation theory, the type of relations between the chairman of the AEAT and its general manager does not allow us to identify the AEAT organisational model with the notion of agency usually considered in the literature on public administration in Anglo-Saxon and Nordic countries.[30] Since its creation in 1991, the appointments of all AEAT general managers show a total political dependence on the State Secretary of Finance, and therefore, on the Minister of Finance. Perhaps what is surprising is that this dependence figures explicitly in the legal organisation chart where it states that the State Secretary of Finance will be the AEAT chairman. Regarding the appointment of their consecutive general managers, every one of them belonged to the body of tax inspectors, the most influential civil servant group of the finance administration and, probably, of the whole Spanish public administration. It

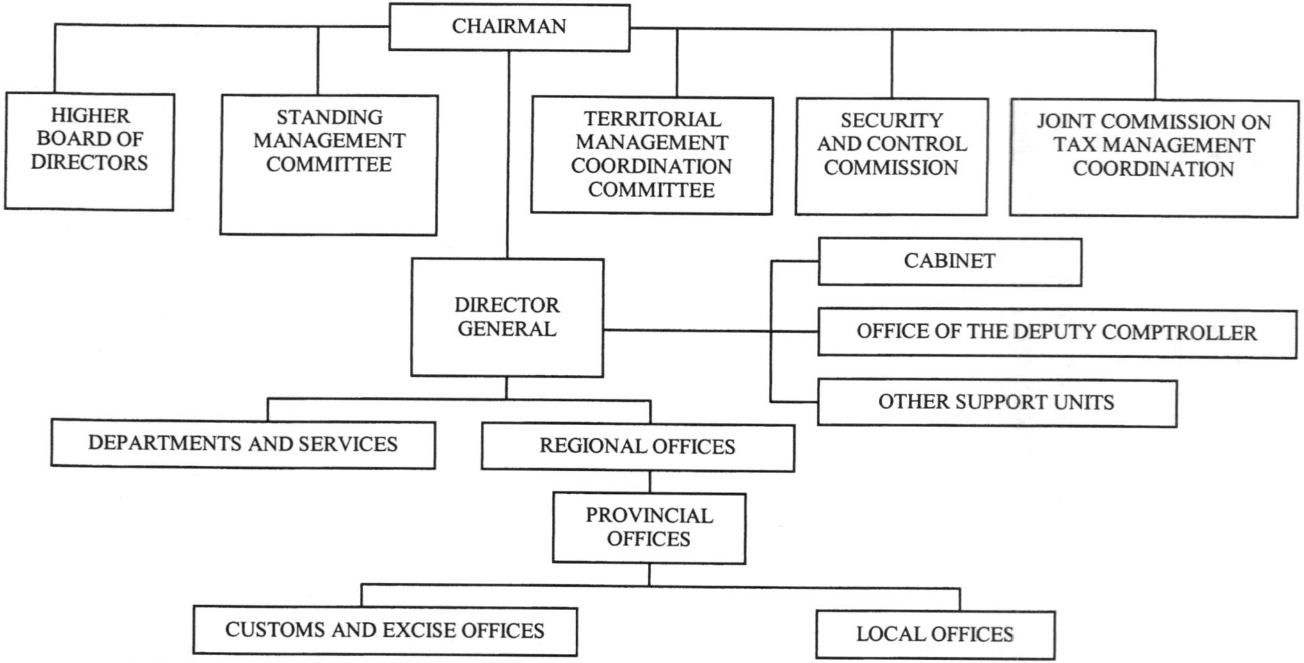

Figure 13.1 Structure of the State Tax Agency (AEAT)

Source: AEAT (2003).

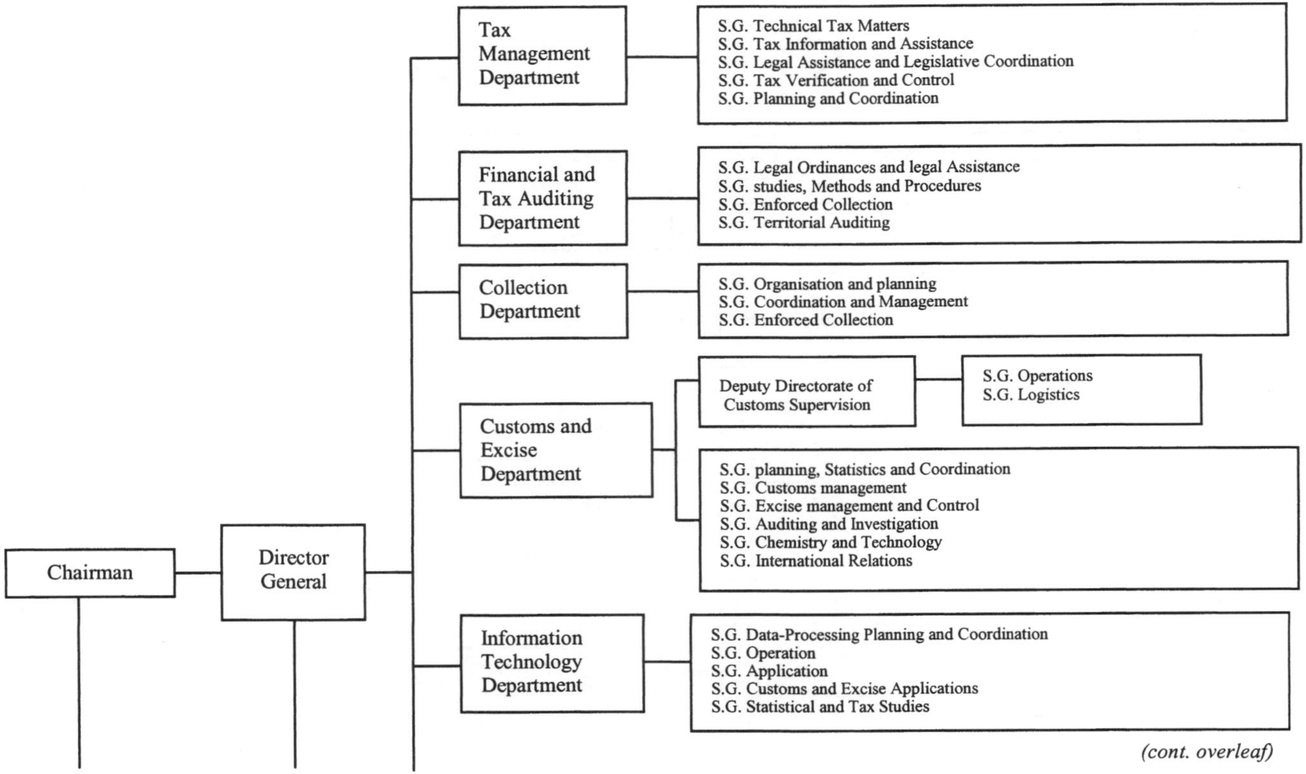

(cont. overleaf)

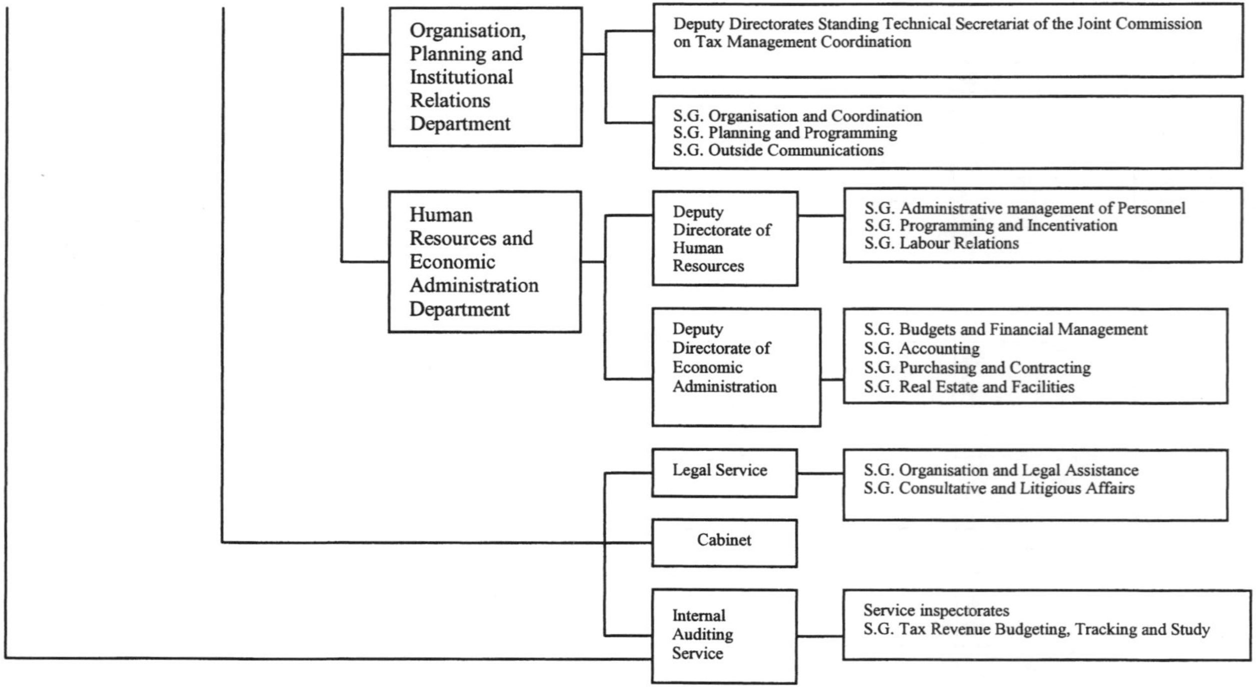

Figure 13.2 Organisation of the Regional Tax Offices

Source: AEAT (2003).

should be pointed out, however, that in spite of this professionalisation of all its members, the aforesaid dependency on political decisions, together with the lack of competition for the post, cause frequent labour disputes and corporative tensions between the board of managers and the inspectors and sub-inspectors who make up its technical staff. This pattern also holds for the regional tax administrations, although within their ambit, the use of the term "agency" has not been that common. Precisely, it is now, with new devolution demands from some historical regions, such as Catalonia or Andalusia, that there is talk about "regional tax agencies", but only with a political motive.

Perhaps the best way to characterise the AEAT is as a semiautonomous model of agency rather than an agency model in the original Anglo-Saxon sense of the term. As we have seen above, the organisational autonomy resides in its wide competences on budgeting, human resources management, and contracting, compared with the regime for most other public agencies. The mentioned dependence on political power has influenced the AEAT performance all along, especially concerning decisions on its priorities, such as the fight against tax evasion. In this respect, internal controversy between the board of managers and the technical staff has been common.

CONCLUSIONS AND FINAL REMARKS

In this chapter, we have reviewed the evolution experienced by the Spanish tax administration from the outset of the democratic transition, way back in 1977, to the present day. Since I think that a long paper should not be overburdened with a very long conclusion, my objective here is simply to emphasise the most relevant points to understand the current situation of tax administration in Spain, and above all, to present the challenges over the next years. In a simple way the current situation of the Spanish tax administration is characterised by the following facts:

- The assistance to taxpayers in the broad sense can be considered the main success achieved by the tax administration, both at state and at regional levels of government. The extensive availability of specific software to fill out tax returns and the implementation of e-tax services has contributed to a significant reduction in tax compliance costs incurred by the taxpayers.
- The excessive casuistry of the Spanish tax laws, together with the broad interpretative ability showed by the administrative tax bodies and by the courts, explains the high levels of litigation existing in

Spain. There is consensus that, in relation to the administration costs, the system has not made as much progress as we would have liked, being largely due to this tax litigation. As it may be presumed, the uncertainty costs related to this situation are considerable.

- Although there is no solvent analysis on the productive efficiency of the tax administration, state or regional, there is a general perception that potential improvements in the human resources productivity are clearly possible. The frequent labour troubles and the corporative tensions between the board of managers and the inspectors and sub-inspectors can help to explain this situation. The use of inadequate schemes of personal incentives, not very compatible with the institutional objectives, and the great mobility of labour also seem to be determining factors of this organisational inefficiency.
- The high level of tax evasion which is very concentrated among the self-employed, freelancers, and small businessmen, as well as in the VAT implementation, is encouraged by the fragmented management of the main state taxes. The relationships between the State Tax Agency and the regional tax administrations in regard to coordination, collaboration, and exchange of information are clearly deficient. The usual political attitudes tending towards maximising territorial tax collections, without taking into account the obvious vertical and horizontal externalities, explain the unsatisfactory situation currently present in Spain. The tax proposals in the last regional elections proposed to reduce or even to abolish some taxes such as the Inheritance and Gift Tax or the Personal Net Wealth Tax. Such proposals do not provide good prospects for improved control of income sources, essential for an efficient application of income taxes.

The current tax decentralisation challenges that Spain faces make it necessary to adopt some reforms as soon as possible. In my opinion, main steps should be taken towards three specific objectives:

- The first one is of an organisational nature: the separation between political and technical responsibilities inside the State Tax Agency. As we have said, this requirement is essential for the incentive schemes to operate correctly. This political independence requires a complex institutional arrangement, where the political parties must renounce the use of the tax administration policy as an instrument to win votes. In this respect, experiences of the Anglo-Saxon and Nordic countries could be very appealing.
- The second one is to achieve an effective integration of regional political decision powers in the AEAT board of directors. If we agree

that there are mutual externalities from central and regional tax administration activities, it is essential to take advantage of collaboration between both levels of government, especially in coordination and exchange of information issues. It is also an organisational question which should not be confused with a simple organisation chart change. It must not be forgotten that behind this efficiency problem, there is an incentive issue. Organisational design should provide an institutional incentive scheme capable of motivating national and regional decision-makers to reveal all their relevant information about tax evasion, inspection and other control plans.

- The third one is essentially a proposal of juridical technique. As we have seen, the Spanish tax codes raise a number of conflicting interpretations. This very negative fact stems from excessively ambiguous tax laws. On numerous occasions, this ambiguity in the law application is a consequence of schemes which distinguish particular cases, circumstances and conditions that are hard to prove. This has led to high administration and compliance costs, as well as to economic uncertainty which encourages tax avoidance. Therefore, future tax reforms should include legal simplification as one of its main aims.

NOTES

* Universidad Complutense de Madrid

1. In addition to the offices in the provincial capitals, five other important non-provincial capital cities had their own tax office.
2. See Sevilla (1979) for a discussion of the original temporary plans for implementing each tax and the subsequent changes.
3. See López-Laborda and Rodrigo (2003) for an extensive discussion of the tax amnesties in Spain. For a specific review and analysis of the implications of the introduction of the *Impuesto Extraordinario sobre el Patrimonio Neto* in 1978, see de Pablos (1990).
4. The Spanish temporary personal net wealth tax was applied from 1978 to 1991. The tax reform of 1991 changed its name, deleting the adjective "temporary", but defining it in similar terms as previously was the case. However, with the passing of time, in effect this tax became a "temporary" tax. Ever since its introduction, succeeding Governments and their tax administrations carried out a highly debatable management of this tax. The eventual transfer of the management and collection in favour of Autonomous Communities in 1980 in the Financing of Autonomous Communities Law (hereafter, LOFCA) was the decisive factor for the Central Government tax administration neglect in improving the management of the personal net wealth tax . We should also note this tax never was included in the tax administration computerisation plans started in the intervening years.
5. See Alba (1997).
6. In those years nearly all the tax returns were filed in hard copy, without electronic process capacity. The first electronic tax returns would not arrive until the early nineties.

As we shall see later, universal use of electronic tax returns has allowed reducing this period about 1 month.

7. Regarding the current Basque and Navarre Foral Regimes' features see López-Laborda and Monasterio's chapter in this book. See also Garcia-Milà and McGuire (2005) for an interesting review about the role of the Foral Regimes in the development of the Spanish fiscal decentralisation system. About the distinctive features of the Basque Tax Administration (which contains the three provincial Foral Tax Administrations of Alava, Guipuzcoa, and Vizcaya) see Órgano de Coordinación Tributaria de Euskadi (2003).
8. In the new territorial division of the country, the regional governments (or Comunidades Autonomas) typically have within their boundaries several provinces; however, in some cases there is only a province with the Comunidad Autónoma.
9. Again, the exceptions were the Basque Country and Navarre, which as mentioned above have their own tax administrations.
10. This result is similar to the one obtained by Alañón and Gómez-Antonio (2004) using other alternative methodology.
11. As a general rule, the Law 30/1984 of Reform of the Civil Service laid down that any civil servant can be promoted to any position with the only restriction of belonging to some civil servants' corps with degree required for each Civil Service access examination. In the Spanish public administration there are five groups in accordance with the education level required: A, university honours degree; B, university general degree (three years); C, secondary education; D, primary education; and E, elementary education.
12. It must be taken into account that Law 30/1984 allowed any civil servant to change his position with hardly any restrictions every two years, including changes between different Departments. The high regard for civil servants belonging to the Ministerio de Hacienda corps meant that these specialists were in great demand in the public sector, with great expectations to improve their wages.
13. 1989 was the first tax year in which this Constitutional Court's sentence was carried out.
14. This was according to the general regulation established in article 6.5 of the *Ley General Presupuestaria* (General Budgetary Law) of 1977.
15. See Sandford, Godwin and Hardwick (1989) for a discussion on the nature of these costs.
16. This percentage was fixed at 16%. Tax liabilities from self-assessments are not included in its calculation.
17. The creation norm also made reference to the tax administration of the European Union's member states, as well as other countries.
18. Law 21/2001 stated mainly changes in reporting procedures between regional tax administrations and AEAT.
19. The inclusion of this new tribute in the Spanish tax system has been explained as a supplementary source of revenues to balance the Public Health budgets in those Autonomous Communities which pleaded lack of resources after taking on the health competences in the year 2002.
20. In this case, the regional tax administrations preserve the jurisdiction for ruling the administrative appeals lodged against the AEAT's inspection proceedings.
21. See Costas-Terrones (1994) about this proposal of tax administration decentralisation and other alternatives.
22. This includes only the "common regime" regions, leaving out the "special regime" regions of the Basque Country and Navarre.

23. See, for example, López-Laborda, Martínez-Vázquez and Onrubia (2004) who analyse the optimal level of decentralisation of tax administration. The focus of this paper is on how well the externalities produced by multiple levels of tax administration can be internalised by different models of organisation of the tax administration (fully centralised, fully decentralised and territorially coordinated).
24. Initially, this tax cut was estimated by the Ministry of Finance at 11% of the IRPF revenues in 1998, whereas Castañer, Onrubia and Paredes (2004) assessed it at 14.7%. Both estimations were done using a no-behaviour microsimulation model which does not incorporate changes in taxpayer population or in the sources of income composition either. After its application in the year 1999, the Ministry of Finance quantified with the real data this tax cut, which was fixed, isolating any behaviour effect, at 14.3% (Instituto de Estudios Fiscales, 2001). Considering the behaviour effects, except population changes and sources of income composition, but including the interactions with indirect taxes and social contributions, González-Páramo and Sanz (2004) have assessed the tax cut between 10.2% per year and 12.6% per year
25. Let's remember that the method applied from 1979 until 1998 fixed the withholding tax rate using a schedule which combined gross salary bracket, marital status, and number of children. Therefore, it is obvious that this system only offered a rough estimate of the final amount of tax to levy.
26. As an additional requirement, it was necessary that all labour income was obtained from a sole employer, since the tax withholding rate is calculated for every employer and, obviously, the IRPF is a progressive tax.
27. The AEAT's excellence in e-tax services was acknowledged at the recent European e-Government Conference held in Como. Spanish tax administration received the Europe e-Government Award 2003 for their e-tax services.
28. In this paper, aggregation of direct monetary costs and economic assessment of time employed provides the estimate of the indirect tax burden. This notion does not include the psychological cost.
29. The average time per taxfiler was 3 hours and 37 minutes in 1998, as against 2 hours and 12 minutes in 1999.
30. On the public agency model features see, among others, Flynn and Strehl (1996) and Horn (1995). Also interesting is the political science view in Miller (2000).

REFERENCES

Aaron, H. J. and J. Slemrod (2004), 'Introduction', in H. J. Aaron and J. Slemrod (eds), *The Crisis in Tax Administration*, Washington DC: Brookings Institution Press.

AEAT (2002), 'AEAT Annual Report 2002', http://www.aeat.es/agencia/memorias/02/ingles/home.html

AEAT (2003), 'AEAT Annual Report 2003', http://www.aeat.es/agencia/memorias/03/ingles/home.html

Alañón, A. and M. Gómez-de-Antonio (2004), 'Evaluación y análisis espacial del grado de incumplimiento fiscal para las provincias españolas (1980–2000)', *Hacienda Pública Española/Revista de Economía Pública*, 171, 9–32.

Alba, C. (1997), 'Modernising Spanish Public Administration: Old Inertias and New Challenges', in W. J. Kickert (ed.), *Public Management and Administrative Reform in Western Europe*, Cheltenham-Northampton: Edward Elgar, pp. 177–198.

Bird, R. M. (1990), 'Expenditures, Administration and Tax Reform in Developing Countries', *International Bureau of Fiscal Documentation Bulletin*, 44(6), 263–267.

Castañer, J. M., J. Onrubia y R. Paredes (2004), 'Evaluating social welfare and redistributive effects of Spanish personal income tax reform', *Applied Economics*, 36, 1561–1568.

Comisión para el Estudio y Prevención del Fraude Fiscal (1990), *Informe sobre el Fraude Fiscal en el IRPF* , Madrid: Instituto de Estudios Fiscales.

Costas-Terrones, J. C. (1994), 'Consideraciones en torno a una Agencia Tributaria única, *Hacienda Pública Española*, 129, 63–71.

De Juan, A., M. A. Lasheras and R. Mayo (1994), 'Voluntary Tax Compliant Behavior of Spanish Income Tax Payers', *Public Finance/Finances Publiques*, 49, 90-105.

De Pablos, L. (1990), *Una Valoración del Impuesto sobre el Patrimonio Neto*, Madrid: Instituto de Estudios Fiscales.

Delgado, M. L., J. Salinas and J. F. Sanz (2001), 'Indirect Tax Burden of the Personal Income Tax: Evidence from the Recent Tax Reform in Spain', *Australian Tax Forum*, 16, 463–482.

Díaz-Yubero, F. (1993), 'Balance del primer año de gestión de la Agencia Tributaria', *Cuadernos de Actualidad. Hacienda Pública Española*, 3, 81–92.

Esteller, A. (2005), 'Incumplimiento fiscal en el IRPF (1993–2000): Un análisis de sus factores determinantes', *Documento de Trabajo*, 227/2005, Fundación de las Cajas de Ahorro.

Flynn, N. and F. Strehl (ed.) (1996), *Public Sector Management in Europe*, Hertfordshire, UK: Prentice Hall.

Fuentes-Quintana, E. (2004), 'Los Pactos de la Moncloa y la Constitución de 1978', en E. Fuentes-Quintana (dir.), *Economía y Economistas Españoles*, 8, 163–238.

Garcia-Milà, T. and T.J. McGuire (2005), 'Fiscal Decentralization in Spain: An Asymmetric Transition to Democracy', in R. M. Bird and R. D. Ebel (eds), *Subsidiarity and Solidarity: The Role of Intergovernmental Fiscal Relations in Maintaining an Effective State in Diverse Countries*, Cheltenham, UK: Edward Elgar, forthcoming.

González-Páramo, J. M. (1997), 'El IRPF en la encrucijada: Entre la convergencia europea y la cesión a las Comunidades Autónomas', 38, 78–97.

González-Páramo, J. M. and J. F. Sanz (2004), *Evaluando reformas fiscales mediante el coste marginal de los fondos públicos: criterios analíticos y aplicaciones a España y otros países de la OCDE*, Bilbao: Fundación BBVA.

Horn, M. J. (1995), *The political economy of public administration: Institutional choice in the public sector*, New York: Cambridge University Press.

Instituto de Estudios Fiscales (2001), *Evaluación de los efectos de la reforma del IRPF en la Ley 40/1998*, Madrid: Instituto de Estudios Fiscales.

Lasheras, M. A. (1990), 'Percepción Social y Politica Fiscal en España. Historia de un compromiso', en *Sistema Fiscal y Administración Tributaria. Análisis de dos realidades España y Argentina*. Madrid: Instituto de Estudios Fiscales.

López-Laborda, J., Martínez-Vázquez, J. and J. Onrubia (2004), Choosing the Optimal Level of Decentralization in Tax Administration, *mimeo*.

López-Laborda, J. and F. Rodrigo (2003), 'Tax Amnesties and Income Tax Compliance: The Case of Spain', *Fiscal Studies*, 24 (1), 73–96.

Martínez-Vázquez, J. and A. Timofeev (2005), 'Choosing between Centralized and Decentralized Models of Tax Administration', Working Paper 05–02, International Studies Program, Andrew Young School of Policy Studies, Georgia State University, Atlanta.
Mauleón, I. and J. Sardá (1997), 'Estimación cuantitativa de la economía sumergida en España', *Ekonomiaz*, 39, 124–135.
Miller, G. J. (2000), ''Above politics': Credible commitment and efficiency in the design of public agencies', *Journal of Public Administration Research and Theory*, 10 (2), 298-328.
Musgrave, R. A. (1969), *Fiscal Systems*, New Haven: Yale University Press.
Órgano de Coordinación Tributaria de Euskadi (2003), *Informe Anual Integrado de la Hacienda Vasca*, Vitoria-Gasteiz: Departamento de Hacienda y Administración Pública, Gobierno Vasco.
Sandford, C.T., Godwin, M.R. and Hardwick, P.J.W. (1989), *Administrative and Compliance Costs of Taxation*, Bath: Fiscal Publications.
Sevilla, J. V. (1979), 'Estructura de las Reformas Tributarias Contemporáneas', *Hacienda Pública Española*, 56, 31–49.
Slemrod, J. B. (ed.) (1992), *Why People Pay Tax: Tax Compliance and Enforcement*, Ann Arbor: University of Michigan Press.

14. The Spanish Tax Reform: Overview and Lessons

Jorge Martinez-Vazquez*[1]

INTRODUCTION

Very few countries in modern history have shown as radical a transformation of society from its political system to its economic institutions and performance as has Spain over the last 30 years. As described in many of the chapters in this volume, the Spanish tax system began an extensive period of reform from 1977 onward, beginning two years after the death of General Francisco Franco. This reform process, which now has been ongoing for the last three decades, has put Spain's public finances on a sound footing and it represents one of the most identifiable key factors behind the "Spanish economic miracle."

This chapter has three main objectives. First, we provide a summary overview of the evolution and performance of Spain's tax system over the last three decades.[2] Although many of the chapters in this volume have looked at different aspects of the reforms and performance of the system, it is desirable to summarise that performance focusing on several aggregate indicators, which may not have been fully integrated in the previous chapters of this volume. Second, the ultimate test of the performance of the fiscal system of any country is to examine how its citizens feel about it. We do that by looking at how "tax morale" among Spanish citizens changed over this period. Even though the average citizen ended up paying considerably more in taxes, it is quite extraordinary that compliance with these higher tax burdens was in large part voluntary, as reflected by the significant increases in tax morale over the years. This has been a long way to come for a country where as early as 1970s tax evasion was not only rampant but also a socially condoned activity. Over the journey of reform, the average Spaniard's willingness to pay taxes voluntarily increased quite dramatically and citizens became more approving of their government's fiscal policies. Third, it is fitting to close this volume by extracting some lessons from Spain's experience with tax reform for other countries. In recent times, countries like Argentina and Mexico have unsuccessfully, because of a variety of circumstances and reasons, tried to reform their tax systems. Although every country has its own features and peculiarities which require highly customised tax reform efforts, we believe that Spain's experience can offer some valuable lessons for what to do and what not to do in carrying out successful tax reform in these and other countries.

THE PERFORMANCE OF SPAIN'S TAX SYSTEM

Several dimensions of the performance of Spain's tax system need to be highlighted. Perhaps the most impressive of these dimensions is the consistent increase in tax to GDP ratio over the last three decades (see Figure 14.1). It is important to clarify that there is no unique or most desirable level of tax effort for a country; how much a country decides to tax itself is eminently a political collective decision that reflects society's preferences toward public goods versus private goods, degree of social solidarity, and so on. There is no right or wrong in this decision. However, it is both important and desirable that a country collect in taxes the right amount of income that it wants to spend through public sector budgets. From the beginning of the transition years to democracy after Franco's death there was a wide consensus in the country, as reflected in the Moncloa Pacts, that the country lacked basic public services, welfare programs for population groups in need, and public infrastructure. In short, there was the political will to spend a significantly higher share of national income through the public sector. To maintain economic stability, this desire to expand the public budgets could only be met with sizeable increases in tax effort.

As can be seen in Figure 14.1, Spain did undergo a considerable increase in tax effort. In 1975 total tax revenues as a percent of GDP stood at less than 20 percent. By comparison, at that time, the OECD average country was collecting in tax revenues 31 percent of GDP. By 2002, Spain had converged to the OECD average with total tax revenues representing over 35 percent of GDP. This overall increase in tax revenues had a mirror image in the "buoyancy" of the tax system vis-à-vis GDP. From 1975 to 2002, the buoyancy coefficient of tax revenues (without social security contributions) was 1.6 and that for social security contributions, 1.1. Naturally, there were significant differences in the buoyancy of different taxes. While the buoyancy for the personal income tax over the same period was 2.4, the one for the corporate income tax was only 0.6. In the case of

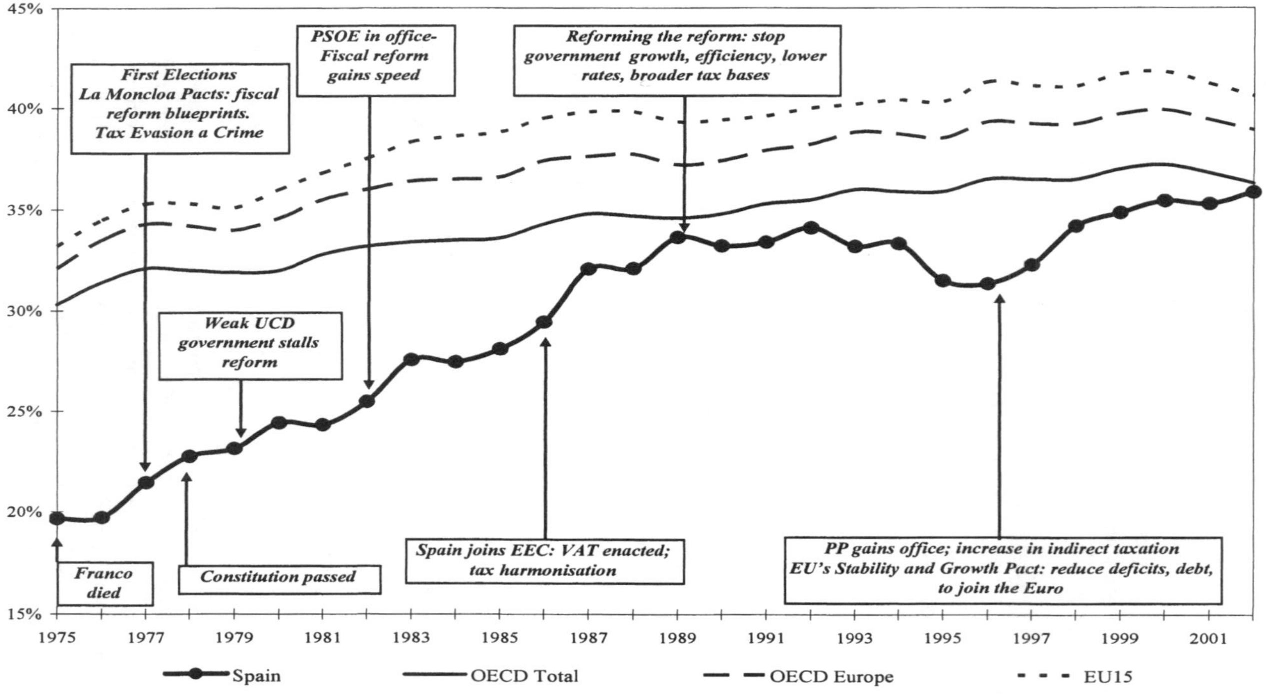

Figure 14.1 Spain's fiscal reform road: selected events (total tax revenue as % of GDP)

indirect taxes, the general consumption tax (VAT) had a buoyancy of 2.3 while that of excise taxes was only 0.3. Taxes on property performed poorly with a buoyancy coefficient of 0.25.

However, as can be seen in Figure 14.1, the rise in tax revenues as percent of GDP was far from steady. At the time of Franco's death in 1975, the Spanish economy was suffering from the aftershocks of the worldwide recession associated with the oil crisis of 1973-74. The critically important Moncloa Pacts provided the blueprints for fundamental tax reform but the politically weak Unión de Centro Democrático (UCD) government elected in 1977 stalled the reforms and only managed to pass some "urgent tax reform measures," while the modernization of the tax administration got frozen. Tax reform finally got in gear with the Socialist Party's (PSOE) ample win in the elections of 1982 and the reformist momentum in policy and administration got a significant push in preparation for Spain joining the European Economic Union in 1986. This required, among other things, the introduction of a modern VAT harmonised with the EEC. The sub-period from 1990 to 1996 saw a decline in tax effort, with an intervening economic recession in 1992-93 and fiscal policy focused on controlling growth in government expenditures and on reducing tax rates and broadening tax bases. Spain had moved swiftly towards reaching the tax paradigm existing in the rest of Western Europe at the beginning of the transition to democracy in the mid-1970s. However, when it reached it by the mid-1980s, the model prevailing in Europe was already under reform, thus moving away from where Spain was going. The fiscal reform blueprint was also in need of reform. After the center-right Partido Popular (PP) won the elections of 1996, the ratio of tax revenues to GDP recovered and resumed growth with the main aim of satisfying the European Union's Stability and Growth Pact and joining the Euro in the areas of budget deficits and overall debt burdens.

In the area of overall fiscal discipline (as measured by government budget deficits and the accumulation of debt) Spain's record over the last three decades shows a more uneven profile but in the long run a rather successful one. The need to close large gaps in capital infrastructure[3] and social programs meant that expenditures often ran ahead of revenue collections. These expenditure demands together with fiscal stabilization policies implemented in recession periods following international macroeconomic shocks pushed the budget deficit into the neighbourhood of 7 percent in the mid 1980s and again in the mid 1990s (see Figure 14.2). However, by 2002 Spain was operating with a balanced budget, as when the country had started the journey of democratization and reform in the mid-1970s. With the approval of the Fiscal Stability Law, which took effect in the 2003 budget, each government level must keep accounts in balance or with a surplus.

The accumulation of government debt during the approximately last three decades offers a mirror image of the evolution of government budget deficits (Figure 14.3). From very low levels of government debt as percent of GDP at the beginning of the journey, government liabilities accumulated at a fast pace especially in the mid-1980s and mid-1990s following the recession periods associated with international macroeconomic shocks. In the mid-1990s, general government gross liabilities as percent of GDP had reached in Spain for the first time the average level of OECD countries. Nevertheless, in preparation for joining the Euro zone, debt levels decreased sharply and Spain was able to meet the Maastricht criterion of an overall debt level of not more than 60 percent of GDP.

Another important dimension of the performance of Spain's tax system has been the evolution in the composition of revenues. In the 1970s Spain's tax system was characterised by a high dependency on social security contributions and indirect taxes. In 1975, as shown in Figure 14.4, social security contributions represented 43 percent of general government revenues, domestic taxes on goods and services, 17 percent, and related "other taxes," 9 percent. On the other hand, direct taxes on income and profits represented only 17 percent of general government revenues. The tax structure was characterised by narrow bases and in some cases, such as social security contributions, by very high rates that yielded less revenue than in other OECD countries.[4] The high dependence on indirect taxation in combination with many special privileges and high levels of tax evasion translated into a regressive tax system, and one that also performed poorly in terms of horizontal equity.[5]

The 1980s and 1990s saw a period of adjustment in tax structure with increases in the relative importance of direct tax collections accompanied also by increases in collections from domestic taxes on goods and services, proper, especially after the introduction of VAT in 1986 (Figure 14.5). By 2002, as shown in Figure 14.6, taxes on income and profits represented 27 percent of general government revenues while domestic taxes on goods and services represented 25 percent. On the other hand, social security contributions had shrunk to 34 percent of general tax revenues. Overall, the significant increase in tax effort over the period was largely accompanied by a fairer distribution of tax burdens and the elimination of large tax distortions that had affected the efficient operation of the economic system. Improvements in tax administration, which allowed the reduction of tax fraud and evasion, together with the elimination of a variety of preferential treatments, increased the progressivity of the tax system and reduced horizontal inequities.[6]

Figure 14.2 Spain's budget deficit (general government net lending)

Source: OECD.

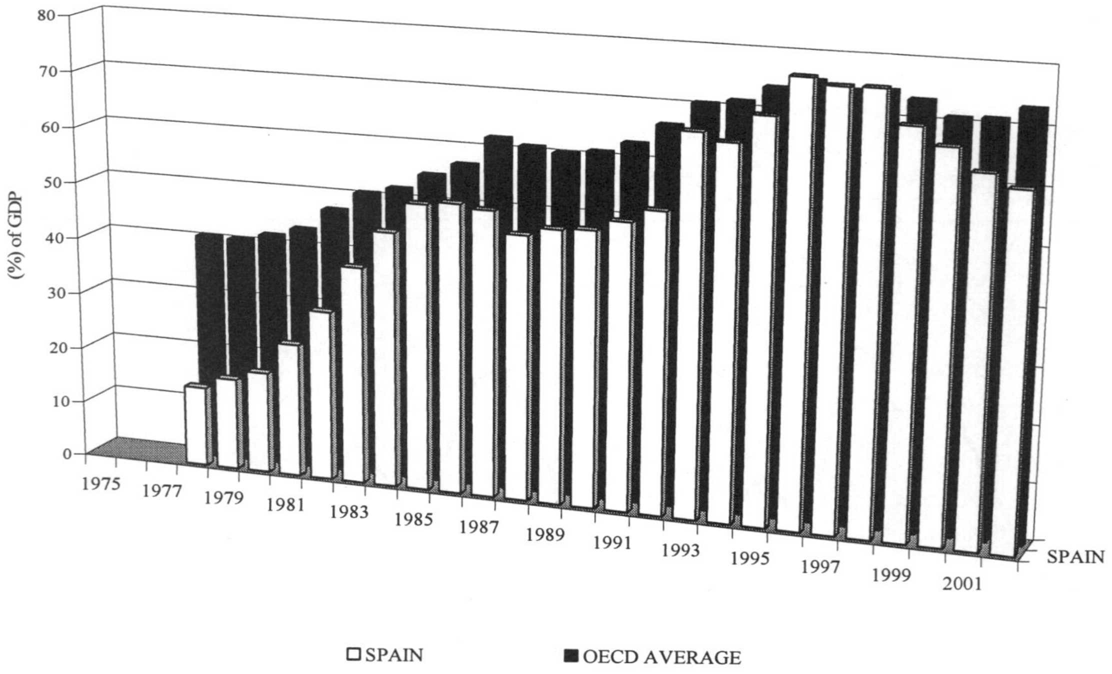

Figure 14.3 General government gross liabilities (as % of GDP)

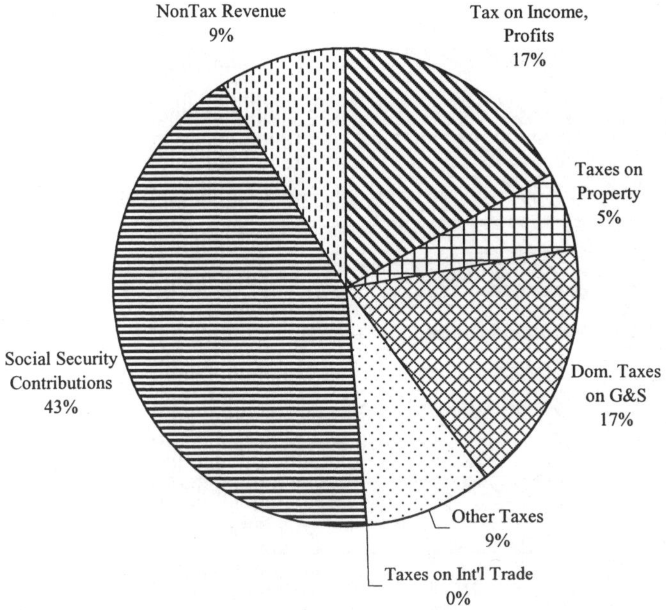

Figure 14.4 General government revenues by source (1975)

However, not everything has been ideal. Despite the rapid process of reform, Spain's tax system has continued to play catch-up with that of its European neighbours. For example, despite better administration and enforcement, tax evasion continues to be relatively high, the tax system is still lagging in international competitiveness, especially in the area of capital income taxation, and tax-induced distortions in labor markets and savings are still present. For better or worse, the tax to GDP ratio lies still below the EU average and the relative importance of income tax revenues still lies below most OECD countries.

Outside the fiscal area, Spain has faced other important economic problems. The government was better able to address the problem imposed by the deteriorating financial position of many public enterprises (ultimately through closings and privatization), than the problems of rising unemployment (particularly among the youth), and the increasing burden imposed by generous pensions and unemployment compensations, especially in light of worsening demographic trends.[7] Labor market rigidities have continued to aggravate the unemployment problem.

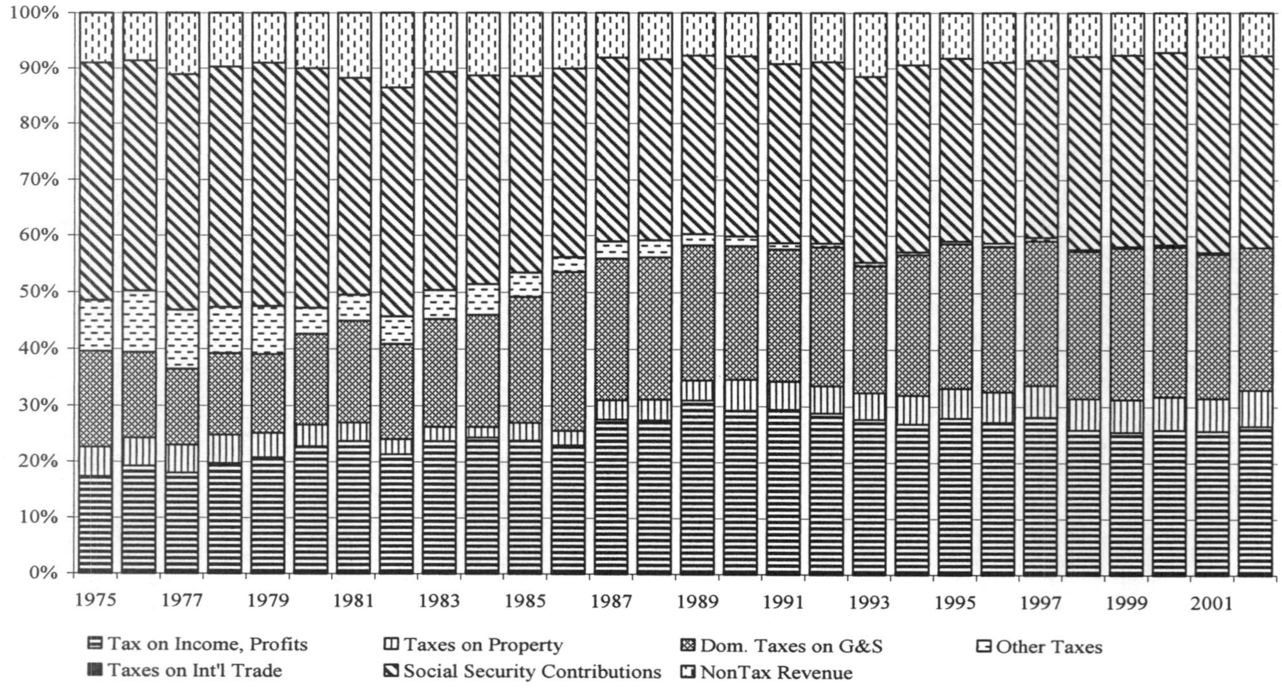

Figure 14.5 Consolidated general government revenue sources (by type)

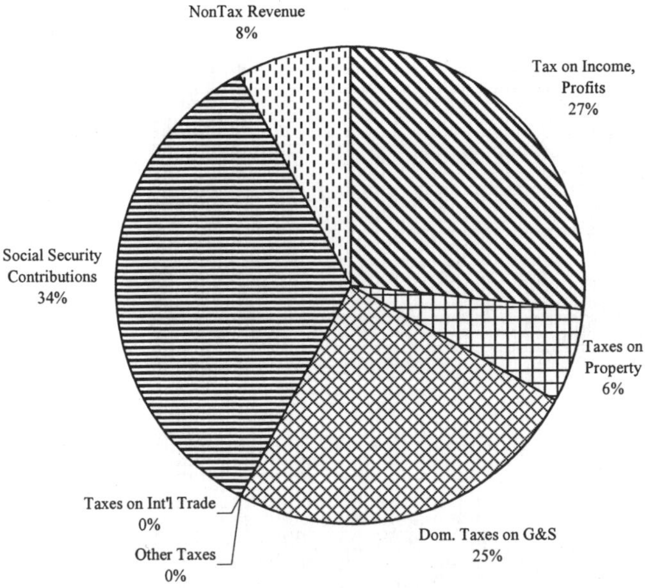

Figure 14.6 General government revenues by source (2002)

One last item in the performance of Spain's tax system is the intergovernmental composition of tax revenues. This is without any doubt the worst performing aspect of Spain's tax system. Despite the fact that Spain has undergone a radical decentralization process, going from one of the most centralised countries in the world in the 1970s to one of the most decentralised today, most of this decentralization has been on the expenditure side of the budget. While the combined share of regional and local governments in total public expenditures is close to 50 percent today, their share in total revenues is just over 30 percent. As shown in Figure 14.7, revenue decentralization, providing regional and local governments with own or autonomous tax sources, has been slow in coming.[8] In 2003, as reported by López Laborda and Monasterio (this volume), 65 percent of all revenues of the regional governments were still coming from tax sharing and other central government transfers. Other than the possibility of using some sort of piggyback personal income tax, with discretion over the rate schedule and credits, all other taxes devolved to sub-national governments are of minor revenue importance.[9] Unfortunately, the heavy dependence on and availability of revenue sharing and transfers has created some sort of soft-budget constraint for regional governments leaving them with little or no incentive to make greater use of their own taxes.

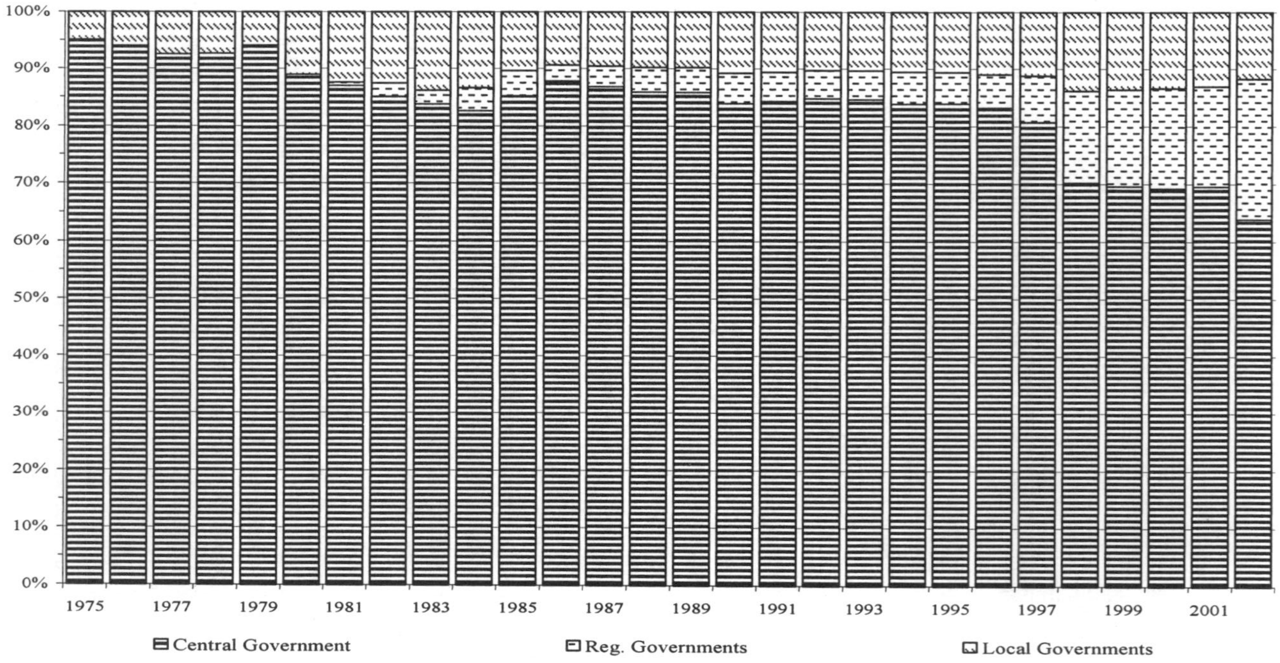

Figure 14.7 Revenue collection by levels of government

Notes: Data from 1998 to 2002 uses gross of transfer figures.

CHANGES IN TAX MORALE[10]

By all counts, at the end of Franco's regime, tax evasion in Spain was rampant.[11] As reported by Comín (this volume) at the end of the 1970s tax evasion in Spain was estimated at 40 percent of tax receipts and above 90 percent of all Spanish taxpayers recognised the existence of fiscal fraud. In addition, at the same time the fiscal system provided ample tax evasion opportunities for the wealthy, there was no political will to prosecute fiscal fraud. In particular, tax evasion was not a criminal offense and evaders only received small administrative sanctions. As in the case of some other Southern European countries, evading taxes had long been acknowledged as one of the most popular "sports" among Spanish citizens. Not paying taxes often was considered a badge of honor and a reason to boast. This clearly was a serious handicap to modernising the tax system and increasing overall tax effort in the country.

Thus, one important question in Spain's transition is whether the fundamental changes the country underwent regarding the role and effectiveness of the public sector since the death of Franco in 1975 affected people's attitudes toward government, and more in particular, their willingness to comply with their tax obligations. Citizens' attitudes toward paying taxes, their "tax morale" or the intrinsic motivation to pay taxes, far from being exogenously determined by cultural traits and mores, appears to have been responsive in other countries to citizens' overall perception of government.[12] The question of the evolution of tax morale in Spain during the last 30 years has been recently examined in Martinez-Vazquez and Torgler (2005) using survey data from the World Values Survey (WVS) and the European Values Survey (EVS). These databases allow the observation of the evolution of tax morale in Spain at four benchmark years: 1981, 1990, 1995, and 1999/2000.[13]

We would expect that the major changes that have occurred in Spain's political and economic system over the past 20-30 years would have impacted (increase or decrease) tax morale. However, isolating the reasons for possible changes in tax morale is not an easy task because of the presence of multiple confounding factors. Using individual response data from the WVS and the EVS helps to control for some of those factors.[14]

The overall picture of the evolution of tax morale in Spain is shown in Figure 14.8 which provides the distribution of aggregate tax morale scores for the years 1981, 1990, 1995, and 1999/2000; the mean values for these four time periods are calculated as the simple average across all individuals in the data sets. Note that the natural cut-off point is at the value 1 because many respondents assert that cheating on tax is "never justified." Therefore, the tax morale variable takes the value 1 if the respondent says that cheating

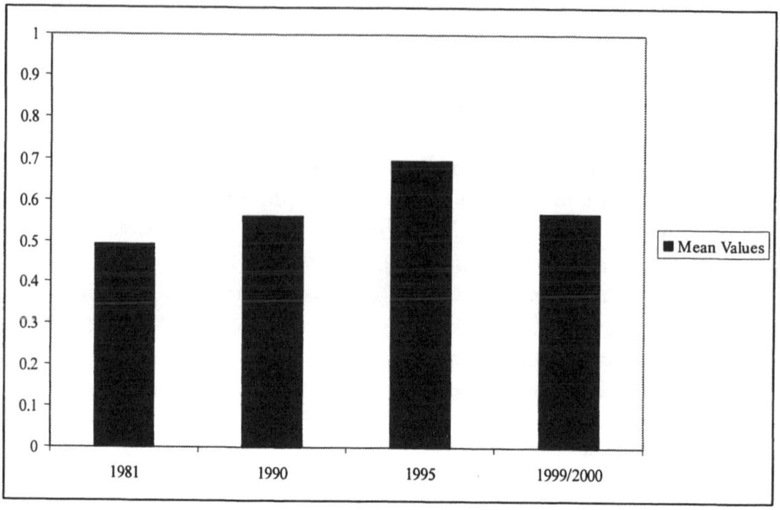

Figure 14.8 Aggregate tax morale in Spain over time (1981-2000)

on tax is "never justified" and 0 otherwise. The interesting result is the strong increase in tax morale in Spain between 1981 and 1990 and a further increase between 1990 and 1995. On the other hand, there is a significant decrease observable between 1995 and 1999-2000.

These changes in the overall level of tax morale would seem to fit well, perhaps up to the observation of 1999/2000, with what has been happening to and around Spanish citizens in the transition years to a democratic regime and thereafter. In 1981 citizens' tax morale was relatively low. By that date, the fiscal system had advanced little from its dismal performance during the late years of Franco's dictatorship. There was still widespread perception of tax evasion, failing economic performance, an inadequate social welfare system, and so on; this overall performance would not have encouraged much intrinsic motivation to pay taxes. The sharp increase in tax morale from 1981 through 1995 is quite consistent with the role of social norms in tax compliance; during those 14 years, the socio-economic conditions for Spanish citizens improved across the board, as the level and quality of public services also improved steadily. The strengthening of institutional structures, in particular the reform of the tax system and tax administration with increased overall fairness, likely produced an affirmation of the public belief in government, at the same time income opportunities improved for a large share of the population. Quite likely, taxpayers reacted favorably to the economic and tax policy changes and public expenditure initiatives that were intended to bring Spain closer to the economic performance of most of its European partners. In summary, the restoration of democracy, the strengthening of social and economic institutions, the process of fiscal decentralization and the creation of a welfare state could have brought a higher level of trust in the state and more positive individual attitudes toward paying taxes through 1995.

The backtracking in the level of tax morale between 1995 and 1999/2000 is harder to explain. Politically, the big change in this period was the change in government when the PSOE lost the elections to the PP in 1996. It is unlikely that this democratic political change is behind the drop in tax morale. More likely, other factors were at play. These may have included the corruption scandals in the last years of the Socialist government, the high unemployment rate during this period, the partial dismantling of the never fully achieved welfare state, or perhaps a growing perception of unfairness associated with the tax reforms aiming at cutting rates and broadening tax bases, which had been introduced around that time.

At any rate, we think it is very relevant for the overall success of Spain's tax reform effort over the last 30 years that tax morale significantly improved over this period even though not in a linear form. We are inclined to believe that the tax and other institutional reforms that got started with the Moncloa Pacts and continued through the accession to the European Economic Community quite likely helped boost Spanish citizens' tax morale. The small but significant decline in tax morale during the second half of the 1990s remains somewhat of a puzzle although some likely causes include institutional changes such as corruption in the public sector, a perception of lower levels of tax fairness, or even high levels of unemployment in the economy. There can be little doubt that the Spanish tax reforms and tax administration modernization efforts resulting in nearly double the tax effort for general revenues, from 22 percent of GDP in 1976 to 39.9 percent of GDP in 2002, has a lot to do with improved tax morale of Spanish citizens. Clearly, tax morale is not something fixed in the culture of the country and keeping tax morale high is a valuable asset for the entire country.

SOME LESSONS

It is, of course, risky to attempt to draw general conclusions and lessons on tax reform, or for that matter on anything else, from the experience of a single country, in this case Spain. However, the Spanish experience with tax reform over the last 30 years, although not without some mistakes and backward steps, also exemplifies what has worked almost universally in other countries that succeeded at fundamental tax reform.[15]

The Role of Careful Study and Preparation

The start of the tax reforms in the late 1970s and early 1980s were preceded by an intense and often frustrating period of careful study and preparation with little or no policy action.[16] However, that work bore fruit; when the time came for reform to be both feasible and also politically desirable, a quite complete and well-documented blueprint for reform was ready. Because of the careful study and preparation, there was much less room for the mistakes and missteps frequently associated with hurried tax reform efforts in many other countries in the past. The preparation for the reforms could have had more depth in empirical estimates of the potential effects of the reforms on revenues, the distribution of tax burdens, and so on. However, the quality of the political debate was enhanced by the availability of the serious work completed up to that point. Because of that, there was less room for some decision makers to assume populist or demagogic positions regarding the reform.

Timing of the Reform

The implementation of fundamental tax reform is more difficult in good economic times. When revenue collections are being propelled upwards by an expanding economy, it is all too difficult to convince the political class to immerse themselves in the difficult and sometimes arcane issues surrounding tax policy reform. Furthermore, tax reform can put at risk political positions by moving the discourse into a territory that at the very least is highly controversial and politically divisive. It is a well known fact among students of tax policy reform that the opportunity for fundamental tax reform becomes more available when the economy is performing poorly and when budget deficits are high on the national agenda. Even more so, the opportunity for fundamental tax reform is enhanced in the presence of political and/or economic shocks. That shock was present in the case of Spain after the end of Franco's dictatorship by the need to catch up for lost time for a period spanning over three decades.

One interesting aspect of Spain's tax reform is that, despite having been implemented by governments with different ideological leanings, overall it has been lineal and persistent. Even though there were temptations to deal with short-term crises, these short-term interventions for the most part never undid or went against the fundamental tenets of the tax reform process set out early in the process. Thus, it is important to differentiate short-term and long-term objectives and to isolate the long-term objectives from temporary pressures and temptations.

Importance of a Comprehensive Approach to *Tax* Reform and the Facilitating Role of Comprehensive *Fiscal* Reform

Much has been written about the virtues and shortcomings of a big-bang versus a sequenced incremental approach to tax reform and it is fair to say that there is little consensus in the literature and among policymakers regarding the most desirable approach. However, there is much less disagreement about the necessity of an explicit blueprint and strategy linking together all aspects of the reform and making the different parts fit together. The lesson from Spain's tax reform is that a sequenced approach to implementation worked well, but perhaps it might have been more desirable to have taken advantage of the window of opportunity provided by the political consensus in the Moncloa Pacts and have implemented much of the reform in a big-bang at that point. But more important for overall success than the speed of implementation of the reforms was the existence of an explicit blueprint and strategy that generally was followed, at least until quite recently, by the different governments in the process of reform. Without a comprehensive blueprint that looked to reform every aspect of the tax system thus making all stakeholders both winners and losers, it would have been so much harder to reach consensus and provide continuity to the different phases of the reform. Thus a comprehensive approach to tax reform was an important ingredient for overall success.

Another important ingredient was that tax policy changes were clearly linked, at least at the beginning of the reforms, with changes in expenditure policy; that is, with fiscal policy reform in the broad sense. There is little question that a broader scope to the reform to include other fiscal reforms on the expenditure side of the budget significantly facilitated acceptance of the tax reform measures. The development of social programs, with a special impact on the welfare of the lowest income groups helped to diffuse some attention for trying more aggressively to attempt to redistribute income through the tax system. Acceptance of higher taxes in any country is generally not forthcoming unless there is a clear sense about how the increased revenues will be used and at the same time, there is general approval for the use of those revenues. This is a lesson that has been frequently ignored in recent attempts at tax reform, for example in Mexico by President Vicente Fox's administration's failed attempt at tax reform at the beginning of his mandate.

Tax Reform Measures Need to Mesh with Other Economic Policy Measures

Tax systems do not operate in a vacuum. Depending on how they are designed, taxes may hinder or enhance the workings of the economy, but clearly there are many other policies (e.g., monetary policy, regulatory policies and so on) that can impact the overall performance of the economic system and ultimately the effectiveness of the tax system. Tax reform efforts are more likely to succeed if they are meshed with other economic policy measures. There is nothing worse for tax policy reform than to be followed by weak and declining tax revenues; the tax reform may have been a technical success for the quality of the measures adopted but would nevertheless appear to be a political failure.

Spain's tax reform program was accompanied by a fairly intensive reform in other areas of public policy, in many cases pushed by the integration agenda with the European Union. However, in some other policy areas, such as labor market liberalization, pension and social security, reforms were slow in coming. Nevertheless, the economy managed to grow at a very healthy pace, although with some vicissitudes, in some cases driven by international economic events.

Reaching a Balance between Efficiency, Equity, and other Objectives in the Reform Package

Tax reform must be a balanced exercise among multiple goals and objectives. There are three possible fundamental objectives behind any tax reform: revenue adequacy, increased efficiency, and a fairer distribution of tax burdens. In the case of Spain's tax reform, the relatively low level of tax effort in the country and the marked needs in social services and public infrastructure meant that a marked increase in tax collections was very desirable. This goal we have seen took precedence but in balanced way with reducing tax distortions in the economy and improving vertical and horizontal equity in the distribution of tax burdens. Although in the initial phases of the tax reform there were signs of pursuing aggressive redistributional policies with high progressive rates, very soon the reform process was channeled toward more modest goals in terms of nominal progressivity with more attention paid to broadening the tax bases. Effective progressivity was increased by reducing the tax burdens on the lower income groups of the population.

Need to Get Tax Policy Right before or at the Same Time as Tax Enforcement and Administration Reform are Tackled

There continues to be a lively debate in the tax reform literature on what should come first, tax administration reform or tax policy reform. It can be argued that improvements in tax administration effectiveness should always be welcome regardless of the presence or not of tax policy reform. On the other hand, stricter enforcement of a tax policy system that is considered unfair and inefficient or exposed to high levels of corruption may be so much harder or even counterproductive. The lesson is to try to get tax policy right, before embarking on a major overhaul of the tax administration system with the goal of significantly increasing tax compliance.

The reform and modernization of the tax administration system were of fundamental importance for the overall success of Spain's tax reform. Although perhaps not entirely intentional, the reform of the tax administration came into being after much of the new tax policy architecture had been designed and to some extent had been put into place. Stricter enforcement of the tax system that was broken and not respected by the people would have been ineffective and counterproductive. Actually, far from causing a taxpayer rebellion, the tough tax enforcement measures, including the criminalization of certain tax offenses introduced in 1977, actually increased tax compliance in an overall atmosphere of increased tax morale. This rather radical change in the effectiveness of tax administration and the turnaround in taxpayer sentiments would not have happened without the reform of the tax system. We must also note that the reform was not only a tax reform but also, as discussed above, a fiscal reform. The changes in expenditure policies and programs actually also played a very significant role in the acceptance of the new tax administration paradigm. It is an important lesson in itself that the very significant tightening in tax enforcement can be accompanied by increases in citizens' tax morale.

Spain's experience comes to highlight the importance of the "small print" in fiscal reform. The improvement of tax administration rarely appears as a significant item in the political agenda; governments tend to pay too little attention to it because it is unlikely to be popular with voters and the results are likely to be seen in the longer run when the incumbent government may be already out of office. However, parallel improvements in tax administration can make the difference between "just on paper" tax reform and real tax reform.

Tax Reform is Not a Once-and-For-All Activity

It is practically impossible to get everything right in a tax reform no matter how integral and fundamental the reform. It is also true that even if we were able to accomplish everything, we should expect the tax system to get partially obsolete as the structure of the economy changes, as evidenced by increasing globalization and the increasing importance of services and e-commerce surpassing more traditional activities in the manufacturing sector. For these reasons, we should expect tax reform to go on over time. However, the need to adapt the tax code to the new economic environment and to correct aspects of the tax laws that are problematic should be balanced with the importance of stability and continuity in tax institutions to avoid confusion and higher costs of taxpayer compliance and administration. Investment and other decisions by economic agents may be put on hold when there is excessive uncertainty about tax institutions.

The Spanish experience with tax reform demonstrates rather well the lesson that tax reform is a continuous process. Having, at least to start with, general blueprints for the direction of the reforms significantly helped keep the process on track. Catching up and adapting Spain's tax system to those of its European partners also helped to provide the reform effort with an internal logic that might otherwise not have been the case.[17] Finally, even though there were a number of tax reform initiatives over the last three decades, these were not so frequent as to impart too much uncertainty and instability in the system.

Original Decisions Cast Long Shadows and are Difficult to Undo

Reaching a consensus on the substance of the reforms is always difficult; compromise and negotiation are usually intrinsic parts of the process. However, one must warn against delaying key points for negotiations. Once new laws are implemented it becomes much harder to re-negotiate or address unsolved issues; "new rights" are acquired and positions are typically hardened. The Spanish tax reform process contains lessons on the dangers of these "original sins." These are most clearly present in the institutional architecture for fiscal decentralization. Three examples will suffice. First, adducing "historic acquired rights," two regions (the Basque Country and Navarre) argued for and got at a time of new beginnings and national consensus special treatment regarding their financial arrangement with the central government.[18] The asymmetric treatment provided these two regions with advantageous financing conditions and represented and continues to represent an unfair and highly inequitable deal for all other regions in the country (those under the general or common regime). Second, revenue assignments initially provided little tax autonomy to the autonomous communities and relied instead on revenue sharing and other forms of transfers for financing the decentralised governments. Over time, as more expenditure responsibilities have been decentralised, the necessary financing has increasingly come more from revenue sharing and transfers, while the modest increases in revenue autonomy provided to the Autonomous Communities has gone for the most part unused, leading to low political responsibility and accountability of regional governments. Third, there has been very little focus since the start on the decentralization at the local level, as opposed to the regional level. This reflects the fact that the Spanish decentralization agenda was, and continues to be, largely driven by political considerations and much less by the efficiency issues typically associated with decentralization policy.

NOTES

* Andrew Young School of Policy Studies, Georgia State University, Atlanta, USA.
1. I am grateful to Gabriel Leonardo for his research assistance.
2. See the essays in Fuentes (1990) and Lasheras and Menendez (1998) for earlier assessments.
3. In the earlier years, much of capital expenditures were fundamentally transfers to public enterprises.
4. See, for example, OECD (1978).
5. In addition, ceilings on wages liable for social security contributions worsened vertical equity.
6. See Onrubia (this volume).
7. See Zubiri (this volume).
8. Note that Figure 14.7 does not properly reflect the level of revenue decentralization after 1998; it was not possible to net out intergovernmental transfers.
9. See Table 11.5 in López Laborda and Monasterio (this volume) for a description of those taxes.
10. This section draws on Martinez-Vazquez and Torgler (2005).
11. See Comín and also Onrubia in this volume.
12. See Torgler (2006), Alm and Martinez-Vazquez (2003) and Bird, Martinez-Vazquez and Torgler (2006).
13. The issue of tax morale so far has not been widely researched in Spain. However, in a recent paper, Prieto Rodriguez et al. (2005) look at the status of tax morale in Spain's Comunidades Autónomas using cross-section data for 1998 from the International Social Survey Programme (ISSP). A main finding of this paper is that tax morale is lower among the supporters of the nationalist regional parties in Catalonia and the Basque Country.
14. These surveys are based on representative national samples of at least 1000 individuals and are conducted via face-to-face interviews at the respondents' homes.
15. See, for example, Harberger (1989), Martinez-Vazquez and McNab (2000), Bird (2004), Bahl (2006).
16. See Fuentes (1973, 1976).
17. See the discussion in González-Páramo and Hernández de Cos (this volume).

18. See the paper by Lopez Laborda and Monasterio in this volume for a full description of the "foral" or special regime.

REFERENCES

Albi, Emilio (this volume). "The Business Community, Policy-Makers and Tax Reform (1977-2004)."

Alm, James and Jorge Martinez-Vazquez (2003). "Institutions, Paradigms, and Tax Evasion in Developing and Transitional Countries," in J. Martinez-Vazquez and J. Alm (eds) *Public Finance in Developing and Transitional Countries*, Cheltenham, UK: Edward Elgar.

Bahl, Roy (2006). " How to Approach Comprehensive Tax Reform," in J. Alm, J. Martinez-Vazquez and M. Rider (eds), *The Challenges of Tax Reform in a Global Economy*, Springer.

Bird, Richard M. (2004). "Managing Tax Reform," *International Bureau of Fiscal Documentation*, February, 42-55.

Bird,Richard, Jorge Martinez-Vazquez and Benno Torgler (2006). "Societal Institutions and Tax Effort in Developing Countries," in J. Alm, J. Martinez-Vazquez and M. Rider (eds), *The Challenges of Tax Reform in a Global Economy*, Springer.

Comín, Francisco (this volume). "Reaching A Political Consensus: The Moncloa Pacts, Joining the European Union and The Rest of the Journey."

Fuentes, Enrique (ed.) (1973), *Informe sobre el Sistema Tributario Español*, 2nd edition, 2002, I.E.F., Madrid.

Fuentes, Enrique (ed.) (1976), *Sistema Tributario Español. Criterios para su reforma*, 2nd edition, 2002, I.E.F., Madrid

Fuentes, Enrique (ed.) (1990). *La Reforma Fiscal y los problemas de la Hacienda Pública española*, Civitas, Madrid.

González-Páramo, José Manuel and Pablo Hernández de Cos (this volume). " Tax Reform in Perspective: The Role of the Public Sector in Spain along the Process of European Integration."

Harberger, Arnold C. (1989). " Lessons of Tax reform from the Experiences of Uruguay, Indonesia and Chile," in Malcolm Gillis (ed.), *Tax Reform in Developing Countries*, Durham: Duke University Press.

Lasheras, Miguel A. and Isabel Menendez (1998). "Spain" in Ken Messere (ed.) *The Tax System in Industrialized Countries*, Oxford University Press.

López Laborda, Julio and Carlos Monasterio (this volume). "Regional Governments: Vertical Imbalances and Revenue Assignments."

Martinez-Vazquez, Jorge and Robert M. McNab (2000). "The Tax Reform Experiment in Transitional Countries," *National Tax Journal*, 53(2) , 273-98.

Martinez-Vazquez, Jorge and Benno Torgler (2005). "The Evolution of Tax Morale in Modern Spain," International Studies Program Working Paper 05-21, Andrew Young School of Policy Studies, Georgia State University, Atlanta.

Onrubia, Jorge (this volume). "The Reform of the Tax Administration in Spain."

Organization for Economic Co-operation and Development (OECD) (1978). *Economic Survey of Spain,* Paris.

Prieto Rodríguez, J., M.J. Sanzo Pérez and J. Suárez Pandiello (2005) "Análisis Económico de la Actitud hacia el Fraude en España," Working Paper, Universidad de Oviedo, 2005.

Torgler, Benno (2006). *Tax Compliance and Tax Morale: A Theoretical and Empirical Analysis,* forthcoming: Edward Elgar.

Zubiri, Ignacio (this volume). "Social Protection and Social Security Contributions in Spain."

Index